# THEIR ACCOMPLICES WORE ROBES

ALSO BY BRANDO SIMEO STARKEY

*In Defense of Uncle Tom:*
*Why Blacks Must Police Racial Loyalty*

# THEIR ACCOMPLICES WORE ROBES

How the Supreme Court Chained
Black America to the Bottom
of a Racial Caste System

Brando Simeo Starkey

DOUBLEDAY
New York

Published in the United States by Doubleday, a division of
Penguin Random House LLC, 1745 Broadway, New York, NY 10019.

DOUBLEDAY and the portrayal of an anchor with a dolphin are
registered trademarks of Penguin Random House LLC.

penguinrandomhouse.com | doubleday.com

Library of Congress Cataloging-in-Publication Data
Names: Starkey, Brando Simeo, [date] - author.
Title: Their accomplices wore robes : how the Supreme Court chained black
America to the bottom of a racial caste system / Brando Simeo Starkey.
Description: First edition. | New York : Doubleday, 2025. |
Includes bibliographical references and index.
Identifiers: LCCN 2025000218 (print) | LCCN 2025000219 (ebook) |
ISBN 9780385547383 (hardcover) | ISBN 9780385547390 (ebook)
Subjects: LCSH: Equality before the law—United States. | Discrimination in
justice administration—United States. | African Americans—Legal status, laws,
etc.—United States. | Race discrimination—Law and legislation—
United States. | United States. Supreme Court. | African American judges. |
Slavery—Law and legislation—United States. | United States. Constitution.
13th Amendment. | United States. Constitution. 14th Amendment. |
United States. Constitution. 15th Amendment.
Classification: LCC KF4757 .S727 2025 (print) | LCC KF4757 (ebook) |
DDC 342.7308/73—dc23/eng/20250114
LC record available at https://lccn.loc.gov/2025000218
LC ebook record available at https://lccn.loc.gov/2025000219

PRINTED IN THE UNITED STATES OF AMERICA
1st Printing

The authorized representative in the EU for product safety
and compliance is Penguin Random House Ireland,
Morrison Chambers, 32 Nassau Street, Dublin D02 YH68,
Ireland, https://eu-contact.penguin.ie.

*Never knew joy before you*
*Haven't known sorrow since you*
*May our Bond forever be Brave*
*Love you forever Wendy*

I prayed for freedom for twenty years, but received no answer until I prayed with my legs.

—FREDERICK DOUGLASS

# Contents

# THEIR
# ACCOMPLICES
# WORE ROBES

# Opening Address

A S I ASSEMBLED THIS BOOK, a complex puzzle depicting the history of a powerful institution conniving with America's omnipresent house guest, White Supremacy, police officers snatched another Black soul.

On March 13, 2020, in Louisville, Kentucky, three White men, plainclothes police officers, exited an unmarked car minutes past midnight and prowled through darkness to an apartment's front door. Inside, a Black woman, Breonna Taylor, and her boyfriend, a Black man, Kenneth Walker III, had settled into bed to watch a movie. The Louisville Metro Police Department was investigating Jamarcus Glover, who had dated Taylor off and on over a few years, for selling drugs from a house miles away. The police obtained a search warrant for Taylor's apartment by lying to a judge, alleging that Glover had received suspicious packages there. Taylor had dozed off on her first day off after a string of twelve-hour shifts working as a hospital emergency room technician. Walker neared sleep too but banging on the front door jolted them both.

"Who is it?" Taylor screamed.

She and Walker heard no response.

"Who is it?" Walker yelled multiple times.

Nothing.

As they stood at the end of the long hallway that led to the front door, Walker fetched his licensed handgun. The officers, meanwhile, unleashed a battering ram.

Thump.

Thump!

THUMP!

The front door burst off its hinges. Fearing that Glover was breaking in, Walker shot toward the door, aiming down to avoid killing the intruder. That round struck Sergeant Jonathan Mattingly's thigh. Detective Brett Hankison returned fire into a window and sliding glass patio door, both shrouded by blinds. Detective Myles Cosgrove and Mattingly also sprayed gunfire inside. Bullets ripped through Taylor's apartment and an adjacent one where a five-year-old child, a pregnant mother, and her boyfriend were slumbering. Taylor, radiantly brown-skinned and cherub-faced, lay on the floor, shot five times, coughing, gasping for air, bleeding.

Her slaying, and the untold numbers of snatched souls whose deaths have echoed the same sorrow since slave ships crisscrossed the Atlantic, illustrate the depravity of America's *racial caste system*— a racial hierarchy enforced through law, rules, and norms that confines the Black population into a subordinate legal, political, and social status, from womb to grave. Devaluation spanning four centuries empowers police, empowers anyone, to vent such violence. Comeuppance too infrequently punishes the hands that break Black skin.

Police victims' families who sue the cities that employ such homicidal officers may witness another way the legal system debases Black life. In wrongful death lawsuits, plaintiffs and defendants hire experts to calculate damages, and they can consider race. In a lead poisoning case concerning a Black male victim, for example, an expert can present calculations reflecting that Black men, on average, earn lower salaries. And courts have accepted them, breeding a perverse incentive where a transgressor, like a toxic waste dump company, should prefer Black targets because courts have recognized them as cheaper victims. Judges condone the appraisal of Black life as literally worth less. Yet, our past bequeathed us the makings of a much fairer present.

In March 1875, the Republican Party relinquished control of a chamber of Congress for the first time since a mortar shot scintillated the sky above Fort Sumter in April 1861. For ten years after the Civil War's close in 1865, Republican legislators, over the complaints of a Democratic Party dedicated to Black subjection, had converted the Constitution from slavery's mercenary into a gatekeeper for liberty. The constitutional *Trinity*—the Thirteenth, Fourteenth, and Fifteenth Amendments—birthed then could have produced complete Black freedom. But a new racial caste system formed instead. And more than the presidency or Congress, the Supreme Court of the United States must be branded as the most indispensable ally of *caste preservationists*, those who establish as an objective the eternal primacy of the White population. The nine black robes have drained The Trinity of its transformational potential, constantly infusing caste preservationists with the special euphoria they experience when relishing triumphs that preserve their coveted White-over-Black world. This has left *caste abolitionists*, those who establish as an objective the destruction of the racial caste system, sullen with unfinished business.

Our sweeping historical journey will stalk the interplay between caste abolitionists, the black robes, and caste preservationists. Whereas caste abolitionists have petitioned the justices to invest The Trinity with enough force to destroy the racial caste system, caste preservationists have insisted that it harbors only the most modest of ambitions. When calling upon the fuller range of legal instruments for complete emancipation that Congress created during Reconstruction, a period lasting from 1863 to 1877, caste abolitionists have frequently beheld justices ignoring their pleas. Caste preservationists have taken note and been emboldened in their pursuit and maintenance of *castework*—caste-producing and -sustaining laws, policies, and actions—believing, correctly, that the judiciary will likely allow their misdeeds. A cycle fueling Black despair.

One cannot overstate the stakes. Unless The Trinity awakens, truly, for the first time, full liberation will never dethrone King Caste. Reform how the Supreme Court *constructs* the Constitution—in other words, what legal effect the Court gives constitutional language—or suffer inside the dungeon that caste built. The boulevard to Black salvation cuts through the Constitution and the Supreme Court.

The Court stole The Trinity away from the cause of freedom, and Black folk paid for that heist. Still do, although they need not always. Ignorance of this theft prevents full comprehension of why the color line has proven stubborn. And ignorance about this renders one unarmed in the battle for racial progress. The Supreme Court *chose* the trail that culminates in Black suffering. The justices could have chosen another.

This book narrates how the Court, for more than one hundred and fifty years, aided and abetted caste preservationists. Best positioned, as the Constitution's final arbiter, to tug the nation into compliance with its purported principles, the Court instead helped a land betray its virtuous self-image. Repeatedly petitioned by Black folk with praying palms to make real the nation's founding conceit—the God-created equality of all—the black robes colluded with the architects of caste. Discover how America reached this predicament, an endeavor that includes directions for how the nation might enter glory.

When the Civil War concluded, Black folk had entertained lofty hopes. Follow me into our past.

# Part I

# Prelude

WELCOME TO THE African Methodist Episcopal Church here in Raleigh, North Carolina, on September 29, 1865, and marvel as enthusiasm bubbles from more than a hundred of America's four million neglected Black souls, and ricochets against the wooden walls.

Back in April, a youthful-looking Union General Ulysses S. Grant and Confederate General Robert E. Lee with his thick white beard, sat ten feet apart in the parlor of a brick home in Virginia. Grant, in disheveled blue, expressed hope that both sides would soon abandon their rifles. In pristine gray, Lee replied that "the emancipation of the negroes would be no hindrance to the restoring of relations between the two sections of the country." After handwriting a letter accepting Grant's surrender terms, Lee shook his hand. By June, gunpowder aroma ceased spoiling the air, and the freedpeople marched about, expecting a legal system that once assessed them like mules to value them as it did White people. Emancipation, they prayed, sowed the death of enslavement *and* all species of racial caste systems.

In late August, a call sounded that exhorted participation in the North Carolina Freedmen's Convention held here now in this unremarkable, white-painted church. The delegates don handmade garments. Only a quarter are literate. And most speak in a dialect you can't decipher. But let their hunger for undiluted freedom define them. One observer will later recall that "a new purpose to labor for their rights" spurs their attendance.

James Walker Hood, the convention's president, addresses the race's gravest need. "[O]ur watchword is 'equal rights before the law,'" proclaims from the pulpit the dark-skinned, wavy-haired reverend. What notes America must play to unlock "equal rights before the law" no one could forecast. Over the next century and a half many will obsess over solutions. In front of a plaster-of-Paris bust of Abraham Lincoln, Hood proposes his own.

Hood demands both the right for Black people to testify in court to "defend our property and our rights" and the right to sit on juries. "It is the right of every man accused of any offence," he says, "to be tried by a jury of his peers. I claim that the black man is my peer, and so I am not tried by my peers, unless there be one or more black men in the jury box." He contends further that "the black man should have the right to carry his ballot to the ballot box." As his speech closes, listen as applause saturates the church, from the carpeted first floor with padded pews that fit three hundred, up to the gallery for one hundred more.

One man reads an address they wish to present to another gathering, one at the state capitol, where White men are convening to reconstitute the state's government. "We most earnestly desire to have the disabilities under which we formerly labored removed," the address declares, "and to have all the oppressive laws which make unjust discriminations on account of race or color wiped from the statutes of the State. We invoke your protection for the sanctity of our family relations. Is this asking too much?"

ABOUT TWO MONTHS LATER, Georgia's provisional governor James Johnson shared nation-altering news. "The [Thirteenth] Amendment," the governor wrote President Andrew Johnson on December 6, 1865, "has passed each branch of the legislature." The *New York Times*'s front page blared, "THE CONSUMMATION! Slavery Forever Dead in the United States," observing that the Thirteenth Amendment had become part of the Constitution.

Abolitionists, for decades, slogged through American hypocrisy struggling to touch this destination. They initially assumed they could reach slaveowners through direct moral appeals. William Lloyd Garrison, a founder of the American Anti-Slavery Society, embodied that belief when vowing that through biblical teachings, America could ditch slavery for a nirvana free from race hatred. "There is power enough in the religion of Jesus Christ to melt down the most stubborn prejudices," he swore, "to overthrow the highest walls of partition, to break the strongest caste, to improve and elevate the most degraded, to unite in fellowship the most hostile, and to equalize and bless all recipients." Anti-abolitionist violence, literature bans, a gag rule that silenced petitions concerning slavery in the House of Representatives, and southerners' devotion to slaveholding, swung the abolitionist pendulum away from individual moral persuasion and toward tactics to command the levers of national power to secure political goals. Abolitionists forsook the pulpit. They rushed the courthouse. Bombarded the statehouse. But only after internecine warfare would a nation founded on liberty feed it to all.

The Thirteenth Amendment reads briskly. Split into two sections, the first states, "Neither slavery nor involuntary servitude, except as a punishment for crime whereof the party shall have been duly convicted, shall exist within the United States, or any place subject to their jurisdiction." The second provides that "Congress shall have power to enforce this article by appropriate legislation." Congress can only enact what the Constitution allows. In Article I, Section 8, the Constitution lists most of Congress's enumerated powers, like the powers to maintain an army and a navy, tax, borrow money, regulate interstate and foreign commerce, coin money, establish Post Offices, and "to make all Laws which shall be necessary and proper for carrying into Execution the foregoing Powers." The Thirteenth Amendment's enforcement clause carried transformational potential, permitting Congress to legislate to ensure Black folk enjoyed the rights provided in Section 1. Those forty-three words, so sweet, so delicious, yet millions force-fed bondage relished their taste only in the afterlife.

The Republican Party, far more supportive of Black rights than the pro-slavery Democrats, imagined the Thirteenth Amendment would stretch beyond ending bondage, and fence the freedpeople from incursions into their fundamental rights. Republican Illinois Congressman Ebon Ingersoll, for example, expected the amendment would "secure to the oppressed slave his natural and God-given rights." Abolitionists argued that enslaved people lacked these rights because the law deemed them property. The new amendment denied state governments, reasoned New York attorney general J. H. Martindale, "a logical argument on which to rest the exclusion of the native-born black man from all the [rights] inherent to citizenship." States could not degrade one "because he is black, any more than they have the constitutional right to classify and degrade white men."

In those days, legal thinkers separated rights among three different buckets—civil rights, political rights, and social rights. The right to enter contracts, the right to sue and be sued, the right to testify in court, the right to inherit, own, and convey property fell into the civil rights bucket. The right to vote went into the political rights bucket. And the social rights bucket involved questions like whether Black people could attend school with White children. Eat at a restaurant alongside White patrons. Marry interracially.

The experiences of Carl Schurz, during a summer 1865 southern tour, indicated those forty-three words would not afford the freedmen equal access to the civil rights bucket.

SCHURZ, A GERMAN-BORN UNION GENERAL whose long beard contrasted with his bookish circular spectacles, conversed with a thirty-something-year-old White man who bellyached with a "resigned helplessness" about his plantation's future. On a steamer carrying him south at the behest of President Johnson, who charged him with taking the post–Civil War temperature of the locals, Schurz implored the former Confederate officer to "make fair contracts with [the people he once owned] and set them to work as free laborers." The man's anger churned. "There was even a slight flurry of excitement in his voice," Schurz recalled. "What? Contracts with those niggers? It would never work." He told Schurz, "Niggers would not work unless compelled to. A free nigger was never good for anything."

This exchange exemplified Schurz's experience. White southerners associated Black skin with slavery—a worldview mass-produced through a centuries-long assembly line of racist thought—and nothing could compel them to disjoin the connection. By the early 1800s, White Americans had demonstrated they viewed Black people as an outsider race. But to the extent that they considered Black people as lower beings, they typically attributed that inferiority to environmental factors that the race could overcome. *Maybe.* When Thomas Jefferson expressed in 1784, "I advance it . . . as a suspicion only, that the blacks, whether originally a distinct race, or made distinct by time and circumstances, are inferior to whites both in body and mind," such extreme thinking had yet to permeate the mainstream.

But as the nineteenth century plodded onward, abolitionists had developed increasingly persuasive arguments for emancipation, provoking slaveowners to answer with a vicious theory of Black inferiority to defend bondage. Slaveowners championed slavery's supposed virtues, describing the African as, biologically, suited perfectly for enslavement and improved by it because proximity to Whiteness gifted him knowledge and culture unavailable to him in his former state of savagery. William Gilmore Simms, a writer and South Carolina politician, spoke for slaveowners when stating, "I do not believe that [the African] will ever be other than a slave, or that he was made to be otherwise; but that he is designed as an implement in the hand of civilization always." Thomas R. R. Cobb, Georgia politician and lawyer, professed that an African's "natural affections are not strong, and consequently he is cruel to his offspring, and suffers little by separation from them," to rebut the charge that slavery unleashed monstrous pain. Society, in fact, needed to continue slavery for the interests of both Black and White since unshackling enslaved people would spark the race's reversion to barbarism, imperiling White society. As Dr. Samuel A. Cartwright promised, "the negro must, from necessity, be the slave of man or the slave of Satan."

On his return north, Schurz advised Johnson that "although the freedman is no longer considered the property of the individual master, he is considered the slave of society, and all the independent state legislation will share the tendency to make him such."

Schurz spoke truth. Beginning in winter 1865, with slavery outlawed, southern states enacted Black Codes. The freedpeople, per the codes, could make contracts, sue, be sued, and testify in court, although some codes restricted their testimony to conflicts involving only Black parties. The rights curtailed, however, defined the codes. Most southern states legally compelled freedpeople to sign labor contracts that they could not breach without risking, often-times criminal, sanction. An implied right not to enter a contract coexists with the right to enter a contract, but the codes refused such liberties. Black folk, overwhelmingly illiterate, would often sign one-sided contracts whose few beneficial terms they struggled to enforce in hostile courts. The Union freed Black folk, but the dilemma of race persisted. Despite those forty-three words, the ghoul that the North Carolina Freedmen's Convention feared most had risen—caste preservationists debuted a new caste system.

Those seeking civil equality for the freedpeople needed a sharper blade.

ON DECEMBER 4, 1865, the first day of the 39th Congress's first session, Republican Pennsylvania congressman Thaddeus Stevens paced toward the South Wing of the U.S. Capitol, shouldering the hopes of Black Americans.

Months before, Stevens feared President Johnson was pursuing a Reconstruction program that would readmit Confederate states to the Union without them exorcising the demon that animated seces-sion. Stevens had articulated his dismay in a Lancaster, Pennsylvania, speech. "The whole fabric of southern society must be changed," the seventy-four-year-old caste abolitionist with blue sunken eyes told an audience in September 1865. "The Southern States have been despo-tisms, not governments of the people. It is impossible that any practi-cal equality of rights can exist where a few thousand men monopolize the whole landed property." He, and other Radical Republicans, the party faction he led that once demanded a prompt end to slavery, committed themselves to clothing the freedmen in the same citizen-ship that White folk wore.

Many colleagues shared his desire to wrestle the administration of Reconstruction from President Johnson, start *congressional* Recon-struction, and restore self-government in the South under leadership that accepted the civil equality of the freedpeople. Below the House

Chamber's stained glass skylight, Stevens pushed for a committee of fifteen congressmen and senators "who shall inquire into the condition of the States which formed the so-called confederate States of America." Stevens joined that committee, which formed nine days later, and it would soon draft an amendment to secure in the Constitution the conditions of the North's victory.

The Senate Judiciary Committee, during this time, focused on burning equality principles into federal law. Committee chairman Lyman Trumbull, Illinois Republican, authored a bill to protect "fundamental rights belonging to every man as a free man." Nearly the entire Republican Party, which occupied about 70 percent of congressional seats, voted for it. President Johnson vetoed it, however, considering it an unfair racial handout. On April 9, Congress overrode his veto, enacting, under the Thirteenth Amendment's second section, the Civil Rights Act of 1866.

STEVENS'S JOINT COMMITTEE, meanwhile, rededicated itself to proposing an amendment. Champions of this endeavor wanted to engrave the 1866 Act into the Constitution. Angst coursed through Republicans—maybe the Supreme Court would rule that the new amendment never empowered Congress to pass the act and pronounce it unconstitutional. Should the Democrats recapture Congress, moreover, they could dismantle it legislatively. If Americans enshrined the act in the Constitution, only a repeal could annul their production. Republicans, though, anticipated failure, having previously stumbled in devising a proposal two-thirds of both houses of Congress supported.

On May 8, 1866, Stevens presented to the House the joint committee's five-sectioned amendment proposal that built on abolitionist thinking. The first section stated, "All persons born or naturalized in the United States, and subject to the jurisdiction thereof, are citizens of the United States and of the state wherein they reside. No state shall make or enforce any law which shall abridge the privileges or immunities of citizens of the United States; nor shall any state deprive any person of life, liberty, or property, without due process of law; nor deny to any person within its jurisdiction the equal protection of the laws." The fifth granted Congress the "power to enforce, by appropriate legislation, the provisions of this article."

"Our fathers," Stevens stated, "had been compelled to postpone the principles of their great Declaration [of Independence] and wait for their full establishment till a more propitious time. That time ought to be present now."

As the congressmen watched from their ornate oak desks and chairs, Stevens said, "the Constitution limits only the action of Congress and is not a limitation on the States. This amendment [fixes] that defect and allows Congress to correct the unjust legislation of the States, so far that the law which operates upon one man shall operate *equally* upon all. Whatever law punishes a white man for a crime shall punish the black man precisely in the same way and to the same degree." This new proposal would cure the illness ailing southern states, Stevens argued, where "different degrees of punishment are inflicted, not on account of the magnitude of the crime, but according to the color of the skin." He championed the proposal because "unless the Constitution should restrain them those States will all, I fear, keep up this discrimination, and crush to death the hated freedmen."

With representatives from the disloyal states still unseated in Congress, New Jersey Democrat Andrew Jackson Rogers articulated their perspective. "I want it distinctly understood that the American people believe that this Government was made for white men and white women," the caste preservationist declared. "They do not believe, nor can you make them believe—the edict of God Almighty is stamped against it—that there is a social equality between the black race and the white." The amendment proposal prevailed anyway, and two years later, on July 28, 1868, Secretary of State William H. Seward certified the Fourteenth Amendment's ratification.

Before this amendment, Congress could not enact legislation to counteract civil rights deprivations committed by states. The Constitutional Convention delegates who met during summer 1787 set out to structure a floundering nation's underdeveloped democracy. The document they created transformed a feckless confederation of thirteen separate mini-republics into a nation of thirteen states under a strong, central federal government, but one whose power was limited by that same document. Those most supportive of a strong federal government convinced the reticent to endorse the Constitution by agreeing to reserve to the states a wide array of powers.

The delegates, therefore, chose not to explicitly grant Congress the authority to act as the custodian of the civil rights bucket. They believed nature, they believed God, granted such basic rights, and allowed the duty to protect them to reside with the states. Already in existence before the Constitution arrived, state governments often did in their constitutions. The 1776 Pennsylvania constitution provided that "no man . . . can be compelled to attend any religious worship," for example. The first ten amendments, the Bill of Rights, operated against federal, not state, intrusion. Simply put, the states safeguarded the civil rights bucket on behalf of their citizens. Southern leaders, however, had long exhibited zeal to invade Black people's buckets.

The Fourteenth Amendment, consequently, reimagined the relationship between the federal government and the states, promoting the former over the latter. Once the federal Constitution could protect civil rights from state infringement, Congress could pass laws enforcing those rights, and Americans could sue in federal court to prevent states from denying them. Per the Republicans who championed it, the Fourteenth Amendment consolidated power in Washington, D.C. Turned the guardianship of civil rights into a national obligation. Strangled the conception that the state could narrow, based on race, an individual's rights. Crushed the South's *states' rights* theory of government.

Two weeks after the Fourteenth Amendment's ratification, the remains of Thaddeus Stevens lay in state in the Capitol Rotunda. Caste preservationists danced, with one newspaper editor penning, "The prayers of the righteous have at last removed the Congressional curse!" Stevens wanted the Fourteenth Amendment to enfranchise Black men but settled for the achievable. The amendment charged the federal government with protecting civil equality. Without the ballot, though, could freedpeople protect themselves?

———

TWO YEARS LATER, on May 19, 1870, from the first-floor cast iron balcony of the six-story Gilmore House, one of Baltimore's finest hotels, Frederick Douglass, in his early fifties, addressed the largest celebration of Black rights in the nation's nearly-one-hundred-year history. A parade of distinguished guests, Union soldiers, musicians, and regular folk promenaded through the red, white, and blue adorned streets to Monument Square, the center of the city's civic life. From Boston to Detroit to St. Louis, Black folk and their allies rejoiced in ornate processions, but Baltimore hosted the grandest affair. Douglass returned to Maryland where he once endured bondage to celebrate what he fathomed lifted Black people to full equality—the Fifteenth Amendment.

A sea of joyous faces blasted energy into the festivities as he began his speech. Before entertaining his stirring words, let's revisit the history that begot this moment.

THE ORIGINAL CONSTITUTION COUNTED enslaved people as three-fifths of a person. The Thirteenth Amendment invalidated the three-fifths clause, meaning the Constitution would recognize the freedpeople as full persons, boosting the number of southern House seats *and* Electoral College votes. If the former Confederacy prevented Black men from voting, emancipation perversely would have fattened secessionists' political strength. Congressional Republicans forced the seceding states to enfranchise Black men as a precondition to reentering the Union, but they doubted the honor code would forever stem the South from reverting the voting booth to a White man's space.

On January 1, 1861, only four of the thirty-four states, Vermont, New Hampshire, Massachusetts, and New York, permitted Black suffrage, and fewer than three thousand Black men could call themselves voters. Nothing sank a political career faster, at the time, than championing Black enfranchisement. The war and its aftermath, however, rearranged many Republican politicians' political convictions, melting this frostiness toward political equality. By 1866, the Radicals sought to curb national disputes regarding Black suffrage through a constitutional amendment. But such idealism trembled before a chilling reality—northern White voters, whenever Black voting rights appeared on referenda, slammed the door on the idea. Republican politicians hesitated to tout a political loser.

During the 1868 national election, the Republican Party united behind requiring suffrage rights for Black men in the South while, in the North, supporting putting Black voting rights on statewide referenda, an incoherent although ultimately popular position. Yet, after the party's electoral triumphs, congressional Republicans worked on another amendment. Black men, they concluded, had proven worthy of the ballot. They shone on the battlefield and inside the precinct. Many would have nodded alongside Schurz as he promoted Black male suffrage when telling President Johnson, "While the Southern white fought against the Union, the negro did all he could to aid it; while the Southern white sees in the national government his conqueror, the negro sees in it his protector; while the white owes to the National debt his defeat, the negro owes to it his deliverance; while the white considers himself robbed and ruined by the emancipation of the slaves, the negro finds it the assurance of future prosperity and happiness."

More crucially, election results showed Republicans they lacked a southern pulse without its Black heartbeat. Particularly worrisome, in Louisiana, where Black men constituted a registered voting majority, Republican presidential nominee Ulysses Grant received less than 30 percent of the vote. White paramilitary groups had exhaled murder and terrorism to produce a White electorate. Spurred by interests in both justice and party, Republicans agreed on a two-sectioned amendment with a first section of thirty-four words: "The right of citizens of the United States to vote shall not be denied or abridged by the United States or by any State on account of race, color, or previous condition of servitude." Section 2 empowered Congress to enforce the first "by appropriate legislation."

Maryland's Democratic governor, Oden Bowie, implored the state legislature to reject the amendment. His criticisms, rooted in states' rights logic, observed that since the nation's inception, states could set voter qualifications. For example, states had once limited voting to landholders. The proposed amendment deprived Maryland, Bowie argued, "of the power of shaping her own internal polity."

He also cautioned against awarding the ballot to "a class of persons whose previous condition renders them wholly unfit, at present, for the intelligent exercise of so delicate and valuable a privilege."

With the phrase "at present," Bowie left possible that Black folk could one day evolve, an idea landing on the more egalitarian side of the caste preservationist thought spectrum. The spectrum's other and more populous side jibed with New York Democratic congressman John Winthrop Chanler, who said, "Black democracy does not exist. The Black race have never asserted and maintained their inalienable right to be a people, anywhere, or at any time." Caste preservationists favored a herrenvolk democracy which blesses the ruling race with democratic rights and smites the ruled race with tyranny. As Alabama politician William L. Yancey told a Boston gathering in 1860, "Your fathers and my fathers built this government on two ideas: the first is that the white race is the citizen, and the master race, and the white man is the equal of every other white man. The second idea is that the Negro is the inferior race."

Maryland's state legislature unanimously rejected the amendment. But when Iowa, on February 3, 1870, ratified it, the Constitution received the Fifteenth Amendment.

THAT WAS THE HISTORY, and beneath the clear skies, Douglass, with a more-white-than-black lion's mane, told the raucous audience for "the last thirty years [I have] often appeared before the people as a slave, sometimes as a fugitive slave, but always in behalf of the slave. But to-day, [I am] permitted to appear before them as an American citizen. How great the change."

The Thirteenth Amendment extinguished slavery. He thought. The Fourteenth sealed his citizenship and civil equality. He thought. Not until the Fifteenth Amendment, though, did Douglass feel fully welcomed into the American family.

"Thirty-five years ago," Douglass said, "[I] was working as a slave in Talbot County and looked forward even then that there would some time come a day when not a fetter should clank or a whip crack over the backs of his fellow men. That day has come at last." Douglass had gained worldwide acclaim for his antislavery prose. He spoke that day as if constitutional amendments had rendered obsolete his abolitionism, first of slavery and now of caste, five years after the war. "The Fifteenth Amendment," Douglass said, "means that hereafter the black man is to have no excuse for ignorance, poverty or destitution. Our excuse for such in the past is swept away from us by the Fifteenth Amendment."

Four years earlier, Douglass and a group of leading Black men had interviewed President Johnson. Please, they implored, support Black male enfranchisement. He replied no. Douglass left disenchanted, expecting that Johnson's opposition "will commence a war of races." Now, Douglass boasted, "We have a future; everything is possible to us."

MAINTAINING A CASTE SYSTEM hinges on White folk commanding the levers of power and prizing their racial interests. In his infamous 1861 "Cornerstone Speech," Alexander H. Stephens, vice president of the Confederacy, announced that this new government emerged from the principle that "all the white race, however high or low, rich or poor, are equal in the eyes of the law. Not so with the Negro. Subordination is his place." The Trinity threatened such thinking.

America, citing its Constitution, depicts itself as a model democracy for guaranteeing liberty. How did caste preservationists, despite The Trinity, reconstitute a racial caste system?

The ensuing pages will trace crimes and controversies, introduce advocates and adversaries, and narrate the stories of Supreme Court cases that tested schemes of racial domination. The *Their* in *Their Accomplices Wore Robes* refers to the caste preservationists whose actions propel this story. The other characters, from caste abolitionists to Supreme Court justices, orbit the caste preservationist star.

Come to our journey's first leg, 1870s West Virginia.

# First Leg:
# The Trinity Conception

W EST VIRGINIA'S SECOND CAPITOL, in downtown Charleston, an Italianate building with Romanesque flourishes, provided coal country architecture fit for Milan. Within its three stories, in February 1873, the Democrat-dominated legislature debated a bill that would help sculpt a post-slavery racial caste system.

Separating from Virginia, a split nearly a century in the making, West Virginia became the thirty-fifth state in June 1863, remaining loyal to the Union. The Republican Party had controlled West Virginia politics since its genesis. Ahead of the 1870 elections, a contingent of West Virginia Democrats asked Delaware Democratic senator Willard Saulsbury how the party could attract Black voters, less than 5 percent of the state's voting population. Saulsbury cautioned that the time remaining until the election seemed "too short to pull the wool over their eyes." He advocated they scream "White man's party" instead because enough "ignorant white men" populated the state "who would [normally] vote the Republican ticket that we can get to vote ours." It worked, and in January 1872, West Virginia held a convention to write a new constitution. Inside a small, run-down Charleston church, seventy-eight delegates, sixty-six of them Democrats, huddled. The most conservative Democrats favored a constitution that restricted Black rights. One Democratic delegate, George Orrick Davenport, a volunteer Union soldier, joined his party's larger contingent, moderates who opposed a constitution that undergirded a racial caste system.

A year later, that strain of anti-Black animus endured and inspired discussion about a White-male-only jury law. The bill appeared destined for history's dustbin—its opponents denounced it as violative of the state constitution. Davenport, also a member of the legislature's lower house, expressed that the constitution he had helped write prohibited such racial exclusion. "If the [state] Constitution don't protect citizens from class legislation," Davenport contended during open debate, "he was sorry that he had been a member of the Convention that framed it and was furthermore sorry that he had voted for it."

Even though he "was as much opposed to [Black jurors] as anybody," the former Army lieutenant believed the 1866 Civil Rights Act, which Congress, in May 1870, reenacted under the Fourteenth Amendment's enforcement clause, "provides there shall be no distinction on this question." Davenport "didn't want to force negroes on juries but thought that under the laws of the United States, they had rights there, and we had no right to debar them." Many White folk shared similar misgivings. In July 1865, Ohio Republican congressman James Garfield confessed privately that he harbored "a strong feeling of repugnance when I think of the negro being made our political equal and I would be glad if they could be colonized, sent to heaven, or got rid of in any decent way. . . . But colonization has proved a hopeless failure everywhere." And thus men like Davenport held their nose and downed their gruel.

After a long day of debating the bill, Davenport, a slender-faced White man with full dark hair and a mustache, sat in a barber's chair. As Black men waited on him, he remarked, "Well, if you niggers know how much I have done for you today, you would wait on me for nothing." Caste preservationists, though, resuscitated the bill. The *Charleston Courier* advised readers that "it was hardly consistent to provide for securing intelligent jurors . . . and then flood the jury boxes with ignorance by admitting negroes indiscriminately."

On February 19, 1873, rancorous debate erupted in the capitol. Representative John J. Thompson commanded the floor and offered his worldview to his colleagues, elbowing them toward the realm of racial subordination.

"Mr. Speaker," he said, "I want it understood that I am opposed to nigger jurors. I will never consent to make them the equal of the white man. I have many reasons for my position; the most important of which is because a nigger is a nigger. . . . For my part, sir, I would rather have no juries at all than to force white men to sit with them."

Representative W. H. Reynolds, in opposition, urged his colleagues to accompany him to the enlightened world. "The doctrine that all men are created equally free has been lifelong with me. I have always believed it and have always maintained it. It is but simply justice, and I propose to stand by it to the last."

These worldviews routed West Virginia toward rival destinations—White-over-Black racial dominance or coequal governance. On March 12, 1873, the legislature limited jury service to "all white male persons, who are twenty-one years of age, and not over sixty, and who are citizens of this state." Caste preservationism triumphed.

Because of the state's poverty, White West Virginians especially cherished the racial caste system. Many poor White people constructed their identity on their supposed superiority over "the nigger." Laws like this one diverted their attention away from a bitter truth—a common oppressor, White men who hoarded a nation's wealth, subjugated the Black folk and the poor White man alike. White Supremacy, evil but ingenious, convinced the poor White man to fixate on cultivating anti-Black hate rather than love for economic self-interest. Henry Wise, pre–Civil War Virginia governor, explained that convincing poor White people of their equality with their economic betters hinged on the caste system. "Break down slavery," he insisted, "and you would with the same blow destroy the great democratic principle of equality among men."

Since West Virginia never seceded, its Reconstruction proceeded as it did in Maryland, Delaware, and Kentucky, loyal border states. Beyond the ending-slavery requirement, minimal federal intervention encumbered those states. That hands-off approach, and a small Black population, enabled the Democratic Party's quick ascent in West Virginia. Just four of the eleven southern states, Tennessee,

Virginia, North Carolina, and Georgia, had returned to Democratic hands when West Virginia passed its jury discrimination law.
Meanwhile, the Republican-led southern states, particularly ones
with large Black populations, like South Carolina, Mississippi, and
Alabama, elected Black men to statehouses that enacted some fairly
egalitarian laws.

But White southerners were salivating to reclaim the crown. The
Supreme Court upholding West Virginia's jury law would suggest
that caste preservationists could install legislation that expunged
Black people from other facets of civic life too. The Civil War and
Reconstruction had destroyed the slave system. Caste preservationists needed an answer: "Can we implement laws that explicitly deny
black people rights in order to water a new fountain of oppression?"

During the state's constitutional convention in 1872, Black citizens had petitioned for a provision that would specifically enable
Black jury service. The convention's chairman waved them off. The
new constitution, he vowed, would prohibit race distinctions. After
the passage of the jury discrimination law, at least two options presented themselves to its foes who believed it violated The Trinity.
Sue the state, arguing that the Constitution barred it, or wait until a
Black criminal defendant raised the issue at trial, a scenario requiring
a crime.

STAND ALONGSIDE ME, on April 17, 1872, in the upstairs back room
of a two-level wooden frame house in Wheeling, West Virginia. The
Ohio River severs this city in two. Taylor Strauder, his wife, Annie,
and her nine-year-old daughter from a previous marriage, Fannie
Green, live in the more populous area, which cradles the river's
coastline, with the Appalachian Mountains looming in the eastern
sky. Spot the bed, lounge, and rocking chair in front of the fireplace.
Notice, on the hearth, that tool normally stored downstairs to chop
wood. A hatchet.

Strauder is leaving their home this night after Annie asked him to
buy yeast. He enters the nearby Miller's Saloon instead. In the back
room, the biracial carpenter sees a Black man named Elijah Pullins.

"You damned son of a bitch, you better go home," Pullins taunts, among dominoes-playing patrons. "I suspect there is someone in bed with your wife now."

Strauder, formerly enslaved in Augusta County, Virginia, doesn't respond. Such cuckold quips often flew in his direction, especially from Pullins.

When Strauder returns home, he opens the front door and swears he sees a White man fleeing through the back door. He confronts Annie, but she denies the accusation, inciting a fight. The two wedded in June 1871, and trouble defined their relationship. He would insist she cheated on him. She had him arrested for threatening her life once, but they reconciled. They always reconciled. This latest tempest stretches into the wee hours of the morning but relents enough for them to sleep on that bed.

The next morning, Annie wakes up and sits in the rocking chair. Strauder, preparing for work, plops on the lounge, awakening Fannie, asleep under the covers. The couple refresh their quarreling.

He asks Annie, "Where are my shoes?"

"I suppose they are where you put them last night."

Nearby, Lucinda Thomas prepares her two small children for Annie, her older sister, to babysit this rainy morning. Lucinda reaches her sister's home at about thirty past six, enters the door, steps in a few paces, and a macabre scene freezes her. Annie seated in a rocking chair. Her head collapsed into her chest and resting on her right arm. A stream of blood rushing down her temple, over her eyes, running off the cliff of her nose, diving onto the floor, and splashing into an expanding crimson pond. About three feet away rests the hatchet with coagulated blood gluing Annie's hair to its hammer side.

Lucinda hurries to the house of the local justice of the peace, Robert Gillespie, who tells her to alert Officer Robert Junkins at his home while he scurries to the crime scene.

Let's mix with the crowd gathering outside the Strauder home. See those twelve White men entering? The ones who look like regular citizens? They will serve on the coroner's jury, which determines cause of death. Gillespie directed the police to summon them. Despite The Trinity, the officers selected only White men. Black men account for 40 percent of the county's male population.

Many have crusaded for the principle that America must bestow to all the same justice. Equal justice. We cherish this principle for various reasons. For one, a matter concerning an individual's rights implicates the rights of an entire group. West Virginia cannot deny Strauder his rights because of his Blackness without infringing the rights of the entire race. For the law to afford Strauder equality, he must have it always, not merely when society sees fit to provide him that. Those twelve White men who serve on this coroner's jury— West Virginia continually replicates this spectacle. But this murder occurred *before* the state will pass its jury discrimination law. In absence of that law, the police *chose* to summon only White men.

"Taylor Strauder killed my mother with a hatchet," Fannie testifies inside the home, her mother's corpse still on the floor. Gillespie issues an arrest warrant, describing Strauder as a "very light mulatto about thirty-two years of age; about five feet ten inches in stature and stoutly built" with a "rather spare face, with high cheek bones, [who] wore when last seen here a scattering beard on his chin."


ON APRIL 25, some Pittsburgh, Pennsylvania, police officers caught the first Wheeling-bound train with Strauder in tow. The officers had arrested him in their city shingling a house the day before. When the streetcar stopped opposite Gillespie's office, the guards removed Strauder from it, allowing an angry mob to punch him with sticks and blast him with insults. Wheeling policemen forged a path through the crowd, and Gillespie ushered Strauder and the guards into his office. Gillespie asked Strauder about his readiness for a probable cause hearing. He replied he could participate the next day.

The guards returned Strauder outside. Cries of "shoot him" and "hang him" flew from the swelling mob. The police formed two lines and, with Strauder placed in between, marched to the jail. Hundreds of onlookers tailed the contingent, berating Strauder the entire way. He passed under the rounded archway of the Ohio County jail and entered his new home, a cell.

The Black members of the mob wanted the justice system to punish the man who had slaughtered one of their own. The system, to produce that outcome, foreshadowed that it would deny Strauder his rights because of his race, a wrong states freely committed when believing courts will pardon them. Black folk would grow accustomed to this posture, seeking protection from a system that deprives them of their rights.

THE NEXT MORNING Strauder sat for his probable cause hearing, held in the jail. Upon learning of Strauder's lack of legal representation, George Davenport entered the jail. Davenport, the state legislator who would the following year oppose the exclusion of Black men from juries, conferred privately with Strauder, christening a bond that would span more years than either could have predicted. Fortune shone on the moneyless Strauder that day when Davenport, a skilled attorney of seven years, agreed to represent him pro bono.

Fortune shone on Davenport too. Strauder's defense presented him, a well-respected member of the state bar, his last best opportunity to leave his mark on the profession. Thirty-one years old, Davenport wouldn't see forty. With no wife or children, he threw himself into lawyering and legislating. A loyal Democrat who called his party "incorruptible," Davenport, smart and honorable, exhibited a "natural kindheartedness and a freedom from malice and wickedness singularly attractive to those who knew him best," a friend remarked. Davenport battled alcoholism—during a legislative session in 1873, the Speaker for the West Virginia House of Delegates had the sergeant-at-arms arrest some legislators, including Davenport, for missing votes. Davenport blamed whiskey for his absence. Four years later, he headed a Christian temperance society. One time Davenport, principled, chastised a judge he felt inadequate and threatened to imperil his career. The judge held him in contempt and sentenced him to five days in jail. On another occasion, Davenport scolded an opposing counsel during open court for untruthfulness. That counsel punched Davenport, who returned the blow.

After Fannie and other witnesses testified, the hearing ended— the state proved probable cause. On May 20, 1872, an all-White grand jury indicted Strauder for murder. Davenport twice asked for continuances, stalling the case a year. Not until May 8, 1873, two months *after* the state legislature passed its jury discrimination law, did Strauder hear a verdict.

"WE THE JURY find the prisoner guilty of murder in the first degree," said the foreman. Strauder "sank to his seat, overcome, his legs refusing to longer sustain him," a reporter observed. Two months later, Judge Thayer Melvin sentenced him to be hanged. The Supreme Court of Appeals of West Virginia, however, reversed his conviction on an arcane technicality, granting Strauder another trial.

Davenport and his thirty-one-year-old mentee Blackburn Barrett Dovener, who assisted him, studied The Trinity with an eye toward invalidating the jury discrimination law. Within the law office of Davenport & Dovener at 174 Fourth Street, they focused on the Fourteenth Amendment. The Thirteenth referred to slavery. The Fifteenth to voting. But the Fourteenth spoke to equality. Two clauses from the amendment's first section must have grabbed them.

First, the Privileges and Immunities Clause: "No state shall make or enforce any law which shall abridge the privileges or immunities of citizens of the United States." The "privileges or immunities of citizens of the United States" refer to the rights Americans possess because of their national citizenship, presenting the opportunity to raise at least two arguments: a narrow one beneficial to Black criminal defendants and a broader one beneficial to the entire Black population. First, they could have argued that Strauder's American citizenship included a privilege, or a right, to a trial with an impartially selected jury panel. Or, second, that the clause granted an immunity from a state treating a citizen as a member of a degraded caste—an individual's immunity from castework—a right which the jury discrimination law had violated. But an obstacle stymied those arguments—in April 1873, nearly a year after Annie's murder, the Supreme Court neutered the Privileges and Immunities Clause in the *Slaughter-House Cases*.

In 1869, the biracial Louisiana legislature passed "an act to protect the health of the City of New Orleans" in response to the squalor, stench, and unsanitary conditions the butchering industry unleashed upon the city. Plying their trade near schools and hospitals, butchers discarded decaying animal carcasses on unpaved roads, in the Mississippi River, wherever, and leaders partly blamed cholera and yellow fever, diseases responsible for thousands of deaths, on such practices. The law forced butchers to relinquish their fly-swarmed shops and pay to operate from the monopoly Crescent City Slaughter-House, located across the river. Some butchers, White men, sued, arguing that the law violated their Fourteenth Amendment rights.

John Archibald Campbell, a former Supreme Court associate justice who had resigned and then served as the Confederacy's assistant war secretary, represented the hundreds of butchers who sued the state. He argued that the slaughterhouse law violated parts of The Trinity, including, specifically, the Privileges and Immunities Clause, because it denied the butchers' right to practice their occupation, what Campbell called a privilege of American citizenship. Campbell spearheaded multiple lawsuits to invalidate laws that Louisiana's Republican-majority legislature enacted. Previously, the legislature passed laws like one forbidding school segregation and another making race discrimination in public accommodations a crime. Such enactments enraged caste preservationists and set them against anything the legislature passed. Campbell chased a transparent objective—harness The Trinity on behalf of White "victims" to undo works of a legislature elected in a majority-Black state.

Writing the Supreme Court's five–four majority opinion, Justice Samuel Freeman Miller, Republican-appointed, ruled against Campbell but awarded caste preservationists an unexpected bounty. The rights implicated in the Privileges and Immunities Clause, Miller wrote, defining them narrowly, included "the prohibition against ex post facto laws, bills of attainder, and laws impairing the obligation of contracts." Miller's argument defied logic—the original Constitution already protected these rights.

Justice Joseph P. Bradley, one of four justices who disagreed with the majority, wrote a dissent that explained the Privileges and Immunities Clause's true meaning. Bradley honored Congress's choice to fundamentally alter American democracy, a choice endorsed by the people who voted overwhelmingly for the Republican Party in the 1866 midterm election, where the Fourteenth Amendment rose above all other campaign issues. Bradley observed that people had state citizenship and federal citizenship. Before the Fourteenth Amendment, state citizenship, the primary form of citizenship, provided citizens protection of their civil rights. Federal citizenship was secondary. The Fourteenth Amendment inverted that, making the federal government the leading guarantor of civil rights.

"If a man be denied full equality before the law, he is denied one of the essential rights of citizenship as a citizen of the United States," Bradley wrote. The privileges and immunities of the citizens—"the right of personal security, the right of personal liberty, and the right of private property"—were fundamental rights. They encompassed the rights in the Declaration of Independence, the right to "life, liberty, and pursuit of happiness," which "belong to the citizens of every free government." Bradley further explained that the rights included in the Bill of Rights, like the right to free speech and peaceable assembly, and against unreasonable searches and seizures, were among those fundamental rights now protected by the Fourteenth Amendment against state intrusion. Simply put, American citizenship had always given the populace a civil rights bucket. Prior to the Fourteenth Amendment, though, the Constitution contained no express grant of power that allowed the federal government to protect that bucket from state intrusions. The Fourteenth Amendment cured that congenital defect.

"The amendment," Bradley wrote, "was an attempt to give voice to the strong National yearning for that time and that condition of things, in which American citizenship should be a sure guaranty of safety, and in which every citizen of the United States might stand erect on every portion of its soil, in the full enjoyment of every right and privilege belonging to a freeman, without fear of violence or molestation."

Seeking to counteract Campbell's gambit to stymie Louisiana's biracial legislature, Miller narrowly interpreted the Privileges and Immunities Clause, revoking its utility for the cause of Black freedom. Contending that the West Virginia law violated "the privileges or immunities of citizens of the United States," would, therefore, slam Davenport and Dovener into a roadblock.

The duo ultimately reached for the Equal Protection Clause: "No

State shall . . . deny to any person within its jurisdiction the equal protection of the laws." The Court most fully untangled that clause in Miller's *Slaughter-House Cases* opinion. "The existence of laws in the States where the newly emancipated negroes resided," he wrote, "which discriminated with gross injustice and hardship against them as a class, was the evil to be remedied by this clause, and by it such laws are forbidden." When West Virginia limited jury service to White men, did it not discriminate with gross injustice and hardship against Black folk as a class? One would think. But if the Supreme Court could impoverish one clause, it could another.

Other West Virginia attorneys, in summer 1874, were exploring the same uncharted and unwelcoming seas on behalf of a Black client. Let's trek eastward, one hundred miles from Strauder's cell, to Martinsburg, West Virginia.

WE WAIT HERE at the corner of Spring and King Streets. The day— August 15, 1874. The time—one in the morning. And the early morning's darkness blankets the town of five thousand. What began twenty-four hours earlier in this ominous three-story Berkeley County jail brought us. Venture within to find the cell belonging to John Toliver, a "dark-skinned mulatto," who described himself to a census taker in 1870 as an illiterate twenty-one-year-old Virginia-born farm laborer. If you scoured the jail, you would not find him. Learn why.

The chain of events ending in Toliver's confinement started on October 7, 1873, after a search party found the remains of twelve-year-old Annie Butler in the woods near her father's farm in the Falling Waters district of Berkeley County. This Annie, unlike Annie Strauder, was White. The night before, she, as was routine, went to corral her father's cows. When she did not return home, a search party combed the area the next morning, finding her, yards from a public road, coated with bruises and the top of her head "mashed into a jelly." Blood covered the murder weapon, a club, about a hundred yards from the murder site. The authorities speculated that her assailant tried to rape her. She hollered. And a bludgeoning quieted the screams. The investigation focused on Toliver based on circumstantial evidence, with his presence near the woods around the same time as Annie offering the strongest piece.

An all-White jury convicted him, and on June 1, 1874, Toliver entered a packed courtroom for sentencing. His attorneys, Henry Blackburn and Ward Lamon, believed him innocent and moved for a new trial, arguing that the jury discrimination law violated Toliver's Fourteenth Amendment rights. The judge disagreed and set a July 31 execution date.

The state supreme court granted Toliver's appeal motion, staying the execution. Since many expected the criminal justice system to uphold the racial caste system, fury grew that retribution had yielded to a Black man's rights. On August 13, murmurs about harm befalling Toliver whisked about town. The mayor raised nary a finger to silence the noise by protecting the jail. At nightfall, calm hung over Martinsburg. Then, around one in the morning of August 14, the jail watched as a horde of about three hundred men, some on horses, others on foot, converged upon it. Some fully disguised, some partially so, and all armed either with a pistol or saber, they collaborated under the command of "the Colonel," who whispered orders.

With each exit secured, the Colonel knocked on the jail's front door. R. A. Blondel, the jailer, stuck his head out of an upstairs window. "Who is there?" he asked.

A hordesman answered, "We have a prisoner for you."

About ten minutes later, Blondel, with his assistant, A. Virtue, opened the front door. A few men rushed in, pistols drawn, demanding the keys to Toliver's cell. After Blondel refused, they grabbed him and Virtue, stole the keys, and stashed the two in a parlor room under guard. Others, meanwhile, hunted for Toliver. After invading his cell, they threw him down, tied his hands behind him, shackled his ankles, dragged him outside, and loaded him onto a one-horse wagon.

The horde left with Toliver, a funeral procession parading to a planned grave. Toliver shed no tears, seemingly at peace. A mile and a half out of Martinsburg, the horde stopped near a hulking locust tree with stout branches. Stout enough to support a body. About thirty encircled their prey. One stepped forward: "John Toliver, we are now waiting to hear your confession."

"Gentlemen," Toliver responded, "I am innocent of this crime. On that day I was at Mr. Tice's, and . . ."

The horde interrupted and one repeated, "John Toliver, we are waiting to hear your confession."

"Gentlemen, I am innocent of this crime," he reiterated. A pause took over before Toliver spoke again: "Will you permit me to pray?"

"Yes, we grant you ten minutes to make your peace with God."

"O! merciful and heavenly Father," Toliver said, "Pardon my executioners, for they know not what they do; and oh! I do pray that little Annie Butler is in heaven. I know she looks down this night and pities me; and now may the blessing of God rest on all my fellow mortals."

One hordesman drove Toliver's wagon under the tree and another fastened a rope around a limb and around Toliver's neck. The horde ordered him to stand.

"John Toliver, will you now confess your guilt, or will you go to perdition with a lie on your lips?"

"Gentlemen, I am innocent of this crime."

"Good-bye, Toliver."

Sorrowfully, he replied, "Farewell, gentlemen."

When the sun rose, Toliver's suspended figure greeted train passengers and the hundreds who journeyed just to consume the spectacle, a Black man swinging from a limb, the strange fruit that grew from trees whose roots fed from soil White Supremacy had poisoned. After the Civil War, when a racial caste system awaited its legal pillars, White folk employed violence to torment the Black masses into compliance.

Four years from now, some newspapers around the country will publish an article that mentions Toliver's lynching. Here's an excerpt from the *Philadelphia Inquirer* on April 16, 1878: "It appeared afterwards Toliver was innocent of the murder of which he was accused."

ON THE MORNING OF NOVEMBER 2, 1874, a jailer returned Strauder to Judge Melvin's courtroom for retrial. Davenport and Dovener petitioned to remove Strauder's prosecution to federal court. The 1866 Civil Rights Act allowed defendants to transfer their cases to federal court if in a state court they couldn't enjoy, based on race, their rights secured to them under the act. Essentially, then, Strauder could remove his case to federal court if West Virginia violated his Fourteenth Amendment rights given that the act and the amendment overlapped. "[B]y virtue of the laws of the State of West Virginia," their petition read, no Black man could serve as a juror and thus Strauder "does believe that he cannot have the full and equal benefit of all laws and proceedings in the State of West Virginia."

In 1871, a North Carolina trial judge considered Lee Dunlap's removal petition. A Black Republican accused of murdering a White Democrat, Dunlap contended that because of his race and party membership, Mecklenburg County's White Democrats cultivated a hostile environment that denied him his right to a fair trial. He further noted that state courts rarely summoned Black jurors. The judge granted his removal petition.

West Virginia legally denied Black men from serving on juries. North Carolina had no such law. Strauder could document local prejudice in West Virginia simply by pointing to the state's statute book. Given that Strauder supplied the stronger case, Judge Melvin could have followed suit, but he rejected the petition. The law did not compel that decision. Melvin chose it.

The proceedings then moved to jury selection. Twenty-eight White men, prospective jurors, entered the courtroom. Davenport and Dovener motioned to quash, or reject, the jury panel as "unconstitutional and void," wanting an impartially selected panel. The West Virginia law, they argued, violated the Fourteenth Amendment, and, accordingly, any panel drawn under it necessarily bore the taint of illegality. Melvin rejected the motion. An all-White jury again convicted Strauder. This time, a composed Strauder accepted the verdict. Melvin again sentenced him to hang.

On March 9, 1875, Davenport met with Alpheus F. Haymond, a West Virginia state supreme court justice. Davenport pursued a simple mission—convince Haymond, who had served in the Confederate Army, to stay the execution and grant an appeal. Davenport argued that Melvin erred in neither granting the removal petition nor quashing the jury panel. Haymond granted the appeal.

But before the state supreme court could decide the case, the direction of national politics swerved. President Rutherford B. Hayes ended Reconstruction.

AT ONE IN THE AFTERNOON of March 5, 1877, the Supreme Court justices exited the bronze doors of the U.S. Capitol and descended the eastern central portico steps, their black robes clashing with the vibrant uniforms of the diplomatic officers who followed. Hayes, Ohio's Republican former governor, trailed the diplomats, the grandiose Capitol behind him. As the crowd spotted Hayes, a stocky, wide-shouldered five-foot-nine man with deep-set blue eyes and a long graying beard, ovation thundered the sky. After the sergeant-at-arms of the Senate finished his opening remarks, Hayes rose, gripping his inaugural address.

Outgoing president Ulysses Grant had sometimes exhibited an instinct to harness the federal government to protect Black rights even if he frequently shrank from the responsibility. At his core, Grant believed southern White folk when their behavior screamed that they would never, without federal compulsion, accept legal equality of the freedpeople. Would the spirit of the predecessor possess the successor? Hayes's inauguration speech would predict how the future would unfold.

As he broached the topic of equal rights, Hayes started auspiciously. "That a moral obligation rests upon the National Government to employ its constitutional power and influence to establish the rights of the people it has emancipated," Hayes told the adoring throng, "and to protect them in the enjoyment of those rights when they are infringed or assailed, is . . . generally admitted."

But Hayes soon kicked Black America into the snake pit, saying, "I am sincerely anxious to use every legitimate influence in favor of honest and efficient local self-government as the true resource of those States for the promotion of the contentment and prosperity of their citizens."

In his diary, Hayes wrote, "the time had come to put an end to bayonet rule," meaning dissolve Reconstruction and remove the remaining troops from the South. He wanted to pivot from interventionism toward a solution he thought solved the quandary of how to include Black men in southern democracy. If the federal government removed itself, he thought, White southerners could return to politics. Economic interests and social strata dissected the White poor from the White rich, the White planter from the White craftsman. White factions, to win elections, would court Black voters to vault their side ahead. And people defend members of their coalitions. White conservatives, the theory predicted, would swoop in to save Black conservatives from White liberals who attempted to violate their rights and vice versa. The winner-take-all incentive structure inherent to two-party politics, consequently, would dull the color line. "The whites must divide before we can hope for good results there," he recorded in his diary. "The blacks, poor, ignorant, and timid, can't stand alone against the whites."

Black Americans, Republicans since emancipation, wept. B. A. Glenn, a Black southerner, sent Hayes a wistful missive. "I am filled with sorrow and shame that you have left the colored people of the South to the tender mercies of those who had proved themselves cruel beyond measure," Glenn penned. "How could you," he questioned, "betray those who most fought for your election[?]" A group of Black Alabamians petitioned Hayes to support the funding of Black folk's emigration to Liberia in wake of his double-crossing. And a Black North Carolinian man wrote to the *New York Times* that "Our people will never forget . . . the cruelty and treachery which prompted Hayes . . . to abandon the colored people of the South."

Republican desertion drove Black Americans to place their hopes with federal courts, particularly the Supreme Court, the site within the federal government best suited to force a nation to abide by its constitutional pledges.

ON NOVEMBER 17, 1877, West Virginia's supreme court handed down its *Strauder v. State* decision. Back in June 1876, Davenport and Henry Mathews, the state attorney general, had argued the case before four justices, all Democrats and three secessionists. Matthews articulated the caste preservationist position that the state had extended Strauder all the rights the Constitution guaranteed him. Seventeen months later, when the court's decision landed, Davenport and Dovener grappled with an argument that threatened not only their chances of victory at the U.S. Supreme Court, but Black people's ability to reap the Fourteenth Amendment's full promise.

Justice Thomas Green penned the unanimous opinion, although White Supremacy, leaving his unmistakable fingerprints on it, deserved credit. "The thirteenth and fourteenth Amendments . . . have little or no other effect," Green wrote, other "than to abolish slavery and declare a negro a citizen, when born in the United States." Not true—the words of both accomplished much more. Enemies of Black freedom, however, wished to disempower The Trinity.

"The mere prohibition of negroes to sit upon the jury which tried him," Green contended, "can not be regarded as the denial of equal protection of the laws to him." Green absurdly claimed the "fourteenth amendment [was not] intended to protect the citizens of any State against unjust legislation by their own State." Because Strauder suffered no denial of "equal protection of the laws," he had no right to transfer his case to federal court. "I can not see why a jury of white men would not be quite as likely to do justice to the prisoner as a jury of negroes," Green wrote. "[B]ut if it were otherwise, it would give him no right to have his case removed to the Federal court for trial."

A savvy legal mind understood the rhetorical sleight of hand. The Supreme Court, in the Slaughter-House Cases, held that the Privileges and Immunities Clause left undisturbed the relationship between states, civil rights, and citizens that had always existed: since only states exercised total control over the civil rights bucket, the federal government had no authority to intervene against state action. Green likened the Privileges and Immunities Clause to the Equal Protection Clause. With a wave of a magic wand, the two clauses melded into one—a neat illusion if White Supremacy could convince judges to perform his trick. The West Virginia justices raised their hands and conjured a ruse the Supreme Court could replicate to spoil the Equal Protection Clause as it had the Privileges and Immunities Clause.

ON APRIL 15, 1878, Davenport convened with Morrison Waite, U.S. Supreme Court chief justice, to discuss Strauder's case. Operating inside the Capitol, lacking personal offices for themselves and with their staff working in cramped offices, the justices lamented their subpar accommodations. The most suitable meeting place, the Court's conference room, provided a comfortable space on the Capitol's ground floor. Two others came in a supportive role, attorneys for the lynched Toliver, Lamon and Blackburn, who would have held a gathering like this, but for a lynching.

Waite, who had opposed slavery and helped establish Ohio's Republican Party, learned the facts of Strauder's case. Davenport requested the Court to consider two possible judicial errors. One, the West Virginia jury discrimination statute violated the Fourteenth Amendment, and two, removal to federal court was therefore proper. The four closed the meeting, and Waite met with the eight associate justices later that day. Four justices needed to agree to hear the case.

By the November 1878 elections, the Democrats had regained control of the entire South, from executive mansions to statehouses, for the first time since the war. Three years prior, Congress passed "An Act to protect all citizens in their civil and legal rights," known as the Civil Rights Act of 1875, which, among other things, prohibited jury discrimination. The West Virginia Supreme Court, in its *Strauder* decision, intimated that Congress lacked power to enact it. Other state courts might proclaim that too. A legal void emerged. Only the Supreme Court could fill it.

Later that afternoon, the Supreme Court notified Davenport of its decision. The case would see its day inside the Court. In the early evening, he then telegrammed Dovener: "A writ of error has been granted by Chief Justice Waite in the case of Taylor Strauder. I will be detained until tomorrow getting papers."

Two other jury discrimination cases would join *Strauder v. West Virginia* on the Court's docket, giving the black robes three early opportunities to supercharge The Trinity.

THE CENTRAL CHARACTER in these two cases, seventy-two-year-old Alexander Rives, served as the federal judge for the Western District of Virginia. Born into a wealthy family with colonial roots, Rives remained loyal to the Union, bucking the social order in Charlottesville, his hometown. The opinion he planned to deliver on November 20, 1878, in the cases of two Black brothers, the Reynolds brothers, convicted by all-White juries, would reverberate throughout and print his name in newspapers nationwide.

In the fall of 1877, the Reynolds brothers fought constantly with three brothers from the Shelton family, poor White folk, on a narrow logging road near a freedmen's school the Black brothers attended in Taylorsville, a rural town. On November 29, Aaron Shelton, twenty-one, pursued Lee Reynolds, seventeen, hit him with a stick and then knocked him over a sawed-off log. Burwell Reynolds, nineteen, stabbed Aaron from behind with a large tobacco knife. Aaron fell instantly and died later. The next morning, the Reynolds brothers' mother hired Andrew Lybrook, married to a daughter of the Reynolds family that once owned her, to defend her boys. Attorney William Martin later joined the defense.

On April 1, 1878, the brothers, each indicted in January by an all-White grand jury for murder, entered the Patrick County courthouse. Lybrook asked that Black men comprise one-third of the jury panel. Judge William Tredway rejected the request. Court officers generally refused to summon Black men in Virginia state courts notwithstanding that the commonwealth's laws opened service to "all male citizens twenty-one years of age, and not over sixty who are entitled to vote and hold office."

Lybrook and Martin then petitioned Judge Tredway to remove both prosecutions to federal court under Section 641 of the Revised Statutes, the federal removal statute's title. The Reynolds brothers "allege," defense counsel argued, "that their race have never been allowed to serve as jurors . . . in the County of Patrick, in any case . . . in which their race have ever been in any way interested." Judge Tredway denied the petition, and on April 3, an all-White jury convicted Burwell of first-degree murder. Tredway, deeming the verdict contrary to the facts, granted a new trial. On April 5, an all-White jury convicted Lee of second-degree murder. Tredway refused to grant a new trial and sentenced Lee to fifteen years. The Virginia Supreme Court, however, overturned the conviction—Lee didn't even stab Shelton—and granted a new trial.

On October 28, 1878, the day the brothers' retrials started, defense counsel again petitioned for an inclusive jury panel. Judge Tredway implored the prosecution to accept the proposition, to no avail. Tredway then denied the removal petition. On October 31, the Burwell jury hung, and Lee was convicted of second-degree murder and given an *eighteen*-year sentence.

As Lee sat in the Patrick County jail, anticipating relocation to the penitentiary, and Burwell awaited his third trial, Lybrook and Martin trekked to Danville. "The purpose [of The Trinity] was to put the negro upon a basis of entire civil equality with the whites all over the Union," Lybrook believed. "[O]f course we of the conquered South did not approve of elevating by one great bound, a chattel we had just owned, to a position of equal citizenship with ourselves, but we had it to do, and more than that, we agreed to do it."

On November 19, Lybrook and Martin offered Judge Rives their removal petition. Rives, expecting it, spent the night mulling it over and the following morning delivered his shocking opinion.

Although Virginia, unlike West Virginia, had no jury discrimination law, Rives still found that the state violated the brothers' Fourteenth Amendment rights. He could have concluded that an equal protection violation required a discriminatory law. Nonetheless, he reasoned that a state acts through its legislative, executive, and judicial branches. Here, the judicial branch transgressed. Rives recalled that Judge Tredway permitted only White men to sit on jury panels. "Was not [this] denial, a denial to the prisoner of the equal protection of the laws?" asked Rives, a learned-looking White man with a long drooping nose, circular spectacles, and a receding hairline.

Days later, a federal marshal and his crew visited the quaint brick Patrick County jail with a writ requiring the state to relinquish the brothers to federal custody. The marshal then carried them a hundred miles away to the Pittsylvania County jail.

ON DECEMBER 4, 1878, inside the neglected, overcrowded capitol building in Richmond, the Virginia Senate passed a resolution asking Governor Frederick Holliday to "communicate to the Senate, as speedily as possible, all the information he has" about the Reynolds brothers affair. Holliday, tracking the events through newspapers, directed the state attorney general, James Field, to investigate.

Reconstruction in Virginia differed from that in West Virginia. Virginia rebels quickly recaptured power after the war, leaving White Republicans and freedpeople openmouthed that the ilk who cleaved a nation in two dusted themselves off and waltzed back into the house as if nothing had happened. Virginia caste preservationists erred twice though. In January 1866, the general assembly, first, enacted Black Codes, drawing Congress's ire, and, second, a year later, almost unanimously rejected ratifying the Fourteenth Amendment. Congress, in response, refused to restore Virginia to the Union. In March 1867, Congress took over Reconstruction from President Johnson and Republicans controlled the state, though only for three years. This saga, nonetheless, taught Virginian caste preservationists a lesson that circumstances didn't compel their West Virginia counterparts to learn—mind the watchful eye of a Republican Congress when designing the new racial caste system. This explained why Virginia never passed a jury discrimination law.

On December 10, Field provided state officials a summary of the case and advice on how to respond. "The right to be tried by a negro jury," Field contended, "is not one of the rights conferred upon the negro race, either by the recent amendments of the Constitution of the United States or the act of Congress known as the civil-rights bill." This misstated the argument—Rives contended that Black folk had a right to an impartially selected jury panel. But the newspapers repeated this distortion, obscuring whether Field willfully attacked a straw man or caste preservationists couldn't comprehend the argument. Field recommended that the state petition the Supreme Court for an order compelling Judge Rives to return the brothers.

LATER THAT DAY, in Charlottesville, Judge Rives, vilified around the country by Democratic newspapers, spoke to a *New York Herald* reporter. Rives, appointed in 1871 by President Grant, told the reporter that he felt obligated to "execute the law of Congress in behalf of the humblest, so as to secure the equal rights of all citizens as guaranteed by the fourteenth amendment."

"But what will the Legislature do about it?" the reporter asked.

"I do not know," Rives responded. "The legislature of the State has been all right, requiring the juries to be summoned without reference to color. The fault is in the courts and officers in my own court. I have always ordered mixed juries and have not discovered that harm has resulted from it; on the contrary, the lawyers seem to prefer them."

Caste preservationists, still championing the states' rights argument despite The Trinity, contended that Rives had "invaded the jurisdiction of the State and her courts and usurped the power and jurisdiction that does not lawfully pertain to him." Virginia attorney general Field called Rives's actions "entirely without justification" and proclaimed that "the peace and good order of society, the protection of the State, the due administration of the law and the public weal demands that redress for the present and security for the future shall be sought through the Legislature of the State and national Government." A Richmond lawyer, W. L. Royall, argued that Rives's "decision strikes a blow at the Sovereignty of the State in all its departments and functions." An editorial in a northern newspaper postulated that "If a [federal] judge can nullify the laws of a sovereign state, set aside the verdicts of her criminal courts and discharge murderers from custody, there will be little reason for the existence of state courts at all."

A few months later, phase two of Rives's assault on the state's exclusionary jury practices landed.

"THE FOURTH SECTION of the Act of March 1, 1875 is in these words," said Rives, addressing a grand jury in his Danville courtroom in February 1879, explaining the law at the center of the prosecution of five state judges.

"That no citizen possessing all other qualifications which are or may be prescribed by law, shall be disqualified for service as grand or petit juror in any court of the United States or any State, on account of race, color, or previous condition of servitude."

Additionally, Rives told the eighteen jurors, seven Black men, six White Republicans, and five White Democrats, "any officer or other person charged with any duty in the selection or summoning of jurors, who shall exclude or fail to summon any citizen for the cause aforesaid, shall, on conviction thereof, be deemed guilty of a misdemeanor, and be fined not more than $5,000."

Per the scuttlebutt, Rives was collaborating with Republican attorney general Charles Devens, Republican Vermont senator George Edmunds, and U.S. District Attorney Warren S. Lurty, the Grant-appointed federal prosecutor who brought the charges. Fingering Rives as the instigator, caste preservationists scolded him in their newspapers. "Why," the Norfolk Landmark rebuked, "should Conservative Virginia be subjected to a shameful outrage?"

"The fact that colored men are seldom seen on Virginia juries raised the presumption that they are, on account of race," Rives instructed the grand jury, "left off of the lists of names . . . from which to draw juries. This is a violation of the laws of the United States, and wherever colored men are habitually left off these lists" the jurors should deem that "evidence that they are so left off on account of race" unless proven otherwise.

Lurty presented damning evidence. Jury lists in Franklin, Patrick, and Charlotte Counties never contained a Black man's name. Same for the jury lists under the Pittsylvania County's sitting judge. And the Henry County judge testified, "No nigger shall ever sit on a jury in my court."

"What is to be taken as evidence of criminal intent?" one juror asked.

Rives answered that "if it were proved that there were negroes in a county competent for jury service, and that the county judge had not had any negroes on his juries, that was sufficient evidence of criminal intent."

Despite all five Democratic jurors voting against it, the grand jury indicted Pittsylvania County judge James D. Coles and four others "for violation of the civil and legal rights of citizens." Rives issued arrest warrants, setting up another Supreme Court fight.

THE JUSTICES HAD ALREADY agreed to hear Virginia attorney general Field's action on behalf of his state to force the Reynolds brothers' return when, on April 8, Chief Justice Waite announced that the Court would hear oral argument on Judge Coles's indictment, which state officials had made a test case. Later that evening, Black Virginians filled the Trinity Methodist Church, a meeting place for Black Richmonders. They congregated inside the downtown church, whose basement once operated as a slave auction house, to discuss their interests.

The Founding Fathers conceived of the jury trial as the truest defender of liberty. The Declaration of Independence, for instance, maligned King George III for "depriving us . . . of the benefits of trial by jury." Before the drafting of the U.S. Constitution, twelve states had their own, all granting just one right in common—a criminal defendant's right to a jury trial. Many of Thomas Jefferson's contemporaries agreed when he remarked, "I consider trial by jury as the only anchor ever yet imagined by man, by which a government can be held to the principles of its constitution."

"[T]he colored citizens of Richmond and of the entire state of Virginia," read a meeting resolution, "owe and hereby gratefully express their thanks to Hon. Alexander Rives for his noble, upright, and courageous course in declaring and sustaining their rights in this vital and all-important matter." Rives didn't imagine himself as extraordinary, although he was—notoriety hounded him for doing what other judges refused. Rives believed that if state judges ceased excluding Black men from juries, federal judges would not meddle. "But if this be not done and a plain duty is evaded under artfully devised and misplaced scruples as to the law," he said, "you will be fomenting further disorders and conflicts." Prohibiting a new caste system from hardening required White Americans like Rives.

The folk in that nondescript two-story brick building believed that the Fourteenth Amendment, and the laws enacted to enforce it, demanded their inclusion on juries. The Supreme Court needed to require Black folk's incorporation in "We the People," to introduce them into the American family, a process starting with constitutional interpretation.

AS YOU LOOK AROUND, if you sense that you're in a basement, that's because you are, that of the State, War and Navy Building on Pennsylvania Avenue in Washington, D.C. While Strauder's health deteriorated, the Reynolds brothers languished in a jail, and federal marshals confined Judge Coles to Pittsylvania County, the Constitution sat here. Take it, four pages of animal skin parchment paper, exquisitely penned with black ink. In your hands rests the nation's governing framework.

In 1787, four years after vanquishing British forces, the union teetered on the edge of catastrophe. The weaknesses of the nation's organizing document, the Articles of Confederation, gridlocked the solving of various problems bedeviling the infant nation. The national government, for example, couldn't even fund itself. The Articles needed revising, yet each state had to agree on alterations, and the minds of thirteen states could never settle on solutions.

Each state, minus Rhode Island, sent delegates to the Constitutional Convention that assembled in Philadelphia in the summer of 1787. James Madison, a Virginian delegate, arrived with a proposal, the Virginia Plan, for a replacement document. Madison believed the convention needed to write a constitution that would facilitate a nation solving problems through the political process—one that the states would vote to adopt. If the convention floundered, a people might have declared independence, wept blood, prevailed in revolution, and seized the opportunity to chart their own course only to capsize less than five years later. They averted calamity when the document you're holding went into effect once New Hampshire became the ninth state to ratify it in June 1788.

"We the People" initially excluded Strauder, the Reynolds brothers, and the Black Virginians disallowed from juries. The Trinity, however, equipped the Constitution with the rations for its redemption, and, along with it, a nation's. Think of the Constitution as a weapon that can help fully emancipate Black people if society chooses to wield it as such. Through constitutional interpretation that redemption happens.

Constitutional interpretation involves two distinct activities, *ascer-*

*tainment* and *construction*. First, we must "ascertain" what the words in the Constitution mean. For example, the First Amendment states, "Congress shall make no law . . . abridging the freedom of speech." To what does "Congress" refer? Just the federal legislative branch? Or is Congress shorthand for the entire federal government? Does speech refer to just oral communication? The answer helps decide whether, say, a president, in the name of national security, can block a newspaper from publishing stolen classified war documents.

Second, one must "construct" the Constitution. The Constitution either prohibits, allows, or requires something. Think of constructions as rules that help determine what the Constitution prohibits, allows, or requires that judges apply in actual cases. In our First Amendment hypothetical, a judge might hold that the First Amendment always prohibits a president from restraining the press. Or a judge might conclude the amendment allows a president to restrain the press when the national security danger is sufficiently pronounced. Or a judge might deem the First Amendment inapplicable, finding that it only restricts Congress. Each is a construction—they tell us what the First Amendment prohibits, allows, or requires. Constructions give constitutional language legal effect. Judges build these constructions on the constitutional framework, turning words into something that impacts people's lives. Judges, throughout history, create, build on, sometimes discard—usually because a subsequent judge concludes a previous judge erred—then re-create constructions.

Some constitutional language reads like rules, other like standards, and some like principles. See Article I, Section 3: "The Senate of the United States shall be composed of two Senators from each State." At the Constitutional Convention, delegates from the least populous states detested the idea of providing the most populous states more power in *both* houses of Congress. The two sides compromised. The House would apportion seats based on population whereas each state would have two senators. The Constitution captured the terms of this bargain with words allowing only one interpretation and the drafters constrained future We the People.

But when the drafters used standards, like the Fourth Amendment's guarantee against "unreasonable searches and seizures," or principles like "equal protection," they allowed future Americans more discretion in what constructions they could build on the constitutional framework. When does a search become "unreasonable"? What constitutes "equal protection"? We the People determine that. Each generation—hash it out. Exchange arguments. Attempt to sway others. Rely on the Constitution as a guide to solve such political problems.

If the drafters couldn't write strict rules but wished to constrain future We the People, they could have embraced historical standards or historical principles. They could have written "no unreasonable searches and seizures according to the understandings of 1791." Such language freezes the meaning of "unreasonable searches and seizures." If people in 1791 understood searching a person's discarded trash without a warrant as reasonable, that would control then, tomorrow, and until amendment. But the drafters didn't write that.

The standards and principles in the Constitution allow each generation to debate which constructions best address the political challenges confronting We the People. To engage in the never-ending struggle to make a more perfect union. Americans must be faithful to the Constitution because it is the highest law of the land, law that articulates rules, standards, and principles. The convention delegates devised a plan that blended constraint and delegation. Sometimes stirring more constraint into the formula, narrowing the range of possible constructions. Sometimes stirring more delegation into the formula, expanding that range. By entering the arena of public debate to express how America can live up to its principles and values, We the People make the Constitution our own.

Even though standards and principles delegate more than rules do, We the People cannot load just any construction onto the framework. Let's say a judge constructed the First Amendment as protecting people not newspapers and then upheld a federal statute forbidding newspapers from criticizing Congress. The framework shatters under the weight of that construction—it betrays the Constitution. Revisiting the past helps determine what constructions the framework can bear. Let's revisit our history and ponder the constructions the Equal Protection Clause may bear.

President Andrew Jackson articulated the most indelible early usage of equal protection when vetoing legislation that would have renewed the Second Bank of the United States. A self-styled champion of the common man, Jackson derided the bank as promoting wealthy northern business interests. "In the full enjoyment of the gifts of Heaven and the fruits of superior industry, economy, and virtue, every man is equally entitled to protection by law," he wrote, adding, "There are no necessary evils in government. Its evils exist only in its abuses. If it would confine itself to equal protection, and, as Heaven does its rains, shower its favors alike on the high and the low, the rich and the poor, it would be an unqualified blessing."

Jackson discussed equal protection in a manner Americans could endorse—the government should not privilege one group above another. Although Jackson, a slaveowner, meant to deny Black skin the warm hand of impartial government, those who supported the Fourteenth Amendment sought to apply it on their behalf. When Michigan senator Jacob Howard presented the Fourteenth Amendment to his colleagues, he said, it "establishes equality before the law, and it gives to the humblest, the poorest, the most despised of the race the same rights and the same protection before the law as it gives the most powerful, the most wealthy, or the most haughty. . . . Without this principle of equal justice to all men and equal protection under the shield of the law, there is no republican government and none that is really worth maintaining."

An amendment needs approval from two-thirds of both houses of Congress *and* three-fourths of the states. Drafters could have precisely worded the Fourteenth Amendment to forbid segregation, enfranchise Black men, permit interracial marriage, bar jury discrimination. Popular opinion, though, cut against those positions, and *that* amendment never would have passed Congress.

But Americans, including federal and state politicians, could support an ambiguous equality guarantee because they disagreed on what equality specifically entailed. Some thought Black men need not the ballot. Others couldn't imagine equality without it. This fomented the need to compromise—engrave an equality principle into the Constitution, delegating to the future We the People which species of racial oppression the principle should eradicate. This would initiate an ongoing dispute about what equal treatment requires.

Although lawyers, judges, and academics have presented various methods of constitutional interpretation, this method, one Yale Law professor Jack Balkin will call framework originalism, best satisfies three goals. First, that we abide by the Constitution's original text. Second, that we abide by its spirit. And third, that we abide by We the People—interpreting the Constitution, a centuries-old document, to satisfy the needs of the living.

The interpretation of the Fourteenth Amendment, of the entire Trinity in fact, that best fulfills these three goals situates anticaste as the animating force. Anticaste constructions build on the premise that no individual should belong to a subjugated caste. Anticaste constructions target processes that relegate an identifiable group to a lower station to protect the rights of the individuals in that group. Anticaste constructions, to serve the individual, train the Fourteenth Amendment to attack castework.

The Fourteenth Amendment empowered Americans to strive for the heavens. To form social movements that clash over what creating an equal society involves. To conceive ideas and arguments regarding what rights an individual must possess in an impartial nation. Victors of that battle will win power to nominate and confirm like-minded judges who will translate arguments into constitutional constructions. The country's foundational text includes a guarantee of equality powerful enough to combat any pathogen of oppression. What it achieves depends on interpretation.

ON OCTOBER 15, 1879, the black robes of the U.S. Supreme Court paraded through a typically crowded public Capitol hallway, entered their Chamber, and sat in their dark leather chairs to hear oral argument for *Virginia v. Rives*, the Reynolds brothers case. For twelve years, Americans had lived with the Fourteenth Amendment, but the extent to which it would protect Black people, no one knew for certain. The amendment, wet clay, waited for finger to mold it.

Days after delivering his opinion in the Reynolds brothers case, Rives sent it to Chief Justice Waite, whom President Grant appointed in 1874 to replace outgoing chief justice, Salmon P. Chase. Some of Waite's colleagues initially doubted his legal prowess, agreeing with

*The Nation*'s dig that he "stands at the front rank of second-rate lawyers." "The question is an exceedingly delicate one," the sixty-three-year-old replied to Rives, concealing his views, "and your opinion certainly presents one side of the case in its strongest light."

The longest-serving justice, seventy-six-year-old Nathan Clifford, a partisan Democrat appointed in 1858 by James Buchanan, espoused the caste preservationist worldview, although failing acuity sidelined his intellect. Seventy-five-year-old Republican Noah Swayne, whom Lincoln appointed in 1862, earned the reputation as the Court's "best lawyer" and most "ardent defender of civil rights." The sixty-three-year-old Republican Samuel Miller, Lincoln's second justice, authored the *Slaughter-House Cases* opinion that negated the Privileges and Immunities Clause. Lincoln tapped Democrat Stephen Johnson Field, sixty-two years old, for his final appointment, selecting him for having opposed secession despite his Democratic Party membership, and because Lincoln, during the war, wanted to keep the western states satisfied inside the Union. In 1859, Field, as a California Supreme Court justice, upheld a state law that provided "No black or mulatto person, or Indian, shall be permitted to give evidence in favor of, or against, any white person."

William Strong, Grant's first appointment, aside from his antislavery views, left few breadcrumbs leading to a firm sense of the seventy-one-year-old's postwar racial politics. Sixty-six-year-old Republican Joseph P. Bradley, Grant's second appointment, dissented in the *Slaughter-House Cases*. Grant's third appointment, Ward Hunt, was absent. Although a stroke enfeebled him, he rebuffed retiring before reaching ten years of service to collect his federal pension. And, born into a wealthy Kentucky slave-owning family, Justice John Marshall Harlan, the Hayes-appointed Republican, had turned forty-six the day before. With just two years on the bench, he had yet to develop a reputation on race. Soon he would.

The attorneys occupied two of three wooden tables facing the justices. Virginia attorney general Field, a former Confederate soldier who left a leg on the battlefield, and William Robertson, a former judge and influential Virginia lawyer, sat at one of the end tables. They awaited their moment to argue why Rives snatching the Reynolds cases, according to the general assembly, destroyed "the right of the people of each State to protect life, liberty and property in their own way, by their own courts and officers." Their adversaries, Attorney General Charles Devens and Westel Willoughby, a Republican judge who formerly sat on the Virginia Supreme Court, represented Rives.

In 1860, the Supreme Court converted its small, damp, and poorly lit chamber—a little old room in the cellar—into a law library and relocated upstairs into a more elegant two-story space, formerly the Senate Chamber. On the white, coffered, half-dome ceiling, five smaller circular skylights bordered a central semicircular skylight, allowing sunlight to burst through and illuminate the plush brown carpet and the spectator benches fitted with red-velvet cushions. A row of green-marble columns glistened behind the justices and a carved-stone bald eagle, perched on the wall high above Chief Justice Waite, watched over the proceedings.

Field moved to the empty middle table, directly in front of Waite, to articulate his case while jousting with the justices' questions. Judge Rives's actions were "wholly without authority," Field contended. Virginia sought to prosecute the Reynolds brothers for a state crime committed on state soil. "We insist that this means an exclusive jurisdiction," Field argued in the brief he and Robertson filed before oral argument, "and under no circumstances can an inferior court, called into existence by act of Congress, ever be clothed with the power to . . . decide any question of controversy with her respecting or arising out of her sovereignty." Disputing the removal statute's applicability, Field insisted Virginia had extended the brothers equality under the law. "The right to have a jury of a particular race or color in whole or in part is not one of the rights which the statute in question secured," he argued.

Willoughby went to the middle table, advancing into the fire. The Fourteenth Amendment, he argued in his brief, guaranteed the right to "a jury constituted without discrimination against his own race or color," a right Virginia refused the Reynolds brothers. "White men may have a jury of their own race and color," he explained, whereas "negroes cannot. White men cannot be subjected to any prejudice against them on account of their race or color; negroes may be. It was just this discrimination which the Fourteenth Amendment was designed to prevent." With the brothers denied their right to equal protection, Rives properly removed their cases to federal court. Willoughby understood why a federal court intruding into affairs normally reserved to states would agitate local passions. But Virginia could avoid that "by a faithful and scrupulous observance on her part of the obligations of the Constitution in all its parts."

THE NEXT DAY, the Supreme Court heard *Ex Parte Virginia*, Judge Coles's case, with many of the same characters inhabiting the stage. The Fourteenth Amendment, Field maintained, granted no one the right to sit on juries. Thus, the Court must invalidate the anti-jury-discrimination provisions of the 1875 Act because "Congress had no power under the Constitution to make" them. Given that Coles was indicted under invalid law, Field contended, he must go free.

Devens and Assistant Attorney General Edwin Smith responded that U.S. District Attorney Lurty secured a grand jury indictment against Coles under a law the Thirteenth and Fourteenth Amendments empowered Congress to enact. Noting that every state granted residents the right to a jury trial, they argued that for the jury trial "to be worth anything, [it] must be impartial and without discrimination." Jury service, they argued, was both a duty and a right. "Without participation in this," Black people were denied "the equal protection of the law." The 1875 Act was good law, Devens and Smith argued, and Rives applied it appropriately.

ON OCTOBER 20, the Supreme Court heard oral argument for *Strauder v. West Virginia*. Davenport and Dovener along with Devens, who filed with the Court to represent Strauder's interests, sat inside the chamber. Robert White, West Virginia's attorney general, and James W. Green, hired to represent the state's interests as special counsel, sat at the opposing table.

Experiencing a career-defining moment with mere months left to live, Davenport argued that the Equal Protection Clause prevented states from enacting laws that explicitly denied racial groups their rights. The Fourteenth Amendment, moreover, granted the right to a jury impartially composed. Since West Virginia denied that right, Judge Melvin erred when refusing to remove the case to federal court.

At the West Virginia Supreme Court, the state's attorney general at the time, Henry Mathews, had argued that a legally mandated all-White jury left undisturbed Strauder's right to a fair trial. The Constitution would require a White man in Strauder's place to accept the verdict of an all-White jury, leading Mathews to rhetorically ask, "Under our law the negro gets all the rights a white man has; can he ask for more?" Yes, a jury "indifferently chosen," Davenport countered at the Supreme Court.

White followed. His legal brief reeked of the unmistakable scent that he considered Strauder's complaint baseless. "Simply because he is a Negro," White argued, "does not make out his case," intimating that Strauder, in wanting an impartially selected jury, requested a handout, illustrating how caste preservationists convert requests for equality into solicitations of charity. According to White, West Virginia excluded from jury duty those unfit for the responsibility, Black men. White noted that West Virginia discriminated against women, children, and men over sixty yet no one seriously suggested that the state denied those groups a constitutionally protected right. What made Black men special?

White and Green, worshippers of states' rights, had pledged allegiance to the Confederacy. This class of men, pained at their humiliating military defeat, grieved as their former property rose to citizen and reveled in a newfound right to equal protection. They balked at the image of the White man and the Black man collaborating as democratic co-partners and championed an openly bigoted worldview. White and Green turned this viewpoint into a construction of the Equal Protection Clause—the Fourteenth Amendment clothed Strauder in citizenship only and did not prohibit state laws that treated him as a member of a lower caste.

Attorney General Charles Devens, closing the case's oral argument, highlighted that the evil of racial oppression, like a boomerang, can hurt White people too: "It is not for a Negro jury that we are contending, nor is it our specific claim that Negroes shall constitute a part of the jury. It is simply that the jury should be impaneled without discrimination against the race of the accused, just as, if the accused were a white person, we would contend against a discrimination against *his* race." Devens completing his argument gave way to the long wait for the three decisions.

Thousands of Black folk, though, refused to wait for the Supreme Court to require White America to respect their equality. Like the Israelites departing Egypt, they journeyed toward their Canaan.

ON JANUARY 27, 1880, J. S. Faulkner, a thirty-year-old brick mason, along with more than twenty other Black folk, all from Kentucky, disembarked a train in Newton, Kansas. People throughout the nation dubbed such Black folk Exodusters, freedpeople who, in large numbers starting in the spring of 1879, fled the South in search of their Promised Land. Lore spread throughout southern Black communities that portrayed Kansas as the land of milk and honey, with forty acres, a mule, and constitutional rights. During the week of March 23, 1879, about 150 from Mississippi and Louisiana dismounted the steamer *Fannie Lewis* at Wyandotte, Kansas. On March 31, the *Joe Kinney* carried 350. A week later, the *E. H. Durfee* delivered 450 more.

The first leg of their journey on the Mississippi River brought some Exodusters to St. Louis. On the city's levee, they huddled around bonfires in the snow and freezing cold, too poor to complete the voyage. They wore inadequate clothing. Some even lacked shoes. And they tugged all their possessions in makeshift luggage. Financial help arrived, largely from St. Louis's Black community, and they completed their travels. As they awaited salvation, they recounted woes from the South.

George Rogers of Madison Parish, Louisiana, described the ever-present reality of fraud: "When you rent land in the South you have to have [your cotton] ginned at the gin of the owners of the land; that is the rule all through the South, and in this way they take all the cotton from the colored people." James Brown, also of Madison Parish, recalled the White man he rented land from telling him before the 1878 elections, "Jim, we are going to carry this thing our way, you God damn niggers have had this thing your own way long enough and we white folks are going to have it our own way or kill out all you God damn Republican niggers." J. D. Daniel remembered the murder of a politically active Black man in Warren County, Mississippi: "[I]t was in the night and they shot him and then burned him." Frederick Marshall of Natchez, Mississippi, admitted he "was afraid of my life all the time, and that is the reason I left the South. When you get to the polls to vote the white men won't let the colored men vote, and say if we go to the box to put the ballot in they will shoot us." John Cummings of Warren County, Mississippi, spoke for many when declaring, "I won't go back to the South again, because there is no living for me there and I can't get my rights there."

Such bitter reports exposed President Hayes's southern strategy, as he later conceded: "It was a piece of policy, but it failed. The conciliation matters came to a bad end but I did it to bring all our people together." He missed that the White South wanted to create a White man's government. Winning an election with Black assistance defied the central conceit of a racial caste system.

"It is not the custom in the South to concede that the negro has any political rights," the *New York Times* observed. "If he has these, the scepter must depart from the hands of the old oligarchy. It has been necessary to keep the negro in his place by forcible means. Is it any wonder, then, that he seeks another and a better country?" The most generous estimates found that twenty thousand fled to Kansas, seeking freedom from the caste system. The Supreme Court could improve the nation for the vast majority who detected no escape.

ON MARCH I, 1880, Dovener entered the Ohio County jail, greeted Strauder, and handed him a telegram revealing the Supreme Court's ruling. White Supremacy, operating through West Virginia's supreme court justices, had plotted to dismantle the Equal Protection Clause before the nine black robes could engineer life into it. If the highest Court sided with caste preservationists, southern legislators would race to their statehouses and pass copies of the West Virginia law. If the Court sanctioned excluding Black people from the jury box, moreover, what could a state not exclude Black people from? The South would test the limits, passing every piece of exclusionary legislation their imaginations conceived. Such an outcome would disfigure the anatomy of freedom Black people had imagined at the war's end. These weren't just jury discrimination cases. They involved all rights. They involved everything.

Strauder read the telegram: "Decision of Court fully in our favor."

When deciding any case, a judge focuses on the issue, or the legal question, sometimes questions, that the case raises. The majority opinion, written by Justice Strong, framed the issues simply: Does a state law limiting jury service to White men violate a right secured to a Black criminal defendant under the Fourteenth Amendment? And if such a right exists, and a state denies it, does the defendant have the right to move the case to federal court? Yes. And yes.

Answering those questions required interpreting the Equal Protection Clause, determining what it required and prevented. One could predict, Strong contended, White folk would marshal anti-Black animosity, post-slavery, toward laws that "perpetuate the distinctions that had before existed." Thus, Congress designed the Equal Protection Clause "to assure to the colored race the enjoyment of all the civil rights that under the law are enjoyed by white persons, and to give that race the protection of the [federal] government, in that enjoyment, whenever it should be denied by the States." The clause, in other words, required that states cease advantaging Whiteness—whatever civil rights White folk retained so too must Black folk.

The Court rebuked the West Virginia Supreme Court's idea that the clause could not invalidate discriminatory state laws. White Supremacy's shell game of pretending away the difference between the Equal Protection and the Privileges and Immunities Clauses failed to hoodwink the black robes. Justice Strong confirmed, however, that the Equal Protection Clause did not entitle Strauder to a jury including Black people. The clause tolerated racial imbalances, if they were not an *intentional* product of the state's scheme. Remember that word for later. *Intentional.* It shall work horrible mischief.

Strong then applied this construction, that the Equal Protection Clause forbade state intentional deprivations of civil rights based on race, to the West Virginia jury statute, finding a violation in the statutory exclusion of Black skin from jury service. Black folk had a civil right to a jury from which their race was not purposefully blocked.

Because Strauder was denied a civil right, Judge Melvin should have granted the removal petition. The Supreme Court reversed Strauder's conviction and sent his case to federal court. The Court chose this interpretation. The justices could have selected another.

Was the right to an impartially selected jury panel *really* a civil right? Before *Strauder*, the question remained unanswered. Traditionally, most deemed the right to sit on a jury a *political* right. Since neither the Civil Rights Act of 1866 nor the Fourteenth Amendment expressly guaranteed a right to an impartially selected jury panel, the Court could have denied that Congress ever created it. The Court, to locate this right, interrogated the idea of equality, arriving at the only logical conclusion—Black folk could not protect themselves absent access to the jury box. In *Strauder*, the Court built a foundational construction on the constitutional framework: a state law that expressly denies a race a civil right faces a nearly irrebuttable presumption of unconstitutionality. This construction still stands. *Strauder* informed states that they cannot pass laws limiting rights or privileges to White people. Caste preservationists would need different stones to rebuild the racial caste system.

Given *Strauder*, *Ex Parte Virginia* proved easy. Again, writing for a Court majority, Strong concluded that since the Fourteenth Amendment guaranteed the right to an impartially selected jury, Congress could enact legislation to curb jury discrimination. The judges were lawfully indicted.

*Virginia v. Rives*, though, went well for caste preservationism. Justice Strong, writing a unanimous opinion, held that the Reynolds brothers had no right to remove their cases to federal court. The removal statute, Strong asserted, "authorizes a removal of the case only before trial, not after a trial has commenced." But, Strong asked, if the state did not by law prohibit Black jury service, how could Black criminal defendants know before the trial that a court would deny their right to an impartially selected jury panel? They couldn't, he concluded. Once convicted, however, Strong allowed that the brothers could argue on appeal that the trial judge had violated their equal protection rights by excluding Black men from the jury pool.

The Court, however, plainly misread the removal statute. It provided that the removal petition must be filed "at any time before the trial or final hearing of the case." The Court disappeared this phrase, effectively fading the statute's virtue—it could force state courts to treat black people equally throughout the entirety of the trial lest they transfer their matters to federal courts.

Yet, a far more ominous part of Strong's opinion overshadowed that blatant misinterpretation. Strong observed that even if the juries that indicted and tried the brothers were all White, and even if Black men never served on Patrick County juries, that does not, by itself, demonstrate an equal protection violation. The brothers would have to prove that in their cases the jury panels were not impartially selected. Judge Rives told the grand jury in the case of the five Virginia judges to infer intentional discrimination from the prolonged absence of Black jurors. Strong spurned this logic. His construction of the Equal Protection Clause—that victims must prove an individual actor intended a discriminatory result—appeared exceedingly difficult to satisfy.

In *Virginia v. Rives*, the Court both neutered the removal statute and outlined an equal protection construction that would seemingly stymie caste abolitionism. This construction could impair Black life far beyond the jury discrimination context. Any Black person claiming to have suffered an equal protection violation would encounter this obstacle. *Strauder* shouted—the path to reconstituting a racial caste system would not proceed through explicitly discriminatory laws. But *Rives* whispered—perhaps another way existed.

A MONTH LATER, Strauder remained in jail as Davenport, thirty-nine years old, neared the end of his tuberculosis battle. He had traveled to the South, hoping the balmy climate would rehabilitate him, but returned just as ill. On April 29, 1880, Strauder wrote to Attorney General Devens for an update: "Mr. Davenport is not expecting to live but a short time. I am very anxious to have the case finally settled, while he is yet alive. I am reliably informed that he will not be able to be at the bar again. I am very feeble myself and am quite anxious to have this case disposed of."

Davenport, not two months after a career-defining achievement, lay on his deathbed. Before his passing, a West Virginia newspaper backed him for the Democratic Party's 1880 presidential nomination: "George would unite all the warring factions of the North and the South would be 'solid' for him. The 'colored troops,' especially, would sweep down all opposition as with a besom of destruction." The moderate Democrat made for an unlikely civil rights fighter but he merited that title. A lesser attorney, a lesser man, a man more like his fellow White West Virginians, might have let Strauder hang from the scaffold, preferring to maintain racial domination above dutifully defending his client and the Constitution. Davenport, with Dovener, a future Republican congressman, formulated a caste abolitionist argument, carried it to the Supreme Court, and won. Although not a caste abolitionist by philosophy, the man who started an excursion with a few years left to live bent his country in a fairer direction in his last days.

Davenport disfavored Black jurors—Black folk were equal under the law, he felt, but perhaps not equal in reality. He nonetheless felt duty-bound to defend the legal principle of Black civil equality because he, in his words, took "an oath to support the Constitution of the United States." On June 8, at his sister's Zanesville, Ohio, home, Davenport passed. His family buried him in the unassuming Northern Cemetery in Barnesville, Ohio, outside of Wheeling. His humble gray headstone reads simply "George Orrick Davenport 1841–1880."

Later that month, the prosecutor dropped the charges against Lee Reynolds. A jury of eight White men and four Black men convicted Burwell Reynolds of manslaughter, sentencing him to five years in prison. The Supreme Court had affirmed the right of an impartially selected jury panel and immediately Black men started sitting on juries, demonstrating the potency of an anticaste ruling from the black robes. On November 17, in his Danville courtroom, Judge Rives directed the prosecution to drop the charges against the five judges. A crowded and surprised courtroom applauded. Rives had made his point—the law forbids the exclusion of Black men from juries. And the Supreme Court validated him.

Per the Supreme Court's decision, West Virginia had to transfer jurisdiction of his case to federal court. On May 2, 1881, more than nine years since Strauder first entered the county jail, Strauder was released from custody. Since the grand jury that indicted him was summoned pursuant to an unconstitutional law, he had never been legally indicted. The federal judge declined to return the case to the Ohio County court and thus West Virginia couldn't retry him. When learning of his freedom, Strauder said, "George Davenport ought to be here to hear this."

The first leg of our journey focused on what The Trinity prevented the state from doing. Our next leg concerns the White masses and puts Justice Bradley at center stage. Remember that in 1873, in his *Slaughter-House Cases* dissent, he gave full effect to the Privileges and Immunities Clause, establishing his willingness to forge anticaste constructions. Two years earlier, in the 1871 case *Blyew v. United States*, he likewise demonstrated a readiness to interpret civil rights law in ways that would best serve the freedpeople.

That case concerned John Blyew and George Kennard, two White men who, on August 29, 1868, chopped a Black family to death in the family's Kentucky home. Because an 1860 Kentucky law prohibited Black people from testifying in state courts against White defendants, Black witnesses couldn't testify against Blyew and Kennard in a state prosecution. Federal prosecutors, under the federal removal statute, transferred the case on behalf of the victims to federal court and secured death sentences against both. A Supreme Court majority found that the federal court wrongly exercised jurisdiction because "only living persons could request removal."

Justice Bradley, in a stirring dissent, explained why he would have upheld the murder convictions. The Thirteenth Amendment, he argued, did more than end slavery—it provided Black folk civil equality, and empowered Congress to conquer the various ways in which the race suffered from legal disadvantages. "The power to enforce the amendment by appropriate legislation must be a power to do away with the incidents and consequences of slavery," he wrote, "and to instate the freedmen in the full enjoyment of that civil liberty and equality which abolition of slavery meant."

Let's proceed to our next leg, which starts just two decades after plucky colonists declared independence.

# Second Leg:
# The Protection Retraction

THIS, THE SECOND LEG of our journey, will climax in 1883 with the Supreme Court case of a Black woman, Sallie J. Robinson. It commences, though, on February 14, 1793, at the nation's capital, Philadelphia, inside the two-story, brick Congress Hall. In this bland, earth-toned first-floor room, we are observing the House of Representatives. Here, congressmen don white-powdered wigs. Work at mahogany desks. Sit on studded leather chairs. The body had shut its galleries earlier, blocking the public from hearing "confidential communications," before opening them, allowing us spectators.

From the second-floor fancier Senate Chamber arrives a message informing the House that yesterday President George Washington, recently reelected, signed "An Act respecting fugitives from justice, and persons escaping from the service of their masters," what the nation will call the Fugitive Slave Act of 1793.

The 1788 kidnapping of John Davis, a Black man living free in Pennsylvania, taken by three White men to Virginia to toil in bondage, sparked the saga that roused Congress to pass the act. The governors of the two states squabbled through letters about Davis's return and the extradition of his three abductors, entangling in their fray the new president who then looped in Congress. Pro-slavery lawmakers exploited this opportunity to invigorate Article IV, Section 2 of the Constitution, the Fugitive Slave Clause: "No Person held to Service or Labour in one State, under the Laws thereof, escaping into another, shall, in Consequence of any Law or Regulation therein, be discharged from such Service or Labour, but shall be delivered up on Claim of the Party to whom such Service or Labour may be due."

In sin-disguising prose, the clause protected slaveowners' property rights. By committing the national government to safeguarding proslavery interests, this clause soothed the southern psyche even as northern sentiment backpedaled from man owning man. When Congress enacted the Fugitive Slave Act of 1793, which provides protocols by which slaveowners can recover runaway enslaved people, the clause served as the basis—remember Congress can pass a law only if the Constitution empowers it.

Yet, the Fugitive Slave Clause does not explicitly grant Congress enforcement power. Such language exists elsewhere in Article IV. Section 1, for example, stipulates that "Congress may by general Laws" require that any state give "Full Faith and Credit" to the "public Acts, Records, and judicial Proceedings of every other State." Given that Article I details legislative power, and the Fugitive Slave Clause appears in Article IV, one could argue, and plenty of abolitionists will, that the Constitution did not extend Congress the power to enforce the clause.

Justice Joseph Bradley's bloodline courses through this era. His sixth great paternal grandfather, Francis Bradley, sailing from England, settled in the New Haven colony in 1638. Bradley's paternal grandfather, in 1791, relocated the family to upstate New York. And a dozen miles southwest of Albany, on March 14, 1813, Philo and Mercy Howland Bradley will welcome a future justice. The eldest of eleven, Joseph grows up in a tight-knit family on a farm in the Helderberg Mountains ensconced by wondrous greenery, the Catskill Mountains beckoning in the distance.

In 1842, three years after Bradley launches his legal career in New Jersey, the Supreme Court will uphold the constitutionality of the Fugitive Slave Act of 1793 in *Prigg v. Pennsylvania*. Justice Joseph Story, writing the majority opinion, affirms Congress's authority to enforce the Fugitive Slave Clause. Ingest his reasoning. By explaining the disposition with which a judge should construct the Constitution, this leg requires understanding it.

How, then, are we to interpret the language of the clause? The true answer is, in such a manner as, consistently with the words, shall fully and completely effectuate the whole objects of it. If, by one mode of interpretation, the right must become shadowy and unsubstantial, and without any remedial power adequate to the end, and by another mode, it will attain its just end and secure its manifest purpose, it would seem . . . that the latter ought to prevail. No court of justice can be authorized so to construe any clause of the constitution as to defeat its obvious ends, when another construction, equally accordant with the words and sense thereof, will enforce and protect them.

*Prigg* concerns Pennsylvania's Personal Liberty law, which prohibits slavecatchers from capturing runaway enslaved people and carrying them beyond state borders without following certain protocols and receiving permission from a state judge. Such laws protect free Black people but complicate slavecatching.

Justice Story will explain that a justice must find the rights the Constitution grants and then choose interpretations that enliven them with muscle and bone. The Court could hold that Congress lacked authority to pass the Fugitive Slave Act of 1793 because of the absence of an enforcement provision in the Fugitive Slave Clause, but chooses an interpretation that helps fortify slaveowners' rights. In defense of its Personal Liberty Law, Pennsylvania articulated a states' rights claim, arguing that a state must have a say in the slave status of the people within its borders. The Supreme Court rejects that argument and invalidates Pennsylvania's law, ruling that its additional procedural protections for accused runaway enslaved people weaken slaveowners' rights and conflict with federal law, the Fugitive Slave Act of 1793.

Decades later, Congress will enact the far more robust Fugitive Slave Act of 1850, which, among other things, obliges the federal government to aid the recapture and prosecution of runaway enslaved people, further entwining federal tentacles into slavery's administration. The law even states that "all good citizens are hereby commanded to aid and assist in the prompt and efficient execution of this law, whenever their services may be required." And any private individual who hinders that execution, like by hiding an alleged escaped enslaved person, faces criminal sanction.

In 1859, Chief Justice Roger B. Taney will write in *Ableman v. Booth* that the Fugitive Slave Act of 1850 is "in all of its provisions fully authorized by the Constitution of the United States." The Supreme Court, in other words, allows Congress to legislate directly against private individuals to protect slaveowners' rights. Remember this. From a clause without an enforcement provision, the Supreme Court chooses to permit Congress to pass broad legislation to protect slaveowners' rights.

If Congress can protect slaveowners' rights by expansively interpreting the Constitution, can it not the same way protect Black rights? In his 1857 *Dred Scott v. Sandford* opinion, Chief Justice Taney will infamously declare that Black people "had no rights which the white man was bound to respect." But a political union that initially excludes Black folk will, a decade after *Dred Scott*, require their inclusion. The Trinity will guarantee the rights necessary to secure complete Black freedom, with each amendment granting Congress the power to enforce that freedom through "appropriate legislation." Black folk will possess the identical citizenship rights as do White folk, and, like northern states that complicate slavecatching, caste preservationists who undermine Black folk's rights will violate the purported terms of the nation's *new* bargain. But will America truly revamp itself to extend Black folk the same protection of rights? Or will America remain a bargain between White folk?

This leg of our journey explores how the Supreme Court evaluates congressional legislation enacted to enforce The Trinity. Justice Bradley, the author of dissents in *Blyew* and the *Slaughter-House Cases*, which expansively interpret the 1866 Civil Rights Act and the Fourteenth Amendment, will author the majority opinion in the 1883 decision concerning Sallie Robinson. The man whose vision for The Trinity in the 1870s meets the exigencies of a battered people crafts the most influential pre-1890s opinion affecting Black freedom.

How fortuitous.

Caste abolitionism will need a justice who grasps how to effectuate The Trinity's potential and prevent the Ku Klux Klan from lynching it as if it has Black skin.

ON THE AFTERNOON OF APRIL 4, 1869, George W. Tillon, a White man in his mid-thirties, stood behind a distillery in New Bern, North Carolina, a city straddling the Neuse River, and drew his sword. Tillon asked Joseph Parrott, a White man in his mid-twenties, along with several others in the group, if they "believed in a white man's government."

Yes, they answered.

Tillon asked "if [they] promised faithfully to labor for the overthrow of the Republican Party."

They did.

Tillon blindfolded each with handkerchiefs, brought them inside the distillery, and made them kneel. All took "a solemn obligation to go to the rescue of a brother member giving a cry of distress, under any circumstances, even to risk [their] own lives; to resist by force of arms if necessary, any aggression of [their] legal rights; to restore this Government to the control of white men, by force if necessary."

After Tillon ordered them to stand, a different man taught them the organization's secret signs, cries of distress, and passwords. They were now, he told them, members of a Ku Klux Klan chapter. Other chapters sprouted up throughout the South following the war, leaving trails of corpses and screeches of fear.

Marjorie Jones, once enslaved in North Carolina, explained that Klansmen "were terrible dangerous. They wear long gowns, touch the ground. They ride horses through the town at night and if they find a Negro that tries to get nervy or have a little bit for himself, they lash him nearly to death and gag him and leave him to do the bes' he can," she remembered. "[T]hem was bad times, them was bad times. I know folks think the books tell the truth, but they shore don't. Us poor niggers had to take it all."

Democracy begs that the loser accept the winner's victory and recognize that even in defeat, both sides share a commitment to a self-governing experiment too vital to rip apart. But after the war, to White southerners, the baby, democracy, wasn't worth nurturing if they had to co-parent with Black folk and carpetbaggers—northerners who relocated to the South after the war to make a new home. The Klan, a vile weed, grew from this terrain. Through carnage, Klansmen sought to foil Reconstruction governments and return the South to its rightful owners. Perhaps Klan gowns would succeed where Confederate uniforms failed.

On March 7, 1870, North Carolina's Republican governor wrote President Grant. "There exists in this State a secret, oath-bound, armed organization, which is hostile to the State government and to the Government of the United States," scribed William Woods Holden. "Bands of these armed men ride at night through various neighborhoods, whipping and maltreating peaceable citizens, hanging some, burning churches, and breaking up schools which have been established for the colored people. These outrages are almost invariably committed on persons, white and colored, who are most devoted in their feelings and conduct to the [federal government]."

Holden's words described much of the South—armed terrorists in sheets on horseback drowning state Republican governments in anarchy. The Klan, the "terrorist arm of the Democratic Party," had caused the defeats of Republican candidates through voter intimidation and brownbeat state officials into discharging their duties in ways the Klan demanded. The Trinity granted new rights but they were only black ink on tan parchment. They lacked muscle and bone. Against masked marauders and other incendiaries, southern law enforcement proved impotent at protecting Black people and their White Republican allies from violent castework.

In the meantime, a black robe falls onto the shoulders of a new justice.


ON MARCH 23, 1870, the day after the Senate confirmed Bradley to the seat vacated by a feeble Justice Robert Cooper Grier, Bradley entered the old Supreme Court Chamber for his swearing in.

A teacher once asked a young Bradley, "Would you rather be a Judge or a King?"

"A Judge," he responded. "Because he sits in judgment of the King."

Recalling his upbringing, Bradley penned, "If one lesson more than any other was stamped upon my early existence, it was the sanctity of home and affections, and absolute justice and charity to all," suggesting an inclination toward a judicial philosophy amendable to the cause of freedom. "Anything mean, deceitful or dishonest was regarded with utmost abhorrence in our family circle, and received prompt and decided condemnation."

Entering Rutgers College in 1833 to prepare for a life in ministry, Bradley found his true calling in the law. *"The choice is before us,"* a conciliatory Bradley advised before the war, "DISUNION, with probable civil war; or CONCESSION and peace." Bradley, a well-respected attorney by then, embraced the latter and in December 1860, proposed two constitutional amendments. His thirteenth amendment would require the prohibition of slavery in territories north of the 36°30′ line and stipulated that after twenty years, each state could choose whether to permit slavery in its own borders. His fourteenth amendment would have compelled a county to return fugitive enslaved people or the slaveowner could sue any noncompliant county in any federal court to receive full compensation. Bradley found many receptive ears after presenting his recommendations to a House of Representatives task force charged with developing a slavery compromise. When the Confederates attacked Fort Sumter, though, Bradley backed the Union, stating "there can be no question or vacillation now" and accepted emancipation for practical and political reasons.

In spring 1867, Bradley, for the first time, visited the South, New Orleans, conceiving strong opinions on its inhabitants. "The Negroes would not stay on the plantations and will refuse to work them," he wrote, "and without them, the plantations will become a desert waste." In White southerners, Bradley smelled a flawed population: "They look upon themselves as a conquered people and I fear will have to suffer still more before they will give up their cherished notions of a great Southern Confederacy."

By 1869, Bradley coveted, above all else, a black robe. A year later, the short, small-framed man stood on the bright red carpet with gold stars, raised his right hand toward the vaulted ceiling, and swore "to never have borne arms against the United States" and "to do equal justice to the poor and the rich." The Supreme Court received a fifty-seven-year-old justice who would supply its most penetrating and methodical intellect in the 1870s and 1880s.

Bradley's face, an observer once wrote about him, "denoted intellectual force and great firmness. In repose it was grave, but the moment that he spoke (and his voice was deep and penetrating) his eye kindled, and his countenance was full of animation." Bradley "had a strong temper," the observer continued, "at times even was passionate, though his passion quickly subsided." He possessed an "old school" manner, meaning he was "reserved toward strangers" and to his friends he was "frank and genial."

During Bradley's first weeks on the Court, Congress debated legislation that would enforce The Trinity and check southern anti-Black violence.

PUT YOURSELF IN THE POSITION of Republican congressmen. Through your party's exertions, you made Black freedom a national responsibility. But bloodcurdling screams from the South awakened you. Hooligans draped in sheets were murdering, burning, and menacing your labors away. And unless you countered terrorism with federal brawn, your enemies would defile your art beyond recognition. You could express your fears simply—violence could prevent the freedpeople from experiencing their civil and voting rights, allowing the Democratic Party to reclaim southern state legislatures and governor's mansions and then, through law, asphyxiate Black freedom. But if you could maintain open voting booths, handcuff the violence, and safeguard Black freedom, you could seal the victories of the Civil War. Here, though, state law and state officials did not ignite the fire you wished to extinguish. No, you want to enact federal laws to snuff the evil perpetrated by private individuals. And you believe The Trinity, which your party masterminded, allows this.

On February 21, 1870, Ohio representative John Bingham, the Fourteenth Amendment's principal author, introduced in the House a bill to enforce voting and civil rights. On May 20, senators considered their version. In the spacious rectangular Senate Chamber, thirty-five feet beneath a cast iron ceiling that showcased twenty-one glass panels that allowed sunlight to burst down, Republican senators debated how to guarantee the freedpeople's rights as Democrats sought to gaslight them into believing they were attempting to cure an imagined disorder. Senators complained about this room. Shoddy acoustics. Poor lighting. But below the unattractive blue-upholstered galleries that wrapped around the walls, Republicans felt the situation bleak enough to deliberate for twenty hours. Two men delivered speeches in the Senate's drafty chamber worth revisiting. John Pool, North Carolina Republican, delivered the first.

"That the United States Government has the right to go into the States and enforce the fourteenth and fifteenth amendments is, in my judgment, perfectly clear, by appropriate legislation that shall bear upon individuals," Pool said.

"I cannot see that it would be possible for appropriate legislation to be resorted to except as applicable to individuals who violate or attempt to violate these provisions. Certainly, we cannot legislate here against States." Congress, in other words, had to target private individuals to address this dilemma. Republicans needed to counteract the villainy of people, not just of state legislation and state actors.

"It matters not whether those individuals be officers [of the state] or whether they are acting upon their own responsibility; whether they are acting singly or in organizations," charged Pool.

"If there is to be appropriate legislation at all, it must be that which applies to individuals."

George E. Spencer, Republican Alabama senator, delivered the other speech. "The condition of the South, political and social, is truly deplorable," the attorney said. "To be a Republican, to advocate of liberty, and a supporter of the [Grant] Administration and its policy, is a heinous crime. It sets a mark upon the brow and a price upon the head. There is no such thing in the South today as freedom of speech, freedom of thought, and freedom of action, except it be in those rare localities where the inhabitants [are] all loyal."

The culture shock must have walloped the New York native. Little had improved in the South where, before the war, antislavery speech provoked antidemocratic frothing. A people not meeting basic norms of democracy, White southerners quite simply did not concede the

right to existence of outgroup members. As South Carolina governor George McDuffie trumpeted, "I would have those who oppose
slavery, if caught in our jurisdiction, put to death without benefit
of clergy." "Who dares go into the southern half of this Union and
speak of the Declaration of Independence except in whispers," abolitionist James G. Birney remarked, "and publicly insist that the object
of the Constitution—to establish justice—ought to be carried out in
practice? No one, unless he has made up his mind to be scourged like
a slave; to die; to be 'hanged like a dog.'"

After the war, that intolerance toward diversity of thought lingered, and Congress, Spencer argued, needed to fumigate the area,
making it hospitable for actual self-governing as opposed to tyranny.
"[I]t is more than manifest," Spencer said, "that in the South the Ku
Klux organization is nothing more nor less than a secret government based upon the ruins of secession, whose hostility is specially
directed against the Union, and whose [goal] is the subversion of the
reconstruction acts and the aggrandizement of political power."

The Klan, in Spencer's view, first sought to control Black labor,
but when Black folk kept true to the Republican Party, "this organization became purely political . . . banded together in the common
purpose of crushing out Republicanism and consecrating the bona
fides of the confederate cause."

"Every mail brings to us the details of some revolting tragedy,"
Spencer reported. "White and colored Unionists seized, murdered,
and their inanimate bodies inhumanly mutilated. No offender is
sought out and punished, and those few good citizens who are opposed to lawlessness tremble, lest some of the outlaws or their sym-
pathizers may guess at or read the secrets of their hearts."

Spencer wanted his party to leverage the law to ensure people's
rights. "Nothing but the most stringent of all laws and regulations
will check this era of bloodshed and dethrone this dynasty of the
knife and bullet."

On May 31, 1870, two months after the Fifteenth Amendment's
ratification, Grant signed the "Act to enforce the Fifteenth Amendment and for other purposes," anticaste legislation. The Enforcement
Act of 1870 made federal offenses of various actions that frustrated
the exercising of civil and political rights. One section punished those

preventing, on account of race, people from voting, or registering to vote. Another made Klan-like activity a crime by outlawing conspiring, banding together, or going in disguise with the intent to deprive another of federally protected rights. A month later, Congress established the Department of Justice, primarily to enforce The Trinity.

While congressional Republicans rose to meet the challenge, Democrats planned a counterstrike.

THE DAY AFTER GRANT SIGNED the 1870 Enforcement Act, 450 members of Ohio's Democratic Party convened inside Comstock's Opera House for the state's party convention. Although the tasks of nominating candidates and framing the party's organizing principles summoned them to Columbus, the new act, what the *Cincinnati Enquirer* labeled "the bill of abominations," overshadowed the proceedings. "[W]e regard the act recently passed by Congress to enforce the 'Fifteenth Amendment,'" the party's platform stated, "as unconstitutional, unjust and oppressive" and an "invasion of the rights of the States, subversive of the best interests of the people, and [we] therefore demand its unconditional repeal."

Nationally, Democrats were grappling with political irrelevance, and winning contests in southern states would assist the party's rescue. In the 41st Congress, which met from March 1869 to March 1871, the Democrats claimed around a quarter of the seats. The states' rights party lacked feasible means to attract southern Black voters, and reducing them to nonvoters would help.

On a stage decorated with flags and Andrew Jackson and George Washington portraits, Lewis Campbell Davis, a fifty-nine-year-old former congressman, presided as the convention chair.

"Fellow citizens," he said, greeting the audience, "[i]t is the mission of the Democratic party to restore to the States the rights that have been wrongfully taken away from them."

Campbell's speech signaled something with which the Republican Party needed to reckon—in the national tug-of-war, the Democrats would strain to stop Republicans from overhauling the original states' rights governing model. They would display an indefatigable spirit in preventing the Republican Party from enlarging the national government's zone of influence in service of Black freedom. The war of wills had already begun.

WATCH AS NEARLY THIRTY MEN on horses coming from various directions converge at the town square here in Eutaw, the seat of Greene County, Alabama. The clock just struck eleven on this Thursday evening of March 31, 1870, about two months before Grant signs the 1870 Enforcement Act. This village of about two thousand, nearly 80 percent Black, sits on the western half of the Black Belt, a region of the American South defined by its fertile dark soil and the Black bodies who farmed it before and after emancipation. The men, armed with guns and sabers, are wearing oversized black robes, a few adorned with gold and silver embellishments. Their faces are covered. Their horses too. As they reach the public square, the few onlookers appreciate they are witnessing the Klan, an active plague here, wrecking Black schools, terrifying teachers. Burning. Killing. The high concentration of Black folk in Eutaw, a well of voters for Republicans, keeps attracting the Klan. By this night, Klan intimidation has drained the county to fewer than a dozen White Republicans.

What brought us here tonight began on December 18, 1869, when Samuel Snoddy, a White Democrat, lay dead on a road with his throat slit ear to ear, his skull wearing multiple fractures, his seventy dollars missing. The police arrested three Black men, Sam Caldwell, Henry Miller, and Caldwell's father, Sam Colvin, who was later released for want of evidence. Somehow, Caldwell and Miller escaped from jail. Caldwell, thereafter, vanished, almost certainly killed. Murder certainly found Henry Miller. And Sam Colvin, already released, hung from a tree, riddled with sixteen bullet holes. Witnesses fingered the Klan specifically for Colvin's lynching. Alexander Boyd, the thirty-five-year-old White Republican Greene County solicitor, investigated these cases, believed he knew who had slayed Colvin, and had let slip that he acquired enough evidence to arrest his executioners. The Cleveland House hotel sits right in front of us. Boyd is inside.

Sleeping.

Using hand signals to keep their prey unaware, the leaders of this Klan posse direct lookouts to stand guard at various points in the vicinity while others dismount their horses in front of the hotel. About a dozen storm inside, head to the main office, and bogart the clerk to escort them upstairs. Once there, they demand the clerk open Boyd's room as a Klansman holds a grass rope.

When the clerk opens the door, men barge in, awakening Boyd. He resists, causing the expected uproar of a man wrestling for survival, scuttling the plot to drag an easily overpowered mark outside and hang him. Then a pistol fires once. After a minute or two of silence more shots bang. Watch as a bleeding Boyd staggers into the hallway where Klansmen unload their final bullets. Three shots to his head. Four to his abdomen. Boyd's remains sprawled along the second-floor hallway. Five minutes after entering, the Klansmen rumble from the hotel, mount their horses, and thunder away. About fifteen miles north of Eutaw, the Klan, that same night, murders James Martin, a politically prominent Black Republican, gunning him down as he flees his house.

Before Boyd's slaying, one citizen pleaded with the Republican governor, William Hugh Smith, for aid: "In the name of God, have mercy and send some protection. I will suggest that our county be put under Marshall [sic] law. Do away with these little civil officers, who are afraid, not brave enough to do their duty." Smith refused, suspecting that would rile the native White folk, a typical political miscalculation of Reconstruction-era Republican governors. They dreamed of coaxing White conservatives into the Republican tent and assumed that requesting federal troops, a strong show of force, would discourage their entrance.

But Boyd's murder convinces Smith to seek federal troops, and, under the command of General Samuel Crawford, ten soldiers will station near Eutaw. Smith also dispatches to Eutaw an investigator, John A. Minnis, who doubts he will ever arrest Boyd's murderers. He's right—no one faces prosecution for the killing because, as one Greene County Republican official explains, "protection from the Ku Klux Klan could not be relied on from the court system because Our Grand Juries indict us & protect them from indictment." Over the next few months, the Klan will slaughter others throughout Alabama ahead of Election Day.

Despite Klan violence, Greene County Republicans will post handbills announcing a Republican rally on October 25 in Eutaw ahead of November voting, with scheduled speakers Governor Smith and U.S. Senator Willard Warner. Democrats will then post handbills announcing *their* intentions to hold a rally the same day, at the same time, at the same location, the county courthouse.

HERE IN DOWNTOWN EUTAW on the morning of October 25, this two-story Greek Revival courthouse will separate the Democratic and Republican gatherings. The Klan, per local lore, burned down the previous courthouse two years ago because it housed records of more than a thousand lawsuits freedmen had filed against White planters. The county rebuilt it at the same location, following nearly the same blueprint, replacing wood with stucco-covered brick.

Yesterday, October 24, Republicans gathered at the courthouse in Livingston, in neighboring Sumter County, likewise a hotbed of Klan degeneracy. At that mostly Black-attended rally, headlined by Governor Smith, Senator Warner, and former governor Lewis Parsons, a group of White Democrats stood off to the side, heckling. When Governor Smith started his remarks, about twelve White men raced through the courthouse toward the rally. One brandished a long knife and stood next to Smith. Keeping calm, he ended his address. The Republican leaders adjourned and eventually boarded their Eutaw-bound train, riding with whiskey-drinking men, some of the same who disrupted the event.

Minutes ago, Republican leaders—County Judge William Miller, uncle of Alexander Boyd, Congressman Charles Hays, and S. W. Cockrell, a local lawyer—sent a note to the Democratic leaders, asking if they wished to debate, seeking an activity that might quell any tempests. "To The President of the Democratic Club," the note read, "We propose to appoint a committee of two to confer with a committee on your part of two, to arrange terms of discussion today." Two Democratic leaders, John Jefferson Jolly, a Klansman, and J. G. Pierce, responded by note spurning the offer, scribing, "the issues as to men or measures in that canvass were not debatable."

Now even more concerned, Governor Smith and the other

Republican leaders solicit help from the sheriff and the military commander, General Crawford. Hays begs the two to post troops in clear view of the courthouse. Parsons and Miller concur. The sheriff thinks that might prove too provocative and, instead, parks troops a half mile from the courthouse. With dread, the Republicans head to the courthouse to begin their rally.

The Republicans place a table outside the circuit clerk's office window, a makeshift speaker's stand, and start twenty minutes after the Democrats commenced their rally about 150 feet away. Once the two-hour Democratic gathering of two hundred closes, some attendees straggle southward to the Republican affair of about eighteen hundred, nearly all Black, as Senator Warner nears the conclusion of his speech. These Democrats yell "damned liar" and "damned carpet-bagger." Parsons follows Senator Warner and takes the stand.

During his speech, a White Democrat shouts, "Let me kill the God-damned old son of a bitch."

"Don't shoot yet," his friends interject. "[I]t's not time."

After Parsons concludes, the final planned speech, Republicans in the crowd goad Hays into speaking, amidst the now rowdy and drunk Democrats menacing near the event's periphery. Hays unnerved White conservatives because the former Democrat and secessionist joined the Republicans in 1867 and won a House seat.

Not long after Hays jumps onto the speaker's stand, a White Democrat yanks him to the ground. The sheriff darts forward to arrest that assailant as Black crowd members approach to defend Hays, a few pulling out knives. A rapid fire of gunshots blasts from inside the courthouse, with some coming from the window directly behind the speaker's table. The bullets zip over the heads of the Black rallygoers, hitting no one.

Jolly screams, "Go in, boys; now is your time."

This round of gunfire flies into the crowd. Black attendees stampede through the fence that surrounds the courthouse. The White Democrats form a line and discharge perhaps as many as two hundred bullets at their backs. The Democrats also point guns at Parsons, Hays, and other Republican leaders, but the sheriff intervenes, keeping all uninjured. Within a few minutes the federal troops rush to the scene, ceasing the bedlam. Senator Warner will later remark:

"a sight so painful as that, to see man after man in that crowd falling and scrambling away with his wounds, while a set of demons stood deliberately firing and shooting them down, is such a spectacle I hope never to see again." Estimates will vary, but the best peg the number of deaths at four and the number of wounded between twenty-four to fifty-four, all Black Republicans.

In the November election, Hays will retain his House seat although he loses Greene County by thirty-five votes. Previously, he had won the county by nearly twenty-five hundred. Governor Smith loses reelection by fewer than fifteen hundred votes. Eutaw alone should have rocketed him past his Democratic challenger. This riot, along with other violent convulsions and widespread Democratic fraud, will help the Democrats recapture the governorship and redeem the state. But with the 1870 Enforcement Act, federal prosecutors could at least imprison perpetrators and dissuade copycats.

EIGHT DAYS AFTER THE RIOT, John Preston Southworth, U.S. attorney for the Southern District of Alabama, indicted twenty-one White Democrats for their involvement. He based his charges on the sixth section of the 1870 Enforcement Act, which made a federal offense of two or more persons conspiring together "to injure, oppress, threaten, or intimidate" a citizen with the "intent to prevent or hinder his . . . enjoyment of any right . . . granted or secured to him by the Constitution or [federal law]." The charges accused the defendants of conspiring to interfere with both the right to peaceably assemble of the Black Republicans in attendance and the right to free speech of the Republican speakers. The defense attorneys, in response, filed a demurrer, or an objection to the charges, that argued that even if the prosecution's factual allegations were true, that would still be insufficient to establish a valid prosecution. More to the point, the defense maintained that the alleged actions violated no rights granted by federal law or the Constitution, and the court should therefore dismiss the charges.

On May 1, 1871, in a federal courtroom inside the granite three-story Classical Revival U.S. Custom House and Post Office in downtown Mobile, two judges heard the arguments on the demurrer, Fifth

Circuit Judge William B. Woods, appointed by President Grant, and Lincoln-appointed district court judge, Richard Busteed. The federal court system split the nation into nine independent circuits. Each had various district court judges. Above them—the circuit judges, one per circuit. And each circuit received one assigned Supreme Court justice. A district court judge alongside the circuit judge heard most circuit court cases. Sometimes a Supreme Court justice heard a case solo or in tandem. Republican lawmakers expected this two-judge system, with one divorced from local passions, would mitigate bias. A week after Justice Bradley took his oath of office, Chief Justice Chase assigned him to the Fifth Circuit, which covered Texas, Louisiana, Mississippi, Alabama, Georgia, and Florida.

After hearing from witnesses, Woods believed that the White Democrats prevented the Republicans at the Eutaw rally from enjoying their First Amendment rights. But Woods fretted that the Supreme Court might disfavor a prosecution of private individuals rather than state actors. Thus, beginning in December 1870, he exchanged with Bradley letters regarding the 1870 Act.

Bradley counseled Woods to focus on motives. The mere act of shooting violated local law, but improper motivation could make a shooting an Enforcement Act case. As Bradley captured in his personal notes, "If this dastardly and savage act was the result of a conspiracy to intimidate the persons attending the meeting from voting at the coming election, it seems to me that it was . . . punishable as a felony under the 6th section [of the Enforcement Act]." The Bill of Rights involve limitations on the federal government. The First Amendment, for example, forbids the federal government, not the state, from infringing religious freedoms. In a letter to Woods, Bradley argued that because of the Fourteenth Amendment, Congress could pass laws to secure those rights against state infringement.

"No State shall make or enforce any law which shall abridge the privileges or immunities of citizens of the United States," Bradley wrote. "Now, the privileges or immunities of the citizens of the United States here referred to," he continued, "are undoubtedly those which may be [deemed] fundamental; and among those I suppose we are safe in including those which, in the Constitution are expressly secured to the people, either as against the action of the Federal Government or State Governments. . . . Viewed simply as a riot, it was offense against the municipal law only; but viewed as a riot to intimidate persons and prevent them from exercising the right of suffrage, guaranteed to them by the Fifteenth Amendment to the Constitution; it was a violation of that."

Woods, in his next letter, asked Bradley "how the Fourteenth Amendment applied to the Eutaw rioters' case." In the previous leg of our journey, we discussed how constitutional interpretation involved two distinct activities: ascertainment and construction. Bradley's response exemplified ascertainment in the context of what "deny" meant in the Equal Protection Clause—"no state shall . . . deny to any person within its jurisdiction equal protection of the laws."

Bradley responded: "Congress has a right, by appropriate legislation, to enforce and protect such fundamental rights, against unfriendly or insufficient State legislation. I say unfriendly or insufficient: for the XIVth Amendment not only prohibits the making or enforcing of laws which shall abridge the privileges of the citizen, but prohibits the States from denying to all persons within its jurisdiction the equal protection of the laws. Denying includes inaction as well as action. And denying the equal protection of the laws includes the omission to protect as well as the omission to pass laws for protection." Consistent with what the congressmen who wrote and voted for the Fourteenth Amendment meant with the word "deny," Bradley ascertained the meaning of deny as impacting states in two ways—forbidding states from not providing protection either through transgression or inactivity.

According to Bradley's construction of the Fourteenth Amendment, the privileges and immunities of the citizens of the United States were fundamental rights, including those conveyed in the Bill of Rights, and, furthermore, the Equal Protection Clause empowered Congress to pass laws to protect those rights should states, either through acts of commission or omission, deny them. Moreover, Congress, because of the Fourteenth Amendment, could pass laws that operate on private individuals. "Since it would be unseemly for Congress to interfere directly with state enactments," Bradley wrote, "and as it cannot compel the activity of state officials, the only appropriate legislation it can make is that which will operate directly on offenders and offenses to protect the rights the Amendment secures."

This dramatically refashioned the relationship between states and the federal government, obliterating the states' rights paradigm. But, Bradley wrote, "it must be remembered that it is for the purpose of protecting federal rights: and these must be protected whether it interferes with the [state] laws or [state] administration of laws." Bradley assured Woods of the constitutionality of the 1870 Enforcement Act and that Congress intended to punish the horror seen in the Eutaw riots.

Before Woods and Busteed heard oral argument for the demurrer, Congress buttressed the 1870 Enforcement Act twice. In February 1871, Congress modestly strengthened the first with the Second Enforcement Act.

Still, the times cried for more.

In spring 1871, President Grant wrote James G. Blaine, House Speaker, begging for something heartier. "There is a deplorable state of affairs existing in some portions of the South demanding the immediate attention of Congress," Grant alerted. "If the attention of Congress can be confined to the single subject of providing means of protection of life and property to those Sections of the Country where the present civil authority fails to secure that end, I feel that we should have such legislation."

Grant's instruction plunged congressional Republicans into effort. Acknowledging that anti-Black violence operated mainly through private individuals and that direct blame could be placed neither at the doorstep of state legislatures nor the feet of state officers, Republicans again legislated against private individuals. Two months after the Second Enforcement Act, Congress passed the Enforcement Act of April 20, 1871, dubbed the Ku Klux Klan Act. It effectively outlawed the Klan and similar organizations that conspired to prevent citizens from enjoying their civil and political rights. The second section, which furnished the act its furthest reach, detailed more than twenty "specific practices defined as illegal, including using force and intimidation to interfere with any citizen's exercise of voting rights in federal elections."

When Justice Woods delivered his opinion denying the demurrer on May 2, 1871, inside the federal courtroom, he cribbed heavily from Bradley's letters. The defendants went to trial in January 1872. The jury of eight White and four Black men deliberated sixty-nine minutes before reaching a not guilty verdict, with the ever-present threat of Klan reprisal possibly preventing convictions. Although enforcement prosecutions floundered in Alabama, in South Carolina they dismantled the Klan, proving that vigorous administration of anticaste laws can thwart White Supremacy's will. As one Black woman who experienced the Klan's fall said, "De Klu Klux Klan sprung right up out of de earth, but de Yankees put a stop ter dat by puttin' so many of dem in jail."

Bradley's view of the Privileges and Immunities Clause, the view he articulated to Woods, succumbed in 1873 in the *Slaughter-House Cases*, a year after the mixed-race jury acquitted alleged perpetrators of the Eutaw riot. But Bradley could restore his deceased vision by cajoling his colleagues to reach the same result by relying wholly on a forceful construction of the Equal Protection Clause. And that's what I want to discuss with you inside the space most connected to The Trinity.

AS WE ENTER THE HOUSE CHAMBER on April 14, 1873, the day the Supreme Court effectively pilfered the Privileges and Immunities Clause, the rostrum at the front of the room summons our focus. Made of white marble, it evokes the ages when the Greeks and Romans manipulated the same material into coliseums and temples. The grandiosity of the rostrum roars, "in this place, we produce great achievements." And with The Trinity, the Republicans did.

When we met inside the basement of the State, War and Navy Building during our previous leg, we concentrated on the "equal" in "equal protection." Concentrated on what creating an equal world entailed. Now, inside the less-than-two-decades-old House Chamber, let's explore "protection," the government's responsibility to *protect* life, liberty, and pursuit of happiness. "Equal protection" contains two words. A proper construction of it allocates meaning to both. Understanding what "protection" embraces begins with the Magna Carta.

Signed by King John of England in 1215, the Magna Carta affirmed the principle that the law bound everyone, including the king. Its fortieth clause reads, "to no one [will we] deny or delay right or justice." These words convey a basic tenet that traces back to medieval Europe—that the head of state owed to all protection over person and property. Leaders have an affirmative obligation to the citizenry. Protection mustn't be denied. Mustn't be delayed.

This thinking excited the pens of English philosophers Thomas Hobbes and John Locke, whose prose developed the leading brains of America's Revolutionary War era. Hobbes and Locke believed that government existed to provide people protection from ruination and open the gates to prosperity. As the Declaration of Independence proclaims, "all men are created equal, that they are endowed, by their Creator, with certain unalienable rights, that among these are life, liberty, and the pursuit of happiness.—That to secure these rights, governments are instituted among men, deriving their just powers from the consent of the governed." When beings combine to forge a society for their mutual benefit, they believe the joint enterprise will protect individual rights. When a government miscarries at providing that protection—an affirmative duty—it breaches a foundational obligation.

Late-eighteenth- and early-nineteenth-century state constitutions embraced this conception of "protection." Take Article X of the Massachusetts constitution, which provided, "each individual of the society has a right to be protected by it in the enjoyment of his life, liberty, and property according to standing laws." The Pennsylvania constitution, similarly, articulated the right of each person "to be protected in the enjoyment of life, liberty, and property." These constitutions establish that "protection" had long embraced an affirmative duty to safeguard fundamental rights. Pro-slavery thinkers endorsed this principle and employed it for their cause, pleading that the government must affirmatively protect their right to own humans and that federal government inaction on that matter denied that protection.

Decades later, abolitionists appropriated this logic on behalf of enslaved people. Charles Olcott, an Ohio abolitionist, said, "What

abolitionists demand as naked justice is, that the benefit and protection of these just laws be extended to all human beings *alike*, to
the colored as well as the white . . . and that all mankind be allowed
the *same* legal rights and protection without regard to color or other
physical peculiarities." Theodore Dwight Weld, Olcott's mentor,
contended that a government carried the duty "to prevent by legal
restraints one class of men from seizing upon another class, and rob-
bing them at pleasure of their earnings, their time, their liberty, their
kindred, and the very use and ownership of their own persons." Put
differently, abolitionists maintained that governments bore responsibility for both providing protection to all persons and preventing
one group from trampling the rights of another. A failure at either
*denied* equal protection. That's what *deny* meant to them. The drafters of the Fourteenth Amendment mined this history, implanting
abolitionist doctrine in the Constitution, giving a nation the arrows
to shoot for a caste-less society.

The people of Alabama formed a government to protect life, liberty, and pursuit of happiness. The Equal Protection Clause reads,
"No state shall . . . deny to any person within its jurisdiction the equal
protection of the laws." Did Black Alabamians, constantly hounded
by Klan sheets, receive that protection from the state?

No, right?

Did that lack of protection embolden the caste preservationists
who shot Black Alabamians as they fled from the Greene County
courthouse?

Yes, right?

You cannot exercise your civil rights without being safe in your
person. Black folk could not move as equals without state protection.
And Alabama failed to provide it, therefore they denied it. As Ohio
congressman William Lawrence explained in this very room, a state
could deny persons of their "absolute rights of life, security, liberty,
and property: either by prohibitory laws, or by a failure to protect
any one of them." Or take New Jersey Republican senator Frederick
T. Frelinghuysen, who affirmed that a "state denies equal protection
whenever it fails to give it." This interpretation of equal protection
lends Congress the means to involve itself with the actions of private

individuals—when the state fails to protect a definable group, like Black folk, from being degraded to an inferior caste, the federal government can interject. Must interject.

The history of the Fourteenth Amendment further demonstrates why we must construct it to empower Congress to legislate directly on private individuals. The second section of the 1866 Civil Rights Act provides "That any person who, under color of any law, statute, ordinance, regulation, or *custom*, shall subject, or cause to be subjected, any inhabitant of any State or Territory to the deprivation of any right secured or protected by this act . . . shall be deemed guilty of a misdemeanor." Notice the word "custom." A person who prevents one from enjoying one's rights by custom can only mean a private individual unconnected to the state—a nonstate actor—violating another's rights by a common practice, like the common practice, or *custom*, of menacing and persecuting Black people to reduce them to second-class citizenship.

Before adopting the 1866 Civil Rights Act, Republicans understood that private individuals, not just state actors and state legislatures, tormented Black existence. Carl Schurz, in a December 1865 report, catalogued how caste preservationists harassed, maimed, and murdered to undermine Black freedom. "It is stated that civil officers are either unwilling or unable to enforce the laws," Schurz wrote, "that one man does not dare to testify against another for fear of being murdered, and that the better elements of society are kept down by lawless characters under a system of terrorism."

Recall that congressional Republicans originally passed the 1866 Act to enforce the Thirteenth Amendment, but some feared the amendment did not empower Congress to enact it. They then conceived the Fourteenth Amendment and re-passed the act under it. Republicans pegged their primary mission as safeguarding Black freedom. And they appreciated that nonstate actors most imperiled that freedom. Hence, they wrote an amendment permitting them to arrest the evil most likely to subvert their objectives.

As we sit at the congressmen's oak desks, designed in an ornate Renaissance Revival mode, let's further explore how to construct the Fourteenth Amendment.

A construction must infuse with meaning both Section 1 and Section 5, which empowers Congress to pass appropriate legislation to enforce Section 1. Given that a law that explicitly denies a race a civil right, like the West Virginia jury discrimination statute, is illegal on its face, Congress would have no need to pass a law to nullify it. If all Section 5 did was allow Congress to nullify bad law or invalidate the misdeeds of state actors, we would consider it superfluous. The federal judiciary can handle those modest tasks.

It must accomplish more.

If the protection in equal protection *required* that states protect their citizens, and Congress could provide that protection when states cannot or choose not to, that construction installs muscle and bone into the Fourteenth Amendment's fifth section, the same muscle and bone the Court gave the Fugitive Slave Clause. Only this construction allows Congress to address all the problems that kept them debating for months. Only this construction endangers all variety of castework and undermines the cementing of a racial caste system. Only this construction allows Black folk to savor the sweet taste of full freedom.

In a few years, the black robes would hear two 1870 Enforcement Act cases where they would respond to requests to infuse meaning into the protection of equal protection.

Kentucky supplied the first.

ON JANUARY 30, 1873, as Kentucky-native William Garner, a twenty-two-year-old biracial brick mason, approached his polling place in Lexington's third ward to vote in the city council elections, he understood his rights. He, to vote, needed to be a man at least twenty-one years old.

Check.

He needed to have resided in the state for two years—check—and be a resident of both the voting precinct and ward for more than sixty days prior to the election.

Check.

Last, he had to have paid the one-dollar-and-fifty-cents poll tax for the previous year. Therefore, on January 15, Garner visited the office of James F. Robinson, the tax collector. Robinson, however, refused payment because of Garner's race. This violated the second section of the 1870 Enforcement Act, which outlawed race discrimination by any official responsible for allowing citizens to perform voting prerequisites. Since, on account of race, Robinson prevented Garner from receiving proof of poll tax payment, per Section 3 of the act Garner could still vote if he swore an affidavit explaining that he would have satisfied all requirements but for race discrimination. He gave the inspectors at his polling place, William Farnaugh, Mathew Faushee, and Hiram Reese, his affidavit. Farnaugh wanted to accept it, but Reese and Faushee overruled him. Garner left without voting.

On March 12, 1873, a federal grand jury indicted Reese and Faushee for Enforcement Act violations. A heavyweight, the septuagenarian Henry Stanbery, President Andrew Johnson's attorney general who espoused the states' rights worldview, agreed to represent Reese and Faushee in federal court.

ON DECEMBER 17, 1873, Gabriel Caldwell Wharton, a handsome, chiseled-face thirtysomething White man, entered the four-story federal U.S. Custom House and Post Office in downtown Louisville. He ascended the grand iron staircase, headed to the eastern side of the second floor, and entered the massive federal courtroom to prosecute Reese and Faushee. Wharton, the Grant-nominated U.S. attorney for the District of Kentucky, had before pressed cases against Klansmen, including one against the sons of influential Kentucky families who had hung two Black people. Wharton's courage courted deadly retribution: "When you strike a Crittenden," the last name of one of the sons, "you strike the State of Kentucky, and his friends will never consent to have justice meted out to him." He tried them anyway.

The Lincoln-appointed District Court Judge Bland Ballard, and the Grant-appointed Sixth Circuit judge, Halmor Hull Emmons, presided over Reese and Faushee's prosecution. Ballard, the judge in *Blyew v. United States*, had previously granted federal jurisdiction over the murder trials of John Blyew and George Kennard, the two White men who hacked to death a Black family, because the state, by law, denied Black people from testifying against White defendants.

Wharton's adversaries, Stanbery and B. F. Buckner, a former Kentucky state legislator, hoped their legal argument would free their clients. Like the attorneys in the Eutaw riots case, Stanbery and Buckner filed demurrers, arguing that the Fifteenth Amendment did not empower Congress to write the third and fourth sections of the 1870 Enforcement Act. Both sections, they claimed, went beyond punishing race discrimination. The two sides debated the issue in the grand pine-floored courtroom. Judge Ballard voted to dismiss the demurrer. Emmons, though, sided with the defense, and because circuit judges were superior to district court judges, Emmons's decision controlled the outcome. Wharton asked the judges to certify their decision to allow a Supreme Court appeal. The judges assented, and the disenfranchisers went free.

AHEAD OF *UNITED STATES V. REESE* ORAL ARGUMENT, a Radical newspaper predicted that the Republican-majority Supreme Court would vindicate the party's view that The Trinity empowered Congress to pass comprehensive legislation that protected Black freedom. Without that vindication, the paper cautioned, "The Democratic party will obliterate every amendment to the Constitution, and every law passed by Congress for their enforcement, that disagrees with the Southern idea of a white man's government. We can only secure freedom and suffrage to the colored people by eternal vigilance."

Before revisiting the arguments exchanged inside the chamber, let's delve deeper into the twenty-three-section 1870 Enforcement Act. Remember, its second section prohibited a person, like a poll tax collector, who must allow a prospective voter to satisfy a voting prerequisite, like paying the poll tax, from racially discriminating. The third provided that when a state officer denies a potential voter from satisfying those prerequisites for reasons "aforesaid," that is, the previously mentioned race discrimination described in Section 2, the potential voter can provide an affidavit stating that he would have been qualified to vote but for the race discrimination. That affidavit makes them an eligible voter. Any state officer who blocked a man with such an affidavit from voting risked not only a civil lawsuit but a fine and possible imprisonment. The fourth section outlawed the actions of any individual, not just state actors, who either by themselves or by conspiring with others, prevented another through "force, bribery, threats, intimidation, or other unlawful means" from either fulfilling any voting prerequisite or from voting. This section likewise employed "aforesaid" to note that the section targeted a racially discriminatory motive. The case hinged on the Court understanding that the relevant sections targeted race discrimination in voting rights.

On January 14 and 15, 1875, Chief Justice Waite and Associate Justices Clifford, Swayne, Miller, Field, Strong, Hunt, and Bradley entered a packed courtroom, filled with congressmen, judges, and lawyers who crammed together for the Supreme Court's first Enforcement Act case. Only one justice present that day would not later hear *Strauder*, *Virginia v. Rives*, and *Ex Parte Virginia*— fifty-nine-year-old David Davis, whom Justice Harlan would replace. "I write the shortest opinions of anyone on the bench," the Lincoln appointee once admitted. "If I had to . . . write legal essays as some judges do, I would quit the concern." Neither of the chief justices he served under, Chase and Waite, trusted the portly Illinoisan to author a meaningful decision like *United States v. Reese*.

U.S. Attorney General George Henry Williams and Solicitor General Samuel Field Phillips represented the Grant administration's pro-enforcement position. In December 1871, Grant selected Williams, former Republican senator from Oregon. In the run-up to the 1872 election, under Williams's leadership, federal attorneys prosecuted Enforcement Act cases throughout the South, hushing Black southern jitters that voting imperiled their necks, putting multiple former Confederate states in Grant's column. As an attorney, notwithstanding, Williams possessed few gifts.

In 1866, as a North Carolina state legislator, Phillips supported the South's first attempt at a post-slavery racial caste system, the Black Codes, but by 1868 he endorsed Black suffrage. When learning that the state's conservatives were threatening to fire Black laborers if they voted Republican, he said, "I am nauseated by all these reports of force, pretendedly defensive, but really . . . *offensive:* intended to make persons vote as otherwise they would not." He later successfully prosecuted Klansmen for Enforcement Act violations as a federal attorney in North Carolina.

Under a thirty-seven-state flag, Stanbery, as "tall as a cedar," and Buckner, short, presented an odd visual pairing inside the chamber where they litigated a narrow case. They argued that the Fifteenth Amendment enfranchised no one, but rather it required that the federal government and states place no race limitations on voting rights. The construction consistent with the text and abolitionist spirit of the Fifteenth Amendment, though, holds that it forbids the federal government and states to deny voting rights based on race, and as with the Fourteenth Amendment, denying includes inaction as well as action. Buckner did, however, correctly observe that the amendment did not enable Congress to enact general voting rights legislation. Congress, for example, couldn't pass a law under the amendment that punished poll workers who denied men older than seventy the ballot. The case, to Stanbery and Buckner, then turned on whether Sections 3 and 4 of the 1870 Enforcement Act limited themselves to the intersection of voting rights and race discrimination.

Section 2, Stanbery and Buckner conceded, dealt with race discrimination, containing an anti-discrimination clause that required officers to perform their duty "without distinction of race, color, or previous condition of servitude." However, neither Section 3 nor 4, they argued, specifically punished race discrimination in voting rights. "There is not the most distant allusion to discrimination on account of race or color," Buckner wrote in his brief. They misunderstood the act, or at least they pretended to. "Aforesaid" obviously incorporated the anti-discrimination clause spelled out in Section 2.

Attorney General Williams, a distinctive-looking man with a receding hairline and bushy beard that circled a bald chin, performed provocatively for his oral argument. Given that Stanbery and Buckner convinced the lower court to sustain the demurrers with a specific argument, he should have simply taught the justices how to read Sections 3 and 4. Instead, Williams delivered unnecessarily sweeping arguments about The Trinity.

Williams insisted that "if the war had settled anything, it had settled the question of states' rights" and that "states' rights were nothing but a breath that had passed out of existence." Its demise benefited all because "it would be impossible for the Union to exist without a strong central government in Washington."

Growing more confrontational, Williams warned "that Congress was the exclusive judge of what was appropriate," telling the black robes that invalidating the 1870 Enforcement Act would be improper—"in only a very few instances had the Supreme Court ever reversed the action of Congress," he claimed. Williams started to list those instances, failing to name half. He cautioned that "the negroes of the South would be disfranchised unless Congress interposed in the most emphatic manner to prevent this wrong" and cited the Court's past, arguing "that if it would go as far in supporting the Fifteenth Amendment, as the judiciary on the same bench had gone in supporting slavery, there was no doubt but what the act of Congress in question would be sustained."

Phillips followed Williams and suggested that because the legal issues in the two cases echoed one another, the Court should defer judgment on *Reese* until hearing a case from Grant Parish, Louisiana, *United States v. Cruikshank*, set to come before the justices a couple months later. Justice Bradley knew the case well. Williams insisted that the Court shouldn't delay *Reese*, exposing how the leading federal attorneys entered the chamber without first resolving their disagreements on cases central to Black freedom. The justices ultimately sided with Phillips.

Let's visit Colfax, a small town along the Red River named after the seventeenth vice president of the United States, and watch the events that produced *Cruikshank*.

SOME ARE FROM GRANT PARISH. Others are from nearby. Some are young. Others are old. Some are wealthy. Others are poor. Some belong to White supremacist groups. Others belong to none. Some have fought in war. Others have fought never. Some once wore Confederate gray. Others once wore Union blue. Some have before tasted blood. Others will taste for the first time today.

On Easter morning, April 13, 1873, a throng of White men departed their various campsites outside Colfax to gather here, their designated rendezvous spot at Bayou Darrow, a water stream in central Louisiana. After the captains assess the battle plan, former Confederate lieutenant Dave Paul, an appointed commander of sorts, reads the muster roll and prepares his men.

"Boys," Paul, also a Klan chief, says, "there are one hundred and sixty-five of us to go into Colfax this morning; God knows how many will come out of it alive."

They all appreciate the objective—evict the Black men guarding the parish courthouse in Colfax about ten miles southeast. Before proceeding to what happens next, learn the backstory.

WILLIAM S. CALHOUN, a wealthy sugar plantation owner, conceived of Grant Parish. Pro-Union during the Civil War, Calhoun embodied the spirit of White Louisiana Republicans who controlled the party postwar—supportive of Black suffrage rights but wanting to circumvent the fraught waters of 1870s racial politics, instead wanting to focus on economic development and innovation to establish a biracial party. Henry Clay Warmoth, the state's Republican governor elected in April 1868, pioneered the party's program for domination. Black folk formed the party's base, and Warmoth hoped to keep them with his left arm while capturing White conservatives with his right.

In 1869, the Republican-dominated legislature, at the behest of Calhoun, also a state representative, created Grant Parish. Drawn to ensure a narrow Black voting majority, the parish was named in honor of President Grant and the parish seat after his vice president, Schuyler Colfax. A new parish needed new appointed civil officers. Warmoth's selections included White Radicals like Delos White as sheriff and William Phillips as parish judge. White conservatives stewed. A former Freedmen's Bureau agent in nearby Winn Parish, Delos White regarded the freedpeople as "sober and industrious" and, with "any kind of favorable chance," he surmised, "they will most assuredly outstrip the whites in material prosperity." Weeks after assuming his position, armed men gave him twenty-four hours to vacate the parish. He stayed. William Phillips, a scalawag—a White southerner who supported Reconstruction and consequently considered traitorous to traditional White-over-Black southern political values—gained a reputation as a Radical for "promising to fight for land, horses, and tools for the freedpeople." His adversaries branded him "the Great Radical Miscegnator [*sic*] and Renegade" for cohabiting with a young biracial woman with whom he had fathered a son.

Groups like the Knights of the White Camellia, an outfit deeply intertwined with the Democratic Party that murdered, in Louisiana, scores of Black folk in advance of the 1868 presidential election, opposed Republican domination in Grant Parish. Much of the local White population, though, rebuffed such militant White supremacists, preferring to collaborate with moderate Republicans. Warmoth, to cultivate a large centrist presence in the party, replaced Sheriff White and Judge Phillips with two Republicans White conservatives preferred. The November 1870 elections proved Warmoth's plan a success in Grant Parish, as Republicans captured nearly 70 percent of the parish vote. Supportive of Warmoth's plan of peace and wealth, moderately conservative White folk mirrored Black voting, believing their place atop the caste system remained assured. The elections left the parish split—both conservative Republicans and Radicals won. William Phillips reclaimed the parish judgeship and Delos White won his recorder race. Alfred Shelby, a White conservative Republican, scored the sheriff election.

On September 25, 1871, the commotion of men on horses and their house burning awakened White and Phillips, who lived together. A fifty-man mob surrounded their place. Men brandishing double-barreled shotguns blocked the exits. Stay and burn. Or rush the door. Two options. They chose the door, and the shotguns blazed. Death arrived fast for White. Playing dead kept Phillips alive. In the yard, the mob left a lit torch atop a twelve-foot pole with a copy of a radical speech Phillips delivered in 1867 attached. Sheriff Shelby headed the mob, Phillips disclosed, along with Deputy Sheriff Christopher Columbus Nash, a Confederate veteran. The message beamed through—White conservatives would no longer tolerate Radicals. A New Orleans grand jury, undoubtedly stocked with caste preservationists, later failed to indict those responsible.

Nash activated an anti-Radical plan, unleashing gangs of armed conservatives on Grant Parish in spring 1872. Radicals divulged that under the threat of violence, conservatives drove them from their homes. Phillips, one victim, fled to New Orleans. Warmoth replaced him with an ex-Confederate conservative Republican. By summer 1872, the luster on Warmoth's plan for a dominant state Republican Party dulled. He then severed himself from the national party, scampering to the Liberal Republicans, a fleeting and ultimately unfruitful political movement that burst onto the scene to oppose Grant's Reconstruction policy. Warmoth called for a Liberal Republican state convention to nominate a full ticket for the fall election under the mantra, "Justice to all Races, Creeds, and Political Opinions." Louisiana's Black and Radical Republicans, however, remained with the national party. Warmoth and his Liberal Republicans ultimately allied with the Democrats, nominating a fusion ticket headlined by gubernatorial candidate Democrat John D. McEnery. Conservative Republicans in Grant Parish likewise enlisted with the Democrats and, together, they fielded fusion candidates. Christopher Columbus Nash received the Grant Parish fusion sheriff nomination and Alphonse Cazabat the parish judge nomination. Grant Parish Republicans ran an interracial, largely Radical, candidate slate.

Fraud defined Louisiana's 1872 November elections. Officials never even announced Grant Parish returns. Both sides there claimed victory although Republicans probably won, given their three hundred registered voter advantage. Sitting governor Warmoth, nonetheless, awarded the Grant Parish races to the fusionists, and in early January 1873, conservatives commandeered the Colfax courthouse and executed office duties. Weeks later, after a protracted dispute regarding who had won the gubernatorial race, Republican William Pitt Kellogg took the governorship. He reversed Warmoth, giving commissions to Grant Parish's Republican candidates, including R. C. Register for judge and D. W. Shaw for sheriff, two White men. That meant two different groups thought they rightfully held elected positions. The Republicans, though, waited to seize their offices.

On March 25, Register and Shaw went to the courthouse, formerly Calhoun's plantation stable, a two-story brick structure built by enslaved people. Finding it locked, they gained entrance through a window, giving them possession. Holding commissions from Governor Kellogg, Republicans deemed themselves the lawful holders of the instruments of power. When Nash and Cazabat learned about losing the courthouse, they discussed reclaiming it and killing every Black man in the parish to keep possession.

On the night of March 31, William Ward, a politically influential Black Radical, remained at home sick. An ally visited his house and informed him that James Hadnot, a local Klan leader, had planned the next day to recapture the courthouse, replace the Republican officials with fusionists, and hang Ward along with other prominent Radicals. Register, Shaw, and other Republicans later met at Ward's home to discuss the rumors. Shaw decided to deputize upward of thirty men, predominantly Black, as special deputies to guard the courthouse.

On April 1, Hadnot and his crew of a dozen stormed into Colfax on horses, brandishing rifles. Shaw's deputies made a show of force. Hadnot and his men retreated. The next day, the two camps exchanged gunfire that hit none, and Hadnot's gang rode off again.

On the morning of April 5, Jesse McKinney, a Black man living near a ferry crossing at Bayou Darrow, was building a fence around his house as a band of White men rode toward him. A White man, with McKinney's wife and six children watching, brandished a pistol and shot McKinney in the head. His wife heard him scream "like a pig." A few in the crew she recognized. Denis Lemoine. Oscar Gibbons. William "Bill" Irwin.

One of the men asked if McKinney was dead. "Yes," someone replied. "He is dead as hell." The men dismounted their horses and danced. Prematurely. McKinney lived six more excruciating hours.

Shortly after the McKinney shooting, Radicals, including William Ward, and White conservatives met in a field for a peace conference. A Black special deputy interrupted to inform his side of what happened to McKinney. The deputy pointed his pistol at the White side, charging them with attempting to broker peace after executing an unassuming Black man. Ward had to whip out his gun to stop the deputy from shooting. The peace conference ended without resolution.

Preparing for battle, the special deputies, now an all-Black outfit with its White members leaving, erected breastworks around the courthouse, and blocked admission into town as the armed White soldiers maintained a home base outside Colfax.

THOSE WHITE SOLDIERS—the White insurgents—mount their horses, cross the bayou, and rage into Colfax, halting in front of Smithfield Quarters, a small all-Black village of cabins a half mile northwest of Colfax. In the distance, the crude and shallow breastwork that the Black guardians built keep the White insurgents about one hundred yards from their prize. The courthouse. Nash, accompanied by two others, each armed with sixteen-shooters, but carrying a white flag, asks to speak with John Miles, a Black man the local White folk like.

"Go tell Lev Allen to come out here," Nash tells Miles, referring to Benjamin "Lev" Allen, a former Buffalo soldier and a local Black leader.

Miles walks to the courthouse, as Nash and his men wait. Miles returns with Allen, who is riding his horse.

"What do you depend upon doing in there?" Nash asks Allen.

"We are doing nothing more than we were before," Allen responds. "Standing still, as we've been standing."

"We want that courthouse."

"We sent an answer to Mr. Hadnot by Mr. Calhoun," Allen counters. "Didn't you receive it?"

"I want you to understand that Mr. Hadnot does not command this company."

Allen replies, "We are going to stand where we are until we get United States troops or some assistance."

"Then go in there and say to your people that I advise them to get out of there. I give you thirty minutes to remove your women and children."

Allen returns to the courthouse and recounts the conversation to the Black guardians. They agree that they should hold steady, believing that, should they acquiesce, the White insurgents would kill them anyhow.

At around noon, the insurgents, using a cannon, launch a lump of iron that lands in front of the breastwork, spraying red soil, starting the engagement. The guardians behind the breastwork, some with Enfield rifles, return fire, but sparingly, conserving ammunition and keeping their heads below their breastwork. This inconsequential combat persists a couple of hours until a squadron of insurgents lugging the cannon, at about two in the afternoon, flank toward the banks of the Red River. The squadron launches iron slugs that penetrate the breastwork. One slices open Adam Kimball. The guardian rushes inside the courthouse, where his intestines plop onto the floor.

With their opponents bursting the stalemate, the guardians, with scant battlefield experience, scurry every which way. Sixty or seventy rush into the courthouse. Some dart into the Red River. Insurgents chase them into the river, shooting all but two. Others bolt into the woods.

Lev Allen yells "halt" to stop his men from deserting. None comply. He then rides into the woods. An insurgent shoots at him but misses. Other horse-mounted insurgents chase the guardians running into the woods, shooting, and killing.

"Master Johnnie," one Black guardian running away cries out, "don't kill me!"

"If you had not been here, you would not have been in this thing," Johnnie Hadnot, James's nephew, barks. "God damn you. I told you what I would do if I caught you here."

Hadnot fires his pistol, and the man collapses to the ground.

Pinckney Chambers, a fiftysomething guardian, is dashing through a field with a friend. A mounted insurgent shoots the friend dead, orders Chambers to freeze, and tells him that he should gun him down too. Chambers begs for his life, pleading that he was pressed into conflict. The insurgent replies that if he is speaking truth, he could live, but if he learns Chambers is lying, he will kill him. Chambers's captor routes him to a warehouse near the courthouse where he sits alongside other captive guardians. William "Bill" Cruikshank, an insurgent, tells Chambers he had heard he was a "good nigger" coerced into battle and would protect him.

The insurgents shift their attention to the courthouse. With their cannon useless against brick walls, leadership turns to Chambers.

"[Here's] a chance to save your life," they advise him. "We are going to light this, and you must take it and put it on the roof."

They hand Chambers a torch wrapped with a ball of cloth dipped in coal oil and threaten that he either ignite the roof or die. With the lit torch, he approaches the courthouse, ten double-barreled shot-guns pointed at him. He touches the roof's cypress shingles with the torch and the wind carries the flames across it as he scurries back. The guardians, eventually aware, hurry into the rafters to knock the shingles off the roof. The insurgents shoot at the roof, forcing the guardians to stop. The roof begins to cave in, and the courthouse will soon succumb to the blaze.

On the second story, Shack White, standing too close to an open window, takes a bullet to the neck. The insurgents dismount their horses and stand near the burning courthouse.

White yells out to an insurgent, "Save me Bill Irwin."

He then tears a sleeve from his white shirt, ties it to a stick and hangs it outside the window. "We surrender," he screams. Another guardian rips a white piece of paper from a book and waves it. The insurgents order them to stack their weapons and exit the court-house. As the first ten or so guardians leave, the insurgents rush the door and shoot. Bill Irwin guns down Shack White up close with his pistol. Insurgents shoot and stab, as bodies, both alive and dead, pile near the courthouse door. Seven guardians retreat into the burning courthouse, lift the floorboards, and hide in the crawl space.

An insurgent spots an older Black man, Benjamin Brimm, lying on the ground, and tells him, "Get up, old man, you're not dead."

That insurgent makes Brimm, a father of five daughters, head to the base of a pecan tree. Meanwhile, insurgents hunt down and kill six Black guardians who ran inside a close by warehouse.

Near the courthouse, insurgents who are loosely gathered in a semicircle as they are shooting at guardians, grow wilder with their volleys. James Hadnot notices and zips forward to urge his side to quit. A bullet then hits him from the side. Another insurgent, Sidney Harris, takes three to the back. Many other insurgents are wounded too, though not mortally.

"Men, save me, I am shot!" someone cries out.

"Cease firing, men," Nash screams. "You are shooting our own men."

At around four in the afternoon, insurgents command Brimm to enter the courthouse and get the remaining guardians, as dead and wounded Black bodies lie all over the one-hundred-acre battlefield.

"Y'all had better come out," Brimm tells them.

"I might just as well to be burned up as to be shot," says the lone holdout who stays behind.

At sundown, rain falls and under the darkness, some Black women in the area sneak toward the courthouse to see about their men.

"Captain Nash, here are your prisoners," someone tells Nash. "What are we to do with them?"

"Now boys," Nash asks the prisoners, "[i]f I take you all and send you home to your cotton, will you go to work?"

Brimm responds, "yes."

"[B]y God, Nash," an insurgent interjects, "if you send these God Dam Negroes home you won't live to see two weeks."

One insurgent who craves more blood pronounces, "Kill the damned niggers."

"Unless these niggers are killed," another warns Nash, "[w]e will kill you."

Luke Hadnot, James's brother, lines up five guardians, shooting each dead. Clement Penn selects Etienne Elzie. Etienne's wife, Annie, lurks a short distance away when Penn takes out his gun. She watches her husband begging for his life.

Pop!

The insurgents spend the rest of the night murdering, slaughtering as many as 150 guardians that day.


ON APRIL 18, JAMES ROSWELL BECKWITH, United States attorney for Louisiana, telegraphed U.S. Attorney General Williams, who responded the next day: "You are instructed to make a thorough investigation of the affairs in Grant Parish, and, if you find that the laws of the United States have been violated, you will spare no pains or expense to cause the guilty parties to be arrested and punished." America would weather such horrors constantly, Beckwith suspected, unless potential perpetrators expected swift and severe punishment. He intended to prosecute, yet by June 1873, authorities had captured none of the eighty he had indicted under the 1870 Enforcement Act. Five months post-massacre, Governor Kellogg provided U.S. marshals a squad of mounted reserves to make arrests. Nine were captured: William "Bill" Cruikshank, Alfred Lewis, Johnnie P. Hadnot, Thomas J. Hickman, William "Bill" Irwin, Austin P. Gibbons, Clement Penn, and Denis and Prudhomme Lemoine. On March 16, 1874, an interracial jury acquitted Lewis, and hung on the others.

Alongside Fifth Circuit Judge Woods, Bradley heard the second trial's testimony, and departed to hear cases in Texas before the Colfax Massacre jury reached its verdict. On June 10, 1874, an interracial jury convicted Cruikshank, Hadnot, and Irwin of violating the sixth section of the 1870 Enforcement Act, the same section the Eutaw rioters were prosecuted under, and acquitted the others.

The defense motioned to set aside the indictments, challenging Congress's authority to even pass the act. Although unavailable for oral argument on that legal issue, Bradley prepared an opinion, perfecting it over two weeks. On the morning of June 24, he boarded a train in D.C., starting his long, hot trek to New Orleans. "There is reason to believe," Beckwith wrote to Attorney General Williams on June 25, "that Justice Bradley will, to what end God only knows, decide the enforcement acts unconstitutional. . . . If he does, his action will [cost] 500 lives between now and November." On June 27, at nine in the morning, Judge Woods delivered his opinion, denying the defense's motion. Woods announced that court would reopen at noon, when Bradley would deliver his.

THE FIVE-FOOT-FOUR JUSTICE BRADLEY entered the massive courtroom and sat alongside Judge Woods, a tall, ruggedly masculine man with a beard. In a calm, steady tone, Bradley read his opinion.

In the Eutaw riots case, Bradley hinged his legal advice to Woods on the Privileges and Immunities Clause. The majority opinion in the *Slaughter-House Cases* shut that spigot. An Equal Protection Clause claim certainly looked appetizing, but Bradley, instead, served a Thirteenth Amendment offering.

That amendment accomplished more than slavery's death, argued Bradley. After emancipation, the freedpeople became citizens and, he said, were "placed on an entire equality before the law with the white citizen."

Under Bradley's construction, the Thirteenth Amendment, therefore, granted complete freedom which also entailed freedom from the "badges of servitude." That phrase, "badges of servitude," referred to the deprivation of rights inflicted upon a person because of slave status. A denial of citizenship was a badge of servitude. A denial of legal equality was a badge of servitude. Because of the Thirteenth Amendment, Black folk enjoyed immunities from all badges of servitude, and the amendment's second section empowered Congress to enforce these immunities, these rights, through legislation. And none could deny that the Thirteenth Amendment operated against private individuals. It, after all, abolished slavery—private ownership of another soul. If the amendment granted citizenship rights and rights to equality as Bradley claimed, Congress could enforce those rights through legislation that targeted private individuals. As Bradley contended, sitting behind the dark wood bench, "Congress had the power to make it a [crime] to conspire to deprive a person of, or to hinder him in, the exercise and enjoyment of the rights . . . conferred by the 13th Amendment."

In the packed courtroom, Bradley illustrated his point through a hypothetical. What if a band of White people prevented a Black man, because of race, from buying property in a White community? "It would be a case of interference with that person's exercise of his equal rights as citizen because of race," Bradley maintained. Congress can enact laws to "remedy and redress" this. Yet if nonracial reasons compelled the preventing of the land purchase, Congress lacked authority to intrude. State law would govern.

Bradley proceeded to the Fifteenth Amendment, which, he contended, provided citizens the right to "not be excluded from voting by reason of race, color or previous condition of servitude." The amendment's second section, furthermore, empowered Congress to enforce this right, and not only against discriminatory law, or discriminatory state officers, but "against outrage, violence, and combinations on the part of individuals, irrespective of state laws," he said, in his steady voice. Denial, in other words, included inaction and action. "Such was the opinion of Congress itself in passing the law at a time when many of its members were the same who had consulted upon the original form of the amendment in proposing it to the states. And as such a construction of the amendment in proposing it to the states."

The Trinity, Bradley argued, equipped Congress with the muskets to quell the "war of race." This evil, "whether it assumes the dimensions of civil strife or domestic violence," Bradley said, "whether carried on in a guerrilla or predatory form, or by private combinations, or even by private outrage or intimidation, is subject to the jurisdiction of the government of the United States; and when any atrocity is committed which may be assigned to this cause it may be punished by the laws and in the courts of the United States," meaning federal law and federal courts.

Bradley's brain, a nimble ballerina, sidestepped the logic of the *Slaughter-House Cases*, pirouetting away from the Fourteenth Amendment and toward the Thirteenth and Fifteenth Amendments to enable Congress to fully protect Black freedom. Please appreciate the situational imbalance between caste preservationists and caste abolitionists. On the one hand, caste preservationists could recite the same old states' rights chorus that they had once sung to defend slavery. No new lyrics needed. Caste abolitionists, on the other hand, needed to argue for new constructions of new amendments, and the most beneficial of these constructions would compel the Supreme Court to permit Congress to exercise power over civil and political rights at odds with American history, particularly at odds because the country once barred the recipient of these rights, Black people, from national citizenship. But Court precedent obliged the black robes to apply the same logic used to secure the rights of slaveowners on Black people's behalf—the Supreme Court must interpret The Trinity to, as Justice Story wrote in *Prigg v. Pennsylvania*, "completely effectuate the whole objects of it" rather than allow rights to turn "shadowy and unsubstantial." Americans who wanted their country to live up to its founding principles of liberty and equality needed minds to construct The Trinity into something that would suppress the pungency of caste. Bradley lent his talents.

After upholding the constitutionality of the 1870 Enforcement Act and broadly conceiving of Congress's powers to protect Black freedom, Bradley moved to the counts of the indictment. Each one he dismissed, offering varying reasons, including that some were "defective on account of vagueness" and others failed to specify that the defendants had violated the rights of Black men because of race.

The decision sent a mixed message. Beckwith correctly predicted Bradley's decision would embolden violent White supremacists as caste preservationists boasted, wrongly, that Bradley had undermined the 1870 Enforcement Act in their effort to claim victory over a crowning Reconstruction achievement. Proud of his opinion, Bradley circulated copies to his Court colleagues, Fifth Circuit district court judges, some senators and congressmen, and Attorney General Williams.

Before the Supreme Court heard the Grant Parish case, Congress debated one more anticaste act, one that Sallie Robinson would rely upon when asserting her civil equality, the constitutionality of which Justice Bradley would evaluate in 1883.

A FEW MONTHS AFTER Bradley delivered his opinion, his Republican Party suffered historic defeats in the 1874 midterm elections, losing ninety-three House and nine Senate seats. Despite an economic depression and Grant administration political scandals, many Republican leaders blamed the drubbing on race politics and supposed that the party must cleanse itself of Reconstruction and deaden the loud, omnipresent ruckus about Black rights in the South. A presidential election two years away, and White northerners wanting sectional reconciliation, many Republicans pushed the party to support the federal government withdrawing from the administration of law and order in the former Confederacy. With weeks remaining until the Democrats controlled the House for the first time since the Civil War, congressional Republicans debated one final bill, what became the Civil Rights Act of 1875.

In the previous leg of our journey, Judge Alexander Rives presided over prosecutions of judges who violated the act's jury discrimination provisions. The act also required equal accommodations in public spaces like inns, public conveyances on land or water, and places of amusement like theaters. "Whereas, it is essential to just government we recognize the equality of all men before the law, and hold that it is the duty of government in its dealings with the people to mete out equal and exact justice to all," the act's first section states, "all persons within the jurisdiction of the United States shall be entitled to the full and equal enjoyment of the accommodations, advantages, facilities, and privileges of inns, public conveyances on land or water, theaters, and other places of public amusement." Violators, per the second section, faced fines and misdemeanor charges.

On February 3, 1875, a month before the 1875 Act's passage, inside the House Chamber, a Black Mississippi congressman, John Roy Lynch, implored his colleagues to acknowledge his humanity and legally require its recognition in public spaces.

"Under our present system of race distinctions," said the distinguished, thin, light-skinned man with chiseled features and big piercing eyes, "a white woman of a questionable social standing, yea, I may say, of an admitted immoral character, can go to any public place or upon any public conveyance and be the recipient of the same treatment, the same courtesy, and the same respect that is usually accorded to the most refined and virtuous. . . ."

"Think of it for a moment," lamented the son of an Irish American plantation manager father and an enslaved mother. "Here am I, a member of your honorable body, representing one of the largest and wealthiest districts in the State of Mississippi, and possibly in the South, a district composed of persons of different races, religions and nationalities. . . ."

"And yet," said the twenty-seven-year-old, one of seven Black House members, "when I leave my home to come to the capital of the nation, to take part in the deliberations of the House and to participate with you in making laws for the government of this great Republic . . . I am treated, not as an American citizen, but as a brute. Forced to occupy a filthy smoking-car both night and day, with drunkards, gamblers, and criminals. And for what? Not that I am unable or unwilling to pay my way. Not that I am obnoxious in my personal appearance or disrespectful in my conduct, but simply because I happen to be of a darker complexion." Grant signed the law on March 1, 1875.

Thus far, we have but dipped our nose into the *Dred Scott* pond. Let's submerge our heads.

In 1834, Dr. John Emerson, who owned Dred Scott, carried Scott from Missouri, a slave state, to Illinois, a free state, and then, two years later, into the Wisconsin Territory, where Congress outlawed slavery, staying there another two years. Emerson returned to Missouri, where ownership of Scott, his wife, Harriet, and their two daughters passed to John Sanford. Seeking freedom for himself and his family, Scott sued Sanford in federal court in Missouri, claiming that their prior residing in a free state and a free territory emancipated them. Federal courts can exercise jurisdiction to hear controversies involving *citizens* of different states. Scott claimed Missouri citizenship and sued Sanford, a New Yorker. Chief Justice Taney framed the central question: "Can a negro . . . become a member of the political community formed and brought into existence by the Constitution of the United States, and as such become entitled to all the rights, and privileges, and immunities, guaranteed by that instrument to the citizen?"

Black people could not be citizens, Taney answered, explaining that the Africans trafficked into America and their heirs, whether bondsmen or freemen, forever existed outside the political community the Constitution contemplated. The "We the People of the United States," Taney wrote, excluded Black people, who were a "subordinate and inferior class of beings," in other words a lower caste, "who had been subjugated by the dominant race." Scott could not sue for his freedom because he had no claim to the rights available to members of the American political community. Black people "had for more than a century before," Taney observed, "been regarded as . . . altogether unfit to associate with the white race, either in social or political relations."

That descriptor—"altogether unfit to associate with the white race"—captured the dilemma of Black life that the 1875 Civil Rights Act could have helped alleviate. The Trinity obliged the nation to annul *Dred Scott*, and the entire racial outlook that animated Taney's reasoning. By ratifying The Trinity, America committed itself to the project of Black *freedom*. The Trinity entrusted all parts of the federal government—legislative, executive, and judicial—to promote Black *freedom*. And The Trinity commanded the states to protect Black folk, affirmatively, to guarantee *freedom* from treatment as a persecuted caste within their borders. Lynch's plight on trains proved that America had yet to overturn *Dred Scott*. Castework continued to checkmate Black freedom. And thus, The Trinity required a national response. With the 1875 Act, Congress complied.

Much of White America, however, stressed little that the executive branch would enforce the act's public accommodation sections. The Grant administration showed scant enthusiasm. The Justice Department, neglecting pleas for instruction and copies of the law, provided federal attorneys and marshals no special guidance on its implementation.

Private individuals, like the White insurgents, on the one hand, sought to convince the Court that Congress couldn't punish them for perpetrating a race massacre. And private individuals, like Sallie Robinson, on the other, sought to convince the Court that Congress could safeguard their right to equal treatment in public spaces. The White insurgents, in *United States v. Cruikshank*, enunciated their arguments first.

ON MARCH 31, 1875, weeks after the Democrats took over the House, the Court heard oral argument for *Cruikshank*. The federal government, which defended the convictions of the Grant Parish insurgents, needed five votes. Given that Bradley, a defender of The Trinity, had already invalidated the convictions on technicalities, finding five justices to allow the convictions to stand appeared most unlikely. Solicitor General Phillips and Attorney General Williams should have pursued a smaller treasure—the Court explicitly affirming the constitutionality of the 1870 Enforcement Act. The defendants' lawyers seated at the opposing wooden table hankered for more than their clients' freedom, coveting an obituary for the enforcement era.

Robert Hardin Marr, on behalf of the convicted defendants, argued that The Trinity did not allow Congress to legislate against private individuals, stressing that "the continuance of the State governments and the liberties of the people were at stake in their decision." A thin man in his fifties with a long pointy nose, Marr, a member of the White League, one of White Supremacy's organizations that committed murders and undermined Reconstruction gov-

ernments, reserved much of his side's allotted time for Justice Field's
older brother.

Seventy years old with thinning, gray hair, David Dudley Field
commanded respect as a preeminent Supreme Court litigator. The
New Yorker argued that at the war's end, two choices lay before
America. Choice one required the nation to "take the blacks specially under the protection of the federal government." The other,
which America selected, involved "declar[ing] that the States, in their
undoubted power to regulate their own affairs, should not do certain
things." This option preserved states' rights, meaning "states must
do some act" to deny Black people their rights "before Congress can
undertake to enact any legislation."

Caste preservationists wanted to disable the Fourteenth Amendment as much as the black robes would tolerate and proposed this
*state action* formula, a shrewd strategy to arrest America's ebb from
the shores of caste. This construction would neuter the Equal Protection Clause—it lifts from states the burden of needing to affirmatively
protect Black folk from the wickedness of private individuals and bars
Congress from carrying that burden on the states' behalf. The judiciary, per this construction, could only invalidate purposeful state discrimination like what the Court would encounter in *Strauder v. West
Virginia*. And Congress could only enforce the Fourteenth Amendment to arrest intentional race-based deprivations of rights by states.
This construction would prove too ineffectual to overturn *Dred Scott*.
White Supremacy, for that reason, cheered caste preservationists for
advocating it.

Justice Miller asked Field about *Reese:* "If Congress had no right to
pass any affirmative legislation, what remedy would have accrued to
the Kentucky negroes whose cases were recently before the court?"

After Field pleaded ignorance of that case's facts, Justice Bradley
explained that in *Reese*, state agents, not the law, denied voting rights.
Miller told Field that his view would leave Black victims without
remedy.

Such victims, Field responded, "had the same remedy as white
men—they could enter their suit in the state courts for damages,"
adding "that if eight hundred thousand voters could not secure the

rights to which they had been declared entitled, then that is the best argument that they are not worthy of them."

In *Prigg v. Pennsylvania*, caste preservationists articulated the opposite viewpoint. When slaveowners' rights dangled from the cliff, they implored Congress to fortify their rights through legislation, and slaveowners' failure to prevent enslaved people from escaping leveled no argument against the propriety of holding stolen Africans. Rather, it confirmed that Congress must draft bills to help recapture their property. States' rights for you. Big government for us.

Field concluded his oral argument by celebrating states' rights, expressing his hope that "the rights of the States would be pronounced just as they were when the oldest member of the court took his seat, except, of course, as restricted by the amendments. Let it still be as from the dawn of our history. *E Pluribus Unum*," referring to America's Latin motto—out of many, one. "These words had been borne upon our flag in every battle on the land and the sea. They were witnesses of the past and pledges of the future. [I] would have them written in this court-room and in every State capitol of this land."

Reverdy Johnson, seventy-three years old with a long drooping face, ended the oral argument for defense counsel. Sanford's attorney in *Dred Scott*, Johnson successfully convinced the Supreme Court that Black people could not claim citizenship. Nearly twenty years later, Johnson returned to the Court to argue that the government's position afforded special privileges to Black people. "It is claimed that under these amendments Congress is clothed with the power to pass any law which in its judgment may be necessary to protect the rights guaranteed to the colored man," Johnson said.

"Where does this lead us?" Johnson asked. "What becomes of that large mass of rights which, from the very nature of our government, must belong to the States? If the assumption is to prevail that the States will not do their duty, it is best to do away with the States altogether. Such legislation sweeps away all that mass of rights which is expressly reserved to the States."

Attorney General Williams closed oral argument and started by reminding the justices of the race massacre. "The parties appearing as defendants in this court," Williams said, "have been tried and convicted. The question is whether these guilty parties should go unwhipped of justice."

As he did during *Reese* oral argument, Williams recounted how the Court had once constructed the Constitution to protect slaveowners' rights and it must again to protect Black people's rights. "If the time ever comes when as liberal a judicial construction shall be given to laws designed to protect human freedom as had always been given to laws designed to protect human slavery," he maintained, "then the doctrine of the government in this case would be admitted."

Building on Bradley's circuit court opinion, Williams argued that the Thirteenth Amendment made no reference to the states, meaning that the opposing argument that Congress could only correct racially oppressive state legislation misled the justices.

Williams went further, contending that the Fourteenth Amendment likewise empowered Congress to pass the 1870 Enforcement Act. He recounted the history of the 1866 Civil Rights Act. He knew it personally as a senator and member of the congressional committee that wrote it and the Fourteenth Amendment. Congress "brought forward" the amendment, he said, "for the express purpose of making [the 1866 Act] valid, to perpetuate it and put it beyond the reach of controversy. Therefore, the identical words of the bill as to citizenship were put in the Fourteenth Amendment. To make assurance doubly sure, after the ratification of the fourteenth amendment, the civil rights bill was re-enacted." Williams's history lesson upended opposing counsel's argument—the 1866 Act allowed Congress to punish private individuals for preventing a person from enjoying rights based on race, and thus the Fourteenth Amendment must allow it too.

But when the justices peppered Williams with questions, his performance exemplified a dilemma Black folk encountered in squeezing the most out of The Trinity—those charged with converting the freedom from caste movement into constitutional constructions oftentimes failed to deliver.

Justice Clifford, a Democrat, said that in his home state, Maine, Black men could always vote. He asked Williams whether if "two indictments were found of conspiracy, one to prevent a colored man and the other a white man from voting, would the [federal courts] have jurisdiction of both cases?"

Williams replied that "they would in the case of the black man. I don't contend that they would in the case of the white man." Wrong answer. The right answer understood that federal courts had jurisdiction over any case involving race-based denials of voting rights.

"Then colored men have more rights in the United States courts," Clifford responded, "than white men."

"That does not follow," Williams countered. "The Constitution does not confer upon white people the right to vote, but it does upon colored people, and thence the power of Congress arises to protect them in that right." Wrong answer. Again. The Fifteenth Amendment merely prohibited the denial of voting rights on account of race. It conferred upon no one the right to vote, something the nation's top attorney should have grasped.

"Suppose the State of South Carolina," Justice Strong questioned, "where the majority of the people are colored, should change its constitution and say that no white man should vote, would a remedy lie in the United States courts?"

Williams responded that he had "no doubt that it would." The correct answer.

The attorney general reiterated that his "idea in the main of these amendments was that any and every right guaranteed by them may be protected in the courts of the United States. Give that construction of these amendments and they are of some value. Give them the other construction, and the freedom [given] to the negro becomes practically a curse. Any doubt as to the validity of this act should be resolved in its favor."

Williams pressed the justices to remember that the amendments and the legislation drawn under them were "practically made by the same hands. Is it to be supposed that those who drew the amendments did not know their scope? According to the arguments on the other side it must be assumed of the Senators and Representatives, either that they violated their oath, or they did not know the meaning of language which they used themselves."

Williams recalled Field's *E Pluribus Unum* sermon, and announced that he "was also here to speak for E Pluribus Unum, and speaking for it, [I] look forward to that day when we can consider ourselves not a nation of inharmonious and warring sovereigns, but a Union whose broad shield shall protect in all and every right of a freeman and a citizen her people from one end to the other."

For the *Reese* and *Cruikshank* decisions, the nation waited nearly a year, until March 27, 1876.

ON JULY 8, 1876, in Hamburg, South Carolina, a small majority-Black town on the Augusta River opposite Georgia, about one hundred White men in a paramilitary terrorist group, the Red Shirts, cornered thirty of the state's Black militia inside a warehouse. This launched a violent White supremacist campaign in South Carolina ahead of the 1876 presidential elections. What transpired inside the Supreme Court Chamber a few months earlier, when Chief Justice Waite announced his opinions in *Reese* and *Cruikshank*, helped embolden such terrorism.

The key question in *Reese*, per Waite, was what legislation Congress could pass under the Fifteenth Amendment. The amendment, he argued, granted citizens a new right—an "exemption from discrimination in the exercise of the elective franchise on account of race, color, or previous condition of servitude." Congress can enforce that right with "appropriate legislation." Did Sections 3 and 4 of the 1870 Enforcement Act qualify as appropriate legislation though? Waite answered no in his opinion, with which six colleagues agreed. "In view of all the facts," he said, "the language of the third and fourth sections does not confine their operation to unlawful discriminations on account of race." Southern lawyers who misread the plain meaning of the act convinced a majority of the nation's most powerful legal minds that a congressional act didn't say something it did.

Justice Hunt, in his dissent, explained the plain meaning of Sections 3 and 4. "By the words 'as aforesaid,'" he wrote, "the provisions respecting race and color of the first and second sections of the statute are incorporated into and made a part of the third and fourth sections." Unless "as aforesaid" conveyed that effect, "they are wholly and absolutely without meaning. No other meaning can possibly be given to them." Recall that in *Virginia v. Rives*, decided in 1880, the black robes misread the federal removal statute and disallowed the Reynolds brothers from transferring their case to federal court. In a span of four years, the Court would weaken two anticaste laws by misconstruing straightforward text. Once—an unforgivable error. Twice suggested an appetite for weakening anticaste legislation.

In his majority *Cruikshank* opinion, signed by Justices Swayne, Miller, Field, and Strong, Waite reiterated the idea, outlined in the *Slaughter-House Cases*, that the states remained the main guardians of the civil rights bucket. He presented this argument as if he were merely describing the Constitution in the only manner one could interpret it, but he *chose* to shrink The Trinity and disregard the plan Congress executed with those three amendments. Attorney General Williams informed the justices that Congress sought to empower the federal government to enforce civil rights against state transgressions and against private individuals, meaning that the justices could have broadly constructed The Trinity to permit Congress to enforce civil rights. Waite pretended those intentions away in an opinion that omitted any mention of White terrorists massacring more than a hundred Black men. Waite did not affirmatively uphold the constitutionality of Section 6, although did not invalidate it either. He hinged his decision to affirm Bradley's prior ruling on poorly written indictments. "They are so defective," he wrote, "that no judgment of conviction should be pronounced upon them."

Justices Clifford, Davis, Hunt, and Bradley dissented and argued outright that Section 6 was a valid exercise of congressional authority. But they agreed with Waite in deeming the indictments too flawed to sustain convictions. Between *Reese* and *Cruikshank*, the chief justice had invalidated key provisions of the Enforcement Act and written opinions completely ignoring that Black people's civil and voting rights—Black people's very lives—lay on the guillotine. Justice Bradley, who had demonstrated the transformational potential of The Trinity, wrote no words.

Back at the Hamburg warehouse, the Black militiamen inside and the White terrorists surrounding it exchanged gunfire. One White man took a bullet to the head and died. The White terrorists, incensed, turned their cannon on the warehouse and blasted away.

Outmatched, the militiamen tried to escape into the darkness. The terrorists caught some and executed four.

Southern caste preservationists took their cues from Waite's opinions, visiting an untold number of horrors on Black souls in the run-up to the election, concluding that the highest Court wouldn't shield Black rights and lives. In 1873, the Grant administration prosecuted more than thirteen hundred enforcement cases. By 1876, the number nose-dove to 152. The era of enforcement had stalled as voters headed to the booths on November 7, 1876.

DURING THE PREVIOUS LEG of our journey, we witnessed Republican Rutherford B. Hayes deliver his March 4, 1877, inaugural address that announced his administration would abandon Reconstruction. We skipped, however, the preceding turmoil.

On election night, Hayes's camp climbed into bed believing the voters had rejected their candidate. Democrat Samuel Tilden's camp awakened the next morning assuming the party's nominee had won and that Democrats would occupy the White House for the first time since James Buchanan vacated it in March 1861. But Florida, South Carolina, and Louisiana sent conflicting returns to Congress, and with one electoral vote from Oregon also in dispute, twenty electoral votes went unallocated. Tilden needed just one. Hayes all twenty. With the Senate in Republican hands and the House under Democratic control, Congress could not decide how to apportion the disputed electoral votes. In January 1877, both parties shook hands to establish a fifteen-member Joint Electoral Commission, with ten congressmen and five Supreme Court Justices, each party selecting five congressmen and two justices, to settle a bitter contest that was inflaming unhealed wounds from the war. The Democrats chose Clifford and Field, the Republicans Miller and Strong. Those justices selected the fifteenth commission member, Bradley, identified as the least political remaining justice.

On February 8, 1877, a month before Hayes delivered his inaugural address, the commission gathered in the Court Chamber and debated who would receive Florida's electoral votes, the first state the commission would decide. A little after two in the afternoon, Bradley read his opinion. Because only he had demonstrated a willingness to vote across party lines at previous meetings, all understood that his judgment would set precedent and name a president. With all eyes fixed on the diminutive silver-haired justice, he gave Hayes Florida's electoral votes. Bradley, a Republican, stayed true to his party. Caste preservationists, watching as the remaining federal troops in the South scampered away after the newly inaugurated president recalled them, resumed regulating the scope of Black freedom unencumbered by fear of federal reprisal. Republicans had concluded that claiming the mantle of Black rights hamstrung their political ambitions. Two years after an electoral bloodbath that lost them the House, the Republicans, through their nominee, campaigned on quitting Reconstruction and won. The Republican Party had shed its old skin and slithered away, stranding Black southerners, like Sallie Robinson, born into slavery in Tennessee in 1850, and left them to fend for themselves.

AT TEN MINUTES PAST THREE in the morning of May 22, 1879, Robinson, a twenty-eight-year-old attractive Black woman waiting at the three-story train depot in Grand Junction, Tennessee, boarded a Memphis and Charleston Railroad Company train with a light-complexioned man with light hair and light blue eyes. The two had bought the first-class tickets to reach their destination, Lynchburg, Virginia. As Robinson and her companion attempted to access the ladies' car, reserved for women with first-class tickets and their male escorts, the train's conductor, C. W. Reagin, blocked the door. Reagin grabbed her arm, bruising it, and denied their entrance.

You "must go in the other car," Reagin demanded, pointing to the smoking car.

They complied but wanted what they had purchased. When the conductor sat down, the companion approached Reagin.

"Why do you people try to force yourselves in that car?" Reagin asked.

They had bought first-class tickets, the companion responded, which entitled their admission into the ladies' car. "[S]he is my aunt," he added.

"She is your aunt—then you are colored too?" replied Reagin.

"Yes, she is my aunt, and I am a colored man," said Joseph Robinson.

"Then you can take her into the ladies' car but wait till we stop at the first station."

Reagin, a longtime conductor, believed from experience that young attractive Black women accompanied by White men often traveled for illicit purposes and that such White men frequently disturbed the peace of ladies' cars. The Robinsons, upset, detrained at Knoxville, spending days there to register complaints with railroad company officials. Unable to address anyone with power, Joseph Robinson penned a letter to the railroad's superintendent. "We wish to give the road no trouble, but do think we are enttitle' [*sic*] to better treatment while passing over your line, and if the managers cannot guarantee and see that we get better treatment, we will resort to other authorities. Let me hear from you immediately on this matter."

Sallie and her husband, Richard, sued the Memphis and Charleston Railroad Company for an 1875 Civil Rights Act violation, seeking $500 in damages. Sallie Robinson and her nephew faced a common indignity for Black folk traveling throughout the South, even after the passage of the 1875 Act. Segregation improved upon the postwar norm of racial exclusion, but Black folk now withstood discrimination in transportation, restaurants, places of entertainment, hotels, truly any public White-operated place. Lower federal courts struggled to consistently interpret the act. Federal officers bungled its enforcement, uncertain of its requirements. Many assumed that clarity would arrive quickly from the nine black robes, but eight years passed before it landed.

ON AUGUST 4, 1880, months after the Supreme Court had decided *Strauder, Virginia v. Rives,* and *Ex Parte Virginia,* jurors deliberated in Sallie Robinson's lawsuit. After several hours, they couldn't reach a verdict and requested further guidance from Judge Ely Shelby Hammond. "The law," Hammond told the jury, "permits a carrier or his agent to temporarily exclude persons suspected by him of being improper characters until he has a reasonable time to investigate or satisfy himself of their real character, so far as is necessary to enforce the rules of the carrier requiring good conduct of the passengers."

This, the last of Hammond's jury instructions, rankled Robinson's attorney, who objected to it. Jury instructions explain legal rules to jurors to help them reach verdicts. With this and other instructions, Hammond, Robinson's attorney believed, nudged the jurors to side with the railroad company. President Hayes appointed Hammond, choosing the former Confederate Army captain for a new district court seat in Tennessee. Southerners detested Grant's carpetbagger and scalawag appointees. Hayes sought to mollify southerners with hopes of wooing them into the party by tapping "true" southern men like Hammond. The jury ultimately found for the railroad company. Hammond ordered the Robinsons to pay the company's attorney fees plus twenty dollars. The Robinsons appealed, the final case of a series of 1875 Act cases that had been appealed to the Supreme Court.

On October 10, 1875, Bird Gee, a thirty-year-old Black farm laborer, sat down to eat at a hotel breakfast table in Hiawatha, Kansas. Allen McCowan, a White man, complained to Murray Stanley, the hotel owner's son. Stanley asked Gee to leave. Gee refused and Stanley forcibly removed him. George Peck, a U.S. attorney, indicted Stanley, but the federal judges sent *United States v. Stanley* to the Supreme Court without a trial. *United States v. Nichols* concerned W. H. R. Agee, a Black man who, on May 22, 1876, was refused a room at Samuel Nichols's inn in Jefferson City, Missouri. James Botsford, a U.S. attorney, indicted Nichols, but federal judges again sent the matter to the Supreme Court without a trial.

On January 4, 1876, George M. Tyler attempted to enter the dress circle, prime seating reserved for White patrons, at San Francisco's Maguire's Theatre. A White doorkeeper, Michael Ryan, refused Tyler on account of race. U.S. Attorney Walter Van Dyke attempted to prosecute Ryan, but the circuit judge dismissed the case. Van Dyke appealed *United States v. Ryan* to the Supreme Court.

On April 21, 1879, a Black woman, M. L. Porter, who had bought a first-class ticket to travel to Lebanon, Tennessee, tried to enter the ladies' car on a Nashville, Chattanooga, and St. Louis Railroad train.

James Hamilton, the conductor, relegated her to the smoking car. A difference in opinion between two federal judges sent *United States v. Hamilton* to the Supreme Court.

On November 22, 1879, William R. Davis Jr., a twenty-six-year-old Black man, went to Manhattan's Grand Opera House, and the doorkeeper, Samuel Singleton, said his ticket was "no good." A policeman who tried to escort Davis off the property told Davis that opera house managers did not admit Black people. "Perhaps the managers do not," Davis replied. "But the laws of the country [do]." Davis filed a criminal complaint against Singleton, whose lawyer argued the act was unconstitutional. The district judge and circuit judge disagreed and sent the matter to the Supreme Court.

Because each case concerned the equal accommodation sections of the 1875 Act, the Supreme Court consolidated them. Before the Court decided the *Civil Rights Cases* in October 1883, however, Bradley's old colleague, in January 1883, delivered a Supreme Court opinion concerning the Ku Klux Klan Act.

OF THE NINE JUSTICES on the Court in 1883, five heard the jury discrimination cases of the first leg of our journey—Waite, Miller, Field, Bradley, and Harlan—meaning four new black robes, all appointed by Republican presidents, graced the chamber: Samuel Blatchford, Horace Gray, Stanley Matthews, and William Woods, the former Fifth Circuit judge. Woods wrote the opinion in the Klan Act case, *United States v. Harris*, which involved the act's most powerful section, the second, which, amongst other things, punished those conspiring "to deprive individuals of the equal protection of the law or to prevent or hinder state authorities from securing the equal protection of the law."

On August 14, 1876, R. G. Harris, in Crockett County, Tennessee, led a mob that attacked four men—Robert R. Smith, William J. Overton, George W. Wells Jr., and P. M. Wells—all while under arrest and in the lawful custody of Deputy Sheriff William A. Tucker. P. M. Wells died from his injuries. U.S. Attorney William A. Murray indicted Harris and others under the Klan Act for conspiring "for the purpose of preventing and hindering the constituted authorities of the State of Tennessee . . . from giving and securing the due and equal protection of the law." The state, according to Murray's legal theory, bore a duty to protect its lawfully detained prisoners. If the state failed to afford that protection from conspiracies to injure them, the federal government could intervene to punish the conspirators. In other words, Murray articulated the theory we discussed in the House Chamber, that equal protection affirmatively requires states to protect its inhabitants and when they don't provide that protection, the federal government can interject.

The justices relied on the submitted written briefs, hearing no oral argument, and took years to decide it, a delay that disappeared many facts. They didn't know that R. G. Harris was the county sheriff, meaning he wasn't a private individual but rather a state actor. And that all the participants, including the victims, were White. On January 22, 1883, inside the Court Chamber, Woods read his opinion, joined by every member minus Harlan. Woods, who had defended the 1870 Enforcement Act as a Fifth Circuit judge, renounced his prior legal reasoning, concluding that none of the three amendments empowered Congress to pass the second section of the Klan Act.

The Fifteenth Amendment pertained only to voting and accordingly was inapplicable. Same with the Fourteenth Amendment, Woods said, because "it is perfectly clear . . . that its purpose . . . was to place a restraint upon the action of the States" and the act's second section ventured beyond state action. "It applies, no matter how well the State may have performed its duty," Woods said. Twelve years before, in the Eutaw riots case, Woods penned that "the fourteenth amendment not only prohibits the making or enforcing of laws which shall abridge the privileges of the citizen, but prohibits the states from denying to all persons within its jurisdiction the equal protection of the laws. Denying includes inaction as well as action." The words of the amendment remained static, but the Republican Party's fidelity to them had strayed. Woods executed his party's new approach to Black freedom.

Last, Congress couldn't resort to the Thirteenth Amendment, because under the act's second section, "it would be an offence for two or more white persons to conspire, etc., for the purpose of depriving another white person of the equal protection of the laws."

A law that could punish White intra-racial violence, in other words, was inappropriate legislation to enforce the Thirteenth Amendment.

Aside from its obvious direct harm to Black people, the decision meant that caste preservationists could continue to intimidate and murder White people into never politically aligning with Black folk, severely frustrating Black people's ability to forge the interracial political coalitions necessary to reap the full fruits of their citizenship. George Spencer, the senator from Alabama who delivered an impassioned speech on the need for the 1870 Enforcement Act, spoke to how Black and White people sympathetic to the federal government feared for their scalps in the South. White conservatives had long responded to opposing political thought with blades and bullets. And state authorities watched with either smiling or helpless faces, unwilling or unable to stanch such bleeding. This necessitated federal intervention to atone for state failure. Eight justices were Republicans. Yet all but one endorsed an interpretation of the Constitution that left their ideological doppelgängers vulnerable. Nothing compelled this decision. They chose it.

While drafting the Fourteenth Amendment, Republicans wanted to suppress the persecution of White Republicans, particularly carpetbaggers who streamed into the South after the Union triumph. Northerners had long fumed about southern states abridging their rights whenever traveling there. One seminal incident occurred in 1844, when a Massachusetts governor sent Samuel Hoar to South Carolina to investigate the selling of free Black Massachusettsans into slavery. South Carolina's government blocked Hoar and his inquiry, and a mob ran him out of the state. Examples of caste preservationists committing outrages against White carpetbaggers and scalawags littered the period between the end of the war and the drafting of the Fourteenth Amendment. Recall that White supremacists burned the home of Delos White and William Phillips in Grant Parish, murdering White and forcing Phillips to vanish to avoid a similar fate. Congress had crafted an amendment that could have also protected them.

The justices could have interpreted the amendment as protecting identifiable classes of persecuted people—lower castes. Black folk met that standard as did White Republicans in the South—native White southerners abused them, through castework, as race traitors.

Such a construction squared with the amendment's history and text. The White victims in *Harris* might not have met this standard and were therefore not deserving of this contemplated protection. That would not have invalidated the Klan Act's second section, but rather have rendered it inapplicable to this controversy. The Supreme Court, instead, narrowly interpreted The Trinity, invalidating the Klan Act's brawniest section, because its terms could have protected White people too, leaving Black folk without its shelter.

Ten months later, those who had mauled the Klan Act dug their claws into the 1875 Civil Rights Act.

THE RACIAL LANDSCAPE in America had shifted drastically from when Bradley wrote his *Blyew* dissent to when he, on October 15, 1883, read his opinion in the *Civil Rights Cases* in the Court Chamber under a thirty-eight-star flag. In 1871, those most dedicated to Black freedom still had reason for hope. Just the previous year, the states had ratified the Fifteenth Amendment, and Frederick Douglass reveled about his people's future. But in 1883, the Reconstruction story had resolved with caste preservationists winning.

In 1882, ex-President Hayes wrote to Chief Justice Waite, reminding him that the Republican Party needed to maintain a friendship with the White South. "With that sentiment right," Hayes scribed, "our cause will advance, with that sentiment wrong, all our efforts will fail." Waite responded, "I agree with you entirely as to the necessity of keeping public sentiment at the south in our favor." The Republican-dominated Court needed to cement a construction of The Trinity that matched Republicans' new race politics. Waite turned to his most trusted ally, the man who had ghostwritten many of his opinions, Justice Bradley, to strike down the 1875 Act's equal accommodation sections.

Bradley launched his *Civil Rights Cases* analysis by assessing the sections under the Fourteenth Amendment. "Individual invasion of individual rights is not the subject matter of the amendment," Bradley said, repudiating his earlier pronouncements. Explicitly discriminatory laws, like West Virginia's jury discrimination law, violated the amendment as did state actors who denied civil rights on account of race, like judges who intentionally excluded Black men from juries. The Fourteenth Amendment, Bradley observed, certainly protected civil rights. And Congress could pass "corrective legislation" to redress their deprivation. Only states, though, could deny rights. A private individual preventing someone from enjoying a right was not tantamount to denying a right. A right exists until a state takes it away.

A state legislature, not Congress, could legally require equal treatment at, for example, theaters. Otherwise, Bradley said, "Congress [would] take the place of the State legislatures and . . . supersede them." Congress cannot legislate on subjects that the Constitution, through the Tenth Amendment, reserved to the states. The equal accommodation sections, Bradley said, were not examples of corrective legislation. That sort of legislation would have limited itself to state-perpetrated wrongs. The sections, instead, forced private businesses and individuals to either affirmatively treat all people equally or risk criminal sanction, regardless of whether the state required unequal treatment. Bradley did seemingly concede that if, say, a state legally required segregation on, say, trains, then that would run afoul of the Constitution. "If the laws themselves make any unjust discrimination, amendable to the prohibitions of the Fourteenth Amendment, Congress has full power to afford a remedy under that amendment and in accordance with it," Bradley said. Remember this for the next leg of our journey.

A decade before, Bradley explained to then circuit judge Woods that "Denying includes inaction as well as action. And denying the equal protection of the laws includes the omission to protect as well as the omission to pass laws for protection." In truth, Congress, through the public accommodation sections, did pass corrective legislation—the sections corrected the inaction of the states. Bradley nurtured a construction, only to orphan it later.

His majority opinion then proceeded to whether the Thirteenth Amendment empowered Congress to require equal public accommodations. Remember, in 1875, Bradley boldly constructed the Thirteenth Amendment, depicting it as a sentinel guarding Black freedom in the "war of race." Eight years later, Bradley reiterated that the amendment established "universal civil and political freedom throughout the United States" and that it allowed Congress to, he said, "pass all laws necessary and proper for abolishing all badges and incidents of slavery in the United States." And under the Thirteenth Amendment, as opposed to the Fourteenth Amendment, Congress could legislate directly upon private individuals. No limitation to corrective legislation under this amendment. The Court's resolution, then, turned on whether "the act of a mere individual, the owner of the inn, the public conveyance or place of amusement, refusing the accommodation, be justly regarded as imposing any badge of slavery . . . ?"

No, Bradley answered, and to suggest contrarily, he said, would be "running the slavery argument into the ground to make it apply to every act of discrimination which a person may see fit to make as to the guests he will entertain, or as to the people he will take into his coach or cab or car." Bradley reaches this result by peeling the White supremacist meaning from the deprivations experienced by Black victims of race discrimination. Hotel managers, train conductors, theater operators denied service to Black folk because White folk considered them, as Chief Justice Taney once explained, lower beings "unfit to associate with the white race." Bradley ignored this and referred to the opprobrium visited upon Black people every day in America as instances of "mere discrimination[s]."

Bradley then uttered one of the more flippant lines from a justice's voice to ever echo in the Chamber's post-emancipation history, saying that "when a man has emerged from slavery . . . there must be some stage in the progress of his elevation when he takes the rank of a mere citizen, and ceases to be the special favorite of the laws, and when his rights as a citizen, or a man, are to be protected in the ordinary modes by which other men's rights are protected." Inside the U.S. Custom House in New Orleans, Bradley's brain danced like a ballerina to avoid the logic of the *Slaughter-House Cases* to protect Black freedom with the Thirteenth Amendment. Inside the Supreme Court Chamber in the *Civil Rights Cases*, his brain sliced like a sword, shredding that amendment while also carving the protection from equal protection.

Bradley was once willing to sacrifice the rights of enslaved people to save the Union, proposing, before the war, amendments that would have continued slavery. Bradley's works reveal a man who, like much of White America, imagined the nation as a political union between White people. During Reconstruction, when much of the party saw itself as needing to protect Black freedom not only out of a sense of moral righteousness, but because Black southern voters facilitated national Republican domination, Bradley was willing to seemingly invite Black folk into the American bargain. But once his party concluded that defending Black freedom hindered electoral goals, he shooed Black folk away.

White Americans had agreed—the nation should remove itself from supervising southern governance, and Bradley played his part, conceiving a construction of The Trinity that captured America's new bargain that excluded Black people. In *Strauder* and *Ex Parte Virginia*, the Court had drawn specific boundaries. States could not enact laws that explicitly denied Black people fundamental rights, and state actors could not directly deny Black people fundamental rights because of race. Three years later, the Court announced that states *could* sit idly by as private individuals relegated the Black population to an inferior station, and Congress could do nothing to enforce these rights—supposedly nationally protected—against state inaction.

Earlier in this leg of our journey, we observed that caste preservationists and White Republicans had sparked a national tug-of-war over Black freedom. Caste preservationists routed the Republicans, wanting to create a racial caste system much more than their foes wanted to enliven caste abolitionism. The Supreme Court, full of Republicans, the theoretical allies of Black Americans, potential vessels for caste abolitionism, wrote the rules that enabled the South to begin sketching the new racial caste system, dispiriting the souls of Black folk, including that of a preeminent leader.

"WHAT DO YOU THINK of the civil rights decision?" a reporter asked Frederick Douglass, in his late sixties, gray-haired, hours after Bradley delivered the *Civil Rights Cases* decision.

"It is rather disheartening, and I regard it as a step backward," Douglass responded in his Washington, D.C., home overlooking the

Anacostia River. "At the close of the war," he continued, "in view of services rendered by colored citizens, there was a disposition on the part of the loyal people of the country to concede to them complete citizenship and equal civil rights in the uses of all public conveyances and institutions, and I regard the decision, as far as I understand it, as part of the general reaction naturally following the increased friendship for the South, which comes of the dying out of the old controversy on the subject of slavery.

"Nearly all the concessions the colored people have received have been the result of the antagonism of the two sections," Douglass said, "and as that antagonism vanishes, I have expected a partial return of the old ideas and usages which preceded the war.

"I have said that I do not despair on account of this decision. It is contrary to the spirit of Christianity, contrary to the spirit of the age, and, as I think, in violation of the Fourteenth and Fifteenth Amendments, and tends directly to make the colored people of the country an aggrieved class, and to weakening that spirit of patriotism which the nation may need for its protection in some perilous hour."

That same night, the manager of the Haverly troupe, blackface minstrel performers, crashed the stage at an Atlanta opera house to read a newspaper report announcing that the Supreme Court had invalidated the 1875 Civil Rights Act. White audience members erupted in a "thunder of applause" that "was never before heard within the walls of the opera house." The hoots subsided, and the manager repeated the news. Again they roared, smiling and congratulating each other. Black attendees occupying the suddenly legal "colored galleries" sat quietly, understanding what the White people cheering understood—the Supreme Court had certified that their citizenship held less value.

A justice on a southern state supreme court messaged Chief Justice Waite, applauding him on Bradley's opinion: "It has done much to confirm me in the doctrine of State Rights, and the probabilities of the revival of that doctrine seem imminent." That grateful justice further wrote that White southerners simply wanted to "use all lawful means to keep the white man supreme in politics." The chief justice, in other words, earned praise for his Court siding with White Supremacy.

In *Harris* and the *Civil Rights Cases*, the Court announced the *state action doctrine*, the construction that the Fourteenth Amendment only curbed the abuses of state law or state actors, pretending away the "protection" in "equal protection." This doctrine exists still, inflicting all manner of havoc and pain as we will later encounter. If the state kept its distance, the White masses could confine Black folk to the basement of society and the federal government could only watch. Caste preservationists considered the state action doctrine essential in the maintenance of the racial caste system.

With The Trinity, Congress wrote words to include the Black population within the American political union. Bradley's opinion, joined by all but one justice, notified that the country reserved muscle and bone for White rights. The case's lone dissenter opened the curtains to an alternate ending.

THE FIFTY-YEAR-OLD JUSTICE John Marshall Harlan had dissented in the *Civil Rights Cases* but hadn't completed his opinion when Bradley delivered his. He had been poring over it for months, ruminating over penning perfection such that "[m]any times," his wife, Malvina, recalled, "he would get up in the middle of the night in order to jot down some thought or paragraph which he feared might elude him.

"It was a trying time for him."

One Sunday morning, Harlan left their Washington home for church. While he was out, Malvina retrieved an attractive antique wooden inkstand that Harlan found that had once belonged to Chief Justice Taney. She cleaned, polished, and filled it with ink. After removing all other inkstands from his study table, she placed Taney's near his papers.

As she looked at it, it said to her, "*I* will help him."

Malvina awaited his return home. As the tall, husky jurist opened the front door, she greeted him.

"I have put a bit of inspiration on your study table," she said in the happiest voice she could muster. "I believe it is just what you need, and I am sure it will help you."

"His pen fairly flew on that day," Malvina remembered, "and, with the running start he then got, he soon finished his dissent."

DONNING THE BLACK ROBE bestows on judges the cloak of objectivity. That silk fabric awards the aura of nonpartisanship and dispassion. In his study, Harlan dipped his pen into the same inkwell as did Taney when he scribed *Dred Scott* and, with his opening paragraph, yanked off that garb of false impartiality. The "opinion in these cases," Harlan wrote, referencing Bradley's majority work, "proceeds upon grounds entirely too narrow and artificial. I cannot resist the conclusion that the substance and spirit of the recent amendments of the Constitution have been sacrificed by a subtle and ingenious verbal criticism." Both the Thirteenth and Fourteenth Amendments, Harlan determined, empowered Congress to enact the 1875 Act's public accommodation sections. His interpretation of The Trinity, unlike that of Bradley, respected Black people as members of We the People.

The Thirteenth Amendment, Harlan contended, established more than amnesty from chains, for it also granted "immunity from, and protection against, all discrimination against [Black people], because of their race, in respect to such civil rights as belong to freemen of other races." Because the Thirteenth Amendment "established universal freedom" in America, "there shall be no discrimination, based merely upon race or color, in respect of the accommodations and advantages of public conveyances, inns, and places of amusement," Harlan charged. The amendment expired the notion that such badges or incidents of slavery should continue tormenting Black life, and Congress could legislate to enforce that immunity.

Bradley considered "public conveyances, inns, and places of amusement" private businesses that could serve whomever and make race distinctions in treatment, not unlike a private citizen could host a private gathering for White guests only. Harlan dismantled that logic, specifying that the nation's legal tradition considered such companies quasi-public. Regarding railroads, for example, the Court, in 1873, expressed that although "the [railroad] was private, its work was public, as much so as if it were constructed by the State." He similarly pointed out the Court's history of deeming inns and theaters as public spaces. They were, Harlan explained, "instrumentalities of the State, because they are charged with duties to the public, and are amendable, in respect of their duties and functions, to governmental regulations." In short, the Thirteenth Amendment empowered Congress to require equal treatment in public accommodations. "I am of the opinion," Harlan wrote, "that such discrimination practised by corporations and individuals in the exercise of their public or quasi-public functions is a badge of servitude the imposition of which Congress may prevent under its power, by appropriate legislation, to enforce the Thirteenth Amendment."

Harlan, moving to his Fourteenth Amendment analysis, explained that the amendment presented Black folk both national and state citizenship, ushering Black people "into the political community known as the 'People of the United States.'" That newfound citizenship afforded an "exemption from race discrimination in respect of any civil right belonging to citizens of the white race in the same State." Congress, therefore, can legislate to protect that right. Harlan disagreed that the Fourteenth Amendment only allowed Congress to negate discriminatory state law or the discrimination of state actors. Limiting Congress to corrective legislation would render Section 5 superfluous. As we discussed during our House Chamber visit, the judiciary could strike down any state law that violated Section 1 of the Fourteenth Amendment. Congress need not legislate to annul state law. Courts can strike down laws that violate the Constitution. That's the province of the federal judiciary. The Fourteenth Amendment granted Congress power to legislate affirmatively and did not simply limit the power of the states. Because the amendment, according to Harlan, conferred the right to exemption from race distinctions with regards to civil rights, Congress could pass laws to enforce and protect that right when it was denied.

Harlan noted that the Supreme Court, to protect slaveowners' rights, allowed Congress to pass aggressive legislation that acted against private individuals. "I insist that the national legislature may," Harlan wrote, "without transcending the limits of the Constitution, do for human liberty and the fundamental rights of American citizenship, what it did, with the sanction of this court, for the protection of slavery and the rights of the masters of fugitive slaves." Harlan, furthermore, explained that the men who penned the Fourteenth

Amendment understood that "the great danger to equal enjoyment by citizens of their rights, as citizens, was to be apprehended not altogether from unfriendly State legislation, but from the hostile action of corporations and individuals in the States." And Republican congressmen wrote the Fourteenth Amendment believing they provided themselves the power to restrain that danger through legislation.

Harlan repudiated Bradley's suggestion that the 1875 Act gifted Black people special favor. "What the nation, through Congress, has sought to accomplish in reference to that race is what had already been done in every State of the Union for the white race—to secure and protect rights belonging to them as freemen and citizens, nothing more." Congress only enacted legislation like the 1875 Act because White people denied Black people their rights. Enacting laws to protect rights wasn't a special favor—it was the purpose of government. It was equal protection. With the 1875 Act, Congress infused meaning into the *protection* in equal protection. But, because of Bradley's opinion, Black folk could not feel the benevolent hand of equal government.

In 1842, Justice Story imparted the principle that "No court of justice can be authorized so to construe any clause of the constitution as to defeat its obvious ends, when another construction, equally accordant with the words and sense thereof, will enforce and protect them." The black robes should have applied Story's principle to The Trinity. But, in a majority opinion written by someone who knew better, America proclaimed its refusal to reform itself to protect Black freedom. Bradley, a man of faith reared to adhere to "absolute justice and charity to all," unmasked himself to be no better than the White masses who supported a racial caste system, providing justice and charity to just some. He could have risen above. Should have risen above. He *chose* not to.

IN 1888, FIVE YEARS AFTER HOLDING that the Fourteenth Amendment didn't affirmatively oblige states to provide equal protection, the Supreme Court held in *Pembina Consolidated Silver Mining Co. v. Pennsylvania* that private corporations qualified as people under the Fourteenth Amendment and therefore were entitled to equal protection. This case demonstrated that the Supreme Court could choose to interpret the Constitution to protect the rights of favored interests. The justices simply disfavored Black people.

Thus far we have learned what the states could not do. State legislatures could not enact law that discriminated on its face nor could state officers intentionally racially discriminate. During this journey, we learned that The Trinity, as interpreted by the Supreme Court, would not impose any affirmative duty to protect Black rights from the misdeeds of private individuals. Caste preservationists were building a durable racial caste system, but one with exploitable fissures. How far could the states go to suture them?

Let's proceed to the next leg of our journey, set in 1890s Mississippi. That state attempted to spearhead the construction of a new durable racial caste system without those fissures. Through the eyes of a Black lawyer, we will explore how Mississippi's leading caste preservationists attempted to achieve their objective.

# Third Leg:
# The Mississippi Inspiration

HERE IN APRIL 1896, Cornelius Jonas Jones Jr., a slim, handsome brown-skinned thirty-eight-year-old freedman, writes a letter to James H. McKenney, the clerk of the U.S. Supreme Court.

"You will certainly pardon me for such informality," the caste abolitionist pens in cursive with black ink on a sheet of lined paper, "but being so deeply interested in cases no. 710 and 711 of John Gibson and Charley Smith from [the] Mississippi Supreme Court, argued and submitted there last December, I crave of you in the strictest professional confidence to know do you think an opinion will be reached in them by the Court at this term[?] And do you surmise any hope for my success[?] You can appreciate my anxiety and can rely on my confidence in the matter."

Born enslaved on August 13, 1858, in Hinds County, Mississippi, Jones practices law from his office here in Greenville, a city nestled along the state's western border. Americans dub this region the Mississippi Delta. Located in the state's northwest, the Delta sits between the Mississippi River to the west and the Yazoo River to the east, and includes portions of Louisiana and Arkansas. Its rich dark soil, providing ideal farming conditions, enticed speculators to buy land, raze trees blanketing the flat topography, and purchase humans to till it. Three decades after the war, Black people comprise a large majority of the residents in the area—part of the Black Belt—lumbering from bondage to sharecropping, yet serving the same overlord, King Cotton.

Gibson and Smith, two Black men convicted of murder by all-White juries, secured Jones for representation. Jones is seeking to reverse their convictions, arguing that, in each matter, court officials practiced jury discrimination, violating the Fourteenth Amendment. You might liken Jones to George Davenport—a lawyer simply striving to protect Black people's right to a fair trial. Don't. Suffrage motivates Jones. Through the Trojan horse of jury discrimination, he believes he can sack the state's Black disenfranchisement scheme, resetting the clock to when Black Mississippians, with their population advantage, decided elections.

For caste preservationists to garden their beloved racial caste system on land The Trinity also inhabits, they must harvest the power of deceit. America yearns to project an image of itself as adhering to the rules of its game. Deceit plays a face-saving role—it enables America to pretend to honor its rules, while defiling them. A society that promises freedom and equality under the law can perpetuate racial trauma and still project an honest face if it lies away its abuses. This anthem—where caste preservationists oppress Black folk, and then, when challenged, lie about it—plays throughout America, throughout history, and especially throughout Jones's Mississippi.

How will the Supreme Court answer such deceit? Will it indulge the deceit? Even refine the deceit? Or will the Court confront the deceit? Maybe expose the deceit? Welcome to the next leg of our journey, where, against the rising tide of deceit, a lawyer armed with the skeleton of an intriguing plan fights to integrate the jury box to integrate the voting booth.

Understanding Jones requires understanding the Mississippi that molded him and his generation of Black southerners. The Mississippi that swelled him with hope. That then siphoned it out. Let's open with a scene from Capitol Hill in winter 1870.


OVER THE COURSE of a few days in February 1870, a light-skinned Black man with a long, pointy nose and a closely trimmed beard sat on a lounge against the back wall of the Senate Chamber. Hiram Rhodes Revels projected silent dignity. Observers crammed into the above galleries to witness the fate of Revels, there to claim his mahogany desk and become Congress's first Black member.

In November 1869, White and Black men in Mississippi, under surveilling Union blue uniforms, voted. Part of the multifaceted Congressional Reconstruction project involved enfranchising Black men, hosting state conventions to draft new constitutions, and electing new state and local representatives. In 1868, nearly 97 percent of Black voting age men in Mississippi had registered to vote. Just about 81 percent of their White counterparts had, with many of them blocked for bearing arms for, or otherwise aiding in, the rebellion. After the final tallies trickled in, Mississippi Republicans reveled in a 76,000 to 38,000 victory, with Black men delivering the Republicans their state legislature majority and ratifying Mississippi's new constitution that guaranteed civil and political equality.

Inside the Senate Chamber, Radical Republican senator Henry Wilson of Massachusetts said, "I present the credentials of Hon-[orable] H. R. Revels, Senator-elect from Mississippi, and I ask that they be read, and that he be sworn in."

Senator Willard Saulsbury intruded: "I object to the reception of that evidence of the election of this man to the Senate of the United States."

Born free in North Carolina in 1827, Revels delivered a prayer in January 1869 to open the Senate session in the Mississippi legislature, making "a deep and profound impression" that inspired his appointment. Until the Seventeenth Amendment's ratification in 1913, state legislatures chose U.S. senators. Five years after the war, Black Mississippians approached a milestone—one of their own joining the world's most deliberative body. But Democratic members connived to exclude him.

"Mr. President," said Maryland Democrat George Vickers, "whenever an individual presents himself to this body for membership in it, and he has been legally and regularly elected to the Senate, and his credentials are properly authenticated, and he be thirty years of age, and be an inhabitant of the State from which he was elected, and has been a citizen of the United States for nine years, I cannot raise any objection to his admission. . . . My objections are all founded upon the Constitution."

The Fourteenth Amendment granted birthright citizenship, overturning *Dred Scott*. The states, however, ratified it just two years prior, meaning the age of Revels's American citizenship, according to Vickers's argument, fell shy of the requisite nine years. Senate Democrats proposed that the Judiciary Committee examine the matter before admitting Revels.

After Democratic senators argued their position, Republican Charles Sumner, perhaps the Senate's most committed caste abolitionist, spoke. In 1849, Sumner represented, unsuccessfully, Sarah Roberts, a five-year-old Black girl proposing to integrate Boston public schools. "The separation of children in the Schools on account of race or color," he argued before Massachusetts's highest court, "is in the nature of *Caste*, and, on this account, a violation of Equality." Seven years later, a congressman nearly bludgeoned him to death with a cane in the Senate Chamber—retribution for Sumner airing an anti-slaveholder screed.

"The vote on this question will be an historic event, marking the triumph of a great cause," said Sumner, a six-foot-four man with a booming voice and stylishly coiffed hair. "From this time there can be no backward step. After prolonged and hard-fought battle, beginning with the Republic, convulsing Congress, and breaking out in blood, the primal truths declared by our fathers are practically recognized. All men are created equal, says the great Declarations, and now a great act attests this verity."

Other senators weighed in. Cheers and jeers ping-ponged between the galleries' warring factions. After days-long discussion, the senators voted along party lines, forty-eight in favor to eight against, with twelve absent votes.

Senator Wilson, elegantly dressed, escorted Revels to the speaker's desk in the front of the room. Those in the galleries stood for a better view. With his right hand raised, Revels took the oath of office, swearing to "support and defend the Constitution."

————

DAYS LATER, at a packed Black church in Baltimore, Revels preached that the "seals of a new era are broken, and we stand tonight in the full radiancy of a period of time which has no counterpart in history," alluding to the Fifteenth Amendment's recent ratification. "Certainly, if the African race ever had just reasons for giving utterance to a glorious paean of universal emancipation, it will be when the passage of that amendment is officially announced."

Black men throughout the nation gained a constitutional right— an exemption from race-based denials of voting rights—and Revels believed that should buoy his people's spirits. Aching under a centuries-long albatross that hunched their shoulders, Black folk might soon feel liberated enough to straighten their spines. Maybe raise their chins. And thus a preteen Cornelius Jones—later a lawyer and the protagonist of this leg of our journey—living in Vicksburg, Mississippi, too young during bondage to have remembered its horror, grew up in a world where a man of his race could become a U.S. senator.

Months afterward, Jones's family visited a Freedman's Bank, chartered by Congress to address the banking needs of the freedpeople. There, he opened an account as did his parents, Cornelius Sr. and Hannah, and his two older sisters, Celia and Sarah, and signed a banking document with an *X*. Though the son of two farmworkers who owned no real property, living in a family with a net worth less than $200, events provided him reason to believe a rigid racial caste system would not confine his future.

But, as we shall soon witness in person, on Saturday, September 4, 1875, evil can disrupt optimism.

SAVOR THE ENTICING AROMA of barbecue. Relish the sun beating against your skin. Survey both the land once worked by enslaved people and the remnants of this home, surrounded by magnolia and pecan trees, that Union boots demolished during the war. Say "hello," to Moss Hill, a twenty-acre plantation gilded by woodland and hills in the outskirts of Clinton, Mississippi, a small, sleepy college town ten miles west of the capital, Jackson.

The local Republican Party is sponsoring a political gathering here, soon to kick off. State senator Charles "Charley" Caldwell, a stern-faced Black man with hulking jowls and a widow's peak hairline, represents this county. Hinds County. He is coordinating the proceedings where more than two thousand Black Republicans, wearing gala attire, will gather. Men and women will listen to speeches. Children will frolic. Entrepreneurs will sell baked goods. About two hundred White Mississippians will attend, including about fifty Democrats. Study the scene here, where Black men will seek to inform themselves on candidates and issues ahead of an election in which they plan to vote without problem. A few months earlier, Justice Bradley sat in a New Orleans courtroom and overturned the convictions in the Colfax Massacre case. U.S. Attorney Beckwith predicted that Bradley's circuit court decision would embolden White supremacists. License them to slay. We have planted our feet in the state most likely to confirm Beckwith's prophecy.

"Charley, this looks bad," remarks Daniel Crawford, a Black shoemaker, before the event starts. "Those four young men—the two Sivleys I know," continues Crawford, referring to four White men, two sets of brothers, nearby. "One I know well and these two Neals—these men, I think they must be that committee."

"O, no," Caldwell, one of five Black men elected to the state Senate in 1869, responds. "I reckon not."

The influential editor of the pro-Democrat *Raymond Gazette*, George W. Harper, inspired Crawford's "committee" anxieties. Harper, who will roam the grounds today, implored Democrats in an editorial to send a committee of White conservatives to any Republican gathering ahead of the November state elections. "[W]henever the radical speakers proceed to mislead the negroes, and open with falsehoods, and deceptions, and misrepresentations," Harper wrote, a committee must "stop them right then and there and compel them to tell the truth or quit the stand."

Before proceeding, we must recount recent Mississippi political history.

BY NOVEMBER 1869, Republicans dominated postwar state politics, but the moderates captained the party. Aside from a public education system that ushered many toward literacy, Black folk, responsible for the party's ascendancy, received crumbs for their loyalty. For instance, in February 1873, Republican governor Ridgley C. Powers summoned every state legislator to the governor's mansion to witness him signing the Civil Rights Law of 1873. Like the federal 1875 Civil Rights Act, Mississippi's variant barred race discrimination in places of public accommodation, building on a law that outlawed segregation in modes of transportation. Powers boasted that the ceremony marked an "advanced step in the enlightened tendency of the time" because Mississippi, he said, earned "the distinction of being the first State in the Union to guarantee, by statutory enactment, full civil as well as political rights to all her citizens, without distinction."

The law flopped. White-owned businesses converted to private establishments and served their customers by invitation only. Within twelve months, those businesses to operating openly as Whites-only enterprises. Very infrequently did Black folk clamor publicly to compel equal treatment, and besides a few occasions on railroads, such bellowing went unanswered. Moderate Republicans failed to enforce the law and the kindling of transformational change petered out. Such limited progress calmed the rage of men like editor Harper, dissuading them from igniting violence to reclaim the state. Yet, he and his ilk reconsidered that approach when, in January 1874, the Radicals, through the candidacy of Adelbert Ames, the former military governor, captured the governor's mansion for the first time.

"The colored people will never be less citizens than they are today," Ames told the legislature during his inaugural address, "and would it not be wiser to recognize their manhood and citizenship with all the rights and privileges which logically and legally pertain thereto?"

Defending Black Mississippians responsible for his election, Ames said, "The colored people ask nothing in charity—they demand but their rights. . . .

"I shall deem myself fortunate if I can be . . . instrumental," he continued, "in removing all causes of distrust, real or imaginary, which may exist between the different classes of our citizens, and I hope the day is not distant when questions of this character shall disappear from our politics. This cannot be, however, until each race shall be secured in every right, civil and political."

In caste preservationists' imagination, they had submitted to six years of carpetbag misrule and now their ultimate adversary, the Radicals, spouting caste abolitionism, won the governor's seat. Worse yet, Black men occupied the lieutenant governor, secretary of state, and superintendent of education offices. Harper guided his kindred spirits to brace for strife: "We must use remedies equal to the emergencies of the case if we desire to arrest the disease."

Assisted by violence that suppressed the Black vote in the South, the Democrats carried the 1874 national midterm elections, earning the party the House of Representatives and exciting Mississippi's caste preservationists—perhaps they too could reclaim power through bloodletting. When Republicans controlled the presidency and both houses of Congress, Mississippi Democrats sheathed their swords, fearing that forcibly retaking the state would provoke Washington's wrath. But a sympathetic House could impede a unified federal response. And events in Louisiana, where White insurgents had slaughtered Black guardians and a Supreme Court justice had just freed the only convicted perpetrators, emboldened them. These circumstances explain why, just days before this Clinton political event, Democratic ruffians dispersed a Republican meeting in Yazoo City and harried the Republican sheriff from town. Caste preservationists in Mississippi, like children, tested the patience of their federal government parents, gauging what would provoke a spanking.

THAT'S THE BACKSTORY, and now, at Moss Hill, Crawford spots six more suspicious-looking White men, youngish, perhaps in their early twenties, donning summer clothing, not the gala attire everyone else is wearing. They join the four who raised his initial concerns. Crawford returns to the forty-three-year-old Caldwell, whom Black people dubbed the meanest man in Clinton for his no-nonsense disposition.

"I do not think we ought to have a meeting here today," Crawford warns. "I feel like as if there is something wrong from these men's appearance. That man would not speak to me. It don't look right now. And they are all armed."

"O, no; I have instructed them not to bring any arms," replies Caldwell, who rose from slavery into the county's most prominent Black leader and one of the state's most influential politicians. "I do not think there will be any fuss, because men not armed are not as apt to risk it as if armed. I have ordered them not to come here armed, and I do not think they will."

At noon, the event starts. The original plan entailed a pure Republican affair. But to conciliate the rabble-rousing Democrats, Amos R. Johnston received an invitation. At about thirty minutes past one, Johnston, a Democratic state Senate candidate, finishes his speech and leaves the speaker's stand erected on a hill in a grove.

Hiram T. Fisher, a White Republican congressional candidate and former Union captain, replaces Johnston to deliver his remarks. Black folk in the crowd yell "Fisher!" to the native Ohioan.

"I happily congratulate the speaker on his conservative tone," Fisher opens, referencing Johnston. "He has made a most remark-able conservative speech, and we have perfect order," he says, the limbs from the surrounding trees deadening his voice and blunting the heat. "I hope the same order course will be maintained at every political meeting that is held this fall."

"Well, we would have peace if you would stop telling your damned lies," a committeeman, about twenty feet away, shouts.

George Swann, a White Republican and a federal court clerk, asks, "Who was it made that remark?"

"It was me," one of the Neal brothers responds.

"That is my brother," the other interjects. "What have you got to say about it?"

Standing in the crowd, Eugene B. Welborne, a Black state leg-islator in Mississippi's lower house, notices this commotion coming from White men a few feet in front of him, nearer the stand. He recognizes one, Frank Thompson, and figures he and the rest came to agitate.

Welborne tells Aleck Wilson, one of about twenty men deputized as a policeman for the event, "Here, I want you to stand here and prevent anything. I see a difficulty brewing here."

Welborne approaches Caldwell, who's behind the speaker's stand, and shares that Frank Thompson was drinking whiskey at this dry event and had been shouting, "Come down! Stop your damned lying there and come down," during Fisher's remarks.

Back in the crowd, Wilson tells Thompson, "While Judge Johnston was speaking nobody interfered. . . . Why cannot Captain Fisher be treated the same way?"

Thompson asks Wilson who he is. Wilson replies he is an officer who will arrest him should his hooliganism continue. The committeemen huddle around Thompson, showing solidarity. One grabs Wilson's collar and drags him down to the foot of the hill. The committeemen and a group of Black men follow, about "seventy-five yards from the speaker's stand and north of it in a little glen surrounded by underbrush and concealed from view."

As the commotion boils, back at the speaker's stand, a man advises Caldwell, "there is a disturbance."

"I will stop it," Caldwell responds. He bolts down the hill armed with but a walking cane.

After arriving, Caldwell asks, "What was the matter?"

"This man," Wilson says, indicating Thompson, "has drawn a pistol on one of the colored men who was marching in the procession" while spewing disrespectful language.

"My young friend," Caldwell says, "for God's sake don't disturb the meeting." Caldwell believes the committeemen are so belligerent that he calls on some other White men to dampen their furor. Caldwell, seeing John Neal, Thompson, and another White man draw their pistols, steps to Neal and tells him, "[T]hat would not do," and repeats that to Thompson. The White men stuff their weapons back into their pants. Disaster ostensibly averted, Caldwell separates the Black men and coaxes them to return up the hill.

Meanwhile, Fisher notices the commotion, pauses his speech, and implores the audience to stay "and listen to me, as my time was limited." Unable to discern exactly what's happening, he figures the fuss will soon subside.

"Go on, go on," chants the audience that remained near the stage.

An obliging Fisher restarts. The band, meanwhile, beats the drums to prod the crowd to return and listen to the speech.

Suddenly, pop! A pistol shot. White smoke from a barrel lifts into the air. Caldwell sees Thompson as the gunman. At least he thinks this. Others eye another committeeman, Martin Sivley. Lewis Hargreaves, one of the Black officers deputized for the day, crumples. A bullet just blew a hole through his skull.

"Fall in, you Raymond crowd!" some committeemen holler.

They form a line and blast away. Black men return fire. The committeemen scatter. Shooting sparks elsewhere. The unrelenting sound of gunfire engulfs the newborn battlefield. The fear. The anguish. The instinct to flee. Those emotions all mushroom. Listen to the shrieks of women and men as they rush up the hill and away from the bedlam. Watch as frantic mothers query a dispersing mass of humanity if it had seen their babies. "I never saw so frightened a gang in my life," one man will later recall. "I have seen soldiers badly panic-struck and running away, but I never saw men get away so quick."

Many Black folk, like Caldwell, will scamper to the federal courthouse in Jackson, the nearest place with stationed federal troops. The swamp will hide others, like Welborne, while a gang of White men raid his home, stealing his livestock and ammunition, and burning down his wagon. When he returns home, he will spot them surrounding it, waiting to execute him.

Within hours, armed White vigilantes will board trains and descend upon Clinton. Over the next few days, caste preservationists will murder Black men, particularly targeting rally attendees. One of the few caste preservationist casualties, Martin Sivley, will lie in rest under a tombstone that reads: "KILLED AT THE CLINTON MISS RIOTS. A BRAVE LIFE SACRIFICED FOR DEMOCRACY." Like the rest, of course, Sivley sacrifices his life to prevent, not protect, democracy. In two decades, the Supreme Court will encounter permutations of this deceit in the cases Jones brings.

The Clinton Riot of 1875 and the litany of other violent outbursts against Black Republicans should convince President Grant to shield them ahead of the November elections. Should Grant fail, a seventeen-year-old Cornelius Jones will witness a coup d'état divesting his people of power.

———

IN THE RUN-UP to the November 1875 state elections, caste preservationists were closing the walls in on active Black Republican Mississippians. Employers fired them. Doctors closed their offices to them. One man recalled, "the colored population were very much intimidated. . . . They appeared to avoid contact with the white people. They held no public meeting. I do not think they had a meeting of the republican club after the Clinton riots."

In mid-October, Governor Ames entered a peace treaty with Mississippi Democratic leaders that required both sides to "abstain from violence, fraud and intimidation," and Ames agreed to disband the state militia he had established to counteract the violent Democratic eruptions bubbling throughout the state. That militia of armed Black men unnerved caste preservationists. Yet, on October 29, Charley Caldwell wrote to Ames, explaining that Democratic leaders were duping him—anti-Black intimidation persisted, and he had deactivated the only outfit that could have protected the state.

A now-spooked Ames exhorted the Grant administration to help subdue the mutineers from murdering and cheating their way into electoral profit. Grant directed the War Department to dispatch troops to the state and instructed Attorney General Edwards Pierrepont on how to deploy the marshals and machinery of the federal judiciary in cooperation with the War Department to secure Mississippi's elections. Unbeknownst to Ames, who expected federal troops on horseback galloping to the rescue, a group of prominent Republicans convinced Grant that Mississippi had already slipped through the party's fingers. And if he swooped in to rescue Black voters from an unsalvageable defeat, the party would also fumble Ohio, the all-important bellwether state. Grant acquiesced, showing how the party nailed Black rights to the cross for the salvation of party politics. Mississippi never welcomed those troops.

Then came Election Day, November 2, 1875. Terrifying cannon fire tore through Hinds County. Democrats, brandishing their sixteen-shooters, drove their horses in squads that slashed through the soil. Persistent gunfire rattled about. In Clinton, three election officers appointed by the board of registration were to supervise the city's polling places and ensure legal compliance. But a cadre of

White men visited each that morning, made them feign illness, and name White Democrat replacements.

Outside a Clinton polling place, Welborne told Caldwell, "I think we might just as well give up; I don't see any use of trying to stay here any longer; we can't do anything here. There these men are riding all about the country with their sixteen-shooters and cutting up in this manner."

"No, we are going to stay right here," Caldwell replied. "You just come right along, and keep your mouth shut. I don't care what they say to you, don't you say a word." Despite witnessing about eighty Black men being denied a ballot, they ventured inside and voted.

Black voting participation crumbled throughout the state, though. In Yazoo County, twenty-five hundred Republican votes were cast in the 1873 election. Two years later, seven. Caste preservationists intimidated Black men from the polls. Killed Black men from the polls. And many who braved the fear still never felt the ballot. Eligible Black voters entered their polling places only to hear, "I cannot find your name here. Stand aside." And fraud often vanished the votes that Black men did cast. About the Black men who trusted him inside a Mashulaville polling place, one White Democrat explained, "They asked me to arrange their tickets for them, which I did just as they told me, and whenever left to me, I always scratched and put the Democratic nominees instead." The former Confederates redeemed the state, implementing the strategy that history remembered as the Mississippi Plan of 1875.

In the aftermath, Mississippi congressman John Roy Lynch, who delivered an impassioned speech in favor of the 1875 Civil Rights Act months prior, met the White House's occupant to vent.

"WHAT SURPRISES ME MORE, Mr. President, is that you yielded and granted this remarkable request," Lynch told Grant, referring to the anti-intervention request the president followed. "That is not like you. It is the first time I have ever known you to show the white feather.

"Instead of granting the request of that committee," Lynch continued, "you should have rebuked the men—told them that it is your duty as chief magistrate of the country to enforce the Constitution and laws of the land, and to protect American citizens in exercise and enjoyment of their rights, let the consequences be what they may; and if by doing this Ohio should be lost to the Republicans it ought to be lost. In other words, no victory is worth having if it is to be brought about upon such conditions as those—if it is to be purchased at such a fearful cost as was paid in this case."

"Yes," replied Grant, "I admit that you are right. I should not have yielded. I believed at the time that I was making a grave mistake. But as presented, it was duty on one side, and party obligation on the other. Between the two I hesitated, but finally yielded to what was believed to be party obligation. . . .

"What you have just passed through in the State of Mississippi is only the beginning of what is sure to follow. I do not wish to create unnecessary alarm, nor to be looked upon as a prophet of evil, but it is impossible for me to close my eyes in the face of things that are as plain to me as the noonday sun."

Caste preservationists, by the year's end, proved Grant prescient.

STAY HOME! Margaret Ann, Charley Caldwell's wife, begged that. But fear hadn't the capacity to bend Caldwell, whose Senate seat went to his Democratic challenger in a stolen election. And thus, on December 30, 1875, he ate dinner and left his house, heading toward Clinton's town center. A blacksmith during slavery, with a free wife and son, Caldwell had enjoyed rare independence for an enslaved man. After the war, he quickly made something of himself. He had another child, a daughter. Owned a home. Amassed a bit of wealth. Could read and write. Became a state senator. Led his people. Caste preservationists loathed him, not only because he dared enter politics and mature into an influential Republican all while having Black skin, but because he killed two White men in self-defense and escaped punishment.

While on his walk, Caldwell encountered a White man, Buck Cabell, his half-brother with whom he shared a genial relationship.

Cabell wanted to celebrate the holiday season over drinks. Caldwell didn't.

"You must take a drink with me," Cabell prodded. "You must take a drink."

Caldwell relented and the two, arm in arm, entered a nearby store and descended into the basement saloon. They lifted their glasses and clanked them together. The White men outside heard their signal— that clank—and shot Caldwell in the back of the head through an open window. He folded onto the floor.

Aware that assassins amassed outside the saloon, Caldwell, wounded, hallooed the name of Judge Edwin Wing Cabaniss. He considered the judge a friend and wanted him to come inside. Cabaniss, among the assassins, remained outside. Caldwell called for the saloon's owner, Charles Chilton. He stayed outside too. Caldwell bellowed for another. No response.

Caldwell chose the next name, Parson Nelson, a pastor.

"Don't shoot me," Nelson said.

"Come in," Caldwell replied. "[T]ake [me] out of the cellar [because I] want to die in the open air and [do] not want to die like a dog closed up."

Nelson carried him to the street where the assassins, among the area's most influential White men, blended with some lower-class White folk, assembled. Caldwell asked that they "take him home to let him see his wife before he died; that he could not live long."

"We'll save him while we got him; dead men tell no tales."

Caldwell stood. Grabbed both sides of his coat. "Remember when you kill me you kill a gentleman and a brave man," he said. "Never say you killed a coward. I want you to remember it when I am gone."

As the thirty to forty rounds minced Caldwell, a seventeen-year-old Cornelius Jones attended Alcorn University. Signing documents with an $X$ at twelve but a second-year student at the state's Black college five years later, Jones took his education at Freedmen's Bureau schools seriously in a way that would enable him to benefit from his American citizenship just as caste preservationists closed opportunity. Participants in democracy in 1869. Confined to a permanent underclass six years later. This somber descent defined the lives of Jones's generation.

For the next fifteen years, Mississippi Democrats retained the throne this way. Fraud. Violence. Terrorism. Economic reprisals. But in 1890, they called a constitutional convention to cement through law what they pilfered through savagery.

THE CASTE PRESERVATIONISTS WHO executed the 1875 plan sought to achieve White political rule through everlasting Democratic primacy. As Democratic senator Lucius Q. C. Lamar wrote in 1879, "The safety of Mississippi lies in the maintenance of the Democratic organization and in its wise direction by conservative leaders who will not forfeit the confidence of the country."

But the interests of White people across the socioeconomic spectrum diverged. White planters in the Delta and White lawyers in the majority-White East should seek differing commitments from their representatives where their interests deviated. Such differences could inspire internal battles. The losers of those battles could leave the party and wage an independent campaign. This theoretical new independent movement could then gather support from an aggrieved and silenced majority of voters, Black men. If an independent opposition party were to field a ticket, the Black vote would prove decisive, and that opposition party could not condone the Democrats abusing Black voters from the polls. A large percentage of White Mississippians, in other words, would teach themselves why and how to oppose castework, a lesson caste preservationists never wanted White folk to learn. Through this conundrum, the defining purpose of Whiteness punches through—it provides people with various interests a shared objective and reason to throw themselves into joint enterprise despite their personal needs.

The Democrats perceived this internal threat and sought to shame their teammates into never turning the key on this nuclear option. James Zachariah George, the chairman of the Mississippi Democratic Party, addressed this at the party's 1877 state convention. "Whatever may happen," George said, "we must settle our disputes and differences among ourselves. We must invite no hostile, no alien arm to give support and weight to one as against another." The convention resolved to treat independent movements "as common enemies to the welfare of the people, and avowed enemies of the Democratic party of the State of Mississippi."

The caste preservationist nightmare became real in the 1881 gubernatorial race between Democrat Robert Lowry and Benjamin King, an ex-Democrat running on a Greenback Party, Republican Party, and Independent Party fusion ticket. Although Lowry won the spirited contest, King reaped more than 40 percent of the vote. This "illustrated in a striking manner the new danger from the enormous negro vote when it was encouraged and supported by a few thousand native white men, who would abandon their own race for the sake of gaining the political offices and political power in the State," wrote Frank Johnston, future state attorney general and a character we will confront later. The mere presence of registered Black voters presented potential independent candidates an opportunity for victory.

After 1875, in no other state did the Black vote evaporate as sharply as in Mississippi, even while Black voters remained a registered majority. In the 1880 presidential election, only a third of registered Black voters cast a ballot, and half supported the Democrats. Republican James Garfield won the presidency despite collecting only 18 percent of the Mississippi vote.

Democrats rode fraud, less so violence, into stable domination. After practically every election season, Democratic wins, particularly those from Black-majority districts, fomented humiliating and factual accusations of fraud from defeated Republicans. The eternal need to swindle to sustain White-minority rule convinced many caste preservationists that the state constitution should disenfranchise Black voters. As one Mississippi judge remarked, "it is no secret that there has not been a full vote and a fair count in Mississippi since 1875—that we have been preserving the ascendency of the white people by revolutionary methods. In plain words, we have been stuffing ballot boxes, committing perjury, and here and there in the state carrying the elections by fraud and violence. . . . [N]o man can be in favor of perpetuating the election methods which have prevailed in Mississippi since 1875 who is not a moral idiot."

The sentiment of drafting a new constitution to purge the electorate of Black voters wafted about time and again. "The state papers," the *Vicksburg Herald* noted in 1877, "are very generally discussing the necessity of a state constitutional convention for Mississippi." The legislature passed a resolution to hold a constitutional convention, but Governor Lowry, in January 1888, vetoed it, arguing that the situation had not yet deteriorated enough to warrant the White ruling class leaping from a fifth-story window. "Quiet reigns throughout our borders," Lowry asserted in his veto message. "The colored people are content and happy . . . Why disturb society . . . ? Why agitate and convulse the country . . . ?" Those holding this anti-new-constitution position reiterated that the party should run the same play—election fraud—that had long been scoring points. In 1873, Black men comprised about 40 percent of the state legislature. After the Mississippi Plan of 1875, that number shriveled to about 14 percent and continued on that course. Most agreed, moreover, with one politician who foresaw that Black disenfranchisement would be "impossible without disqualifying tens of thousands of white men."

In November 1888, however, Republicans landed the presidency and Congress. In 1889, President Benjamin Harrison "asked for new measures to protect the black franchise." That same year, the majority-Black Mississippi Republican Party fielded candidates for state offices before withdrawing them after Democratic saber-rattling. Such factors nudged many remaining holdouts into supporting a constitutional convention. And besides, as one Confederate colonel remarked, "The old men of the present generation can't afford to die and leave their children with shot guns in their hands, a lie in their mouths and perjury on their souls, in order to defeat the negroes. The constitution can be made so this will not be necessary." Caste preservationism remained the central commitment, just enclosed inside a durable, yet genteel casing.

In October 1889, James George, now a U.S. senator, explained to the state legislature why a White supremacist future depended on a successful constitutional convention. In the same space, Representatives Hall, where the convention would convene a year later, George forewarned that the ever-increasing Black population hurtled the state toward crisis. "For the first time in many years," the big, unkempt man with a long goatee told the state legislators, "all of the departments of the [federal] government are in unfriendly hands. The check on bad legislation, coming from a Democratic House of Representatives, is gone." Presuming the Republican-led Congress would "pass a law taking the federal elections from the control of the state," he said, "our first duty . . . is to devise such measures, consistent with the constitution of the United States, as will enable us to maintain a home government, under the control of the white people of the State."

In February 1890, with Governor John M. Stone's blessing, the legislature established that a constitutional convention would assemble on August 12, to disenfranchise Black voters "legally," not because of any alleged ignorance. No, because of race. "If every negro in Mississippi was a graduate of Harvard," wrote a *Clarion-Ledger* correspondent, "and had been selected as class orator he still would not be as well fitted to exercise the right of suffrage as the Anglo-Saxon farm laborer." "The convention is called," the *Raymond Gazette* informed in June 1890, "for the purpose of divising [*sic*] means by which the negro can be constitutionally eliminated from politics."

ON SEPTEMBER 2, Robert C. Patty, the chairman of the convention's Franchise Committee, responsible for concocting a Black disenfranchisement scheme, presented to the convention the proposal his committee had hatched. Most White Democrats wanted all Black, but no White, men disenfranchised. The obvious, however, cut through quickly—none could produce an honest, coherent proposal that would achieve that result. Therefore, the committee created one figuring to bear far more heavily on Black men that would also be dishonestly applied.

The multilayered plan hinged on disenfranchising Black men by prohibiting or dissuading them from even registering. Under it, a prospective voter, to register, had to have resided for a year in the election district and two years in the state. Black people, heavily leveraged in agriculture, lived transiently, sniffing constantly for better employment inside and beyond state lines. "Each sane male citizen," Patty told the convention, "who has paid a poll tax of $2 on or before the first day of February" for two consecutive years, cleared another eligibility hurdle. Black folk, largely poor, would disproportionately struggle to pay months in advance for an election likely bereft of attractive candidates. A detractor described it as "like buying a ticket to a show nine months ahead of time, and before you know who is playing or really what the thing is all about." One could register without paying the poll tax but couldn't vote, meaning those who anticipated an inability to afford the poll tax would likely spare the effort of registering.

Clearing the most crucial hurdle, Patty explained, required one "to read any section of the state constitution; or to be able to understand the same when read to him, or give a reasonable interpretation thereof." This hurdle, the understanding clause, would whisk to the clouds when a Black man approached it, but thwack to the soil when a White man did, because the state would coach registrars to generally accept the performance of White, but not Black, prospective voters.

This plan elicited initial ambivalence—some delegates dreaded the disenfranchisement of many uneducated White men, the very men who sent them to the convention. Amid uncertainty, on September 15, 1890, inside the Greek Revival capitol, under its copper dome and between its wooden interior walls, a freedman seized the rostrum. Isaiah Montgomery. The chance to enter the state's architectural crown jewel and possibly tank the plan fell to him, short and slightly built, with skin as "black as the ten of spades," Jefferson Davis, the president of the Confederacy, once described. The convention's only Black delegate addressed the 133 others, imploring them to compose a constitution he believed would most benefit *his* race.

ONLY ONE BLACK MISSISSIPPIAN in the 58 percent Black state could have finessed himself into that convention. Once owned by Joseph Davis, Jefferson's elder brother, Montgomery grew up enslaved on Mississippi's renowned Davis Bend plantation. There, he enjoyed a private education, learning how to read and write, receiving private tutoring alongside his master's seeds. By the age of twelve, he earned the plantation's de facto accountant position. Post-emancipation, Montgomery, a Republican, largely eschewed Reconstruction politics, supposing the boulevard to Black liberation circumvented the electoral coliseum. The White Mississippian treasured the racial caste system, and Montgomery concluded that Black folk should acquiesce to castework in exchange for space to chase economic progress free from meddlesome White fingertips.

Montgomery and his father, Ben, had long pined for the same fantasy—grinding a shovel into the dirt of an all-Black town. He learned of the Louisville, New Orleans, and Texas Railroad laying tracks from Memphis to Vicksburg and hawking "rich, alluvial land" along the new line. In the spring 1887, his father ten years passed, Montgomery dumped his financial interests and convinced his cousin to follow suit. Together they bought 840 acres of Delta land for a place they named Mound Bayou.

Three years after founding his refuge, Montgomery told the delegates that his "mission here is to bridge a chasm that has been widening and deepening for a generation," referring to Mississippi's racial strife, "to divert a maelstrom that threatens destruction to you and yours, while it promises no enduring prosperity to me and mine."

Montgomery, shy and confident seemingly only when speaking about Black folk, said that "the deliberations of the Franchise Committee have reached the conclusions embraced in their report after prolonged debate which fully developed all the conflicting interests, all of which have due care. Mutual sacrifices of opinions and interests have been made on all sides. I confidently believe, sirs, that it is the safest measure for this convention to adopt."

He sided with *them*. The enemy. His persecutors. In the stately chamber, Montgomery endeavored to get a ploy to disenfranchise Black Mississippians stitched into Mississippi's constitution.

Montgomery noted that Black voters had a more than seventy thousand registration edge. But that mattered not, he said, because the "white people determined that the best interests of the State and their own protection demanded that they should rule.

"The methods employed to produce this result," he continued, "have introduced into the body politic every form of demoralization— blood shed, bribery, ballot-stuffing. Corruption and perjury stalk unblushingly through the land. The good people of Mississippi stand aghast at the spectacle."

According to Montgomery, the committee's plan would disen-franchise about 12,000 White men but over 123,000 Black men, leaving a more than 48,000 White majority.

"It is a fearful sacrifice laid upon the burning altar of liberty," Montgomery said. "I wish to say to my people, Nay, we have not taken away your high privilege, but only lifted it to a higher plane and exalted the station of the great American birthright. I wish to tell them that the sacrifice has been made to restore confidence, the great missing link between the two races; to restore honesty and purity to the ballot-box, and to confer the great boon of political liberty upon the Commonwealth of Mississippi."

He spellbound the delegates. And convinced them. "The effect of this speech was electric," the *New York World* reported. "The crisis of the Convention was passed. That which the culture and the polish of Mississippi's proudest had vainly tried to effect had been accom-plished by this once slave—the exponent of a despised race. He had united the Convention. Henceforth there was little debate, except upon matters of detail."

On November 1, the convention ratified the new constitution. "Restricted by the Federal Constitution, we have tried to secure a more enlightened franchise without discrimination or injustice," said convention chairman Solomon Calhoon. "There is but one sovereign by divine right. That sovereign is mind. I look in vain for any instance of African contribution to the disclosure of undiscovered truths tend-ing to ameliorate the individual or social condition of man." Calhoon deemed the Black race "unfit to rule," echoing the *Dred Scott* deci-sion. "I do not hesitate to declare the opinion that there is nowhere a better Constitution than the one you now establish."

Calhoon dissolved the convention, completing what history remembered as the Mississippi Plan of 1890.


ON OCTOBER 21, 1890, Frederick Douglass delivered a race speech inside D.C.'s Metropolitan AME church, a former Underground Railroad stop. Seventy-two years old with snowy-white hair, Doug-lass fired indignation inside the two-story church, red-brick with granite trim, detailing how America, with the aid of a Black man, reneged on the promise of freedom.

Below the colored stained glass windows gracing the building's High Victorian Gothic exterior, Douglass told the packed church that Montgomery "has surrendered to a disloyal State a great franchise given to himself and his people by the loyal nation. . . . He has virtually said to the nation: 'You have done wrong in giving us this great liberty. You should give us back a part of our bondage.' He has surrendered a part of his rights to an enemy who will make this surrender a reason for demanding all of his rights. He has conducted his people to a depth from which they will be invited to a lower deep, for if he can rightfully surrender a part of his heritage from the National Government at the bidding of his oppressors, he may surrender the whole."

Montgomery predicted "no opposition to the plan from any of the colored people of the State." A falsehood. John Lynch, then an ex-congressman, raged that the "entire scheme is a fraud, a sham and a swindle, the sole purpose of which is to perpetuate the ascendancy of the Democratic party in the State." Sidney D. Redmond, a Black Mississippi politician, predicted Montgomery would become "the Judas of his people." Another prominent Black Mississippi politician surely detested Montgomery's speech—one Cornelius Jonas Jones Jr.

In 1878, Jones, at twenty, graduated from Alcorn University. For two years, he worked as an agent for the Mississippi Cotton Seed Association where, near the Yazoo River, New Orleans businessmen allocated him more than $400,000 to purchase cottonseed. Thereafter, he crossed the border into Louisiana where he taught schoolchildren. On January 5, 1881, he married Bettie Julien, an educated and intelligent Black woman, in her father's home. Reporting on the marriage, the *Vicksburg Herald* described Jones as a man with a "fair education and the good sense to make money and to know how to hold it." In 1884, Bettie died, and his mother began raising their two daughters, Gertrude and Quincella. In 1885, Jones helmed a school in Mayersville, Mississippi, a Delta town on the Mississippi River, as its principal. Showing dedication to Black progress, in 1886 he served as a secretary of a group that endeavored to start a Black high school in Lake Providence, Louisiana, across the river from Mayersville.

In the early 1880s, Jones, during his time as a teacher, started studying law under the guidance of a former Louisiana Supreme Court justice. After returning to Mississippi, he continued his legal education under politically influential brothers, the McLaurins, one of whom, Anselm J. McLaurin, later won the governorship. On January 28, 1888, Jones passed the bar. The committee that examined him reported that "he showed a fine knowledge of the law." Living in Ben Lomond, Mississippi, a town in Issaquena County, the county with the nation's highest Black-to-White population ratio, seventeen-to-one, he launched his practice. From that county, in 1889, he won a state legislature race, one of six Black men elected that year, all to the lower house. Mississippi Democrats tolerated Black Republicans like Jones, running to represent the Blackest districts, winning elections. Those piddling triumphs left the Democrats' domination intact.

On January 24, 1890, before the state legislature passed its constitutional convention bill, Jones delivered a strong speech against it and was, per the *Clarion-Ledger*, "complimented by all who heard him." The telegraphed plan, he argued, would injure poor people of both races, and leave White men disgruntled if the convention thieved their voting rights. The plan, he said, would send the state "tottering upon the verge of her ruin." Jones ran to represent the 94 percent Black Issaquena County at the convention, a perilous choice. A White Republican who pursued a delegate seat was murdered for rallying Black Republicans to oppose their disenfranchisement. Threatened violence coerced Republicans to pull a nomination of a Black delegate. Jones lost his delegate race, and Issaquena County "elected" White delegates to the convention.

Although the new disenfranchisement scheme would not operate until 1892, it immediately dispirited Black souls. Three days after the convention closed, Mississippi held state elections. Only about 30 percent of the regular Black vote was cast. One Democratic newspaper opined that Black folk shifted to "their material interests and domestic betterment and [left] politics alone," the response White Mississippians desired, what Montgomery thought best.

In 1891, Jones didn't win reelection and pivoted, full-time, to the legal profession, becoming one of the Delta's few Black attorneys. Privately, Jones vowed to convince the United States Supreme Court to invalidate the 1890 constitution. He could have launched a Fifteenth Amendment crusade. After all, it secured voting rights. Instead, Jones premised his legal assault on the Fourteenth Amendment, implementing a shrewd strategy that would catch caste preservationists unaware.

Per the new constitution, only registered voters current on their poll tax payment could serve on juries. As the convention debates made plain, despite devising a scheme containing nary a mention of race, the delegates intended to terminate Black politics. Thus, the state practiced jury discrimination, indirectly. Jones would represent Black criminal defendants. After all-White juries convicted them, he planned to convince the Court that Mississippi limited jury service to White men, infringing the Equal Protection Clause. If he swayed a Court majority, he believed he could cancel Mississippi's disenfranchisement ploy and return the ballot to Black men's hands. Black America would shower with adoration the Black Mississippian who toppled the beast.

The previous leg of our journey chronicled how the Supreme Court eviscerated congressional legislation enacted to enforce The Trinity against the castework of private individuals. After the shotgun barrel and the Klan sheet disrobed Black men of political power, Democrats redeemed the South, opening the opportunity for them to cement the racial caste system through the drafting of new state constitutions, a process that Mississippi pioneered. But, during the 1870s and 1880s, the Supreme Court reiterated that The Trinity prevented states from denying rights based on race, meaning that the Court should invalidate the Mississippi Plan of 1890. Knowing that, Mississippi would have to harness the power of deceit to convince the black robes to rubber-stamp its castework. The Mississippi attorney general couldn't waltz into the Court Chamber and admit that the state intentionally bounced the Black man from the voting booth. He needed to lie. And when he did, how would the Supreme Court respond?

Jones launched his attack with two cases involving Black criminal defendants: Charley Smith, accused of the shooting death of Wiley

Nesby, a Black man, during a house party on May 6, 1893, and John Gibson. His alleged crime warrants recounting.

AT ABOUT FOUR in the afternoon on Saturday, January 9, 1892, Robert Stinson, the White assistant manager on the Refuge plantation, part of businessman Edmund Richardson's vast cotton empire, gathered Black day laborers inside the plantation store to pay their wages. Gibson, among those clustered behind a short partition wall in the store's rear, drove a wagon on the Washington County property in the Delta. Stinson docked Gibson, and a few others, twenty cents.

"What for?" the twenty-five-year-old Gibson asked.

"Because you didn't do as I said for you to do," Stinson replied inside the crowded place.

Gibson, who sported a tuberculosis scar under his left ear and a knife wound on his left collarbone, war marks from a violent, disease-ridden era, complained to the bookkeeper, who refused to intervene. Demanding his money, the five-foot-nine, 160-pound brown-skinned Black man repeatedly returned to a flippant Stinson, who repeatedly shooed him away.

"[I do] not want to have any fuss," Stinson said.

Gibson disengaged from this unfruitful, repetitive back-and-forth and huddled around the fire-heated stove at the store's center where Black laborers were congregating on the frigid day.

"The son of a bitch. If you dock me twenty cents me or you, one, will go to hell tonight," Gibson spat aloud.

T. D. Apple, a White salesman, called Gibson to him and demanded that he "not talk that way to a white man" and "to get away from there."

As the sun slipped behind the horizon, Stinson left for the house of the plantation's manager, Captain W. H. Drummond, where Stinson resided in a room that doubled as an office. Gibson headed to a nearby saloon.

A while later, inside Stinson's room, Drummond was working at a desk, tending to plantation business, as Stinson warmed himself at the fireplace. Gibson knocked on the window.

"Well," Drummond said after raising the window, "Mr. Stinson knows what he is doing, and I am not going to have anything to do with that."

Stinson then rose from his seat: "I have done all I am going to do, and I am not going to pay you another cent."

"You have got me to pay, and I am going to have my pay," Gibson demanded.

"If you don't go away, I will kill you."

"All right come ahead. One of us will die tonight."

"Go away from here," Drummond said. He shut the window and returned to work.

When Stinson left the room, Drummond reviewed the payment ledger—Stinson *had* marked Gibson twenty cents less than warranted. Stinson, meanwhile, asked Drummond's daughter for her father's pistol and left the house, heading toward the front gate.

Fifteen or twenty minutes later, gunshots sounded. Drummond rushed toward the booms. At the front gate, he found a fallen Stinson with one gunshot wound near his heart. Drummond and others carried Stinson inside the house and laid him on his bed where he gasped a few final breaths. Armed bands immediately formed to hang from a tree the man who had committed what newspapers called an "assassination."

Months passed. The temperature climbed and fell again. Until November 1893, when Gibson turned up in Kansas City, Kansas. His cousins there had helped him hide, allowing him to sleep at different homes every day. In custody, Gibson insisted he acted in self-defense. Stinson drew his revolver, he claimed. The two wrestled over it. And it went off while in Stinson's hands. Gibson fled into the woods and escaped to Kansas City, he insisted, never knowing Stinson's fate.

Gibson, unlike Charley Smith, who certainly committed first-degree murder, could present a viable self-defense claim given that Stinson hurried to the front gate with a gun after announcing intentions to kill. But Gibson had little right to self-defense against a White man in America, much less in Mississippi. The rest of the South ogled as that state disenfranchised Black men and would surely sample their constitutional lyrics if the Supreme Court validated them. Only 6 percent of Black men, after the constitution went into effect, remained registered voters. This saddled Jones with immense

pressure. Convincing the Court to invalidate the Mississippi constitution could not only save the lives of his clients, it could repel a danger poised to undermine the freedom of Black southerners. Jones's
ambition, however, required an exquisite legal performance.

Let's visit a scene that captures but a parcel of the grim landscape
Black Mississippians traversed in the 1890s and inhabit that setting
to discuss what Jones, auditioning for the role as the most influential
early Black civil rights attorney, the role of caste abolitionist savior,
needed to do to win.

LINGER WITH ME outside the Copiah County home of Doc Thompson on a March 1893 night. Inside, the Black farmer lives with his
wife in this sparsely populated rural part of southwest Mississippi.
Unbeknownst to him, a violent band of White men are assembling
in his yard.

As the North had already snatched the future by embracing the
industrial age of factories and big cities, much of the South, including Mississippi, clung to an economically decrepit agrarian existence.
Economic distress choked Mississippi's farmers during the early
1890s. Farm operation costs soared. Crop values plunged. Desperate
and moneyless, farmers opened lines of credit, driving them toward
the crop lien system where farmers obtained credit, and the credit
holders, merchants, placed a lien on farmers' ungrown crops. Merchants demanded that farmers grow cotton and loaned them money
at steep interest rates. The inevitable appeared—default notices and
merchants seizing farmers' properties.

The merchants frequently hired Black workers to farm such foreclosed land, generally absent White supervision. Down-on-their-
luck White Mississippians, in other words, surrendered their acreage
and witnessed Black families work it. Violent paramilitary groups
called White Caps, in response, formed. Whitecappers initially targeted only Black folk on merchant-owned land, intimidating them
off property and out of the county, out of the state sometimes. But
soon Whitecappers rolled through southwestern Mississippi, attacking Black folk inhabiting any land, even land they owned, forcing
desertion. These men outside Thompson's home are Whitecappers.

Watch as they venture into his chicken coop and create noise to coax him to open his front door. Once he does, E. D. Smith, a local White man, along with a few others, riddles his body with bullets, as his wife watches.

Black southerners like Thompson are trying to live, trying to enjoy the freedom The Trinity theoretically provides them. But men like Smith refuse to allow them to enjoy that freedom. Black folk's right to exist, to this sort of White man, hinges on their usefulness to White folk's financial well-being. For this reason, Whitecappers in Lawrence County, Mississippi, exhorted "white farmers" to "combine forces and gain control of the negro labor, which is by right ours." Their paramount objective, the group stipulated, was "to control negro laborers by mild means, if possible; by coercion if necessary."

A decade ago, a twenty-three-year-old Jones encountered such White supremacist violence. On October 28, 1881, hidden men lying in wait, with double-barreled shotguns, fired upon Black men traveling to a fusion political gathering at a Sharkey County, Mississippi, plantation. Jones, at the time an advocate for the fusionist cause, was scheduled to speak there. Three died. Several others suffered wounds. The next day, an interracial group of citizens met at the county courthouse. Jones, who addressed the meeting, previewed the fearlessness he displayed when challenging the state's disenfranchisement scheme. "[C]old-blooded villainy was committed to intimidate you," he said, "that you will thereby fail to poll a full Fusion vote, but I think it is high time that you were showing your manhood by hurling this deed back in the teeth of the bush-whackers. 'Tis true we cannot provide against a mob of vile cut-throats, but make this our theory, the more that fall by the savages in ambush, the more ambitious the survivors must rally." Should Jones fail at regaining the ballot for his people, a want of courage would not deserve the blame.

But success requires a legal strategy rooted in the current legal realities. Jones, helpfully, will receive assistance. On October 21, 1895, he travels to Washington, D.C., just as Hiram Revels had twenty-five years prior. Instead of seeking a Senate seat, Jones journeys to partner with Emanuel Molyneaux Hewlett, a Black attorney, to devise a strategy to invalidate the suffrage provisions of the Mississippi constitution. Born free in Brooklyn in 1850, Hewlett, forty-five with a receding hairline and a handlebar mustache, experienced a far better upbringing than did Jones. His mother and father, Aaron, the first Black instructor at Harvard University, reared Hewlett in Cambridge, Massachusetts. Graduating from Boston University School of Law in 1877, Hewlett became the law school's first Black alumnus. In July 1890, President Harrison appointed him as a D.C. justice of the peace.

Their planning must start with *Strauder v. West Virginia*. As you remember, the Court held in *Strauder* that West Virginia's jury discrimination law violated the Equal Protection Clause because it denied Black men a civil right. In *Virginia v. Rives*, the Court required that, in the absence of a discriminatory law, Black criminal defendants had to prove that the state intentionally excluded Black prospective jurors to establish an equal protection violation. After those two cases, the Court decided four that Jones and Hewlett must master.

The Supreme Court decided the first a year after *Strauder*.


ON MARCH 31, 1880, the headline "A Revolting Crime" blared from the front page of Wilmington, Delaware's, *Morning News*, informing readers of a rape allegation leveled by Margaret Gosser, a twenty-five-year-old White woman. Her husband finished breakfast and left for work on the snowy morning of March 29. According to her, at around noon, a Black man knocked on her door. She granted the freezing stranger's plea for admission into her small one-room home to warm his feet. While inside, she claimed, the man threw a towel over her head, strangled and raped her, a horror lasting ten minutes. After hearing the description of her alleged assailant, her husband helped secure an arrest warrant for John Neal, a short and skinny Black man, who, despite illiteracy, became a minister. An all-White jury indicted him.

Before Neal's trial, his attorney, Ivy-educated Anthony Higgins, argued to a panel of three Delaware Supreme Court justices that state officials excluded Black jurors from the grand jury that indicted his client, violating the Fourteenth Amendment. "There must be discrimination somewhere," Higgins insisted, "for there has never yet been a colored man summoned upon any jury in the State Courts of Delaware." The judges, however, unanimously rejected Higgins's position. Chief Justice Joseph Comegys wrote that "none but white men were selected is in no wise remarkable in view of the fact—too notorious to be ignored—that the great body of black men residing in this State are utterly unqualified by want of intelligence, experience, or moral integrity to sit on juries."

An all-White jury convicted Neal. A *Morning News* editorial pontificated that he "was convicted of the crime of being a 'nigger' rather than of the crime with which he was charged." On May 2, 1881, the Supreme Court granted the formerly enslaved defendant a new trial. Justice Harlan's majority *Neal v. Delaware* opinion gave Jones and Hewlett reason to start their mission confidently.

Before the trial, Higgins motioned to void Neal's indictment, claiming intentional jury discrimination, and filed an affidavit detailing the argument. Delaware's attorney general agreed to treat the affidavit as true to expedite matters, meaning the state waived its right to later refute it. Since Neal made an allegation, and Delaware essentially consented to its veracity, Justice Harlan found that Delaware risked that the Court would deem the affidavit as evidence of jury discrimination. Harlan then assessed local demographics, observing that Black folk "exceeded twenty thousand in 1870, and in 1880 exceeded twenty-six thousand, in a total population of less than one hundred and fifty thousand," yet none had ever served on a jury in a state court. Harlan argued that this supported an inference of unconstitutional jury discrimination. Chief Justice Comegys's remark that Black men failed to meet minimum standards for jury service further buttressed Neal's case. Thus, an unusual confluence of events—the affidavit that the state agreed to treat as true, that no Black man had ever served on state juries, and Comegys's remark—satisfied the evidentiary burden of proving that Delaware had violated Neal's equal protection rights.

In September 1881, a grand jury that included the first Black man ever called as a juror in a Delaware state court, indicted Neal, demonstrating how Supreme Court decisions can spark quick, positive change. Three Black men sat on the venire from which the trial jury was drawn. None served though. In December 1881, as the fore-man read the verdict, Neal trembled. When hearing the words "not guilty," he "began to straighten himself up as if life, after all, had not lost its charms," a reporter observed. "He was literally overwhelmed with joy and could with difficulty restrain his feelings."

Even before Margaret Gosser's alleged rape, another jury dis-crimination case had been meandering to the Supreme Court, *Bush v. Kentucky*, decided in 1883. If *Neal* supplied Jones and Hewlett opti-mism, *Bush* triggered dread.

IN 1878, John Bush and his wife, both formerly enslaved, were hired as servants for the Van Meters, a prominent White family in Fay-ette County, Kentucky. On the evening of January 13, 1879, James Van Meter, the family patriarch, returned home intoxicated and accused Bush's wife, Mary, of spreading rumors about his wife. Dur-ing an ensuing fight, Bush claimed that James Van Meter attempted to shoot him but accidentally hit Van Meter's seventeen-year-old daughter, Annie, instead. Physicians figured she would survive, but Annie died after a doctor with scarlet fever treated her wounds. Van Meter told the police that Bush had shot Annie after she ended their romantic tryst. The police bought Van Meter's tale and charged Bush with murder.

On February 5, 1879, an all-White jury indicted Bush. Fourteen days later, the trial jury hung. The state retried and convicted him, but a Kentucky appellate court tossed the conviction—the jury was not informed that if scarlet fever had caused Annie's death, Bush wasn't culpable. Before the next retrial, Llewellyn P. Tarlton Jr., Bush's court-appointed attorney, petitioned the state judge to remove the case to federal court because authorities convened the grand jury that indicted Bush under Kentucky law, which limited grand jury service to White men. Relying on *Strauder*, the state court judge decided "that the law was for the defendant," and transferred Bush's case to federal court. The federal judge quashed the first indictment and discharged Bush. Fayette County police then rearrested him, and on November 19, 1880, again indicted him, with an all-White jury. For Bush's trial, the prosecutor ordered Sheriff W. D. Nicholas to assemble seventy-five prospective jurors without reference to race. Nicholas returned with seventy-five White men, twelve of whom found Bush guilty. The judge sentenced him to be hanged.

Justice Harlan, penning the Court's majority opinion, found in Bush's favor because Kentucky had twice enacted jury discrimination laws after the Fourteenth Amendment's ratification. The Kentucky Court of Appeals, relying on *Strauder*, invalidated the more recent iteration of that law. But the grand jury that reindicted Bush was drawn before that decision. Harlan assumed that the local sheriff, therefore, followed Kentucky law and intentionally excluded Black jurors.

Although Bush received a new trial, a couple of warning signs screamed from the opinion. First, Harlan rejected that because the jury panel that convicted Bush was all-White, the sheriff excluded Black jurors. "It may have been true that only white citizens were selected and summoned," Harlan wrote, "yet it would not necessarily follow that the officer had violated the law and the special instruction given by the court 'to proceed in his selection without regard to race, color, or previous condition of servitude.'" In Fayette County, 4,300 White citizens and 3,400 Black citizens were at least the age of twenty-one. Drawing an all-White sample from this population should have struck the justices as highly improbable. Kentucky served deceit—that it did not limit jury service to White men—and the black robes lapped it up.

Even more disturbing, the justices reflexively assumed local officials obeyed the law. Bush won his case because the law required Black exclusion. If the law required inclusion, then the justices would have assumed that state officials complied, an assumption revealing dumbfounding naïveté. In fact, Chief Justice Waite, in his dissent, wrote that his colleagues should have assumed that Kentucky's officers followed *Strauder* even though Kentucky law required them to only select White men for the jury. A chief justice assuming that state officials would comply with the Court's decisions smelled odd given that the judicial system exists because people violate laws. Jones and Hewlett, nonetheless, needed to develop a strategy responsive to these two points.

Bush's triumph only postponed the inevitable. An all-White jury reconvicted him, and the black robes refused his appeal. On November 21, 1884, moments before his execution, Bush told the gathered audience that James Van Meter "did not tell you he destroyed his infant before its time." This secret—Van Meter's involvement with his wife's abortion—caused the maelstrom that ended in his daughter's death. Bush left behind a widow and seven children.

ONE FINAL CASE that Jones and Hewlett needed to understand concerned neither jury discrimination nor Black people at all, *Yick Wo v. Hopkins*, decided in 1886. During California's Gold Rush era, Chinese immigrants filled a void in the marketplace by operating commercial laundries. About thirteen hundred folk of Chinese descent in San Francisco worked in laundries by 1870. From 1870 to 1884, the San Francisco Board of Supervisors regulated Chinese laundries tightly. In 1880, the board passed an ordinance that prevented the operation or building of wooden laundries in the city absent permission. Although appearing racially neutral, the law was unevenly enforced. The board denied all two hundred Chinese folk who petitioned for permission, but only one of the eighty non-Chinese petitioners. The Tung Hing Tong, the Chinese American launderers' trade association, directed members to defy the ordinance. Lee Yick was convicted, ordered to pay a fine for operating an unauthorized wooden laundry, and imprisoned after defaulting. When the California Supreme Court upheld the law, Yick appealed to the Supreme Court, arguing that the administration of the law violated the Equal Protection Clause.

In *Yick Wo*, Justice Matthews, writing for a unanimous Court, ruled that although the ordinance was facially neutral, its enforcement violated the Equal Protection Clause. "Though the law itself be fair on its face," Justice Matthews penned, "and impartial in appearance, yet, if it is applied and administered by public authority with an evil eye and an unequal hand, so as practically to make unjust and illegal discriminations between persons in similar circumstances . . . the denial of equal justice is still within the prohibition of the constitution."

Here the Court found an equal protection violation in the absence of proof establishing discriminatory intent. The statistical disparities clearly indicated race discrimination. Yet, San Francisco presented a race-neutral explanation for those disparities—only Chinese launderers used roof scaffolding to dry laundry. The black robes could have accepted that explanation. But here, unlike in the jury discrimination cases, they reached a different, more racially just, result. Had an epiphany struck the justices? And how should Jones and Hewlett formulate their plan considering these cases?

Let's delve into that now.

AS JONES TOURED D.C.'S COURTS during his visit, he observed that Black "lawyers are not treated in any part of the South by the judges with such contempt as I found them treated [here]." In Washington, with Jones leading the charge, two early Black civil rights attorneys would attempt to formulate a caste abolitionist legal strategy.

The light of precedent—a court decision that becomes authority for subsequent cases with comparable facts—guides lawyers. Say the Supreme Court ruled in the hypothetical *Federal Money Case*, a dispute regarding whether the federal government could print and circulate a five-dollar bill, that the Constitution empowered Congress, and only Congress, to enact a law to issue paper money. Then imagine if two years later the New York state legislature passed a law to issue paper currency in five-dollar increments. The Court should invalidate that law, following the precedent of the *Federal Money Case*, finding that the Constitution forbade states from issuing currency. If Congress subsequently passed a law issuing fifty-dollar bills, however, the Court should uphold the law because the currency denomination difference isn't relevant. If the relevant facts are similar, precedent tells courts to reach similar rulings. If the facts differ, precedent tells courts to reach different rulings.

Jones and Hewlett should have pegged *Strauder, Virginia v. Rives, Neal, Bush,* and *Yick Wo* as the relevant precedents. Since the Court decided *Strauder, Neal, Bush,* and *Yick Wo* favorably, they would want to argue that the facts in *Charley Smith* and *Gibson* matched the facts in those four cases, and the Court should therefore decide them similarly. Conversely, they would want to differentiate *Charley Smith* and

*Gibson* from *Virginia v. Rives*, arguing that the relevant facts in those diverged from those in the Reynolds brothers case.

After studying the precedents, Jones and Hewlett should have realized the mission necessitated a four-pronged strategy. First, they had to substantiate that the officials who selected and summoned jurors, jury commissioners, intentionally excluded Black men from the juries that indicted and convicted Gibson and Smith. The Court, particularly in *Virginia v. Rives* and *Bush*, had articulated that a mere absence of Black men from the jury would not by itself prove intentional exclusion. This evidence gathering would have to happen at trial. Jones, who defended Charley Smith during his trial and helped oversee John Gibson's various trials, would need to call witnesses, particularly jury commissioners, to prove the argument. Perhaps, on the stand, Jones could coax a commissioner to confess. Or he could find other witnesses or documentary support. No matter what, Jones needed evidence.

Second, Jones, at trial, needed to supply numerical evidence showing that Black men rarely or never served on Mississippi juries, recreating the stark numerical disparities that convinced the Court to rule against San Francisco in *Yick Wo*. And Jones couldn't just merely assert that Black men never served. Pretrial, Jones had to call witnesses, maybe judges, lawyers, jury commissioners, or court clerks, and ask them how many Black men served on juries in their counties. He needed to show an absence of Black jurors that would force the state to disprove, with evidence, his claim. The state could not rebut this, allowing victory on this point.

Third, Jones and Hewlett needed to connect the race discrimination their clients suffered to what happened at the 1890 constitutional convention, the trickiest prong. Courts typically rule on the narrowest grounds, meaning judges ordinarily avoid discarding two laws if discarding one suffices, and generally won't strike down a law if they can implicate individual actors. By merely holding that the state officials in Gibson's and Smith's cases violated The Trinity, the Court could decide for Jones's clients without invalidating the Mississippi Plan. Thus, Jones and Hewlett needed to advance a strong argument—that one could not separate the behavior of the state officials from the pertinent constitutional provisions, that the discrimination of the officials was dictated by those provisions, and that unless they were invalidated, such discrimination would continue.

And fourth, Jones and Hewlett needed evidence that the convention delegates wrote the 1890 constitution to target Black citizens and that it produced discriminatory results, by far the easiest prong to satisfy. The convention delegates blabbed about their intentions incessantly. And the registration numbers proved the strategy's success—only 6 percent of the voting-age Black male population, but 58 percent of the White male population, were registered to vote. If Jones and Hewlett executed these four prongs, they would best position themselves.

Jones and Hewlett had only one venue for success—inside the two-story semicircular room, before the eight Ionic marble columns, in front of the nine black robes. If all-White juries acquitted Gibson and Smith, Jones would have nothing to appeal, meaning he needed the state to convict his clients and for the Mississippi Supreme Court to reject his arguments on appeal.

That happened.

Gibson's case took longer to reach the U.S. Supreme Court. In March 1893, the Mississippi Supreme Court reversed his first conviction on a technicality. Gibson's January 1894 retrial closed with a hung jury, which, in that era, in that state, signaled innocence. Gibson heard the "guilty" verdict at the close of his third trial. The Mississippi Supreme Court reversed the conviction, though, citing three reversible trial judge errors, including barring a witness from testifying that as Gibson approached the gate, Stinson warned, "You had better go, or I am either going to whip you or kill you." In January 1895, an all-White jury convicted Gibson, and he was again sentenced to hang "by the neck until he is dead."

Charley Smith's December 1894 trial closed with a quick guilty verdict and a death sentence set for the following month. The Mississippi Supreme Court heard both cases in summer 1895, finding no constitutional rights violations. Jones petitioned the U.S. Supreme Court to hear both appeals. As the wooden planks for the scaffolding to hang Gibson came together, the Court granted an oral argument for both, scheduling each for December 1895, staying their executions.

What happened in the South Carolina capitol days before Jones and Hewlett argued their cases raised the stakes even more.

IN 1876, THROUGH FRAUD AND VIOLENCE, White Democrats retook the South Carolina government and thereafter reigned over the majority-Black state through its old guard conservative leadership. Then, in 1890, Benjamin "Pitchfork" Tillman won the governorship. A violent White supremacist and author of many Black murders, Tillman, who participated in the Hamburg Massacre detailed in our previous leg, melded anti-Black rabble-rousing and economic anxiety among the poor White masses into a political insurgency that hijacked the state Democratic Party and the executive mansion in Columbia. "The whites have absolute control of the State government," the one-eyed Tillman proclaimed at his December 1890 inaugural address, "and we intend at any and all hazards to retain it. The intelligent exercise of the right of suffrage . . . is yet beyond the capacity of the vast majority of colored men."

By 1892, some conservatives flirted with pulling Black voters into their coalition to oust the Tillmanites. But the train of thought never gathered steam. Two years later, more pondered it, yet not enough hopped aboard to propel it forward. The same anxieties that aroused support for a constitutional convention in Mississippi—disunion among White Democrats leading to the activation of a silenced Black majority—triggered the Tillmanites.

The constitution drafted at the 1868 convention where seventy-six Black and forty-eight White delegates enacted a document that implemented "a free public school system in which racial discrimination was not permitted . . . and enlarged the electorate by providing for universal male suffrage" still organized the state's government. Tillman spearheaded a movement to supplant it with one that would, he hoped, "disfranchise as many Negroes as [possible] without disfranchising a single white man, except for crime." Persistence fulfilled his wishes, and on September 10, 1895, the sitting Tillmanite governor, John Gary Evans, opened a constitutional convention, saying, "We have seen that white men can divide, and it is your duty, in view of such division, to so fix your election laws that your wives, your children and your homes will be protected and Anglo-Saxon supremacy preserved."

A month into the convention, fifty-six-year-old Robert Smalls, a Republican freedman, rebuked Tillman's plan. "[T]his Convention has been called for no other purpose than the disfranchisement of the Negro," said Smalls, a former member of Congress, while standing on the floor of the hall of the House of Representatives inside the still-under-construction Greek Revival capitol. Smalls, one of six Black delegates, opposed the aims of the 106 White delegates who wanted to retrace the footprints Mississippi left in the sand five years before.

"We served our masters faithfully, and willingly, and as we were made to for 244 years. . . . Why should you now seek to disfranchise a race that has been so true to you?" asked Smalls.

"Since Reconstruction times 53,000 have been killed in the South, and not more than three white men have been convicted and hung for these crimes," said Smalls, who liberated himself during the Civil War by sailing a Confederate boat to freedom. "I want you to be mindful of the fact that the good people of the North are watching this Convention upon this subject. . . . I hope that we may be able to say when our work is done that we have made as good a constitution as the one we are doing away with."

When the convention adjourned on December 4, South Carolina had ratified a constitution that duplicated Mississippi's. Whether other states could follow depended on the U.S. Supreme Court.

DAYS AFTER THE SOUTH CAROLINA CONVENTION CLOSED, Jones and Hewlett argued *Gibson* and *Charley Smith*. Their opposition, Frank Johnston, Mississippi's attorney general, remained in Mississippi. On December 11, 1895, he telegraphed McKenney, the Court's clerk. "Impossible for me to leave here at this time," he wrote. "Ask the court to grant me ten or twelve days to file briefs in Gibson and Smith cases. I did not know the cases had been advanced."

Johnston, the son of Amos Johnston, the Democratic speaker at the Clinton Riot, served as an 1890 convention delegate. He knew his state kept juries all-White and disenfranchised Black men. He endorsed it. He voted for it. But his sort veiled such intentions before the nine black robes. Johnston, to keep the justices from annulling castework, would turn to deception. Convince the justices that the caste preservationists in the Magnolia State never committed the transgressions to which they had repeatedly confessed.

Johnston had already displayed talent in the art of deceit. In 1875, Johnston, then a thirty-one-year-old attorney, arrived in Clinton hours after the initial gun battle alongside scores of White men from neighboring locales who swept into town armed and ready to kill. By the time he left Clinton, he saw Black corpses strewn about the town's soil and White men indiscriminately spraying bullets into flee-ing Black backs. In the aftermath, James George, then the chairman of Mississippi's Democratic Party, asked him to produce propaganda about the Clinton Riot that painted Black folk as the instigators.

Johnston composed a report with Judge Edwin Cabaniss, a co-conspirator in Charley Caldwell's assassination. In Johnston's rendi-tion, a White man accidentally shot the ground at the Republican meeting, sparking bedlam from the Black side. Johnston, further-more, defended the slaughter of Black men in the ensuing days because "it was subsequently reported that the negroes threatened to attack the town" and thus White men "who were indignant at the murder and mutilation of their white friends" had to kill "seven or eight negroes," a gross underestimation of the number of Black fatalities. In alleging this, Johnston enlivened a popular deceit—the tale of Black barbarians assembling to menace the countryside—necessitating preemptive White carnage.

SINCE OUR LAST COURT CHAMBER VISIT, the Waite Court had dissolved.

Thirty minutes before noon on March 28, 1888, in Washington, D.C., the first in a carriage caravan approached the Capitol under a muted stillness. As men took a coffin out of a hearse, the Supreme Court associate justices, wearing their black silk robes, observed from the sidewalk. Up the stairs and into the House Chamber the casket went, as national leaders, including Democratic president

Grover Cleveland, nearly six-foot and portly, waited for the funeral to commence. About seven months ahead of the presidential election, Cleveland would appoint the next chief justice to replace Morrison Remick Waite, who unexpectedly succumbed to pneumonia days before.

Observers anticipated a close presidential race. Cleveland hoped the appointment opportunity would assist his reelection against Benjamin Harrison, Republican senator from Indiana. Meanwhile, the Republicans controlled the Senate narrowly—thirty-nine to thirty-seven—compelling Cleveland to tap a replacement that would cost the Republicans should they spurn his choice. Cleveland landed on Melville Weston Fuller, a successful but largely obscure attorney from Illinois, a pivotal swing state. "So unknown" was Fuller, who had never served in a federal office, the *New York Herald* reported, "his name does not appear in the latest works of contemporary biography."

Fuller, born in 1833 in Augusta, Maine, spent his impressionable years under the tutelage of his grandfather, a judge and evangelist for the politics of President Andrew Jackson, an avatar for expanded suffrage among White men, laissez-faire economics, western expansion, and Native American genocide. Fuller attended Harvard Law School for six months before gaining admission to the Maine bar in 1855. A year later, he headed to Chicago, a city charging toward commercial dominance in the West.

Fuller, like most New Englanders, detested slavery, although he thought the federal government lacked the authority to curtail it. Despite supporting the Union during the war, he distrusted Lincoln's stewardship of it. As a Democratic delegate at the Illinois 1862 constitutional convention, Fuller supported blocking both Black folk's future entry into the state and their right to vote there, castework etched into the constitution's final version. As a state legislator, he pushed for the adoption of the Corwin Amendment, a proposed constitutional amendment Congress passed in 1861 that, if the states had ratified it, would have prevented the federal government from interfering with slavery. And about the Emancipation Proclamation, Fuller said it was "predicated upon the idea that President may so annul the constitution and laws of sovereign states, overthrow their domestic relations, deprive loyal men of their property, and disloyal as well without trial or condemnation." In the 1860s, then, Fuller treated American democracy as a bargain between White men.

Fuller considered the Constitution the people's document, meaning that, in his own words, "constitutional theories, whatever their merits in the abstract, cannot prevail in the long run against the judgment of a majority of those for whom the Constitution was framed." Put another way, he reasoned that the Constitution received its power from the people and mustn't thwart their will. His Democratic Party membership, adherence to states' rights, and Corwin Amendment support predicted a sympathy toward constitutional constructions that facilitated caste preservation.

Jones and Hewlett would soon test that.

ON DECEMBER 13, 1895, two Black attorneys entered the highest courtroom in the land to argue *Charley Smith v. Mississippi*, among the small handful of Black attorneys to argue a case before the Supreme Court before the twentieth century. As they stood in the chamber, before a forty-four-star American flag, the justices understood the South's story. Black men once voted. White men, with bloodstained gloves, pilfered their ballots. Mississippi began the disenfranchisement voyage, first walking the beach. South Carolina followed those footprints. And the black robes surely fathomed that other southern states would too should they uphold the Mississippi Plan of 1890.

The seventy-nine-year-old Stephen Johnson Field, on the bench since 1863, was the longest-serving justice, then John Marshall Harlan, sixty-two, and Horace Gray, sixty-seven. Democrat Grover Cleveland appointed two justices during his first term, spanning 1885 to 1889. His first, Lucius Lamar, replaced Justice Woods. Lamar, a former Mississippi Confederate, was confirmed in 1888 but died in 1893. Cleveland's second, Chief Justice Fuller, five-foot-six with long white hair and a signature thick white mustache, occupied the middle chair.

Republican Benjamin Harrison succeeded Cleveland in March 1889. His first appointment, David Josiah Brewer, replaced the deceased justice Matthews, and arrived with an origin story that suggested receptivity toward caste abolitionism. In 1837, Brewer was born in Smyrna, Asia Minor, the son of missionary parents who raised him in Connecticut. In his youth, Brewer dove into abolitionism, and at twenty-one relocated to Kansas, one of many antislavery New Englanders who stormed the state to prevent slavery's westward expansion. He stayed and became a Kansas Supreme Court judge. From that position, he penned a decision upholding the right of a Black citizen to vote. On another occasion, Brewer reiterated Black folk's rightful place in America, saying, "the Constitution was framed to secure the blessings of freedom and citizenship to all who wished them, and though its authors were compelled to bend a little to peculiar interests, they laid the foundation and bade America prepare for universal citizenship." And in an 1892 address, he reaffirmed Black humanity. "This is not an Anglo-Saxon, not a Teutonic, not even a Caucasian nation," Brewer said. "The blood of all races mingles in that of the American people." Yet, while a jurist on Kansas's highest court, he wrote, "I dissent entirely from the suggestion that under the 14th amendment of our Federal Constitution, the State has no power to provide for separate schools for white and colored children."

On December 23, 1890, Harrison appointed Henry Billings Brown to the seat Justice Samuel Miller's death emptied. From South Lee, Massachusetts, Brown was born into affluence in 1836. After studying law at Yale and Harvard, he relocated to Detroit to practice law. The Republican's first appointment was as a U.S. attorney in Michigan. In 1875, Brown, ambitious, successfully solicited a Michigan district court judgeship from President Grant. He repeated the same strategy fifteen years later, securing his Court seat. Lacking a racial track record—he flourished as an admiralty law expert—he left little indication regarding his possible complicity with constructing the Constitution to permit castework, although in a few months, he would pen one of the Court's most infamous opinions on the matter.

Harrison's next appointment, George Shiras Jr., replaced Justice Bradley. For months, Bradley had been sick, preventing him from attending oral arguments before his January 1892 death. Shiras, born in Pittsburgh in 1832, had never served in public office before joining the Court, having built a prosperous practice in corporation law, representing industrial and railroad interests, the sort of law that features little thought regarding constructing The Trinity.

Cleveland defeated Harrison in 1892. The so-called Lodge Bill, which would have enforced the Fifteenth Amendment by empowering the federal government to protect Black voting rights in the South, loomed as a pivotal campaign issue. Cleveland opposed it. Harrison endorsed it. Keeping hold of the Solid South, Cleveland made inroads in the North and the new western states. After the defeat, many Republicans concluded the party should, as it had in the 1876 election, eschew protecting Black rights.

Cleveland's first Court appointee of his second term, Edward Douglass White, replaced Republican appointee Samuel Blatchford. White, the son of a Louisiana governor, was born into money and privilege. At fifteen, White returned home from Georgetown University for Confederacy enlistment. After the war, he immersed himself in Louisiana's Democratic politics, participating in the state's redemption and serving in one of the military companies that temporarily ousted an elected Republican government. White's journey bore all the marks of a man who would wear the black robe and swallow caste preservationist deceit.

The Court's most junior member, Rufus Peckham, another Cleveland appointee, took his spot a few days before oral arguments in Jones and Hewlett's cases, replacing Howell Edmunds Jackson, who died months before. Born in 1838, the Albany, New York, native grew up in a family of lawyers. As the nation hurried toward the Civil War, he told his brother, "I am proud I believe in no negro equality." As the war trudged along, Peckham fretted that "the radical abolitionists" were erring in "making it a war for the freedom of the slaves, in spite of the Constitution and if necessary in spite of the Union." Like Cleveland's other two sitting justices, Peckham seemed eager to rebuff caste abolitionist arguments. Yet, Jones and Hewlett had a mission—present the best version of their case and force the Court to either accept their facts or side with obvious deceit.

Attorneys generally cannot introduce new issues on appeal that were not articulated in the moment during the pretrial or trial. As the builder must lay the proper foundation for a sturdy home, then, Jones had to raise the jury discrimination issues at the proper time to enable later success. And he largely did in *Charley Smith*.

After an all-White grand jury indicted Smith, Jones moved to quash the indictment, arguing that the "grand jury . . . was purposely selected of the white race . . . for the purpose of procuring this indictment against defendant," violating the Fourteenth Amendment. Jones, furthermore, sought to remove the case to federal court, although he would surely lose given that Mississippi had no jury discrimination law. In his removal petition, he stated that in Bolivar County, the site of the crime and prosecution, "1,300 or more duly registered [were] colored voters in said county and 300 [were] white voters upon the registration roll of said county." Jones proffered incorrect numbers, citing pre-convention data. Under the new constitution, Bolivar County had 163 registered White voters to 116 registered Black voters, meaning the new constitution disenfranchised more than a thousand Black men in the county, but fewer than two hundred White men. The premise of Jones's argument should have been that the convention delegates intended to and *did* disenfranchise Black men. His numbers suggested that the convention produced no discriminatory effect.

Jones also moved to quash the trial jury panel because "persons of [Smith's] race and color were purposely, on account of their color, excluded by said officers of the law." State law required jury commissioners to follow specific protocols that involved using the registered voter rolls to create a list of potential jurors. The commissioners, Jones believed, simply selected White men without referencing the rolls. Jones asked the trial judge to allow him to subpoena the commissioners to interrogate them under oath. The judge denied him that chance, blocking him from proving his case. Nonetheless, because Jones raised the proper constitutional issues at trial, Jones and Hewlett could raise them on appeal, leaving the possibility open for the four-part strategy essential to victory.

Jones argued *Charley Smith*, although he executed the plan both had devised. They, therefore, both wore the failures. The argument they brought before the Supreme Court fulfilled none of the four prongs. They raised some of the right points but their misreading of *Neal v. Delaware* tanked their endeavor.

Remember, in *Neal*, the defendant's affidavit charged the state with jury discrimination, and the state agreed to treat the affidavit as true. Seeking to prove that Mississippi intentionally excluded Black men from the juries, Jones offered the trial judge a sworn affidavit from Charley Smith that merely affirmed that Smith believed his accusation that the state racially discriminated against him. "The record will show the sufficiency of the affidavit," Jones and Hewlett wrote in their brief, further insisting that Smith's affidavit "was materially stronger than the one in the case of *Neal vs. Delaware*." But Mississippi district attorney Walton Shields never agreed to treat Smith's affidavit as true. Jones and Hewlett likened the facts in Smith's case to those of Neal, but they misunderstood the Court's *Neal* reasoning. Worse, they failed to even compare their case to *Yick Wo*. And worst, they introduced no facts from the 1890 convention to establish its discriminatory purpose. Yet, given that the judge denied Jones from even subpoenaing jury commissioners, thereby foreclosing the prospect of substantiating a Fourteenth Amendment claim, the black robes should've granted Smith another trial.

Johnston, in his brief, correctly observed that because Mississippi had no law limiting jury service to White men, Charley Smith, like the Reynolds brothers but unlike John Bush and Taylor Strauder, had no right, per precedent, to remove his case to federal court. Regarding the motions to quash the indictment and void the jury panel, Johnston contended that "No evidence was introduced, and none was offered by the accused on the hearing of the motion, nor was the accused denied the process of the Court by which to secure the attendance of witnesses, or the production of books or papers to prove the averments made in his motion." Johnston erred—the judge did deny Charley Smith the process to present witnesses.

And last, Johnston dismissed Jones and Hewlett's *Neal* comparison, noting that the state did not agree to treat Smith's affidavit as true. Thus, Jones had to provide "independent evidence" proving his accusations, which, Johnston observed, Jones failed to present. Johnston left unspoken the full truth that the state excluded Black men from jury pools because White Mississippians wanted them expelled from civil society. But because Hewlett and Jones presented a substandard argument, Johnston didn't even need to employ the full measure of deceit.

Hewlett presented the oral argument for *Gibson*, but the proper foundation was not laid. At trial, only a petition to remove the case to federal court under the federal removal statute was brought, and the judge denied the request to subpoena jury commissioners to support that petition. No petition arguing that the state excluded Black men from the grand or petit juries was brought either. Because those Fourteenth Amendment claims went unarticulated at trial, Jones and Hewlett couldn't even execute the four-part strategy in *Gibson*. That strategy hinged on reserving *constitutional* claims to appeal. Gibson's case was botched, and a man no jury should have convicted would swing from a rope.

A LITTLE AFTER NOON on a Saturday, a barefoot John Gibson stood on a wooden scaffold, around twelve feet above ground. His heels planted on a trapdoor. Hands tied behind his back. A black hood over his head. And around his neck a noose. More than a year after Jones and Hewlett had exited the U.S. Supreme Court, then located in the Capitol, after poorly arguing his case, Gibson tasted his final gasps.

Justice Harlan's unanimous opinion that sealed Gibson's death arrived on April 18, 1896, days after Jones wrote his letter to the Supreme Court clerk that opened this leg of our journey. Jones and Hewlett lost *Gibson* for an obvious reason—the Court had long interpreted that the right to remove a case to federal court for jury discrimination existed only if the state, by law, racially discriminated. The Court acknowledged that Jones sought to subpoena the jury commissioners. But, Harlan reasoned, even if the commissioners had confessed, that would not support removal but instead a motion to quash the indictment or the petit jury panel. And no such motions were brought. In their *Gibson* brief, Jones and Hewlett wrote, "could it be probable or reasonable to suppose that all the names so drawn to the number of two hundred [in the venire] would have by chance been all names of white men." But trial failures rendered this observation moot.

The Court rejected Charley Smith's appeal too. Writing another unanimous opinion, Harlan distinguished the case from *Neal*: "The facts stated in the written motion to quash, although that motion was verified by the affidavit of the accused, could not be used as evidence to establish those facts, except with the consent of the state prosecutor or by order of the trial court. No such consent was given." Harlan's opinion ignored that the trial judge refused Jones's request to subpoena jury commissioners. The justices had no argument to support refusing Charley Smith a new trial based on this refusal, and thus they simply ignored it. They indulged Mississippi's deceit. Despite two chances, Jones and Hewlett swayed nary a justice.

Don't allow Jones's and Hewlett's miscues to distract from the nine black robes attaching their names to opinions that sullied American democracy. Neither the underlying facts, the law, nor the arguments the counsels made compelled these outcomes. Ineffective lawyering doesn't confine justices. They, especially Justice Harlan, who had expansively interpreted The Trinity in his *Civil Rights Cases*, could have reached different outcomes. They could have realized, although Gibson was tried a handful of times, no Black person ever sat on his juries, something that could not have occurred but for jury discrimination. They chose to forsake wisdom, alerting caste preservationists that the Court allowed them to disregard the Constitution.

And even though Jones and Hewlett failed to compare their cases to *Yick Wo v. Hopkins*, a four-year-old decision didn't elude the justices' memories. If they believed their construction, that uneven application of a facially neutral law violated the Equal Protection Clause, that should have applied in *Gibson* and *Charley Smith*. The Court could have stopped Mississippi from executing two men who received sham trials. In his briefs, Johnston, a man who considered race traitors White men who ran for office on independent tickets, swore that Mississippi engaged in no race discrimination in its courts, a deceit. Instead of confronting the deceit, the justices indulged it, allowing the ultimate punishment.

In the 1890s, Mississippi, oftentimes, held executions near the county jail before an audience. The state conducted Gibson's in private, though. At twenty-six minutes past noon on May 1, 1897, a sheriff pulled the lever on the trapdoor. Gibson plunged but the rope around his neck stopped his thudding to the ground. On seven different occasions, the state had set his execution date. And each time, he ducked the gallows. Not this time.

Death, cruelly, waits during hangings. Victims can struggle for minutes. Gibson swung for twenty before the doctor pronounced him dead. Twelve hundred seconds, enough time to stew over America negating his citizenship. Gibson's life confirmed that Taney's *Dred Scott* analysis still operated. If Mississippi permitted Black men on the juries, Gibson could only wonder whether he would have heard "guilty." The world, however, parked him on the wrong side of the color fence. Death was his penalty. His final words rang out: "I'll meet you all in heaven."

Jones, without Hewlett's assistance, returned to the lab, seeking another opportunity to force the Supreme Court to make Mississippi honor the nation's Reconstruction promise of universal freedom. A month after the *Gibson* and *Charley Smith* decisions landed, the Court announced another that further protected the maturing racial caste system, a decision signaling that even should Jones perfectly execute the four-pronged strategy—unlikely given his prior deficiencies—he might never catch triumph.


THE WORDS THAT JUSTICE BROWN READ from his short majority opinion delivered on May 18, 1896, garnered little national attention at the time. Nearly every newspaper that reported on it cribbed from the same cursory Associated Press write-up that explained the Court upheld the constitutionality of a southern law. Perhaps the judgment struck the masses as too predictable to warrant a fuss. The case stemmed from a June 7, 1892, event. A question began it all.


"ARE YOU A COLORED MAN?" J. J. Dowling, a train conductor, asked a light-skinned man in a Whites-only seat inside the mahogany-interior East Louisiana Railroad train.

"Yes," replied Homer Adolph Plessy.

On the warm but cloudy afternoon, the twenty-nine-year-old shoemaker walked two miles from his home in the downtown New

Orleans Faubourg Tremé neighborhood. To the Press Train Depot he went. Bought his first-class ticket to Covington, Louisiana. Passed the train cars reserved for "coloreds." Sat down in the Whites-only car. And waited for that question. The steamboats and dockworkers on the New Orleans River, meanwhile, performed background noise.

"Then you will have to retire to the colored car," Dowling replied.

The Separate Car Act, passed by the Louisiana legislature on July 10, 1890, required all train companies to afford "equal but separate" seating inside their cars, splitting Black from White passengers. Those failing to remain in their race's assigned accommodations risked a twenty-five-dollar fine or a twenty-day maximum sentence.

New Orleans Afro-Creoles, who, because of their mixed-race ancestry and distinct culture, distinguished themselves as a discrete ethnic group, helmed the charge against the law. In September 1891, leading Afro-Creoles formed the Comité des Citoyens, to undertake a legal challenge. "This obnoxious measure is the concern of all our citizens who are opposed to caste legislation and its consequent injustices and crimes," the committee said in its plea. "We therefore appeal to the citizens of New Orleans, of Louisiana, and of the whole union to give their moral sanction and financial aid in our endeavors to have that oppressive law annulled by the courts."

The committee selected Plessy, a quiet member, born on March 17, 1863, in Union-occupied New Orleans to test the law's legality. Endeavoring to expose the absurdity of the state entrusting railroad companies with determining racial identity, an especially mercurial concept in a city brimming with mixed-race persons, the committee found in Plessy, one-eighth Black, a racially ambiguous man Black enough to be arrested for riding in a train's White section.

When Dowling demanded that Plessy move to the Colored car, Plessy, adhering to the plan to get arrested, responded that, as a first-class ticket buyer, he would keep his seat. The White folk in the car roused. Dowling directed him to leave once more. Plessy persisted. Into the depot Dowling went, returning with Christopher C. Cain, an off-duty police officer.

Cain, whom the committee had hired to arrest Plessy, cautioned Plessy: "If you are colored you should go into the car apart for your race. The law is plain and must be obeyed."

Plessy remained resolute. Cain arrested him and hauled him to the nearest jail. The number eight train proceeded to Covington as Plessy was booked, then quickly released on bond.

On November 18, 1892, Criminal District Court Judge John Howard Ferguson—the Ferguson in *Plessy v. Ferguson*—upheld the Separate Car Law: "There is no pretense that he was not provided with equal accommodations with the white passengers. He was simply deprived of the liberty of doing as he pleased, and of violating a penal statute with impunity." The *Times-Democrat* rejoiced. "We are glad to see that Judge Ferguson has decided the separate car act constitutional, and thus put a quietus to the efforts of some negro agitators to disobey it and sweep it aside."

JUSTICE BROWN, writing for a seven-to-one majority, found that the Thirteenth Amendment ended slavery and involuntary servitude but allowed segregation on trains. Brown regarded the truth of this "too clear for argument." Precedent, however, painted a different portrait. In the *Civil Rights Cases*, the Court, speaking through Justice Bradley, stated that the amendment prohibited slavery *and* established "universal civil and political freedom throughout the United States." Now, with no explanation, the Court surrendered that position. Brown said a "statute which implies merely a legal distinction between the white and colored races," like the Separate Car Act, "has no tendency to . . . reestablish a state of involuntary servitude." The Louisiana law consequently did not violate the Thirteenth Amendment.

Brown concluded that the Fourteenth Amendment, likewise, tolerated the state mandating racial separatism on trains. He conceded that the goal of the amendment "was undoubtedly to enforce the absolute equality of the two races before the law," but the Separate Car Act implicated social, not civil, rights. "Laws permitting, even requiring, their separation in places where they are liable to be brought into contact do not necessarily imply the inferiority of either race to the other," Brown claimed. He distinguished *Plessy* from *Strauder*—the latter featured "a discrimination which implied a legal inferiority in civil society, which lessened the security of the

right of the colored race, and was a step toward reducing them to a
condition of servility."

Brown likened the Separate Car Act to school segregation or theater segregation laws, which he considered likewise constitutional
exercises of a state's police power. The Tenth Amendment reserves
to the states whatever powers not delegated to the federal government. A state's police power—the power to provide for the welfare,
health, and safety of the public—emanates from this amendment.
Brown concluded that a state legislature could separate the races on
a train by law to promote its citizens' general welfare.

Plessy's attorneys argued that the law marked Black folk with a
badge of inferiority. "If this be so," Brown responded, "it is not by
reason of anything found in the act, but solely because the colored
race chooses to put that construction upon it. . . . If one race be inferior to the other socially the Constitution of the United States cannot
put them upon the same plane." The Court constructed the Equal
Protection Clause to allow for segregation in public spaces because
racially separating the races did not deny Black people equality.

When Congress debated the 1875 Civil Rights Act, the bill's
detractors admitted that a state law requiring racial segregation in
places like trains would violate The Trinity, and those detractors
strongly denied, correctly, that any state had passed such a law. Furthermore, Bradley premised his *Civil Rights Cases* majority opinion on the 1875 Act forcing private business to treat races equally
rather than barring states from mandating that private businesses
treat the races unequally. The implication of his argument pierces
through—if the 1875 Act had prevented states from requiring segregation in accommodations, the black robes would have upheld it.
Whereas the *Civil Rights Cases* decision tolerated persecution, *Plessy*
facilitated it. Emboldened it. The Louisiana legislature, having
deprived Black men of the ballot through violence, enacted a law that
stamped the race as inferior. Louisiana pretended that the law had
no involvement with fortifying a racial hierarchy through law, something that should obviously breach The Trinity. The Supreme Court
refined Louisiana's deceit, constructing the Constitution to abet
castework.

Justice Harlan, unlike the Court's majority, refused to indulge

Louisiana's deceit, bashing the position that Louisiana premised the Separate Car Act on anything other than the sentiment that Black people constituted an inferior caste whose presence should not disgrace the White race on trains. "Everyone knows," he explained in his dissent, "that the statute in question had its origin in the purpose, not so much to exclude white persons from railroad cars occupied by blacks, as to exclude colored people from coaches occupied by or assigned to white persons." Harlan understood that this law budded from the mindset outlined in *Dred Scott* that presumed Black people as "lower beings" and "altogether unfit to associate with the white race." Defining the case as one involving "social equality" belittled the stakes. *Plessy* concerned personal liberty. *Plessy* concerned civil rights. "If a white man and a black man choose to occupy the same public conveyance on a public highway, it is their right to do so, and no government, proceeding alone on grounds of race, can prevent it without infringing the personal liberty of each."

Harlan's dissent supported the position that he would have seen the law as castework. "But in view of the Constitution," Harlan said, "in the eye of the law, there is in this country no superior, dominant, ruling class of citizens. There is no caste here." Harlan then proffered a line we will encounter in the second part of our journey, nearly a century later. "*Our constitution is color-blind,*" he said, "and neither knows nor tolerates classes among citizens. In respect of civil rights, all citizens are equal before the law."

The Court, through its majority *Plessy* opinion, invited Jim Crow to overrun America, increasing the gravity of Jones's mission. Black folk, to parry caste preservationists, needed the ballot—voting rights furnish a vital, if penetrable, shield against state-sponsored oppression. Without the shield, Tennessee passed the first Jim Crow railroad law in 1881. Florida followed in 1887. Then Mississippi in 1888. Texas in 1889. Alabama, Arkansas, and Georgia in 1891. Kentucky in 1892. Segregation, like disenfranchisement, helped build the racial caste system. The South depicted Jim Crow as a supportive friend, sequestering races that preferred isolated spheres. In reality though, he menaced as a brute bred to degrade.

Brown and Harlan at least agreed that The Trinity protected civil and political equality, precisely the point of Jones's legal campaign.

If the black robes truly believed that, perhaps Jones just needed to prosecute a stronger case.

ON JUNE 15, 1896, Jones stood inside a courtroom on the second floor of the brownstone courthouse in Greenville, representing a new client, Henry Williams, for the murder of Eliza Brown. Jones returned to revive his legal crusade, needing his talents to match his dedication to a supposed American principle—liberty—while living in the midst of people, White Mississippians, unable to respect it.

In December 1895, Theophilus, Eliza's brother, reached into a pile of clothes while in her home, searching for a pair of pants. He moved a rag, uncovering his sister's lifeless face.

District attorney B. G. Humphries charged Williams, her boyfriend, with her strangulation death. A biracial man with a violent past, Williams faced charges for murdering a woman in 1893, but the chief witness disappeared, an unavailability authorities suspected him of prompting. "Williams is a notorious character," the New Orleans *Times-Democrat* reported, "having been charged with the murder of three women, two of whom were victims of strangulation." On May 25, an all-White grand jury indicted him for murder.

Before Williams pleaded not guilty, Jones moved to quash the indictment. Black citizens, Jones argued, were "denied the right to be selected as jurors," an equal protection violation. This time, Jones directly attacked the 1890 convention, arguing that delegates drafted the constitution "for the specific purpose of depriving the majority of the citizens and electors of the State, of the full, free, and impartial enjoyment of the rights of elective franchise, because of their race." Jones excoriated the state's scheme of drafting a constitution that appeared evenhanded by its terms but that entrusted White folk, like voter registrars and jury commissioners, with oppression duties. Mississippi's constitution, Jones argued, violated Williams's Fourteenth Amendment rights.

Jones provided three affidavits, one signed by Williams, another by Jones himself, and another by John Dixon, a Black murder convict Jones was representing. The affidavits, mimicking each other, stated that the argument in the motion—that the 1890 constitution discriminated against Black Mississippians—was true, establishing that Jones misunderstood why he had failed previously. The Court's opinions in *Gibson* and *Charley Smith* should've taught Jones the worthlessness of those affidavits. Judge R. W. Williamson overruled Jones. On June 19, 1896, an all-White jury convicted Williams. Jones moved to set aside the verdict on Fourteenth Amendment jury discrimination grounds. Williamson overruled Jones again and sentenced Williams to be hung on July 30.

Jones prepared to take Williams's case to the state supreme court. In the meantime, he had an election.

ON AUGUST 1, Mississippi's Republican Party held a rally in Greenville to support Jones's candidacy for Mississippi's 3rd Congressional District. "Let every old soldier who fought for the country and every Republican who voted before he was disfranchised by the New Constitution," stated the leaflet advertising the event where Jones spoke. "Every Republican is called to duty."

Ex-Confederate general Thomas Catchings, Jones's opponent, first won the seat in 1884. Jones needed the Black vote, but ahead of the 1892 elections, fewer than 9,000 Black men held voter registration in Mississippi, down from 190,000. "[T]he political map of Mississippi no longer contains a black belt," the Jackson *Daily Clarion* bragged, adding that the "proportion [of black voters] . . . is worth nothing—for it represents the degree of success of the central and supreme motive and idea of the convention: the reduction of the negro vote to a harmless minority."

After losing, Jones contested his defeat, petitioning the House of Representatives to deem *him* the rightful winner because, among other reasons, Mississippi's understanding clause, the requirement that voters who could not read instead demonstrate understanding of a passage read to them, violated The Trinity. In his deposition for the disputed election, he claimed the clause "was enacted for but one purpose, and that was a scheme or plan to throttle the suffrage of a majority of the voters of the State" and that it "has been used to the means desired, resulting in the extensive disfranchisement of about 180,000 male citizens of the United States." He argued that without it, he, not Catchings, would have received more votes. If the House agreed, it could have awarded him the seat.

Given that the Republicans controlled the House, Catchings had reason to fret. On Catchings's behalf, Mayre Dabney, an 1890 convention delegate, toured the district to dispute the veracity of Jones's contentions.

"Upon inquiry of the circuit clerks in the several counties," Dabney alleged, "I ascertained . . . that it was a rare occurrence for any person, white or black, to be denied the right to register when he applied.

"One clerk said that he had refused to register only one man on account of the understanding clause; others said they had refused very few for any cause; and others still said that they had never refused one because he could not read or write or could not understand a clause of the Constitution when read to him."

The explanation for the grand reduction of Black voters, Dabney claimed, lay with the poll tax. "I found," Dabney maintained, "that a very small percent of the negroes had paid their taxes, consisting, save in a few exceptional cases, of only a poll tax of $2.00, before February 1st of the year 1896, and indeed did not pay the tax at all." For every White person delinquent on the poll tax, Dabney estimated that eight to twenty Black men were. Prospective voters could register without having paid the poll tax. They just couldn't vote, explaining why Black registration numbers shriveled—having no intentions to pay the poll tax rendered pointless the act of registering.

Delegates to the convention probably assumed the understanding clause would be most effective at scrubbing the registration rolls of Black names. If Dabney was correct, that assumption seemed, at least initially, false. Nearly half the voters who registered under the understanding clause were Black.

"Only 1.56 percent of the total white voters registered under it," Dabney said, "while a much more significant 11.86 percent of the total black voters registered in this manner."

According to Dabney, Jones's argument condemning the understanding clause for disenfranchising Black voters missed the mark. But Jones's larger point, that delegates modeled the 1890 constitution to establish minority White rule, remained true, and Dabney's numbers demonstrated the effort's success. Moreover, although Dabney implicated the poll tax for these results, it, like the understanding clause, fit into the larger disenfranchisement subterfuge.

The House rejected Jones's contest, another data point illustrating Republicans' abandonment of Black voters. In the 1896 presidential election, Republican William McKinley defeated Democrat William Jennings Bryan by nearly a hundred electoral votes, despite Bryan sweeping the South. After the 1874 midterm elections, the Republican Party had decided to ditch Black southerners and profited electorally. Republicans' hopes, in the party's estimation, hinged on deserting The Trinity, and Republican Supreme Court justices constructed the Constitution accordingly.

Given that both parties now recoiled at the prospect of protecting Black rights, Jones needed strong evidence proving the racial exclusionary intentions of the Mississippi Plan of 1890—something damning enough to shake the justices awake. And from the unlikeliest of places, it appeared.

THE STATE CAPITOL IN JACKSON housed the Mississippi Supreme Court. Jones had litigated inside the elegant second-floor courtroom before. Faced the three justices and the tall spectacular windows from which sunlight beamed. On November 30, 1896, just months after Jones rededicated himself to his mission, from that room, where the state's racial caste system received a patina of lawfulness, came a decision that could blow open his efforts. From where Mississippi seceded and drafted its new constitution, arrived a dynamite stick— a decision written by the court's chief justice, Tim Cooper, in *Ratliff v. Beale*, a case concerning the state's poll tax.

Mississippi's attorney general, Wiley Nash, Frank Johnston's successor, championed efforts to make the poll tax compulsory. That tax financed public schools. Because few Black folk paid it, White Mississippians believed they bankrolled Black children's education, while their children could benefit from the increased funds a more commonly paid poll tax would generate. Johnston opposed Nash's plan, as did Solomon Calhoon, the convention's president, and Senator James George. They all feared that a compulsory poll tax meant more Black men would pay it, vote, and threaten White political dominance.

Nash, trusting that a compulsory poll tax would not produce a Black renaissance, initiated a test case with the help of W. T. Ratliff, tax collector for Hinds County, and Ambus Beale, a Black factory worker. Beale had not paid his poll tax in 1895 and owned no real property. Nash wanted the state supreme court to allow tax collectors to place liens on nontaxable property, property that wasn't a home or land, to compel poll tax payment. Ratliff seized Beale's bedstead with the intention of auctioning it to pay the poll tax.

"With a large negro majority," Johnston argued, representing Beale, "elections were accompanied by disorders and race conflicts until the adoption of the present constitution. It is part of the history of the state that the purpose of the legislature in calling the constitution convention was to provide, within the limits of constitutional power, a scheme of suffrage that would secure an electoral body in the state from which the elements of ignorance and incompetency should be, as far as practicable, excluded." Johnston implored the justices to bar county tax collectors from seizing personal property to repay delinquent poll taxes. "The design," Johnston said, "in making the payment of the poll tax a qualification of the elective franchise, and then exempting nontaxable property from its payment, was to leave payment optional with that large class of voters who owned no taxable property, as an inducement to them not to vote."

Nash and John H. Campbell, a former state supreme court justice, represented Ratliff. Campbell planned to trap the court. The state's highest tribunal would surely avoid admitting that the 1890 convention delegates intended to disenfranchise Black men. "Can it be that the poll tax was imposed to exclude negroes from voting?" Campbell asked rhetorically. "The constitution says it was to aid common schools. Is that a lie?"

The court answered "yes," and Nash lost. "Within the field of permissible action under the limitations imposed by the federal constitution," Cooper wrote for a unanimous court, "the convention swept the circle of expedients to obstruct the exercise of the franchise by the negro race." In short, the chief justice corroborated Jones's argument that Mississippi intended to disenfranchise Black men.

Cooper deemed straightforward why the convention embraced a poll tax, writing, "the clause was primarily intended by the framers of the constitution as a clog upon the franchise, and secondarily and incidentally only, as a means of revenue." The court prohibited Nash from empowering county tax collectors to compel payment of the poll tax by seizing personal property. "It is evident that the more the payment of the tax is made compulsory," Cooper wrote, "the greater will be the number by whom it will be paid, and therefore the less effectual will be the clause for the purpose it was intended."

Cooper blessed Cornelius Jones. The state's leading jurist divulged, in writing, that the 1890 convention delegates set their minds to disenfranchise Black men. The editor of the Jackson *Clarion-Ledger* understood the crisis, writing, "this decision will yet be used . . . in an effort to nullify the franchise article of the constitution of Mississippi, for the court says that the object of this section was to disqualify the negro as a voter."

Cooper's opinion in Henry Williams's case, released a few weeks prior to his *Ratliff v. Beale* opinion, exhibited shameless inconsistency. In that opinion, Cooper wrote that "we have no power to investigate or decide upon the private, individual purposes of those who framed the constitution." But at the month's end, to protect the state's disenfranchisement scheme in the poll tax case, he had the power to investigate those "individual purposes." In upholding Williams's conviction, Cooper hid behind the constitution's neutral language, asserting that the convention targeted negative characteristics, not color, and that more Black folk lost their suffrage rights because "a greater number of the more fortunate race is found to possess the qualifications which the framers of the constitution deemed essential for the exercise of the elective franchise."

During our previous leg, Frederick Douglass told a reporter after the *Civil Rights Cases* decision that as bitterness between North and South dissolved, so too would White northerners' concern about southerners' flagrant abuse of The Trinity. At the height of northern antipathy toward the secessionist South, the North supported congressional Reconstruction. But once those antagonisms faded, the appetite for interfering with southern administration of law and justice to correct wrongs done to Black people faded, especially as the North inflicted its own trauma on Black skin. As Jones appealed *Williams v. Mississippi* to the Supreme Court, the nation, an estranged family, found another reason to release sectional grudges.

WAR WAS THAT REASON, or its approach. The February 1898 sinking of the Navy battleship USS *Maine* in Cuba's Havana Harbor doused the nation in anxiety and frenzy—America appeared to be hurtling toward war with Spain, stirring feelings of patriotism among many White Americans as the country crawled out of the economic depression of the mid-1890s. That same specter of war offered Black folk hope. The terrors of Jim Crow, disenfranchisement, and lynching left Black folk scouring for a strap to pull that would liberate them from despair. War offered an opportunity to pace the battlefield. Display American allegiance. And hopefully coax requited love. Yet should Black folk shed blood for a country that made them shed tears?

On March 7, 1898, George Henry White, a North Carolina Republican, addressed his House colleagues. As Congress's only Black member, the forty-five-year-old shouldered the burden of articulating a race's ambitions and grievances during the most harrowing decade since the Civil War's resolution. Swinging from trees. Denied the ballot. Segregated to the fringes of society. All manner of castework, from private individuals and state actors alike, stampeded Black Americans.

"The nation has not at all times given us that protection to which our loyalty has entitled us," White said. "This is painfully evidenced by the almost daily outrages chronicled, showing lynchings, murders, assassinations, and even criminations of our people all over the Southland," explained White, who won his seat by forging interracial alliances, living proof of the fears that drove the southern constitutional convention movement. "But, regardless of the faults of this grand old Union of ours, we love her still, and if the nation should find it necessary to resort to arms and our present strained relations with Spain should develop into a war, I pledge you that the black phalanx is ready to be mustered in, one-half million strong." Much of the Black press ultimately concurred that Black America had much to gain through exhibiting loyalty during international strife. As the

Black newspaper *Washington Bee* exhorted, "the crime of the Maine must be avenged."

Another Black newspaper proved prophetic, though, writing, "the Negro might as well know it now as later. The closer the North and South get together by this war, the harder [Black folk] will have to fight to maintain a footing."

On March 18, 1898, weeks before the seven-month Spanish-American War started, Jones brought *Williams v. Mississippi* to the Supreme Court.

AS THE JUSTICES FILED into their chamber on March 18, 1898, under a forty-five-state flag, only one new black robe greeted Jones. Democrat Justice Field retired in December 1897, providing Republican president McKinley the prospect of reshaping the Court. He selected Joseph McKenna, former Republican California congressman and sitting U.S. attorney general. Many federal judges warned Chief Justice Fuller about McKenna, formerly a Ninth Circuit judge. McKenna, the judges cautioned, possessed an inadequate legal mind, performed uninspiringly as a judge, and lacked fitness for the black robe. Fuller investigated the accusations, even raising them with McKinley, but the president stuck with McKenna.

Born to an Irish immigrant father and an English immigrant mother, McKenna grew up in Philadelphia, a city rife with narrow-minded anti-Irish and anti-Catholic bigotry. Given the anti-Chinese discrimination he pursued as a congressman, having endured provincialism didn't prevent him from reproducing it.

Jones, this time, centered the 1890 constitution convention in his attack, arguing that the delegates devised it "with the purpose and intent to discriminate against the negro voters of the State because of their race." Jones spoke truth here, though providing accurate numbers detailing how the constitution obliterated Black voting would have invigorated his presentation. Instead, he contended that "190,000 negroes of the State ... have been ... stricken from the body of suffrage in the State," an inflated figure. This time, Jones, wisely, likened his case to *Yick Wo v. Hopkins*. Mississippi's constitution mirrored the San Francisco laundry ordinance in *Yick Wo*, Jones maintained, in that both were seemingly neutral yet were enforced unequally.

Nonetheless, Jones misstepped a few times. For one, he ignored *Strauder, Virginia v. Rives, Neal,* and *Bush,* blundering particularly in not drawing analogies to *Neal.* In *Beale,* the Mississippi Supreme Court insisted that Black folk faced disproportionate disenfranchisement because of their negative traits that made them less fit for suffrage rights. This statement echoed the chief justice of the Delaware Supreme Court's remark in *Neal* "that the great body of Black men residing in this State are utterly unqualified by want of intelligence, experience, or moral integrity to sit on juries." Jones, moreover, did not attempt to subpoena jury commissioners. Given that the Supreme Court did not punish Mississippi for denying his subpoenas in *Charley Smith* and *Gibson,* one can understand his decision, although he did err here. An attorney should blow out every candle.

Yet, in *Beale,* the Mississippi Supreme Court had already conceded Jones's central claim. He argued that the convention delegates wrote the constitution to disenfranchise Black men. And the state supreme court justices conceded this. What more could the black robes require?

The opposing counsel chair in the courtroom sat empty. In his January 1898 message to the state legislature, Governor Anselm McLaurin, under whom Jones studied law, said, "[t]here has been no more important case before the Supreme Court of the United States carried from this State since its admission into the Union in 1817." Because the state attorney general couldn't dedicate all his energies to the matter, Mississippi paid $500 to Charles B. Mitchell to write a brief defending the state but didn't foot the travel bill to D.C. The *Clarion-Ledger* called Mitchell, a state senator during Reconstruction, among the "faithful band of white men then members of the Legislature [who] were on constant vigil and compelled to resort to all sorts of tactics to outwit the black horde that held sway in both houses." In other words, a caste preservationist.

Mitchell used the constitution's neutral language as a fig leaf, writing, "nothing can be found, not a line or word, which in any manner whatever discriminates against any citizen because of his race, color or previous condition." And although more Black men lost their voting rights under the new constitution, that was because "a greater number of the more fortunate race is found to possess the qualifications which the framers of the Constitution deemed essential for the exercise of the elective franchise."

Rather than finding an argument to defend the motives of the convention delegates, Mitchell pretended they were unknown. "It is true that the plaintiff in error has a good deal to say as to the motives which actuated the framers of these laws," he wrote. "[W]e think the surest way to arrive at their motive is by a proper Construction and interpretation of the laws themselves, and these laws have been favorably construed by all the Courts in the country, and simply to impugn the motives of the action of a sovereign State is no argument whatever and we think should not be indulged in without sufficient grounds."

Mitchell wrote a deceitful brief, but the state's supreme court had already admitted the facts necessary to invalidate the 1890 constitution. In the previous leg of our journey, the Supreme Court struck down legislation that punished private individuals for interfering with Black people's enjoyment of rights. The Fourteenth Amendment only applies to state action, the black robes exclaimed. In an honest America, the *Ratliff v. Beale* decision, where a state supreme court admitted that the state endeavored to restrict Black rights, would have settled the matter.

The Court decided *Williams v. Mississippi* while Louisiana held its constitutional convention. The opinion could erase the footprints in the sand. Let's head to New Orleans to explore the Court's decision.

HERE ON MAY 12, 1898, inside this two-story room with intricately coffered ceilings and an imperial staircase set against the back wall, Ernest Benjamin Kruttschnitt addresses the convention delegates. Three decades ago, White men slaughtered Black folk outside this building, the Mechanics Institute, staining the streets with blood during the New Orleans Massacre of 1866. The constitutional convention, like those in Mississippi and South Carolina before, was, as the New Orleans *Times-Democrat* stated, held "(1) to secure white [domination] for all time in Louisiana, and (2) to assure honest elections and put an end to the frauds which have so long debauched the public sense of the State." The convention's president, Kruttschnitt, a chunky-faced White man with droopy eyes, is addressing the gathering on its final day.

After much debate on which disenfranchisement scheme to adopt, the convention selected something similar to Mississippi's although Louisiana's delegates adopted a so-called grandfather's clause that exempted from onerous voting preconditions any man who was entitled to vote before January 1, 1867, or a man who was the grandson or son of such a man, a scheme that obviously excluded Black men. Many thought that the grandfather's clause too transparently flouted the Fifteenth Amendment, that the convention could achieve its ends without such a blatant artifice. Kruttschnitt, on the convention's final day, occupies the rostrum to buoy his people's spirits much like Senator Hiram Revels did at a Black Baltimore church to herald the Fifteenth Amendment's ratification two decades ago.

"We have not drafted the exact Constitution that we should like to have drafted," he admits, "otherwise we should have inscribed in it, if I know the popular sentiment of this State, universal white manhood suffrage, and the exclusion from the suffrage of every man with a trace of African blood in his veins.

"We could not do that, on account of the Fifteenth Amendment to the Constitution of the United States, and, therefore, we did what has been so well expressed by the Supreme Court of Mississippi, and what has been referred to approvingly by the Supreme Court of the United States, in the late case of Wilson vs. the State of Mississippi."

Kruttschnitt says "Wilson" but means *Williams v. Mississippi*, decided April 25. Fuller tapped McKenna to write the unanimous opinion. McKenna would never receive the full confidence of fellow justices as his weak *Williams* opinion explains. Jones succeeded in centering the constitutionality of the suffrage provisions of the state's constitution. The Court rejected his argument, nevertheless, writing that the provisions "do not on their face discriminate between the races, and it has not been shown that their actual administration was evil; only that evil was possible under them."

McKenna refused to extend *Yick Wo*'s Fourteenth Amendment construction—that a race-neutral law applied in a discriminatory fashion violates the Equal Protection Clause—to Mississippi's constitution. In his *Williams* opinion, McKenna merely asserted that the *Yick Wo* principle "is not applicable to the constitution of Mississippi and its statutes." The opinion addressed the Mississippi Supreme Court's *Beale* decision too. McKenna, in fact, quoted this passage from *Beale* in his opinion:

"By reason of its previous condition of servitude and dependence, this race had acquired or accentuated certain peculiarities of habit, of temperament, and of character, which clearly distinguished it as a race from that of the whites—a patient, docile people, but careless, landless, and migratory within narrow limits, without forethought, and its criminal members given rather to furtive offenses than to the robust crimes of the whites. Restrained by the federal constitution from discriminating against the negro race, the convention discriminated against its characteristics and the offenses to which its weaker members were prone."

Yet, McKenna, oddly, concluded that "nothing tangible can be deduced from this." In reality, the Court could easily deduce that the state intentionally disenfranchised Black voters. Because Jones did not establish that jury commissioners purposefully excluded Black men from the juries that indicted and convicted Williams, the Court found no equal protection violation.

In 1890, White Mississippians, displaying an inability to abide by basic democratic behavioral standards, purposefully expelled Black men from politics. Worse yet, the state conceded this, and the Supreme Court of the United States turned its head. At the beginning of this journey, I asked, "How will the Supreme Court answer such deceit? Will it indulge the deceit? Even refine the deceit? Or will the Court confront the deceit? Maybe expose the deceit?"

We have our answer.

When the *Williams* decision landed during the convention, Louisiana Democrats rejoiced. "It is a declaration that the State can attach conditions to the suffrage," the *Semi-Weekly Times-Democrat* celebrated, "and the fact that these conditions shut out a great many negroes, and even that they were adopted for the specific purpose of shutting out the negroes, does not make the provision unconstitutional and in conflict with Federal Law." "Such a doctrine, emanating from the highest judicial authority," the *Times-Picayune* cheered, "provides safety for the institutions of the country against the dreadful consequences that were intended to flow from the enactment of the fourteenth amendment of the constitution."

Kruttschnitt, finishing his speech, tells the delegates to celebrate their achievement. "What care I whether the test we have put be a new one or an old one? What care I whether it be more or less ridiculous or not? Doesn't it meet the case? Doesn't it let the white man vote, and doesn't it stop the negro from voting, and isn't that what we came here for?"

The Fourteenth and Fifteenth Amendments, a southern newspaper had declared in 1875, "may stand forever, but we intend . . . to make them dead letters on the statute-book." By the end of the nineteenth century, caste preservationists had fulfilled their mission. Jones will concede as much in a 1901 letter. In a Supreme Court case where "the decision will in any manner cloud the prospect for perpetual white [domination] in the South," Jones writes, "the result thereof is too well known to us." Unable to live as a full citizen, Jones will, in the early 1900s, relocate to Muskogee, Indian Territory.

Here in the 1890s, the Court allows states to deny civil rights based on race, all while professing that the Equal Protection Clause still prohibits states from denying civil rights based on race. How can the Court disappear something while claiming to still hold it? The answer—the Court is stealthily overturning precedent, stealthily canceling equal protection. The Court has heard cases brought by Black victims denied equal protection and is simply disregarding race-based deprivation of rights, indulging and refining deceit by refusing to treat denials as denials.

The Court, in our previous leg, created the state action doctrine that defeated congressional legislation that enforced The Trinity against private individuals. During this leg of our journey, we saw that the Supreme Court wouldn't even honor its construction. John Gibson and Charley Smith asked the Court to stop the state from denying their rights. The Court responded that they didn't prove a rights denial. Homer Plessy asked the Court to stop the state from denying his rights. The Court responded that he wasn't denied a right. Henry Williams, while holding the state's confession, asked the Court to stop the state from denying his rights. The Court responded that the confession didn't mean anything. The Court, in reality, concocted the state action doctrine as an artifice because, in that moment, it facilitated caste preservationism. During this leg, the doctrine undermined caste preservationism, convincing the Court to jettison it, inviting more states to leave their footprints in the sand.

"AND WHAT IS IT that we want to do?" asked John Barnett Knox, on May 22, 1901, inside the hall of the House of Representatives during Alabama's constitutional convention. "What it is, within the limits imposed by the Federal Constitution, to establish white [domination] in this State," said the convention president. "This is our problem, and we should be permitted to deal with it, unobstructed by outside influences, with a sense of our responsibilities as citizens, and our duty to posterity."

With *Williams v. Mississippi*, the Supreme Court had empowered caste preservationists to compose constitutions that reflected their unwillingness to commit to freedom, equal justice, and free and fair elections. Knox, and the other delegates who wanted to disenfranchise Black men, had displayed an inability to abide by the requirements of inhabiting a democracy. And the black robes did not force them to reform. Did not squelch their contravening the nation's supposed rules. The justices, instead, bent those rules to condone castework. When Knox expressed that "outside influences" must permit them to enshrine White Supremacy's objectives in the state's constitution, he was articulating a want he knew the nine black robes had already given in *Williams v. Mississippi*.

"We are reunited. Sectionalism has disappeared," said the reelected president, William McKinley, weeks prior during his inauguration.

Sectionalism had indeed disappeared. Enough that slavery reappeared.

# Fourth Leg:
# The Slavery Reintroduction

L ET'S OPEN THIS LEG OF OUR JOURNEY with a vignette—its salience will soon strike you. Field laborers in the turpentine business toiled in the wilderness, insects buzzing about, gashing open longleaf pine trees native to the Southeast. Resin oozed from the wounds which was then collected for the making of various products, including the caulk used to seal holes in wooden ships. As the tide of modernization swept across most industries, turpentining remained anchored to antiquity, as laborers lugged rudimentary equipment before sunrise, tending to thousands of trees until sunset, as though when they slogged in darkness through mud into forests, they stepped back in time a century. The industry once employed more Black laborers in the region than any other. White men refused to drudge alongside them. That was, they spit, "nigger work."

On May 19, 1900, William Moore, the head of a turpentine farm in Molino, Florida, and C. I. Joiner, Moore's teenaged White employee, journeyed twelve miles searching for three Black laborers, Will Smith, Will Thomas, and John Irving, who, Moore claimed, left his employ owing him money. Moore and Joiner found them in the Pensacola, Florida area at a turpentine farm operated by William Proctor.

Laborers like Smith, Thomas, and Irving, as in many southern industries dependent upon Black labor, received an advance upon signing a twelve-month contract and repaid that advance with deductions from their piddling monthly salaries. The unpaid advance rekindled in White businessmen the sensation of ownership over Black bodies. Turpentine laborers frequently ended their contracts owing their employer. The camp commissary store sold price-inflated goods, helping keep workers ensnared in the quicksand of indebtedness. Since laborers could always reenlist, indebtedness most affected those craving fresh employment opportunities. When indebted laborers left, employers commonly hunted them down, as if the Fugitive Slave Acts remained good law, sometimes culminating in disaster. Months prior, Moore had shot and killed Jeff Griffin, a Black laborer who deserted Moore's farm. A grand jury, no doubt all White, decided against indictment.

The two turpentine operators had agreed, when Moore left Proctor's commissary store after an hour-long discussion, that Proctor would pay Moore what Will Smith owed, five dollars, shifting Smith's indebtedness from Moore to Proctor. This allowed Smith to continue on Proctor's farm. But Moore refused payment for Irving and Thomas. He wanted their labor and planned to return them to Molino to extract it.

As Moore and Joiner mounted their horses, their captives Irving and Thomas in tow, several Black laborers on Proctor's camp emerged from a wooden frame house—laborers typically dwelled in dilapidated shacks on turpentine campgrounds—to prevent Irving and Thomas's kidnapping. A gunfight erupted.

America remembers this period as the Progressive Era. A spirit of reform defined the times. Capitalism burgeoned, introducing circumstances and dilemmas to which government was called upon to respond. People of varied backgrounds knew in their marrow and sinew that unscrupulous capitalists, corporate monopolies, and venal politicians had vanished the fair economic play and good government they believed had once existed. The injustice that Will Smith, Will Thomas, and John Irving endured—involuntary servitude—was just one sort chronicled by the Progressive Era's muckraking journalists. This injustice and others that were mainly experienced by Black people launched legal controversies that sometimes reached the Supreme Court.

This leg of our journey will focus on Black people's labor, specifically, Black people's natural, God-given right to own their own labor, something Moore treated as his until a bullet entered the right side of his neck, gored his carotid artery, and exited his left lung. Joiner, his accomplice, survived a gunshot to his leg.

The era's most prominent Black leader extolled labor as *the* building block for Black salvation and advanced a caste abolitionist strategy he believed could untether his people from the knot of wrongs like this one unfolding in the piney woods. Let's meet him on Harvard University's campus one June 1896 day.

HERE INSIDE THE PACKED SANDERS THEATRE, a wooden Gothic space that radiates a cathedral's aura, the crowd belts out its loudest hurrahs when Charles William Eliot, Harvard's president, extends an honorary Master of Arts degree to the forty-year-old Booker Taliaferro Washington. Eliot introduces him as a "Teacher, wise helper of his race; good servant of God and country." The star power of the country's most influential Black man dwarfs that of telephone inventor Alexander Graham Bell and the other honorary degree recipients.

Weeks earlier, a letter arrived at the Alabama school that Booker T. heads as president, the Tuskegee Institute, founded to train Black teachers and provide Black students an industrial education. "Harvard University desires to confer on you at the approaching commencement an honorary degree," he read while sitting on his veranda surrounded by his wife, Margaret, and three children. Booker T. will call receiving the letter "the most surprising incident" of his life.

After a tour of Harvard's campus, the honorary degree recipients sit for the Alumni Dinner where two hundred graduates and their invited guests will hear speeches. Booker T. delivers one, although not one as indelible as that which catapulted him into prominence three years before.

IN 1893, THE WORLD'S COLUMBIAN EXPOSITION drew 27 million to Chicago. An envious Atlanta sought to host a similar extravaganza on behalf of the "New South," a coinage meant to promote the region as open for industrial development. Local businessmen expended $2 million, covering eleven acres with buildings and exhibits that displayed the South's best creations. Atlanta organizers, to avoid the accusations of race exclusion that dogged Chicago's event, erected a building for Black southerners to exhibit their accomplishments and offered Booker T. a speaking slot during the opening ceremony of the Atlanta Cotton States and International Exposition.

On September 18, 1895, Washington, about five-foot-seven and medium-brown-complexioned, sat on a stage inside the overly hot Exposition Hall, sweating, fearing the moment when his name would fill the space, signaling him to deliver the first address by a Black man before an interracial audience in the South. "I was determined from the first not to say anything that would give undue offense to the South and thus prevent it from thus honoring another Negro in the future," Booker T., born into slavery on a small plantation in Hale's Ford, Virginia, on April 5, 1856, later remembered. "And at the same time, I was equally determined to be true to the North and to the interests of my own race." Upon hearing his name, he stood to utter the words he had rehearsed repeatedly. The White members of the packed crowd largely muted themselves, stillness clashing against the acclamation from Black members.

The sun flooding through the windows and into his piercing gray eyes, Booker T., a thin man, stood on the stage and implored Black folk to "cast down your bucket where you are" and seize opportunity in the South. He likewise urged White southerners to "cast down your bucket where you are" and help elevate Black southerners, a people who had forever proven loyal. With the fates of the two races intertwined, both forced to inhabit the same region, White southerners, he argued, would never fulfill their promise without helping Black people fulfill theirs.

Booker T. paused after leveling each point. Held his hand high above his head, fingers stretched apart. "In all things that are purely social we can be as separate as the fingers, yet one as the hand in all things essential to mutual progress," he proclaimed, balling a fist to complete the demonstration.

In exchange for this assistance, Booker T. argued that Black folk should prove themselves worthy of the political rights that had been pillaged decades before. "The wisest among my race understand that agitation of questions of social equality is the extremest folly," he said, "and that progress in the enjoyment of all the privileges that will come to us must be the result of severe and constant struggle rather than of artificial forcing. No race that has anything to contribute to the markets of the world is long in any degree ostracized. It is important and right that all privileges of the law be ours, but it is vastly more important that we be prepared for the exercise of those privileges."

When Booker T. finished, Rufus Bullock, Georgia's Reconstruction-era Republican governor, bolted across the stage and congratulated him. Cheers flooded the hall. Handkerchiefs waved about. Heaved hats cascaded from the ceiling. "Your words cannot fail to delight and encourage all who wish well for your race," later wrote the sitting president, Democrat Grover Cleveland, "and if our colored fellow citizens do not from your utterances gather new hope and form new determinations to gain every valuable advantage offered them by their citizenship, it will be strange indeed." Booker T. reaped praise as a Moses-like figure, and influential Black newspaperman T. Thomas Fortune dubbed him "The new Frederick Douglass," an inheritor of the legacy left behind by the icon who had passed in February 1895.

A year later, inside Harvard's Memorial Hall, Booker T. sampled from his greatest hit.

"I FEEL LIKE A HUCKLEBERRY in a bowl of milk," he quips, engendering laughter.

"If through me, an humble representative, seven millions of my people in the South might be permitted to send a message to Harvard—Harvard that offered up on death's altar, young Shaw, and Russell, and Lowell and scores of others," he says, referring to Harvard men who died in the Civil War, "that we might have a free and united country, that message would be 'Tell them that the sacrifice was not in vain. Tell them that by the way of the shop, the field, the skilled hand, habits of thrift and economy, by way of industrial school and college, we are coming. We are crawling up, working up, yea, bursting up. Often through oppression, unjust discrimination, and prejudice, but through them all we are coming up, and with proper habits, intelligence and property, there is no power on earth that can permanently stay our progress.'

"We are to be tested in our patience, our forbearance, our perseverance, our power to endure wrong, to withstand temptations, to economize, to acquire and use skill; our ability to compete, to succeed in commerce, to disregard the superficial for the real, the appearance for the substance, to be great and yet small, learned yet simple, high and yet the servant of all. This, this is the passport to all that is best in the life of our Republic, and the Negro must possess it, or be debarred," says Booker T., enrapturing the audience, as he does most everywhere he speaks. While a student at Hampton Normal and Agricultural Institute, he refined himself. Curated his presentation. Practiced public speaking and expunged the "plantation" from his voice, consuming Abraham Lincoln's great addresses to emulate the facilities of a magnetic orator.

"In working out our destiny, we shall need, the help, the encouragement, the guidance that the strong can give the weak. Thus helped, we of both races in the South, soon shall throw off the shackles of racial and section prejudice and rise as Harvard University has risen and as we all should rise, above the clouds of ignorance, narrowness, and selfishness, into that atmosphere, that pure sunshine, where it will be our highest ambition to serve MAN, our brother, regardless of race or previous condition."

Loud applause pours when Booker T. concludes, and President Eliot grabs his hand. "[Yours] was the best speech of the day," he says.

In 1881, White men in Macon County, Alabama, wrote Civil War general Samuel C. Armstrong, Hampton Institute's head, requesting the name of a White man who could lead a normal and industrial school like Hampton in their area. Local White folk feared Black folk joining the Exoduster movement and thought a school might stem a population drain. "The only man I can suggest," Armstrong countered, "is one Booker T. Washington a graduate of this institution, a very competent capable mulatto, clear headed, modest, sensible, polite and a thorough teacher and superior man. The best man we ever had here." A week later, the reply telegraph arrived: "Send him here at once."

On June 24, 1881, a twenty-five-year-old Booker T., looking eighteen despite his handlebar mustache, disembarked a train in Tuskegee, a small town of two thousand, expecting to find "a building and all the necessary apparatus ready for me to begin teaching." He "found nothing of the kind," he said. "I did find, though, hundreds of hungry, earnest souls who wanted to secure knowledge." He mashed tireless fundraising, ingenuity, and persistence into the bricks that built a thriving hub of instruction.

Booker T. prays to the god of industrial education, believing the Black masses would discover salvation in mastering the skills and knowledge useful to vocations within an industrial economy. "I plead for industrial education and development for the Negro not because I want to cramp him, but because I want to free him," he once wrote. "I want to see him enter the all-powerful business and commercial world." Booker T. joins his industrial instruction with teachings on cleanliness, morality, and work ethic. Some would rather shepherd the Black masses toward a liberal arts education that the good White folk provide their kin. Slighting that path for his people, Booker T. had remarked that a young Black man in unclean clothes, living in a filthy, neglected cabin while reading a French grammar book presented one of the saddest spectacles he had ever encountered. He tells Black folk that if presentable, pious, and hardworking, they could prosper in the South.

Inside Harvard's Memorial Hall, as in Atlanta and wherever else, Booker T. preaches respectability politics. This racial progress strategy implores Black people to disprove, through their behavior, caste preservationists' justification of racial inequality on account of supposed biological or cultural inferiority. Disciples of respectability politics champion this gospel for two reasons. First, they hope White folk will notice when Black folk reach respectability and treat Black people better. Second, they seek to further Black folks' own interests, regardless of White approval. As Booker T. will write later in life, "I tried to emphasize the fact that political agitation alone would not save the Negro, that back of politics he must have industry, thrift, intelligence and property; that no race without these elements of strength could permanently succeed and gain the respect of its fellow citizens." In respectability politics, Booker T. found his strategy for caste abolitionism.

Booker T.'s respectability politics grew from pre-1840s abolitionism. The South treated the tribulations of free Black people in the North as proof that slavery best suited the race. Abolitionist William Lloyd Garrison stated, "It would be absurd to pretend, that, as a class, they maintain a high character," referring to free Black northerners. Abolitionists, though, contended that unbearable oppression prevented Black people from ascending the economic ladder and meeting a nation's moral standards. "I do not hesitate to assert," Garrison maintained, "from an intimate acquaintance with their condition, that they are more temperate and more industrious than that class of whites who are in as indigent circumstances, but who have certainly far greater incentives to labor and excel."

Respectability politics offered abolitionists a solution to slavery and an answer to the northern caste system—prove yourself, Black northerners, and crumble the partition barricading your people from freedom and equality. An editorial from *Freedom's Journal*, the nation's first Black newspaper, posited that "the further decrease of prejudice, and the amelioration of the condition of thousands of our brethren who are yet in bondage greatly depend on our conduct. It is for us to convince the world by uniform propriety of conduct, industry, and economy, that we are worthy of esteem and patronage." Similarly, the author of an 1832 piece in the *Liberator*, Garrison's abolitionist newspaper, entitled "What Can the Free Colored People Do for Themselves?," lectured Black folk that after they demonstrate their worth, "they need not fear but what prejudice will die away, and their equality will be acknowledged, and soon no difference will be known between the colored man and the white."

Nineteenth-century abolitionists urged Black northerners to climb and become beacons of virtue—a mountaintop White boots did not kiss—to receive equal rights, in the face of conditions that cinched together their ankles. Populations act rationally. People work hard and follow the rules if they believe they can win. Black northerners understood the White man rigged the game and then considered their defeats as demonstrating inferiority. Abolitionists

told Black folk to win anyway and believed the strategy would succeed, a perception inspired perhaps by a recognition that should it
sink, nothing would float. Respectability politics surfaced from the
pond that drowned all other strategies.

Booker T., in his own life, saw reason to trust in respectability politics. When he arrived at Tuskegee, White folk there, he said, "never
even began to have confidence in me until we commenced to build a
large three-story brick building; and then another and another, until
now we have eighty-six buildings which have been erected largely by
the labour of our students, and today we have the respect and confidence of all the white people in that section."

Booker T. repurposed respectability politics for a southern climate that simulated what Black northerners endured before the war:
supposedly free, undeniably a degraded caste whose second-class
citizenship drew sustenance from written law. As the nation tiptoed
into a new century, Booker T. emerged as the hero America needed,
a leader who could advocate for Black people's aims because he won
White people's respect. One who could appeal to Black and White
folk alike, as neither extreme to the latter, nor inauthentic to the former. One who could barter a racial compromise and convince both
races to unite around mutual economic advancement. Justice Field
wrote in his *Slaughter-House Cases* dissent that the "property which
every man has in his own labor, as it is the original foundation of all
the property, so it is the most sacred and inviolable." Booker T. petitioned the Black masses to leverage their most valuable property to
forward their cause. The strategy failed—Booker T. planted it in soil
White Supremacy had long ago contaminated. This leg of our journey explores why the seed of respectability politics never flourished
in the first two decades of the twentieth century.

We must treat the 1899 Supreme Court case *Cumming v. Richmond County Board of Education* as prologue. Justice Harlan, after his
*Gibson* and *Charley Smith* decisions, further charring his bona fides as
a racially enlightened justice, wrote the unanimous opinion. He concluded that the Fourteenth Amendment did not bar a school board
from maintaining a public high school for White students but none
for Black students. The Richmond County, Georgia school board
allocated all funds reserved for Black education toward elementary

schooling. The district offered public high school options for White students only. *Cumming* gifted constitutional cover to the South, which refused to provide public education to Black pupils past grade school, mocking *Plessy*'s separate but equal farce, ridiculing the state action ruse. Thus, economic opportunities relying upon education stood beyond the Black masses, kicking them toward laboring for the White man, fingernails manipulating the dirt, much the way their parents and grandparents did during the days of *Dred Scott*. In *Cumming*, the Supreme Court furthered the White South's aspirations to narrow Black people's economic avenues.

This wouldn't completely torpedo Booker T.'s program though. After all, Black folk could still prove themselves through the work open to them. The story of how this turned fruitless begins right after the war.

IN SEPTEMBER 1865, fifty-one-year-old botanist and owner of the Berkeley County, South Carolina, Pooshee Plantation, Henry William Ravenel, expressed one of White Supremacy's most durable and destructive theses. "There must be stringent laws to control the negroes," he penned in his diary, and "require them to fulfill their contracts of labour on the farms." Ravenel believed no planter "will venture to engage in agricultural operations without some guarantee that his labour is to be controlled & continued under penalties & forfeitures. Without these, there would be certainty of loss. It behooves those who have brought about such a state of things to devise a system which will secure to the negro subsistence & a home, & to the white an equitable profit."

The Union Army legitimated this thesis. Early in Reconstruction, General Oliver Otis Howard, commissioner of the Freedmen's Bureau, opined that the freedpeople needed "wholesome compulsion" to work and backed requiring them to sign labor contracts or face criminal punishment, issuing the blueprint—one-year contracts signed around New Year's for the upcoming year—that would define southern labor arrangements. Freedpeople in the months following the war, however, frowned at continuing the sixteen-hour workdays of their bondage and expected respectful treatment from employers.

After the 1865 planting season, many desired fresh starts far from their former masters. Planters, in response, browbeat state governments into legislating to control Black labor. Carl Schurz, who toured the South after the war at President Johnson's behest, reported that, to White southerners, "the negro exists for the special object of raising cotton, rice and sugar *for the whites*, and that it is illegitimate for him to indulge, like other people, in the pursuit of his own happiness in his own way. Although it is admitted that he has ceased to be the property of a master, it is not admitted that he has a right to become his own master."

On October 27, 1865, provisional South Carolina governor Benjamin Franklin Perry implored state legislators to enact "A Bill to establish and regulate the domestic relations of Persons of Color, and to amend the law in relation to Paupers, Vagrancy and Bastardy," promising that it was "necessary for the protection of colored persons and the enforcement of their labor. Without it there will be the greatest confusion, idleness and crime at the beginning of the next year." Take note of the word *crime*—White Supremacy activated the fear of Black folk's purported criminality to vindicate what we'll observe during this leg of our journey.

In December 1865, the legislature passed it. The law designated Black workers as "servants" and their employers as "masters." A servant who deserted work without cause committed vagrancy. A jury of three White men could assign a vagrant to a master for compulsory labor. The law stipulated that servants must labor "from sun-rise to sun-set" and restricted them from leaving their master's premises without permission. Once a servant contracted to work for a master, none could hire the servant away, an "anti-enticement" provision. House servants had to "be especially civil and polite to their masters, their families and guests," obliging Black people to adhere to antebellum social etiquette. The code, moreover, prevented Black people from working as an "artisan, mechanic or shop-keeper, or any other trade employment or business on his own account and for his own benefit" absent a judge-issued license. Caste preservationists defended the code as necessary to protect White *and* Black folk from the latter's inferiority.

The 1866 Civil Rights Act invalidated southern Black Codes.

Radical Reconstruction's most ardent supporters, from Congress to southern statehouses, focused on securing political rights, opening access to courts, providing public education, and passing federal laws to enforce The Trinity. Labor rights received less attention during this period, a calamitous oversight because the Black Codes presaged what White southerners "will do if they should again obtain control of this Government" as Josiah Thomas Walls, a Black Reconstruction–era Florida congressman, predicted. After recapturing southern statehouses, caste preservationists concocted various schemes to control Black labor, some written in law, others carried out by customs that the southern legal system rubber-stamped. Not until the end of the century did the Supreme Court begin to hear cases concerning these schemes.

Let's meet the complicated protagonist of the first such case in a Georgia jail.

ON JANUARY 15, 1900, Madison County deputy sheriff Richard B. Aycock guides an *Augusta Chronicle* reporter into a cell where Robert A. Williams, a White man in his fifties with a wooden leg, lies on a pallet.

The reporter asks Williams, an emigrant agent, one who recruits laborers for employment beyond a state's borders, "what he proposed to do?"

Williams responds that he wants to test the constitutionality of Georgia's 1908 General Tax Act that requires an emigrant agent to register and pay a $500 fee in each county where the agent recruits labor.

"I have whipped this law in Alabama and North Carolina," he boasts, "and I will whip it in Georgia."

After the Civil War, hundreds of thousands of Black folk migrated from lower-wage states like Virginia, Alabama, Georgia, North Carolina, and South Carolina to Mississippi, Arkansas, Louisiana, and Texas for higher wages. Emigrant agents informed potential recruits of job opportunities, advanced relocation money, and some even paid off debts.

"Do you realize the intensity of the feeling against you here?" the reporter asks, referring to the White folk who hated him for enticing Black laborers.

"Yes," Williams replies. "I had an interview with representatives of a committee of citizens last night, who told me of the situation. I shall do whatever my attorney, Colonel James Davison, of Greensboro, says. If he says leave this section, I shall do so."

For longer than a decade, Williams had been working toward landing himself in a Georgia jail. Learn his backstory.


ROBERT A. "PEG-LEG" WILLIAMS, the "king of labor agents," fought in Nathan Bedford Forrest's Confederate calvary, replacing the leg he lost in battle with a wooden peg. By 1890, the Democrat and native Mississippian professed to have relocated more than eighty thousand Black laborers in the previous seven years. Either he or a subagent would slip into heavily Black-populated areas, visit potential recruits in their homes or churches, and inform them of higher-paid opportunities. Williams would slide into town at night and, with a supportive railroad line, have a series of extra cars lined up, what he called his Montezuma Special, waiting at the train depot. Southwestern planters paid him per laborer, and "the Moses of the Carolina Exodus" would subtract the train fare from that and net about three dollars per worker in some cases.

In 1891, a North Carolinian complained to his state representatives: "We are bothered by people from other states persuading away our laborers, which ought to be a criminal offense." The legislature passed a law that required emigrant agents in specified heavily Black-populated counties to pay a thousand-dollar tax for any county where they operated. In 1893, the North Carolina Supreme Court invalidated it under the state constitution.

Williams wanted to recruit in the state where he lived, Georgia. "I shall employ able counsel and show that the law is invalid. It's unconstitutional," he told a reporter. "It amounts to saying that a man can't leave the state if he chooses—at least, that he shan't be given information or help. The law is unconstitutional on the face of it."

Nine years later, Williams was emigrating labor to the Mississippi Delta from drought-stricken Greene County, Georgia. A reporter asked an old Black Georgian man, "Why are you going?" The old man answered, "To better our condition." Initially, Williams agreed to recruit only those under no contract. Some predicted that his work would prompt labor shortages. The Greene County prosecutor, James Davison, who represented Williams, refused to prosecute him for operating without paying the tax. A prominent planter, nonetheless, helped secure a warrant and authorities arrested Williams on December 16, 1899. Williams posted bond and resumed emigrating labor.

News of Williams's arrest spread, increasing awareness of his trade. Black laborers were rebuffing overtures to sign new contracts, flirting with emigrating instead. Starting in November 1899, on Wednesdays and Saturdays, Black folk would walk from as far away as twenty-five miles to Williams's train cars at Madison, a Morgan County town in central Georgia. Laborers leaving gave those who remained a better bargaining position, boosting wages. When Williams went to Greensboro, the county seat of Greene County, he learned of officials' plans to arrest him for not paying the tax. Following the advice of his attorney, Davison, Williams paid the tax and established a Greensboro office.

On the morning of January 14, 1900, Black folk assembled at the Madison train depot, a one-story yellow-brick building, awaiting Williams and his Montezuma Special. A Morgan County judge, unbeknownst to Williams, had granted an arrest warrant for him the previous day for "the offense of acting as emigrant agent without a license." Before the train reached the depot, Sheriff Edgar Fears arrested him. At the behest of Governor Allen Candler, Fears surrounded the jail with guards. Responding to threats, Williams released a statement to "All Colored Farm Hands" that read, "To those of you who are expecting to go to Mississippi my advice is to return to your homes and make arrangements for the year, as the railroads have refused to furnish me trains which to transport you. Therefore, there will be no more emigrant trains this season."

THE EMIGRANT AGENT LAW fit into an interlocking system devised to deny Black people ownership of their labor. Another part of that

system, anti-enticement statutes, outlawed hiring laborers employed
by another. Like emigrant agent laws, anti-enticement laws targeted,
mainly, the actions of White folk, illustrating the difficulty White
Supremacy faced in keeping his legion rowing in the same direction.
Anti-enticement laws came into vogue because White employers
hired Black laborers away from one another, hiking the price of labor.
State legislatures intervened, creating an environment that reduced
Black people's capacity to leverage their labor to improve their material conditions. Vagrancy laws, which essentially made unemployment a crime, strengthened the system, strong-arming Black people
into jobs regardless of desirability. When planters suffered labor
shortages, sheriffs would round up idle Black people, convict them,
and funnel them to White employers.

Southern legislatures masterminded a system that effectively
regranted White folk property rights in Black labor. With local law
enforcement assistance, caste preservationists denied a key facet of
freedom—labor ownership.

Now let's return to inhabiting Peg-Leg Williams's story.


ON JANUARY 16, 1900, the day after the *Augusta Chronicle* reporter
visited Williams in jail, Judge John Hart is holding a hearing in
Union Point, Georgia. Many are crammed inside this small office
while onlookers gawk from outside the window. Williams's attorney, Davison, filed a habeas corpus petition, arguing that the state
must free Williams because the emigrant agent law violates the
Constitution.

"This is not a question for regulation by police power," Davison
says, "but is a question concerning the civil rights and liberties of the
people—those inalienable rights granted by the Constitution of the
United States." Davison is arguing that the state's emigrant agent law
exceeds Georgia's police power and infringes the basic rights of Black
folk seeking employment opportunities outside state lines.

E. W. Butler, Morgan County solicitor, counters Davison: "I cannot see how the great state of Georgia can permit one . . . to come
into a community and at the dead hour of midnight, by promises and
persuasions, induce an ignorant and wholly irresponsible population

to leave their peaceful homes and thereby disrupt the labor conditions, without bearing his share of the burdens of taxation."

Judge Hart sides with Butler. "I can see a vast difference between an emigrant agent, in one sense, and one who seeks to procure laborers under contract," Hart concludes. "[W]hen a man comes into a community and takes all—from the grandfather to the babe—then he comes in under the head of an emigrant agent. I respect the opinions cited by able counsel for defense, but feel constrained to declare the law constitutional."

On April 11, 1900, Williams will lose his appeal, unanimously, at the Georgia Supreme Court. The U.S. Supreme Court agrees to hear his case. In this era, the nine black robes will not adjudicate an anti-enticement or vagrancy law dispute, meaning the emigrant agent law stands in for a range of laws devised to control Black labor.

Before the nine black robes would hear *Williams v. Fears*, Booker T. visits a race conference in Alabama. There, he hears the gamut of White America's racial thinking, including virulently racist thought, what many White folk wanted to inform the Supreme Court's approach to matters involving Black labor.

IN EARLY MAY 1900, visitors streamed into Montgomery, a city hugging the Alabama River, and snagged nearly all available hotel rooms to absorb eighteen lectures at a conference sponsored by a new organization, A Southern Society for the Promotion of the Study of Race Conditions and Problems in the South.

More than two thousand lingered inside a newly constructed auditorium, a point of pride for Montgomery, for the opening day of the conference. From the Jim Crow galleries of about four hundred, Booker T. ingested speeches. The night's last speaker, Hilary Herbert, a Democrat who had represented Alabama in Congress from 1877 to 1893, received a cordial reception when he stepped forward to deliver "The Problems That Present Themselves." The Navy secretary under President Cleveland addressed a question crucial to White Americans: "How will the Negro affect the white man's civilization, and to what extent will the presence of each race influence the welfare of the other?" His answers reflected the moderate White southern viewpoint.

"Negro suffrage has failed," Herbert, sixty-six years old with silver hair, said. "It has brought weakness instead of strength to the political party that conferred it," and, he argued, increased "the debt of every State where it was dominant" because the representatives whom Black voters elected increased spending on public programs. Enfranchising Black men, Herbert concluded, "has not bettered the condition of the black man or the white."

Resulting from the Black population's purported failures, "White men in every State have obtained control and they must keep it, if they mean to preserve Anglo-Saxon civilization," declared the former Confederate soldier.

"The Negro is not equal to the white man," Herbert claimed, something American culture taught people to assume. "Science and history alike proclaim this truth. The Negro's skull is thicker, his brain is smaller than the white man's," Herbert said, cloaking his racism with the shroud of academic discipline to sell it as a settled fact.

"Here the races are side by side and cannot get away from each other. We must raise him. . . . We must work it out, or God only can tell what is to become of us. It is a mighty task, but it can be accomplished, if we but enter upon it with courage and faith in ourselves and our people." Herbert believed that despite Black folk's inferiority, White people should help them because the inferior race would otherwise clip the wings of White America's soaring civilization.

Although Herbert's endorsement of Black biological inferiority no doubt unnerved Booker T., other speeches enunciated even more horrific views. Paul B. Barringer, a professor at the University of Virginia whose speech fit the aggressively White supremacist mold, maintained that "all things point to the fact that the Negro as a race is reverting to barbarism with the inordinate degradation of that state. It seems, moreover, that he is doomed at no distant day to ultimate extinction."

Somehow, Booker T. expressed hope after the conference. "The negro," he wrote, "suffers very often in reputation because few of those who make damaging statements have ever taken the trouble to visit him in his place of business, his home, his school, and his church, where the higher and more encouraging side of his life may be seen. More and more of the American people must come to judge the negro much as they do other races—by the best types, and not by the worst."

A few months later, a reporter would visit a Black couple and return with a harrowing tale exposing what could happen to those seeking to improve their circumstances by hopping aboard Peg-Leg Williams's Montezuma Special.

ON NOVEMBER 30, 1900, a month after the Supreme Court heard oral argument for Williams's case and ten days before it would announce its decision, a Black preacher informed a reporter about a woman in the "colored" waiting room at the Atlanta train station. Shortly before noon, the reporter crossed the color line and noticed a crowd of Black folk surrounding a "yellow negress," Mary Scott, alongside Ed, her "black shadow of a husband." They were waiting for a train to Athens where they had lived before a westward misadventure.

Months prior, George Daniel, a Black man and subagent for Williams, persuaded Black folk in Scott's town to emigrate to Arkansas. Daniel read from circulars promising wonders. Men could fetch a dollar and a half to three dollars a day in logging camps or on plantations. Women could pocket twenty to thirty dollars a month fulfilling domestic duties. Households would receive a free cabin and a garden. Only the head of the household would need to repay the eleven-dollar train fare to the family's new home and only after securing profitable work. The diligent, Daniel vowed, could buy land and a home within two or three years.

The Scotts were among 250 Black people on their train. Upon crossing the Mississippi River, a White man boarded and counted them like bales of cotton. At every post-Memphis station, White men would retrieve some of them from the train. She and her husband, along with a "score" of other Black folk, were taken from a train station near Pine Bluff, Arkansas, and driven on foot as a man on horseback herded them to a logging camp deep in the piney woods. Although promised cooking work, she was handed an axe and forced to hack trees alongside men as guards surveilled them. Ed was promised fifty cents a day and Mary forty cents, but after purchasing supplies from the commissary store, they owed money, including the cost of their train tickets. Ed earned just a quarter, the only money they had received.

Mary attempted to communicate with friends back east, to no avail. After becoming sick, she was permitted to go to the nearest town for care. Ed escaped to join her. A Black Pine Bluff church gathered funds to pay their train tickets back home. She and her husband freed themselves, but many remained behind in slave conditions. Daniels, she believed, collected three dollars a head for each worker he convinced to emigrate.

While waiting in the Atlanta station, she stood, pointed to the yellow signs across the street in front of Williams's office, and shouted condemnation. The reporter captured her remarks this way: "Dere's his place—dat Peg Leg Williams, what totes po' niggahs out ter de woods in Arkansas an' sella um inter slav'ry wussern dat in Georgy foh de wah. If yo' black folks heah know'd what I knows you'd make him clean out o' heah, if he bees white."

At the Supreme Court, Davison, Williams's attorney, argued that the emigrant agent law violated the Fourteenth Amendment because it "restricts the right of the citizen to remove from one State to another and abridges the privileges and immunities of the citizen" and "impairs the natural right of the laborer to labor." Georgia passed the statute, Davison maintained, "to impose a burden on laborers, to prevent them from leaving the state." James M. Terrell, the state attorney general, however, likened the emigrant agent law to a normal tax, one that funded education, paid down the interest on the public debt, and compensated injured Confederate soldiers and their widows. Terrell eschewed the argument proffered by the Morgan County solicitor, who had framed the law as necessary to prevent men like Williams from taking an "ignorant and wholly irresponsible population" from a state that needed labor.

Thus far in our journey, we have interacted with two Fourteenth Amendment clauses, the Equal Protection Clause and the Privileges and Immunities Clause, that the nine black robes have sabotaged. Let's visit the height of abolitionism to examine a different clause potent enough to ensure that racial identity wouldn't limit one's ability to labor freely, should the Court choose to interpret it that way, the Due Process Clause.

ON MAY 12, 1835, inside the Third Street Presbyterian Church, on the corner of Houston and Thompson Streets in Manhattan, an abolitionist, James Gillespie Birney, excoriates Washington, D.C.'s, most diabolical pestilence. Attendees inside this church have convened for the American Anti-Slavery Society's second annual meeting. With two expansive galleries, the large church accommodates members of the nation's leading abolitionist organization. Birney, a forty-two-year-old politician and attorney from Kentucky, crams an uncomfortable truth down the throats of attendees—they, those most devoted to slavery's ruination, elect politicians who aid in prolonging it in the nation's capital.

"Look at the state of things in the District of Columbia," he says. "Are you not as much participants in the slavery existing there, as the people of Kentucky are in Kentucky? The people of Kentucky elect legislators who pass laws confirming slavery in that State: and you elect legislators who confirm the continuance of slavery in the District of Columbia. Where is the difference? Slavery exists by your permission; this never could have been but by the aid of northern votes: and to him who knoweth to do good and doeth it not, to him it is sin."

Carved from Maryland and Virginia, two slave states, the nation's capital has allowed slavery since its 1791 inception. As Birney speaks, the District of Columbia serves as a depot for a legion of enslaved people, as so-called slave pens, where slavers store Black souls before auctioning them, dot the city. Defeating slavery in D.C. would thrill the abolitionist movement, delivering it a tremendous victory, the unshackling of 3,200. Given that the capital is not a state, abolitionists believe they can skirt the argument that the Constitution blocks Congress from subverting slavery in the states. Congress wields complete legislative power over those sixty-eight square miles— abolitionists like Birney believe they can ban slavery there through legislation.

Foot soldiers for slavery will craft a response rooted in the Constitution, more specifically, the Due Process Clause. Included in the Fifth Amendment, which limits the power of the federal government, the Due Process Clause states: "No person shall . . . be deprived of life, liberty, or property, without due process of law." Pro-slavery forces contend that this clause protects the property rights of D.C.-residing slaveowners and therefore prohibits Congress from outlawing slavery in D.C.

Henry Laurens Pinckney, a South Carolina congressman, in a congressional committee report, will argue that men come together to form government to safeguard individuals' natural and unalienable rights. And one can find no right more sacrosanct than that of property. Pinckney concedes that the Constitution grants Congress exclusive power to legislate within D.C., but the Constitution "does not," he clarifies, "and could not, confer unlimited or despotic authority over" D.C. The Constitution limits Congress here—the right to legislate is "qualified," he protests, "by the provision that 'no man shall be deprived of life, liberty, or property, without due process of law.'" Declaring slaveholding illegal would strip the slaveowner of his property, a due process violation. "We lay it down as a rule," Pinckney proclaims, "that no Government can do any thing directly repugnant to the principles of natural justice and of the social compact. It would be totally subversive of all the purposes for which government is instituted." Additionally, "Congress," Pinckney insists, "is not only restrained from the commission of any act by which these objects may be frustrated, but that it is bound to sustain and promote them." Stated differently, government has both a duty to not deny a person "of life, liberty, or property" and an obligation to affirmatively protect "life, liberty, and property," for if it doesn't, society can collapse. Depriving includes inaction as well as action.

When Pinckney hoists due process onto the pedestal as the great protector of slavery in D.C., he presses abolitionists to hoist due process into the clouds, compelling them to compose a counternarrative. Connecticut abolitionist Theodore Dwight Weld will volunteer to father this reasoning, forging abolitionist thinking that informs what the drafters of the Fourteenth Amendment will produce. Weld flips the pro-slavery camp's formulation, arguing that enslaved people too are persons under the Fifth Amendment who shall not "be deprived of life, liberty, or property, without due process of law." Weld writes that "every slave in the District has been deprived of liberty *unconstitutionally*, and is therefore *free by the constitution*." Per Weld's argument, due process encompasses a substantive right—a right to life, liberty, and property—and a procedural right—a right to not have that life, liberty, and property deprived without a fair procedure, like a trial for instance. Abolitionists depict the Due Process Clause as a tool to free enslaved people and secure equality under the law and in the courts.

According to abolitionists, furthermore, the Due Process Clause requires that the government supply due process. It both restricts governmental power and obliges government to give protection against the actions of private individuals who deny others of their life, liberty, and property. Slaveowners in D.C. denied enslaved people their liberty, and Congress's nonintervention denied enslaved people a fair procedure, or due process, to have their voices heard before their liberty was taken.

For the next three decades, abolitionists will view due process this way. And once the chance to install the God-driven beliefs in the equality of all His children into the Constitution arrives, Republican congressmen insert a Due Process Clause into the Fourteenth Amendment that applies to states: "No state shall . . . deprive any person of life, liberty, or property, without due process of law." This carries the twin duties of nondeprivation and the obligation of the government to supply due process should a private individual take it away. Again, depriving includes inaction and action. This recalls the argument for equal protection that we discussed during the second leg of our journey, no? Equal protection commands the state to not only treat people equally but to affirmatively protect them from unequal treatment.

This conception of due process can shelter Black folk from caste preservationists who seek to steal their labor. Georgia passes its emigrant agent law to infringe both Black folk's right to move about the country to find work and their right to contract with faraway employers, denying their liberty to relocate, denying their property right in their labor, denying their right to make contracts. The same holds true for vagrancy laws and anti-enticement statutes—the South will institute both to deny Black people their liberty and their property rights in their labor.

In addition to this abolitionist history, by the time the Supreme Court hears Peg-Leg Williams's case, *Williams v. Fears*, the nine black robes will have already developed thinking in other contexts that they can easily apply to the cause of caste abolitionism.

In 1884, for example, in his concurrence in *Butchers' Union Co. v. Crescent City Co.*, Justice Bradley writes, "The right to follow any of the common occupations of life is an inalienable right, it was formulated as such under the phrase 'pursuit of happiness' in the declaration of independence, which commenced with the fundamental proposition that 'all men are created equal; that they are endowed by their Creator with certain inalienable rights; that among these are life, liberty, and the pursuit of happiness.' This right is a large ingredient in the civil liberty of the citizen." Then in 1897, Justice Peckham writes in his unanimous opinion in *Allgeyer v. Louisiana* that "liberty" includes "the right of the citizen to be free in the enjoyment of all his faculties, to be free to use them in all lawful ways, to live and work where he will, to earn his livelihood by any lawful calling, to pursue any livelihood or avocation, and for that purpose to enter into all contracts which may be proper, necessary, and essential to his carrying out to a successful conclusion the purposes above mentioned."

Thus, when the Court hears *Williams v. Fears*, it will have ample basis to construct the Due Process Clause into a protector of Black laborers' rights. Unscathed from the Court's disastrous race jurisprudence thus far, the Due Process Clause can salvage bits of the Fourteenth Amendment's lost promise.

ON DECEMBER 10, 1900, when, inside the Supreme Court, Chief Justice Fuller delivered his opinion in *Williams v. Fears*, Peg-Leg Williams had already found a new headquarters on Wall Street in Atlanta for his emigrant agent business. He had already informed the county tax collector that he intended to not pay the tax, expecting to win his appeal. He, in fact, lost.

Fuller, sixty-seven years old, explained in his eight-to-one majority opinion that the Court addressed one main issue, "whether a state law taxing [emigrant agents]," he said, "is invalid . . . because [it is] in conflict with the Federal Constitution."

Through the Due Process Clause, the Fourteenth Amendment protected the right to contract, Fuller concluded, relying on *Allgeyer v. Louisiana*. Fuller, however, found that Georgia treated emigrant agents as it treated other occupations, levying a tax the state deemed appropriate to raise money to fund the government. The General Tax Act of 1898, in addition to taxing emigrant agents, taxed various other commercial enterprises, including circus companies and clock and stove sellers. Fuller said that the "general legislative purpose is plain," which was to levy taxes to finance state government. The Court focused on how the law treated Williams, in other words, and found it constitutional. The Court failed to subject to analysis how the law affected Black laborers. Justice Harlan dissented but offered no written opinion.

Fuller's opinion disregarded what incited southern state legislatures to tax emigrant agents. Georgia attorney general J. M. Terrell said the Court's decision "would virtually put a period to the immigration business in Georgia," revealing the actual motivation. The state set the goal as no one paying the tax, the exact opposite of raising revenue. Understanding that emigrant agents needed to work in multiple counties to make the enterprise feasible, Georgia set the entry fee high to dissuade anyone from entering the profession.

As the Court ignored that the Mississippi legislature pursued a scheme to disenfranchise Black voters, it ignored the behavior the Georgia state legislature sought to change—Black people contracting with distant employers. In *Allgeyer v. Louisiana*, decided just three years prior, the Supreme Court struck down a Louisiana law that essentially forbade the state's citizens from purchasing insurance from out-of-state insurers. The Court could have likened the emigrant agent tax to that Louisiana law—both were instituted to limit whom citizens of a state could contract with—but the Court chose not to, further weakening The Trinity and wasting an opportunity to strengthen a Fourteenth Amendment clause not yet sapped of its potential.

The emigrant agent tax spawned from the slaveowner mindset that forbade Black folk from serving as the masters of their own labor. And the Court's decision spawned from the mindset that jurists should disregard how White Supremacy motivated state legislatures. White southerners dismissing the thought that they should respect Black people as laborers augured poorly for Booker T.'s respectability politics caste abolitionist strategy.

After *Williams*, Alabama, Florida, North Carolina, and Virginia enacted emigrant agent laws as those of Georgia and South Carolina remained on the books. And although vagrancy laws and the anti-enticement statutes never reached the Court, *Williams* indicated an unreceptiveness to challenges of them. The nine black robes disregarded the realities on the ground, and the denial of Black freedom they incited.

SAMUEL M. CLYATT, the manager of the Clyatt & Tift turpentine distillers in Waterloo, Georgia, had informed H. S. Sutton, the Levy County, Florida sheriff, that he would be traveling to his town. Clyatt wanted Sutton to execute arrest warrants for Black laborers who had deserted his employment. At around five in the afternoon on February 10, 1901, Clyatt, E. T. Ford, and another White man named Mr. Taylor, all carrying guns, arrived at the train station in Bronson, a small North Florida town, and coincidentally ran into Sutton. Not expecting Clyatt in that moment, Sutton told him he couldn't execute his warrants but wrote a note to give to Deputy Sheriff William Yearty, who perhaps could.

Clyatt and his men rode to Yearty's house, arriving hours later in darkness. Clyatt handed Yearty Sutton's note and told him about the warrants he wanted to execute for men who had run off to work, he thought, at a local distillery operated by James R. Dean. Yearty, not wearing his glasses, saw the warrants but couldn't read what crime the men were accused of and assumed the warrants were for stealing. Gambling, instead, was the manufactured charge.

They arrived at Dean's place at four in the morning. Yearty went to Dean's door and briefed him on Clyatt's dilemma. Dean responded that four of the Black laborers did work for him and escorted Yearty, Clyatt, and his men to his commissary office to settle the matter. Clyatt allowed Dean to keep two of the laborers, but, Clyatt said, he "wanted to make an example of Will Gordon and Mose Ridley" and carry them "back to Georgia." Once Dean paid the debt of the two whom Clyatt had allowed him to keep, Dean retrieved Gordon and Ridley, bringing them inside his commissary.

At sunrise, Clyatt, not a law officer, tried to handcuff them. Gordon resisted, saying that he owed nothing.

Clyatt pointed his gun at Gordon, who raised his arms. "I reckon you will go," Clyatt said.

The two captives, handcuffed, were put into Yearty's buggy, while Clyatt, Ford, and Taylor followed on foot. As they left Dean's camp, Yearty notified Gordon and Ridley, who had left behind all their possessions, that he was hauling them to the county jail. They begged to return to Georgia with Clyatt. As they neared the train station, Yearty relented, releasing the men to Clyatt, who paid him five dollars for his efforts, compensation like what slavecatchers received a century prior.

Fred Cubberly, a U.S. commissioner, told the U.S. attorney for the Northern District of Florida, John Eagan, that Clyatt's actions would make for an ideal federal prosecution test case. Cubberly explained that similar incidents "are almost every day occurrences in this locality." W. O. Butler, a Florida Panhandle attorney, detailed for Eagan how turpentine distillery owners and local law enforcement officials trapped Black laborers "in a worse state than when they were slaves, for the first thing one of these turpentine men do when they hire a negroe [sic] is to make an advance in money or goods, mostly always in goods." Owners created a labor arrangement that started with indebtedness and exploited that to extract labor in near perpetuity. Laborers, forced to toil, could be "held at the muzzle of a gun and worked on extremely short rations," Butler told Eagan, "and when he happens to do anything that does not suit them they are tied up and beat most outrageously." If the laborer fled, the employer could easily attain a fraudulent arrest warrant from a local unscrupulous magistrate as did Clyatt. Sometimes employers, like William B. Moore, whose story launched this leg of our journey, would track down their laborers on their own and forcibly return them to work, knowing law enforcement acquiesced to their whims, despite such illegality.

You probably assumed that no matter how much rotten fruit—disfranchisement, Jim Crow, civil rights deprivations—the nation shoved into their maws, Black folk could at least savor the sweet forty-three words of the Thirteenth Amendment without fear that the prohibition against slavery may too spoil. Not true. Booker T. Washington understood the crisis, writing, "colored people on these plantations are held in a kind of slavery that is in one sense as bad as the slavery of ante bellum days." From a stage in Atlanta, he implored his people to "cast down your bucket where you are" only for White southerners to repossess their buckets. If he wanted Black folk to prove themselves through labor, they must own that labor. Booker T., to improve the situation for these unfree souls, needed good fortune. A few months later, it arrived in tragedy.


AT THIRTY MINUTES PAST THREE in the afternoon on September 14, 1901, Secretary of War Elihu Root, whose long nose hung over his salt-and-pepper mustache, stepped forward in the green-painted library in a Buffalo, New York, mansion.

"Mr. Vice President, I—," he said, choking up, tears swamping his eyes.

After steadying himself, Root finished: "I have been requested by all of the members of the Cabinet of the late President who are present in this city of Buffalo, all except two, to request for reasons of weight affecting the Administration of the Government, you should proceed to take the constitutional office of President of the United States."

Republican president William McKinley's cabinet members, save Secretary of State John Hay and Treasury Secretary Lyman Gage, filled the library, where the sun invaded through a stained glass window, falling onto the dust covers that protected chairs. Vice President Theodore Roosevelt, a barrel-chested man of about five-foot-eight with short brown hair, wearing trademark pince-nez eyeglasses before his blue eyes, vacantly stared ahead.

Roosevelt bowed to Root, cleared his throat, and said, while hesitating with his high-pitched voice, "I shall take the oath of office at once." As he fought back tears, his voice grew stronger with each word, speaking in his typical staccato speech pattern: "In this hour of deep and terrible National bereavement, I wish to state that it will be my aim to continue absolutely unbroken the policy of President McKinley for the peace, the prosperity, and the honor of our beloved country."

"Theodore Roosevelt, raise your right hand," said local federal judge John Raymond Hazel.

McKinley had been shot twice in the abdomen on September 6, at the Pan-American Exposition in Buffalo, by an anarchist, Leon Czolgosz, clutching a revolver. Initial reports that the president would pull through calmed the country, but infections vanquished his system. "It is useless, gentlemen," said a resigned McKinley. "I think we ought to have a prayer." Early in the morning of September 14, he passed.

Roosevelt, the nation's youngest president at forty-two, repeated after Judge Hazel: "I do solemnly swear that I will faithfully execute the office of the President of the United States."

Roosevelt directed his secretary, William Loeb, to write perfunctory cancellation letters for his vice presidential obligations. "I am directed by President Roosevelt to express deep regret that he cannot come," Loeb wrote. Roosevelt took a piece of paper with "Executive Mansion" letterhead and personally addressed a man he had long admired.

The South scorned Roosevelt. Five months into his vice presidency, Mississippi's Jackson *Daily Clarion-Ledger* jeered him: "Three years ago he was a great hero. Now he is a very ordinary man whose faults are glaring even to the vision of his best friends. . . . Teddy has reached the topmost rung of his political ladder. It is useless to climb any further." Suddenly, two bullets wrested the White House from a Republican president southerners liked and delivered it to an adversary. Alabama novelist John Henry Wallace recalled that McKinley's speeches throughout the South "caused the Southern people to weep tears of joy and the great Southern hearts to bound with gladness." In truth, White southerners fancied McKinley because he ignored the sobs of Black southerners while placating White southerners who prayed for a White man's government, although such conciliation won him nary a southern electoral vote in 1896 and 1900. The

Republican Party, nonetheless, continued yearning for a southern Republican Party with a new, White heartbeat. Roosevelt inherited this mission. He coveted guidance.

"When are you coming North?" Roosevelt wrote Booker T. Washington. "I must see you as soon as possible. I want to talk over the question of possible appointments in the South exactly on the lines of our last conversation together. I hope that my visit to Tuskegee is merely deferred for a short season."

Roosevelt had visited Tuskegee Institute before where he proclaimed, "the salvation of the Negro lay in the development of the Booker Washington theory." He considered Booker T. "a man for whom I have the highest regard and in whose judgment I have much faith." Roosevelt appreciated that Booker T. understood the South, and, wanting voters to elect him to serve his own term, needed counsel.

Despite his high regard for Booker T., Roosevelt held a low opinion of Black people. "I entirely agree with you," he once told a friend, "that as a race and in the mass [Black people] are altogether inferior to the whites." Roosevelt, like many White folk, wished for an all-White America but conceived of no feasible method to manifest that. A prolific writer of race thinking, Roosevelt considered Booker T. a member of a youthful race, one nearer savagery than civilization. Although expressing confidence Black folk could evolve, he reasoned such progress would advance slowly. Given the race's limitations, he considered Black men generally unfit for suffrage rights but believed America should grant exceptions. Individuals warranted judgment on their own merits, he thought, even while trusting that Black folk inhabited an inferior station. The chief executive, notwithstanding, would soon receive Booker T. at the White House.

ONE SPRING 1865 MORNING, a nine-year-old Booker T., valued at $400, walked to the big house alongside the other Black souls the Burroughs family owned. A federal officer stood on the porch and read a long document as the Burroughses hovered. Booker T. perceived "deep interest or perhaps sadness, on their faces, but not bitterness." His mother, Jane, cried, kissed him and his siblings, and explained the officer's message.

They were free.

On September 29, 1901, two Black servants steered Booker T. through the White House's quiet executive office space into Roosevelt's library for a nine o'clock meeting. Booker T., who had long dodged the political limelight, understanding that White southerners detested Black folk trespassing into politics, the White man's playground, debated even coming: "I felt that I must consider seriously the question whether I should allow myself to be drawn into a kind of activity that I had definitely determined to keep away from."

Roosevelt wanted to discuss southern political appointments. Republican presidents, Roosevelt reasoned, had erred in appointing to southern political offices the sort—Black people and White Republicans—whom native White southerners had resented. Moreover, party loyalty, Roosevelt claimed, not qualification drove choices. Roosevelt distrusted southern Republicans, deriding them as "a set of black and white scalawags, with a few commonplace, decent men, who have wrangled fiercely among themselves and who make not the slightest effort to get any popular votes," and as men "whose venality makes them a menace to the whole party." With their most loyal voters disenfranchised, southern Republicans could rarely win elected office. They did, however, exercise real clout in deciding the party's presidential nominee and accordingly devoted themselves to receiving political appointments and courting affections at quadrennial presidential nominating conventions.

Roosevelt confided in Booker T. that he wanted to offer political appointments to the best candidate for the job, irrespective of party, or race, meaning he could nominate White Democrats in the South and Black Republicans in the North. Tapping Black folk to northern posts especially intrigued Booker T., who later wrote, "not a single coloured man had ever been appointed, so far as I know, to a Federal office in any Northern state."

Booker T. recommended that Roosevelt appoint Democrat Thomas Goode Jones, former Alabama governor, to replace Judge John Bruce, a federal district judge in Alabama who would soon reach the mandatory retirement age. At the Alabama constitutional convention that assembled in May 1901, Jones supported Black suffrage. "The Negro race is under us," Jones declared at the convention. "He is in our power. We are his custodians. . . . If we do not lift them up, they will drag us down."

"I will offer this place to Jones," Roosevelt told Booker T., "provided you will act as my messenger. I want you to go to him and say to him that you are authorized to offer the place to him and to say to him that if he is appointed, it will be solely on your recommendation."

They agreed to meet again to further consider appointments and Booker T. returned to Alabama. Somehow, southern newspapermen learned about the two connecting. The Jackson *Daily Clarion-Ledger* reported that "Washington told [Roosevelt] if he wished to make the Republican Party in the South respectable he should appoint respected white men to office, even if they be Democrats. It remains to be seen if the President takes the advice."

ON OCTOBER 1, 1901, Booker T. traveled to Montgomery to evaluate Jones. When he got there, news of Bruce's sudden death had surfaced, infusing urgency into his mission. After gauging Jones's fitness, Booker T. wrote Roosevelt. "I saw ex-Governor Jones yesterday, as I promised," Booker T. explained, "and he is willing to accept the judgeship of the Middle District of Alabama. I am more convinced now than ever that he is the proper man for the place. . . . He stood up in the Constitutional Convention and elsewhere for a fair election law, opposed lynching, and he has been outspoken for the education of both races."

Booker T. boarded a train to Mississippi for a speaking tour while his personal secretary, Emmett Jay Scott, headed to D.C. to hand his boss' letter to Roosevelt. The cooperation between Booker T. and Roosevelt blossomed as telegrams ping-pong between them.

ROOSEVELT'S SOUTHERN STRATEGY STARTED auspiciously. On the morning of September 21, 1901, a week after his swearing in, legislators filed into the White House, once beautiful, now tumbling into dilapidation, to congratulate the new president on his pre-oath-of-office remarks. "That simple declaration," said Senator Nathan Scott, a West Virginia Republican, referring to Roosevelt's commitment to continue the policies of his predecessor, "immediately restored confidence in the business world."

"The South will support you most heartily," North Carolina Republican Senator Jeter Connelly Pritchard told Roosevelt. "The Democratic newspapers are predicting good for you and of you, and the feeling of all the people for you, irrespective of party, is most kindly."

"I am going to be President of the United States and not of any section," Roosevelt replied. "I don't care for sections or sectional lines."

Roosevelt told Mississippi Democratic senator Hernando Money, another among the long visiting line, "I am half Southerner and I have lived in the West, so that I feel that I can represent the whole of the country." Roosevelt considered himself a "half Southerner" because of his Georgia-born mother, Martha, who supported the Confederacy while the family lived in their five-story Manhattan brownstone.

On October 7, taking Booker T.'s advice, Roosevelt appointed Jones, further pleasing southerners. The *Montgomery Advertiser* delighted that Roosevelt "demonstrates in the most emphatic way that he is not merely the President of one Party or of one section, but of all parties and all sections." "I question," Booker T. thought, "whether any appointment made in the South has ever attracted more attention or created more favourable comment from people of all classes than was true of this one."

Weeks later, during his Mississippi tour, Booker T. learned Roosevelt had requested another meeting. Fretting about inviting even more attention to his behind-the-scenes political maneuvering, Booker T. discussed the matter with a friend traveling with him. Deciding to meet again with Roosevelt, Booker T. explained that he and his friend "decided that the only policy to pursue was to face the new responsibilities as they arose, because new responsibilities bring new opportunities for usefulness of which I ought to take advantage in the interest of my race. I was the more disposed to feel that this was a duty because Mr. Roosevelt was proposing to carry out the very policies which I had advocated ever since I began work in Alabama."

ON OCTOBER 16, 1901, Roosevelt dictated a note to his secretary inviting Booker T. to the White House for a seven-thirty dinner. Moments later, Roosevelt questioned himself—should he summon a Black man to dine with his family? That same day an Alabama newspaper reported that "it looks like Booker Washington is to be the prime adviser in the matter of dispensing pie in Alabama. Our republican friends should make a note of this." Mississippi politician James Vardaman bristled because Roosevelt "should be able to find enough white men without calling Booker T. Washington. It will be better for the country in the end." Roosevelt wrote a friend, "it seemed to me that it was natural to ask him to dinner to talk over this work, and the very fact that I felt a moment's qualm on inviting him because of his color made me ashamed of myself and made me hasten to send the invitation."

When Booker T. arrived at the D.C. home of Whitefield McKinlay, a mulatto real estate agent who hosted him during his stay, he found the president's invitation. Booker T., apprehensive, discussed the matter with McKinlay. Booker T. had dined with White folk in the North and received honored guest treatment. He also had recently returned from Europe where he sipped tea with Queen Victoria at Windsor Castle. Yet, he grasped that a Black man who dined with a White family violated southern racial etiquette and surely recalled President Cleveland suffering criticism for hosting Queen Lili'uokalani of Hawaii in the White House in 1895.

Booker T. took a sheet of Tuskegee stationery. "My dear President," he wrote. "I shall be very glad to accept your invitation for dinner this evening at seven-thirty." He accepted because "recognition of the race and no matter what personal condemnation it brought upon my shoulders I had no right to refuse or even hesitate."

Wearing a pressed formal black suit, Booker T. rode a mile and a half south in McKinlay's carriage to the White House. After entering the circular drive, he climbed out, ascended five steps, and stood in front of the entrance. Men accompanied him inside and escorted him beyond the colorful screen that separated the White House's public space from its living quarters. Small and badly needing renovation, the living quarters paled in comparison to the Manhattan mansion of Roosevelt's youth. Despite the White House's rat infestation, it vastly outshone the rickety one-room, dirt-floor, cracked-wall cabin that Booker T. called home during bondage. Before freedom, he had never slept on a bed. Never sat to eat meals. He nibbled here and there, sometimes on the food pigs had turned down.

At dinner, Booker T. ate around an oval table with Roosevelt, his wife, Edith, young sons Archie and Quentin, and Roosevelt's friend Philip Stewart, a Colorado mining and utilities executive. Roosevelt typically dominated conversation. Edith would often whisper, "Theodore! Theodore!" and a talkative but embarrassed Roosevelt would reply, "Why, Edie, I was only—." Booker T. tended to speak cautiously, carefully plucking each word. When Archie and Quentin went to bed, the men retired to the Red Room, a vividly painted parlor room, to discuss politics over coffee. With more appointments to make and seeking to win the 1904 Republican nomination, Roosevelt needed advising. At around ten, Booker T. said good night and darted off to the train station to catch the last New York–bound locomotive. A reporter perused the White House's social register and wrote for his newspaper that "Booker T. Washington, of Tuskegee, Alabama, dined with the President last evening."

WEEKS LATER, Booker T. traveled through Florida. "In some way it became pretty generally known along the railroad that I was on the train, and the result was that at nearly every station a group of people would get aboard and shake hands with me," he remembered. "At a little station near Gainesville, Fla., a White man got aboard the train whose dress and manner indicated that he was from the class of small farmers in that part of the country." Booker T., abiding by Jim Crow, typically purchased a compartment on trains divided from White folk.

Booker T. shook the man's hand.

"I am mighty glad to see you," the man said. "I have heard about you and I have been wanting to meet you for a long while." He looked

Booker T. over and continued, "Say, you are a great man. You are the greatest man in this country!" Booker T. downplayed the praise, but the man shook his head and reiterated, "Yes, sir, the greatest man in this country."

Roosevelt, Booker T. responded, deserved that honor.

"Huh! Roosevelt?" he replied. "I used to think that Roosevelt was a great man until he ate dinner with you. That settled him for me."

On October 17, the day after the dinner, the *Atlanta Constitution* simply called Booker T. "Probably the First Negro Ever Entertained at the White House." The next day, the *Constitution* flashed a headline more satisfying to the White South's bigoted palate: "BOTH POLITICALLY AND SOCIALLY, PRESIDENT ROOSEVELT PROPOSES TO CODDLE DESCENDANTS OF HAM." Southern caste preservationists fumed. "The action of President Roosevelt in entertaining that nigger," South Carolina senator Ben Tillman said, "will necessitate our killing a thousand niggers in the South before they will learn their place again."

A tornado in the South, it was a whisper in the North. Reporters hounded Booker T. for comment. Silence greeted them. Never again would Roosevelt dine with a Black man in the White House. Seeking to put the matter behind him, Roosevelt defended himself from accusations of insufficient genuflection to White Supremacy by noting that he had appointed fewer Black people and more White Democrats than any Republican president.

The dinner happened during the run-up to Alabama's constitution ratification vote. Alabama, unlike Mississippi, sent its constitution to the people for approval. The new constitution's supporters campaigned on the dinner and its underlying threat of social equality. Per one influential Alabama Democrat, "Roosevelt ate with Booker T. Washington, and that is about the only reason I can give why you should vote to ratify the constitution we made in Montgomery." The voters complied, and on Thanksgiving Day, the governor proclaimed that the state had a new constitution, one that followed the Mississippi Plan of 1890.

Despite Democratic pressure to reject it, Jones accepted the judgeship, a seat in an area rife with Black labor exploitation.

ONE DAY AROUND 1906 in an Alabama court, Ray Stannard Baker, a mild-mannered, unassuming White man, observed as a Black man accused of stealing cotton appeared before a magistrate.

"Does anybody know this Negro?" asked the magistrate.

Two White businessmen rose to say yes. The magistrate fined the Black man twenty dollars and court costs. The two businessmen then argued about which would pay what the Black man owed.

The magistrate asked the Black man, "Who do you want to work for, George?"

After picking, George and the man signed a written contract that the magistrate formally sanctioned. The man paid George's fines, and George agreed to repay him with four months of labor—an arrangement facilitated through the state's criminal surety law. It allowed the buying of labor from the state by paying the fines of someone convicted of certain misdemeanors. The criminal surety law required that misdemeanants perform the contract or face reconviction, another fine, and an even longer compulsory labor period. The businessman was always White. The misdemeanant nearly always Black. The crime often fictional. The trial usually a sham. Baker, one of the Progressive Era's most renowned muckrakers, toured the South in the early 1900s, watching this and other scenes, and reported that freedom appeared illusory for many Black southerners.

"[T]he larger landowners and employers of the South," Baker wrote, "want the black man to work for them. More than that, they *must have him:* for he has a practical monopoly on labour in the South. White men of the employing class will do almost anything to keep the Negro on the land and his wife in the kitchen—so long as they are obedient and unambitious workers."

*Anything*, including denying them liberty. "The natural tendency," because of the high demand for Black labor, Baker revealed, "is to convict as many negroes as possible."

Before Thomas Goode Jones's nomination, hopefuls courted Booker T., thinking he could influence Roosevelt to select them instead. One hopeful, William C. Oates, Jones's successor as governor, implored Booker T. to focus on the courts. "With the impending sentiment among a large class of the white people in the South," Oates said, "the greatest bulwark of protection to your race is to be found in the federal judiciary." Booker T. understood this well. In Jones, Booker T. thought he had helped elevate someone who would inhibit the theft of Black sweat and muscle.

A year and a half into his judicial tenure, Jones was poised to make a wise man of Booker T.

THE EIGHTEEN-YEAR-OLD FEDERAL POST OFFICE and Courthouse dominated the intersection of Dexter and South Lawrence Streets in downtown Montgomery, near where Booker T. had consumed race speeches. The post office occupied the first floor of the mammoth building made with pressed brick beneath a French château roof and ninety-foot tower, a gorgeous execution of architecture set behind a chaotic spiderweb of telephone wires, telegraph wires, electric light wires, and the electric streetcar wires that zigzagged across the roads. U.S. marshals ascended stone steps or a handsome elevator to reach their second-floor offices. On the night of March 21, 1902, Deputy U.S. Marshal Byron Trammell spoke with a *Montgomery Advertiser* reporter inside the building about arrests he made the day before.

"I left Montgomery Thursday night . . . to Goodwater, Coosa County," he told the reporter, referring to the remote town of about seven hundred in central Alabama. "I had in my possession papers for the arrest of Jesse L. London, a Justice of the Peace of that county; L. A. Grogan, bailiff and constable; William T. Joiner, Robert Franklin, John McDonald and T. M. Pruitt," all prominent citizens of the area. "We arrested all except Pruitt, whom we could not find. From Goodwater we took the prisoners to Birmingham this morning where they were released on $2,000 bond each to appear at the next term of the court."

The federal government charged the men in connection with the kidnapping of Madison Davis, a Black man, and the selling of him to Elijah Turner, who oversaw a limestone mining operation near Calcis, Alabama. Davis apprised federal authorities of the twenty-seven others Turner kept in involuntary servitude. Unlawfully arrested,

Davis went through a farce trial for obtaining goods under false pretenses, a fictitious charge. London, the magistrate, fined him. Turner paid Davis's fine and worked him for months.

"If the evidence corroborates the allegations of the negro," Judge Jones told the reporter, "it means that the slave traffic has revived in Alabama. The government, however, now has the affair in hand and it will be sifted to the end."

That same day, Judge Jones wrote Philander C. Knox, United States attorney general, about "a systematic scheme of depriving negroes of their civil liberty, and hiring them out [that] has been practiced for some time" in Alabama. Knox learned additional facts from a local who explained that "the enslavement of the colored people in Alabama" was "carried on by that class of men who by reason of their party prominence in the community where they live have so exercised influence over juries and public officials as to make the local courts . . . powerless to enforce the law." They were "protected in their brutal and inhuman conduct by that class of Democrats who believe that no law, moral or otherwise, is violated in the enslavement of Negroes."

Warren S. Reese Jr., U.S. attorney for the Middle District of Alabama, informed Knox that the "conditions of the 'black belt' in this district are more deplorable as the investigations of the grand jury proceed. It is now being revealed that hundreds of negroes are held in peonage and involuntary servitude of the most vicious character. Men and women are arrested on the flimsiest charges," and "they are brutally whipped, worked and locked up without let or hindrance. The tortures inflicted" on them "are severe and sometimes result in total disability or death." Per Reese, "Some counties in this district are honey combed with these slave practices." Reese had lived in Alabama all his thirty-seven years but, he wrote, "I never comprehended until now the extent of the present method of slavery."

Reese told Knox that the magistrate and the businessman almost always operated in concert. And after the sham trial, which the magistrate typically kept no record of, the businessman dragged his new paid-for labor to his new home where he was "locked up at night in a cell, worked under guards during the day from 3 o'clock in the morning until 7 or 8 o'clock at night, whipped in a most cruel manner, [and] is insufficiently fed and poorly clad." When "the time of a good working negro is nearing an end," Reese reported, "he is rearrested upon some trumped up charge and again carried before some bribed [magistrate] and resentenced to an additional time." If the captives flee, "the dogs are placed upon their track," Reese said, "and they are invariably retaken and subjected to more cruel treatment." By June, a concerned President Roosevelt requested a report from Attorney General Knox, who promised "vigorous and uncompromising prosecution."

As Secret Service agents and federal marshals sprawled through rural central Alabama, digging up facts, many caste preservationists not directly involved in these schemes, on the one hand, diminished whatever federal investigators unearthed as isolated instances wholly unrepresentative of the labor market. The scheme's participants, on the other hand, defended the legality of their actions. Elijah Turner, for example, told a Birmingham reporter that he violated no rights of Madison Davis. "I do not deny that I work negroes at Calcis Lime Works," he conceded, "but I have always done so. . . . This negro Davis did work there last year. He did so under contract signed by himself voluntarily, and this contract is witnessed by F. M. Pruitt and R. N. Franklin, of Goodwater."

Judge Jones wanted to eradicate this practice. Yet, Jones confronted an issue. Although Congress forbade slavery with the Thirteenth Amendment, it passed no law that explicitly empowered the federal government to prosecute slaveholders. The closest Jones found, an 1867 federal statute, targeted something called peonage, a mode of involuntary servitude once rampant in the New Mexico Territory. Jones pushed for federal investigations of men who possibly violated this statute. The prosecution of Alabama's new slaveocracy started with the education of a grand jury.

"WHAT IS MEANT BY HOLDING or returning a person 'to a condition of peonage'?," Judge Jones asked a little after noon on June 15, 1903, inside the massive federal courtroom occupying the third and fourth floors of Montgomery's federal building.

"At the time of the passage of the act of Congress to which your attention will presently be called, a system of service popularly called 'peonage' existed in New Mexico," said Jones, "which spoke of the relation as that of master and servant.

"It derived the institution from Mexico," he continued beneath the twenty-three-foot-high ceiling, "which, in turn, inherited it from Spain. Peonage was not slavery, as it formerly existed in this country. The peon was not a slave. He was a freeman, with political as well as civil rights. He entered into the relation from choice, for a definite period, as the result of mutual contract. The relation was not confined to any race. The child of a peon did not become a peon, and the father could not contract away the services of his minor child, except in rare cases," explained Jones, a bit over six feet tall with dark eyes and black-and-silver receding hair.

"The peon, male or female, agreed with the master upon the nature of the service, the length of its duration, and compensation. The peon then became bound to the master 'for an indebtedness founded upon an advancement in consideration of service.'" In other words, peonage started with a mutual agreement between a peon and master.

"The improvidence and the needs of laborers and servants, the greed of employers, and the exercise, often corrupt, of almost irresponsible power of local magistrates," Jones told the jurors, "resulted in citizens becoming bound, in constantly increasing numbers and length of service, to compulsory 'service or labor' to coerce payment of debt or compel the performance of real or pretended obligations of personal service."

In response, Congress endeavored "not only to destroy the system as it existed in New Mexico, but to prevent in the future in that territory, or 'in any other territory or state' of the Union, the reappearance or re-establishment of the evil conditions which the system created. Accordingly, by the act approved on the 2d day of March, 1867," Congress enacted the federal peonage statute. "Congress," Jones said, "not only annulled all legislation attempting to uphold peonage as a legalized institution, but went further and provided for the punishment of every person instrumental in holding, arresting, or returning 'of any person' to a 'condition of peonage.'"

Crucially, Jones interpreted the statute broadly. Debt peonage, a term of art, refers to a specific form of involuntary servitude, one where a person is compelled to labor for another because of indebtedness. The federal peonage statute specifically outlaws the "involuntary service or labor of any persons . . . in liquidation of any debt, *or obligation.*" The word *obligation* expands the scope, meaning the statute also targeted a landowner who, for instance, held a laborer in involuntary servitude because the landowner simply felt that the laborer was obligated to work, regardless of debt.

Peonage appeared mainly in three places. First, in the Cotton Belt, a region spanning from Texas to the Carolinas. Second, turpentine farms in Mississippi, Alabama, South Georgia, and North Florida. And third, railroad construction camps. Peonage ripped through the South like a wildfire, burning Black freedom, restoring White ownership of Black labor. Not until the early 1900s did the federal government confront this decades-long dilemma.

Booker T. told Oswald Garrison Villard, abolitionist William Lloyd Garrison's grandson, that "we owe to Judge Thomas G. Jones . . . a great debt of gratitude for what is being done in regard to exposing the peonage system in Alabama." When addressing the National Afro-American Council, Booker T. further exalted Jones, saying, "Though their voices may not be often or loudly lifted, there are in this country, North and South, men who mean to help see that justice is meted out to the race in all avenues of life. Such a man is Judge Thomas G. Jones, of Alabama, to whom more credit should be given for blotting out the infamous system of peonage than to any other."

Jones offered an early interpretation of the peonage statute, but Judge Charles Swayne's Tallahassee federal courtroom held the first peonage prosecution, that of Samuel M. Clyatt, which resulted in a conviction. The men Clyatt held in peonage were never prosecuted for a crime, although Clyatt did procure a fraudulent arrest warrant from a magistrate. But his seeking to force his victims to labor because of a debt, real or imagined, satisfied the definition of peonage. His case would reach the Supreme Court, providing the nine black robes their first chance at grappling with the practice.

ON APRIL 11, 1904, inside the City Court Hall in Tifton, a remote South Georgia town inching toward modernity, where dirt roads encountered newly installed electric streetlights, the mayor presided over a mass meeting. The attendees were fundraising for attorneys to represent Clyatt before the Supreme Court. A man named W. M. Hammond said that the legal matter that assembled them "is not one involving the liberty of Mr. Clyatt alone, but it personally interests every one engaged in the sawmill and lumber business, the turpentine industry, and in fact, everyone who employs labor. It is a question involving the right of contracts and also of state rights."

Three years earlier, on November 21, 1901, a federal grand jury indicted Clyatt on two counts under the peonage statute. The first charged Clyatt with "unlawfully and knowingly return[ing]" Will Gordon and Mose Ridley to a state of peonage. The second alleged that Clyatt had "caused and aided in returning Gordon and Ridley" to a state of peonage. Remember the word "return."

Gordon and Ridley had disappeared, last seen with Clyatt and his men, after Clyatt had vowed to make examples of them. On March 25, 1902, the trial jury convicted Clyatt. Seeking leniency, Clyatt told Judge Swayne that he "acted in good faith, and had no intention of violating the laws of Georgia, Florida or the United States." Clyatt proclaimed his innocence "of any willful violation of the law." Judge Swayne replied "that he could not see why Mr. Clyatt and his men, not being officers of the law, should come into Florida in the night time, armed with guns and revolvers, and forcibly carry off citizens of this State, without due process of the law." Swayne sentenced him to four years' hard labor in the Atlanta federal penitentiary.

Clyatt's counsel petitioned Swayne to stay the punishment until the Supreme Court could assess the legality of prosecuting his client under the peonage statute. Swayne agreed, and Clyatt went free pending appeal. In March 1904, the Fifth Circuit Court of Appeals in New Orleans sent the case to the Supreme Court to focus on two issues. First, whether peonage could exist in the absence of state law. Second, whether Clyatt violated the federal peonage statute. Hammond told those gathered inside Tifton City Court Hall that he had just come from Valdosta, Georgia, where $5,000 had been pledged to secure "the best legal talent in the country" to convince the black robes to resolve those issues in their favor.

Roosevelt's Justice Department understood that the sawmill and turpentine industries considered the peonage statute a menace to their economic viability. U.S. Attorney Alexander Akerman informed Attorney General Knox that the sawmill men reasoned that unless they "were permitted to control their labor as they saw fit, without any interference from the federal authorities, they would be unable to carry on" their businesses. "Every turpentine operator and saw mill man, as well as everyone employing labor in this section," the *Atlanta Constitution* reported, "feels that they are affected by Judge Swayne's construction of this law, and take a vital interest in the case."

Clyatt's supporters helped secure Senator Augustus O. Bacon and Congressman William G. Brantley, two Georgians, for his defense. At the Supreme Court oral argument in December 1904, Bacon and Brantley argued that the Thirteenth Amendment did not empower Congress to pass laws that acted upon individuals and that peonage couldn't exist in the absence of state law.

When writing their briefs, Henry Hoyt, Roosevelt's solicitor general, and William Henry Moody, his attorney general, dipped their pen in Black misery, forefronting the pain of the descendants of enslaved people who became practically enslaved themselves. "We think that we may truthfully say that upon the decision of this case hangs the liberty of thousands of persons," Moody wrote, "mostly colored, it is true, who are now being held in a condition of involuntary servitude, in many cases worse than slavery itself, by the unlawful acts of individuals, not only in violation of the thirteenth amendment to the Constitution, but in violation of the law which we have here under consideration."

Moody defended the federal peonage statute as an appropriate measure to enforce the Thirteenth Amendment and urged the justices to uphold it. Because federal judges were awaiting the Supreme Court's assessment of the peonage statute's constitutionality, Moody explained that the executive branch felt "practically paralyzed" in protecting Black southerners. "Since the certification of this case to the Supreme Court," Hoyt explained, "several of the circuit and district courts in the fifth circuit, in which numerous prosecutions for violation of the peonage statutes are pending, have refused to try any of the cases, but have postponed them to await the decision of the court in this case." On December 13 and 14, 1904, the Court heard oral argument for *Clyatt v. United States*. On March 13, 1905, the Court delivered its opinion.

JUSTICE OLIVER WENDELL HOLMES ONCE TEASED Justice David Josiah Brewer for his "itch for public speaking." The man loved a captive audience. On March 17, 1905, Brewer found one inside the Sunday school house of the Calvary Baptist Church on the corner of 8th and H Streets in Washington, D.C., four days after the sixty-seven-year-old announced his majority opinion in *Clyatt v. United States*. The balding, portly justice delivered a speech on his favorite topic, Christianity. Inside the red-brick Gothic church with a 140-foot-tall iron tower, Brewer addressed 150 who donned formal attire for a Baptist Sunday school banquet. Brewer titled his talk "Religion and Patriotism."

"The man who is the best Christian makes the best patriot," Brewer said, "and the man who is the best patriot is likely to make the best Christian."

Brewer discussed some national problems—the greedy combination of wealth that generated massive monopolies, on one side, and the unscrupulous leadership of labor unions on the other. "Such evils cannot be met by courts, by legislation, by judicial decisions, or executive proclamation," he contended. "I sometimes see the papers calling out for decisions against trusts, and I can but smile to think how futile all the larger part of such effort will be. The remedy is not in judicial decisions, but rests in the introduction into the hearts of the men of the nation of the spirit of the Golden Rule."

*Do unto others as you would have them do unto you.* Most consider the Golden Rule as imploring people to act with benevolence—treat others as you wish to be treated. But the rule, as Brewer, a devout Christian, certainly understood, embraces a larger demand. The Golden Rule calls on us to also reflect on how our actions affect others. It calls on us to love all of God's children equally. In the context of *Clyatt*, the Golden Rule instructed Brewer to imagine how he would feel if he were, because of the color of his skin, living under the peril of having his liberty and labor stolen.

In his *Clyatt* opinion, Brewer scrapped Judge Jones's broader construction of the peonage statute by ignoring the phrase "or obligation." In our journey, we have encountered the Court's weakening federal statutes by pretending words away. It happened again here. Brewer narrowed the statute to just debt peonage despite some manifestations of the new slavery arising from situations unconnected to debt. Justice Brewer, nonetheless, deemed the peonage statute constitutional based on both long-standing precedent that the Thirteenth Amendment enabled Congress to pass legislation directly affecting private individuals and the recognition that peonage was involuntary servitude, which the amendment expressly forbade.

Brewer had long needled his colleagues for their willingness to reverse the sentences of convicted criminals. In a 1903 article, he championed eliminating criminal appeals entirely to reduce lynching, contending that White folk would find fewer reasons for lynching Black people accused of heinous crimes if the specter of a judge delaying a final resolution disappeared. Responding to the condemnation he received for this position, he called the appeals process a "statutory privilege" that enabled the guilty to escape punishment. Thus, Brewer had built an anti-conviction-reversal persona. For Clyatt, he shed it.

U.S. Attorney Eagan charged Clyatt with returning Gordon and Ridley to a state of peonage. Brewer believed Eagan provided ample evidence showing that Clyatt "caused the arrest of Gordon and Ridley on warrants issued by a magistrate in Georgia." But Brewer concluded Eagan's evidence failed to prove "that Gordon and Ridley were ever theretofore in a condition of peonage." Returning a person to a state of peonage means, implicitly, that the person was before in a state of peonage. Brewer found, however, that the trial testimony didn't establish prior peonage, even though if Clyatt thought Gordon and Ridley could not leave they were by definition in a state of peonage before their desertion. Through this specious hairsplitting, Brewer determined that the trial judge erred in sending the case to the jury because the prosecution did not establish at trial that Clyatt had kept Gordon and Ridley in a state of peonage before hunting them down. Brewer concluded this despite reading just a *summary* of the trial testimony. The Court overturned Clyatt's conviction on a baseless technicality.

Justice Harlan assailed Brewer's opinion, noting in his dissent that Clyatt's defense counsel never objected to the case's submission to the jury, nor did defense counsel request that the judge vacate Clyatt's conviction based on insufficient evidence. Recall in the previous leg of our journey that the Supreme Court, in *Charley Smith v. Mississippi*, ignored Cornelius Jones's timely objection to the trial judge denying Jones the opportunity to subpoena jury commissioners, refusing to even consider it as a reversible error. Here, the justices *on their own* overturned a conviction, an inconsistency that cut in favor of caste preservationism, as nearly every inconsistency did in this era. Also recall that in *Gibson v. Mississippi*, the Court refused to consider Jones's Fourteenth Amendment argument because of the failure to object to the state excluding Black men from the juries that indicted and convicted John Gibson. These justices had proven to be sticklers for details. Yet here, Brewer, a justice who had chided his colleagues for supporting the appeals process in the context of Black criminal defendants, suddenly switched sides, benefiting a White neo-slaver. Harlan wrote, "it is going very far to hold in a case like this, disclosing barbarities of the worst kind against these negroes, that the trial court erred in sending this case to the jury."

With its obvious victims, obvious villains, obvious stakes, peonage furnished journalists with all the threads for riveting storytelling that perfectly fit within the Progressive Era ethos—the need to spotlight ills that begged for cures. One notorious villain, John Pace, faced prosecution in Judge Jones's Alabama courtroom. A northern newspaper called the 270-pound Pace "a combination of feudal baron and wholesale slavedriver" and an "animal-like person, with two feet almost eaten off with disease, with fingers which are expected to drop away within a year" who was "quite like the slave-shipping characters of 'Uncle Tom's Cabin.'" Judge Jones worked with Booker T. to splash such narratives onto northern front pages, informing the masses and the powerful about the Black agony allowed to fester in the South that northern silence aided and abetted. As President Roosevelt said, "The absence of protest from the north has undoubtedly . . . had a bad effect in encouraging" peonage.

Given that the Justice Department invited the Court to apply a racial lens to the case, Clyatt and his gunmen crossing state lines to arrest Black men for exercising their right to leave, allowed the Supreme Court to acknowledge the suffering of members of their own society, to acknowledge that their countryfolk, because of their race, couldn't even enjoy the Thirteenth Amendment. Yet, a Court majority evaded these facts and signed on to an opinion written by a man who preached on Christianity, patriotism, and the Golden Rule—three things Brewer professed to lean on but withheld from his *Clyatt* opinion, withheld from Black peons. The Court disregarded that this case reflected widespread deprivation of due process inflicted on Black Americans, because of their Blackness, just as it had in *Williams v. Fears*. In both cases, arms of the state, the legislature in *Williams* and police officers and magistrates in *Clyatt*, deprived Black laborers of liberty in violation of the Due Process Clause, and the Court developed no legal analysis that responded to this racial emergency.

Archibald H. Grimké, a caste abolitionist who climbed from slavery to Harvard Law School, excoriated Justice Brewer's *Clyatt* opinion. "He told those young men that the Golden Rule introduced into the hearts of the people was a better remedy for National ills than the 'big stick.' But he failed to inform them that the 'big stick' of righteous laws is one of the most effective instruments for preparing the world for the reign of the Golden Rule."

The *Clyatt* case produced one triumph: Roosevelt's Justice Department had successfully defended the peonage statute's constitutionality. The department thereafter directed federal attorneys to draft indictments more precisely. The federal attack on peonage sputtered after *Clyatt* though. The few prosecutions that did trickle forward typically arose from the impetus of individual federal prosecutors or after a particularly egregious set of facts surfaced. With Ridley and Gordon still missing, the Justice Department dropped its prosecution of Samuel Clyatt, who later became Tifton's mayor. "[J]ustice delayed," Justice Brewer wrote in his piece maligning criminal appeals, "is often justice denied." Indeed.

Before proceeding to our next case, let's delve deeper into a leading reason why a nation was so willing to let the South exploit Black labor, using a Roosevelt speech as a gateway to this larger discussion.

AT A QUARTER PAST SEVEN on the evening of February 14, 1905, President Roosevelt arrived at Manhattan's Waldorf-Astoria, one of the world's largest, most grandiose hotels. As Roosevelt found his seat in the ballroom venue for the Nineteenth Annual Lincoln Dinner of the Republican Club of the City of New York, loud cheers honored the man who had won a landslide victory in November, thumping Democrat Alton B. Parker, despite carrying no southern states.

Just before ten at night, Roosevelt stood in his typical bravado—one hand in his pocket and gesturing forcefully—as he delivered remarks on race.

"In the first place, it is true of the colored man, as it is true of the white man," Roosevelt said, "that in the long run his fate must depend far more upon his own effort than upon the efforts of any outside friend. Every vicious, venal, or ignorant colored man is an even greater foe to his own race than to the community as a whole. The colored man's self-respect entitles him to do that share in the political work of the country which is warranted by his individual ability and integrity and the position he has won for himself. But the prime requisite of the race is moral and industrial uplifting," he claimed, endorsing Booker T.'s program.

"Laziness and shiftlessness, these, and above all, vice and criminality of every kind, are evils more potent for harm to the black race than all acts of oppression of white men put together. . . . If the standards of private morality and industrial efficiency can be raised high enough among the black race, then its future on this continent is secure," said the president, hinting at support for respectability politics.

When discussing the Black population, Roosevelt segued into crime. White folk coupled Black and criminality as they coupled White and superiority. The White masses felt compelled to formulate a code to account for supposed Black frailties. Extralegal levers needed to be pulled to turn lesser beings into a tolerable presence, many White folk assumed, and if the federal government denied them those levers, then Black people, through crime and laziness, would capsize White civilization.

Booker T., through appeals to their economic interests, tried to coax White folk to abandon the denials of rights and the anti-Black violence that much of White America condoned as a tool to bring Black folk to heel. In a 1904 piece entitled "A Protest Against the Burning and Lynching of Negroes," for instance, he wrote that "the rule of the mob destroys the friendly relations which should exist between the races and injures and interferes with the material prosperity of the communities concerned."

Booker T. reasoned that anti-Black violence hurt White people economically. But even if sometimes true, it wasn't always. As Peg-Leg Williams's tale shows, self-interest often divided White folk. In that vein, because Black labor cost less, White businessmen sometimes preferred it, leading to White laborers harnessing violence to dictate which trades Black people could pursue, as our next legal dispute establishes.

THOMAS DIXON JR., notorious for his racist novel *The Clansman* that later hit theaters as *The Birth of a Nation*, loathed Booker T.'s program for industrial education. "Industrial training gives power," he asserted. "If the Negro ever becomes a serious competitor of the white labourer in the industries of the South, the white man will kill him." In 1901, Georgia governor Allen Candler echoed Dixon, remarking that although Booker T. was a "good negro ... I am opposed to putting negroes in factories and offices. When you do that you will cause dissatisfaction between the two races and such things might lead to a race war. The field of agriculture is the proper one for the negro."

Such words exposed dissension among White people. Some thought that Black folk needed to be raised lest they undermine American society. Others predicted that raising the race would instigate labor competition that could produce White losers. The latter mindset resisted Black people proving their respectability, believing that outcome antagonistic to White working-class interests.

At ten in the morning of August 17, 1903, fifteen White men, many of them prosperous planters in Poinsett County, Arkansas, barged into a northern Arkansas sawmill owned by two White men but operated solely by Black laborers, demanding that the eight Black men there leave. They complied. Local newspapers termed this Whitecapping, referring to anti-Black intimidation and terrorism, common in Arkansas, common throughout the South.

The fifteen plantation owners probably wanted Black laborers farming, rather than working in factories. Black men, as Ray Stannard Baker chronicled, held a virtual monopoly on agricultural labor—if they didn't tend to the fields, few would. But sawmill owners and railroad companies, because of cost, often preferred Black labor, opening more vocational options to Black men. White laborers, in response, sometimes battered and threatened Black competitors into rejecting these options, which they thought belonged to White men. Black laborers, therefore, confronted threats from various segments of the White population. White employers in Arkansas who preferred low-cost Black laborers wanted to protect them and pushed the federal government to prosecute Whitecappers.

William G. Whipple, a U.S. attorney in Arkansas, indicted the fifteen men with "knowingly, willfully and unlawfully" conspiring to "oppress, threaten and intimidate" the Black sawmill laborers, in violation of Section 5508 of the Revised Statutes, part of the First Enforcement Act, meant to enforce the Thirteenth Amendment. Whipple indicted them, more specifically, with prohibiting, because of race, a Black worker's ability to earn under a labor contract. The defendants filed demurrers, arguing that they should go free because the Constitution did not grant the right to contract and thus Congress could not legislate to safeguard it. Jacob Trieber, federal judge for the Eastern District of Arkansas, dismissed the demurrers. A German immigrant who favored leveraging The Trinity to defend Black rights, Trieber identified the right to contract as a "fundamental or natural" right secured by the Thirteenth Amendment. The McKinley nominee believed southern states would not protect these rights and, therefore, the federal government should. The trial jury convicted William Clampit, Wash McKinney, and Reuben Hodges, who then appealed their convictions to the Supreme Court. When Attorney General Moody took the case over, it involved one matter—whether Congress could legislate to protect Black folk from efforts to prevent them, because of race, from performing under labor contracts.

On April 23, 1906, Moody entered the Court Chamber to defend the constitutionality of the law that Whipple convicted the men under. If the Court followed its precedent, Moody, a fifty-two-year-old lifelong bachelor from Massachusetts, would successfully defend the rights of the eight Black Arkansas laborers, save a law that protected freedom, and inform caste preservationists that the federal government could punish them for violating Black people's contract rights. Let's watch his performance.

THE COURT'S COMPOSITION HAS CHANGED since our last visit. Republican appointees still claim most spots, six, although the party's desertion of Black folk renders party affiliation of marginal utility. Chief Justice Fuller, seventy-three with his snow-white mane, maintains the center seat. Justice Harlan, once the youngest member, now the longest-serving, sits as a wise seventy-two-year-old. Justice Brewer, sixty-eight, still occupies a seat. Same with seventy-year-old Justice Brown. The sixty-year-old Justice White, the second-longest-serving Democratic nominee, survives, as does sixty-seven-year-old Rufus Peckham, another Cleveland appointee. McKinley nominee Justice McKenna, sixty-two, who, with his *Williams v. Mississippi* opinion, wrote the shallow opinion that green-lit Black disenfranchisement, also keeps a chair.

Born in Boston on March 8, 1841, Oliver Wendell Holmes Jr., Roosevelt's first appointee, replaced Justice Gray. After graduating from Harvard College in 1861, Holmes, an abolitionist, enlisted with the Union Army. After the war, he attended Harvard Law School, graduating in 1866. Holmes, brilliant, added new vision and perspective to legal thought through various articles, treatises, and lectures. Just a few months after his Harvard Law professor appointment, the governor of Massachusetts tapped him for the state's highest court.

On December 8, 1902, Holmes became a U.S. Supreme Court justice.

Roosevelt's second appointee, fifty-seven-year-old William Rufus Day, who replaced Justice Shiras, hails from Ohio. A longtime McKinley friend, Day shuttered his practice to move to D.C. after McKinley won the presidency, serving as the assistant secretary of state before climbing to the head of the State Department. McKinley appointed Day, a skinny, quiet man who spoke with a low voice, to the Sixth Circuit Appeals Court where he stayed four years before replacing Justice Shiras in March 1902.

"It is inconceivable, your honors," says Moody, a small man in the big room, "that the conduct which is set out in this indictment would not be regarded as a crime in any community not made up of barbarians. I have no doubt whatever that it is a crime under the laws of the State of Arkansas. The question here is, whether it also is a crime against any law of the United States, constitutionally operative [in] Arkansas."

Moody, with his serious and dark eyes, reads the statute under consideration: " 'If two or more persons conspire to injure, oppress, threaten, or intimidate any citizen in the free exercise or enjoyment of any right or privilege secured to him by the Constitution or laws of the United States, or because of his having so exercised the same,' . . . they shall be punished in the manner prescribed in the statute."

Moody asks the most pertinent question. "Has a negro the right to contract for his own personal labor and in the execution of that contract the right to be exempt from concerted force and intimidation because of his race, secured by the Constitution of the United States and protected by any law of the United States passed in pursuance of the power conferred upon Congress by the Constitution?"

"Do you draw any distinction," Justice Brewer interjects, "between the right of a negro to make a contract and the right of a white man?"

"No, sir," Moody responds, trying to steer the discussion back to the heart of the case: Black people being prevented from enjoying fundamental rights—the right to contract for labor and the right to execute that contract free from racial intimidation. "Is the denial to a negro of the right to labor, a denial based upon his race alone, a denial inspired by race hostility—the denial of a right secured to him by the Thirteenth Amendment to the Constitution?" Moody asks. "The position of the government is this: Where a man is forcibly denied, on account of his race or color, the right to earn his own bread by the sweat of his own brow, he is denied one of the essential rights of freedom, and to that extent is forced into a position of involuntary servitude."

Moody returns to Brewer's question. He reminds the justices that the Thirteenth Amendment "was more than an act abolishing the institution of slavery. In the words of Mr. Justice Bradley, its reflex action established affirmatively in every person residing within the jurisdiction of the United States the right to be free." The ability to contract with another to sell labor sits at the very heart of freedom. If the federal government must sit idly as White folk bully Black people, on account of race, from working, then the federal government can't defend Black freedom, and America ratified a viper, the Thirteenth Amendment, lacking fangs and venom.

Moody invokes "the well-settled doctrine of this court" that Congress, under the Thirteenth Amendment, "may protect the people against what are sometimes called 'badges,' sometimes 'incidents,' sometimes 'essential characteristics' of slavery or servitude." Justice Bradley's *Civil Rights Cases* opinion articulated this principle. "Is, then, a denial of the right to labor on account of race an incident of slavery, a badge of slavery, an essential characteristic of slavery?" Moody asks.

"You think the concerted action of individuals denying the right of another to labor is putting him in a condition of slavery?" Brewer asks, missing the point.

"Concerted action against another person, on account of his race, to deprive him of one of the essential rights of freedom, the right to labor, is a violation of the Thirteenth Amendment," Moody replies. The three convicted men stormed into a sawmill and demanded the Black workers cease working because of color. Moody is arguing that's a violation of a right guaranteed under the Thirteenth Amendment.

"The language of the thirteenth amendment is slavery or involuntary servitude," Brewer counters, his remark suggesting that he wants to limit the Thirteenth Amendment to barring slavery and involuntary servitude, as Justice Brown did in his *Plessy* opinion, as opposed to guaranteeing freedom.

Moody replies, "Yes, sir," to Brewer, conceding that the Thirteenth Amendment speaks of slavery and involuntary servitude.

"Now," Brewer asks, "is it not an essential element of slavery that there should be a master to whom the involuntary service is rendered directly?"

"I am relying here upon the well-settled doctrine," a patient Moody explains again, "stated clearly in the *Civil Rights Cases* to which I shall hereafter refer, in language which, in part, was quoted and approved in the recent *Clyatt* case, that 'badges,' or 'incidents,' or 'essential characteristics' of slavery or involuntary servitude are forbidden by the Thirteenth Amendment equally with slavery or involuntary servitude themselves." Moody knows that Brewer authored the *Clyatt* opinion and is reminding him that he cited the *Civil Rights Cases*, three times in fact, in it.

Moody reads from Bradley's circuit court *Cruikshank* opinion to underline how the Thirteenth Amendment altered America: "The war of race, whether it assumes the dimensions of civil strife or domestic violence, whether carried on in a guerilla or predatory form, or by private combination, or even by private outrage or intimidation, is subject to the jurisdiction of the Government of the United States." Moody is ably countering the caste preservationist, states' rights argument. That argument holds that the Thirteenth Amendment merely guaranteed a limited right to neither be enslaved nor subjected to involuntary servitude and did not involve what Moody called " 'badges,' sometimes 'incidents,' sometimes 'essential characteristics' of slavery or servitude."

Holmes, with his long angular face and distinctive white handlebar mustache, says, "You might say wherever a race hostility against the negro arises or threatens involuntary servitude, that under those circumstances it is within the protection of the laws to which you are referring, and yet a racial hostility or an overt act of a precisely similar character against other races might exist and under those circumstances might not be within them."

In this moment, Moody should know that Brewer and now Holmes are trying to lull him into defending a position the Court can eas-ily swat away. Holmes is a brilliant man, the smartest on the bench probably, certainly smart enough to know that based on the Court's precedent, Section 5508 of the Revised Statutes, is constitutional. But how can justices who wish to eschew precedent do that while maintaining a façade of adherence to it? One way is to cow Moody into framing the statute as constitutional because Congress drafted the Thirteenth Amendment as a special gift to protect Black folk. If Moody argues this, Brewer and Holmes could then support an opin-ion that turns on whether the Thirteenth Amendment granted Black people special rights, which enables Congress to pass the law at issue. But Moody sidesteps this trap, and repeatedly hurls precedent into the justices' faces, demanding they follow it.

Moody draws a hypothetical. Imagine White people in the west had said to the Native Americans, "'You shall not work; you are Indian or you are a Mexican; you shall not work on account of your race;' . . . would there be any distinction between such action directed against the Indian or Mexican and the same action directed against the negro? I submit there is no distinction between the cases." Through this hypothetical, Moody frustrates the effort to attack a straw man.

Moody once more refers to the *Civil Rights Cases* to bolster his position. "We have in that case a clear definition of what the majority of the court understood to be essential characteristics of slavery—badges and incidents of slavery." Moody then quotes the opinion that lists the right "to make contracts" as one of the incidents. Brewer and Holmes sit silently as Moody bests them.

Moody ends by appropriating the moderate White southern viewpoint that Booker T. heard at the Montgomery race conference to convince the Court to produce an anticaste decision. "If the negro who is in our midst can be denied the right to work and must live on the outskirts of civilization," Moody says, "he will become more dangerous than the wild beasts, because he has a higher intelligence than the most intelligent beast. He will become an outcast lurking about the borders and living by depredation. . . .

"If the nation has not the power at the very threshold to say to those who declare against this or other races, that as a race it shall not have one of the most essential rights of a free man, it is powerless indeed. I submit that it has that power. It was given to the nation by the Thirteenth Amendment, and this case is brought within it."

ON MAY 28, 1906, the day the Court decided *Hodges v. United States*, Justice Brown conveyed his goodbye message inside the Chamber. With blindness sacking one eye and invading the other, Brown thought the country deserved someone competent to render performance befitting the nation's highest tribunal.

Bidding his farewell, Brown boasted that "the now universal acquiescence in [the Supreme Court's] decisions, though sometimes reached by a bare majority of its members, is a magnificent tribute to that respect for the law inherent in the Anglo-Saxon race, and contains within itself the strongest assurance of the stability of our institutions." This remark demonstrates how thoroughly White Supremacy had conquered the White psyche—a justice felt comfortable delivering a racially exclusionary remark inside the hallowed courtroom. Although the justices had decided the case, the Court held the *Hodges* majority opinion text until October 24, 1906, after the dissenting justices filed theirs.

By a seven-to-two vote, the Supreme Court ordered the lower court to dismiss the indictments, holding that Congress lacked authority to enact Section 5508 of the Revised Statutes. Justice Brewer, author of the majority opinion, wrote that the Thirteenth Amendment purged the nation of slavery and involuntary servitude, nothing more. "The meaning of this is as clear as language can make it," he contended. In other words, Brewer interpreted the Thirteenth Amendment as terminating involuntary servitude and slavery, a narrow construction of the amendment articulated in *Plessy*, as opposed to guaranteeing freedom, a broader construction the Court had adopted in the *Civil Rights Cases*.

Brewer argued that, clothed in the right to not be enslaved, Black people thereafter stood on the same plane as White people and needed to do what White people had long done—turn to the states for protection of their rights. Preventing Black people from performing contracts because of race was not the federal government's concern. Brewer reasoned that the Court accepting Moody's construction of the Thirteenth Amendment was tantamount to treating the amendment as a special bodyguard solely reserved for Black folk's defense. In other words, after Brewer and Holmes tried to badger Moody into saying this during oral argument, seven justices simply put the words in his mouth and attacked their straw man. "It is for us to accept the decision [of Congress]," Brewer wrote, "which declined to constitute them wards of the nation or leave them in a condition of alienage where they would be subject to the jurisdiction of Congress, but gave them citizenship, doubtless believing that thereby, in the long run, their best interests would be subserved, they taking their chances with other citizens in the states where they should make their homes."

Brewer cited only one case substantively, the *Slaughter-House Cases*. In fact, he quoted that case but replaced the line that the Thirteenth Amendment was "a declaration designed to establish the freedom of four million of slaves" with ellipses, confirming that the devout Christian knew the Court had long interpreted the amendment as embracing the broader construction of guaranteeing freedom. The Court majority simply abandoned it.

Recall that Justice Bradley in his majority opinion in the *Civil Rights Cases* wrote that Congress could not outlaw private segregation in places like hotels and opera houses under the Thirteenth Amendment because staying overnight in an inn or sitting in the prime seat of an auditorium was not a badge or incident of slavery, unlike not being able to file a lawsuit or work under a contract. Justice Bradley wrote this promise. Twenty years later, when following that logic would have provided Black folk a measure of freedom, the Court repudiated its own interpretations.

Brewer's opinion further restricted the federal government from punishing private individuals who, on account of race, imperiled Black folk's fundamental liberties. Judge Trieber, the Arkansas district judge who upheld the statute, understood that southern states neglected to defend Black rights. He supported the federal government stepping forward to remedy states' failures. Justice Brown, in his goodbye message, praised the Anglo-Saxon race for its respect of law, yet by forsaking precedent, while avoiding a clear articulation of why, he disrespected the law. Justices Harlan and Day dissented, endorsing Moody's argument.

In *Hodges*, the Court again impaled the Thirteenth Amendment. Meanwhile, the amendment bled its power in another way: after the Civil War, the former slave states returned to selling Black people. One 1866 newspaper advertisement, for example, informed of the "Public Sale" of a "negro man, named Richard Harris," who was convicted of larceny, "to be sold as a slave" by an Anne Arundel County, Maryland, sheriff.

Caste preservationists insisted that Congress left a loophole in the Thirteenth Amendment, that a guilty verdict reset the calendar to 1850, and Black people, provided they had been convicted of a crime, could be sold. As John T. Morgan, a former Confederate general, said in 1866, "[since] the constitution of the United States [gives] the power to inflict involuntary servitude as a punishment for crime, a suitable law should be framed by the state jurists [to] enable them to sell into bondage once more those Negroes found guilty of certain crimes." Perhaps you figure Morgan correctly interpreted the Thirteenth Amendment. But let's interrogate that. Here's the text:

"Neither slavery nor involuntary servitude, except as punishment for crime whereof the party shall have been duly convicted, shall exist within the United States, or any place subject to their jurisdiction."

It forbids slavery and involuntary servitude except where it exists "as punishment for crime whereof the party shall have been duly convicted." This barred slavery or involuntary servitude unless it had been meted out to punish a person who had been convicted of a crime. For instance, a judge sentencing a criminal to hard labor inside the prison for burglary met this standard. A prison warden, however, who leased that same criminal to a turpentine distillery to raise state revenue violated this construction of the Thirteenth Amendment. This practice, convict leasing, a miserable fate many Black southerners fell into, filled southern states' coffers. The state leased convicts for reasons having little to do with punishing crimes, most often to generate money, but also to enrich private firms, discipline prisoners, dishearten prisoners into accepting their lowly status, and to prepare convicts for labor market reentry. Such rationales for convict leasing violated the text of the Thirteenth Amendment and its abolitionist origins.

Under convict leasing, the state, or the lessor, leased a convict to an individual or a firm, the lessee. The state pocketed the money. The lessee received labor and bore responsibility for feeding, clothing, and sheltering the leased convict. "Wherever I found the lease system in the South," Collis Lovely, who investigated southern convict labor, reported, "I found convicts in a hopeless state of slavery, more cruel and inhuman than chattel slavery ever was . . . because under chattel slavery the slave owner had a property right in the slave." Under convict leasing, a living convict could replace a dead one, motivating lessees to squeeze every ounce of life from a leased convict before receiving another.

Once this news, that Black people returned to the auction block, found Republicans, many of them hissed that their former enemies had contrived a ruse to defy the results of the war. "I cannot imagine," said Maryland Republican senator John Creswell in 1867, "that any reasonable interpretation given to the phraseology used in the constitutional amendment could justify any such practice as has been attempted and acted out in Maryland," referring to early instances of convict leasing. According to Creswell, "the words 'unless for crime' . . . signified only that sort of involuntary servitude which a culprit may be obliged to render to the State, and never intended to authorize any individual, by reason of a decree of court or a public sale, to hold any other human being in bondage." Republicans, with the Thirteenth Amendment, wanted to supplant slavery with free labor throughout the South. Thus, the selling of convicts to replace free labor violated a foundational party principle. Republicans never would have written or ratified an amendment they believed allowed for such practices.

Nonetheless, the caste preservationist construction of the Thirteenth Amendment won without a real fight ever happening. For decades, states leased Black convicts, encouraging southern criminal justice systems to springboard into the convict business, allowing White people to continue treating Black labor as their property. In addition to infringing the Thirteenth Amendment, convict leasing should have been considered a Fourteenth Amendment violation—it was castework. An intentional scheme to steal labor from a people based on race. But the Supreme Court effectively stole from Black people the dream the amendments could have secured. And because the Court had undermined The Trinity, convict leasing never faced a serious legal challenge. The Court had thoroughly limited people's imagination of what The Trinity could achieve. How could Booker T. Washington's rose, respectability politics, bloom in such a hostile climate?

Although no one took this matter to the courtroom, one woman did decide to fight for humans treated like property. She captured the attention of the nation and the president.

IN OCTOBER 1906, a year before she would die of uterine cancer, Emma Maitland Stirling, a sixty-six-year-old Scottish woman, seized her last moment to express righteous indignation about human suffering.

After creating child welfare services in Scotland and promoting child emigration to Nova Scotia, Stirling retired, in 1895, to Coatesville, Pennsylvania, and summered in the Tampa, Florida, area. There she learned facts that inspired her to tell the president startling information—the enslavement of men, both Black *and* White. Stirling feared speaking about it because "murder," she said, "is a small crime in many portions of southern Florida, and that arson and similar crimes are frequently resorted to as punishment for talking about what is going on." Nonetheless, she sounded off and previewed for a *Washington Times* reporter her findings regarding the "barbarism, atrocity and cruelty" of South Florida slave camps.

"I don't like to talk too much about this matter yet," she told the reporter inside a D.C. apartment on October 14, the day before she met with Roosevelt. "I want first to get it in the hands of the President and enlist his help. The Humane Association of Florida proposes to put a stop to this slave-holding and it has sent me here to present to the powers that be every fact which will aid them in prosecuting the guilty parties.

"Those responsible for these helpless black and white slaves are not residents of Florida," she continued, "but come from a far distant state. The convict labor in itself is nothing but slave-holding, for the treatment meted out to them by those who buy them for a term of months or years, as though they were purchasing cattle, is inhuman in the extreme." The men toiled for turpentine, lumber, and phosphate rock mining companies that, she reckoned, northern interests owned.

"We are trying to stop that thing, but the State delights to traffic in this sort of business," she said. "[W]e are fighting now to free gangs of men who are held absolutely in a state of bondage, who were carted into the State like mules and are kept under lash at hard labor, and who are given barely enough to live on." Bosses with guns guarded them as they worked, preventing their escape.

"I know that it will take some mighty power in this government to end the slavery, that I know to exist and that's why I came to Washington to interview the President." State officials felt powerless to counteract the problem, partly because of law enforcement's complicity. U.S. Attorney Joseph N. Stripling tried to investigate the matters but lacked manpower. The federal government needed to devote extra resources.

President Roosevelt had already been apprised of the South's peonage sewer. Judge Jones three years prior, after all, had been presiding over peonage cases, and Roosevelt's Justice Department had been investigating peonage just as long. Thus, when Stirling told him her story in the White House on October 15, he could not have been shocked. Her words, nonetheless, excited him to have his administration probe further. After his meeting with Stirling, Roosevelt announced that his administration would investigate. "In regard to the so-called 'peonage' practice existing in some of the Southern states," Roosevelt's statement read, "I have decided to send Assistant Attorney-General [Charles W.] Russell to Florida and elsewhere in the South to look after the various prosecutions and other matters connected with compulsory labor there. I have selected Mr. Russell because of the fact that he is a Southern man, a Democrat, and familiar with the conditions existing in the South." Russell headed south, where, for the next two years, his flashlight illuminated depravity.

In Knoxville, Tennessee, "Negroes were held in slavery and brutally beaten by foremen at railroad construction camps 36 miles from an existing railroad," Russell discovered, "and a mountain gorge through which runs a small river, down which the bodies of negroes occasionally floated from this or some of the other construction camps (there were 11 in all)."

The guilty parties almost always trapped Black folk, Black men especially. Yet, businesses often could not satiate their thirst with them and therefore sometimes nabbed White men. Misbelieving that this depravity only infected Black skin, White Americans allowed it to spread to them. Russell discovered that European immigrants would disembark in New York and hear melodies about journeying to "the land where it never snows" for high-paying, abundant employment. "They would go down there and would not be allowed to leave," Russell reported. "If they did, they could expect to be brutalized or even murdered."

Regarding the West Virginia Ritter Lumber Company, he revealed that "the white workmen were held in peonage on railroad work in the southern part of the State. They were guarded night and day by mountaineers, and two of those who escaped were caught by a young railroad watchman named Hatfield, who wounded one in the face with a blow with his pistol and tied the two with a rope and brought them back by train." Justice Harlan's cousin, William Harlan, manager of a lumber company, even implicated himself. "These men kept constantly trying to escape after they got here," he confessed. "Of course[,] we keep bloodhounds to trail down men who jump their contracts."

Russell expressed "no doubt . . . that the chief support of peonage is the peculiar system of State laws prevailing in the South, intended evidently to compel service on the part of the workingman." One state at the vanguard in the fashioning of laws to compel labor was Booker T.'s Alabama.

ON APRIL 6, 1908, inside the office of Boling Chapel Young, a Montgomery magistrate, a Black man named Alonzo Bailey sat through a preliminary hearing. The state accused Bailey of "obtaining fifteen dollars under a contract in writing with intent to injure or defraud his employer." At his hearing near the federal courthouse, H. C. Borden, manager of the Riverside Company, testified that in front of him, on December 26, 1907, Bailey signed a labor contract to work for a year at the Scotts Bend Place, a large Montgomery County plantation. Bailey received a fifteen-dollar advance, which he was to repay through $1.25 deductions from his twelve-dollar monthly salary. Bailey worked throughout January and a few days into February 1908 and quit. His employer had him arrested for violating the state's revised false pretenses law.

The original 1885 version outlawed signing a labor contract that included an advance with the intent to defraud. The Alabama Supreme Court, when interpreting the law, held that a laborer quitting without repaying the advance didn't prove that the laborer had fraudulent intentions when signing the contract. The court required the state to establish that the laborer had entered and broken the contract with fraudulent intentions. The state legislators learned that proving intent carried an onerous burden—what Cornelius Jones learned in our previous journey, what we will learn much later as well—and, in 1903, revised the law.

The revised law stipulated that for contracts that came with an advance, a laborer's failure to complete the contract, or refund the advance, provided "prima facie evidence of the intent to injure or defraud his employer." In other words, abandoning a job without repaying the advance was evidence of intent to defraud. North Carolina, Florida, Georgia, Mississippi, Arkansas, and South Carolina passed similar statutes. In 1907, Alabama's legislature revised it again to bring tenant farmers under its provisions. An Alabama evidentiary rule that barred testimony "as to [a defendant's] uncommunicated motives, purpose, or intention," prevented defendants from even testifying on their behalf. Therefore, once laborers accepted a job with an advance, they needed to finish the contract, refund the advance, or face near automatic conviction.

This law, through facially neutral language, targeted Black people, the overwhelming majority of those who filled agricultural jobs, the industry that followed the yearlong-contract-plus-advance paradigm. Employers could foster unbearable working conditions and extract every ounce of Black output, and the law forced laborers to suffer or risk criminal penalty. Booker T. remarked that the law "simply means that any white man, who cares to charge that a Colored man has promised to work for him and has not done so, or who has gotten money from him and not paid it back, can have the Colored man sent to the chain gang." Caste preservationists endorsed the law as necessary to account for Black folk's dishonesty and shiftlessness. Without the law, they contended, Black folk would fleece employers and live off dishonestly obtained funds.

William H. Thomas, a Montgomery City Court judge, declared the false pretenses law unconstitutional, but the Alabama Supreme Court reversed him. On January 17, 1907, Thomas griped to Booker T. that the U.S. Supreme Court would have sided with his legal reasoning had it heard the matter. Thomas attempted to coax Booker T. to help that case reach the black robes, but Booker T. dawdled on the sidelines.

After his hearing, Bailey was jailed. Eight days later, his wife visited Edward S. Watts, a young White attorney in Montgomery. On April 14, 1908, Watts filed a habeas corpus petition in Thomas's court, arguing that the false pretenses statute violated the Equal Protection and Due Process Clauses and the Thirteenth Amendment because it reduced Bailey to involuntary servitude. Restrained by the Alabama Supreme Court's prior rulings, Thomas ruled against Bailey. Watts appealed. Thomas tried again to convince Booker T. to spearhead an effort to purge the state of its false pretenses law.

INSIDE DOROTHY INDUSTRIAL HALL, a two-story brick building on Tuskegee Institute's campus, teachers instructed women on certain gendered duties, like dressmaking, laundry, and millinery. In one of the sewing rooms, students would perform at their wooden chairs and desks and perfect the craft, by hand or with machines, as a teacher guided them and sunlight fell into the room from the windows overlooking the two-thousand-acre campus. Dorothy Hall also featured two high-grade kitchens, where students learned how to cook, not fancy meals, but the common dishes that regular Black folk ate every day. Attendants always kept classrooms neat and sweet-smelling. Flowers and open windows allowed sweet smells and fresh air to circulate as male students walked around in their cadet-style dark blue uniforms. Exemplary respectable Black people roamed Tuskegee. Booker T.'s soldiers, "tidy and neat," would pass through the institute and enter society as model citizens demonstrating Booker T.'s pledge that Black folk could meet a nation's standards for respectability. Here, Booker T. coordinated a legal attack against Alabama's false pretenses law.

Booker T. and a group of White folk, including Montgomery City Court judge William Thomas and federal district judge Thomas Jones, all pulling strings in the shadows to conceal their involvement, combined to support Bailey's legal challenge. Booker T. sent Ernest Atwell, the Tuskegee Institute's business agent, to connect with Judge Thomas. On June 24, 1908, Atwell relayed to Booker T. that "the court official in Montgomery," clandestinely referencing Judge Thomas because all knew Booker T.'s mail was monitored, believed they would likely get Bailey's case heard by the Supreme Court if they could raise enough funds. Thomas projected they needed $200 to $300 and urged that Booker T. hurry as the state supreme court would soon hear the case. "[Thomas] is very anxious," Atwell told Booker T., "that you not be known in the transaction, and that his connection with it be kept secret." On June 30, the Alabama Supreme Court affirmed Thomas's ruling, reiterating that the law's purpose was "to punish fraudulent practices, not the mere failure to pay a debt."

Judge Thomas's former law partner, Fred Ball, joined Bailey's defense team. Booker T., meanwhile, solicited money from Oswald Garrison Villard, the editor of the *New York Evening Post*. Villard answered that he had been "squeezed dry" too. "You see," he told Booker T., "this is precisely the kind of a case for which I want my endowed 'Committee for the Advancement of the Negro Race.'" A year later, Villard helped found the National Association for the Advancement of Colored People.

On October 2, 1908, Judge Jones wrote President Roosevelt two letters. In one, he confidentially revealed that Watts and Ball were capably stewarding Bailey's case. "If the case is won," he wrote, "I want these young lawyers to get all the credit, and therefore want to keep my letter to you off the files, and as far as possible to keep myself in the background." He did, though, alert the president to having helped formulate the legal arguments. In his official letter, he warned Roosevelt that "if this statute, with the *presumption* of leaving and fact which it authorizes from the mere fact of *quitting the service*, is upheld, we will at last have a constitutional system of peonage."

As Booker T. successfully raised money, he wrote the attorney general, Charles J. Bonaparte who took over for Moody who had replaced Justice Brown on the Supreme Court. Booker T. told Bonaparte of the work begun by "philanthropic white men of this state" yet questioned "if it will be possible for the Attorney General's office to interest itself in some way so that the matter may be thoroughly probed." Bonaparte, sympathetic to the anti-peonage cause, although mainly out of favor toward European immigrants, responded that the "Bailey case had already been brought to the attention of the Department by the President, and I have instructed a competent Attorney to review it carefully and to give me a memorandum as to appropriate procedure on the part of this Department."

The Court didn't hold oral argument for *Bailey*—it was submitted on briefs. On December 21, 1908, Justice Holmes wrote the majority opinion. The case, he concluded, was not ripe and therefore the Court could not settle the underlying legal questions. Bailey hadn't sat for a jury trial, and thus how the law affected his prosecution wasn't known. Booker T. and his team of secret agents had to start over.

In February 1909, Bailey had the jury trial that the Supreme Court required before it would settle the constitutionality of Alabama's false pretenses law. Borden, manager of the Riverside Company, testified, but Bailey couldn't because of the Alabama evidentiary rule that prohibited him from testifying to his uncommunicated motives. The all-White jury convicted him, and the judge fined him thirty dollars and assessed court costs of nearly forty-seven dollars more. With Bailey unable to pay, the court sentenced him to hard labor for 136 days. The fundraising on his behalf recommenced as the Alabama Supreme Court upheld the law. In October 1910, the U.S. Supreme Court heard oral argument for the second *Bailey v. Alabama*, with the Court lacking a chief justice. Fuller had died on July 4, 1910, and Roosevelt's successor, Ohio Republican William Howard Taft, had not yet replaced him.

Alexander Garber, Alabama attorney general, and Thomas Martin, Alabama assistant attorney general, defended the false pretenses law as a constitutionally permissible mechanism by which to punish fraud, denying that the state intended to compel labor in defiance of the Thirteenth Amendment. Presuming fraud after a contractual breach was a natural conclusion one could draw, they argued, and a state must be free to fashion evidentiary rules to solve state problems. Denying an intent to target Black laborers, the attorneys underscored the law's facial neutrality.

Watt condemned the Alabama statute as violating the Equal Protection and Due Process Clauses, the Thirteenth Amendment, and the peonage law. "The real object of the statute," Ball wrote in his brief, was "to enable the employer to keep the employee in involuntary servitude by overhanging menace of prosecution which he knows must be successful on account of the artificial presumption or rule of evidence making the quitting prima facie evidence of the crime, which is practically conclusive because the defendant cannot testify in his own behalf as to his unexpressed intent."

ON OCTOBER 10, 1910, ten days before oral argument for *Bailey v. Alabama*, Charles Evans Hughes, a Taft nominee, traded the New York governor's mansion for the seat Justice Brewer vacated upon his death. Days prior to delivering his majority opinion in *Bailey*, which he did on January 3, 1911, Hughes brought it to Justice White's Washington, D.C., home. Because of White's poor eyesight, Hughes, the son of an abolitionist clergyman father, read it to him.

"We at once dismiss from consideration the fact that the plaintiff in error is a black man," said Hughes, a man with a serious face, thinning tresses, and a graying beard, reading from his opinion. "The statute, on its face, makes no racial discrimination, and the record fails to show its existence in fact."

Alabama enacted the statute to re-create White ownership of Black labor. The Court should have identified this as a deprivation of due process, given that the statute denied people a stock ingredient of liberty—the right to choose not to work free from fear of criminal prosecution. The Court, moreover, should have identified this as an equal protection deprivation. George Wickersham, Taft's attorney general, wrote in his brief, "It is common knowledge that Alabama is chiefly an agricultural State and that the majority of laborers upon the farms and plantations are negroes." Each reported legal dispute regarding the false pretenses law, Wickersham noted, "is that of a farm laborer." The Justice Department presented a strong case that Alabama instituted the false pretenses law to subjugate Black people. Hughes *chose* to disregard it.

Yet, Hughes told White, listening on with a warm, round face, he held Alabama's law unconstitutional. Key to Hughes's reasoning was the timeline of the law's origins. Only after prosecutors floundered at proving fraudulent intent under the original version did the state revise it. The law convicted Bailey, Hughes reasoned, not facts presented at trial, which denied him procedural due process. In other words, the process by which the state took Bailey's liberty was a sham, falling below necessary standards. "Had it not been for this statutory presumption," Hughes read, "no one would be heard to say that Bailey could have been convicted." The state presented no evidence of Bailey's purported fraud at the time he signed the contract. Rather he worked for "upwards of a month."

But the law provided that the state only needed to establish that Bailey left his employment and failed to repay his advance in order for the jury to convict. "Was not the case the same in effect as if the statute had made it a criminal act to leave the service without just cause and without liquidating the debt? To say that he has been found guilty of an intent to injure or defraud his employer, and not merely for breaking his contract and not paying his debt, is a distinction without a difference to Bailey." Worse yet, the state evidentiary rule barred Bailey's testimony to his uncommunicated motives. Once he signed the contract and pocketed his advance, the law required that Bailey labor, or be convicted of a crime if he did not repay the advance. The statute compelled him to work because of indebtedness, which constituted peonage and violated the Thirteenth Amendment.

Once Hughes finished reading, White said the opinion "Cannot be improved on—clear, convincing and in my opinion unanswerable." Justice Harlan read a copy, responded, "I am with you through

& through. . . . You may well be proud of this opinion," and returned it without change.

After the Court formally announced its ruling, Booker T. saluted the "great victory." He made *Bailey* happen, although outsiders never learned of his involvement. *Outlook*, a magazine edited by Lyman Abbott, a clergyman and social reformer, who had received information about the case from Booker T., called *Bailey* "One of the most important decisions of the Supreme Court in recent years."

In *Bailey*'s aftermath, the Justice Department attacked another pillar buttressing pervasive involuntary servitude. In Judge Thomas Jones's federal courtroom, the White men behind peonage fell into the crosshairs. But the statute they executed peonage under, Alabama's criminal surety statute, survived. In *United States v. Reynolds*, decided in 1914, the Supreme Court finally struck it down. In his majority opinion, Justice Day reasoned that the criminal surety statute forced one to work under the threat of imprisonment to pay off a debt, a method of involuntary servitude. "Compulsion of . . . service by the constant fear of imprisonment," Day, who spoke with a soft low voice, said while reading his opinion, "is in violation of rights intended to be secured by the Thirteenth Amendment."

But the Court, again, ignored the original racial sin that flashed like a warning sign in *Reynolds*—that the criminal surety law fit into a larger whole. This leads us to the central judicial failure of the first part of our journey. Cases came to the Court Chamber, each depicting a solidifying racial caste system, and the black robes failed to articulate a construction of The Trinity that responded to it, that could have helped sketch a new reality for Black people, that could have painted a constitutional landscape consistent with a country that fancied itself as a moral beacon. The black robes, during this leg, could have harnessed the Due Process Clause to create a robust imperative for Black freedom and liberty. They focused on a narrower sight instead: the right of a person to not be subjected to involuntary servitude. A half century of cases afforded the Court all the facts necessary to convince a fair-minded observer that Black life had a cannon pointed at it. The Court's jurisprudence showed no signs that the Constitution's final interpreter saw any cannon at all.

If the justices somehow believed that, for example, Mississippi's

disfranchisement scheme was anything other than a poorly camou-
flaged ploy to defy the Fifteenth Amendment, then what we explored
during this leg, Black people being dragged back into quasi-slavery,
should have disabused them of that. Like a lightning bolt, an epiphany should have jolted the justices—*castework is afoot!*—compelling
them to devise constitutional constructions to thwart caste preservationists. These justices could have compensated for the delinquen-
cies of their predecessors. The constitutional system required them
to construct The Trinity to involve Black Americans as full members
of the national polity. When justices take the oath of office, they are
agreeing to protect the rights of all people, including Black people,
just as the Court once protected the rights of slaveowners. Instead,
the justices continued to promote the desires of caste preservationists as though The Trinity were some trifling nuisance. The justices
dishonored the black robe. They *chose* that outcome. And that choice
explains why they wrote peonage decisions that landed like a whim-
per that disturbed little, rather than writing decisions that rocked
the South like a hurricane, destroying the foundations of involuntary
servitude.

Harry M. Daugherty, attorney general under Republican president Warren Harding, wrote in his 1921 report, "Peonage . . . still
continues in many of the Southern States. The victims are almost
always extremely poor, ignorant, and friendless. Many times it appears
that county officers conspire with the employers to force these unfor-
tunates into bondage, which is worse than outright slavery. . . . Some
of the cases reported in the hundreds of reports received have been
extremely aggravated and in several instances the poor victims have
been murdered when it was discovered by the employer that this
bureau was conducting an investigation." Well into the 1940s, the justices were strikng down replicas of Alabama's false pretenses statute
that refused to die because the Court sided with caste preservationists
and facilitated Black folk becoming a powerless degraded people. A
race lacking its fundamental rights cannot claim freeman status. And
not until December 1941 did the federal government outlaw convict
leasing. Black folk kept regressing into quasi-slavery because they
lived on its slippery precipice. Caste preservationists wanted them on
unstable footing. The Supreme Court helped them make it so.

A brief vignette featuring William Moore, who endeavored to steal Black labor but fell to a bullet, opened this leg of our journey. To understand why Booker T.'s respectability politics gambit had no chance, let's return there.

AFTER MOORE'S DEATH, eight Black men—Dave Powell, Amos Clark, James Tarrance, Charles Robinson, Judson Moore, W. C. Green, Marshall Boyd, and Will Smith—were indicted by an all-White jury in Escambia County, Florida, for third-degree murder. Isaac L. Purcell, their attorney, a Black lawyer who practiced in the county, argued that the state violated the Equal Protection Clause by practicing jury discrimination. The trial judge rejected his claim. The all-White jury convicted the "Molino Eight," tried jointly, of third-degree murder, and the judge handed them each a fifteen-year sentence.

Black necks charged with ending White life rarely avoided the rope unless White jurors doubted guilt. Those hearing this case should have. White men under the same circumstances—defending two kidnapping victims—never would have been arrested, let alone indicted and convicted. Purcell lugged the jury discrimination argument to the Supreme Court. On February 23, 1903, Justice Brewer, writing the unanimous opinion in *Tarrance v. Florida*, concluded that Purcell failed to prove intentional jury exclusion.

In May 1903, a thirty-seven-year-old Dave Powell, languishing behind bars, wrote to the black robes, seeking help, apparently not fully grasping that they had already affirmed their convictions. In his letter that showed he had very little education, what the South wanted for Black people, Powell wrote, "We are not guilty of it at all," referring to Moore's killing, suggesting that the eight were not even the ones who participated in the shootout. Powell explained that "we believe that you [honorable] judges will see that we get [justice] and if we get [justice] we go free! . . .

"We are a long ways from home," he continued on behalf of the six living Molino Eight, "and no friends to speak a word for us[.] We are down south and are colored. . . . We can't get [justice] down [here.]"

And that line—*we can't get justice down here*—encapsulates why Booker T. Washington's respectability politics never gained traction. Respectability politics couldn't flourish because caste preservationists wanted it to founder—they gagged at the specter of Black people proving their equality—and the Supreme Court helped shape the environment for caste preservationists to transform their wants into reality.

Although respectability politics did not help abolish caste, it achieved something quite destructive. It taught Black folk to see themselves through the eyes of those who sought to oppress them. Through the eyes of those who refused to acknowledge their humanity. For when a people believe that their success depends not on internal characteristics, but on external evaluations of those characteristics, the jaundiced thought of the tormentors infiltrates the self-evaluations of the tormented. Black people thought *less* of themselves because caste preservationists thought *nothing* of them.

The Supreme Court stole The Trinity, the culmination of the abolitionist crusade. Caste preservationists yearned to degrade their fellow citizens into a lowly status, not wanting them to ascend from slavery into their civic equals. They continued to embrace an old concocted White supremacist worldview, once articulated in *Dred Scott*, that depicted Black people as lesser beings with the capacity for barbarity and shiftlessness that would subvert a nation, a worldview that justified maintaining a racial caste system. Imagining themselves as stewards of the American experiment, caste preservationists convinced each other that limiting Black freedom best satisfied national interests. They thought that Black folk inhabiting the lowest rung satiated American economic, political, and social needs. And the Supreme Court justices, through constitutional interpretation, guided caste preservationists in creating a racial caste system that the justices could feign was consistent with a nation that professed to live by the ideals of liberty and equality. A nation required to live by those ideals because of The Trinity.

Don't absolve the other branches of government, but rather identify the Supreme Court as the main point of failure. When the Democratic Party recaptured the House of Representatives in March 1875, ending Republicans' complete control of the national government during Reconstruction, a network of constitutional amendments and enforcement laws existed that could have legally required Black freedom. But the Supreme Court constructed the Constitution to leach that network of its transformational potential.

While visiting New York City in fall 1915, Booker T.'s health rapidly declined. After doctors informed him that he would not survive his malady—inflammation of the kidneys caused by hypertension—he hurried back to Alabama. He wished to die at the school he founded with a dilapidated church and $2,000, which, thirty years later, received a half-million-dollar valuation. His train arrived a bit after midnight on November 14, 1915. A few hours later, Tuskegee lost its leader. When Booker Taliaferro Washington died, his people stood in no meaningfully better position than when he took the stage inside Exposition Hall in Atlanta in 1895. Don't attribute the failure of his program to him though. It failed principally because the Supreme Court answered the prayers of caste preservationists. Their accomplices wore robes.

# Part II

# Prelude

S TAND WITH ME HERE in the early morning of July 10, 1964, at this dark and lonely intersection, where U.S. Route 29 meets Georgia State Route 72 in northern Athens. Here, two events will unfold. One within moments. The other within twenty-four hours. As we watch, we will retrace America's race odyssey after Booker T.'s passing. Let's begin with the first event.

Clarence Ellington, his wife, Parolee, and their two sons, Black citizens of Fort Pierce, Florida, along with the family dog, had packed into their 1962 Oldsmobile to visit Parolee's parents in Abbeville, South Carolina, just across the Georgia border. Now, at about thirty minutes past one in the morning, Ellington is driving north on 29, looking for the turn onto 72 right before us. A bit ago, Ellington spotted a car tailing him.

The exit to enter the state highway, an abrupt right-hand turn, surprises Ellington. He veers. The trailing car, at the same time, speeds up to ride beside him. That car's bright lights impaired Ellington's vision, adding even *more* imprecision to his driving, thereby forcing the speeding car to likewise botch the turn. Suddenly, three shotgun blasts wallop Ellington's driver's side door, leaving more than a hundred pellet holes about eighteen inches below the window. The shooter's car darts off. After reaching Abbeville, Ellington alerts authorities to what just befell his family in Klan country.

———

WORLD WAR II FURNISHED White Americans with ample reason to eliminate racial lawlessness.

On November 4, 1944, the deafening cheers of a raucous crowd of forty thousand electrified the chilly air inside Fenway Park, home of the Boston Red Sox. Spotlights shadowed a black four-door 1939 Lincoln convertible as it glided through the ballpark, inched up a wooden ramp erected at the center of the baseball field, and rested on a ten-foot-high platform. The man of the evening waved his worn gray fedora from the backseat, and the adoring throng bellowed, "We want Roosevelt," the thirty-second president, Democrat Franklin Delano Roosevelt.

The crowd roared until the clock struck nine, the scheduled time for Roosevelt's closing speech of the 1944 presidential election campaign.

Japan's attack on Pearl Harbor had thrust the U.S. into World War II. The success of the invasion of Normandy that commenced in June 1944 had catapulted the Allied forces onto a victory trajectory. Battling Nazi Germany, a state predicated on ethnic superiority and opposition to liberal democracy, incited America to self-identify as its antithesis—a nation committed to egalitarianism, personal freedom, individual rights, and democratic governance. In service of this goal, FDR ended his campaign heralding American inclusivity.

"Religious intolerance, social intolerance, and political intolerance have no place in our American life," said the commander in chief, days before drubbing his challenger. "And thinking back a good many hundred years here in New England you have been fighting bigotry and intolerance for centuries. You know that all of our people—except pure blooded Indians—are immigrants or descendants of immigrants, including even those who came here on the Mayflower," FDR said, spurning the nativist impulse to treat recent immigrants as less American than those whose familial trees burrowed deeper into the soil while also overlooking that the story of thirteen million neglected souls kicked off with an unplanned boat ride.

"Today in this war our fine boys are fighting magnificently all over the world. And among those boys are the Murphys and Kelleys, the Smiths and the Jones, the Cohens, the Carusos, the Kowolskis, the Schultzes, the Olsens, the Swobodas and right in with the rest of them—the Cabots and the Lowells," FDR said.

"Our young men and young women are fighting not only for their existence, and their homes, and their families. They also are fighting for a country and a world where men and women of all races, colors, and creeds can live, work, speak, and worship, in peace, freedom, and security," FDR declared, miscasting America as a nation free of a racial caste system, an America actually keeping with the abolitionism that inspired The Trinity.

In March 1933, during the Great Depression, FDR entered the White House after trouncing sitting Republican president Herbert Hoover. FDR implemented the New Deal, massive government spending geared to revive a flatlining economy. Through his first term, FDR shrank from addressing civil rights and championed a New Deal that offered Black people less assistance, by its terms and through its administration. Despite his denial of equal protection, FDR's economic policy nourished Black folk, a disproportionately starving population amongst broad deprivation, instigating a Black political realignment. In 1932, about 65 percent of Black voters cast a ballot for Hoover. In 1936, 76 percent went for FDR. Because of southern disenfranchisement, northern cities provided nearly all these votes. The Democratic Party, once the watchdog for the slaveocracy, had nabbed the Black vote. And would keep it.

In 1942, FDR established the Office of War Information to educate Americans on the necessity of winning the war and to implore the citizenry to view the clash as an ideological struggle for tolerance and liberal democracy against a possible intolerant and autocratic blitzkrieg. Convincing the citizenry to imagine the country as committed to equality, impartiality, and fair play could unlock opportunities for oppressed castes. As one OWI official reasoned, "By making this a people's war for freedom, we can help clear up the alien problem, the negro problem, the anti-Semitic problem."

The OWI, to further this domestic propaganda mission, disseminated posters explaining the need for, as one version implored, "Cooperation between racial and ethnic groups." Another encouraged that "TEAMWORK among all nationalities, groups and creeds made America great. That same teamwork *now* will speed our Victory." FDR, to avert a march on Washington, an embryo fathered by civil rights organizer A. Philip Randolph to protest race discrimination in the war effort, signed Executive Order No. 8802, which outlawed such discrimination in the defense industries. An OWI explanatory poster taught that "[i]t is the duty of employers and labor organizers to provide for the full participation of all workers without discrimination because of race, creed, color, or national origin." During World War II, the executive branch sold the idea that tolerance and unity described the true American spirit, helpful for winning the war and forging a prosperous postwar future.

The World War II–era propaganda efforts, and the war itself, helped fully integrate southern and eastern European immigrants. Warfare thrust Americans of varied European ancestries into a melting pot forged amidst aerial bombing and submarine missiles. As Paul Piscano, an Italian American architect, reflected, the war marked a turning point: the "Italo-American stopped being Italo and started becoming Americans." National policy blocked the Black caste, however, from such proximity-begets-advancement possibilities. Black women's desires to volunteer to service the war effort fell victim to the color line. Black men, operating in segregated units, had little opportunity for advancement in the armed forces, and received scant chances to prove their mettle in the trenches. Whereas open arms embraced the Cohens, the Carusos, the Kowolskis, the Schultzes, a turned back shunned the Black Smiths and the Black Joneses.

In his 1944 magisterial treatise, *An American Dilemma: The Negro Problem and Modern Democracy*, Gunnar Myrdal, a Swedish sociologist, observed how an American creed—the belief system that the Great Maker created all persons equal, that all deserved opportunity—conflicted with the Black experience of racial oppression. The dilemma, Myrdal argued, "acquired tremendous international implications" for a nation that endeavored to sell itself as an inspirational Western-style capitalist democracy that other nations, particularly nations with significant populations of people of color, should imitate for peace and prosperity. "The situation is actually such that any and all concessions to Negro rights in this phase of the history of the world will repay the nation many times," Myrdal wrote, "while any and all injustices inflicted upon them will be extremely costly." For "international prestige, power, and future security," America, Myrdal contended, needed to welcome Black folk into the body politic.

Let's advance to the second event, which will reveal how well America met that need.

FORT BENNING, A UNITED STATES ARMY POST near the Alabama-Georgia border, sits about 180 miles from our intersection here. On July 10, 1964, hours after an unknown shooter blasted Ellington's Oldsmobile, a forty-nine-year-old Black man, Lemuel Penn, a lieutenant colonel in the Army Reserves, had just completed a two-week field-grade officers' refresher course. Penn had told his wife the day before that he remained at Fort Benning the entire time, electing to avoid the "racial unpleasantness" of the early 1960s.

Penn, along with two other Black reservists who too were D.C. public school teachers, Major Charles E. Brown, and Lieutenant Colonel John D. Howard, decide to carpool home. Minutes after midnight on July 11, 1964, they, in Brown's white 1959 Chevrolet Biscayne four-door sedan, exit Fort Benning's gate. Upon reaching Atlanta, they fill up the tank at a Texaco gas station. Penn retrieves a map, seeking a shortcut. He finds a route that would steer them through our intersection here. They opt for it.

AFTER THE WAR, in late July 1947, the grievances of Black protesters pelted the White House's painted sandstone façade. Black Americans, during World War II, championed a Double V campaign. Victory over fascism abroad. Victory over White Supremacy at home. Black troops helped vanquish the Axis powers in faraway theaters yet returned to the same ugliness. The same in that it resembled what they were just fighting abroad. The same in that it was what they had confronted all their lives in America.

On July 17, 1946, Maceo Snipes, a Black World War II veteran, voted in the Democratic primary in Taylor County, Georgia, the only Black soul in his district who flouted the Klan edict for Black residents to cede their Fifteenth Amendment rights in that election. The next day, World War II veteran Klansmen descended upon his family farm and shot him in the back, murdering him. Eight days later, outside Monroe, Georgia, White men lynched two Black couples, Roger and Dorothy Malcom and George Dorsey, a World War II veteran, and Mae Murray Dorsey, seven months pregnant. As many as twenty strapped them to trees, pummeled them, and drowned their bodies in bullets. No one involved in either horror faced prosecution. A Morehouse College student wrote the *Atlanta Constitution*. "We want and are entitled to the basic rights and opportunities in education, health, recreation, and similar public services; the right to vote; equality before the law; some of the same courtesy and good manners that we ourselves bring to all human relations," seventeen-year-old Martin Luther King Jr. expressed. The abominations that incited King garnered national attention, triggering demonstrations, including some in front of the White House, occupied by Missouri Democrat Harry S. Truman.

Three days after the Monroe lynchings, the National Negro Congress, a communist-affiliated racial justice organization, rang the alarm: "The civil rights of all people of the Nation are endangered and unless we act now to stop police brutality in Washington, lynchings in Monroe County, Ga.; rioting in Columbia, Tenn., and shooting of innocent persons in Freeport, Long Island, we will find ourselves enslaved as the people of Nazi Germany were under Hitler." The following day, more than a thousand appeared at Washington Union Station and marched to 1600 Pennsylvania Avenue. Their placards cut through the warm summer's air. "Pass the Anti-Lynch Bill Now." "Outlaw All Race Hatred Groups." "What the Hell Did We Fight for—Lynchings?" From the White House, protesters streamed to the Justice Department and presented their demands—anti-lynching legislation, anti–poll tax legislation, and a plan to erase the Klan—to Attorney General Thomas C. Clark before rumbling to the Capitol.

In the short time since the Axis powers flapped the white flag, world events had reshuffled American racial politics. America, before, could subjugate Black people without incurring much penalty. Now, caste preservationism imperiled the country's new and main objective, a foreign policy objective—restraining the spread of communism and blunting its leading evangelist, the Soviet Union. On March 12, 1947, President Truman, at an address to a joint session of

Congress, laid out the stakes of acquiescing to Soviets gaining influence. On a podium inside the House of Representatives, Truman spoke to Americans, exaggerating the case to scare them to his side.

"At the present moment in world history nearly every nation must choose between alternative ways of life. The choice is too often not a free one," Truman said, a forty-eight-star flag posted behind him, radios feeding a populace his words. The choices, he maintained, were, on the one hand, "distinguished by free institutions, representative government, free elections, guarantees of individual liberty, freedom of speech and religion, and freedom from political oppression," versus, on the other hand, an existence under a regime that "relies upon terror and oppression, a controlled press and radio, fixed elections, and the suppression of personal freedoms." Humanity stood at a "fateful hour," he proclaimed, reading his speech from a binder, looking up intermittently. "The free peoples of the world look to us for support in maintaining their freedoms. If we falter in our leadership, we may endanger the peace of the world—and we shall surely endanger the welfare of this Nation." Viewing itself in a cold war against communism and totalitarianism, the federal government contemplated how domestic realities touched the pursuit of success, learning that its racial caste system marred its chances.

America implored countries to copy its, not the Soviets', blueprint. Tormenting Black citizens, however, tarnished the nation's image, hindering the viability of selling Western-style capitalist democracy to Asian, African, Caribbean, and South and Central American countries. An opportunistic Soviet Union ably shaped Black anguish into worldwide propaganda. One atrocity the Soviets propagated involved Black World War II sergeant Isaac Woodard. A South Carolina police chief, Lynwood Shull, peppered Woodard with nightstick blows, blinding him. After an all-White jury acquitted Shull, the crowd in the packed courtroom celebrated, an embarrassing spectacle for a U.S. government that, at the time, was prosecuting Nazis in Nuremberg.

American leaders pushed for civil rights gains to satisfy Cold War objectives. On December 5, 1946, Truman, by executive order, established a Committee on Civil Rights "to," the order read, "inquire into and to determine whether and in what respect current law-enforcement measures and the authority and means possessed by federal, state, and local governments may be strengthened and improved to safeguard the civil rights of the people."

In 1911, a twenty-seven-year-old Harry Truman, a corporal in the Missouri National Guard, had penned his future wife. "I think one man is just as good as another so long as he's honest and decent and not a nigger or a Chinaman," he wrote. "I am strongly of the opinion that negros [*sic*] ought to be in Africa, yellow men in Asia and white men in Europe and America." Truman hailed from Dred Scott's Missouri, which, perhaps more than any non–Deep South state, clung to White Supremacy's teachings. Realities, though, pressured Truman to unlearn them, and he did. Somewhat. Probably more than most White men born in 1884 would. "My stomach turned over when I learned that Negro soldiers, just back from overseas, were being dumped out of army trucks in Mississippi and beaten," he acknowledged. "Whatever my inclinations as a native of Missouri might have been, as president I know this is bad. I shall fight to end evils like this."

On June 29, 1947, on the National Mall in Washington, Truman addressed the NAACP. The first president who did. "Many of our people still suffer the indignity of insult, the harrowing fear of intimidation, and, I regret to say, the threat of physical injury and mob violence," he told members of the association seated before the reflecting pool. "The prejudice and intolerance in which these evils are rooted still exist." The audience listened as a white marble memorial of Abraham Lincoln overlooked Truman. "The conscience of our nation, and the legal machinery which enforces it, have not yet secured to each citizen full freedom from fear. We cannot wait another decade or another generation to remedy those evils." A month later, Truman signed an executive order that barred segregation in the armed forces, revoking 170 years of codified castework. A president, finally, considered doing right by Black people a national interest. And acted on it.

AT ABOUT THIRTY MINUTES past three in the morning, the three reservists reach downtown Athens. Brown parks on Broad Street, about four miles from our intersection, stopping the car a few feet from the arched gateway to the University of Georgia and near the Athens Confederate Monument, located on the street's median strip. This, in the darkness of the early morning, is where three out-of-town Black men pull over, amidst the racial turbulence that marked the summer of 1964.

Brown, the driver, needs a break. Penn offers to relieve him, and Brown takes the passenger seat. Howard stays in the back. Friendly-faced with big warm eyes, Penn presses his brown oxford shoe on the gas pedal and the wheels spin toward our intersection. Exceeding the speed limit, Penn has every reason to rush home. He has a beautiful family with a wife and three kids and will soon receive his third degree, a PhD from New York University.

As Penn winds through a small sleepy town, Colbert, just north of Athens, he zips past a night policeman, Billy Smith. The car is speeding, Smith determines, and he begins to pull them over but relents. Penn isn't driving recklessly. Around four in the morning, the horizon still impeding the sunrise, watch as Brown's white Chevy hums by us and then the cream-colored Chevy II station wagon, driven by a White man and his two friends, that stalks a couple of hundred yards behind.

ON OCTOBER 23, 1947, sixteen years and eight months before Penn takes the exit onto Georgia Route 72, a small NAACP delegation headed by Walter White, the association's executive secretary, and W. E. B. Du Bois, its director of special research, entered the United Nations building in Lake Success, New York, a small village on Long Island. Formed in 1945 in the shadows of the Second World War to prevent a third, the United Nations operated in its temporary home, a large office building, outside of which the fifty-five flags of the member nations formed a circle. Days before, White had written a column that addressed how American racism undermined national interests. "A Scandinavian journalist tells me that throughout Europe," White wrote, "the Communists are utilizing treatment of the Negro in the United States as their major weapon in attempting to prove that the United States is hypocritical in saying it believes in human freedom while it permits lynching, disfranchisement and economic injustice against colored persons to continue."

Having leapt to the forefront as America's leading caste abolitionist organization, the NAACP celebrated its thirty-eighth year in 1947, boasting more than fifteen hundred branches and more than a half million members. On this day, at an official ceremony, in front of two high-ranking U.N. officials, Henri Laugier and Dr. John P. Humphrey, the NAACP took one of the boldest steps for Black freedom in the mid-twentieth century. White and Du Bois formally requested the United Nations to intervene on behalf of Black Americans. White, a fifty-four-year-old Black man who could pass for White, delivered the introduction.

"Because freedom is indivisible and can be denied to no human being anywhere on the face of the earth without abridgment of the freedom of all other human beings," White said, "[b]ecause injustice against black men in America has repercussion upon the status and future of brown men in India, yellow men in China, and black men in Africa, we submit that no lasting cure of the causes of war can be found until discrimination, based on race or skin color is wiped out in the United States and throughout the world."

With a face weathered by age and racism, Du Bois formally presented a document he spearheaded and edited, "An Appeal to the World: A Statement on the Denial of Human Rights to Minorities in the Case of the Citizens of Negro Descent in the United States of America and an Appeal to the United Nations for Redress." "This protest," the seventy-nine-year-old Harvard-trained academic said, "is a frank and earnest appeal to all the world for elemental Justice against the treatment which the United States has visited upon us for three centuries. . . . It is to induce the nations of the world to persuade this nation to be just to its own people, that we have prepared and now present to you this . . . documented statement of grievances, and we firmly believe that the situation pictured here is as much your concern as ours."

"I was humiliated," Attorney General Thomas C. Clark said, "to realize that in our America there could be the slightest foundation for such a petition. And that the association could conclude that amongst all of our honorable institutions there was no tribunal to which such a petition could be presented with hope of redress."

The Soviets requested a copy, as did Czechoslovakia, Egypt, Pakistan, Mexico, Denmark, India, Liberia, Haiti, and Poland. The U.N. rejected the NAACP's intervention plea. Humphrey informed the delegation that the U.N. "has no power to take any action in regard to any complaints concerning human rights."

In December 1947, Truman's Committee on Civil Rights released its final report. Across nearly 180 pages, *To Secure These Rights* charged that racism undermined the country's anticommunist efforts and prevented the "promise of freedom . . . to be reached." It corroborated the work that Du Bois had introduced at the U.N. The Truman administration explained the depths of the wounds and encouraged the nation to heal them, something that conflicted with the worldviews of the three caste preservationists trailing Penn, Brown, and Howard.

AROUND FOUR IN THE MORNING, James Lackey, a twenty-nine-year-old White gas station attendant with insecurities about his misshapen head, is driving Cecil Myers's cream-colored Chevy station wagon accompanied by Myers, a twenty-five-year-old textile mill laborer, sitting in the passenger seat, and Joseph Howard Sims, a forty-one-year-old machinist and gun collector, in the back. As the three White men cruise Athens, they spot Brown's Chevrolet and its rear D.C. license plate.

"That must be some of President Johnson's boys," Sims says, referring to President Lyndon Baines Johnson.

Myers tells Lackey to tail the car. Sims instructs him to hang back to escape detection. As Penn turns onto Georgia Route 72 and next onto Georgia Route 172, Lackey follows far away enough that Penn doesn't notice.

"What [are you] going to do?" Lackey asks.

Sims replies, "I'm going to kill me a nigger."

Each belongs to the Klan, members of its third wave. After the second wave of the 1920s waned, the Klan resurfaced in the 1950s to counteract the Civil Rights Movement much as the first iteration emerged to crush Reconstruction.

Georgia Route 172 appeared like a major highway on the map when Penn, Brown, and Howard were choosing their itinerary at the gas station. In reality, they chose a two-lane back road through a desolate area, a narrow artery cutting through small farms among barren reddish clay hills. Penn turns widely around a chicken farm. Moments later, Lackey does too. The end of the turn transitions into a straight drive down a long hill that leads to a concrete bridge over a gorge in the Broad River. As they descend that hill, Sims and Myers direct Lackey to speed up and ride alongside the Chevy. This is the final leg of the Black officers' back road shortcut. At about fifteen minutes until five, Lackey accelerates next to Penn.

ON THE MORNING OF MARCH 12, 1956, the prospect of the caste system's demise activated southern Democratic senators.

In advance of oral argument for *Brown v. Board of Education*, the Justice Department, under Republican president Dwight Eisenhower, filed a brief with the Supreme Court supporting the plaintiffs, Black schoolchildren represented by NAACP attorneys. Segregated public schools, the plaintiffs argued, violated the Fourteenth Amendment. The Justice Department brief agreed and invoked the expense segregation exacted on foreign policy as an additional rationale for overturning *Plessy*. "The segregation of school children on a racial basis is one of the practices in the United States that has been singled out for hostile foreign comment in the United Nations and elsewhere," the brief underscored. In *Brown*, decided May 17, 1954, a unanimous Supreme Court, speaking through Chief Justice Earl Warren, wrote, "We conclude that, in the field of public education, the doctrine of 'separate but equal' has no place. Separate educational facilities are inherently unequal," invalidating de jure school segregation, or segregation by law, in twenty-one states. The North's battlefield victory ignited the first Reconstruction. The NAACP's courtroom victory launched the second.

On May 31, 1955, the Supreme Court announced its *Brown II* decision. In that case, the Court required de jure segregated school districts to desegregate "with all deliberate speed," delivering a one-two punch, the gravest hazard to systemic racial oppression that caste preservationists had encountered since the ratification of the Fifteenth Amendment. Many defiant congressional southern Democrats refused to concede defeat, wanting to articulate rage about the Court upending precedent. A smaller minority preferred silence. Folk in both camps, though, understood that their White constituents expected them, their national representatives, to counterattack.

South Carolina senator Strom Thurmond preferred that the southern caucus sound a strident call to arms for White southerners who wished to enlist with the oppositional forces. Thurmond had long acted as a leading custodian for the racial caste system. In 1948, southern Democrats formed the States' Rights Democratic Party, the so-called Dixiecrats, and nominated Thurmond as their presidential candidate. Truman's pro–civil rights posture, most especially military desegregation and the civil rights plank Truman supported at the Democratic National Convention, sent southern Democrats searching for new quarters. Thurmond won Alabama, Louisiana, Mississippi, and South Carolina. Truman, nonetheless, eked out a surprising victory. Through a fleeting political movement, Thurmond and the Dixiecrats ignited the South's recommitment to states' rights and foreshadowed southern Democrats splitting from the national party.

In early February 1956, Virginia senator Harry F. Byrd endorsed Thurmond's idea. "If we can organize Southern states for massive resistance," Byrd declared, "I think that in time the rest of the country will realize that racial integration is not going to be accepted in the South." Byrd and Thurmond had composed three response drafts to the school desegregation decisions, but their words failed to convince fellow southern senators to support interposition, the defiant viewpoint that states could disobey federal laws and judicial pronouncements should states deem them unconstitutional. A determined Thurmond and Byrd, nonetheless, blustered that they would issue an acerbic statement on their own. Walter George, the eldest southern senator, filled the leadership vacuum. He called a southern caucus meeting, which culminated in an informal committee of southern Democratic senators, Georgia's Richard Russell, North

Carolina's Sam Ervin Jr., and Mississippi's John Stennis. They tailored a response designed to convince the nation to back down from requiring the South to disavow Jim Crow education, "The Declaration of Constitutional Principles," better known as the Southern Manifesto.

Attuned observers understood what would happen inside the Senate Chamber on March 12, 1956. That morning, Florida Democratic senator Spessard Holland had appeared on NBC's *Today* show, explaining the Southern Manifesto to Americans watching at home on their bulky television sets. Newspapers across the country, furthermore, had printed it in full. At around eleven, the Senate Gallery, where busts of esteemed deceased lawmakers fit into the niches of the walls, admitted journalists, staffers, and wives of senators to watch history.

Vice President Richard M. Nixon, seated before a black marble rostrum, asked, "Is there further morning business?"

Attention swung to the front row where Walter George, seventy-eight years old, slowly rose from his wooden desk and spoke without Nixon even recognizing him.

"Mr. President," George said, his feet planted on thick red carpet, "the increasing gravity of the situation following the decision of the Supreme Court in the so-called segregation cases, and the peculiar stress in sections of the country where this decision has created many difficulties, unknown and unappreciated, perhaps, by many people residing in other parts of the country, have led some Senators and some Members of the House of Representatives to prepare a statement of the position which they have felt and now feel to be imperative."

George's provocative introduction incited commotion. Whispers whipped through the gallery. Murmurs from pro-*Brown* senators bounced off the red Levanto marble pilasters. California Republican William Knowland, Senate minority leader, called for order. Nixon banged the gavel, quelling the ruckus.

"I present the declaration," George said beneath the recently installed stainless steel and plaster ceiling.

"The unwarranted decision of the Supreme Court in the public school cases is now bearing the fruit always produced when men substitute naked power for established law. . . . We regard the decision of the Supreme Court in the school cases as a clear abuse of judicial power," George said, speaking deliberatively in the red and tan room in the Capitol's North Wing. "It climaxes a trend in the Federal Judiciary undertaking to legislate, in derogation of the authority of Congress, and to encroach upon the reserved rights of the States and the people. The original Constitution does not mention education. Neither does the 14th amendment nor any other amendment. The debates preceding the submission of the 14th amendment clearly show that there was no intent that it should affect the system of education maintained by the States. The very Congress which proposed the amendment subsequently provided for segregated schools in the District of Columbia," George said, correctly relating the history, and leveling a basic, though specious point—something deemed constitutional in 1868 must remain that nine decades later.

"Every one of the 26 States that had any substantial racial differences among its people," George continued, "either approved the operation of segregated schools already in existence or subsequently established such schools by action of the same law-making body which considered the 14th amendment.

"As admitted by the Supreme Court in the public school case," George said, referring to *Brown*, "the doctrine of separate but equal schools 'apparently originated in Roberts v. City of Boston (1849), upholding school segregation against attack as being violative of a State constitutional guarantee of equality.' This constitutional doctrine began in the North, not in the South, and it was followed not only in Massachusetts, but in Connecticut, New York, Illinois, Indiana, Michigan, Minnesota, New Jersey, Ohio, Pennsylvania, and other northern States until they, exercising their rights as States through the constitutional processes of local self-government, changed their school systems. In the case of *Plessy v. Ferguson* in 1896 the Supreme Court expressly declared that under the 14th amendment no person was denied any of his rights if the States provided separate but equal public facilities. This decision has been followed in many other cases."

George finally reached the manifesto's dismount: "We pledge ourselves to use all lawful means to bring about a reversal of this decision which is contrary to the Constitution and to prevent the use of force in its implementation."

One hundred and one of the region's 128 congressmen and senators signed the document, each hoping it would demonstrate the South's commitment to caste preservationism enough that the nation would capitulate. Winning such a significant victory with *Brown*, though, had pumped confidence into caste abolitionists. They believed more would come.

WHEN THE STATION WAGON PULLS alongside the Chevy at about fifteen minutes before five in the morning, neither Penn, nor an asleep Brown, nor Howard in the backseat, notice.

Bang! Bang!

Brown awakens, figuring his car had blown two tires. His Chevy, now with orange-sized holes in the front *and* rear driver's side windows, veers uncontrollably. It caroms into the bridge wall then back onto the road. The taillights of the station wagon, meanwhile, vanish into the fog.

ON JULY 3, 1964, eight days before Brown's sedan thudded against a concrete bridge, Attorney General Robert F. Kennedy, in the East Room of the White House, chatted with Speaker of the House John W. McCormack, a Massachusetts Democrat. Inside the beautifully ornate space, caste abolitionist heroes like now-reverend Martin Luther King Jr. and Roy Wilkins, head of the NAACP, intermingled with Washington politicos in the massive room with gold curtains and gold-trimmed mirrors hanging on decoratively molded walls.

At fifteen minutes before seven in the evening, President Johnson, wearing a black suit and tie, strode past his jubilant guests. He sat at a wooden desk and signed the Civil Rights Act of 1964. Before the bill's passage in the House, Virginia Democrat Howard Smith, an old bespectacled caste preservationist, conceded defeat: "When the roll is called, you will vote this monstrous invasion of civil and constitutional rights of all the 180 million people of this country into the law of the land. It will contain implements of oppression upon the people of this country unmatched in harshness and brutality and raw dictatorship never before witnessed since the tragic days of reconstruction following the War between the States."

White southerners denounced the bill as tyrannical legislation that would deprive them of their God-given rights. Southern Democratic senators had packaged such language with prolific use of the filibuster to block anticaste legislation for decades. They reached again into the bag to perform the trusty illusion and discovered the magic had lost its enchantment. At seven, Johnson addressed a national audience on television, informing them of a momentous occasion.

"We believe that all men are created equal," Johnson said, looking straight ahead into his teleprompter and a television camera. To his right, his guests. To his left, the media. "Yet many are denied equal treatment. We believe that all men have certain unalienable rights. Yet many Americans do not enjoy those rights. We believe that all men are entitled to the blessings of liberty. Yet millions are being deprived of those blessings. Not because of their own failures, but because of the color of their skin. The reasons are deeply embedded in history and tradition and the nature of man. We can understand without rancor or hatred, how this all happened, but it cannot continue. Our Constitution, the foundation of our republic forbids it. . . .

"The purpose of this law is simple; it does not restrict the freedom of any American, so long as he respects the rights of others. It does not give special treatment to any citizen. It does say the only limit to a man's hope for happiness and for the future of his children shall be his own ability. It does say that there are those who are equal before God shall now also be equal in the polling booths, in the classrooms, in the factories, and in hotels, and restaurants, and movie theaters and other places that provide service to the public. . . .

"Let us hasten that day when our unmeasured strength and our unbounded spirit will be free to do the great works ordained for this nation by the just and wise God who is the father of all."

Johnson later shellacked Republican Arizona senator Barry Goldwater in the 1964 presidential election, indicating broad popularity for his civil rights agenda. But Louisiana, Mississippi, Alabama, Georgia, and South Carolina handed their electoral votes, by wide margins, to

Goldwater, who vehemently opposed the 1964 Act. Asserting that the party had abandoned his kinsmen, Strom Thurmond became, ahead of the election, a Republican, triggering a political realignment. According to White southerners, Johnson had betrayed them. He backed civil rights. He concussed their racial caste system. Once a conduit for sustaining a White man's government, the Democratic Party ceased supplying a political high command for caste preservationism. The Republicans, since Reconstruction, had long pined for White southern support, even double-crossing Black voters for it, but receiving nothing. That love came, a century later, once the Democratic Party backstabbed allegiance to caste.

PENN'S HEAD FLOPS FORWARD. His glasses dangle from one ear. His hands release the steering wheel. Brown and Howard, in the darkness of the early morning, lurch toward Penn to support him and grab control of the wheel. Brown feels warmth on his arm.

Blood!

One of the shotgun blasts entered through the back window, nearly hitting Brown, ultimately causing only car damage. The other entered through the driver's side window, blowing the left side of Penn's head off. Three children lost a father. A wife lost a husband. And White Supremacy poached another Black life to preserve caste.

Brown wrenches control of the wheel and stops the car on the other side of the bridge. He and Howard fear traveling in the same direction as the station wagon that shot at them went. Then, through the fog, they think they see that vehicle driving back toward them. Yes! It's the same car. Brown rushes back toward Athens. As he drives up the hill that Penn drove down, Brown continuously looks into the rearview mirror. When passing a stop sign on the road, Brown thinks he sees the station wagon's lights gaining on him. Brown asks Howard the time.

"5:15 a.m."

While driving on Georgia Route 172, he misses the turn back onto Route 72 and barrels into a ditch. As they stand out on the bank of the highway, Brown notices Penn's blood has soaked his clothes. Eventually a motorist spots them and gets help, Billy Smith, the officer who spotted Penn darting through Colbert. After the police question them, Brown calls Georgia Penn, informing her that Lemuel had been murdered. Learning of the slaying, President Johnson orders an FBI investigation.

EIGHT MONTHS AFTER PENN'S DEATH, the Senate Judiciary Committee convened inside the New Senate Office Building, seven stories of white marble diagonally across from the Capitol. The Johnson administration's next bill to secure Black freedom occupied the day's docket. The attorney general, Nicholas Katzenbach, demystified its necessity to Americans and promoted it to senators inside a wood-paneled hearing room.

During the Eisenhower administration, Congress passed its first civil rights act since Reconstruction, the Civil Rights Act of 1957. It empowered the attorney general to sue on behalf of citizens who had been denied voting access on account of race. The act also established the Civil Rights Division inside the Justice Department to oversee such lawsuits. The Civil Rights Act of 1960 strengthened the 1957 Act. Still, the times cried for more.

The Fifteenth Amendment, Katzenbach told the committee, "has not been . . . successful against more 'sophisticated' techniques for disenfranchising Negroes. While, in theory, the Amendment devitalizes these techniques, in fact, they flourish. It is now apparent that its promise is yet to be redeemed, and that Congress must meet the obligation, expressly conferred by the Amendment, to enforce its provisions."

"In Alabama," he said, "the number of Negroes registered to vote has increased by only 5.2 percent between 1958 and 1964—to a total of 19.4 percent of those eligible. This compares with 69.2 percent of the eligible whites. In Mississippi, the number of Negroes registered to vote has increased even more slowly. In 1955, about 4.3 percent of the eligible Negroes were registered; today, the approximate figure is 6.4 percent. Meanwhile, in areas for which we have statistics, 80.5 percent of eligible whites are registered. In Louisiana," he continued in painstaking detail, "Negro registration has scarcely increased at all. In 1956, 31.7 percent of the eligible Negroes were registered. As of January 1, 1965, the figure was 31.8 percent. The current white percent is 80.2 percent. . . .

"The Negroes of Dallas County, Alabama, of which Selma is the seat, have been the victims of pervasive and unrelenting voter discrimination since at least 1954," Katzenbach said. "Dallas County has a voting-age population of approximately 29,500, of whom 14,500 are white persons and 15,000 are Negroes. In 1961, 9,195 of the whites—64 percent of the voting-age total—and 156 Negroes—1 percent of the total—were registered to vote in Dallas County."

For weeks, Selma dominated national attention. On March 7, 1965, Bloody Sunday, six hundred Black folk exited the red-brick and white-stone-trimmed Brown Chapel AME Church and marched through downtown Selma and toward the Edmund Pettus Bridge, the beginning of a planned Selma-to-Montgomery march against disenfranchisement. As footsteps neared the steel-arched bridge, the waters of the Alabama River rippling a hundred feet below, state troopers slung batons and unleashed tear gas in front of recording cameras. That night, ABC planned to air *Judgment at Nuremberg*, a Hollywood production about Nazi trials. The network interrupted it to show footage of White officers bludgeoning Black protesters. The parallels aligned too well for White Americans to ignore, no matter how much they may have wanted.

Katzenbach explained why the existing legal tools flunked the test. On April 13, 1961, the Justice Department, under Democratic president John F. Kennedy, sued the Dallas County Board of Registrars for discrimination in voting registration, a scheme effectuated largely through literacy tests. "Two and a half years later, the court of appeals granted an injunction against discriminatory registration practices," Katzenbach said. "Two months later, Department personnel inspected and photographed voter registration records at the Dallas County Courthouse. These records showed that the same registrars whom the district court had earlier given a clean bill of health were engaging in blatant discrimination. With a top-heavy majority of whites already registered, standards of applicants of both races had been raised. The percentage of rejections both for white and Negro applicants for registration had more than doubled since the trial in May 1962. The impact, of course, was greatest on the

Negroes, of whom only a handful were registered. Eighty-nine percent of Negro applications had been rejected between May 1962 and November 1963.

"Of the 445 Negro applications rejected, 175 had been filed by Negroes with at least 12 years of education, including 21 with 16 years and one with a master's degree," Katzenbach detailed, illustrating that Dallas County registrars sought to exclude Blackness, not illiteracy.

In March 1964, the Justice Department sued the county registration board again. The October 1964 trial produced evidence establishing "795 Negroes had applied for registration but that only 93 were accepted," Katzenbach said. "During the same period, 1,232 white persons applied for registration, of whom 945 were registered. Thus, less than 12 percent of the Negro applicants but more than 75 percent of the white applicants were accepted." On February 4, 1965, the district court entered a second decree. "The court enjoined use of the complicated literacy and knowledge-of-government tests and entered orders designed to deal with the serious problem of delay."

Through this process, Black registration had scarcely progressed. "After four years of litigation," Katzenbach said, "only 383 Negroes are registered to vote in Dallas County today. The Selma-to-Montgomery march demonstrates that, understandably, the Negroes are tired of waiting."

Katzenbach's main adversary in the room, sixty-eight-year-old senator Ervin, hammered away at the bill. A jowly man with white hair and black eyebrows, Ervin, who cowrote the Southern Manifesto, defended his hostility to civil rights legislation as a principled dedication to a limited, small federal government, not a cultural devotion to restraining Black freedom. Ervin, a former North Carolina Supreme Court justice, possessed the acumen helpful to southern conservatives who sought to wield legalese to advance caste preservationism. Ervin argued that the voting rights bill deprived states of a power inherent to statehood—the right to set voter qualifications—but deprived only certain states, ones alleged to have an extensive record of disenfranchising Black voters. This, Ervin argued, violated the Constitution.

"There is nothing in this law that is destroying that right of States that haven't abused [the right to set voter qualifications]," Katzenbach said, replying to Ervin's position. "How can you take the position that because States can give the qualifications, they can use that provision to violate the Fifteenth Amendment?"

"You are forcing us to give up literacy tests which have been upheld in the court," Ervin countered.

"These states are not giving up anything they are now doing because they already register illiterates—illiterate whites," Katzenbach replied, pointing out that southern states sought to disenfranchise based on race, not qualifications. The Johnson administration conceived the voting rights bill to plunder that treasured right.

ON AUGUST 6, 1965, in the Capitol Rotunda, President Johnson announced the passage of the Voting Rights Act of 1965.

"Three and a half centuries ago the first Negroes arrived at Jamestown," Johnson said in a slow, stilted pace. "They did not arrive in brave ships in search of a home for freedom. They did not mingle fear and joy, in expectation that in this new world anything would be possible to a man strong enough to reach it. They came in darkness and in chains. And today we strike away the last major shackle of those fierce and ancient bonds. Today the Negro story and the American story fuse and blend."

On April 12, 1941, Lemuel Penn married Georgia Cornelia Fountaine in Washington, D.C. America, shortly thereafter, shipped him off to war, demanding that he fight for the freedom he and his people never enjoyed. For his homeland he fought anyway. Then returned. Built a life. Earned his slice of the American dream that was not cut for him. That was *never* cut for *anyone* who looked like him. And caste preservationism snatched it all away. His wife told friends, "It is a pity that he could live through World War II and not be able to return home and live within the boundaries of his own country in safety and security." But like her husband, she never witnessed the nation pass the Voting Rights Act. On July 20, 1965, inside George Washington University Hospital, just a year after her husband's murder, Georgia Penn died at fifty-two of a rare type of arthritis. Her friends said she could not move on. A broken heart, they reckoned, killed her.

By the mid-1960s, the weakening of White Americans' commitment to caste preservationism, an outcome inextricably linked to the Cold War motivating them to support racial progress for their own self-interest, had transformed the country. Congress, in this environment, had enacted new anticaste legislation. The Supreme Court, moreover, had overturned among the most racially destructive precedents in its history. The nation, as it had when Democrats retook the House in 1875, possessed the tools to enforce Black freedom from life as a subjected caste. And perhaps now the will. Accompany me to the new Supreme Court Building for the fifth leg of our journey.

# Fifth Leg:
# Thurgood and the Caste Dereliction

TODAY, DECEMBER 8, 1953, the cool Washington, D.C. air bites us amid the score of others who likewise fancy a warm seat inside. At the 250-foot-wide oval plaza outside the United States Supreme Court Building, everyone gathered here, including some who camped out overnight, hopes to attend oral argument for a lawsuit initiated to obliterate the southern racial caste system's most weight-bearing pillar. Before we witness a Black attorney, the man whom we will shadow for the next three legs of our journey, represent his race before the nine black robes, behold these stunning stone creations. Stay alert. Their aura of hypocrisy can suffocate you.

The fifty-three-step stairway leading to the grandiose Greek-styled courthouse, completed in 1935 under then–chief justice Charles Evan Hughes's guidance, and its surrounding marble statues, present ornaments of fairness befitting the land's highest tribunal. This veneer, however, taunts the Black caste. An irony-soaked fig leaf too skimpy to conceal that the judicial system, spearheaded by what transpires inside, sacrifices the progeny of formerly enslaved people to help White people forever maintain the pole position of society. Today, one such progeny, forty-five-year-old attorney Thurgood Marshall, a tall light-skinned Black man with dark slicked-back wavy hair and a mustache, marches into this shrine to milk it of its duplicity.

Born in Baltimore on July 2, 1908, the same year the city passed an ordinance requiring separate "Colored" and "White" toilets on trains and ships, Marshall enters the chamber to advocate for Black schoolchildren from South Carolina, Virginia, Delaware, Kansas, and Washington, D.C. Their parents rose when the NAACP blew the clarion that beckoned Black parents weary of their children attending neglected, legally mandated separate schools. For your offspring, their offspring, for the entire race, the call exhorted, attach your names to class-action lawsuits. Help rescue our people.

Marshall and his phalanx of co-counsel believe winning *Brown v. Board of Education* will finish the caste abolitionist crusade for complete freedom. The bigwigs at the NAACP predict that the demise of *Plessy v. Ferguson* and segregation will usher Black folk into full citizenship. With a downed Jim Crow, they assume Black folk will reap unconditional autonomy to soar to the sky or spill to the soil, no different than White folk. Recall that more than a century ago, abolitionists trusted that Black folk proving their equality would smother all beasts of racial oppression, showing how often caste abolitionists delude themselves into buying that White Supremacy could possibly succumb to one well-heaved grenade. As the abolitionists experienced, events will expose NAACP leaders' naïveté. White Supremacy manufactured segregation to disembowel hope from Black dreams and can and will assemble other menaces to achieve the same.

This moment inside the courtroom, nonetheless, arrives because the NAACP, for two decades, plotted for it.

The NAACP commissioned Nathan Margold, a sage New York attorney, to devise a legal strategy to topple *Plessy*. The short, slender Romanian-born Jewish man started in October 1930 and submitted his 218-page report in May 1931. Margold wrote that "if we boldly challenge the constitutional validity of segregation if and when accompanied irremediably by discrimination, we can strike directly at the most prolific sources of discrimination." *Plessy* permits separation but requires equality. Thus, when a state segregates Black schoolchildren but provides them unequal education, the state violates *Plessy*'s "separate but equal" construction of the Equal Protection Clause. Margold's strategy, if successful, would've compelled Jim Crow states to fund White and Black education equally. The NAACP predicted that those states, to avoid maintaining a prohibitively expensive dual school system, would've desegregated voluntarily. "The Association does not intend to endorse the principle of segregation," an internal 1934 memorandum explained, "but to fight segregation by making it so expensive to the State that there will be a disposition on the part of the taxpayer to do away with it." The Margold Report inspired the NAACP's eventual Jim Crow assassination plot.

After becoming the NAACP's lead attorney in 1935, the refined and brilliant Black Harvard Law graduate Charles Hamilton Houston inaugurated the association's school desegregation efforts. A year later, Houston, the former dean of Howard Law School, hired a tall and lean twenty-eight-year-old Marshall, the top student in Howard Law's 1934 class, as an assistant special counsel. Marshall worked alongside Houston inside the 69 Fifth Avenue Manhattan NAACP headquarters. "I don't know of anybody I would rather have in the office than you or anybody who can do a better job of research and preparation of cases," wrote Houston to his former pupil. Before that, Marshall scraped by from his one-room Baltimore office with but a desk, phone, old rug, and few paying clients.

Houston contended that confining Black folk to separate, neglected schools kept them undereducated and therefore easily subjugated. "Discrimination in education is symbolic of all the more drastic discrimination which Negroes suffer in American life," Houston once observed. Caste preservationists wanted to indoctrinate Black folk into accepting second-class citizenship as normal. The way things should be. The way they would be always. Checkmating segregated education, to Houston, would confiscate the enemy's strongest mind-controlling sedative.

Back in 1933, Marshall first worked with Houston, at the time Howard Law's dean, on the criminal defense of George Crawford, a Black man charged with murdering two White women in Virginia. They saved Crawford from a death sentence, an improbability given the circumstances. After graduation, Marshall accompanied Houston during an investigation of dilapidated southern Black schools with mud floors and porous roofs. "A lawyer," Houston once told his Howard Law students, "is either a social engineer or a parasite on society." In Marshall, Houston discovered his greatest social engineer, what Houston described as "a highly skilled, perceptive, sensitive lawyer who [understands] the Constitution of the United States and [knows] how to explore its uses in the solving of problems of local communities and in bettering conditions of the underprivileged citizens." The social engineer, Houston admonished, could make America, for Black people, a more hospitable place to call home. "The lawyer was there to bear the brunt of getting rid of segregation," Marshall observed, the grasshopper imparting the sensei's wisdom. "And Houston made public statements that Black lawyers he trained at Howard would become social engineers rather than lawyers. That was our purpose in life." Cornelius Jones operated as a proto-social engineer. Houston, as a lawyer, bested him in every way.

Rather than attack public education for schoolchildren, Houston, with Marshall as his lieutenant, started at the graduate and professional school level, targeting states that lacked equal educational opportunities for Black adults. In Houston's first segregation case to reach the Supreme Court, *Missouri ex rel. Gaines v. Canada*, Missouri, a state with no public Black law school, offered to pay Lloyd Gaines's law school tuition in an adjacent state. In 1938, the Supreme Court held that Missouri providing no Black in-state option violated the Equal Protection Clause. A state, the Court ruled, couldn't offload its constitutional obligation onto another. Caste preservationists, in response, threw together Jim Crow professional schools.

In 1940, Marshall succeeded Houston as the NAACP's chief attorney, assuming control over the desegregation strategy. He produced, winning in *Sipuel v. Board of Regents of the University of Oklahoma*, decided by the Court in 1948. The University of Oklahoma's law school, Marshall successfully argued, had to admit Ada Lois Sipuel because the state offered no legal education for Black Oklahomans, violating the Equal Protection Clause. In *Sweatt v. Painter*, decided in 1950, Marshall convinced the Court that the Equal Protection Clause required the University of Texas's all-White law school to enroll Heman Sweatt because it, from educational quality to prestige, massively outshone the state's hastily assembled Jim Crow law school. The Court, in other words, required the South to satisfy the equality obligation in separate but equal.

The Court's opinion in *McLaurin v. Oklahoma State Regents*, decided the same day as *Sweatt*, flashed another smile across Marshall's genial face. George McLaurin attended the University of Oklahoma to pursue his doctorate but endured disparate treatment. Sat in segregated classroom seating. Sat at a separate chair in the library. Sat at a designated spot in the cafeteria. The Court ruled that Oklahoma withheld equal protection. After *Sipuel, Sweatt,* and *McLaurin,* where the Supreme Court weakened its separate but equal construction of the Equal Protection Clause, the NAACP finally plotted to take Jim Crow's heart, deciding to attack separate but equal directly and at the precollegiate level. "We are going to insist on nonsegregation in American public education from top to bottom—from law school to kindergarten," said Marshall after a late-June 1950 two-day conference at the association's headquarters.

Marshall argued inside the Court Chamber in December 1952, representing his schoolchildren clients. He told the justices that "racial segregation in and of itself was . . . a denial of equality." After that oral argument, the justices concluded that in a case that could disrupt social and legal arrangements affecting millions, they must avoid speaking with multiple, separate voices, grasping that returning with a nonunanimous decision would weaken the Court's esteem and sow discord. The Court requested that the parties return for reargument, which we will soon witness.

The defendant Jim Crow jurisdictions, in their briefs, argued that the Court correctly decided *Plessy* in 1896. Their attorneys, headlined by an elderly white-haired John W. Davis, former solicitor general for President Woodrow Wilson and one of the most accomplished living Supreme Court litigators, noted that the postwar Congress that penned the Fourteenth Amendment supervised segregated schooling in D.C. and that segregated education predominated before, during, and after the amendment's ratification. The minds behind the 1866 Civil Rights Act and the Fourteenth Amendment, they argued, pursued humbler aims—safeguarding only the most fundamental of rights—like the right to testify, own and sell property, and make contracts. Nothing more. An amendment that once tolerated segregated education, a practice which existed not to demean Black folk, but rather to facilitate orderly living between the races, could not suddenly prompt its extinction.

That the specific intentions of the drafters and many of the ratifiers of the amendment better supported their opponents' Fourteenth Amendment conception rankled Marshall and his team. Yet, they argued anyway in their briefs that the drafters intended to eliminate segregated schooling. Since Reconstruction, the Supreme Court has dulled The Trinity, siphoning off its transformational nectar. As the Supreme Court's anti-Black decisions poured forth spanning The Trinity's first ninety years, caste abolitionists allowed the sweetness of the Fourteenth Amendment to sour even in their own imaginations. NAACP attorneys, therefore, functioned within an environment where the legal community misconceives of that amendment as of limited service to Black freedom.

But excuses free no souls from chains—the NAACP lawyers must reimagine The Trinity. Allow the light of its abolitionist, anticaste origins to illuminate a new, more emancipatory path. Americans are not bound by the specific intentions of the men who wrote the Constitution, or how they expected it would apply in any given context. The words themselves bind Americans, words that support an anticaste construction of the Fourteenth Amendment. The NAACP pines for *Plessy*'s ruination. The words and the underlying principles of the Fourteenth Amendment support the mission. Marshall must focus on that. Only that. The amendment's abolitionist conception fleshed it with the muscle of anticaste. Americans had convinced themselves that segregated education could exist in an equal society. Decades of evidence proved them fools. In the eight-thousand-square-foot courtroom under a forty-eight-state flag, Marshall must inject caste into the case. Must argue that Jim Crow education violates the Equal Protection Clause because it assists in the maintenance of a racial caste system. The Trinity, he must hammer, forbids castework!

But he fails.

"As I understand [opposing counsel's] position, their only justification for [schools segregated by race] being a reasonable classification is, one, that they got together and decided that it is best for the races to be separated and, two, that has existed for over a century," Marshall says at the lectern in the center of the crowded and exquisite courtroom.

"Neither argument, to my mind, is any good," Marshall tells the nine White faces behind the raised mahogany bench.

"They can't take race out of this case. From the day this case was filed until this moment, nobody has in any form or fashion, despite the fact I made it clear in the opening argument that I was relying on it, done anything to distinguish this statute from the Black Codes, which they must admit, because nobody can dispute, saying anything anybody wants to say, one way or the other, the Fourteenth Amendment was intended to deprive the states of power to enforce Black Codes or anything else like it.

"We charge that they are Black Codes," Marshall continues, in a stirring argument as the new chief justice, Earl Warren, seated in the middle, looks on. "They are obviously Black Codes if you read them. They haven't denied that they are Black Codes, so if the Court wants to very narrowly decide this case, they can decide it on that point. So whichever way it is done, the only way that this Court can decide this case in opposition to our position, is that there must be some reason which gives the State the right to make a classification that they can make in regard to nothing else in regard to Negroes; and we submit the only way to arrive at that decision is to find that for some reason Negroes are inferior to all other human beings."

In five months, the Court will return and speak with one voice.


EIGHT MINUTES BEFORE ONE in the afternoon on May 17, 1954, Chief Justice Warren, a white-haired, rectangular-faced man, begins delivering the Court's unanimous *Brown* opinion. Marshall, sitting in the lawyer's section, fixes onto the eyes of Justice Stanley Reed because of a rumor that Reed, a Kentucky native who Marshall most fears will head a block of justices to uphold *Plessy*, hired a law clerk to write such an opinion. Reed, who did employ such a clerk, reciprocates the glare.

"Does segregation of children in public schools solely on the basis of race, even though the physical facilities and other 'tangible' factors may be equal, deprive the children of the minority group of equal educational opportunities?" asks Warren.

"We believe that it does.

"To separate them from others of similar age and qualifications solely because of their race generates a feeling of inferiority as to their status in the community that may affect their hearts and minds in a way unlikely ever to be undone," Warren proclaims, reading from his short opinion written plainly to allow the average American to understand it.

"We conclude that in the field of public education the doctrine of 'separate but equal' has no place. Separate educational facilities are inherently unequal."

Look as happiness washes over Marshall. Self-satisfied, Marshall, who attended Baltimore's Jim Crow schools, believes he's the nation's best attorney, having succeeded, he imagines, in toppling Black Americans' chief tormentor. Marshall turns to George Hayes and James Nabrit Jr., two NAACP attorneys: "We hit the jackpot." He tells the press that the South, he thinks, won't "buck the Supreme Court." And when he departs the chamber, he picks up a small White child, the son of a Texas attorney, and frolics through the marble halls.

Warren's opinion supports, but does not require, an anticaste construction of the Fourteenth Amendment. The conclusion that separate education demeaned Black people and empowered the conglomerate that denied them full citizenship, though, best explains the decision. *Brown* will seize the title as *the* flagship opinion in American case law, the Court's creation that best reflects its commitment to the tenet "Equal Justice Under Law" carved into its building. Legal minds will squabble about what *Brown* means for the Constitution. Nearly all will attest that their way of interpreting the document fits with *Brown*'s underlying logic. Scrutiny sinks an interpretive methodology that produces the wrong result in *Brown*.

Throughout our journey, the Supreme Court has scrubbed the Fourteenth Amendment of its abolitionist origins. The NAACP's campaign against *Plessy* afforded Marshall the moment to restore The Trinity's lost promise by helping introduce anticaste as its animating force. Marshall won the battle over *Plessy*. But will the terms of his victory make winning the war for Black freedom harder? And how will caste preservationists respond to this victory?

After The Trinity's ratification, caste preservationists threw themselves into the work of nullifying it, convincing the Court to interpret the amendments in a way that helped them build a post-slavery racial caste system. After the Civil Rights Movement—the Second Reconstruction—caste preservationists would, like their forefathers before, throw themselves into the work of nullifying The Trinity once more. The next battle will unfold on the beachhead of how to construct The Trinity post-*Brown*. More specifically, the next two legs of our journey will focus on whether the Court would construct the Fourteenth Amendment as enabling reformers to redress Black subjugation through race-conscious policies.

Before exploring that battle, let's probe the era's race politics.

LATE IN THE EVENING on New Year's Eve 1964, Daniel Patrick Moynihan, assistant secretary of labor for policy planning and research, called his two closest aides, Ellen Broderick, his personal secretary, and Paul Barton, his staff researcher, into his office. The bookish thirty-seven-year-old briefed them on their next project— helping him produce a report on Black families. National unemployment rates dwindled. Congress had enacted sweeping civil rights legislation that appeared impossible to pass a decade prior. An observer might sniff the hints of a country solving the riddle of how to supplant a decaying caste system with an egalitarian, multiracial democracy.

Yet, the statistics measuring the socioeconomic vitality of Black folk in urban ghettos unexpectedly angled downward. Moynihan, a PhD historian, wanted to explain why and directed Broderick and Barton to dive into the data on the nexus between the Black family and unemployment. Given the sensitive nature of the mission, he directed them to investigate in the shadows. In March 1965, the team emerged with a seventy-eight-page report, *The Negro Family: The Case for National Action*. Moynihan piggybacked on the scholarship of two leading Black academics, Kenneth Clark and E. Franklin Frazier, to arrive at his thesis—the breakdown of the Black family, provoked by past and present racial oppression and marked by fatherlessness and a matriarchal structure, fomented the tribulations in urban ghettos. "[U]nless this damage is repaired," he warned, "all the effort to end discrimination and poverty and injustice will come to little."

Moynihan forecast that this Black familial crisis, unless addressed, would confine the Black underclass inside a doom loop of devastation, writing that "most Negro youth are in danger of being caught up in the tangle of pathology that affects their world, and probably a majority are so entrapped. Many of those who escape do so for one generation only; as things now are, their children may have to run the gauntlet all over again." He alerted that "the present tangle of pathology is capable of perpetuating itself without assistance from the white world. The cycle can be broken only if these distortions are set right."

The Court should have interpreted the Fourteenth Amendment as requiring states to abstain from castework, affirmatively defeat the castework of private individuals, and ensure lower castes did not exist within their borders. State and local governments, instead, intentionally walled off the Black population from liberty and the pursuit of happiness. Miami, for example, employed zoning regulations to create "Colored Town," a segregated neighborhood that isolated Black people from resources and opportunity. Meanwhile, the city government cheered on private loan companies for denying Black Miamians home loans, meaning they could build neither generational wealth nor flourishing communities. This one-two punch coldcocked Black folk throughout America.

The Supreme Court, through an appropriate construction of The Trinity, could have helped block both blows. But the black robes allowed governments and private caste preservationists to work collaboratively, a left and right hand relegating the Black caste to environments inhospitable for the growth of optimism yet fertile for the sowing of despair. Evidence to believe that skin color would limit their life outcomes surrounded Black folk as they moved through a broader society whose policies enabled White progress. Every second of every day since the ratification of The Trinity, because of the very existence of a relentless caste system, states had been denying Black people equal protection, spawning all sorts of maladies, including damaged psyches, inherited hopelessness, and a wobbly family structure. Black people struggled, not because they were Black, but because they were a people whom people condemned, for generations, to an environment that bred struggle. The Fourteenth Amendment's enforcement clause empowered congressional intervention, and a new national commitment to Black freedom demanded it. Yet, the legislative branch could do little even if inclined to fully right these wrongs because the judicial branch invented constitutional roadblocks. The Supreme Court streamlined Black agony.

Moynihan hoped to disabuse the Johnson White House of the assumption that anti-discrimination legislation, like a crane, would lift the Black underclass and conveniently deposit them into a comfortable middle-class existence. Policy, Moynihan believed, needed to act specially on Black folk's behalf to undo centuries of persecution, centuries of equal protection denial, centuries of castework. "The policy of the United States is to bring the Negro American to full and equal sharing in the responsibilities and rewards of citizenship," Moynihan wrote, articulating his ideals. "To this end, the programs of the Federal government bearing on this objective shall be designed to have the effect, directly or indirectly, of enhancing the stability and resources of the Negro American family."

Three months after Moynihan polished his report, President Johnson delivered a historic speech that demonstrated Moynihan had convinced him of his thesis.


ON JUNE 4, 1965, Johnson stood on a temporary platform overlooking the main quadrangle on Howard University's Washington, D.C., campus. Wearing academic robes and in front of a building named after Frederick Douglass, Johnson proclaimed at the historically Black university that "You do not wipe away the scars of centuries by saying, 'Now you are free to go where you want, and do as you desire, and choose the leaders you please.' You do not take a person who, for years, has been hobbled by chains and liberate him, bring him up to the starting line of a race and then say, 'you are free to compete with all the others,' and still justly believe that you have been completely fair. Thus, it is not enough just to open the gates of opportunity."

Johnson, addressing a crowd of five thousand, mostly Black students and their families gathered for commencement, continued his speech. "All our citizens must have the ability to walk through those gates," he said in his Texas twang. "This is the next and the more profound stage of the battle for civil rights. We seek not just freedom but opportunity. We seek not just legal equity but human ability, not just equality as a right and a theory but equality as a fact and equality as a result. For the task is to give twenty million Negroes the same chance as every other American to learn and grow, to work and share in society, to develop their abilities—physical, mental and spiritual, and to pursue their individual happiness." America becomes truly free, truly equal, per Johnson, not when the laws merely affirm equality, but when even the murmurs of the caste system quiet.

"Thirty-five years ago," Johnson said, expounding on the dilemma,

> the rate of unemployment for Negroes and whites was about the same. Tonight, the Negro rate is twice as high. In 1948, the eight percent unemployment rate for Negro teenage boys was actually less than that of whites. By last year that rate had grown to twenty-three percent, as against thirteen percent for whites unemployed. Between 1949 and 1959, the income of Negro men relative to white men declined in every section of this country. From 1952 to 1963, the median income of Negro families compared to white actually dropped from fifty-seven percent to fifty-three percent. In the years 1955 through 1957, twenty-two percent of experienced Negro workers were out of work at some time during the year. In 1961 through 1963 that proportion had soared to twenty-nine percent. Since 1947, the number of white families living in poverty has decreased twenty-seven percent while the number of poorer nonwhite families decreased only three percent. The infant mortality of nonwhites in 1940 was seventy percent greater than whites. Twenty-two years later it was ninety percent greater. . . .
>
> Of course, Negro Americans as well as white Americans have shared in our rising national abundance. But the harsh fact of the matter is that in the battle for true equality too many—far too many—are losing ground every day.

Passing anti-discrimination legislation, to Johnson, still left an unpaid debt. America, in arrears, owed equality as a reality and commanded the rehabilitation of centuries-old injuries. A majority of White voters had backed him, a president who insisted the nation needed to pay penance. Such progress, many assumed, would soothe Black rage. As Johnson exited the platform, the Howard choir sang "We Shall Overcome," the sanguine Civil Rights Movement gospel anthem. But many Black folk chuckled at the song's rosy lyrics and those who believed America would tolerate Black people prevailing over White Supremacy. A couple months later, the cynics would seem wiser.

THE NEXT MONTH, on August 17, 1965, Martin Luther King Jr. landed in a smoldering Los Angeles torched by riots in Watts, a Black neighborhood in south L.A. Some young, militant Black South Angelenos warned King against visiting—they loathed his nonviolent program that, in their eyes, achieved little beyond publicly maligning Black people. "By the end of the week," one Black college student groaned, "old liver lipped Martin Luther King will come in here and everybody will be talking about how he came in and soothed the savaged beasts. He'll come in here with that old mess about 'Violence whether black or white, is wrong.' Just wait, he'll be here." The rage in places like Los Angeles or Chicago, which still relegated Black folk to a subordinate class, initially confounded King, who had concentrated on capturing equal rights for Black southerners. After meeting with Black leaders, he held a news conference.

"I believe, and have said on many occasions, that violence is not the answer to social conflict, whether it is engaged in by white people in Alabama or Negroes in Los Angeles," King said, wearing a black suit and tie, before a bed of microphones.

"Violence is all the more regrettable in this period in light of the tremendous non-violent sacrifices that both Negro and white people together have endured to bring justice to all men. But it is equally clear, as President Johnson pointed out yesterday, that it is the job of all Americans to right the wrongs from which such violence and disorder spring. The criminal responses [that] led to the tragic outbreaks of violence in Los Angeles are environmental and not racial,"

King remarked as Bayard Rustin, his mentor on nonviolent protest, stood over his right shoulder smoking a cigarette.

"The economic deprivation, social isolation, inadequate housing, and general despair of thousands of Negroes teeming in Northern and Western ghettos are the ready seeds [that] give birth to tragic expressions of violence," King observed, displaying an understanding of how racial oppression, melded with denial of opportunity, produced an alloy of despondency and fury in a capitalist system. "By acts of commission and omission none of us in this great country has done enough to remove injustice," King said, unwittingly indicting the nation for a denial of equal protection as abolitionists and the Fourteenth Amendment framers had intended—denial included inaction as well as action. "I therefore humbly suggest that all of us accept our share of the responsibility for these past days of anguish."

King called the riot, in his southern Baptist preacher cadence, "a sort of blind and misguided revolt against society and authority on the part of people who, for many reasons, feel alienated from their nation, from their families in many instances and from themselves and out of self-hatred, self-rejection, frustration, seething desperation. Because of that plight, they unconsciously and consciously turn to these methods. I don't think there was any individual or group that organized the riot."

The Watts Riot schooled King on how the Civil Rights Movement, centered on certain grievances—codified segregation and disenfranchisement in particular—of southern Black folk, offered meager sustenance to Black folk outside the South. Those in the North and West often framed their oppression in economic terms. "When all is finally entered into the annals of sociology; when philosophers, politicians, and preachers have all had their say, we must return to the fact that a person participates in this society primarily as an economic entity," King later wrote with the Watts Riot in mind. "When persons are for some reason or other excluded from the consumer circle," King continued, "there is discontent and unrest." On the heels of the storm that challenged King to incorporate economics into his program for freedom, Moynihan's research snagged the spotlight.

THE SAME DAY THAT KING landed in Watts, White House press
secretary Bill Moyers distributed copies of *The Negro Family* to the
White House press corps. Reporters solicited answers explaining
why Southern California burned. Moyers thought it provided them.
The next day, August 18, conservative journalist Robert Novak, in a
syndicated column, revealed that "some administration officials view
the report as a political atom bomb."

Some liberals welcomed *The Negro Family* for encouraging
national leaders to transition from a focus on formal equality—the
legal requirement to treat races equally—to guaranteeing that Black
folk *experienced* equality. After all, caste preservationists could hardly
achieve near-absolute Black oppression through honest maintenance
of unequal rules. When Black folk beat the systems stacked against
them—like when they met the requirements of a literacy test—their
tormentors still refused their registration. Thus, why would the
country limit its reparation to formal equality when it did not limit
its subjugation to formal inequality?

Other liberals, though, assailed Moynihan for blaming the victims. A related line of criticism censured Moynihan for furnishing
caste preservationists with new anti-Black arguments. The old racist trope defended Black folk's lowly station as proper for a biologically inferior race. That now rankled ears as taboo speech. Moynihan,
his detractors contended, provided the logic to relocate inferiority
from blood to culture, a relocation White America deemed socially
acceptable to communicate. Other caste preservationists argued that
Moynihan's work confirmed that Black folk were undeserving of
government assistance, which couldn't solve their myriad problems.
Black folk, they vowed, needed to fix their own issues. The storm over
*The Negro Family* ripped for weeks. On December 12, 1965, Moynihan appeared on NBC's *Meet the Press* to unpack *The Moynihan Report*.

"When the report was originally released it won warm praise from
a great many of people," said the show's host Lawrence E. Spivak, a
bookish White man with black circular glasses, from a Washington,
D.C., television studio. "I think the president used it as the basis for

his famous speech at Howard University. What's your explanation that it's being criticized for fostering a new racism?"

"Any issue raised in this sensitive and important area naturally gets criticized and should be examined and studied," replied a passionate Moynihan, a tall, burly man, leaning in his chair, hulking over a small microphone. "But I think you'll find, Mr. Spivak, that the overwhelming response from American scholars, American civil rights workers, and I certainly hope to count myself one, and persons interested to solve this great wrong of American life, has been that the report is accurate and compassionate and useful, and the question is what to do about the problems it raises."

"You start the report, and these are your words," Spivak said, "'The U.S. is approaching a great new crisis in race relations.' What do you mean by new crisis? I thought we were in a continuing crisis."

"This was written last winter," responded Moynihan, who spoke with a lisp. "And I felt that the great crisis having to do with the protections of liberties of Negro Americans in the South were probably coming to an end. We were passing these bills. We were going to get this work done. If we had to pass many more, we would do so. It seemed to me we would now turn to the northern ghettos, the northern slums where just passing a law wasn't going to change things. Where problems were much more difficult, and much less responsive to simply feeling right about them. You had to do hard, difficult, slow things."

"One of the major conclusions you come to in your report is that the Negro family has deteriorated. How is that generalization justified in view of the great growth of the negro middle class?" Spivak asked.

Moynihan conceded that some Black folk had reached the middle class. "But," he explained, "the slums are also filling up with lower class people. Unemployed, ill-educated, ill-housed, for whom the cycle of no jobs, bad education, and bad housing just reproduces itself and [undermines Black life]."

Spivak quoted William Ryan, a Harvard psychologist, who criticized Moynihan's work. "'The implicit point is that negroes tolerate promiscuity, illegitimacy, one parent families, welfare dependency and whatever else that is supposed to follow.'" Spivak asked, "How do you answer those charges?"

"I'm not responsible for the fact that he can't read," Moynihan snorted. "As E. Franklin Frazier said, and I quoted from him at some length, there is a lot of evidence that when the Negro middle class ... gets its opportunity, gets its bearing, they seem more stern, more rigid than most. But the evidence is simply clear—Negro Americans are like any other Americans, and when they're forced into the ghetto and forced into disorganization they have no better protection than anyone else."

"Mr. Moynihan," said Robert Novak, a member of the show's panel who represented the conservative viewpoint, "in your report you say, 'equality of opportunity almost ensures inequality of results.' Are you proposing preferential treatment in the hiring of Negroes?" Novak laced his question with an audible taint of astonishment, as though no reasonable person would endorse such.

"I believe this country owes the American Negro his back wages," Moynihan retorted, speaking in metaphor, ducking the question.

"Should the federal government support preferential treatment for Negroes then?" Novak asked.

"I believe what President Johnson said in his Howard University speech," Moynihan answered, referring to the speech he helped write. "You cannot keep a man in chains for three centuries and take the chains off him and say suddenly you are free to run the race of life as anybody else. People have to be given the opportunity to compete with effective resources and I believe we should make a special effort."

Urban riots unveiled that a national, not just a southern, racial pestilence afflicted America. Most White people shied away from articulating old biological racism. They insisted, instead, that cultural pathologies, exacerbated by welfare policies, made Black folk dependent on the governmental teat and reticent to work, and *that* explained Black folk's presence in the socioeconomic cellar. This worldview contradicted that racial oppression meaningfully impaired Black opportunity. Whatever racism existed, this argument held, resided in the minds of isolated bad actors. Nothing systemic was afoot. Moynihan had unwittingly fed a worldview that supported the racial caste system.

AMID THIS RESHAPING of the racial landscape, a new justice received his robe.

On the morning of June 13, 1967, more than sixty years after Booker T. Washington inflamed White southerners for defiling the White House with his skin and dignity, a tall stately Black man, Clifford Alexander, the chair of the Equal Employment Opportunity Commission, entered the Oval Office. Alexander found President Johnson in his wooden rocking chair. Seated in the middle of the room at a round marble coffee table, Johnson held the names of senators and Chief Justice Warren written on large white index cards in one hand and a telephone in the other. Johnson was informing Vice President Hubert Humphrey of his choice to replace Associate Justice Thomas C. Clark, Truman's former attorney general. Alexander watched as Johnson then called Mississippi segregationist senator James Eastland. "I know you must agree," Johnson said in a monotone, "that this is the best-qualified person." Johnson called more senators, concluding each conversation with "I am sure with this distinguished record that you will support this nomination."

Another Black man, Louis E. Martin, the deputy chairman of the Democratic National Committee, entered and stood alongside Alexander. Johnson telephoned Chief Justice Warren, who said he supported the choice. Johnson asked Martin and Alexander to wait outside while he talked with the man he had selected. The night before, at Justice Clark's retirement party, Johnson tricked that man into believing that he had decided to nominate someone else. The man, incensed, laughed it off, resisting the itch to argue. Barely.

Now the man entered the Oval Office five minutes after eleven, spotting Johnson hunched over a news service ticker-tape machine. As he waited, the man scanned the room, spotting a slew of index cards and papers on the marble coffee table with some scattered on the mint-green rug beneath the rocking chair. The man coughed to get the president's attention. Johnson turned around, feigning surprise.

"Oh, hi, Thurgood. Sit down, sit down."

The two exchanged pleasantries until Johnson looked to Marshall, fifty-eight years old and a bit heftier than two decades before when he argued *Brown*, and said, "You know something, Thurgood. I'm going to put you on the Supreme Court."

A shocked Marshall, with graying slicked-back hair and thick black-rimmed glasses, blurted, "Oh yipe!"

Johnson laughed and then brought back in Martin and Alexander. Marshall sat on an off-white couch across from Martin and Alexander. Johnson told Marshall that he chose him because "you are very much like me—brought up in poverty . . . not a Harvard boy like Cliff." Although not reared in poverty, Marshall affected humble upbringings. For about an hour, a joyous Marshall told jokes with Martin and Alexander as Johnson telephoned enthusiastic civil rights leaders about nominating the first Black man to the Supreme Court. Johnson had planned for this moment once he appointed Marshall as the solicitor general in August 1965, the position he held after his four-year stint on the Second Circuit Court of Appeals. "I did not tell Marshall of my intentions. . . . But I fully intended to eventually appoint him to that body," Johnson later recalled. "I wanted him to serve as Solicitor General as an advocate to prove to everyone, including the President, what he could do."

At noon, Johnson and Marshall exited the French doors behind the president's Resolute Desk and strolled into the sunlight and toward a lectern. The gathered reporters understood that Johnson had tapped Marshall.

"I have just talked to the Chief Justice and informed him that I shall send to the Senate this afternoon the nomination of Mr. Thurgood Marshall, Solicitor General, to the position of Associate Justice of the Supreme Court," Johnson said, wearing a gray suit and squinting on the sunny day. "He is qualified by training and by very valuable service to the country. I believe it is the right thing to do, the right time to do it, the right man, and the right place."

Joining the Court offered Marshall the opportunity to try to rectify his not employing the anticaste framework while litigating *Brown*. He would have the chance, from behind the mahogany bench, to respond to whatever caste preservationists would concoct to undermine The Trinity once more, just as the nation began implementing policies to remedy its inaction and action in the conservation of the racial caste system.

ON MAY 20, 1968, some attendees of the Seattle-based University of Washington had spent much of the day demonstrating outside the five-story Administration Building, an exemplar of Gothic architecture with haunting gargoyles and pointed arches. At twenty minutes past five in the evening, a predominantly Black group of about sixty stormed the building and charged into the university president's suite of offices. The students, members of the Black Student Union, operated under the leadership of E. J. Brisker, an assertive Black student with black-rimmed glasses and a short Afro.

For months, Brisker and the BSU had clamored for racial improvements at the university, including the recruitment of students of color and the money to tutor them, more faculty of color to serve as teachers and role models, and the development of a Black Studies program. In the late 1960s, militancy nabbed the imaginations of young Black folk. The aggressive Black Power leadership spirit ascended, composing the soundtrack of the era against the backdrop of the Civil Rights Movement's failures to improve the material conditions of Black people trapped in ghettos. On May 6, 1968, the BSU drafted a letter for President Charles Odegaard that listed demands and called the university "a racist institution" that "has sent white and black students into society with the racist notion that white, middle-class, Western ideals and practices are superior."

Odegaard's reply endorsed many of the BSU's goals and communicated willingness to collaborate. Two weeks of silence, however, embittered the BSU, sparking their barging into the meeting. Black college students had evolved mightily since Marshall attended Lincoln University, an HBCU in rural Pennsylvania. As an undergraduate, Marshall voted, like most of the student body, against integrating the all-White faculty. His schoolmate, Langston Hughes, later a leading Harlem Renaissance writer, badgered Marshall about his apathy toward the matter. He convinced Marshall to appreciate the necessity of Black inclusion on the faculty. A wiser Marshall subsequently helped propel a successful second referendum.

The BSU had plotted to confine Washington governor Dan Evans, who was visiting campus that day, and President Odegaard, until the two met their demands. But the governor had already left the campus. Instead, the students interrupted a mundane Faculty Senate Executive Committee meeting. Upon entering, some students began the sit-in while others barricaded the suite. The subject of the meeting swung to their grievances. By forty minutes past six, discussions ended, and Odegaard, along with most of the thirteen administrators, fled to an inner office. The students remained in an outer office, joined by some of the administrators who supported their goals. By seven-thirty, the Seattle police controlled the building's perimeter.

At fifteen minutes past eight, university vice president Donald K. Anderson and UW police chief Ed Kanz delivered an ultimatum to the protesters: leave within fifteen minutes or be forcibly removed. But heavy oak office doors that separated the students from the police deprived that shotgun of cartridges—the cops would struggle to get to them even if they tried. Minutes before the deadline, Brisker and five other protesters went to the offices where President Odegaard and some faculty members had retreated. Brisker, blocked from entering, stood in the open doorway and bargained with Odegaard. At fifteen minutes before nine, the two sides struck a deal and Brisker announced that Odegaard had signed the BSU's proposal, ending the protest. The gambit succeeded as various improvements came to the school, including the increase of minority students and faculty, a critical step toward greater inclusivity.

At other colleges and universities, campus student groups adopted militant tactics to spark advancements. Other university officials, like Odegaard, responded positively, backing plans that promoted minority inclusion. Generations of racial oppression had driven racial underrepresentation in higher education. College administrators, in response, endeavored to mend injustice through affirmative action programs in college admissions, instituting policies that would ensnare them in legal battles about what the Fourteenth Amendment permitted.

MONTHS LATER, amid this spirit of reform, Thurgood Marshall visited the University of Wisconsin Law School. On September 21, 1968, during a year marked by assassinations, Robert Kennedy in June, Martin Luther King in April, urban riots, and antiwar protests, Marshall addressed an audience of eight hundred and discussed the Fourteenth Amendment on its centennial.

"[T]he ratification of the Fourteenth Amendment," Marshall said inside the University of Wisconsin Memorial Union Theatre, "marked the beginning of [a] revolution, one in which this law school and especially its students must play a vital role.

"This revolution has continued only fitfully over the last century," observed Marshall, wearing a suit and tie and his now-signature black thick-framed glasses, his eye health on its downturn. "Yet its goals are precisely the same as those which underlie the Fourteenth Amendment. The ideals of fairness, justice, and equality which prompted the adoption of that amendment stand now as yet unfulfilled promises to new generations of men. If the history of the last century proves anything, it proves that these promises are not self-fulfilling. The drafters of the Fourteenth Amendment placed them in the Constitution so that later generations would lack power to negate them. And yet decades of inaction and backsliding followed. The Fourteenth Amendment and its grand ideal of equality under the law have meant no more than succeeding generations were willing for them to mean. The responsibility for making the amendment mean what it says fell anew to each generation. Through the years, most failed."

With the Fourteenth Amendment, Marshall said, America received "the power to make certain that the fundamental rights of all individuals were respected. It was not a time for defining those rights with any precision; it was a time for creating institutions which would guarantee their maintenance. Without the power to enforce basic human rights, they would become mere paper promises."

Despite decades of dereliction, Marshall said, "I'm not discouraged and I'm sixty, the great-grandson of a slave and the first Negro appointed to the Supreme Court."

Feeling improvement, Marshall claimed, "Today, the legislatures, the courts, the bar, and the people of this country are demonstrating a concern for fairness and justice unparalleled in the history of our nation." But, he thought, the people had to fight complacency. He more than anyone.

"And so the task was left to us, the lawyers, judges, legislators, and citizens of the future. Without committed action by committed individuals, without persistent use of the legal and political tools created in 1868, the amendment could not be expected to match its promise. What is essential now if this promise is to be kept is a new kind of activism, an activism in the pursuit of justice. And as we pursue these goals, there is no reason to shy away from the word 'activism.'"

The depths of the American dilemma, as Marshall argued, necessitated policymaking activism. Transcending the caste system would require America to heal the bones and skin it had snapped and lacerated. At least some of the policies that would reverse the damage would mention race. This meant that the justices would need to interpret the Constitution as allowing legislators and policymakers to remedy the effects of racial oppression through race-conscious governing. If redressing past and ongoing oppression didn't justify such policies, then the most effective versions would either never go into effect or live with insecure futures.

Like many colleges and universities, University of Washington implemented such a policy, an affirmative action admissions program that admitted minority students with, on average, worse standardized test scores and grade point averages than their White counterparts. Rejected White applicants grumbled that such programs turned them into new victims of racial injustice. Marco DeFunis, one such applicant, graduated from the University of Washington and sought admission to the university's law school. After rejections in 1970 and 1971, he sued, contending that the school's admissions program racially discriminated, denying him equal protection. He won his lawsuit in state court and was admitted fall 1971. The school appealed to the Supreme Court. After oral argument, the Court, in February 1974, released a short opinion that sidestepped the legal issues of his case because it didn't present a live dispute. DeFunis, already enrolled for years, would have graduated in a matter of weeks. With Justice Marshall dissenting, a five-to-four majority considered the legal question involved moot—the school had admitted him and regardless of the Court's decision, DeFunis would finish his legal education.

The Court ducked the controversy, while a matching one hurtled toward its docket.

WHEN WORKERS ASSEMBLED three green prefabricated buildings on a pasture, the new medical school at the University of California, Davis, cleared a final hurdle in the preparation for its inaugural class. In late September 1968, forty-eight students—forty-two men and six women—striving toward a professional degree and a six-figure salary gathered for orientation at the school's temporary home in Yolo County, a rural agricultural area in Northern California, fifteen miles west of Sacramento. That year, as the wails from mourners of King's assassination vibrated through the national consciousness, the Association of American Medical Colleges counseled medical schools to boost the number of underrepresented minorities in their classrooms. A year later, an association committee advocated that by the 1975–76 academic year, Black folk should occupy 12 percent of the seats reserved for first-year medical school students. Yet, during Davis medical school's infancy, minorities filled only 3 percent of the spots.

In 1970, when only about eight hundred minority students attended U.S. medical schools, Davis debuted an affirmative action admissions program, one like those popping up at more than a hundred other medical schools. Davis started the program for a few reasons, including wanting to redress America's legacy of racial oppression. Davis established a two-track admissions program. Under the regular process, members of the admissions committee whittled the applicant pool down to a manageable bunch, interviewed the most promising candidates, and graded each on a hundred-point scale, based on the interview, GPA, Medical College Admission Test scores, personal essay, letters of recommendation, and extracurricular activities. Regular admissions candidates nabbed forty-two of fifty spots. The responsibility for filling the remaining eight fell to the special admissions committee. Students who opted for consideration under this process needed to demonstrate they had faced an economic or educational disadvantage. Although outwardly open to all, the special admissions committee, comprised predominantly of members of color, admitted no White applicant who sought consideration. In 1971, the school doubled its class size to one hundred and the number of special admissions seats to sixteen. Special admissions admittees generally had lower GPAs and test scores.

In 1971, a thirty-one-year-old White man, Allan Paul Bakke, a NASA engineer at the Northern California Ames Research Center, wrote the Davis medical school. The 1962 University of Minnesota graduate wanted to know how his age might compromise his candidacy. Dr. Alexander Barry, an associate dean at Davis, responded that despite setting no maximum age, "the Committee does feel that when an applicant is over thirty, his age is a serious factor which must be considered. One of the major reasons for this is that such an applicant can be expected on an actuarial basis to practice medicine for about ten years less than the applicant of average age. The Committee believes that an older applicant must be unusually highly qualified if he is to be seriously considered for one of the limited number of places in the entering class."

Davis, on November 26, 1972, received Bakke's application, one of more than twenty-six hundred. Bakke, who finally submitted all the accompanying materials to complete his application in early January 1973—caring for his wife's ailing mother delayed him—also applied to thirteen others. As the youngest school to which he applied, Davis, with the thinnest reputation, offered him, one of forty thousand medical school applicants across the country, perhaps the best chance at one of the fourteen hundred seats for first-year medical school students. Additionally, Davis could let the father of two learn close to his ranch-style home in Sunnyvale, a San Francisco suburb, at a more affordable in-state price.

On March 21, 1973, a nervous Bakke drove north one hundred miles, through bustling big-city highways to the quiet backcountry, for his on-campus interview with Dr. Theodore West, a Davis faculty member. Bakke impressed West, who later described him as a "well-qualified candidate for admission whose main handicap is the unavoidable fact that he is now 33 years of age." Bakke, West found, "articulated well in all areas except in his response to my request that he express his reasons for changing from engineering to medicine.

During this phase of his conversation, he was more halting, more introspective, and I sensed an air of frustration and emotion which I attribute to his concern about the impact of his age and the fact that this probably is about the last chance for him to apply."

A Davis rejection letter landed at Bakke's home in May. Every school denied him, his age sinking his prospects. Two weeks later, Bakke wrote George Lowery, Davis's associate dean of admissions, requesting that he be placed on the school's waitlist, allowed to register for classes, and enroll until a spot opened. "Your letter denying me admission to Davis was a tremendous disappointment," Bakke confided, "but I'm not yet willing to give up my commitment to becoming a physician." No answer came.

On July 1, Bakke, feeling jilted, punched out another letter on his typewriter. Considering the "inexorable passage of time," Bakke wrote, "I feel compelled to pursue a further course of action. My commitment to becoming a physician and serving in medicine requires it." Once fretting about his age, Bakke now pivoted after learning about the special admissions program. "Applicants chosen to be our doctors should be those presenting the best qualifications, both academic and personal," Bakke wrote. "Most are selected according to this standard, but I am convinced that a significant fraction of every current medical class is judged by a separate criterion. I am referring to quotas, open or covert, for racial minorities. Medicine needs the ablest and most dedicated men in order to meet future health needs. I realize that the rationale for these quotas is that they attempt to atone for past racial discrimination. But instituting a new racial bias, in favor of minorities, is not a just solution."

Bakke decried race preferences as illegal and divulged his intention to consult those "in both Federal and state government" about mounting a legal challenge. "My main reason for undertaking such action," he warned, "would be to secure admission for myself. I consider the goal worth fighting for in every legal and ethical way." Bakke concluded by thanking Lowery and stating, "I do still hope to be accepted to medical school. I won't quit trying." More than forty years before, Thurgood Marshall, who coveted a seat at the University of Maryland's law school, might have wanted to shoot off such a letter. He never even applied, though, knowing that the school *refused* people of his race. Bakke did not experience that—the vast majority of Davis's admittees were White.

On July 18, 1973, Peter Storandt, who managed Davis's admissions office, wrote Bakke. Storandt brooded about the admissions process. The special admissions program, the thirty-two-year-old White man griped, equated disadvantage with racial and ethnic minority identity. And high-level medical school officials directed him to admit at least sixteen applicants based on personal or political connections. In his letter, Storandt informed Bakke that he nearly gained acceptance and encouraged him to reapply for early admissions in the fall. "In the event that our decision is [a rejection] you might consider taking my other suggestion, which is then to pursue your research into admissions policies based on quota-oriented minority recruiting." Enclosing a summary of the special admissions program, Storandt wrote, "I don't know whether you would consider our procedure to have the overtones of quota or not, certainly its design has been to avoid such designation, but the fact remains that most applicants to such a program are members of ethnic minority groups." Storandt mentioned DeFunis's lawsuit, not yet even argued at the Court, and also provided Bakke the names of two lawyers interested in contesting affirmative action in education. He closed by spurring Bakke to "make a second shot at Davis."

On August 3, 1973, at around four in the afternoon, Bakke visited Davis to meet Storandt, who had invited him for a discussion. Storandt waited for Bakke in one of the green temporary buildings the school operated from as permanent facilities on the western side of the four-thousand-acre campus neared completion. Bakke, a stocky blond-haired man with a comb-over who stood a bit under six feet, shook Storandt's hand. The administrator offered his guest coffee and tried to prompt some small talk, but Bakke just wanted to discuss matters concerning his candidacy. He peppered Storandt with questions regarding the special admissions program, seeking no information about those who gained admission through personal and political connections. "Bakke was a man who felt as strongly as anyone I've ever known about his potential as a healer of the sick and as a benefactor of the community," Storandt later remembered. "He struck me as a character out of a Bergman film—somewhat humorless, perfectly straightforward, zealous in his approach; it was really striking; he was an extremely impressive man and I felt he deserved a straight answer."

Bakke wrote Storandt on August 7, explaining that he would apply early and sue the medical school even should Davis admit him. "Our discussion was very helpful to me in considering possible courses of action," Bakke wrote. "I appreciate your professional interest in the question of moral and legal propriety of quotas and preferential admissions policies; even more impressive to me was your real concern about the effect of admissions policies on each individual applicant." Six days later, Bakke applied to Davis, one among thirty-one hundred competing for the eighty-four regular admissions program spots. "I know my motivation is as strong and honest toward a career in medicine as that of any applicant," he conveyed in his personal essay, "more than of anyone else in the world."

On August 30, 1973, for his admissions interview, Bakke again trekked to Davis, where his litigation threats had drawn scrutiny. Lowery interviewed Bakke himself, finding some of his views "disturbing." Bakke, Lowery reported, "had very definite opinions which were based more on his personal viewpoint than upon the total problem. He was very unsympathetic to the concept of recruiting minority students so that they hopefully would go back to practice in the neglected areas of the country. . . . My own impression of Mr. Bakke is that he is a rather rigidly oriented young man who has a tendency to arrive at conclusions based more upon his personal impressions than upon thoughtful processes using available sources of information." Davis rejected Bakke under early admissions. The regular admissions committee in the spring did too. Thirty-two White applicants with better numbers than Bakke had likewise received rejections. After learning of his fate on April 1, 1974, Bakke hired an attorney experienced in fighting affirmative action, Reynold Colvin, a former assistant U.S. attorney. The San Francisco litigator once convinced a federal court to invalidate the city's board of education plan to demote White administrators and replace them with racial minorities. Davis, Bakke and Colvin thought, had rejected a man because he was White.

Allan Paul Bakke was born on February 4, 1940, in Minneapolis, Minnesota, to Orine and Charles Bakke. Charles, a mailman. Orine, a teacher. They moved to South Florida before Allan's tenth birthday. When Bakke graduated from segregated Coral Gables High School in 1958, the American experiment, for three and a half centuries, had steeped Whiteness in advantage. Slavery, segregation, disenfranchisement—White Supremacy's handmaidens—all operated as elements of a scheme to advance Allan Bakkes in most every facet of their lives. Even in the decade prior to Bakke's birth, the federal government, through New Deal programs, enhanced the value of White skin.

The Social Security Act of 1935 guaranteed post-retirement income for millions. Social Security initially denied benefits to agricultural laborers and domestic servants, employment held largely by Black folk. Scores of Black maids and sharecroppers, bulldozed into a lifetime of menial low-income work, struggled to care for themselves in their final years. Instead of inheriting wealth, their offspring inherited poverty. The Wagner Act, passed in 1935, empowered unions to collectively bargain. These unions, though, excluded Black folk, blocking them from good-paying jobs, health care, job security, and pensions. The Federal Housing Administration paved a lily-White road to homeownership. From 1934 to 1962, White folk received 98 percent of the more than $100 billion in federally backed home loans, racial reparations for no racial injury. The FHA deemed too risky the guaranteeing of homes in Black neighborhoods. From 1934 to 1962, 350,000 homes were built with federal assistance in Northern California, where Bakke lived. Black folk received fewer than 100 of them.

During the depths of the Great Depression, America chartered rescue boats for White folk, while largely stranding Black Americans. The original race preference tree, planted in 1619 and nurtured ever since, bore fruit reserved for White mouths. And it sustained them, for centuries, nourishing millions of White families into the middle class. When President Johnson observed in his Howard speech the widening gap between Black and White, he omitted how the hands of policy wrenched the two races apart. Unsurprisingly, White folk brought no lawsuits against the federal government to the Supreme

Court for unjustly enriching them, or unfairly denying them the opportunity to eat solely from the trees they planted themselves.

Congress passed laws, and the Supreme Court interpreted The Trinity, to stop segregation and other instruments of the racial caste system. In response, White plaintiffs, on behalf of White people, sought to harness the Equal Protection Clause to lock in the White racial advantages that they had amassed since colonial America. If federal and state governments could not atone for their wrongdoing, White folk would continue earning interest on White Supremacy's past investments in them. Bakke's case was the next step in resolving the constitutional question of whether racial oppression justified race-conscious remedial policies.

ON JUNE 20, 1974, two months after the Supreme Court skirted the constitutional issue in *DeFunis*, Colvin filed Bakke's lawsuit in the Yolo County Superior Court. Petitioning for Bakke's admission to Davis medical school, Colvin argued that Davis violated Bakke's equal protection rights. In late November 1974, Judge F. Leslie Manker agreed, deeming the special admissions program a racial quota that violated the Fourteenth Amendment. "No race or ethnic group," Manker advanced in his opinion, "should ever be granted privileges or immunities not given to every other race." Manker refused to order Bakke's admission, though, crediting Davis's contention that Bakke still would have been rejected without the special admissions program. In March 1975, Manker ordered the medical school to cease consulting race in admissions, halting a program that, between 1968 and 1974, increased the number of Black students twelvefold. Donald Reidhaar, the general counsel for the University of California nine-campus system, appealed to the California Supreme Court as did Bakke, who petitioned the court to order his admission.

On September 16, 1976, the Supreme Court of California decided the case that would soon captivate a nation and foment White resentment against "reverse discrimination." "The Equal Protection clause," Chief Justice Stanley Mosk wrote in the court's majority opinion, "applied 'to any person,' and its lofty purpose, to secure equality of treatment to all, is incompatible with the premise that some races may be afforded a higher degree of protection against unequal protection than others." The court sided with Bakke, agreeing with both Judge Manker's "racial quota" descriptor of the special admissions program and his conclusion that it infringed the Fourteenth Amendment. The court went further than did Manker, ordering Bakke's admission. The governing board of the University of California school system, the board of regents, appealed to the U.S. Supreme Court, which agreed to hear the case, staying the supreme court of California's orders to admit Bakke and cease using race in admissions. Observers understood that *Regents of the University of California v. Bakke* would become a landmark decision, pulling the president of the United States into the most controversial post-*Brown* equal protection case.

THE DEMOCRATIC PARTY REVAMPED the nominee selection process for the 1976 primaries, transferring power in picking the nominee from party bosses to the people. Georgia governor James Earl Carter Jr. best grasped how these modifications altered the race, and, with a superior game plan, slayed better-known challengers. In the aftermath of Republican president Richard Nixon's Watergate scandal, the cadence of the fresh-faced erstwhile peanut farmer who radiated honesty and integrity better matched the nation's anticorruption tempo. On July 15, 1976, months before the California Supreme Court decided *Bakke*, the once obscure governor, wearing a navy suit and a red tie, strode down an aisle in Madison Square Garden, parting a sea of applause. He had arrived to collect his prize, the Democratic Party's nomination for president.

When the blond-haired Carter climbed the burgundy carpeted stairs to the top of the rostrum, the fifty-two-year-old looked out to hundreds of delegates, all praying that he could recapture the White House for them. Nixon's electoral successes in 1968 and 1972 disconcerted the Democratic Party's bigwigs, who had grown accustomed to winning presidential elections since 1932. Only Dwight Eisenhower, a moderate war hero, interrupted Democratic domination. But Nixon's achievements, propelled by the cunning deployment of the Southern Strategy, an ongoing political project to teach White voters to structure their political identities and commitments with their anti-Black antipathies, appeared to tilt the presidential election playing field in Republicans' favor. Heading a multiracial party forced Carter to perform a daunting balancing act to win the general election—appeal to Black voters carrying centuries of anger at a system that denied them freedom and new expectations that the nation would address their concerns, while courting White voters carrying both newfound fears that meager Black gains came from their account and old feelings of racial antagonisms toward people of color.

"We can have an America that provides excellence in education to my child and your child and every child," Carter said, head moving side to side as he read his acceptance speech from two teleprompters. "We can have an America that encourages and takes pride in our ethnic diversity, our religious diversity, our cultural diversity—knowing that out of this pluralistic heritage has come the strength and the vitality and the creativity that has made us great and will keep us great," he claimed while pumping his right hand as the multiracial audience exploded into cheers. "We can have an America where freedom, on the one hand, and equality, on the other hand, are mutually supportive and not in conflict, and where the dreams of our nation's first leaders are fully realized in our own day and age." But what percentage of White folk believed that equality for Black folk posed no threat to what they considered their freedom?

Four months later, Carter narrowly defeated incumbent Gerald Ford, suturing together the New Deal coalition that FDR forged in the crucible of the Great Depression—labor union members, religious minorities, Black people, White southerners, and White blue-collar voters. His reelection hopes hinged on keeping the fragments intact.

*Bakke* entangled Carter, in his first year as president, in a race controversy that split his coalition. Carter cautiously navigated the choppy political affirmative action waters, while one White cabinet member, a forty-six-year-old from Brooklyn, goaded the administration to shout into the bullhorn that states could remedy systemic racism with race-conscious solutions.

ON JUNE 7, 1977, Joseph A. Califano Jr., the secretary of health, education and welfare, and about twenty leaders representing eight Jewish American interest groups, gathered around his large round office table, leaving it half filled, inside the minimalist South Portal Building in D.C. Comments he uttered weeks prior championing Davis's special admissions program incensed them. They wanted to unload their displeasure to his face. Califano considered serving as head of HEW an honor—it extended him the opportunity to aid the most needful. And who needed more than White Supremacy's centuries-long prey? For more than a decade, Califano, a Harvard Law graduate, backed policies to relieve the consequences of the racial caste system. He clung to his beliefs just as tightly as his visitors did to theirs.

When Johnson delivered his Howard speech, Califano served as a Department of Defense liaison to the Johnson White House. He endorsed Johnson's pro-affirmative-action message then. A decade later, his personal stance endured. On March 17, 1977, shortly after his confirmation, Califano told a *New York Times* reporter, "How am I, as Secretary of the H.E.W. ever going to find first-class black doctors, first-class black lawyers, first-class black scientists . . . if these people don't have the chance to get into the best [schools] in the country?" Regarding the *Bakke* case, which the Court would soon hear, he said, "it is important that we not lose the ability to have affirmative action programs which would give minorities . . . the opportunity to get into the major graduate schools and universities in the country."

The next morning, a *Times* headline blasted that "Califano Says Quotas Are Necessary to Reduce Bias in Jobs and Schools." Califano did tell the reporter that he supported quotas but meant it as shorthand for affirmative action. The former, in the popular imagination, generally referred to a set number of opportunities reserved for underrepresented groups regardless of the qualifications of the specific recipients whereas the latter concerned opening opportunity to individuals belonging to historically underrepresented groups who did meet a qualification threshold. The word *quotas* irked many as contravening notions of fairness, creating a mental space where many fabricated images of undeserving Black folk rejoicing with their unmerited bounties.

Two weeks later, nearly fifty educators from top universities sent President Carter a public letter demanding that Califano renounce quotas. "For if it is permitted to discriminate against whites . . . today," the letter scolded, "it is permitted to discriminate against anyone else tomorrow." The educators maligned Califano's position as in "flagrant defiance of law." Califano reengaged the *Times* to retract his quota endorsement. "It's obviously a nerve-jangling word," he conceded. Nonetheless, he affirmed his embrace of affirmative action, expounding that "either because of past or ongoing discrimination against minorities" the nation needed "affirmative action to rectify the situation."

Meeting with Jewish American leaders afforded Califano another occasion to clarify his beliefs. He understood their qualms. During the 1920s and 1930s, prestigious universities like Harvard, unnerved by the number of Jewish enrollees, capped their presence with quotas. Califano told them he sided with Davis and that the Supreme Court should declare its admissions program constitutional. The quotas of yesteryear shut the gates on Jewish people. Davis opened them for people of color. The guests who gathered around his office table accused him of supporting quotas even for unqualified Black students. He replied that he "thought the administration had to support affirmative action programs and universities which were willing to provide access to minorities." After the meeting, the Jewish American leaders disparaged Califano for "inflexibility" and "insensitivity."

Affirmative action programs proliferated in the late 1970s, as did responsive White antipathy. "For much of white middle America," Califano later wrote, "the sympathetic images of black schoolchildren in the segregated South had been tarnished by the violence of life at black-dominated urban high schools. Leading colleges accepted only a small fraction of those whites who applied, so each space given to a black under an affirmative action program was seen by white parents and students as having been taken from them." The sentiment that Black folk were culturally inferior, bolstered by the caste preservationist reading of *The Moynihan Report*, became a dominant White belief, provoking more anti-affirmative-action ire.

In advance of *Bakke* oral argument, attention switched to what position the Carter administration would defend. At a July 28 press conference, Carter said Califano and Attorney General Griffin B. Bell "will prepare our position" while affirming that he supported affirmative action in principle although it could "contravene the concept of merit selection." Califano implored the administration to articulate an equal protection interpretation that permitted affirmative action generally and Davis's specific program. Weeks of administration wavering flustered Califano, who built, among his colleagues, a reputation as self-important and pushy. The first draft of the administration's *Bakke* brief sparked Califano's stewing exasperation that bubbled over at a cabinet meeting.

ON SEPTEMBER 1, Attorney General Bell, a fifty-eight-year-old White lawyer from Georgia and a reliable supporter of civil rights while a federal appellate judge, delivered the eighty-eight-page first draft to President Carter. "Rumors circulated today among civil rights lawyers that the draft essentially took Mr. Bakke's side," the *Times* reported, "and would attempt to guide affirmative action policies away from quotas such as were part of a minority recruitment program in the California school." Given that, historically, the Court often adopted whatever argument White House administrations defended, Califano understandably stressed over the brief. He read it and found it even more disappointing than he had feared. The "brief presented no legal or intellectual endorsement of affirmative action," he groaned, "and flatly argued that 'racial classifications favorable to minority groups are presumptively unconstitutional.'" The draft disowned the position that the Court should distinguish laws and policies geared to repair the aftereffects of the racial caste system, like affirmative action, from those responsible for creating and maintaining it, like segregation.

On September 6, Califano called Bell to condemn the brief. Bell suggested that he consult Solicitor General Wade McCree, and Califano did the next day. Inside the Greek Revival Justice Department Building, McCree, an elegant Black man born in 1920s Iowa, sat alongside two young White conservative lawyers, Nixon administration holdovers. Any race-conscious program, the two holdovers told Califano, was "presumptively unconstitutional." A dismayed Califano watched as McCree, a former Sixth Circuit judge, volunteered no counterpoint. "My God," Califano thought. "[McCree's] bending over backward." Califano remembered that when President Johnson put the first Black man on the Federal Reserve Board, Andrew Brimmer, Johnson said, "I want to be Goddamn sure he hasn't forgotten what it's like to be black." Califano regarded McCree as a once quality jurist but figured wariness about appearing partial toward Black folk throttled his voice.

During the meeting, one of the holdovers expressed skepticism about the possibility of writing a brief endorsing Davis's special admissions program.

"Like hell it's impossible," Califano retorted. "I don't have any problem writing it. A lot of people in this country have worked for years to try to get equality for blacks, to develop affirmative action programs, to remedy past discrimination. We're not going to have that work thrown out the window by a couple of young lawyers."

Increasingly nervous about the brief undermining civil rights, Califano handwrote President Carter a memo:

> Mr. President, I believe you will make the most serious mistake of your administration in domestic policy to date if you permit the Justice Department to file the Bakke brief in the form I read it and under present circumstances. . . .
>
> The brief I have read proposes new, uncharted law in your administration's name—and distinctly pernicious social policy. Race-sensitive programs are not "presumptively unconstitutional," as that brief asserts. . . .
>
> There are few, if any, more persistent, significant, or intractable problems that will touch your presidency at home than the problem of race in America. There may be no more significant signal you will send on this subject than the *Bakke* brief you eventually approve.

The Justice Department revised the brief, but the improvements fell short of Califano's expectations. The new version ditched the "presumptively unconstitutional" language but still asserted that "race-sensitive admission programs have a special burden of justification, not unlike those in invidious racial classification cases." *Invidious* discrimination refers to injurious or malicious discrimination that the law mustn't tolerate, like West Virginia's jury discrimination law in *Strauder* or Louisiana's Separate Car Act in *Plessy*. The brief recommended that the Court interpret the Fourteenth Amendment to bar a program that set aside a certain number of seats for minorities, as the Davis program effectively did, because "affirmative action programs must use race as a way of eliminating unfairness, not perpetuating it."

Califano bashed the brief to Stuart Eizenstat, Carter's domestic affairs advisor, and called on Eizenstat to support the Justice Department lawyers huddling with HEW lawyers to perfect it. Eizenstat hesitated to back such a summit, telling Califano the Justice Department was "climbing the walls" because of his meddling that also distressed White House counsel Bob Lipshutz.

"If you won't call the meeting, at least use our memoranda to argue against [the Justice Department's handling of the brief]," Califano implored.

Eizenstat pushed the Justice Department to change the brief again, mollifying Califano. Somewhat. The D.C. media, meanwhile, speculated that Carter would side with Allan Bakke. As these matters played out, Carter offered his administration little inkling as to his position. Then on September 12, the day of a scheduled cabinet meeting, a page one *New York Times* story carried a headline that alarmed Califano: "Carter Said to Back Bar to Race Quotas." Califano concluded that he must raise the matter at the meeting.

IN THE CABINET ROOM, located in the White House's West Wing, Califano sat in his leather chair that featured his name-engraved brass plate on the back. Carter called on Andrew Young, the ambassador to the United Nations and civil rights leader.

Young, a forty-five-year-old Black man with a short Afro, addressed the lawsuit that grabbed national attention. "The Bakke case is perceived as a betrayal of the black community by the judicial system," Young said. "Bakke has been denied admission by twelve other medical schools—some of which had no blacks or Chicanos—on the basis of his age."

Califano chimed in, telling President Carter that the *Bakke* brief would be the administration's most read brief. He restated the points he had articulated in his memo and urged Carter to "take a strong stand in favor of affirmative action."

Califano looked at Bell, who he thought appeared uncomfortable. Bell said that Solicitor General McCree had been completing a final version.

Days later, to learn the contents of that final brief, Califano had to send someone from his staff to the Justice Department. Califano picked Richard Beattie, HEW's general counsel. After viewing it, Beattie reported back that "it's not quite how you would have written it, but it's a win for our side." On September 19, 1977, the administration filed it.

*Bakke* would force the Court to decide how to resolve the claims of White people who contended that a state policy implemented to remedy past racial oppression violated their equal protection rights. Let's visit a scene from one of the most shameful chapters of twentieth-century America to explore how the Court evaluated cases involving race distinctions, in other words, disputes concerning actions by government that treat races differently, and what that history tells us about how the Court might approach *Bakke*.

ON DECLARATION DAY, May 30, 1942, fallen soldiers, from beyond the grave, bask in the gratitude of the living. Meanwhile, World War II engulfs the globe. I have dragged us to this depressing backdrop, a horse stall inside the Tanforan Racetrack, which sits in San Bruno, a small town on the San Francisco Peninsula, thirty miles from where Bakke will live one day. Spiders, mice, rats, fleas, the stink of manure, and a family. They all simmer inside this cramped stall beautified with dirty, cracked walls. In this space, for reasons that will soon grab you, we shall wade through the twentieth-century history of how the Court grapples with race distinctions.

The Equal Protection Clause, here in 1942, still leaves Black life without friend in the Constitution. When the drafters molded the Fourteenth Amendment, they shaped the Equal Protection Clause as the strongest. Mightier than the Due Process Clause. Beefier than the Privileges and Immunities Clause. But through construction, the black robes have reduced to a carcass a potential forceful ally for the alienated. The NAACP, through sheer determination, will perspire vitality into it, making the clause a real companion with *Brown v. Board of Education.* Starting in the 1970s, however, caste preservationists will summon it to rescue their White racial advantages from the tyranny of a caste-less society.

Laws, inherently, discriminate. A twenty-year-old can't buy liquor. A twenty-one-year-old can. On land zoned for commercial use, a home developer may not build. But a commercial developer may. To declare something illegal is to also declare something legal, and laws distinguish between the two behaviors. An ordinance in early-twentieth-century New York City, for example, forbade privately operated buses, but not delivery trucks, from presenting outward-facing advertising. Private bus businesses lamented this supposed unfair discrimination. In 1911, the Supreme Court upheld the ordinance in *Fifth Avenue Coach Co. v. New York*, reasoning that the city government could treat businesses falling into one class, buses, differently from those falling into another class, delivery trucks. City officials believed they acted in the best interest of the citizenry when passing the ordinance, and the justices deferred to that judgment. This makes sense, no? When elected leaders enact a law, shouldn't judges allow that law to operate absent a strong reason not to? But what constitutes a strong reason?

In the early twentieth century, the Supreme Court lived on the wrong side of this balance, striking down social welfare laws it should have let stand. For instance, the Court invalidated minimum wage and maximum work hours laws that legislators enacted to improve their constituents' lives. Justices who opposed such regulations used odd legal reasoning to construct the Constitution to prohibit what they politically detested. In the 1930s, however, responding to political pressure and FDR's threats to add seats to the Supreme Court, the black robes flinched, allowing social welfare laws to survive review. *United States v. Carolene Products Co.*, decided in 1938, signified this reversal. This case concerned a federal law, the 1923 Filled Milk Act, that prohibited the shipment across state lines of food products that contained filled milk, a "skimmed milk compounded with any fat or oil other than milk fat." Prosecuted for selling a filled milk product across state lines, Carolene Products argued that the law was unconstitutional.

When deciding whether to invalidate a law, courts typically use tests. If the law passes the test, it survives but dies if it fails. In *Carolene Products*, the Court evaluated the law under the rational basis test. A law is constitutional, under this test, if it furthers a legitimate state interest, and a rational relationship exists between the interest and the means used to achieve that interest. Said differently, judges ask whether the law makes sense given the stated goal. The Filled Milk Act distinguished between products containing filled milk and those containing milk fat. Under the rational basis test, judges should allow the law if they can conceive any sensible reason why Congress would treat the two differently. Chief Justice Harlan Stone found that Congress passed the law to protect consumer health. Banning filled milk products, which supposedly posed health risks, from being sold across state lines, Stone concluded, was reasonably related to that goal. The law passed the rational basis test and therefore survived. A rational basis test, an extremely deferential standard, presents the lowest level of judicial scrutiny.

On December 7, 1941, six months ago, Japan bombed Pearl Harbor. Those of Japanese ancestry in America—alien and citizen alike—understood that war with the empire would rupture their sense of normalcy. Hours later, FDR declared all Japanese immigrants older than fourteen "alien enemies." The next day, Congress declared war on Japan. Without evidence of impropriety, politicians representing the Pacific Coast, where most people of Japanese ancestry resided, begged the federal government to address the supposed Japanese problem.

On February 14, 1942, Lieutenant General John L. DeWitt, the military commander of the West Coast and neighboring inland states, wrote Secretary of War Henry L. Stimson, conveying an often-expressed message. "The Japanese race is an enemy race and while many second and third generation Japanese born on United

States soil, possessed of United States citizenship, have become 'Americanized,' the racial strains are undiluted," he charged. "It, therefore, follows that along the vital Pacific Coast over 112,000 potential enemies, of Japanese extraction, are at large today. . . . The very fact that no sabotage has taken place to date is a disturbing and confirming indication that such action will be taken." Bigoted. Illogical. Extremely American.

On February 19, 1942, FDR issued Executive Order No. 9066. It granted the war secretary, along with military commanders like DeWitt, powers to prevent espionage and sabotage. More specifically, the order permitted military leaders to divide America into military zones, and subject suspected threats therein to curfews and even removal. DeWitt quickly exercised his authority, instituting a curfew order applying to Italian and German immigrants and all persons of Japanese ancestry on the West Coast. Then, from late March to August 1942, DeWitt issued more than one hundred orders that required the exclusion and evacuation of all persons of Japanese ancestry in California, Oregon, Washington, and parts of Arizona.

On March 24, 1942, DeWitt declared a curfew order covering where Gordon Hirabayashi, a senior at the University of Washington, lived. Born in Seattle in 1918 to Japanese immigrant parents, Hirabayashi resided in a dorm on the same campus where the Black Student Union will conduct a sit-in protest. Hirabayashi initially obeyed the order. While studying at the library at night, he had grown accustomed to hearing, "Gordon, it's five to eight," a reminder of the directive to remain home from eight in the evening until six in the morning. He would then scurry to his dormitory, Eagleson Hall, another of the campus's Gothic buildings, two blocks away. But one night he pondered, "I can't do that. I have to change my philosophy or I can't do this, or I'm not true to myself, and if I'm not, I'm not a very good citizen to anybody. Why am I dashing back and those guys are still down there, and I could stay longer and get some more work done, too?" Gordon began defying the curfew order.

Shortly after the curfew order's announcement, the government began sticking official proclamations on telephone poles and post office bulletin boards throughout Seattle. "NOTICE," the Civilian Exclusion Order No. 57 shrieked, "all persons of Japanese ancestry, both alien and non-alien, will be evacuated from the above [specified areas] by 12 o'clock noon, P.W.T., Saturday, May 16, 1942." On May 13, 1942, Hirabayashi penned, "Why I refuse to Register for Evacuation." It explained his intention to flout the exclusion order. "I consider it my duty to maintain the democratic standards for which this nation lives," he wrote. "Therefore, I must refuse this order for evacuation."

On May 16, 1942, Hirabayashi entered the local FBI office to present it. An agent confiscated his briefcase containing his diary.

"You know, there was another restriction you faced. What did you do about that?" the agent asked.

"What's that?" Hirabayashi responded.

"The curfew restriction. It's in your diary. Were you out after eight last night?"

"Yes. Like you and other Americans, so was I."

"Oh, then you violated the curfew, too. That would be a 'count two' violation."

Days prior, on May 3, 1942, DeWitt issued Civilian Exclusion Order No. 34, requiring persons of Japanese ancestry in parts of southern Alameda County, California, to register with the Army for exclusion from the area by noon, May 9, 1942. "I felt angry and hurt and confused about my future," Fred Korematsu, a twenty-three-year-old Japanese American, recalled. "I could not understand how the United States Government could do this to American citizens, who were interned while Americans of German and Italian descent were allowed to be free."

On May 8, 1942, Korematsu's family complied with the exclusion order while he stayed behind. "I didn't feel guilty 'cause I don't think I did anything wrong. I'm not like a criminal. I didn't do any criminal act," he thought. But American policy treated him not as an individual, but as part of a mass aligned with the enemy. Right now, on Declaration Day, thirty miles away from the horse track, an officer is stopping Korematsu and Ida Boitano, his girlfriend of Italian descent, as they are walking down Estudillo Avenue in San Leandro, California, in the East Bay. Korematsu, who had recently undergone cosmetic surgery in an attempt to conceal his ethnicity, says he is "Clyde Sarah" before acknowledging his Japanese extraction. The officer throws him in jail. Meanwhile, his mother, Kotsui, his father, Kakusaburo, and his brothers, Harry and Joe, are inside this stall with us. Others languish in stalls here. Welcome to a Japanese internment camp, one of ten such horrors scattered across the West, trapping more than 120,000.

Two days from now, June 1, 1942, the Supreme Court will announce its *Skinner v. Oklahoma* decision. That case concerns the aptly named Oklahoma Habitual Criminal Sterilization Act, which enables the state to sterilize "habitual criminals." Jack T. Skinner, a White man convicted four times of theft crimes, will resist Oklahoma's effort to sterilize him, complaining that the law violates the Equal Protection Clause. The Court, as a threshold matter, must decide what test applies. Because sterilization affects the right to reproduce, a fundamental right, the Court subjects the law to "strict scrutiny," a test much stiffer than rational basis. The law fails strict scrutiny because the Oklahoma legislature lacks a strong reason for not treating like things alike. The state can sterilize a grand larcenist although not an embezzler, despite the criminal equivalence. "When the law lays an unequal hand on those who have committed intrinsically the same quality of offense and sterilizes one and not the other," Justice William O. Douglas, a liberal legend, writes for a unanimous Court, "it has made as invidious a discrimination as if it had selected a particular race or nationality for oppressive treatment." In *Skinner*, the Court simply demands equal treatment. "Oklahoma could continue to sterilize habitual chicken thieves," Douglas explains, "as long as it was willing to sterilize embezzlers as well."

A year from now, on June 21, 1943, the Court will decide *Hirabayashi v. United States*. Hirabayashi, convicted of violating the curfew and exclusion orders, receives two ninety-day sentences to run concurrently. The Court *should* regard both orders as the most recent and egregious instances of anti-Japanese castework. Early Japanese immigrants shoved their hands into western soil and farmed it with practices from their homeland. Their success unnerved White folk who grew increasingly scared about the potential disruption of the region's social and economic order. Politicians appeased them, enacting state and federal laws that curbed Japanese emigration and prohibited Japanese noncitizens from purchasing land, confining persons of Japanese ancestry to a lower caste, protecting White racial advantages.

A unanimous Supreme Court, speaking through Chief Justice Stone, *could* hold—*should* hold—that since the orders exemplify castework, they must pass strict scrutiny. Instead, Stone reasons that because of the war, residents of Japanese ancestry, regardless of citizenship, might subvert national interests, a particularly hair-raising prospect in western states, given the many venues for national defense located there. The Court upholds the curfew order as a war necessity and refuses to subject it to a strict scrutiny analysis. The justices determine that they need not review the exclusion order given that Hirabayashi will still face a three-month sentence regardless of its constitutionality. Stone does write, though, that "[d]istinctions between citizens solely because of their ancestry are by their very nature odious to a free people whose institutions are founded upon the doctrine of equality. For that reason, legislative classification or discrimination based on race alone has often been held to be a denial of equal protection."

This defies logic. Stone should trace the invidiousness of the curfew order not to race distinction, but to the reduction of Japanese folk to a caste using race distinction. Stone confuses the disease, the maintenance of caste, with the symptom, a racial classification. Like every other justice up until this point, possibly excepting Justice John Marshall Harlan, Stone misunderstands what marks America's treatment of racial minorities as abhorrent. People of color wince, not from classification, but from the boot on their throats. The black robes adopt the shallowest, least erudite framework—classification—one that conveniently obscures their moral depravity as co-conspirators in persecution. Abolitionists imparted the knowledge, but disinterest isolated the black robes from it. Nonetheless, Stone's focus on classifications becomes a part of American case law. Any justice could subsequently cite it to fortify a malignant Equal Protection Clause construction.

On December 18, 1944, in *Korematsu v. United States*, the Court, speaking through Justice Hugo Black, will affirm the constitutionality of the Japanese exclusion orders, upholding internment as a war necessity. Like *Hirabayashi*, *Korematsu* leaves behind language that could guide the justices in *Bakke*. "It should be noted," Black writes for the six-to-three majority, "that all legal restrictions which curtail the civil rights of a single racial group are immediately suspect. That is not to say that all such restrictions are unconstitutional. It is to say that courts *must subject them to the most rigid scrutiny*. Pressing public necessity may sometimes justify the existence of such restrictions; racial antagonism never can." Justice Black's analysis falters because he fails to specify that a legal restriction that curtails the civil rights of just one racial group constitutes castework. The maintenance of caste, not the classification, poses the dilemma. In two anti-Japanese restrictions cases, seminal equal protection disputes, the Court neglects caste, overlooking what should animate the Constitution's equality guarantee. Each Court decision, a block, builds on the previous. These blocks help form the foundation. In *Hirabayashi* and *Korematsu*, the Court lays an unsound base.

In 1954, the Court in *Bolling v. Sharpe* will further solder strict scrutiny and racial classification. A companion case to *Brown*, *Bolling* deals with segregated education in Washington, D.C. *Bolling* teases the brain—the Court, in *Brown*, relies on the Fourteenth Amendment, which restrains *state* behavior. What constitutional provision, if any, nullifies *federally* managed Jim Crow schools? Chief Justice Warren writes that the Fifth Amendment's Due Process Clause contains an implied equal protection guarantee. He adds to our discussion when writing, "Classifications based solely upon race must be scrutinized with particular care, since they are contrary to our traditions and hence constitutionally suspect." Here, Warren focuses on the method of caste maintenance, classification, rather than the caste maintenance itself. The Court continues to ignore caste and accentuate classification.

In 1964, the Court will decide *McLaughlin v. Florida*, which concerns a law forbidding interracial cohabitation between nonmarried Black and White persons of the opposite sex. Relying on the Supreme Court's unanimous 1883 *Pace v. Alabama* decision, Florida defends the law. The *Pace* Court upheld an Alabama statute that outlawed "any man and woman [who] live together in adultery or fornication" and levied harsher punishments for transgressors who broke this law interracially. Writing for a unanimous Court in *McLaughlin*, Justice Byron "Whizzer" White invalidates the Florida law, overturning *Pace*. The Florida law violates equal protection principles, White reasons, because it contains racial classifications that are inherently "constitutionally suspect," meaning laws containing racial classifications must pass strict scrutiny. White contends that the Florida law, to pass strict scrutiny, must show an "overriding statutory purpose" or it is "invidious discrimination forbidden by the Equal Protection Clause."

Last will come *Loving v. Virginia*, which the Court decides in 1967. Mildred Jeter, a Black woman, and Richard Loving, a White man, contest a Virginia law forbidding interracial marriage. Chief Justice Warren writes the unanimous opinion nixing it. Invoking *Hirabayashi*, Warren writes, "this Court has consistently repudiated '[d]istinctions between citizens solely because of their ancestry' as being 'odious to a free people whose institutions are founded upon the doctrine of equality,'" illustrating how the serpent, faulty analysis from the past, slithers into the future. Because the anti-miscegenation statute racially classified, the Court holds that it must pass strict scrutiny, which requires that a law be "necessary to the accomplishment of some permissible state objective." Insulating the White race from the taint of Black admixture, the purpose of anti-miscegenation laws, isn't a permissible state objective, and the statute fails strict scrutiny. But the decision *should* have turned on anti-miscegenation laws regarding Black people as untouchables—a people tainted by birth—a hallmark of caste legislation.

This survey of cases establishes that the black robes will produce precedent that reflects that they poorly conceive the nature of oppression. For more than a hundred post-Trinity years, the Court helps caste preservationists implement a caste system all while not discerning, one, that they were supporting castework, and, two, what made castework invidious. They fail to comprehend that actions that help reduce a race to a lower station, not classification, is the actual evil all along.

As we refocus on our surroundings—people living in squalor, enclosed by fences, watched by armed guards—let's concentrate on what triggers strict scrutiny. The Court, in the cases we just explored, selects racial classification as the trigger. And, superficially, one can understand, although should not excuse, the error. Passing laws that mention race provides the easiest way for caste preservationists to subjugate racial minorities. Although castework should trigger strict scrutiny, classification and castework intertwine tightly enough that employing racial classification as the trigger often leads to the same result. But what happens when White people complain about a race-conscious policy implemented to remedy the preservation of caste. Is a medical school admissions program to enroll more Black students *really* akin to school segregation or anti-miscegenation laws? A hypothetical can illustrate the pitfalls of reducing an equality guarantee to anti-classification.

Let's imagine two identical Americas. In both, a plague ravages the population. In America One, the plague can kill White people but only produces mild flu-like symptoms in people of color. In America Two, the plague can snuff everyone. Both Americas enact a law requiring that White people receive lifesaving medicine, in short supply, first. A proper course of action in America One, this practice would horrify in America Two. Yet, if racial classification triggers strict scrutiny, courts would treat the law as a similar scourge in both Americas, a foolish approach. In America One, the law allocates medicine to those most in need whereas in America Two, the law values people of color as less worthy to live.

In the real world, in *Bakke*, would the Court realize that, in hindsight, perhaps the anti-classification principle made superficial sense but is an improper trigger for strict scrutiny? Would the justices appreciate that racial classification is a potential indication of oppression, but caste is proof of oppression? Would the justices understand that America needed to stamp out Jim Crow laws, for example, not because they classified, but because they reduced Black folk to second-class citizenship? Or would the Court continue protecting White racial advantages?

In September 1977, one of Marshall's law clerks, Ellen Silberman, will write her boss a memo about "what level of scrutiny must be applied" under the Equal Protection Clause in affirmative action cases. The question before the Court, she writes, "is whether this unconventional racial classification which discriminates against whites, requires [strict scrutiny]." She continues: "are we going to put an end to all attempts to bring minorities and particularly Negroes out of the lowest level occupations and into the mainstream of American life. If this program is struck down by the Court, so much else will go with it." In his *Brown* arguments, Marshall errs in not at least attempting to install anticaste principles as the backbone of the Fourteenth Amendment. The black robe blesses him with another opportunity from the other side in the battle over *Brown's* legacy.

ON THE MORNING OF OCTOBER 12, 1977, hundreds line up on the marble steps outside the Supreme Court Building, re-creating a twenty-four-year-old scene from *Brown*. Some arrived as early as four in the morning, then huddled in blankets and sleeping bags, protection against the cold, to capture one of four hundred seats to watch oral argument for *Bakke*. Pro-affirmative-action protesters chanted "Defend. Extend Affirmative Action!" as others carried placards, inspiring a sporting-event-like atmosphere. Before watching the main event, let's explore the dueling legal arguments as detailed in the respective briefs.

The regents of the University of California school system plucked a legend from Harvard Law's faculty, Archibald Cox, the former Kennedy-appointed solicitor general, to defend the special admissions program. Davis implemented it, principally, Cox argued, to counteract racism, both past and present, which had depressed the life outcomes of people of color. Cox also presented additional supportive reasons. For one, the school strove to compose a diverse student body to provide a rich learning environment that included students of varied racial backgrounds. The special admissions program, Cox further contended, would improve "medical care in underserved minority communities," eliminate "historic barriers to medical careers for disadvantaged minority racial and ethnic groups," and produce an "increased aspiration for such careers on the part of minority students." Only through a race-conscious admissions program, Cox claimed, could the school achieve these worthy goals.

A large percentage of the nation's Black doctors graduated from two historically Black medical schools, Howard University and Meharry Medical College. But post-*Brown*, those schools admitted meaningful numbers of White students. As the amount of qualified minority medical school applicants swelled, that of White applicants ballooned. If the Constitution disallowed schools from considering race, many applicants of color would stand little chance of acquiring a medical education. "The Davis program," Cox wrote in his brief, "like its counterparts nationwide, represents a voluntary effort by a medical school faculty to further the process initiated in *Brown v. Board of Education*." Cox framed affirmative action, a policy to dismantle racial barriers, as the natural progression of the story the Court wrote in 1954 to forge an egalitarian society.

Cox needed to convince the Court to replace the anti-classification principle with another *mediating principle* for the Equal Protection Clause. He proffered what he called "stigmatic harm." Cox distinguished *Bakke* from cases like *McLaughlin* and *Loving*, noting that the special admissions program didn't demean a race. *McLaughlin* and *Loving*, Cox clarified, concerned laws that emanated from a worldview that held that the blood of dark inferiors mustn't contaminate that of their White superiors. Essentially, then, a line connects Chief Justice Taney's remark in *Dred Scott* that described the Black caste as "altogether unfit to associate with the white race" to stigmatic harm. Given that Davis's special admissions program instigated no stigmatic harm—the idea that Davis thought him racially inferior would never strike Bakke—the Court should apply the rational basis test. Cox cautioned that affirming the California Supreme Court's decision would "stand as one of those rare but tragic instances in which the judiciary has contributed to the continued subordination of racial minorities." Untrue. Those instances happened habitually.

Cox's adversary, Reynold Colvin, maintained that the case turned on whether Davis excluded Bakke "solely because of his race as the result of a racial quota admission policy which guarantees the admission of a fixed number of 'minority' persons who are judged apart from and permitted to meet lower standards of admission than Bakke?" Colvin answered yes. "Because state-imposed racial discrimination is constitutionally suspect," Colvin wrote, "persons victimized by it have always been afforded vigilant judicial protection; such discrimination is unlawful unless the government demonstrates that it is strictly necessary to promote a compelling state interest."

Petitioning the Court to hold the special admissions program to strict scrutiny analysis, Colvin insisted that the reasons Davis offered fell short of that high bar to justify a racial preference policy. And, if the Court rejected his positions, the Equal Protection Clause would afford White folk a weaker bodyguard. Equal protection, Colvin posited, "no longer would be available to every individual, but would depend upon the race of the person asserting it. Advancement by way of individual achievement would be replaced with the rule that rights and benefits can be awarded according to ancestry." The Court, if following this logic, must treat Bakke's claim like those of the Black plaintiffs in *Sweatt, McLaurin, Sipuel,* and *Canada.* "His claim is the right not to be discriminated against because of his race," Colvin wrote. Davis's special admissions program blocked Bakke from competing for sixteen spots because of his race. But for this unconstitutional race discrimination, Colvin declared, Bakke would have received admission and thus, the Court should require it.

Justices and their clerks study briefs before oral arguments. Marshall could preview in them caste preservationists' strategy for reconquering The Trinity—appropriate the work of civil rights litigators, appropriate his own work, and sic it, like police canines, at those marching the nation away from the racial caste system. They would portray White people as the new victims and affirmative action as a policy akin to White Supremacy's works, like Jim Crow schools, that fell years prior. Caste preservationists rode an old horse, the anti-classification principle, into this new conflict.

In the first four legs of our journey, we saw the nine black robes teaching caste preservationists how to subdue the Fourteenth Amendment's caste-killing capabilities, allowing the pot of White racial advantages to further fill. Now caste preservationists have devised a plan for the robes to harness that same amendment to safeguard those White racial advantages and therefore preserve the caste system. Opposing affirmative action did not mean one was a caste

preservationist, but all caste preservationists opposed remedial policies for no larger reason than that they feared such policies would
undermine the caste system. Would the grandchildren succeed as the
grandparents had?

Let's watch this new war's first battlefield.


"THE FIRST CASE ON TODAY'S CALENDAR is Regents of University
of California against Bakke," says the white-haired Chief Justice
Warren Earl Burger. "Mr. Cox, you may proceed whenever you're
ready."

"This case here," says Cox, speaking with an aged voice and
professorial cadence from the lectern inside the packed chamber,
"presents a single vital question: Whether a state university, which
is forced by limited resources to select a relatively smaller number of
students from a much larger number of well-qualified applicants, is
free voluntarily to take into account the fact that a qualified applicant
is Black, Chicano, or Asian, or Native American in order to increase
the number of qualified members of those minority groups trained
for the educated professions and participating in professions from
which minorities were long excluded because of generations of pervasive race discrimination.

"The answer which the court gives will determine perhaps for
decades whether members of those minorities are to have the kind
of meaningful access to higher education in the profession which the
universities have accorded them in recent years or are to be reduced
to the trivial numbers which they were prior to the adoption of
minority admissions programs."

As sixty-five-year-old Cox speaks, Justice Marshall nears his
tenth anniversary on the Court. The tall, medium-built man who
had argued *Brown* has aged into a heftier version, with a double chin
and graying hair. The wit he commanded to disarm bigots in hostile
southern courtrooms while defending his clients, from alleged rapists to schoolchildren, remains sharp. As just one black robe, Marshall cannot, singly, defeat caste preservationist plans to appropriate
his legal work and use it against policies he supports. He can shep-

herd. But others must join his flock. The freshness of the legal questions presented in *Bakke* complicates predicting which robes might accompany him should he plot a footpath.

Marshall's closest friend and ally, the elfish William Brennan Jr., has served the longest among active justices. Born in Newark, New Jersey, on April 25, 1906, to Irish immigrant parents, Brennan graduated from the University of Pennsylvania and then Harvard Law. Ahead of the 1956 presidential election, Republican president Eisenhower appointed Brennan in October 1956. A faithful liberal, Brennan conceives of the Constitution as a living document that must both evolve to meet the needs of the people and promote the fairness necessary to function as a legitimate document that organizes a democratic society. Marshall shares his viewpoint wholeheartedly. The two operate in tandem. Brennan, gregarious and charming, shouldering the persuasion responsibilities. Marshall lighting the fire when their fellow robes disregard how their decisions affect people in the real world.

Potter Stewart, sixty-two years old with a prominent nose and receding dark hair, has sat on the bench the second longest. Born on January 23, 1915, Stewart grew up in Cincinnati and graduated from Yale College and Yale Law. After Justice Harold Hitz Burton retired, Eisenhower tapped Stewart, who on October 14, 1958, took his seat. In 1974, he voted with the five-to-four majority in *Milliken v. Bradley*, the decision that blocked a Detroit, Michigan, plan to bus students across district lines to create racially diverse, integrated public schools. *Milliken* holds perhaps more predictive value than any recent case for how the justices might decide *Bakke*. Because of *Milliken*, northern White parents could flee cities and head to the suburbs to defeat integration and *Brown*.

President Kennedy's only appointee, Byron White, a big, imposing six-foot-one man born on June 8, 1917, hailed from Colorado. After graduating from the University of Colorado, he led, in 1938, the National Football League in rushing. Following World War II naval service, he earned a law degree from Yale, playing football to pay his way. When Justice Charles E. Whittaker retired in 1962, Kennedy chose White. The fifty-nine-year-old joined the liberal justices Marshall, Brennan, and Douglas in *Milliken*, supporting inter-district busing to integrate public schools.

Conservative president Nixon sought to swing the Court to the right with his four appointees. Chief Justice Warren Burger, Nixon's first, was born on September 17, 1907, in St. Paul, Minnesota. The St. Paul College alumnus graduated from law school at the University of Minnesota. In 1969, Nixon nominated Burger to replace Chief Justice Warren, ending the famed Warren Court, which oversaw a fifteen-year liberal judicial revolution. For various reasons, Marshall dislikes Burger, who wrote the *Milliken* decision, including that the chief justice habitually assigns him to write the decisions for the least interesting cases, rarely if ever for those that will echo through time.

Nixon's second appointee, Harry Blackmun, born November 12, 1908, likewise grew up in St. Paul, Minnesota. In 1950, the Harvard College and Harvard Law graduate became counsel at the Mayo Clinic in Rochester, Minnesota. When liberal justice Abe Fortas retired, Nixon first selected South Carolina native Clement F. Haynsworth Jr., whose nomination failed because of ethics, civil rights, and anti-labor concerns. The nomination of Nixon's second choice, G. Harrold Carswell of Georgia, crashed after a segregationist speech of his surfaced. Nixon turned to Blackmun, an Eighth Circuit judge since 1959, whom Chief Justice Burger had recommended. Blackmun joined the majority in *Milliken*, opposing inter-district busing.

Nixon's third justice, Lewis Franklin Powell, a bony man with a gaunt face, was born in Suffolk, Virginia, on September 19, 1907. Powell graduated from Washington and Lee University for both undergrad and law school before attending Harvard for his Master of Law degree. Nixon nominated him in 1971 to replace Justice Hugo Black. Powell, who once wrote an amicus brief opposing school busing, reminds Marshall of educated and genteel southerners who adorned their anti-Blackness with a bow of paternalism. Given that he joined Burger's majority opinion in *Milliken*, Powell presents as an unlikely ally.

Nixon's last appointee, William Hubbs Rehnquist, was born in Milwaukee, Wisconsin, on October 1, 1924. Since his youth, Rehnquist admired Republican presidential nominees and strongly opposed Democrats, particularly FDR. He graduated from Stanford with an undergraduate, a master's, and a law degree. While clerking for Justice Robert Jackson during the Court's 1952–53 term, Rehnquist wrote a memo concerning *Brown* entitled "A Random Thought on the Segregation Cases." "I realize that this is an unpopular and unhumanitarian position for which I have been excoriated by 'liberal' colleagues," he wrote, "but I think *Plessy v. Ferguson* was right and should be re-affirmed." After his clerkship, he relocated to Arizona where he jumped into Republican Party state politics, campaigning for Barry Goldwater. Rehnquist, during his confirmation hearings, confronted questions about his *Brown* memo. "I believe that the memorandum," he professed, "was prepared by me as a statement of Justice Jackson's tentative views for his own use," a transparent canard for various reasons, none more salient than that he wrote the memo in the first person. And initialed it. Rehnquist voted with the majority in *Milliken*, shares Nixon's commitment to jostle the Court toward conservatism, and offers Bakke his surest vote.

The most junior black robe, John Paul Stevens, was born in Chicago on April 20, 1920. Stevens graduated from the University of Chicago and earned the highest grades ever at Northwestern Law School. Stevens clerked for liberal justice Wiley Rutledge before returning home to practice at prestigious firms. When liberal justice Douglas retired in 1975, President Ford chose him, a moderate Sixth Circuit judge. The Senate unanimously confirmed Stevens in December 1975.

Cox, a lanky White man with dark bushy eyebrows and graying hair, highlights three truths he believes support the constitutionality of the special admissions program. First, the number of qualified medical school applicants dwarfs the number of spots. Second, racism has defined American life, "much of it," he says, "stimulated by unconstitutional state action" that "shut [Black folk and other peoples of color] out of the most important and satisfying aspects of American life including higher education and the professions." And third, he contends, "there is no racially blind method of selection which will enroll today more than a trickle of minority students in the nation's colleges and professions. These are the realities which the University of California, Davis Medical School faced in 1968."

"Mr. Cox," Rehnquist interjects, "what if Davis Medical School

had decided that since the . . . minority population of doctors in California was so small, instead of setting aside sixteen seats for minority doctors, they would set aside fifty seats until that balance were
redressed and the minority population of doctors equal that of the
population as a whole. Would that be any more infirm than the program that Davis has?" Rehnquist is trying to push Cox to specify how
far a school can take an affirmative action program. If a sixteen-seat
set-aside should survive, why not fifty?

"I would say that as the number goes up," Cox responds, "the
danger of invidiousness or the danger that this is being done not for
social purposes but to favor one group as against another group, the
risk if you will of a finding of an invidious purpose to discriminate
against is greater and therefore I think it's a harder case but I would
have to put the particular school in the context of old schools."

"Can you give me a test," Justice Stevens asks, "which would differentiate the case of 50 students from the case of 16 students?"

After Cox vomits a garbled answer, Stevens interrupts, teaming
up with the most conservative justice: "But in Mr. Justice Rehnquist's
example, he was assuming precisely the same motivation that is
present in this case, the desire to increase the number of black and
minority doctors and the desire to increase the mixture of the student
population. Why would that not justify the fifty?"

Cox finally defends the hypothetical program, stating that "if it's a
solidly based then I would say fifty was permissible." Given that Cox
backed the anti-stigmatization principle, he answers correctly.

Wade McCree, Carter's solicitor general, replaces Cox at the lectern. After graduating from Harvard Law in 1944, McCree moved
to Detroit where none of the city's prestigious firms would hire him,
notwithstanding his terrific academic profile and his letter of recommendation from Harvard Law's dean. Michigan, as all states, did
nothing to arrest such pervasive employment discrimination. All
Black folk of McCree's age suffered from state denial of equal protection, through inaction and action. The other side contends that Bakke
stomached a similar wrong. McCree grimaces at the suggestion.

"The interest of the United States of America," McCree, a
brown-skinned man with high cheekbones, says, representing the
Carter administration, "stands from the fact that the Congress and

the executive branch have adopted many minority-sensitive programs. They take race or minority status into account in order to achieve the goal of equal opportunity. The United States has also concluded that voluntary programs to increase the participation of minorities in activities throughout our society, activities previously closed to them, should be encouraged and supported. Accordingly, it asks this Court to reject the holding of the Supreme Court of California that race or other minority status may not constitutionally be employed in affirmative action and special admissions programs properly designed and tailored to eliminate discrimination against racial and ethnic minorities as such discrimination exists today or to help overcome the effects of past years of discriminations." McCree insists that "if the ultimate social reality is the irrelevancy of race, the present reality is that race is very relevant. Accordingly, it would appear that to be blind to race today is to be blind to reality."

"Mr. solicitor general," Chief Justice Burger asks, "is there any evidence in this record that this university, its medical school at Davis, has ever engaged in any exclusion or discrimination on the basis of race?" McCree and Cox want the Court to accept general societal discrimination as justifying affirmative action admissions policies. But what if the black robes conclude that racist legacy matters not? What if they deem whether the institution that seeks to administer an affirmative action program has discriminated in the past as the only relevant consideration?

"There is no evidence in the record that this university has, and, indeed, I would be surprised to have found it," McCree responds. "We suggest that it is not enough merely to look at the visible wounds imposed by unconstitutional discrimination based upon race or ethnic status, because the very identification of race or ethnic status in America today is itself a handicap. And it is something that the California University at Davis, Medical School, could and should properly consider in affording a remedy to correct the denial of racial justice in this nation. And we submit that the Fourteenth Amendment, instead of outlawing this, indeed, should welcome it as part of its intent and purpose."

McCree "conclude[s] that this is not the kind of case that should be decided just by extrapolation from other precedents," cautioning the justices against comparing Bakke's complaint to that of Black claimants like Gaines, Sipuel, and Sweatt. "That we are here asking the Court to give us the full dimensions of the Fourteenth Amendment that was intended to afford equal protection and we suggest that the Fourteenth Amendment should not only require equality of treatment but should also permit persons who were held back to be brought up to the starting line where the opportunity for equality will be meaningful," McCree maintains, sampling from President Johnson's Howard speech, and ending his oral argument. McCree utters the key point—that the Court should treat the oppression of people of color as justifying race-conscious remedial policies.

Next comes Colvin, replacing McCree in the spotlight and insinuating himself into the role of Thurgood Marshall on a stage containing the man. Marshall litigated more equal protection cases than perhaps anyone. For one of his first, on June 17, 1935, Marshall stared down the state of Maryland in a Baltimore courtroom. He represented Donald Murray, a Black man seeking to level the color barrier at the University of Maryland School of Law, the school Marshall had once yearned to attend. At trial and on appeal, Marshall successfully argued that excluding Murray while not offering Black students a separate law school violated the Fourteenth Amendment. Bakke's supporters envisioned him as undertaking a similar struggle, fighting a school that had, on account of race, rebuffed him.

Marshall understood the defining difference between the two lawsuits. Maryland, on the one hand, had refused to admit Black students, a policy fitting into a larger racial caste system. At Davis Medical School, on the other hand, White students constituted a majority. The affirmative action admissions programs sought to amend what the segregationist admissions program had effected. Caste preservationists, by stripping the two policies from historical context, manufactured a moral equivalence to pursue the same ends that the University of Maryland once sought—the maintenance of White racial advantage.

"Allan Bakke's position is that he has a right and that right is not to be discriminated against by reason of his race," says Colvin, a white-haired man, as his voice raises, and he pounds the lectern. "And that's what brings Allan Bakke to this Court."

"Well," Justice White says, "what's your response to the assertion of the university that it was entitled to have a special program and take race into account and that under the Fourteenth Amendment there was no barrier to its doing that because of the interests that were involved. Now what's your response to that?"

"Our response to that is fundamentally that race is an improper classification in this situation," Colvin replies, "because the concept of race itself as a classification becomes in our history and in our understanding an unjust and improper basis upon which to judge people." Bakke, Colvin argues, had an individual right to compete for every seat, and Davis denied him that on account of race. Colvin solicits the justices to endorse the anti-classification principle.

"Your client did compete for the eighty-four seats, didn't he?" Justice Marshall questions.

"Yes, he did."

"And he lost."

"Yes, he did."

"You're talking about your client's rights," Thurgood says, "don't these underprivileged people have some rights?"

"They certainly have . . . the right to compete," Colvin answered. "They have the right to equal competition."

Colvin's remark pretends that America hosts an equal competition. It doesn't. Never has. The competition, for Bakke, kicked off at his birth. Raised by parents favored in the job market. Attended segregated White schools as Black children attended neglected Jim Crow schools and lived in neglected neighborhoods. American policy blew the wind into his sails his entire life. His culture taught him how to not feel it. How to not sense he was even in a sailboat. How to trick himself into believing his muscles grew weary from rowing. Colvin performs a patented caste preservationist two-step. First, he disappears White racial advantages and second, treats measures to counteract those advantages as undermining an otherwise fair process. He nails the choreography and returns to his seat.

"Mr. Cox," Chief Justice Burger says, "do you have something further?"

Cox revisits the lectern to close out the day. "The first main proposition that I would assert is that the racially conscious admissions program at Davis and any racially conscious admissions program designed to increase the number of minorities to their professional school, is fully consistent with both the letter and the spirit of the Fourteenth Amendment," Cox says, before outlining three subsidiary points.

"We say first that there is no perceived rule of color blindness incorporated in the Equal Protection Clause."

In the third leg of our journey, we confronted Justice Harlan's *Plessy* dissent that expounded, *"Our constitution is color-blind"* to strike down the Louisiana Separate Car Act. After the Court rejected Harlan's views and helped state governments develop a durable racial caste system, Cox must disclaim that the Constitution is color-blind to allow the state to remedy the ills that the Court facilitated in the first place. Please do keep color-blindness top of mind.

"We say second," Cox continues, "that the educational, professional, and social purposes accomplished by a race conscious admissions program are compelling objectives or to put it practically, they are more than sufficient justification, for those losses, for those problems that are created by the use of race. We don't minimize them, but we say that the cost is greatly outweighed by the gains.

"And third . . . we submit that there is no other way of accomplishing those purposes."

Cox closes a passionate two hours, and the race case that dominated the national news like none since *Brown* goes to the justices.

DAYS LATER, they met inside their elegant Conference Room to discuss their viewpoints on the case and determine their votes. When the justices shuffled out, no majority had formed, clarifying that *Bakke* would require time. Marshall wrote on his yellow legal pad that he only needed one more vote, gathering that Brennan, Stewart, and Powell agreed to uphold the special admissions program. The needed fifth vote, he posited, would come from White. This initial meeting uncorked the bottle, and internal jockeying gushed forward, with the justices attempting to persuade their colleagues to adopt their outlooks through typed, sometimes fiery, interoffice memoranda that bounced between justices' chambers.

On November 10, 1977, Rehnquist dispatched a memo that unraveled his thinking. "The University's admissions policy in this case," the staunch conservative wrote, "seems to me to make its 'affirmative action' program as difficult to sustain constitutionally as one conceivably could be." Rehnquist, who had two decades before advanced that the Equal Protection Clause tolerated segregation, flipped, arguing now that the Fourteenth Amendment prohibited race classifications. "I think it as a postulate that difference in treatment of individuals based on their race or ethnic origin is at the bull's eye of the target at which the Fourteenth Amendment's Equal Protection Clause was aimed." Here, Rehnquist articulated an early example of how caste preservationists interpreted the Equal Protection Clause post-*Brown*. After defending the constitutionality of segregation, they abruptly insisted on color-blindness the moment institutions began redressing past and ongoing castework.

Brennan's memo landed two weeks later. "I don't have to debate the question whether the Fourteenth Amendment protects whites as well as blacks. Surely it does. The difficult question is deciding what triggers the protection. If I thought for a moment that Davis' failure to admit Bakke represented a slur of whites," Brennan wrote, "then I would not hesitate to apply the strictest of scrutiny. But we all know that Davis' action represents absolutely nothing of this." Brennan, in other words, espoused Cox's anti-stigmatization principle. The admissions program, per Brennan, survived review because Davis implemented it to increase minority doctors, a short-term goal, and it facilitated the long-term goal, he wrote, "to reduce the degree to which California and American society are overall racially conscious societies."

Expressing a moderate viewpoint, Justice Powell maintained that although the special admissions program violated the Fourteenth Amendment, an admissions program could treat minority racial identity as a plus if race counted as one among many factors. The Davis plan, he charged, overstepped the constitutional line. It treated race as decisive in admissions decisions—race determined viability for a special admissions seat.

On December 9, the justices, minus Blackmun, held up at the Mayo Clinic for prostate surgery, met again inside the Conference

Room, near the chief justice's chambers. The eight sat in their hand-made green leather and mahogany chairs, as a member of the Court's police force, as convention, stood outside the door to prevent disturbances. There Marshall sat, before a large twelve-foot mahogany table, the first Black person allowed inside such a room on equal footing, lugging along with him the burden of completing *Brown*'s unfinished business. Beyond his legal aptitude and experience, Marshall brought much to the room, where walls lined with American oak, built-in bookshelves, red volute carpet, and a black marble fireplace established a dignified setting. As the descendant of enslaved people, Marshall lived inside the racial caste system. During conferences Marshall weaved humor with experience into stories that taught his colleagues what their White skin shielded from them, what they would hardly perceive unless a Black person pointed it out, and how White skin afforded its owners invisible wages. Marshall implored his colleagues to interpret the Constitution as allowing the redressing of racial oppression. "He spoke with such conviction," Justice White once observed. "It was conviction that came out of experience. He could embellish his points with examples that would scare you to death, experiences he had trying cases in the South." Marshall uttered perhaps the most insightful remark of the conference: "this is not a quota to keep someone out—it's a quota to get someone in."

At the end of the conference, three—Brennan, White, and Marshall—wanted to side with Davis. Four—Burger, Stewart, Rehnquist, and Stevens—supported striking down the special admissions program. Powell wanted to outlaw that specific program but reverse the injunction on using race altogether as an admissions factor. Other admissions programs that considered race, Powell reasoned, could survive judicial review. Just not that one. And Blackmun, recuperating from prostate surgery, had yet to reveal his views. The justices deferred the vote and agreed to continue exchanging memos.

Brennan and Marshall disagreed with Powell, who wanted to employ strict scrutiny to evaluate the constitutionality of Davis's special admissions program. Wanting to reserve that standard for cases concerning actions that stigmatized and demeaned a racial group, Brennan championed an intermediate scrutiny test, one more searching than rational basis but less onerous than strict scrutiny to evaluate remedial actions like affirmative action. Marshall likewise rebuffed strict scrutiny, favoring a more flexible standard. In a memo, Marshall wrote that the "legality of affirmative action simply could not be resolved without consideration of the historical, legal, and sociological context of past racial policies and practices."

By January 1978, the thorny issues involved left the justices hopelessly split, as they awaited Blackmun's voice. Meanwhile, Marshall's agitation with his colleagues and their inability to understand the Black plight festered. "I repeat, for the next to last time," he vented in a memo, "the decision in this case depends on whether you consider the action of the Regents as *admitting* certain students or as *excluding* certain students." If they thought this case was about admitting students, "then this is affirmative action to remove the vestiges of slavery and state imposed segregation by 'root and branch.' If you view the program as excluding students, it is a program of 'quotas' which violates the principle that 'the Constitution is color-blind.'" In *Plessy*, the Court explicitly rejected the conception of the Constitution as a color-blind document and announced that, Marshall wrote, "Ours was a nation where, by law, individuals could be given 'special' treatment based on race." He continued: "For us now to say that the principle of color-blindness prevents the University from giving 'special' consideration to race when this Court, in 1896 licensed the state to continue to consider race, is to make a mockery of the principle of 'equal justice under law.' . . . We are not yet all equals, in larger part because of the refusal of the Plessy Court to adopt the principle of color-blindness. It would be the cruelest irony for this Court to adopt the dissent in *Plessy* now and hold that the University must use color-blind admissions."

No justice responded. Not even Brennan.

On May 1, Blackmun, finally well enough to engage, told his colleagues by memo where he stood, locking in the last vote. The Court had finally settled *Bakke*. Opinion drafts circulated. Then, on June 28, 1978, the black robes, one by one, filed into their chamber.

"THE JUDGMENT AND OPINION of the Court in Regents of the University of California against Bakke, will be disposed of in this way,"

Chief Justice Burger said, watchful press members in attendance locked into every word. "Mr. Justice Powell will announce the Judgment of the Court."

Justice Powell failed to convince four others to join his entire opinion. Burger, Rehnquist, Stevens, and Stewart joined the parts that affirmed the ruling from the California Supreme Court that the special admissions program violated the Equal Protection Clause. That five also affirmed the order that Davis admit Bakke. Brennan, Marshall, Blackmun, and White joined the parts of Powell's opinion that reversed the portion of the prior ruling that prohibited the use of race in future college admissions processes.

"I am authorized to announce only the Judgment of the Court," said Justice Powell. Typically, the Court releases Opinions of the Court. But in cases like *Bakke*, when a majority cannot agree with any opinion in totality but could agree on an ultimate resolution, the Court releases a Judgment of the Court that will be included in one justice's opinion. Powell, who considered his *Bakke* opinion his most meaningful, had decided early that he would vote to uphold affirmative action, believing that outlawing it would undermine the addressing of racial inequality. But, he concluded, Davis had stretched the limits of what the Equal Protection Clause allowed.

"The facts in this case are too well known to be re-stated this morning," Powell continued. "Perhaps no case in modern memory has received as much media coverage and scholarly commentary."

The first section of the Fourteenth Amendment guaranteed individual rights, Powell reasoned. Personal rights. Not rights belonging to groups. Allan Bakke had the same equal protection rights as did Mildred Jeter. Same rights as did Lloyd Gaines. "The guarantee of equal protection cannot mean one thing when applied to one individual and something else when applied to a person of another color," Powell wrote. "If both are not accorded the same protection, then it is not equal." Powell maintained that the special admissions program, regarded as a racial classification because Davis fashioned it to admit minority applicants, should trigger strict scrutiny. He failed, however, to convince a majority to support this position. "Racial and ethnic distinctions of any sort are inherently suspect," he wrote, relying on *Loving* and *McLaughlin,* "and thus call for the most exacting judicial examination."

But believing that strict scrutiny should apply didn't automatically invalidate the special admissions program. Strict scrutiny merely required that the program pass a rigorous test. But exactly what test? The Court had long dithered in detailing its exact parameters. The special admissions program should fail, Powell contended, because Davis lacked a "substantial" justification for racially classifying. Powell rejected that remedying America's legacy of oppression in a way that would harm innocent persons like Bakke afforded states a substantial justification for racially classifying. Five justices agreeing would have stripped states of the central rationale for affirmative action and protected White racial advantages.

Also rejecting that "improving the delivery of health-care services to communities currently underserved" was a persuasive enough reason, Powell believed that Davis *could* remediate specific instances of its own race discrimination. But nothing in the case record indicated any such misdeeds. Limiting affirmative action programs to cure only specific instances of discrimination would've provided meager tools to solving the problem. America needed broad policies, not a piecemeal approach too weak to shut the systemic, pervasive gaps that Johnson's Howard speech had chronicled.

Enrolling a diverse student body likewise met Powell's standard for a substantial justification. Powell mentioned Harvard's admissions program that counted minority racial identity as a plus in admissions decisions but required all applicants to compete for each spot. "The applicant who loses out on the last available seat to another candidate receiving a 'plus' on the basis of ethnic background," Powell wrote, "will not have been foreclosed from all consideration for that seat simply because he was not the right color or had the wrong surname." But treating racial diversity as the justification for remedial policies strips reformers of the central rationale that activated them, leaves such policies on unsteady ground, and limits the type of solutions that could be implemented.

Per Powell, Cox was prodding the Court to hold that White folk warranted less equal protection. "It is far too late," Powell wrote, "to argue that the guarantee of equal protection to all persons permits the recognition of special wards entitled to a degree of protection greater than that accorded others." This line struck Marshall as insensitive at least and at worst racist.

Although colleges and universities retained the space to use race in admissions, Powell's opinion contained warning signs. Disaster awaited if the justices adhered to the anti-classification principle, particularly if they rejected that remedying past racism met whatever justification necessary to employ a racial classification. Many policies to upend the racial caste system would racially classify. Such policies would vanish if five justices endorsed anti-classification as the Equal Protection Clause's mediating principle. White racial advantages, then, would outlast the living. *Bakke* infused urgency into the fight—Marshall would need to proffer a new construction of the Equal Protection Clause, or caste preservationists would win *Brown*'s legacy and all the spoils, including the Fourteenth Amendment. A few months later, a disheartened Marshall broke a rule he had heeded for years.

ON NOVEMBER 18, 1978, forty-four years after his graduation, Marshall returned to Howard to celebrate Wiley A. Branton, a veteran civil rights lawyer and longtime friend, becoming the law school's dean. Marshall breached his self-imposed prohibition against publicly speaking on race, which lasted longer than ten years, delivering a biting address inside Cramton Auditorium, a drab brick building that hosted musicians on Howard's campus. A sitting justice who once thought after *Brown* that the NAACP had won the clash for complete Black freedom, explained, a month post-*Bakke*, why the fight endured.

Marshall, whose voice grew leathery with age, cautioned his largely Black audience of five hundred to reject "the myth" of Black progress. "Be careful of the people who say, 'You've got it made. Take it easy. You don't need any more help,'" he advised. "Today we have reached the point where people say, 'You've come a long way.' But so have other people come a long way. Has the gap been getting smaller? No. It's getting bigger. People say we're better off today. Better off than what?"

Marshall said that sometimes he fielded requests to travel the nation to inspire Black children. "For what?" he asked rhetorically. "These Negro kids are not fools. They know that if someone says they have a chance to be the only Negro in the Supreme Court, the odds are against them."

In his *Bakke* opinion, Marshall likewise scoffed at the concept of Black progress. More valuably, his opinion noted how the anti-classification principle contradicted the Fourteenth Amendment's origin story. His best evidence, that the Congress that passed the Fourteenth Amendment enacted legislation, most notably the Freed-men's Bureau, for the specific benefit of the freedpeople, exposed how the Fourteenth Amendment's drafters did not adhere to an anti-classification principle. The Freedmen's Bureau, a federal agency created mainly to help the formerly enslaved transition to freedom, "was regarded, to the dismay of many Congressmen, as 'solely and entirely for the freedmen, and to the exclusion of all other persons,'" Marshall wrote. "Indeed, the bill was bitterly opposed on the ground that it 'undertakes to make the negro in some respects . . . supe-rior . . . and gives them favors that the poor white boy in the North cannot get.'" Marshall continued: "Since the Congress that consid-ered and rejected the objections to the 1866 Freedmen's Bureau Act concerning special relief to Negroes also proposed the Fourteenth Amendment, it is inconceivable that the Fourteenth Amendment was intended to prohibit all race-conscious relief measures."

The same congressmen also passed a law for "the relief of desti-tute colored women and children." And before, during, and after the ratification of the Fourteenth Amendment, they appropriated money for "colored" Union Army soldiers. Those who wrote the Fourteenth Amendment enacted remedial legislation that contained racial clas-sifications, proof that they imagined they had written an amendment that allowed such lawmaking. Of course, this specific history did not bind the justices deciding *Bakke.* But caste preservationists treated anti-classification as the drafter's purpose, a falsity, and held that falsehood as a shield against having to defend their choice.

Marshall omitted evidence that would have bolstered his posi-tion. Through the Fourteenth Amendment, Congress endeavored to constitutionalize the 1866 Civil Rights Act, which stated that all citizens "of every race and color . . . shall have the same right . . . as is enjoyed by white citizens." Marshall should have noted that this framing adopted the language of anticaste—it operates from the assumption that White people, as a group, enjoy a baseline level of citizenship and requires that all others, as a group, enjoy the same. By mentioning "white citizens" it contains a classification, and thus offended an anti-classification framework. The 1866 Act might have stated "laws that mention race are forbidden." The drafters chose different words. For a reason. And that reason became clear when they wrote laws specifically for the benefit of an oppressed Black population.

"While I applaud the judgment of the Court that a university may consider race in its admissions process," Marshall wrote in his *Bakke* opinion, "it is more than a little ironic that, after several hundred years of class-based discrimination against Negroes, the Court is unwilling to hold that a class-based remedy for that discrimination is permissible. In declining to so hold, today's judgment ignores the fact that for several hundred years Negroes have been discriminated against, not as individuals, but rather solely because of the color of their skins."

Righteous indignation pervaded Marshall's *Bakke* opinion. But he needed to translate that into a construction of the Equal Protection Clause that would dethrone the anti-classification principle. For reasons we will learn in the penultimate leg of our journey, the anti-stigmatization principle, although workable on this front, would prove utterly useless in stopping another method of Black subjugation. Anticaste furnished the answer. The only answer: *the Equal Protection Clause guarantees that no state shall allow any individual to belong to a lower caste.*

Castework triggered strict scrutiny. California, in the 1970s, fulfilled its obligation to Allan Bakke, but not to its Black inhabitants. Marshall should've defended affirmative action's constitutionality on the ground that it didn't reduce White folk to a lower caste. It didn't aid in the maintenance of an anti-White caste system. Yes, the Fourteenth Amendment grants individual rights. Not group rights. The amendment guarantees, therefore, that the state will protect, affirmatively, all individuals from becoming a member of a subordinated people. The state will not, of its own will, produce and maintain the existence of caste and will not, through inaction, allow lower castes to endure. Abolitionism insinuated this promise into the Constitution. By embracing anticaste, We the People dispel the ghosts of *Dred Scott.* We the People embrace everyone, regardless of race.

Losing in *Bakke* left the seventy-year-old Marshall distraught. He took the loss as a sign that time and events had evaporated his once ample pool of influence. His friends, other justices, and his clerks reported that he seemed depressed. He mismanaged his moment in *Bakke.* Yet, another chance to articulate the anticaste principle and slant the battlefield in the favor of Black freedom from caste would soon find him.

BORN IN 1922, Parren Mitchell, like Marshall, grew up in segregated Baltimore, one of seven children. The cruelest works of White Supremacy touched his thinking early in life when his older brother, Clarence Mitchell, at the time a reporter for a Black newspaper, recounted, for him, the gruesome October 1933 lynching of George Armwood in nearby Princess Anne, Maryland. Clarence detailed how White folk mutilated Armwood, a mentally challenged Black man accused of raping a seventy-one-year-old White woman. Later serving as an NAACP anti-lynching congressional lobbyist, the older brother labored, with little success, to prevent such atrocities through the passage of federal law. Decades afterward, the little brother joined the other side as a congressman, winning a seat in 1970 to represent a majority-White district in Baltimore, the first Black politician to win such a congressional district. Parren Mitchell, a Democrat, doggedly pushed the federal government to expand economic opportunity for Black folk, who, he once wrote, "must have equitable ownership and/or control over the production, distribution and consumption of goods and services in this nation's economic system."

In July 1976, amid high unemployment and an otherwise wobbly economy, Congress passed the Local Public Works Capital Development and Investment Act of 1976, which doled out $2 billion to help state and local governments fund public works projects. By February 1977, the money had been spent and Congress sought to extend the act, wanting to disperse even more in the first year of Carter's presidency. As Congress debated, on February 24, 1977, Mitchell addressed his colleagues from the House Chamber's plush carpeted floor, aiming to attach an amendment to the bill that would redress invidious race discrimination in the construction industry.

"I want to commend the chairman and the members of the committee who have done a great deal to make this public works bill far more equitable than it was last year," said Mitchell, a thin, brown-skinned man who spoke with a soft voice. "But there is one shortcoming that I see in the bill that I am attempting to address through my amendment.

"That shortcoming is that there will be numerous contracts awarded at the local level for various public works projects, but in that there is no targeting—and I repeat—there is no targeting for minority enterprises," reiterated Mitchell, one of eighteen Black members of the 95th Congress. "Let me tell the Members how ridiculous it is not to target for minority enterprises. We spend a great deal of Federal money under the [Small Business Administration] program creating, strengthening, and supporting minority businesses and yet when it comes down to giving those minority businesses a piece of the action, the Federal Government is absolutely remiss," said Mitchell, the first Black graduate of the University of Maryland to take all his classes on campus, earning a master's degree in sociology.

"The average percentage of minority contracts, of all Government contracts, in any given fiscal year, is 1 percent—1 percent. That is all we give them."

Mitchell proposed that for all contracts granted, Congress require that a certain percentage be set aside for minority contracting firms, ensuring that the federal bounty fed people of color too.

"I would point out also that this concept of a set-aside is becoming increasingly popular," Mitchell added. "Many states and many local subdivisions have moved into the process of setting aside contracts for minorities. That is because that is the only way we are going to get the minority enterprises into our system."

The House adopted Mitchell's Minority Business Enterprise provision, and on May 13, 1977, Carter signed the Public Works Employment Act of 1977. Under Mitchell's MBE provision, construction firms, almost always White-owned, would bid on the opportunity to fulfill a public works project, say the building of a neighborhood park. A firm, to receive a contract for the project, had to submit a bid and that bid needed to specify how at least 10 percent of the contract's value would go to a minority-owned firm. The provision defined the minority categories as "Negroes, Spanish-speaking, Orientals, Indians, Eskimos, and Aleuts." If no such minority firm could feasibly fulfill the obligation, the state or local government conducting the bidding could apply for a waiver from the federal government. Mitchell's MBE provision, which contained the first instance of a federal law "of general application containing an explicit racial classification," garnered scant national attention. The *Baltimore Sun*, Mitchell's hometown daily, merely noted that he had "won approval of a modified amendment designed to ensure that Black firms receive a portion of the construction allocated under the bill."

Five months later, private individuals, construction contractors, and subcontractor associations operating in New York filed suit to halt the enforcement of Mitchell's MBE provision. Its racial classification, they claimed, harmed White-owned businesses, violating both the equal protection component of the Fifth Amendment and the Equal Protection Clause. In December 1977, a district court judge upheld the provision. In September 1978, the Second Circuit affirmed that ruling, finding that "even under the most exacting standard of review the MBE provision passes constitutional muster." The plaintiffs, led by named party H. Earl Fullilove, appealed to the Supreme Court. On the morning of November 27, 1979, the justices heard oral argument for *Fullilove v. Phillip Klutznick*, the commerce secretary.

A small bespectacled Black man, Drew Days III, assistant attorney general for the Justice Department's Civil Rights Division who had also helped write the *Bakke* brief, represented the Carter administration inside the Court Chamber. Defending the constitutionality of the MBE provision, Days, born in Jim Crow Georgia, argued that Congress, through the provision, sought to remedy past racial inequities in the construction industry and wanted to guarantee that federal dollars spent on public works projects went to minority contractors whom the process had long excluded. Congress correctly identified this as a worthy goal, and only such a provision could address the problem. Congress bore a special duty, Days argued, given the enforcement clauses of the Thirteenth and Fourteenth Amendments, to stamp out racial injustice. Therefore, judges should defer to Congress when assessing that body's legislative fulfillment of its duties. True, White-owned firms typically would not be able to compete for 10 percent of these contracts. Yet, they could still bid on the remaining 90 percent. And although some White-owned firms might lose out to minority competitors who entered with higher bids, asking that White contractors share the burden of ameliorating past wrongs did not deny them equal protection. Given that the law did not stigmatize White folk, Days contended the MBE provision only had to survive the rational basis test. In other words, Days followed Archibald Cox and Justice Brennan in advocating the anti-stigmatization principle.

Let's visit a quadrennial political event in Detroit, Michigan, to discuss how the Court resolved the matter.

ON THE EVENING OF JULY 17, 1980, as we, among a sea of White faces, await when the headline speaker will waltz across the vividly blue stage inside the newly built yet dull Joe Louis Arena, the home of the National Hockey League's Detroit Red Wings, let's discuss the *Fullilove* decision.

Chief Justice Burger wrote the opinion, handed down July 2, that contained the Judgment of the Court, which affirmed the lower court's ruling that upheld Mitchell's MBE provision. In *Fullilove*, Burger scrambled to avoid replicating the *Bakke* disarray of the Court—producing no majority opinion and consequently fomenting confusion in lower courts and the nation. "Would it not be better to try for a 'united front,'" Burger wrote to Powell, "instead of a cluster of concurring opinions—a practice of which I increasingly receive complaints from judges all over the country." As in *Bakke*, however, no opinion garnered the full support of five robes. Disagreements, particularly over what test to apply, strict scrutiny or some intermediate test, left the six justices voting to affirm—Burger, Brennan, White, Marshall, Powell, and Blackmun—unable to coalesce around one opinion. The dissenters—Stewart, Stevens, and Rehnquist—

concluded that the provision, a purported racial quota, violated the White plaintiffs' equal protection rights.

In his opinion, Burger wrote that any "preference based on racial or ethnic criteria," because such policies necessarily racially classify, must "receive a most searching examination." Yet, he didn't specify which test—strict scrutiny, rational basis, or something in between—a racial preference policy must survive. Burger simply stated that Mitchell's MBE provision would survive even the strictest. Remember in *Bakke*, no majority formed to support Davis seeking to remedy general societal racial oppression as a strong enough justification for a racial classification in college admissions. In *Fullilove*, however, a majority agreed that Congress remedying more specific past race discrimination in public contracting met the standard to justify the racial classification.

Burger reasoned that the Fourteenth Amendment's enforcement clause empowered Congress to remedy invidious race discrimination. "Congress had abundant evidence," Burger wrote, "from which it could conclude that minority businesses have been denied effective participation in public contracting opportunities by procurement practices that perpetuated the effects of prior discrimination." Despite the availability of minority firms to participate in public works, they reaped little opportunity because of "the existence and maintenance of barriers to competitive access which had their roots in racial and ethnic discrimination, and which continue today, even absent any intentional discrimination or other unlawful conduct." Congress wielded the power to counteract this. And the flexible nature of the set-asides—the federal government could issue waivers—enabled the MBE provision to survive.

True, some White-owned firms would lose to minority-owned firms with higher bids. Nonetheless, Burger wrote, "it was within congressional power to act on the assumption that in the past some nonminority businesses may have reaped competitive benefit over the years from the virtual exclusion of minority firms from these contracting opportunities." In other words, given that Congress had concluded that White-owned firms received unjust enrichment because of past pro-White preferences, Congress could offset that history. Six black robes agreed that the Constitution empowered

Congress to implement race-conscious remedies for past and present invidious discrimination and to prevent its recurrence, rejecting the claim that affirmative action amounted to reverse discrimination and that the Constitution required color-blindness.

The main reason why the same justices reached a different decision in *Fullilove* than in *Bakke* was that Congress, specifically entrusted with the duty to enforce the Fourteenth Amendment, did the policymaking here. That Congress was counteracting more specific instances of race discrimination as opposed to general historical discrimination strengthened the case. And because the waiver protected against White firms losing out on opportunity simply because a suitable minority firm could not be located, it further convinced the justices to vindicate Mitchell's provision. In *Fullilove*, nonetheless, caste abolitionism seemed to recover ground lost in *Bakke*.

Marshall penned a lackluster concurrence that took no effort to reintroduce anticaste into the heart of the Fourteenth Amendment, missing *another* opportunity. Still, he will soon have reason to rejoice. Based on *Fullilove*, state and lower federal courts will uphold state minority set-aside programs and other affirmative action programs in education and employment. Federal courts, moreover, will approve other congressional set-asides. But Drew Days, years later from his perch on the faculty of Yale Law School, will warn that lawmakers are failing to exercise proper care when enacting these set-aside plans, writing that "many plans appear to be the products of hasty decisions to 'do something.' No effort was made to identify the problem and to examine various alternative remedies, or to apply explicit racial criteria only after other solutions were proven inadequate to the task."

Our review of *Fullilove* now concludes, and a dark-haired sixty-nine-year-old White man wearing a black suit takes to the rostrum. As celebratory horns blare and a university fight song pumps through the hockey arena on the Detroit River, "Thank you, thank you very much," the man shouts with a wide toothy grin, seeking to calm the raucous crowd.

"With a deep awareness of the responsibility conferred by your trust, I accept your nomination for the presidency of the United States," says the former governor of California, Republican Ronald Wilson Reagan.

# Sixth Leg:
# Thurgood and the Ignorance Observation

O N MAY 26, 1937, at the eighteenth-century English-style Court of Appeals Building in Annapolis, Maryland, defeat taught a twenty-eight-year-old Thurgood Marshall a lesson about ignorance. The case that concluded there originated in Baltimore County, which surrounded Marshall's hometown city of Baltimore like a crescent moon. Black folk, comprising nearly 10 percent of the population of the rural county, mainly huddled in three areas. Catonsville. Towson. Sparrows Point. The rest sprinkled themselves throughout the countryside.

A young Black girl, Margaret Ordarlee Williams, born in September 1921, completed the seventh grade in June 1934 at her one-room school, "Colored School #21," in Cowdensville, a small Black community southwest of Baltimore. Her report card noted her promotion to the eighth grade and that her teacher deemed her a "very good student." White skin would have opened one of the county's eleven all-White high schools to her. The county school board commanded Black students, however, to surmount a special obstacle to obtain a public education beyond the seventh grade. In the 1920s, the county stipulated that Black students who graduated from seventh grade with the requisite performance would receive a publicly funded post-seventh-grade education in the form of tuition to attend a Jim Crow high school in Baltimore, *if* they passed a competitive examination. This represented progress. Before this, Baltimore County offered *no* public higher educational opportunities for Black schoolchildren. After failing the test, Margaret returned to her one-room school to repeat the seventh grade, she and her parents praying that more training would ready her to outmatch her nemesis. Yet it bested her again the following year, making casualties of 71 percent of the Black children who attempted it. Black residents swore that the county made the test needlessly challenging to restrict the number of costly scholarships.

On September 12, 1935, Joshua Byard Williams Jr., his daughter Margaret, and their pastor entered the all-White Catonsville High School. The principal, David Zimmerman, received them. Marshall waited outside the three-story red-brick building, a suitable education space, unlike Margaret's one-room wooden frame schoolhouse. A few months before, Marshall had won the trial for *Murray v. Pearson*, a lawsuit to integrate the University of Maryland School of Law. The oral argument for the appeal at the Court of Appeals of Maryland loomed two months away.

When Williams presented Margaret's report card, Zimmerman politely refused Margaret's enrollment on account of race. "As per instructions," Marshall wrote Charles Hamilton Houston, who oversaw the case from Manhattan, "Williams showed the record of his daughter to the principal, and the principal made the statement in the presence of another witness that her record was good enough for admission to any high school." Just not her color.

Houston and Marshall feared potential blowback if they initiated a lawsuit on Margaret's behalf before the Court of Appeals had decided *Murray*. White Marylanders might extrapolate that the NAACP was plotting against all segregated schools, down to kindergarten, inciting the court to rule against Donald Murray to bottleneck any advancement that might culminate in the unimaginable—little Black boys attending school with little White girls. On January 15, 1936, Marshall won the *Murray* appeal. With victory in hand, on March 14, 1936, Marshall sued Zimmerman, the county superintendent, and the Baltimore County School Board, demanding that the court force county school officials to admit Margaret to her nearest high school. The petition argued that the Constitution afforded Margaret, as a county public elementary school graduate, the same right to receive a post-seventh-grade education as White students received.

Although framing the lawsuit as a frontal attack on secondary school segregation, the NAACP hunted a different, humbler objective—Baltimore County establishing a Black public high school. An NAACP press release stressed this: "It is recognized by both the white and colored people here that this sort of legal action is for the purpose only of securing high school education for Negroes and is not to be construed as a movement having for its ultimate object the forcing of Negro pupils into white high schools." Debate about whether integrated schools even best satisfied the needs of Black children pervaded Black discourse, from the ivory tower to the ghetto, with one camp urging that because White folk cared only about White kids and loathed Blackness, they would compromise the education of Black youths in integrated institutions.

During the September 1936 trial for *Margaret Williams v. David Zimmerman et al.* inside the Greek Revival Baltimore County courthouse in Towson, Marshall thought Judge Frank Duncan "leaned very far to the other side." Marshall, a month before accepting a full-time position with the NAACP, cautioned Houston: "We are in for a real battle." At trial, Marshall reiterated that the lawsuit emanated not from Margaret's "desire to enter that school," but that the county, offering no Black high school, an equal protection violation, deprived them of requesting any other remedy. The county's counsel answered that the dearth of Black students, dispersed throughout the county, vindicated not establishing what would amount to a prohibitively expensive Black high school. Marshall wrote to Houston, describing opposing counsel as "exceptionally mean, nasty and arrogant." They "injected prejudice throughout the argument," he relayed, "pleading that there was a Negro girl trying to crash into the white school and trying to break down the traits of the state of Maryland."

Opposing counsel supported their argument with only one case, *Gong Lum v. Rice*, where the Supreme Court, in 1927, upheld a Mississippi school district forbidding a Chinese American girl's admission to a White school and assigning her to a Jim Crow school instead. Not *Plessy*, a more relevant case. Not *Cumming v. Board of Education of Richmond County*, the most relevant case. And Marshall even had to provide his underprepared adversaries *Gong Lum*'s citation. The county's lawyers, furthermore, proudly affirmed that the state enforced segregation to relegate Black skin to an inferior status. Judge Duncan ruled for the school board, nonetheless, finding that Margaret's failing the test rendered her ineligible for a high school education. She experienced no rights denial, he concluded, and was not entitled to remedy.

In the Maryland Court of Appeals courtroom where we began, Chief Judge Carroll Bond affirmed Duncan's ruling. Bond weaseled away from the primary issue—the constitutionality of Baltimore providing Black children with no public high school education options. Instead, Bond centered Marshall's behavior, in particular his supposed mistake of not seeking either one of two remedies—requiring that the county fix the test or end its testing requirement—as though permitting the county to keep a gentler version of its scheme of forcing Black children to travel to another city with no public transportation equaled the education given to White students. The loss convinced the NAACP to shelve for more than a decade any operations targeting primary and secondary segregated education. The outcome drilled an uncomfortable lesson into Marshall. The racial mood of the time can swamp fidelity to law and facts and more ominously, fidelity to rational thought.

Marshall devoted himself to the democratic experiment even though it existed only in the imagination. Never in the soil. And certainly never for his caste. He endeavored to breathe virtue into the experiment, even braving threats to his hide. In November 1946, for instance, he narrowly escaped a lynch mob in Tennessee after successfully defending several Black men falsely accused of instigating a race riot. Through the fog of anti-Blackness, though, Marshall could still detect a scenario where the Stars and Stripes could transcend its tainted birth. He believed America could habilitate itself, but only if it accepted the reality of its past. Understood the nature of Black oppression. Studied how oppression touches all facets of society. And then devoted itself to righting the congenital sin. America, he knew, needed to adopt constructions of the Constitution that unlocked Black freedom. And that required judges to root their work in knowledge.

Jurists throughout history, though, have marshaled the absence of knowledge—ignorance—in decisions that promote caste preservationism. The first four legs of our journey documented this. In our first leg, the Supreme Court misread a federal removal statute, reducing its usefulness to Black people seeking to transfer cases to federal courts and away from hostile state courts. In our second leg, the black robes missed the obvious known fact that the word "deny" in the Equal Protection Clause embraced inaction as well as action and flubbed the meaning of the word "aforesaid," leading to the invalidation of crucial Enforcement Act sections. During our third leg, in upholding Mississippi's 1890 constitution, the Court likewise wielded ignorance. Mississippi called a constitutional convention to disenfranchise Black men, and the black robes behaved as if they had no inkling about the intentions to annul the Fifteenth Amendment, despite that the convention transpired in the light and was chronicled in newspapers throughout the country. In our fourth leg, White capitalists, with states provisioning the whips and chains, reduced Black folk to quasi-slavery, denying the right to life, liberty, and the pursuit of happiness, yet somehow the Court did not connect this uniquely racial trauma to the Fourteenth Amendment's Due Process Clause, which protects the right to life, liberty, and the pursuit of happiness.

In Margaret Williams's lawsuit, Judges Duncan and Bond likewise dispensed what we'll call *ignorant legal analysis*. They obtusely followed formal legal rules, disregarded readily known facts, and exhibited inexcusable obliviousness to obvious social realities. True— Margaret failed the test. But reducing the case to whether she passed a test displayed a blind obedience to formal legal rules without regard to whether the rules made sense to apply. Baltimore County maintaining eleven high schools for White pupils, but zero for Black pupils, meant the latter endured inferior treatment. But the judges disallowed such simple truths from informing their work. Baltimore County reduced Black residents to second-class citizenship—a lack of a Black high school exemplified that. The judges operated as if an omnipotent force had disappeared all trace of the caste system, blocking them from perceiving the reality they lived in and helped create.

Perhaps you interpret this as indicating dishonesty, that these judges sought to uphold Jim Crow and pursued whatever route, however inane, that maneuvered them to their predetermined destination. The judges would, publicly at least, dispute any nefarious motives. They can deny what they can hide, their inner thoughts. But they cannot hide the words they wrote. We see them. They cannot hide that those words lacked intellectual rigor. The funk of folly, in the legal arena, often accompanies the funk of fraud.

Turning the crank on the Gatling gun of ignorant legal analysis, the Supreme Court throughout the 1980s delivered victories for caste preservationism in the battle over the Fourteenth Amendment, protecting White racial advantages. Ignorance powered the scheme that bested Justice Marshall and his vision for an America unsullied by White Supremacy. The descendants sampled the music of the ancestors to win a modern fight. Follow me to the Supreme Court Chamber to listen to the remix. Hear how closely the music mimicked the original. Let's flash forward to June 28, 2007, a year after Margaret Williams's death, to hear an opinion as ravaged by ignorant legal analysis as that written in her case.

"I HAVE THE ANNOUNCEMENT," the seventeenth chief justice, fifty-two-year-old John Roberts, says, "in Parents Involved in Community Schools v. Seattle School District No. 1 and Meredith v. Jefferson County Bd. of Education. The Parents Involved case comes to us from the Ninth Circuit," he continues in a professorial monotone, "and concerns the adoption and implementation by the Seattle School District of a student assignment plan that requires all students to identify themselves as either White or non-White. Seattle then uses the racial classifications to help ensure that the racial balance at certain schools falls within a predetermined range based on the racial composition of the school district as a whole. Seattle's assignment plan allows incoming ninth graders to choose from among any of the district's high schools, ranking the schools in order of preference. If too many students list the same school as their first choice, the district employs a series of tiebreakers to determine who will fill the open slots at the oversubscribed school." One of those tiebreakers, Roberts says, "is based on race. If the school is racially imbalanced under Seattle's plan and it has too many non-White students, then White students will be selected for admission. If the school has too many White students, then non-White students will be selected to move the school closer to the desired racial balance.

"Petitioner Parents Involved, the group of parents whose children have been or may be denied assignment to their chosen school in Seattle solely because of their race, challenged the constitutionality of Seattle's assignment plan under the Equal Protection Clause of the Fourteenth Amendment."

The outrage of a White mother, Kathleen Brose, kick-started the lawsuit. In 1999, her eighth-grade daughter, Elizabeth, applied to high schools. A resident of an upscale White neighborhood in a heavily segregated city, Kathleen wanted her daughter at nearby Ballard High School. They ranked it first. Ballard had recently reopened after a $35 million renovation. Housed in a modern brick building with solar panels and situated on thirteen acres of land with cherry-blossom-filled courtyards and state-of-the-art facilities, the school provided students an excellent educational opportunity. Elizabeth wasn't selected for Ballard, though. Or her second and third choices. She got her fourth choice, Franklin High School, which Brose described as a "heavily black school with lower test scores." Brose told a reporter, "I just thought it was terribly unfair. It was a violation of our children's constitutional rights. I just felt that the school district needed to quit focusing on placing kids in schools based on their skin color." She helped start the group Parents Involved in Community Schools for this legal challenge.

The *Meredith* case, also concerning a White mother and child, emerged from Louisville, Kentucky, and involves a local school assignment process, which, Roberts says, "classifies its students as either black or other and makes a school assignment based on among other factors the district's racial guidelines which require all schools to maintain black enrollment of between 15 and 50%.

"Petitioner Crystal Meredith enrolled her son Joshua, a kindergartner in Jefferson County's schools, upon moving to the district. And after he was assigned to a school far from home, she thought to transfer Joshua to a nearby elementary school. Jefferson County denied Joshua's transfer application, even though the school he wished to attend had available space, because his transfer would have had an adverse effect on his current school's compliance with the racial guidelines. Meredith challenged Jefferson County's use of the racial guidelines under the Equal Protection Clause and the Sixth Circuit upheld the school district's assignment policy."

The Seattle and Louisville education boards pursued a voluntary desegregation plan that, naturally, consulted race to facilitate a goal of *Brown*—interracial educational environments. "I got the feeling on hearing the discussion yesterday that when you put a white child in a school with a whole lot of colored children, the child would fall apart or something," said Thurgood Marshall when arguing *Brown* inside this room more than a half century ago. "Everybody knows that is not true."

Because the two cases involve the same legal issue, the Court decided them jointly. Chief Justice Roberts wrote the plurality opinion that contained the Judgment of the Court. Twenty-seven years after holding in *Fullilove* that Congress could racially classify to undo near racial exclusion in federally funded public works projects, the Court held that by allowing race to inform school assignment decisions, both school districts violated the Equal Protection Clause. Worse yet, Roberts's opinion misconstrued both the NAACP lawyers' arguments in *Brown* and the *Brown* opinion. The Court gifted caste preservationism a victory by adopting arguments that embezzled the work of the Civil Rights Movement and funded the protection of White racial advantages.

In his written opinion, Roberts argues that the spirit of the White plaintiffs from Seattle and Louisville, who *opposed* measures that integrated schools, more closely resembled the spirit of the Black schoolchildren plaintiffs from *Brown*, who fought *for* integrated schools. You must inhale his funk of folly:

> The parties . . . debate which side is more faithful to the heritage of *Brown*, but the position of the plaintiffs in *Brown* was spelled out in their brief and could not have been clearer: "[T]he Fourteenth Amendment prevents states from according differential treatment to American children on the basis of their color or race." What do the racial classifications at issue here do, if

not accord differential treatment on the basis of race? As [Robert L. Carter of the NAACP] who appeared before this Court [on December 9, 1952] for the plaintiffs in *Brown* put it: "We have one fundamental contention which we will seek to develop in the course of this argument, and that contention is that no State has any authority under the equal-protection clause of the Fourteenth Amendment to use race as a factor in affording educational opportunities among its citizens." There is no ambiguity in that statement. . . . What do the racial classifications do in these cases, if not determine admission to a public school on a racial basis? Before *Brown*, schoolchildren were told where they could and could not go to school based on the color of their skin. The school districts in these cases have not carried the heavy burden of demonstrating that we should allow this once again—even for very different reasons. . . . The way to stop discrimination on the basis of race is to stop discriminating on the basis of race.

According to Roberts's logic, Elizabeth and Joshua suffered the same injury as did Linda Brown—their districts assigned them to a school based on race. One must concede that in each matter, the state considered race. Yet, equating the plaintiffs provides a flagrant instance of ignorant legal analysis. Elizabeth and Joshua, on the one hand, experienced the disappointment of not attending their preferred school because their local representatives prized children attending school with kids from all walks of life. Linda, on the other hand, suffered the weight of the state deeming her racially inferior and engraving that into her young psyche. If *Brown* turned merely on racial classification, Black and White students in Jim Crow states endured comparable harms. After all, Jim Crow statutes classified White as well as Black students. Imagine if a White boy in the 1950s sued. How would his lawyers relay his injury? That the board of education did not stack the deck *enough* in his favor? The idea that both races withstood comparable harms lampoons rational thought.

Calling *Brown* a case about racial classification misinterprets, embarrassingly, Chief Justice Warren's words in one of the simplest opinions in the Court's history, an opinion Warren wrote plainly to allow even the unlearned to follow. Yet, the nation's leading jurist put his name on something that argued *Brown* centered not on the state purposefully disadvantaging Black people but rather the state merely racially classifying. Roberts winds the crank and sprays bullets of ignorance for forty-one pages.

Roberts reproduces blunders similar to those that sank Justice Henry Billings Brown's majority *Plessy* opinion. Justice Brown presented Louisiana's Separate Car Act of 1890 as just another humdrum law, one unconnected to the hell engulfing Black existence. His opinion misunderstood that the state legislature passed the act to enforce a racial hierarchy. Misunderstood how laws can legally confine a population to a lesser station. Misunderstood how laws can train the inferior caste into accepting that station. Misunderstood how this fortifies the caste system. Misunderstood that the caste system, helped by restricting the ballot, produces lawmaking that keeps the caste system's blood flowing. Consider it a feedback loop for Black misery.

Through ignorance, Justice Brown crafted an opinion that concluded that a state passing a law to cement and signify Black folk's legal and social disability did not violate a constitutional guarantee of equality. In Justice Brown's retelling, the Separate Car Act merely divided the races on trains and singled neither race out for special scorn. Nothing to see here, the black robe said. Of course, one might detect strategic deceit in both Roberts's and Brown's opinions. But the words also contain substandard analysis, confusion of history, cluelessness about methods of oppression, and an obliviousness to facts, all errors that a competent jurist would never commit. Yet they did, and their colleagues co-signed them. That Court observers rarely connect the Court's deeply flawed race jurisprudence to ignorance demonstrates how this nation sees caste preservationist decisions as unremarkable and familiar, something perhaps warranting criticism, not something to evaluate as to whether they meet minimum cognitive standards. During this leg, we explore just how much the production of ignorant thought complicates the abolition of caste.

In *Parents Involved* and *Meredith* the five-to-four majority hands caste preservationism a highly coveted win. White parents understand that one of the most salient racial advantages they can bequeath in a nation that supposedly prizes merit, high-quality K–12 educational opportunities, sets their children up for future success. In a nation that supposedly prizes merit, White children "earn" the right to attend schools that Black children have less access to absent race-conscious decision-making like that implemented in Seattle and Louisville. Public school educational quality intertwines with the wealth of the neighborhood in which it sits. White wealth, the sweet fruit of White Supremacy, dwarfs that of Black wealth, and that wealth opens educational opportunities. White Americans continue reaping what White Supremacy planted hundreds of years ago. And caste preservationists want to protect their right to continue dining on those apples and pears, while hiding, even sometimes from their own consciousness, the fruits' origins.

Thurgood Marshall, having died on January 24, 1993, cannot censure Chief Justice Roberts for misappropriating the NAACP's work. But some of Marshall's co-counsel in *Brown* will explain how Roberts's opinion warps history. Robert L. Carter, a ninety-year-old federal judge in Manhattan, repudiates Chief Justice Roberts for distorting his words. "All that race was used for at that point in time was to deny equal opportunity to black people," Carter says, referring to the pre-*Brown* days. "It's to stand that argument on its head to use race the way they use it now." Jack Greenberg, an eighty-two-year-old Columbia law professor, calls Roberts's opinion "preposterous." "The plaintiffs in *Brown* were concerned with the marginalization and subjugation of black people," Professor Greenberg says. "They said you can't consider race, but that's how race was being used." In other words, the NAACP attorneys arguing *Brown* were denouncing racial classifications used by the state to oppress a race. Oppression, not racial classification, elicited their fury. William T. Coleman Jr., another former NAACP attorney, calls Roberts's opinion "100 percent wrong."

Caste preservationist arguments inform the Fourteenth Amendment interpretations that ultimately win the battle over *Brown* and protect White racial advantages. The movement appropriated the labor of civil rights litigators, appropriated Marshall's own labor, and pointed it, like a water hose, at the march toward remedying the effects of the racial caste system. This leg of our journey will chronicle how the Court adopted ignorance, particularly ignorant legal analysis, and how that stunted caste abolitionism. We will commence by following a person who helped lay the groundwork for this outcome, the grinning man we saw onstage inside the Detroit hockey arena.

ON THE MORNING OF AUGUST 4, 1964, a thirty-six-year-old White FBI agent, Jay Cochran Jr., stood on a freshly filled earthen dam for a small pond on a cattle farm in Philadelphia, Mississippi. He pointed a stick at the dirt and said, "We'll start here."

Using a bulldozer and other excavation equipment, FBI personnel started digging at the Old Jolly Farm, owned by a White Klansman. After the 106-degree heat broiled the workers for hours in the densely wooded area, the stench of rotting flesh punched through the soil. Fourteen feet and ten inches below where Cochran once stood, three bodies, side by side, lay facedown. James Chaney. Twenty-one years old. Andrew Goodman. Twenty years old. Michael Schwerner. Twenty-four years old. Three civil rights workers, participants in Freedom Summer, a campaign to register Black voters in Mississippi against the will of those obedient to White dominance. Their loved ones had clung to hope for forty-four days until their corpses burned themselves into the national memory. Many indeed cannot ponder Philadelphia, Mississippi, without these gruesome murders hijacking the psyche.

Sixteen years later, on the morning of August 3, 1980, a festive mood percolated through the nearby Neshoba County Fair Grounds. More than four hundred wooden family cabins, some pink, others green, orange, or blue, festooned with pennants and American flags, housed many of the attendees for the fair held annually in Philadelphia, a small town of about six thousand in central Mississippi. These vividly painted cabins surrounded a red-clay racetrack. In the middle of this oval track, fair activities, like carnival rides, game booths, and food stations entertained and catered thousands each year.

Loud applause and "We want Reagan" chants from the fifteen thousand, almost all White, attendees greeted an eleven-car caravan. Wearing an open-neck white shirt and red clay–stained shoes, Ronald Reagan took to the grandstand, a raised sheltered platform inside the racetrack, for his first official post-convention campaign event. Standing on this Mississippi stage, where the crowd clapped to a high school band playing "Dixie," demonstrated that Reagan, a Californian, would challenge Carter, a southerner, on his home turf. The Reagan campaign wanted to re-create the Nixon coalition, requiring the candidate to formulate his own Southern Strategy. Democrats struggled to remain connected with White voters who wavered at joining a political coalition that claimed 90 percent of the Black vote. The Reagan campaign appreciated how leveraging White animosity would benefit the candidate.

"I believe in states' rights," Reagan says, "and people doing as much as they can for themselves. We've reached this distorted balance in our nation by giving too many powers to the federal government." States' rights had long served as a rallying cry for supporters of racial caste systems—from the original antebellum version to its post–Civil War sequel. Reagan endorsing states' rights tickled the erogenous zones of those who wanted to confine Black people to their rightful, lower place.

The Reagan campaign discerned how to charm racists through encrypted language after openly racist language had surrendered much of its political value decades ago. Lee Atwater, a leading Reagan political strategist, regurgitated the game plan: "You start out in 1954 by saying 'Nigger, nigger, nigger.' By 1968 you can't say 'nigger'—that hurts you. Backfires. So you say stuff like forced busing, states' rights, and all that stuff. You're getting so abstract now [that] you're talking about cutting taxes, and all these things you're talking about are totally economic things and a by-product of them is [that] blacks get hurt worse than whites." The Reagan campaign coupled dog whistles with political positions that would comfort those who could hear the whistles and cherish their sounds.

After Reagan clobbered Carter by nearly 10 points and 440 electoral votes, Marshall felt the nation jetting toward a philosophy that reminded him of what he thought he had vanquished in 1954.

ON NOVEMBER 4, 1980, Democrats lost the White House and turned a fifty-eight to forty-one Senate majority into a forty-six to fifty-three minority. The next day, reports surfaced that Republican Strom Thurmond, the former head of the States' Rights Demo-cratic Party, would chair the Judiciary Committee, replacing liberal lion Ted Kennedy. Federal judge nominees, including Supreme Court justices, would pass through a committee helmed by a man who joined the Republican Party after the Democratic Party proved insufficiently allegiant to White Supremacy.

When Justice Brennan heard the Thurmond news, he visited Mar-shall's chambers to commiserate. They knew. A conservative move-ment barreling toward them was poised to obliterate their vision for America and the Constitution. After their conference of woe, they skulked arm in arm out of Marshall's chambers. Martha Minow, a Marshall clerk, stood in the hallway, watching the two old men, Marshall, tall and wide, Brennan, short and thin, pace through the marble hallway. "You could just see there was a sense of everything they had worked for being turned around," Minow remembered. A November 6 front-page headline in the *New York Times* captured the mood: "Reagan Buoyed by National Swing to Right."

President Reagan soon encountered accusations of personal big-otry. "No matter how you slice it," he once responded, "that's just plain baloney." As a sports announcer in the 1930s, he alleged, he was "one among a handful in the country who opposed the banning of blacks from organized baseball." He regaled audiences with the tale of how he invited a Black college football teammate, William Frank-lin Burghardt, to stay at his home overnight after a segregated hotel refused him. Reagan assured Americans that his parents reared him "in a household in which the only intolerance I was taught was the intolerance of bigotry," even recounting how his father prevented him from watching the movie *The Birth of a Nation*. And in 1948, he campaigned fervently for Harry Truman, he said, and supported the civil rights policies of the era.

Reagan excluded, however, that since the mid-1960s, on the key race policies, he had espoused the caste preservationist perspec-tive. He bad-mouthed the Civil Rights Act of 1964, avowing that he would have voted against it if in Congress. He derided the Voting Rights Act for violating states' rights, considering it "humiliating to the South." During his 1966 California gubernatorial campaign, he applauded state Proposition 14, which allowed a real estate holder to deny renting or selling property "to any person as he chooses," a measure to permit housing discrimination. "If an individual wants to discriminate against Negroes or others in selling or renting his house," he contended, "he has the right to do so." The Fair Housing Act of 1968, a federal housing anti-discrimination measure— Reagan deprecated it as violative of property rights. And he certainly omitted that in 1971 he spewed invective to President Nixon about Black Africans. "To see those, those monkeys from those African countries—damn them," Reagan mocked on his telephone call to Nixon. "They're still uncomfortable wearing shoes!" With Reagan wearing the caste preservationist team colors in the Oval Office, Marshall faced an emerging strategy to convince the Supreme Court to interpret the Fourteenth Amendment to protect White racial advantages.

Marshall could identify the Reagan administration officials storming his beach. Inspect with me a moment from Reconstruction-era South Carolina. During this flashback, we will discuss the ignorance-wielding foe Marshall could not see encroaching on his conception of racial progress.

BEAUFORT COUNTY SPANS much of southeastern South Carolina, an area embellished by the majestic South Carolina Sea Islands. Because we arrived here in June 1869 to witness the administration of justice, roam the Barnwell Castle with me. The county operates its courthouse inside this four-story monstrosity built during the Revolutionary War. As we enter the gated property and venture into a courtroom, we spot a *New York Times* correspondent here to feed northerners craving news on the South's progress under biracial governance. A remarkable sight shocks him. "[P]erfect equality," he will later write, "in the Courts of Justice. . . . The sensation is peculiar . . . to see a Court in session, where former slaves sit side by side with their old owners on the jury, where white men are tried by a mixed jury, where colored lawyers plead, and where white and colored officers maintain order. But this is done at every Court, and justice is not overwhelmed. Of course, there are those who have feelings of deep, silent repugnance; but no one is shocked in his innate sense of justice or in his instincts of moral propriety."

Eleven months after South Carolina became the twenty-eighth state to ratify the Fourteenth Amendment, making it part of the Constitution, the South Carolina legislature, the first majority-Black legislature in American history, passed a law requiring that the racial composition of a jury mirror that of the voting population of the county where the jury sits. The former law, which contained no racial classification, required selecting prospective jurors from property tax rolls, which underrepresented largely propertyless Black men. The new law uses voter rolls, a far more inclusive list in a state that enfranchised Black men. Therefore, less than a year after the legislature ratified the Fourteenth Amendment, it passed a law that racially classified, demonstrating that the lawmakers did not conceive of the Fourteenth Amendment as prohibiting race-conscious law-making. Forcing Black folk to sit for trials with disproportionately White juries reeked of unfairness that a race-conscious law could foil. The legislators focused on eliminating injustice and if a law that racially classified could satisfy the state's obligation of providing equal protection, why not pass it? They clearly thought the Fourteenth Amendment condoned their enactment. South Carolina's caste preservationists preferred the former law. "It made no discrimination," they cried. But in 1895, this same ilk will draft a new state constitution to disenfranchise Black men. *They support color-blindness, in other words, when it promotes caste preservationism.*

As we remain in this Reconstruction-era moment, in this Revolutionary-era courthouse, let's explore how the enemy Marshall could hardly see creeping forward will emerge.

In 1980, amid the stone sculptures and wood carvings of the Sterling Law Building at Yale Law School, Steven Calabresi, a conservative student, will feel disconnected from his liberal classmates and the school's liberal faculty. Through the New Deal, the Civil Rights Movement, and Johnson's Great Society antipoverty programs, liberals act on their conviction that government must soothe a wide array of economic and social maladies. Calabresi's undergraduate friends from Yale who now attend the University of Chicago Law School, Lee Liberman and David McIntosh, share his qualms that liberals, through devotion to big government, are undermining not just personal and property rights, but the Constitution itself. They malign, for instance, the Warren Court and its supposedly wayward constitutional interpretation, its way of inventing rights not spelled out in the text of the document. They found a student organization as a vehicle for their outlook. The Federalist Society.

In late April 1982, Black Yale Law alumni will meet for a conference, "Under Color of Law: Equality or Its Semblance," at the university's biology building. Three blocks away, the Federalist Society holds a three-day symposium in the law school. Around two hundred, including high-profile conservative scholars like Antonin Scalia, a University of Chicago law professor; conservative rockstar jurists, like D.C. Circuit Judge Robert Bork; and Reagan Justice Department figures, like Theodore Olson, an assistant attorney general, attend the dryly titled "A Symposium on Federalism: Legal and Political Ramifications." The specter of a conservative revolution sends the attendees into spasms of excitement. As they congregate inside the school's largest lecture hall and outside it for meals and drinks, the sensation that the broader conservative movement can erase the supposed liberal constitutional order thrills them. They picture their team as the protagonist in a political melodrama, eager to relish the happy ending when their vision for the Constitution pervades the American imagination, from the courtroom to the dining room. Within a year, seventeen Federalist Society chapters will form on other law school campuses. With conservative gospel and political donations as its stucco and brick, the Federalist Society forges its place as the nation's most powerful legal network.

The Federalist Society most changes American legal behavior by selling their ever-changing recipes of originalism as *the* true way to interpret the Constitution. Although conservatives will cook various originalisms, all share a similar stock—that courts must interpret constitutional language in keeping with some aspect of that language's original quality. Original intent of the drafters—what they meant when they wrote it. Original expected application of those living at the time of ratification—how did they expect it to apply in a given situation. The original understanding of the ratifiers—what the state legislatures thought they were agreeing to when they voted for it.

On and on the variations go. Originalism, no matter what though, fixes in time the Constitution's meaning. Originalists believe that their philosophy restrains judges. Disciplines judges. They believe that it prevents them from interpreting the Constitution to fit their personal political preferences. The Reagan administration latches on to originalism and clothes most every legal argument in supposedly originalist apparel. Conservative originalists, post-*Brown*, engineer the claim that the Fourteenth Amendment forbids race-conscious decision-making into a core pillar.

And therein lies why I summoned you to this castle in 1869. Reagan administration lawyers will champion originalism, but they will never ask, let alone answer correctly, what the freedpeople thought the Fourteenth Amendment meant. If you truly cared about what "equal protection" meant in 1868, would you not at least investigate what it meant to the people it was primarily drafted for? Black legislators voted to ratify the amendment. What did the amendment mean to them? Might you at least consider the question?

No one can say definitively what the Fourteenth Amendment originally meant for no other reason than it meant different things to different people. The Constitution has more than one original meaning. Reagan administration lawyers will proffer arguments that misunderstand this and treat the Fourteenth Amendment as if it has one well-defined conception. And that one conception aligns perfectly with their political preferences. The interpretative methodology that supposedly disciplines judges and keeps them from making the law say whatever they want perversely allows just that. Actually, emboldens just that. Self-styled originalists turn dead men into marionette dolls and make them say whatever they want without having to defend their personal politics.

Caste preservationists need Reagan to install a legal apparatus to execute the plan. And that plan needs an architect. Enter William Bradford Reynolds. In September 1983, he will deliver an ignorance-laden speech at the National Housing Center in D.C. that revealed the caste preservationist endgame for the Fourteenth Amendment.

————

NEARLY TWO YEARS BEFORE Reynolds's ignorant speech, in May 1981, a few months into Reagan's presidency, Attorney General William French Smith announced in a speech of his own that the Justice Department would no longer support quotas to remedy employment discrimination. Previous administrations would sue local public sector organizations, say a fire department, under the 1964 Civil Rights Act after uncovering evidence of employment discrimination. If the department failed to implement sufficient reforms, those administrations would support remedies that forced the department to hire minority applicants, generally until they filled a specified percentage of the workforce. The Reagan administration dubbed beneficiaries of such remedies as "nonvictims of discrimination" who warranted no redress. Only "actual victims of discrimination," applicants truly discriminated against, should benefit from remedial programs. Along those lines, the administration labeled White workers who lost out on employment opportunities because of remedial programs as "actual victims." Both limiting the ramifications for employers who commit castework and contorting the definition of "discrimination victim" were strategic linchpins of the effort to warp the Fourteenth Amendment into an instrument of White racial advantages.

This viewpoint flowed from a startling level of ignorance. When that hypothetical fire department refused to hire Black folk, the entire Black population suffered. The managers of that fire department, by excluding Black people from opportunity, played their role in maintaining the caste system. The caste system exists because people, each day, choose to keep it operational. Each instance of castework contaminated the reservoir that sustained Black life. Per the 1980 census, 27 million Black people lived in the United States. Caste victims all. Nonvictims none. Let's say that every employer in a state refused to hire Black people. And the state legislature, in response, provided equal protection by compelling employers to hire a specified percentage of Black employees. The Reagan Justice Department, if following its logic, would have considered all White members of the workforce actual victims of discrimination because of a policy meant to address rampant castework. Knowledge would have taught department officials the perversity of this mindset. Ignorance taught them the opposite.

Attorney General Smith called both busing and quotas "ineffective" measures in his speech, speaking on behalf of Reagan, who had campaigned against them. A "more practical and effective approach to the problem of equal educational and occupational opportunity," he maintained, should supplant both. After Smith's speech, the *Washington Post* reported that in "practical terms, the change in policy will probably mean that the department will no longer intervene in school desegregation cases in favor of mandatory busing as it has done, often decisively, many times in previous administrations." The *Post* added that Justice Department "sources said it probably also means that there will be no more advocacy, in the Supreme Court or anywhere else, of affirmative action plans which include quotas or remedies that amount to quotas." Busing and quotas, Smith asserted, denied White people opportunities, and violated the color-blindness principle. Policies designed to relieve Black oppression fell into disfavor for supposed ineffectiveness, and, most crucially, for harming White people.

Reworking the pertinent question of "how to remedy America's troubling legacy of anti-black racism" into "how to protect white people from such remedies," created the ideal environment to turn the Fourteenth Amendment into the safekeeper of White racial advantages. On the one hand, designating Black people as nonvictims would mean that the Equal Protection Clause afforded them limited utility unless they could isolate an individual state actor who discriminated against them, as in our third leg when the Supreme Court required that Cornelius Jones point to some malfeasant jury commissioner to prove that his clients had experienced jury discrimination. Any individual White person, on the other hand, could potentially claim victimhood status from a remedial policy, meaning the state could never enact them, and thus the clause would afford White skin significant protection.

Around the time of Smith's speech, Reagan selected William Bradford Reynolds to helm the office, assistant attorney general for the Civil Rights Division, that Drew Days III, who successfully argued *Fullilove*, had occupied under Carter. Reynolds, a Yale and

Vanderbilt Law School graduate born into wealth, marketed himself as a disruptor. When a *New York Times* reporter asked him to defend his qualifications for the position, he replied that he would give the "issue of remedies in the civil rights arena" a "hard, fresh look."

Reynolds sold Reagan on a plan for remaking the federal judiciary, believing that Reagan could appoint three Supreme Court justices and restock nearly half of district and circuit court seats. Reynolds advised Reagan to appoint conservative jurists who could answer liberal counterparts supposedly creating rights to satisfy their political proclivities, like a right to privacy that protected abortion rights, not enumerated in the Constitution. Reynolds fancied judges who both passed a conservative ideological purity test and possessed professional competence and technical legal prowess. Only those who met this standard could win his confidence in their willingness and ability to execute the caste preservationist strategy for the Fourteenth Amendment.

In September 1981, Reynolds alerted the House Subcommittee on Equal Opportunities that the Justice Department would "no longer insist upon, or in respect support the use of quotas or any other statistical formulae designed to provide nonvictims of discrimination preferential treatment on the basis of race." By that he meant even employers proven to have engaged in castework needn't redress their misdeeds. Benjamin L. Hooks, the NAACP's executive director, excoriated that reversal. "The Reagan Administration acts as if the white male is the minority," he complained. Reynolds, referring to quotas as a "morally wrong" policy that had "created a racial spoils system in America," agitated for a "color blind" administration of civil rights laws, and branded affirmative action programs as instances of racism. "That means," he insisted, "that we cannot tolerate a society where we are going to condemn discrimination on the one hand and condone discrimination on the other hand. To use race to get beyond racism make no more sense than to prescribe alcohol to get beyond alcoholism." The Reagan administration preferred recruitment goals, wanting employers to develop a pool of minority candidates, without external pressure to hire any.

Regarding school desegregation, the administration vowed to interfere only when presented with "direct evidence of pervasive intentional discrimination." With Reynolds at the helm, the goal became removing "remaining state-enforced racial barriers to open student enrollment," not desegregation. "We are not going to compel children who do not want to choose to have an integrated education to have one," Reynolds once professed. Naturally, he also rejected busing, remarking, "We continue to believe that it is far better to desegregate dual public school systems through the use of transfer programs that depend on non-mandatory measures." Such measures, though, left school segregation undisrupted. These individual notes, these sounds against race-conscious integrated schooling, found their way into Chief Justice Roberts's opinion in *Parents Involved* and *Meredith*. Anger at the Reagan administration boiled hotly enough in the civil rights community that the National Urban League's annual report in 1982 bemoaned that "[a]t no point in recent memory had the distance between the national government and black America been greater than it was in 1981, nor had the relationship between the two been more strained."

On September 12, 1983, Reynolds delivered that ignorant speech entitled "Civil Rights Goals for the Year 2000 and the Means for Achieving Them" at a conference for the U.S. Commission on Civil Rights, an independent federal agency created to study civil rights policy and advise the federal government how to improve it. Inside the National Housing Center, located in the National Association of Home Builders building in downtown Washington, D.C., he explained why the Reagan administration, not its opponents, had inherited the cape and cowl of the civil rights superhero. Former protagonists in the struggle for racial equality once wore it. He proclaimed that for championing two supposedly seminal constitutional principles—anti-classification and color-blindness—members of the Reagan administration deserved the honor as its rightful heirs.

Reynolds, a tall and skinny forty-one-year-old White man with balding blond hair, opened boldly: "The choice we face, as I see it, can be succinctly stated. It is a choice between an officially color-blind society, on the one hand, and a government-supported, race-conscious society, on the other."

With this salvo, Reynolds hinted at a grievance that caste preservationists would repeat throughout the Reagan era—that race-conscious remedies tugged the nation toward immoral governance. That considering race, even to remedy past oppression, routed America down the same choppy waters already sailed during Jim Crow. Black leaders who supported such policies, therefore, warranted disparagement for becoming what they once condemned. The claim that Black folk's cultural inferiority explained their predicament reinforced the position that their wanting race-conscious remedial policies indicated moral failure. Black folk, per this argument, wanted policies to account not for a country's miserable legacy but for a population's current ineptitude. In the 1980s, America's anti-Black toxicity worsened. Castigating a people and their culture no longer satiated caste preservationists. Their craving for White dominance compelled them to graduate to impugning Black folk's goodness.

"America's first enduring step towards providing equality for all races was, of course, passage of the Thirteenth, Fourteenth, and Fifteenth Amendments, which abolished slavery, guaranteed to all citizens equal protection under the law and protected the right to vote from racial discrimination," Reynolds said. "History faithfully records that the purpose of these Amendments was to end forever a system which determined legal rights, measured status, and allocated opportunities on the basis of race and to erect in its place a regime of race neutrality. Thus, in the 1866 debates on the Fourteenth Amendment, the Equal Protection Clause was described as 'abolish[ing] all class legislation in the States [so as to do] away with the injustice of subjecting one caste of persons to a code not applicable to another.'"

On the Senate floor on May 23, 1866, Republican senator Jacob Howard delivered the words Reynolds quoted. Reynolds meant to support the originalist contention that the drafters of the Fourteenth Amendment conceived it as an anti-classification amendment. He, however, failed to include the next line from Howard's speech: "[The Equal Protection Clause] prohibits the hanging of a black man for a crime for which the white man is not to be hanged." In 1866, the beast that Congress endeavored to tame—the Black Codes—instilled fear in freedpeople not because they racially classified, but because they reduced them to a subordinate caste using racial classifications. Some Black Codes levied different punishments based on the race of the accused, arguably their most pernicious aspect. This was an example of "class legislation" in that it treated one group as an inferior caste. Reynolds seemed to equate, wrongly, opposition to "class legislation" to opposition to laws that racially classified. Exhibiting ignorance of the historical period, Reynolds misinterpreted the point of Senator Howard's words—that the state could no longer engage in castework because of the Fourteenth Amendment.

"Thirty years later," Reynolds continued, "in 1896, a Supreme Court Justice, the elder Justice Harlan, correctly recognized that these Civil Rights Amendments had 'removed the race line from our governmental systems.' In *Plessy v. Ferguson*, he declared: 'Our Constitution is color-blind and neither knows nor tolerates classes among citizens. . . . The law regards man as man, and takes no account of his surroundings or of his color.'"

Caste preservationists, for a century, sneered at Harlan's articulation of color-blindness, burying it under a mountain of castework. But the moment society turned to redressing that trauma, they dusted off Harlan's dissent. It suddenly warmed their hearts because it, superficially, bolstered the position that racial classifications violate a Constitution that required color-blindness. But to truly understand Harlan's plea, we must examine the entire passage:

> The white race deems itself to be the dominant race in this country. And so it is, in prestige, in achievements, in education, in wealth, and in power. So, I doubt not, it will continue to be for all time, if it remains true to its great heritage, and holds fast to the principles of constitutional liberty. But in view of the Constitution, in the eye of the law, there is in this country no superior, dominant, ruling class of citizens. There is no caste here. Our Constitution is color-blind, and neither knows nor tolerates classes among citizens. In respect of civil rights, all citizens are equal before the law. The humblest is the peer of the most powerful. The law regards man as man, and takes no account of his surroundings or of his color when his civil rights as guaranteed by the supreme law of the land are involved.

Harlan argued that the law cannot assist a racial hierarchy. Put differently, he conceived of a color-blind Constitution as an anticaste Constitution, not an anti-classification one. The use of the phrase "color-blind" continued Harlan's visual metaphor of "in *view* of the Constitution, in the *eye* of the law, there is in this country no superior, dominant, ruling class of citizens." The Constitution cannot see—in other words, it cannot support and help perpetuate—a racial caste system.

If Justice Harlan endorsed an anti-classification construction of equal protection, he would have dissented from, not written the unanimous opinion of, *Cumming v. Board of Education of Richmond County*. Recall, in that case, the Supreme Court upheld a school board maintaining public high school education for White students only. Harlan also joined the unanimous opinion in *Pace v. Alabama*, where the Court upheld a law that punished interracial fornication more harshly than such intra-racial intimacies. His stances in both cases dovetail with the common worldview of the period that regarded matters touching education and sexual dalliances as implicating social rights. The laws in *Cumming* and *Pace*, according to this viewpoint, did not bear upon fundamental rights and therefore did not involve the state in caste maintenance. Harlan erred—these laws certainly performed castework. But Harlan surely understood that in both matters, the state racially classified. If Harlan espoused Reynolds's conception of color-blindness, he would have dissented in both cases. Reynolds's ignorance informed his mistaking the conservative movement as championing the flavor of color-blindness found in perhaps the Court's most palatable dissent.

"In *Brown*," said Reynolds, reading from his speech, "the Supreme Court finally laid to rest the separate-but-equal doctrine. The Court acknowledged with eloquent simplicity that the Equal Protection Clause requires race neutrality in all public activities. 'At stake,' declared Chief Justice Warren for a unanimous Court, 'is the personal interest of the plaintiffs in admission to public schools on a [racially] nondiscriminatory basis.' Race consciousness as a tool for assigning schoolchildren was flatly and unequivocally condemned," Reynolds said, misstating the point of *Brown*, delivering lyrics that would decades later inspire Chief Justice Roberts.

"This judicial insistence on colorblindness in our public school systems was precisely the conclusion urged by the school children's attorney, Thurgood Marshall," Reynolds claimed. "Expressly rejecting the notion that the Constitution would require the establishment of 'non-segregated school[s]' through race-conscious student reassignments, Mr. Marshall argued to the Court that: 'The only thing that we ask for is that the State-imposed racial segregation be taken off, and to leave the county school board, the county people, the district people, to work out their own solution of the problem, to assign children on any reasonable basis they want to assign them on.' So long as the children are assigned 'without regard to race or color . . . nobody,' argued Mr. Marshall, 'would have any complaint.'"

Justice Marshall, of course, disputed that the Fourteenth Amendment demanded color-blindness as Reynolds meant it. The nation, in December 1952, when he spoke the words Reynolds quoted, used race to subjugate Black people. Reynolds translated "don't refer to my race to oppress me" into "don't refer to race to relieve my oppression." Nonetheless, by failing to anchor his Fourteenth Amendment analysis with the hook of anticaste, Marshall conveyed easily misappropriated messages.

"Remedial goals, quotas, or set-asides based on race," Reynolds said, "perpetuate the very evil that the Fourteenth Amendment seeks to remove: they erect artificial barriers that let some in and keep others out, not on the basis of ability, but on the basis of the most irrelevant of characteristics under law—race." This of course was false. The old-style anti-Black oppression kept Black people out. Remedial policies allowed Black people to enter. "They turn upside down the dream of Dr. Martin Luther King, Jr.," Reynolds claimed, "the dream that someday society will judge people 'not by the color of their skin, but by the content of their character.'"

Reynolds invoked King's "I Have a Dream" speech and peddled even more ignorance—the position that King opposed affirmative action. In his book *Why We Can't Wait*, King wrote, "Whenever the issue of compensatory treatment for the Negro is raised, some of our friends recoil in horror. The Negro should be granted equality, they agree; but he should ask nothing more. On the surface, this appears reasonable, but it is not realistic." A King biographer quoted King as saying, "A society that has done something special against the Negro for hundreds of years must now do something special for the Negro." King backed affirmative action.

"Professor William Van Alstyne," Reynolds said as he neared his conclusion, "pointed in the right direction in his *Chicago Law Review* article 'Rites of Passage: Race, the Supreme Court and the Constitution.' As he there stated:

> "one gets beyond racism by getting beyond it now: by a complete, resolute, and credible commitment never to tolerate in one's own life—or in the life practices of one's government—the differential treatment of other human beings by race. Indeed, that is the great lesson for government itself to teach: in all we do in life, whatever we do in life, to treat any person less well than another or to favor any more than another for being black or white or brown or red, is wrong. Let that be our fundamental law and we shall have a Constitution universally worth expounding."
>
> If we follow that sound advice, there is every prospect that by the Year 2000 the evil of discrimination that has plagued us for so many years can begin to be discussed largely as a problem of the past. . . . If we do not, but rather choose the course of color-consciousness, my prediction is that as benign as the intent may be—we will some twenty years from now be no closer to a realization of the dream of Dr. Martin Luther King, Jr. than we are today.

After Reynolds's final word, the commissioners and members of the fifty-state advisory committee in attendance pounced. One dismissed his speech as "rhetorical claptrap" because it distorted the "history of the civil rights movement and 25 years of litigation." Another called it "a demonstration of how the devil can quote Scripture for his own purposes." Someone else maligned it as "a preposterous insult to his audience of civil rights leaders." A fourth said, "We object to, resent and reject that kind of rhetoric."

Reynolds listened with folded arms. "If the Administration's alternative is inadequate," he replied, "then instead of yelling at each other, we should try to come up with something that's more effective."

Reynolds and like-minded Reagan administration officials taught the conservative movement, which included Supreme Court justices, that it should convert the Fourteenth Amendment into a tool to protect White racial advantages and showed how to accomplish the feat while wearing men like Howard, Harlan, Marshall, and King as masks, appreciating that this presented an avenue to promote their constitutional vision with the public. What better way to convince the populace to buy your constitutional product than by marketing it as consistent with the amendment's drafters *and* icons for Black justice? Ignorance sold the product.

Meanwhile, an atypical case was heading to the black robes— a lawsuit initiated by White public school teachers who depicted themselves as victims of the state persecuting them because of their color, much like a Black educator Marshall had once represented.

ON NOVEMBER 15, 1939, inside the six-story Neoclassical United States Post Office and Courthouse in Baltimore, where the United States District Court of Maryland sat, Marshall's prey trapped himself in the guillotine.

His client, Walter Mills, a Black principal at the segregated Camp Parole elementary school in Anne Arundel County, sued the county school board. Mills made $1,058 per year, $800 less than the county's average White principal. White teachers there took home $1,250. Black teachers with equal qualifications—$550 less. Although Black folk represented a third of the county's population, only one-fifth of the education spending went to Black children. "I felt that what we were doing was just as important as the white principals and that we should be equally paid for it," Mills later recalled. "As a matter of fact, our facilities were very much worse than the white schools, but we did just as well."

The NAACP filed this lawsuit and similar ones, highlighting another inequity in Jim Crow education—pay compensation castework. This particular phenomenon underlined a caste system conceit—that White folk deserved more because Whiteness held more value.

Judge William Calvin Chestnut, a Hoover appointee, asked George Fox, the county school superintendent, whether anti-Blackness explained unequal pay. "Can you sit there and tell me that the racial factor did not enter into this state of affairs?" he questioned from the bench.

Fox testified that "his poorest white teacher was a better teacher than his best colored teacher."

Marshall offered no response, allowing Fox's own words to prove the NAACP's argument. Marshall asked why Black but not White teachers had to clean classroom floors.

Fox, angry, replied through a grimaced face, "this had always been blacks' work."

"The crucial question in this case," Chestnut wrote in his opinion released a week later for *Mills v. Board of Education of Anne Arundel County*, "is whether the very substantial differential between the salaries of white and colored teachers in Anne Arundel County is due to discrimination on account of race or color. I find as a fact from the testimony that it is." This lawsuit pushed the state to level statewide pay for the 1940–41 school year. Additional NAACP lawsuits resulted in equal pay for Black teachers elsewhere. Fifty years later, the Reagan administration would advocate for White teachers who sued their school board, claiming that courts should resolve their claims no differently than that of Mills.

IN NOVEMBER 1985, Tom Bearden, a reporter for *The MacNeil/ Lehrer NewsHour*, a PBS television news program, traveled to Jackson, Michigan, about eighty miles west of Detroit. He visited White teachers who had sued the Jackson Board of Education. Inside a drab, earth-toned living room with mismatched furniture, four of the eight teachers behind the lawsuit recounted their anxiety of constant joblessness.

Adopted in 1972, Article XII of the collective bargaining agreement between the teachers' union and school board stipulated that if "it becomes necessary to reduce the number of teachers through layoff from employment by the Board, teachers with the most seniority in the district shall be retained, except that at no time will there be a greater percentage of minority personnel laid off than the current percentage of minority personnel employed at the time of the layoff." Because of this provision, the school district retained Black teachers with less seniority and cut more senior White teachers. As the economy struggled through the 1970s, and Jackson's population shrank, the tax base shriveled right as the demand for teachers dwindled, sparking ever-present worry of layoffs. Virtually every year as summer break neared, some teachers received notice of their discharge, and would then wonder for months if the district would rehire them for the fall. On April 7, 1981, the eight White teachers learned that they would not have employment for the 1981–82 school year and possibly beyond. In September, they filed suit in federal court, framing Article XII as "a naked racial preference" that violated their equal protection rights.

Susan Diebold, one of the White teachers, told Bearden, "The whole time I was on layoff, every day I was worried. It was awful."

"I'm being discriminated against because of my color," said Susan Lamm. "I am continually laid off because I'm white."

Lamm, who endured nine layoffs spanning twelve years, told Bearden, "We're not doing anything different than a Black person would do if they were laid off because of their color. We're standing up for our constitutional rights. And I don't think that that's being racist."

On November 6, 1985, when the Supreme Court heard the case, *Wygant v. Jackson Board of Education*, seven of the teachers had regained their jobs but didn't know how long they would keep them. "We stand to lose again and again," Wendy Wygant said. The defenders of these teachers portrayed them as victims not unlike Walter Mills, teachers shortchanged because of race, a description that ignored the school district's history. Ignored American history. A description, in other words, rooted in ignorance.

IN 1981, CLEOMAE DEAN DUNGY, a Black teacher at Jackson High School, like the White teachers who sued, lost her job. "The main problem is the money crunch," the 1980–81 Jackson High yearbook explained, "which has put the public school system in a very tight spot." Born just across from Detroit in Amherstburg, Canada, in 1920, Cleomae settled in Jackson, Michigan, with her husband, Wilbur L. Dungy, a World War II Tuskegee Airman. The same year they married, 1953, the Jackson school district hired sixty-one teachers, including Carrie Hannan, its first Black teacher. The pace of minority hiring snailed along, and by 1961, minorities filled only ten of the 515 positions. As teachers of color trickled into Jackson schools— one this year, zero the next—Cleomae and Wilbur welcomed four children. For a few years, the family resided in East Lansing, as Wilbur completed his doctorate, and Cleomae earned a master's degree in speech. They returned to Jackson, and in 1967 the Jackson school district hired Cleomae to work at Jackson High School where she taught English, public speaking, and a popular Shakespeare course, as her husband took a professorship at Jackson College.

In 1969, minorities were 15 percent of the student body in Jackson schools, but only about 4 percent of the faculty. Of the nine all-White schools, eight featured all-White faculties. Half of the district's Black teachers taught at two 70 percent Black schools. In April 1969, the NAACP's Jackson branch filed a complaint with the Michigan Civil Rights Commission detailing discrimination pervading Jackson public schools, particularly in the largely segregated elementary schools. The school board, the NAACP argued, preferred White teachers and generally restricted the few Black teachers to Black schools. The complaint further alleged that the district meted out harsher punishments to Black students, administered a racially biased curriculum, and fostered poor relationships with Black parents. White teachers, the complaint charged, "have lower expectations of black students . . . [and] teachers and administration interact negatively with black students on the basis of preconditioned methods and techniques of dealing with black students." One of Cleomae's daughters, Lauren, endured a year of a White woman elementary schoolteacher failing to teach her class. The teacher behaved as though she must control, not educate, Black children.

The Michigan Civil Rights Commission's preliminary report substantiated the NAACP's assessments. The school superintendent, in response, formed a committee whose preliminary report likewise found systemic troubles. "Jackson needs more qualified minority group teachers, administrators and counselors," the committee's report stressed. "Minority group students . . . need to associate with persons of their own ethnic extraction who have proven levels of achievement." The role model theory. "White students have to grow up in schools where successful minority group professional people are more frequent because the attitudes these students form in their school years are the attitudes they carry through life."

An example corroborating the role model theory comes from Cleomae's family. Her oldest son, Tony, quit the football team ahead of his senior year at Jackson Parkside High School after learning that he had been voted a team captain but not his best friend Bobby, also Black. The two had starred on the team since their sophomore year, and Tony suspected the predominantly White school intervened to select a White player as the other captain. After learning about Tony's decision, Leroy Rockquemore, a Black assistant principal at Frost Junior High School where Tony had attended, invited Tony to his home. Rockquemore had developed a relationship with him and other kids, eating with them during lunch and taking them to sporting events to show that he cared.

"You can't quit," Rockquemore told Tony. "You're not going to make things better by quitting." Tony's father had said the same, but hardheaded teenage boys often need to hear the words from another voice. Tony followed the advice of a Black educator hired around the time the NAACP lodged its complaint, rejoining the team. He later accepted a football scholarship to the University of Minnesota and played in the NFL, where he won a Super Bowl ring before becoming a coach. *That* Tony Dungy was the first Black head coach to lead his team, the Indianapolis Colts, to a Super Bowl victory.

The report urged that "within a year each of the 22 elementary schools in Jackson should include at least two minority members on the school staff" and noted that local racism, like housing discrimination, scared off minority teachers. In the late 1930s, the federal government redlined Jackson, producing investments and home-ownership in the White parts of town, poverty and dereliction in the

Black parts. The committee advised that "affirmative steps be taken to deal with those problems and to recruit minority teachers."

Rather than deal with a lawsuit, the school board, teachers' union, and the superintendent's committee worked cooperatively to tackle these problems. One solution involved a pledge to "take affirmative steps to recruit, hire and promote minority group teachers and counselors as positions become available." Over the next two years, the minority teaching percentage rose to nearly 9 percent, still below the 16 percent of minority students though. Layoffs in spring 1971, however, disappeared much of those gains. The collective bargaining agreement had required discharges based on seniority.

In February 1972, White students at Cleomae's Jackson High, where 10 percent of the fifteen hundred students were Black, instigated a brawl with Black students stemming from a voluntary, Black-history-themed assembly. White students mistook it for a "Black Power" gathering and thought it intimidating. "The blacks were being pushed down their throats," one White boy complained, articulating learned behavior. "This is just too much too soon." The next day, forty-four Black students who attended Northeast Junior High School refused to enter their school, demanding a special assembly to discuss the Jackson High events. At Jackson Parkside High School, a race fight erupted among upward of twenty kids.

The violence roused the school board into renewed action. On February 17, 1972, the district's Citizens Advisory Committee recommended both full integration of the district's elementary schools in the fall of 1972 and that each have at least two Black teachers. The school board debated and ultimately agreed to it. And to avoid a repeat from the previous year of the district losing many minority teachers, the teachers' union, 85 percent White, voted for Article XII, the target of the White teachers' lawsuit. Without a court hounding it, the Jackson School Board willingly implemented what received adulation as a model affirmative action process, what the *New York Times* described as "a voluntary program negotiated as a labor agreement between the school board and the teacher's union."

During layoffs in 1974, the school board disregarded Article XII. The union and two laid-off minority teachers sued. The judge deemed Article XII constitutional and concluded that the school board had violated it, finding for the plaintiffs. Following this decision, the board followed Article XII each year, including in spring 1981, sparking *Wygant v. Jackson Board of Education.*

District Court Judge Charles Joiner, a Nixon appointee, granted the school board's motion for summary judgment in *Wygant*, ruling against the White teachers without holding evidentiary hearings. This meant that appeals courts would receive a case record lacking a robust documentation of the history that compelled the school board's remedial actions. The Sixth Circuit three-judge panel, which included another Nixon appointee, unanimously affirmed Joiner's ruling, holding that the school board and the teachers who entered the collective bargaining agreement had a legitimate interest in remedying past and ongoing misdeeds committed in the school district.

This meant that two Nixon appointees had rejected anti-classification and color-blind principles. Stewards of the conservative legal movement, men like William Bradford Reynolds, wanted to prevent similar judges from ever again receiving lifetime judicial appointments from a Republican.

On November 6, 1985, the Supreme Court heard oral argument. Let's watch.

AS WE WALK THROUGH the heavy oak doors into the Court Chamber and gaze at the raised mahogany bench where the justices sit, the Reagan administration has already influenced this event.

In June 1985, administration attorneys, including Reynolds, acting solicitor general Charles Fried, and a thirty-five-year-old assistant attorney to the solicitor general named Samuel Alito Jr., submitted a brief to the Court that translated the ignorance from Reynolds's National Housing Center speech into legal arguments. On behalf of the White teachers, the government attorneys informed the justices how the conservative team should analyze such matters. The brief argued that *Brown* specified that the Fourteenth Amendment "forbade all legal distinctions based on race or color," stripping racial oppression from the explanation of what actually animated the Court's decision. The NAACP lawyers, the brief further maintained, agreed that "the Fourteenth Amendment prohibits a state from making racial distinctions in the exercise of governmental power," mistaking how the NAACP warred against a lived experience—racial oppression—achieved through race distinctions. No tears fell from Black eyes merely because of a classification. No Black person whimpered, "stop mentioning my race." They screamed, "remove your dagger from my spine!" And, of course, the brief misrepresented Justice Harlan's "[o]ur Constitution is color-blind" line, simplifying it beyond recognition, replicating a Rembrandt portrait as a kindergartner's finger painting.

By providing legal analysis barren of logic and intellectual depth, by rooting their thought in ignorance, caste preservationists can transform the Equal Protection Clause into a guardian of White teachers who sustained no racial oppression. The Jackson Board of Education endeavored to retain minority teachers—it did not reduce White people to an inferior status. Each teacher remained an individual of a caste that retained many of the racial advantages, big and small, that it had enjoyed for centuries. The board simply wanted to create a better educational environment for all children, particularly Black children whose life outcomes suffered, for decades, because of the district's castework, because of the state's castework, because of the nation's castework. Reagan's lawyers pitched ignorance to the black robes in hopes that they would translate it into equal protection constructions.

Administration attorneys, though, will take no part in the oral argument set to begin. An attorney from the Mountain States Legal Foundation, a right-wing public law center in Colorado, will. In 1977, conservatives founded MSLF, which took over the case after the Sixth Circuit defeat. Other well-funded legal organizations formed around the same time to likewise push the courts to serve caste preservationist ends. MSLF opposed race-conscious remedial measures as much as the Reagan administration did and entered the lawsuit to win a key victory for the cause. "If this system is allowed to stand, it will institutionalize discrimination for discrimination's sake," said Diane L. Vaksdal, one of MSLF's five lawyers. "What they're saying is that black children can't learn from white teachers. That's like saying you or I couldn't learn from Gandhi or Martin Luther King."

Vaksdal, like Reynolds, peddled ignorance. After all, if the Jackson board thought that Black children couldn't learn from White teachers, the board would have supported school segregation and hired only Black teachers for Black schools. Jerome Susskind, the board's attorney, dubbed the MSLF a "stalking horse" for the Reagan administration.

"MR. CHIEF JUSTICE," says K. Preston Oade Jr., a tall, burly White man with thick glasses and silver hair, "we are here today because the individual petitioners have suffered what we deem to be the constitutional injury by being laid off on numerous occasions from their employment as tenured public school teachers with the Jackson School District in Jackson, Michigan. . . .

"The reasons for these layoffs are because of a race-based system for layoff contained in a labor contract between their employer and their union. We submit that this is an explicit use of race imposed and sponsored by the state itself," Oade said, "and as such we submit that it must be justified by the state and that justification must be of the most compelling nature."

The Court had never approved the use of a race-conscious remedial policy absent a judicial finding of prior race discrimination. And no such judicial finding existed here. Oade frames Article XII as a measure to bring racial parity between the student body and the teaching staff. White teachers, he argues, have a constitutional exemption from having their race considered for layoffs, but "students," he wrote in his brief, "do not have a constitutional right to attend a school with a teaching staff of any particular racial composition." And the school board's role model theory rationale for affording minority teachers extra layoff protection did not justify a race preference under a strict scrutiny analysis.

For the first time, a woman wears a black robe. Sandra Day O'Connor replaced Justice Stewart in September 1981. Born in El Paso, Texas, on March 26, 1930, the precocious and studious Day proceeded to Stanford after graduating from high school at sixteen. The same year she earned her law degree, 1952, she married John Jay O'Connor III, whom she met while on the *Stanford*

*Law Review.* Later, she and her husband moved to Arizona where her active involvement in Republican politics raised her profile. She won a race for a state Senate seat and then a state judgeship on the Maricopa County Superior Court. After she declined a gubernatorial run in 1978, the Democratic governor appointed her to the Arizona Court of Appeals. On August 19, 1981, Reagan nominated her to the Supreme Court, fulfilling his campaign pledge to put a woman on the Court.

O'Connor, fifty-five years old with graying hair, interjects first to ask in a stilted cadence, "do you think that a school board has the right to look at its employees overall and to look at the number of black employees it has and the number of black employees available in that immediate area for employment in jobs in the school and conclude for itself that the school hasn't done as much as it should have to employ black employees and develop a program to implement some effort to hire more black employees?"

O'Connor laces her reasonable-sounding question with ignorance. Her premise omits that the school board introduced affirmative action measures, in part, to remedy its previous preference for White teachers. By ripping the case from its backstory and framing the board's decisions as concerning a simple desire for racial balance, she misrepresents the case in a way that delights caste preservationists. Skinning the historical context from the dispute reproduces the ignorant legal analysis found in *Plessy* and that follows in *Parents Involved* and *Meredith*.

"Justice O'Connor," Oade replies, "we agree with that, and we think that as a predicate for properly conceived affirmative action that is exactly what any employer must do."

"Well," O'Connor asks, continuing her questioning based on an unserious premise, "could it, as part of the program, adopt some kind of layoff policy like this if it felt it were necessary to complete the implementation?" The question foregrounds a peculiarity about the case. Affirmative action typically concerns hiring. White people who believe they are victims of an affirmative action hiring plan lose nothing they possess when not hired. This case involves *layoffs*. The White teachers *had* employment and then didn't, they supposed, because of Article XII.

"We think that there are some differences between affirmative action recruiting and what an employer may do to incumbent employees," Oade answers, framing the case as especially problematic because the White teachers lost actual employment. "We think to take two public employees, one white and one black, and to treat them differently because of their race must, as I've said, bear a most extraordinary justification."

"Yes. Do you think it is possible under the kind of inquiry I suggested?" O'Connor asks.

"I think, Justice O'Connor, there are, for example, school desegregation cases where the courts have found that in order to remedy on-going constitutional violations in segregated school districts and in order to have effective desegregation that it may be necessary to make layoffs by race, but only if strictly necessary to remedy constitutional violations. And, of course, there are no such constitutional violations in this case. We say there is no balancing to be done. Individuals, says the Constitution, have a right to equal protection under the laws. If there is some injury that must be remedied or some other compelling constitutional value, then there is a balancing test to be done, but in this case before the Court, we pled in the complaint in the lower courts in paragraph 21 of our complaint that . . . and I quote, 'There has been no finding of past employer discrimination in the hiring of teacher personnel on the part of the Jackson School Board by a governmental agency competent to rule on such matters.' "

Oade is right. But misleading. No finding of past discrimination exists because the district court granted the school board's summary judgment motion before discovery, and because the school board, after the NAACP filed its complaint with the Michigan Civil Rights Commission in 1972, decided to address the problem voluntarily. If the board had ever fought integration, a court would have certainly made such a finding.

"Isn't it true," Justice Marshall asks, referring to the education board's long-standing pro-White hiring preference, "that some of the teachers in your group got their jobs solely because of the color of their skin?" the failing voice of the seventy-seven-year-old trailing off.

Marshall highlights a crucial point—the White teachers want the Court to invalidate a collective bargaining agreement provision that harms them, which would leave in place the benefits they've enjoyed all their lives that are invisible to them. The White teachers were born into an environment that made employment success far easier. And for decades, the Jackson School Board had preferred to hire them as the slow pace of minority hiring continued until the NAACP's complaint. The Jackson board functioned as part of the caste system, violating the equal protection rights of Black residents through both inaction and action. Atoning for that through race-conscious measures did not reduce the teachers to members of an inferior caste.

"No, we reject that, Justice Marshall," Oade replies, denying that the teachers benefited from being White.

"Is there anything in the record to prove it?" Marshall asks.

"There is nothing to prove . . ."

Marshall interrupts: "Didn't you have segregated schools in Jackson?"

Oade hesitates. A direct answer would divulge that the school board's efforts to diversify its faculty helped redress a specific injury the board had inflicted. The Court not having this knowledge—ignorance—helps the plaintiffs. A cagey Oade starts his answer, "We think . . ."

Marshall interrupts, "Didn't you?"

"We don't believe that is correct, Justice Marshall."

"You never had segregated schools in Jackson?"

"The record goes back in this case to 1953 and we know one thing about the Jackson School District in 1953 . . ."

"My phrase was ever," Marshall reiterates.

"It—"

Marshall's impatience swells: "Did you ever have segregated schools in Jackson?"

"I can't answer that question, Justice Marshall. The record does not answer that."

"But, did you look that up?" Marshall asks. "Were you interested in finding out?"

"I was very interested in finding out."

"Well, did you find it?" Marshall asks, lathering his voice with incredulity, given that Oade could have easily found the answer to the question.

"We have data . . ."

"Is the answer yes or no?" Marshall asks again, tired of Oade ducking the obvious answer.

"The answer is the record does not show that."

"And, you didn't find it?"

"And, I did not find it."

Oade regains his footing when he scathes Article XII. "It uses race to determine and assign job rights without any utilization analysis of its work force," he laments, "without any determination that they are not hiring or retaining minorities according to the available supply, without any goals and timetables to place some kind of appropriate limit on what is being done here."

Marshall responds that the layoff provision resulted from collective bargaining between the school board and an overwhelmingly White union. "Well, I don't see how much clout twenty has over eighty percent. I have great difficulty in finding that clout," Marshall sputters through his raspy voice.

"Justice Marshall, first of all, we want to upset it because it is unconstitutional, and it deprives the petitioners before this Court of their constitutional rights, and we object to any characterization that this was carefully negotiated." Oade ends his argument, and the school board's attorney follows.

"Mr. Chief Justice, and may it please the Court," says Jerome A. Susskind, a short man with a nasally voice. "By 1972, this Court had charged school boards to step up to their Fourteenth Amendment duties to end discrimination and integrate their schools, advising boards to evaluate the total facts and to review a wide range of factors. This is exactly what the Jackson Board did as a part of a comprehensive, four-year study. The Board knew that the district had discriminated against students and faculty. The Jackson Board further knew minority teachers would be necessary for faculty integration and were educationally essential to aid students who will live in the society. The educational policy was sound, and the governmental interest was compelling. Article XII was but a part of total integration. It was arrived at bilaterally. All the teachers' views were represented. It is clearly designed so that the gains made would not be in vain and destroyed in the event of a decline in total student enrollment."

Susskind is arguing that the Jackson board's action to integrate its faculty promotes *Brown*'s logic. The effort resulted from the well-founded conclusion that Jackson's own discrimination caused the lack of Black teachers and that this harmed students, particularly Black students. When the school adopted a desegregation plan, therefore, it forged another plan to integrate its faculty. "Absent Article XII, the district," Susskind wrote in his brief, "would have very few minority teachers and the Jackson Board's effort to integrate its school system would be frustrated. The Fourteenth Amendment does not require this result."

"Has there ever been any judicial decision of discrimination by the board?" asks Justice Powell in an aged voice, seeking to understand whether any court had found that the school board had discriminated in the past.

"No judicial. But the board, the board, I think . . ."

Powell interrupts. "Has there ever been any judicial decision?"

"You have, of course, the NAACP," Susskind replies.

"The answer with respect to this board is no, isn't it?"

"Your Honor," Susskind says, "there has been no judicial determination, and it was a voluntary effort to integrate, and there was no reason for a trial."

"So, there has been no judicial determination?"

"That is correct for those reasons," responds Susskind. "Now, let me also say as to the facts and the stipulated record, Justice Powell, that Jackson surely knew what was going on there, but didn't want to flail itself publicly either," Susskind says. "So, I guess the main fault we seem to have here is that we don't have a really good record because we voluntarily integrated. Now, had we been like Dayton or like Columbus or Detroit and refused to integrate, did not obey this Court's order until somebody sued us and made us do it, we would have the record you would want. But Jackson voluntarily integrated and, therefore, it doesn't have the record. So, we are sort of in a Catch-22 situation on that."

O'Connor fixates on whether the Jackson board had a compelling state interest to pursue a race-conscious remedy. "Now, what is the compelling interest that the school board asserts here?" she asks. "Is it to maintain a faculty/student ratio or is it some other purpose? What do you rely on today?"

Susskind replies that the school board "was looking at the fact that it had to integrate, to look at the faculty and the students. I am talking about the students by placement and the need for integration and where the faculty was placed and what they would have to address on that issue. But, at the same time they were dealing with the question of integration, they also were dealing with the issue of educational soundness, for a diversified faculty, and dealing with that problem. Now, if you are asking me which is more important, they were both equally important."

"So," O'Connor responds, "the Board does rely essentially on faculty/student ratio and the role model rationale."

"Justice O'Connor, I didn't say that, and I didn't mean that. I think what I was looking at specifically was what was its duty to integrate, how to go about that integration, and certainly at the same time . . . and we make no apology for it . . . educationally—"

"You are talking about hiring employees, integrate hiring?" she asks.

"I would just like to, if I may for you, lay out some facts that I think the Court should be looking at," he says. "Two hundred and fifty teachers were hired during the '50s. One of them was a minority teacher. In 1961, you had twelve thousand six hundred eleven students, five hundred fifteen teachers, and ten of them were minority. Now, by 1971, and this is stipulated to in the record, they went on an intensive recruitment program to bring teachers in. Now, in 1972, okay, you actually had the integration plan which now went to busing and went to the allocation of the faculty. You just had those hiring gains. Now, the reason it is addressed in Article XII is if you are not going to do something about layoffs is it going to be considered by the public as a good faith effort to integrate?"

"Maybe I can't get an answer," O'Connor says, rather remarkably, "but I really would like to know what the compelling state interest is that you are relying on for this particular layoff provision in a nutshell."

Ignorance describes the state of lacking knowledge. Susskind just revealed the compelling justification—remedying segregation and the once near-exclusion of minority teachers. Confronting that complicates the matter for caste preservationists who would rather treat history as unknown and irrelevant for constitutional construction.

The justices will soon hold a conversation that helps Chief Justice Roberts write his *Parents Involved* and *Meredith* opinion.

DURING THEIR CONFERENCE to discuss *Wygant*, the justices continued their near decade-long debate on the proper standard of review for remedial race-conscious policies. Customarily dressed in business attire for these assemblages, the justices huddled around the large mahogany table near the black fireplace in the spacious, though sparsely furnished, Conference Room. Chief Justice Burger, seated on the eastern end of the table, his back to a tall window overlooking Second Street, remarked first.

"Societal discrimination has never commanded a court here," he stated, meaning the Court had never deemed general societal discrimination reason enough to support race-conscious remedies.

In 1984, the Supreme Court reviewed a Florida judge's decision to strip a White mother of custody of her daughter. The father, White, sought full custody because the mother, his ex-wife, was cohabitating with a Black man. The trial judge, believing that the social stigma of interracial relationships would scar the daughter, bowed to the father's wishes. In *Palmore v. Sidoti*, the Supreme Court reversed the trial judge and proclaimed that racial "classifications are subject to the most exacting scrutiny; to pass constitutional muster, they must be justified by a compelling governmental interest and must be 'necessary . . . to the accomplishment' of their legitimate purpose." But in *Wygant*, the Sixth Circuit administered a less rigorous test. Burger expected the Court to apply the same test to evaluate Article XII as it did in *Sidoti*.

"Close scrutiny," Burger told his colleagues below the high ceiling, "searching examination is the test—a compelling state inter-est must be shown, and the court of appeals said 'reasonableness.' Without a finding of actual discrimination, you cannot sustain the contract. A school board is not like Congress or a state legislature to decide these questions." Burger sided with the White teachers.

The senior-most associate justice, Brennan, seated across from Burger, said the Court should follow *Steelworkers v. Weber*. In that 1979 case, the Court upheld a private employer's affirmative action hiring plan as legal under the Civil Rights Act of 1964. "Because I believe *Weber* applies," Brennan remarked, "and that the state has compelling interests in remedying past discrimination and creating a diverse faculty, the remaining question is whether the means chosen here are acceptable. I think they are." Brennan backed the Jackson Board of Education.

"The desire to have a diverse faculty does not, without more, jus-tify what is done here," White said, disagreeing with Brennan. "I don't find any conclusion of discrimination, societal or otherwise." The teachers received another vote.

Marshall, a vote for the education board, countered White. "It is not clear whether this was done solely on race. There were segre-gated schools when this contract was made," contradicting Burger and White's view that the Court should operate from the position that no race discrimination had occurred before Article XII because no court had found that to have been true.

Blackmun, another vote for the board, reflected similarly. "I stand with my *Bakke* and *Weber* decisions and affirm. This was a plan to desegregate." In both cases, Blackmun endorsed affirmative action as a permissible remedy to past and present discrimination.

"The classification is based solely on race," Powell countered. "It must be justified on compelling state interest grounds and the means adopted must be the least restrictive. There is no showing here that meets even the intermediate level of scrutiny."

Rehnquist, another vote for the teachers, added that "the redress of societal discrimination requires far more evidence of actual dis-crimination than we have here."

"I disagree with everyone," said Stevens, spinning the conversa-tion anew. "I don't rely on societal discrimination to justify this racial classification. I don't like having separate levels of equal protection. This was just an effort to integrate its faculty and student body. The idea was educational—to teach kids that whether you are black or white, everyone has a chance to be a teacher. So, there is a legitimate government interest, and if they need Article XII to do that, it is also legitimate." The board had four votes. O'Connor, the junior-most justice, went last, as custom.

"This Court has fashioned a standard of scrutiny for racial discrimination—strict scrutiny," O'Connor said. "The Sixth Circuit is wrong in applying a standard of reasonableness." O'Connor sided with the teachers.

On May 19, 1986, the Court announced its decision. As in the previous remedial race preference cases, a majority failed to coalesce around one anti-classification opinion, for which the Reagan Justice Department had pined. Powell wrote the plurality opinion that contained the Judgment of the Court, which found that Article XII violated the White teachers' equal protection rights. Burger and Rehnquist joined in full. O'Connor joined in part. White joined just the judgment. Thinking that the layoff provision passed constitutional scrutiny and wanting the case remanded for further fact-finding, Marshall dissented, as did Brennan, Blackmun, and Stevens.

Powell argued that state-sponsored racial classifications, regardless of their asserted remedial purpose, must survive a two-pronged strict scrutiny test, the test that would eventually win over competing strict scrutiny variants, the test that Chief Justice Roberts would apply twenty years later. First, the racial classification "must be justified by a compelling governmental interest." And second, the "means chosen by the State to effectuate its purpose must be narrowly tailored to the achievement of that goal." Compelling and narrowly tailored—that became the test. Powell identified neither a compelling governmental interest nor a narrowly tailored means.

Powell rejected that the role model theory met the compelling interest standard. Giving the theory the Court's blessing, Powell contended, would permit education boards to pursue policies, like the one under review in this case, far into the future—it offered no definitive stopping point. "The role model theory," he wrote, "allows the Board to engage in discriminatory hiring and layoff practices long past the point required by any legitimate remedial purpose." Furthermore, he insisted, it could empower a largely White area to hire no minority teachers, equating, oddly, an education board seeking an inclusive, diverse, integrated faculty to one *excluding* Black teachers. Powell also disregarded the education board's conviction that Black teachers in the classroom improved the educational outcomes of Black students. A wealth of social science research, however, has corroborated the role model theory. One study found that a Black child having two Black teachers by the third grade increased the college enrollment likelihood by 32 percent. Powell supplied no evidence disproving the role model theory. He simply discounted it based on the absence of knowledge.

Powell likewise considered remedying general societal discrimination an inadequate justification. "This Court never has held that societal discrimination alone is sufficient to justify a racial classification," he wrote. "Rather, the Court has insisted upon some showing of prior discrimination by the governmental unit involved before allowing limited use of racial classifications in order to remedy such discrimination." The Court had previously set a goal that school districts, voluntarily, should cleanse their segregated messes before a lawsuit arrived. Here, a district did just that, and the black robes punished it.

"Carried to its logical extreme," Powell argued, regarding the education board's desire to hire more Black teachers, "the idea that black students are better off with black teachers could lead to the very system the Court rejected in *Brown v. Board of Education.*" Powell repeated what a lawyer from the group representing the White teachers said before oral argument, showing how the ignorance that buttressed caste preservationism wormed its way into Supreme Court opinions. The Jackson Board of Education wanted layoff protections for minority teachers because students, particularly Black students, would fare better in a school with a diverse faculty. If the district believed that Black students needed to be taught only by Black teachers, then the district's decision to integrate made little sense. Powell balanced his opinion on shaky, illogical arguments. Ignorant legal analysis.

Powell also deemed that the school board failed to narrowly tailor the layoff policy given how significantly it burdened the White teachers who had committed no transgressions yet incurred a hefty price. "In cases involving valid hiring goals, the burden to be borne by innocent individuals is diffused to a considerable extent among society generally," Powell wrote. "Though hiring goals may burden some innocent individuals, they simply do not impose the same kind of injury that layoffs impose." In cases involving layoffs, "the entire burden of achieving racial equality [falls] on particular individuals, often resulting in serious disruption of their lives. That burden is too intrusive," Powell argued.

*Wygant* stood for the principle that equal protection required limiting the negative ramifications affirmative action programs could inflict on what Powell termed "innocent parties." The Jackson Board of Education openly stated its goal—create and maintain a diverse faculty, particularly considering its own previous anti-Black hiring policies, to better teach children. And the Supreme Court struck a central part of the plan down because it hurt "innocent parties" as though Black children were not "innocent parties" of America's—and Jackson's—race legacy. The Court protected White racial advantages and deserted Black children.

In his dissent, which Brennan and Blackmun joined, Marshall expressed his preference that the Court return the case to district court for discovery to gather all the facts. Nevertheless, he would have found for the education board on the merits. "I believe that a public employer, with the full agreement of its employees, should be permitted to preserve the benefits of a legitimate and constitutional affirmative-action hiring plan even while reducing its work force," he argued. He even exposed Powell's opinion. "The real irony of the argument urging mandatory, formal findings of discrimination lies in its complete disregard for a longstanding goal of civil rights reform, that of integrating schools without taking every school system to court," Marshall wrote. "Our school desegregation cases imposed an affirmative duty on local school boards to see that 'racial discrimination would be eliminated root and branch.'" If Marshall had steeped his argument in the anticaste principle, he would have authored a more powerful dissent that appropriately distinguished between what the White teachers experienced and what his client Walter Mills had decades earlier.

On May 27, 1986, Chief Justice Burger announced his retirement, granting Reagan the opportunity to further remake the Court.

"MY NAME IS JAMES J. BROSNAHAN," testified a balding White man in his sixties on August 1, 1986, to the Senate Judiciary Committee. "Between April 10, 1961, and February of 1963, I served as an assistant United States attorney, prosecuting federal criminal cases in Phoenix."

Brosnahan narrated how on November 6, 1962, he investigated illegal voting obstruction complaints. "One of the complaints frequently voiced on that day," Brosnahan recounted, "was that Republican challengers would point out a black or Hispanic person in the voting line and question whether he or she could read. . . . Arizona law required that a voter be able to read English. According to the complaints," Brosnahan continued, "these challenges were confrontational and made without a factual basis to believe the person challenged had any problems reading. The U.S. Attorney's Office was advised that because the challenges were so numerous, the line of voters in several precincts grew long and some black and Hispanic voters were discouraged from joining or staying in the voters' line." U.S. attorneys interviewed voters and polling place workers and concluded these complaints fit into a Republican effort to depress minority voting.

"I received a complaint on Election Day and went with an agent of the Federal Bureau of Investigation to a polling place in south Phoenix. . . .

"When we arrived, the situation was tense. At that precinct I saw William Rehnquist, who was serving as the only Republican challenger. The FBI agent and I both showed our identifications to those concerned, including Mr. Rehnquist. We both talked to persons involved and the FBI agent interviewed anyone having information about what had occurred at the polling place. In fairness to Justice Rehnquist, I cannot tell the Committee in detail what specific complaints there were or how Mr. Rehnquist responded to them. The complaints did involve Mr. Rehnquist's conduct. Our arrival and the showing of our identifications had a quieting effect on the situation and after interviewing several witnesses, we left. Criminal prosecution was declined as to all participants in the incidents at various precincts that day. Prosecution was declined as a matter of prosecutorial discretion." Reportedly, Rehnquist committed similar transgressions at other minority precincts that day.

Rehnquist participated in the Arizona Republican Party's Operation Eagle Eye, a 1960s voter suppression campaign that involved harassing Black and Brown folk while they stood in voting lines, attempting to disqualify and discourage them from voting. During the third leg of our journey, we discussed Charley Caldwell and Eugene Welborne in Hinds County, Mississippi, confronting voting harassment at a precinct in 1875. Conservatives repurposed such tactics in milder form to achieve the same ends—White rule. Rehnquist and others challenged Black and Hispanic voters to test their ability to read the Constitution in English, what poll workers believed he did to intimidate people from voting, something federal civil rights laws outlawed.

This behavior matched his views. As a clerk for Justice Jackson, he defended separate but equal and pushed Jackson to uphold Jim Crow education. In a written memo to his boss, he contended that Black folk had deserved only the rights that the White majority saw fit to give them, echoing Chief Justice Taney in *Dred Scott*. In one of his *Brown* memos, he wrote, "it is about time the Court faced the fact that white people in the South don't like the colored people; the constitution . . . most assuredly did not appoint the court as a societal watchdog to rear up every time private discrimination raises its admittedly ugly head. To the extent that this decision advances the frontiers of state action and 'social gain,' it pushes back the frontiers of freedom of association and majority rule." Rehnquist, along those lines, defended the constitutionality of excluding Black people from Democratic primaries. In 1964, he testified against a proposed Phoenix ordinance that would have forbidden "local merchants from refusing to serve black patrons because of race," calling the law a "mistake" that violated the freedom and the property rights of White business owners who wished to discriminate. And in 1967, he wrote a letter to the *Arizona Republic* against school integration proposals. He supported neighborhood schools "which [have] served us well for countless years."

"I have read the testimony and letter supplied by Justice Designate William Rehnquist to this Committee in 1971," Brosnahan told the senators. "On pages 71 and 72 of his testimony, he describes his role in the early 1960s as trying to arbitrate disputes at polling places. That is not what Mr. Rehnquist was doing when I saw him on Election Day in 1962. At page 491 of the 1971 Record in his letter, William Rehnquist stated: 'In none of these years did I personally engage in challenging the qualifications of any voters.' This does not comport with my recollection of the events I witnessed in 1962 when Mr. Rehnquist did serve as a challenger." Despite Brosnahan and others offering similar testimony, the Senate confirmed Rehnquist as chief justice.

In a 1986 article, Rehnquist pinpointed "original intent" as the bedrock principle of his constitutional philosophy. Original intent originalism, to him, required a search for "what the words [the framers] used meant to them." Rehnquist claimed that the Fourteenth Amendment prevented "invidious discrimination." The man who snubbed the anti-classification principle when it meant invalidating anti-Black laws flipped to support it when it could invalidate race-conscious remedial programs. Earlier, we toured the Barnwell Castle in Beaufort and discussed the caste preservationists who supported the state's former race-neutral jury selection law, celebrating its color-blindness, cursed the race-conscious replacement, maligning its color consciousness, and then endorsed Black disenfranchisement, praising its effectiveness. Rehnquist aped those men's mental gymnastics.

Reagan also appointed a new associate justice, Antonin Scalia, who attended the 1982 Yale Federalist gathering. Born in Trenton, New Jersey, on March 11, 1936, to a Sicilian immigrant father and a first-generation Italian American mother, Scalia excelled at school, graduating magna cum laude from both Georgetown University in 1957 and Harvard Law School in 1960. In 1974, Scalia served as assistant attorney general for President Nixon's Office of Legal Counsel.

In 1977, he joined the University of Chicago Law School's faculty where he became a leading conservative scholar. In 1979, his article assailing affirmative action that referred to Black folk as a "creditor race" delighted conservative lawyers. After Reagan nominated him to replace Rehnquist as an associate justice, the Senate confirmed him on September 17, 1986. Scalia styled himself as an originalist. "It's what did the words mean to the people who ratified the Bill of Rights or who ratified the Constitution," he remarked, describing his process, although Black ratifiers' thoughts never entered his judicial equations. Scalia strongly repudiated the notion that judges should interpret the Constitution as a living document, despite sharing William Bradford Reynolds's Fourteenth Amendment framing, one that lacked historical basis.

With Rehnquist and Scalia, the caste preservationist program for seizing control of the Fourteenth Amendment proceeded. The next key case involved one of the nation's most racist police forces. Caste preservationists would side with that force to further their aims.

ON JULY 7, 1986, Morris Dees, the head of the Southern Poverty Law Center, a small liberal public interest law firm headquartered in Montgomery, Alabama, walked across the hall into the office of his newly hired legal director, J. Richard Cohen. A thirty-one-year-old from Richmond, Virginia, Cohen had just litigated a case against dangerous White supremacists in North Carolina. Dees told him that the Supreme Court would hear a controversy the center had been litigating for years involving the Alabama state troopers. Every step of the way, the Justice Department, through previous presidential administrations, had sided with the SPLC and against the notorious troopers who had stonewalled integration efforts. But the Reagan Justice Department opposed the SPLC's efforts to compel the Alabama state troopers to promote Black troopers. Those efforts injured White troopers, the department complained.

Just two months prior, Cohen, a University of Virginia and Columbia Law School graduate, left a small D.C. firm, scouting a new adventure. When Dees offered him the position, Cohen jumped at the offer to do work that touched his soul. But Cohen questioned whether he could meet the challenge Dees tossed at him—argue the Alabama state troopers case at the Supreme Court. He had never even handled an appeal and believed Dees could pick a veteran hand who would better meet the moment. Yet when Dees asked if he would do it, Cohen responded:

"Of course."

On March 16, 1968, Oscie Lee DeVance, a twenty-two-year-old Black man, sat in his car outside a nightclub near Notasulga, Alabama. Suddenly, Notasulga police chief Bobby Singleton approached him. Singleton arrested DeVance for disorderly conduct and hauled him to jail. During booking, Alabama state trooper James Bass called DeVance a "nigger" and kicked him repeatedly. Singleton and Bass drove DeVance to the police shooting range where Singleton held a gun to his head as Bass bludgeoned him. They then shot at his feet while Singleton demanded that he dance. The Alabama state troopers helped enforce the racial caste system and would continue absent compulsion, meaning Cohen needed to win an affirmative action case before increasingly hostile black robes.

Inside his beautiful office, where he could look out onto the Alabama Department of Public Safety building, the troopers' headquarters, he studied the litigation that commenced in the 1970s.

ON BLOODY SUNDAY IN 1965, the Alabama state troopers had no Black members. None the following year. None in 1967. None the next year. And the next. In 1970, Frank Minis Johnson Jr., a federal district court judge, found that the Alabama Personnel Department, which allocated support staff to the Alabama Department of Public Safety, had practically barred Black applicants from employment. "From 1963 until the commencement of this lawsuit in June, 1968," Judge Johnson wrote, "federal officials made repeated but unsuccessful efforts to persuade defendant officials and their predecessors to adopt a regulation expressly prohibiting discrimination on the ground of race or color. . . . Defendants have repeatedly refused to adopt such a regulation. *Alabama is the only state among the fifty states which has refused to adopt such a regulation.*" In *United States v. Frazer,*

Johnson enjoined the Alabama Personnel Department from committing employment discrimination.

In 1972, the NAACP, on behalf of Black state trooper hopefuls, sued the Alabama Department of Public Safety. Judge Johnson concluded that the department had "engaged in a blatant and continuous pattern and practice of discrimination in hiring in the Alabama Department of Public Safety, both as to troopers and supporting personnel." In its thirty-seven-year history, the department had employed zero Black troopers. "This unexplained and unexplainable discriminatory conduct by state officials," Johnson stressed, "is unquestionably a violation of the Fourteenth Amendment."

Johnson required the department to "hire one black trooper for each white trooper hired until blacks constituted 25% of the state trooper force." In March 1972, the department hired its first three Black state troopers. In 1974, Black plaintiffs returned to Johnson's courtroom, complaining of continued efforts to foster a space for White troopers only. The following year, he found that the department had virtually closed the hiring spigot to stymie integration and had pursued other nefarious schemes to preserve a lily-White force. "[T]he high attrition rate among blacks," Judge Johnson observed, "resulted from the selection of other than the best qualified blacks from the eligibility rosters, some social and official discrimination against blacks at the trooper training academy, preferential treatment of whites in some aspects of training and testing, and discipline of blacks harsher than that given whites for similar misconduct while on the force." Johnson reaffirmed the hiring order and enjoined the department from continuing its noncompliance ploys.

In 1977, the Black plaintiffs returned to court, this time to lament promotion practices. After a long discovery period, the two sides, in February 1979, entered into a partial consent decree which required, among other things, that the department develop within one year a promotion procedure that would have "little or no adverse impact upon blacks seeking promotion to corporal." Five days after the judge approved that decree, the department sought clarification for the 1972 hiring order. The department argued that the requirement that Black folk fill 25 percent of the trooper force should apply only to entry-level positions, maintaining that for 25 percent of the state trooper force to be Black, nearly 38 percent of the entry-level positions needed to be Black. This, the department contended, would have resulted in more promotion-eligible White applicants being passed over than the Constitution allowed. Judge Johnson again sided with the Black plaintiffs, writing, "The Court's [1972] order required that one-to-one hiring be carried out until approximately twenty-five percent of the state trooper force is black. It is perfectly clear that the order did not distinguish among troopers by rank." As of November 1, 1978, not one Black trooper had reached the rank of corporal.

In 1983, the Black plaintiffs returned to federal court, wanting to force the department to promote Black troopers to the rank of corporal "at the same rate at which they have been hired, 1 for 1" until the department implemented a nondiscriminatory promotion process. The judge endorsed this plan, citing the need to redress both past exclusion of Black troopers and continuing efforts to frustrate progress. The Eleventh Circuit upheld the ruling, finding that the promotion plan would remedy the discriminatory "effects, which, as the history of this case amply demonstrates, 'will not wither away of their own accord.'" The courts employed the anti-discrimination principle to frame the ills at issue when, as we've seen before, the anticaste alternative provided a better framing. The department's efforts to keep the state troopers all White fit into a larger effort to use the troopers to maintain racial domination over the Black population. Think of Oscie Lee DeVance. By framing the dilemma as merely concerning discrimination, the judges invited specious comparisons between the race-conscious decision-making that locked Black folk out and the race-conscious decision-making that unbolted doors.

The Reagan Justice Department appealed the ruling on behalf of White troopers who lost promotion opportunities, contending that the one-for-one promotion plan turned White troopers into discrimination victims in violation of the Equal Protection Clause. William Bradford Reynolds had been itching to get involved with a race-conscious promotion plan case. The Alabama state troopers dispute, *United States v. Paradise*, offered him the opportunity.

As Cohen prepared, he understood *Paradise's* uniqueness. "The case presented a novel question," he wrote. "The Supreme Court had ruled that affirmative action orders were acceptable under certain circumstances when it came to hiring. But the Court also had ruled that affirmative action orders were probably never acceptable when it came to layoffs. Promotions fell somewhere in between. How would the Court see it?" As Cohen practiced his oral argument, fighting on behalf of Black Alabamians who he understood to have suffered on the bottom of the racial caste system since the Civil War, Thurgood Marshall, no longer willing to muzzle himself as he had through the first ten years of his Court tenure, raised his voice against the new push to reconquer the Fourteenth Amendment.

DURING THE PREVIOUS LEG of our journey, we explored how, in September 1968, Marshall celebrated the Fourteenth Amendment's centennial. "I'm not discouraged and I'm sixty, the great-grandson of a slave and the first Negro appointed to the Supreme Court," he told the audience. He lauded legislators, judges, and lawyers for "demonstrating a concern for fairness and justice unparalleled in the history of our nation."

A few months later, Nixon won the White House. The Civil Rights Movement, the Second Reconstruction, wheezed to an end. A conservative political renaissance launched and climaxed with the Reagan presidency. Marshall's swelling hope deflated throughout the 1980s. Reagan's landslide 1984 reelection afforded conservatives the power to further bend a nation and its courts. The likes of William Bradford Reynolds wielded it.

Black folk of Marshall's age, accustomed to losing the big fights, knew to pivot to the next goal, imbibing the intoxicating elixir of telling the enemy off. On September 5, 1986, in New York City at the annual judicial conference for the Second Circuit, Marshall told the enemy off. Each year since *Bakke*, Marshall had delivered remarks at the conference, bashing the Court's rightward lurch. Often, he maligned his conservative colleagues about criminal justice matters. This time, against a well-concerted effort to harness the power of the Fourteenth Amendment to protect White racial advantage, Marshall, overweight, slowly moving, and jowly, explained the ignorance undergirding the color-blind principle.

"Obviously, I too believe in a colorblind society," he told the judges and lawyers, "but it has been and remains an aspiration. It is a goal toward which our society has progressed uncertainly, bearing as it does the enormous burden of incalculable injuries inflicted by race prejudice and other bigotries which the law once sanctioned, and even encouraged. Not having attained our goal, we must face the simple fact that there are groups in every community which are daily paying the cost of the history of American injustice." Marshall thought these uncomfortable historical truths should inform constitutional interpretation. His adversaries culled a superficial lesson from history—that race consciousness was always morally wrong. Problematic when it abused a Black person. Problematic even when it relieved that abuse.

"The argument against affirmative action is but an argument in favor of leaving that cost to lie where it falls," the seventy-eight-year-old said. "Our fundamental sense of fairness, particularly as it is embodied in the guarantee of equal protection under the law, requires us to make an effort to see that those costs are shared equitably while we continue to work for the eradication of the consequences of discrimination. Otherwise, we must admit to ourselves that so long as the lingering effects of inequality are with us, the burden will be borne by those who are least able to pay." In *Wygant*, the Court let the cost lie with Black schoolchildren to protect White teachers, helping produce school faculties with fewer Black teachers, leading to fewer Black college students in the future.

"For this reason, the argument that equitable remedies should be restricted to redressing the grievances of individual victims of discrimination completely misses the point. The point is that our government has a compelling interest in dealing with all the harm caused by discrimination against racial and other minorities, not merely with the harm immediately occasioned when somebody is denied a job, or a promotion, by reason of the color of his skin," Marshall declared. His conservative colleagues denied that remedying past societal discrimination presented a compelling reason to racially classify. Had he preached the anticaste gospel as ardently as his opponents did anti-classification, he would have proffered the ideal framework for differentiating illicit uses of race from those he thought America needed to embrace. His recipe still would have flopped in the era of Reagan, but he would have bestowed better ideas to the next generation.

"It has been argued that the use of affirmative race-conscious remedies inflicts an immediate harm on some, in the hope of ameliorating the more remote harm done to others. This, it is said, is as abhorrent as the original discrimination itself. Some have compared the use of such race-conscious remedies to using alcohol to get beyond alcoholism or drugs to overcome a drug addiction, or a few more cigarettes a day to break the smoking habit," Marshall remarked, a slap at Reynolds's anti-affirmative-action metaphors. "I think the comparison is inappropriate and abhorrent. Affirmative action is not, as the analogies often imply, a symptom of lack of social willpower; when judiciously employed, it is instead an instrument for sharing the burdens which our history imposes upon all of us."

Marshall believed the persistence of racial inequality evidenced a suboptimally performing democracy. Caste preservationists attempted to impugn the morality of Black Americans who supported remedial affirmative action programs. Marshall reversed the accusation, alerting them that no, *they* committed the moral transgression—of forcing Black folk to dig themselves out of a pit in which White oppression mired them. Marshall articulated a righteous argument. Let's strengthen it.

We take our countries as they are. The good. The bad. We relish the virtues. We endure the pitfalls. For centuries, America, through White people operating as a collective, has purposefully advantaged Whiteness and handicapped Blackness. The betterment of both living White people and the White people yet conceived motivates this collective, producing a world where Black people experience fewer of the virtues and more of the pitfalls. The caste preservationist goal is to leave that imbalance alone. Let it remain. The proffered solutions, they swear, punish innocent White people. And that mustn't stand for the same reason why it shouldn't have stood when Black people were the target. But the White collective's racial domination pervaded so thoroughly, so successfully, for so long—and continues still—it long ago prevented the concept of innocence for We the

People. For when you become part of We the People, by birth or by choice, solving the problem becomes your responsibility. The Trinity guarantees a caste-less society. And all have failed. No innocence can survive in a sea of sin. Innocence can only come after we drain that sea. When we abolish caste as The Trinity demands of us. No American, no matter the race, can claim innocence. Not Thurgood Marshall. Not William Rehnquist. Not Allan Bakke. Not Wendy Wygant. We are but individuals who are still wading in that sin, individuals who have yet to drain the sea. We the People can bask in innocence once we have. But not until then. Not until we have complied with The Trinity. Thus, when the Court implicitly or explicitly regarded White plaintiffs as innocent victims of remedial policies, they misidentified them twice. None are innocent. And none can be a victim of an appropriate remedy to sin, a remedy that doesn't reduce a people to a caste, that didn't introduce new sin to the sea.

A few months after Marshall's speech, the Court heard oral argument for *Paradise*.

ON THE MORNING OF NOVEMBER 12, 1986, Cohen rode with Morris Dees to the Supreme Court. Cohen had gotten little sleep the night before, and a bout of mental fogginess overwhelmed him. As they cruised past Union Station in D.C., intense anxiety pushed him to consider belly-rolling out of the car, hopping on a train, and disappearing. He had been practicing for months. Holding moot sessions. Fielding advice from more seasoned appellate litigators. Cohen understood the White troopers' frustration about the one-for-one promotion remedy. But he also understood that because the state had subjugated Black folk for so long, courts needed to uproot the oppressive system that the state troopers helped pilot. Cohen had contemplated handing the case to an experienced hand. But once his eyes met the white marble and granite, a nervous Cohen entered the Supreme Court Building primed to defeat Solicitor General Charles Fried. Cohen slipped into the office of the clerk of the court, Joseph Spanion Jr., who made sure to greet attorneys who had never argued a case at the Court to check whether they had dressed appropriately and knew the rules. After passing inspection, Cohen entered the Court Chamber and conversed with Solicitor General Fried. He then chatted with Reynolds, whom he knew well.

"Oyez Oyez Oyez" rang out and thirty-year-old Cohen, thin, about six-foot-two with curly hair, stood up and the nine justices filed in, including Marshall, whom Cohen viewed as an awe-inspiring character. A legend. Cohen most fretted about O'Connor's vote. Thinking her a swing vote, he had planned to treat her questions with care.

"We will hear argument first this morning," Chief Justice Rehnquist said, for "*United States against Phillip Paradise.*"

Fried starting his argument eased Cohen's nerves. Fried offered a simple argument—that the "quota" discriminated against innocent White state employees "for no independently justifiable remedial purpose." The district court pursued this race-conscious policy to achieve racial balance at each rank of the police force. "This . . . goes well beyond a proper remedial purpose and cannot be justified under the Court's decisions," he argued, inviting the Court to follow *Bakke* and *Wygant* and discard an affirmative action plan.

Cohen listened to Fried and thought, "I got this guy. He doesn't sound like a lawyer to me. He sounded like a law professor."

ON FEBRUARY 25, 1987, Cohen received a call from the Supreme Court informing him of the decision. He darted across the hall to Dees's office.

"Good guys win again," he boasted.

Justice Brennan wrote the plurality opinion that provided that the "race-conscious relief imposed here was amply justified and narrowly tailored to serve the legitimate and laudable purposes of the District Court." Cohen paid little attention to O'Connor's dissent, but it taught two lessons—first, how ignorant legal analysis infected the Court in ways that predicted *Parents Involved* and *Meredith*, and second, how the Reagan Justice Department's language had invaded the Court.

O'Connor backed the position that race-conscious remedial policies must pass strict scrutiny. She conceded that the federal government, through the district court, had compelling reasons to remedy past and ongoing discrimination by the department, but denied that the judge devised a narrowly tailored promotion plan. The judge, she insisted, could have championed a solution that harmed White troopers less. She vented that "the one-for-one promotion quota used in this case far exceeded the percentage of blacks in the trooper force, and there is no evidence in the record that such an extreme quota was necessary." She glossed over, however, that numerous lawsuits had hit the department and the department's long record of filibustering orders to embrace inclusive hiring practices.

O'Connor preferred to bubble-wrap the White troopers, unwilling to let more than a minute cost of castework fall on them. She proposed that the judge should have chosen a less onerous remedy, writing, "the District Court could have found the recalcitrant Department in contempt of court, and imposed stiff fines or other penalties for the contempt." And herein lay the ignorant legal analysis. As Brennan's opinion observed, "the Department had been ordered to pay the plaintiffs' attorney's fees and costs throughout this lengthy litigation; these court orders had done little to prevent future foot-dragging." O'Connor advocated for solutions that had already proven ineffective. O'Connor could tolerate continuing castework against Black troopers but not impairing the promotions of White troopers.

Cribbing from Reagan Justice Department's language, O'Connor branded the Black troopers, whom the Alabama Department of Public Safety never wanted to exist and then oppressed the moment they did, "nonvictims." But she called the White troopers who received no promotions because the department had failed to devise a nondiscriminatory promotion policy actual victims. In other words, she contrived a world that defined the White troopers as real victims because courts blocked the department from continuing to persecute the Black fake victims. This ignorance mirrored one of the many logical pitfalls that contaminated Justice Roberts's opinion in *Parents Involved* and *Meredith*. That by striving to grant all children a better education, Seattle and Louisville had violated the rights of White children. Yet, courts should view a system wherein Black children generally received a worse education as irrelevant under the Equal

Protection Clause. They didn't want to drain the sea. They wanted to add more sin.

*Paradise* presented Marshall with a respite, a dollop of water to a thirsty desert wanderer. Yet, the underlying reality remained. Caste preservationists held more power than caste abolitionists and the political mood of the era showed scant indications of reversal. Marshall, in response, sharpened his public remarks and assailed the man most responsible for the Court's trajectory.

FOR A LOCAL WASHINGTON, D.C., television show that aired in September 1987, Carl T. Rowan, perhaps the nation's most prominent Black journalist at the time, interviewed Marshall. The justice discussed presidents and their race policies.

"I don't think Roosevelt did much for the Negro," Marshall said. "But I think Truman is going to come out on top. Eisenhower, I don't think did anything, except to try to undermine [*Brown*]—which he did. Kennedy was held back by the Attorney General, his brother. His brother said don't do anything for the Negroes because you won't get re-elected—wait until you're re-elected and then do it. And then he got killed.

"But Johnson, his plans were unbelievable, the things he was going to do. But he was too far out for Negroes and civil rights. He wasn't thrown out because of Vietnam; they just used that as an excuse to get rid of him." Regarding Carter, Marshall said, "I think his heart was in the right place. But that's the best I can do with him."

"What about Reagan?" asked Rowan about the sitting president.

"The bottom."

"The bottom?"

"Honestly," Marshall replied, "I think he's down with Hoover and that group. Wilson. When we really didn't have a chance."

"Yet he's been one of the most popular presidents the country ever had in the polls."

"Is he more popular than the average movie star?"

"A young fellow like me is not going to get mad at an old fellow like him," quipped the seventy-six-year-old president about the seventy-nine-year-old justice when asked for a comment. After reporters pushed for him to reply earnestly, Reagan said, "I hope he will be informed that isn't my record, not only in the administration but also as governor of California. In fact, I was raised in a household in which the greatest sin was prejudice. I just wish he had known that. From boyhood on, I have been on the side of civil rights and no discrimination, and I am just sorry that he is not aware of that."

Reagan arranged a White House meeting with Marshall. In the upstairs living quarters, the two spoke. "I literally told him my life story," Reagan later recorded, "how Jack and Nelle had raised me from the time I was a child to believe racial and religious discrimination was the worst sin in the world, how I'd experienced some of it as the son of an Irish Catholic in a Protestant town; how as a sports announcer I'd been among the first in the country to campaign for integration of professional baseball; how'd I'd tried as governor to open up opportunities for blacks. That night, I think I made a friend."

Reagan made no friend. Marshall subsequently griped, "I wouldn't do the job of dogcatcher for Ronald Reagan," who "started the downhill slide which is proceeding as planned in civil rights. You just get the feeling that it's hopeless." White America loved Reagan and Marshall derogated him, rare criticism from a sitting justice about a sitting president. A few weeks later, Marshall knocked the luster off White men White America treasured even more.


RETIRED CHIEF JUSTICE BURGER, the chairman of the Constitution's bicentennial celebration, which stretched throughout 1987, invited Marshall to participate in a reenactment of its signing in Philadelphia. "If you are going to do what you did two hundred years ago," a defiant Marshall remarked, "somebody is going to have to give me short pants and a tray so I can serve coffee." On May 6, 1987, Marshall addressed a legal conference in Hawaii instead.

"I do not believe that the meaning of the Constitution was forever 'fixed' at the Philadelphia Convention," Marshall said inside the luxurious Kapalua Bay Hotel. "Nor do I find the wisdom, foresight, and sense of justice exhibited by the Framers particularly profound." Marshall swung the cleaver at originalism, ascending at the time. If the framers lacked the special sagacity often attributed to them, then allowing their intentions or understandings propel constitutional interpretation centuries later disobeyed logic.

"To the contrary," Marshall said, "the government they devised was defective from the start, requiring several amendments, a civil war, and momentous social transformation to attain the system of constitutional government, and its respect for the individual freedoms and human rights, we hold as fundamental today. When contemporary Americans cite 'The Constitution,' they invoke a concept that is vastly different from what the Framers barely began to construct two centuries ago." Marshall told the audience at the patent and trademark conference that the citizenry's, albeit uneven, willingness to address national problems sparked those advancements. The founders deserved no credit.

"While the Union survived the Civil War, the Constitution did not. In its place arose a new, more promising basis for justice and equality, the Fourteenth Amendment, ensuring protection of the life, liberty, and property of all persons against deprivations without due process, and guaranteeing equal protection of the laws. And yet almost another century would pass before any significant recognition was obtained of the rights of Black Americans to share equally even in such basic opportunities as education, housing, and employment, and to have their votes counted, and counted equally." Here, Marshall outlined the knowledge that the conservative justices ignored—that for nearly a century after the Civil War, a color-conscious Constitution enforced a racial caste system.

"[T]he true miracle was not the birth of the Constitution, but its life, a life nurtured through two turbulent centuries of our own making, and a life embodying much good fortune that was not," Marshall maintained. "I plan to celebrate the Bicentennial of the Constitution as a living document, including the Bill of Rights and the other amendments protecting individual freedoms and human rights."

Failing health—overweight, wearing a hearing aid in both ears, and glaucoma in both eyes—diminished the lively character who argued *Brown*. The seventy-eight-year-old understood that the America he thought he had secured when he floated out of the Court Chamber on May 17, 1954, had not arrived and would not in his lifetime. During conferences, he castigated his colleagues for their crucial role in keeping Black people trapped by the evil the Constitution once countenanced and still did, yelling at the justices he believed undermined Black Americans. As decisions came down that he vehemently rejected, particularly *Wygant*, he grew angrier.

The next key case started with a Richmond, Virginia, city council meeting on the night of April 11, 1983.

"GOOD EVENING. MR. MAYOR, members of Council, my name is Stephen Watts. I am an attorney with the law firm of McGuire, Woods, and Battle here in Richmond, and I'm appearing tonight on behalf of my client, Associated General Contractors of Virginia, or AGC, in opposition to the proposed ordinance."

Per data compiled in early 1983, for the previous five years, Richmond had awarded White-owned firms nearly 100 percent of the public money spent on construction projects, totaling approximately $124 million. The majority-Black city council, in a 50-percent-Black city, had invited feedback from the community on whether to adopt a minority set-aside program mimicking what the *Fullilove* Court approved. Richmond's remedial plan required prime contractors who received a construction contract to outline how minority firms would receive at least 30 percent of the contract value.

"AGC is a Virginia non-profit organization," Watts explained, "composed of some six hundred general contractors, subcontractors, material, and service suppliers, located throughout Virginia. . . . AGC believes the ordinance represents bad policy and may be unlawful. AGC is opposed to any classification or preference based on race in the awarding of public construction contracts," Watts stated. "The effect of this ordinance will be to exclude nonminority contractors and subcontractors from a significant portion of the total dollar value of Richmond's construction projects."

Henry Marsh III, a Black councilman, said, "you indicated that one of the organizations you represented, Associated General Contractors, had six hundred general and subcontractors in Virginia?"

"That's correct."

"What number of that six hundred would be black?"

"At the moment, I think the answer to that question is none," Watts answered. "There have been some in the past. There are none now."

"Have you contacted any minority organizations or minority contractors?" Marsh asked.

"No, sir," Watts answered.

At the end of the hearing, the city council enacted the set-aside. On October 5, 1988, more than five years later, the Supreme Court heard oral argument regarding its constitutionality.

"WE'LL HEAR ARGUMENT NEXT," said Chief Justice Rehnquist, "[for] the *City of Richmond v. J. A. Croson Company*. Mr. Payton, you may proceed whenever you're ready."

In 1983, the J. A. Croson Company, a mechanical plumbing and heating contractor, won the bid to install stainless steel urinals and water closets in the Richmond city jail but couldn't locate a minority-owned subcontractor to fulfill 30 percent of the contract. When Richmond rebid the contract, the company sued, arguing that the minority set-aside violated the Equal Protection Clause. The Fourth Circuit, applying strict scrutiny, agreed. Richmond appealed.

The chamber had a new justice, Anthony McLeod Kennedy. Born on July 23, 1936, the Sacramento native earned degrees from Stanford and London School of Economics before graduating from Harvard Law School in 1961. In 1966, he helped draft an antitax proposition for Governor Reagan, who took an immediate liking to him. In 1974, when a Ninth Circuit seat opened, Reagan urged President Gerald Ford to appoint Kennedy, who then proved a reliably conservative federal jurist. After Justice Powell's retirement announcement, Reagan first chose Judge Robert Bork, a conservative firebrand on the D.C. Circuit Court. His history on various matters, including race, derailed his candidacy. Reagan, afterward, selected Kennedy, a safer choice.

"Mr. Chief Justice, and may it please the Court," said John A. Payton, representing the city of Richmond, speaking in a smooth, polished cadence, "the sole issue in this case is the constitutionality of the ordinance enacted by the city of Richmond, to remedy the effects of racial discrimination in its construction industry." Payton, a light-skinned Black man with thinning dark brown hair and a full beard, practiced at a high-powered D.C. law firm.

"By enacting this ordinance," said the forty-one-year-old in a dark suit, "Richmond was attempting to address one of the most difficult problems confronting our nation and its cities and states. Identified racial discrimination is a scourge of our society. Richmond focused on discrimination in the construction industry and proceeded to try to remedy that discrimination."

Payton argued that no matter what level of scrutiny the Court applied, the set-aside should survive. The ordinance, as an attempt to correct the ramifications of race discrimination in the construction industry, satisfied the compelling interest requirement, he said, although Richmond did not stipulate that it had perpetrated that discrimination. And, he explained, Richmond narrowly tailored the ordinance. "It is a temporary, flexible plan that is designed to fit its remedial purpose and have minimal impact on the interests of non-minorities," Payton wrote in his brief.

"Mr. Payton," Justice O'Connor interrupted. "Is there any indication that the city considered any race-neutral alternatives before enacting a percentage set-aside requirement?"

"Well, the city was well aware of other efforts, especially efforts by the United States Congress, to deal with this problem," Payton replied. "The problem that the city was faced with wasn't that there was a group of minority contractors out there who were simply having trouble with bonding requirements or bidding requirements . . . not to say that those aren't problems, but they are, I think, secondary problems. The problem was that we had a business system that had precluded measurable minority participation."

O'Connor questioned whether the "state and local government have as much authority and power to act in this area as Congress does, with its express grant of authority under the Fourteenth Amendment?" Burger's plurality *Fullilove* opinion seemingly relied on the idea that the Fourteenth Amendment granted Congress special duties to combat these sorts of problems. Likewise, in *Wygant*, justices seemed to balk that the judiciary should green-light an education board in racially classifying. O'Connor's query forced Payton to defend why a city council should wield such power.

Payton followed a simple strategy—convince the Court to follow *Fullilove*. He, therefore, needed a persuasive answer for O'Connor. In his brief, he compared the city council to Congress, his only option. "Like Congress," Payton wrote, "the Richmond City Council had good reason to believe that there could be no change in the status quo without race-conscious affirmative action to break down barriers to minority opportunity in its public works program."

During oral argument, he told O'Connor, "I think that state and local governments have greater responsibility. These are problems that are very difficult to solve. We haven't come up with magic bullets for racism, or vaccinations to prevent it, and localities have to deal with these problems that they see every day in their contracting dollars, for example. And I think that it's not possible for Congress to come up with remedies that affect various localities in ways that will actually deal with these problems."

An equal protection construction that imposed an affirmative duty on states to dismantle the racial caste system would have supported the position that the Fourteenth Amendment empowered Richmond to level the stark racial imbalances in question. Given that the Court had axed this construction in the 1870s, however, Payton could not restore it in the Reagan era. Decisions written during a time when White Americans widely accepted the biological inferiority of Black people still shaped the legal landscape a century later.

"The Fourteenth Amendment was precisely designed to prohibit States from taking action on the basis of race, wasn't it?" O'Connor asked.

"I think the Fourteenth Amendment was designed in a way to require States to treat people fairly," Payton replied. "And I think this Court has dealt in the past, on several occasions, with whether or not States can take action that would be characterized as affirmative action, and I think the analysis is, there are disagreements on the edges, but the analysis is, if there is a sufficient or compelling state interest, and the means are sufficiently related or narrowly tailored, that it is authorized for a state to do that, and for the state's political subdivisions to do it as well."

Walter H. Ryland, a Richmond-born attorney, represented the Croson Company. The Reagan administration's brief, written by Solicitor General Fried and Reynolds, nonetheless, contained the Croson Company's most meaningful representation. The ordinance racially classified, the brief argued, and no different than an anti-miscegenation statute, it thus must pass strict scrutiny. The brief asked the Court to, for the first time, write a majority opinion that held that courts must evaluate remedial uses of race the same as it did invidious racial classifications—that "the racial classification must be 'narrowly tailored' to achieve a 'compelling' governmental interest."

The brief denied that the near-zero Black participation in local public construction projects, absent any proof that Richmond had caused those racial imbalances, presented a viable basis for a race-conscious remedial policy. "[Richmond] has at most identified race-neutral conditions perpetuating the effects of past discrimination," the brief stated. "Accordingly, the ordinance cannot be justified as a remedy for unlawful discrimination by others in the local construction industry." Fried and Reynolds, furthermore, denied that Richmond narrowly tailored the ordinance given that the city tried no race-neutral alternatives first. The 30 percent set-aside, moreover, "bears no relation to the percentage of qualified minority group members in the relevant pool of those able to participate as subcontractors." Per the brief, Richmond had passed an ordinance that helped nonvictims and turned White-owned firms into actual victims.

On January 23, 1989, the Supreme Court handed down its decision. The next day, *New York Times* reporter B. Drummond Ayres, a bespectacled White man in his fifties, visited the former capital of the Confederacy to appraise its impact.

JUSTICE O'CONNOR COMPOSED the majority opinion that invalidated Richmond's set-aside. Only Brennan, Marshall, and Blackmun dissented. For the first time, a majority held that race-conscious remedial programs must pass strict scrutiny, the lyrics Marshall had fought to never hear from the mahogany bench since *Bakke*. O'Connor found neither a compelling reason, nor a narrowly tailored means. Richmond defended the set-aside as a benign policy enacted to help subjugated peoples, not punish White folk. O'Connor countered with among the most destructive ignorant legal analyses in the Court's history. She defended strict scrutiny as the solution to the nonexistent problem of distinguishing between policies geared to ameliorate past injustice and those implemented to subjugate Black people. You must inhale her funk of folly:

> Absent searching judicial inquiry into the justification for such race-based measures, there is simply no way of determining what classifications are "benign" or "remedial" and what classifications are in fact motivated by illegitimate notions of racial inferiority or simple racial politics. Indeed, the purpose of strict scrutiny is to "smoke out" illegitimate uses of race by assuring that the legislative body is pursuing a goal important enough to warrant use of a highly suspect tool. The test also ensures that the means chosen "fit" this compelling goal so closely that there is little or no possibility that the motive for the classification was illegitimate racial prejudice or stereotype.

Judges, according to this illogic, would struggle to distinguish the purpose of this set-aside from, say, an anti-miscegenation law, without applying strict scrutiny. But Brennan's anti-stigmatization principle would have solved the issue. The set-aside did not treat White people as inferior. And the anticaste principle would have solved the issue. The set-aside did not treat any White firm owner as a member of a degraded caste. Caste preservationists wanted courts to evaluate remedial policies as they did Jim Crow laws and O'Connor produced a rationale to support the thinking. And her reference to "simple racial politics" seemed like a barb thrown at Richmond, a half-Black city with a majority-Black city government, suggesting that base racial political calculations, not high-minded governing considerations, motivated city officials.

With these lines, Chief Justice Roberts would create a new song in *Parents Involved* and *Meredith* that equated Jim Crow education to school integration efforts in Louisville and Seattle. In protecting White racial advantages, justices orchestrated the argument that the worst instances of state-sponsored racial oppression looked the same as policies formulated to uproot the vestiges of that oppression.

Marshall's dissent blistered O'Connor's opinion. "A profound difference separates governmental actions that themselves are racist, and governmental actions that seek to remedy the effects of prior racism or to prevent neutral governmental activity from perpetuating the effects of such racism," he wrote. A justice with eyes could see the difference between a law premised on the inferiority of a racial group and a law premised on remedying a long-standing race oppression. "In concluding that remedial classifications warrant no different standard of review under the Constitution than the most brutal and repugnant forms of state-sponsored racism," Marshall penned, "a majority of this Court signals that it regards racial discrimination as largely a phenomenon of the past, and that government bodies need no longer preoccupy themselves with rectifying racial injustice."

Until the Fourth Circuit invalidated it, Richmond's set-aside succeeded. The seas drained some, showing a proof of concept for other cities. Black folk received 30 percent of construction contracts, before returning to receiving less than one percent after the Fourth Circuit nixed it. "We had been making good progress in race relations in Richmond, but now I worry," Councilman Marsh told Ayres, the *Times* reporter. Marsh pegged economic opportunity as the direst issue for Black Americans and the Court preventing the state from implementing race-conscious solutions snuffed the possibility for progress. "We were just beginning to get a number of black contracting firms steady on their feet," Marsh revealed. "Getting blacks into this country's economic mainstream is the key race issue for the rest of this century," he believed. "One of the best ways to cut black unemployment is to build up black businesses, and we were doing that, making real progress. A court decision like yesterday's is very, very damaging." Caste preservationists lusted after a Supreme Court decision like *Croson* because they understood how helpful it would prove in thwarting Black upward mobility.

*Croson* "scarred" Justice Marshall until his death. A wise mind understood the Court's majority would use strict scrutiny to kill almost every racial remedial policy. Through a construction of equal protection that protected White racial advantages and maintained White economic supremacy, the Court kneecapped the state from subverting the racial caste system. Marshall thought the nation needed to use race to get beyond race to enjoy a true democracy free from racial stratification. Until 1954, the Court had effectively repealed the Fourteenth Amendment. With the anti-classification and color-blind principles, the Court again awarded caste preservationists the interpretation of the Fourteenth Amendment that they treasured. In 1995, four years after Marshall's death, the Supreme Court, in *Adarand Constructors v. Pena*, overruled *Fullilove*, requiring that even federal remedial policies that racially classified needed to pass strict scrutiny.

Before we advance to the next leg of our journey, let's return, on May 30, 1942, to the Tanforan Racetrack in San Bruno, California, to discuss the seminal instance of ignorance that Thurgood Marshall could not correct.

HERE, AGAIN, inside the squalid horse stall, recall *Hirabayashi* and *Korematsu*, two seminal cases in which the Court will hand down opinions that will avoid the true toxin—racial oppression—that poisons life for people of color. If the black robes acknowledge racial oppression and the maintenance of caste as the actual dilemma, excusing curfews and internment then becomes an impossible assignment. The justices would have to justify subjecting an entire people without evidence of malfeasance. If the justices can reduce those curfew orders and internment to government actions that merely racially classify, however, they can proffer legal analysis that veils the grotesque face of what they condone. And what they leave behind, anti-classification, calcifies into a bedrock principle. Those two opinions, those twin jarring notes, resonate in all the music that follows. We must, then, identify the anti-classification principle as foundational ignorant legal analysis. Justices rise to the Court despite, or perhaps because of, their racial illiteracy. The responsibility for constructing the Constitution's equality guarantee falls on them. And the ignorant birth ignorance.

Decades later, when remedial policies reach the Court, the black robes will call on the sorcery of the anti-classification principle—that once allowed the moral abomination suffered here at this racetrack—to preserve White racial advantages. The watershed moment strikes in *Brown v. Board of Education*. It offers the best, perhaps only, moment where Marshall can convince the black robes to axe the anti-classification principle, although caste preservationism might ultimately win regardless. Marshall secures a once impossible victory for caste abolitionism in convincing the Court to declare separate but equal unconstitutional. But he does this through arguments that can superficially buttress the anti-classification principle.

That will work all manner of horror. An anticaste construction of the Equal Protection Clause, what Marshall should champion carries transformative potential, enabling state governments and the federal government to redress what the racial caste system inflicts. The anticaste principle finding no home in Supreme Court precedent helps ignorance drown Chief Justice Roberts's *Parents Involved* and *Meredith* opinion. And it prevents *true* reform. The Fourteenth Amendment demands that states affirmatively provide equal protection and allows Congress to come forward whenever the states fall behind. The existence of the racial caste system demonstrates the miscarriage of duty. Both the federal government and the states, therefore, are failing We the People, a failure that must be solved fully to comply with The Trinity's national edict to guarantee Black freedom.

Yet, perhaps the most perverse aspect of the last two legs of our journey has slipped our surveilling eye—that the policies discussed will be insufficient to the task. Affirmative action presents an ineffective, lazy option to remedying caste. Not enough. Not nearly enough. But these early solutions, like set-asides and special admissions programs, quickly rise to salience and quickly face political and judicial attack. This hostile environment chokes out the breathing room to devise better, more creative solutions, solutions that will almost certainly take race into account. Caste abolitionists should have one goal—convincing the Court to allow past and ongoing general societal oppression to serve as a sufficient justification for race-conscious remedies. Caste preservationism, though, wins. Sin still pervades the sea. And We the People still bathe in it.

IN THE PREVIOUS LEG OF OUR JOURNEY, I divulged that the anti-stigmatization principle might have generated suitable results in race-conscious remedial policy cases but offered nothing in other key types of Fourteenth Amendment controversies. Those concern the flip side to the equal protection conundrum: What happens when governments engage in behavior that produces results that appear like intentional castework, but the alleged Black victim cannot prove that intent? Let's explore that question next.

This leg tackled the funk of folly. Time now for the funk of fraud.

# Seventh Leg:
# Thurgood and the Two-Faced Deception

WELCOME TO 1920S SEGREGATED BALTIMORE, where a fifteen-year-old Thurgood Marshall delivers hats for the Schoen-Russell Millinery Shop, a women's hat and dress boutique on Charles Street. Ripping north to south, the road vibrates laughter, tunes, energy, and horse-drawn wagons through this city on the Patapsco River. The boutique, owned by a Jewish man, Mortimer Schoen, an avatar for Marshall of a fair-minded White person, enriches a section of the segregated metropolis where many among the city's Black community spend coins on food and fun.

One day during five o'clock rush hour traffic, Marshall, the son of a Pullman-porter father, William, and a schoolteacher mother, Norma, waits for one of the countless streetcars that clack through the roads and connect the city. As he hops aboard one, struggling to maneuver among bodies while lugging a stack of four hatboxes, Marshall, skinny and tall, grazes against a White woman. A White hand yanks his shirt collar and jerks him back onto the street.

"Don't push in front of a white lady!"

Baltimore operates unsegregated streetcars, producing a rare locus of relative social equality. The law not enforcing the caste system in that space arouses some White folk to speak on the system's behalf through indignities and violence spewed against Black skin.

"Damn it, I'm just trying to get on the damned [car]," Marshall vents.

"Nigger, don't you talk to me like that."

William Marshall, a light-skinned man with blue eyes, instilled into his sons, Aubrey, a future doctor, and the younger Thurgood, that they should give respect and demand its return. "If anyone ever calls you a nigger, you not only have my permission to fight, you have my orders to fight him," the father admonished. "Either win or lose right then and there." Marshall obeys, setting down the hatboxes. Then and there, he fights. And wins.

Marshall, the lawyer, will learn how best to battle the brainchildren of White Supremacy that smite his people during his formative years—the various mutations of overt racism. Segregation enactments. Voter disenfranchisement hustles. Jim Crow justice. Marshall will explain in his *Bakke* opinion five decades later, "It is unnecessary in twentieth-century America to have individual Negroes demonstrate that they have been victims of racial discrimination; the racism of our society has been so pervasive that none, regardless of wealth or position, has managed to escape its impact." Experience teaches Marshall to conceive of oppression as the highly visible output, of highly visible hands, inflicting highly visible traumas.

But as Marshall's caramel skin wrinkles, his hulking jowls droop, and white tresses overrun his mane, White Supremacy will advise his disciples to change and become more silent, teaching them that castework can and must persist absent readily identifiable nefarious actors intending to subjugate Black people. Centuries of anti-Black machinations means caste preservationism can, on many occasions, proceed on autopilot. Just sit and allow it to happen. In post–civil rights America, the racial caste system will therefore endure without the once deafeningly loud gears grinding away.

What constitutional constructions could undermine this new, far more subtle, method of oppression? Marshall's Korean War experience will provide a preview of the sort of revamped antagonist he will combat from the Court.

BLACK AMERICAN SOLDIERS STATIONED in Japan post–World War II, by virtue of their American identity, enjoyed a higher social status than they did back home. The Japanese people, weary from death, destruction, and upheaval, considered them less as a degraded caste and more part of a much welcomed effort to rebuild their economy and government and ready their nation for peace and prosperity. The soldiers' reprieve from the Black man's emotional and mental trauma expired when, on June 25, 1950, North Korea invaded South Korea. President Truman hurried troops stationed in Japan to the screeches of artillery thunder at the 38th parallel, the line demarcating the two countries on the peninsula. One of the first dispatched units, the 24th Infantry Regiment of the Army, all-Black, initially collected flowers for their heroism. However, as for most others at the conflict's outset, the regiment sustained heavy casualties against the larger North Korean legions.

Soon thereafter, letters from thirty-six soldiers of the 24th and their families flooded the NAACP. The Army charged the soldiers with misbehaving before the enemy—in other words, for cowardice and shirking assigned duties. The *New York Times* covered the story of one court-martialed man, Lieutenant Leon A. Gilbert. The thirty-one-year-old, who commanded Company A of the 24th, received the death sentence for flouting an order, a month into the war, to captain his men into battle. "I did not refuse to obey the order," he professed. "I was trying to explain why it couldn't be carried out. There were twelve men in my command. Then I considered it my duty as an officer to show why the order meant certain death." The NAACP's Board of Directors sent an eager Marshall to the Pacific to investigate what befell the thirty-six. In January 1951, three years before *Brown*, Marshall arrived in Tokyo to delve into what he described at the time as "the most important mission of my career."

From 1945 to 1952, the Allied nations of World War II occupied Japan and headquartered inside the Dai Ichi Building in downtown Tokyo. Douglas MacArthur, the chief of the Far East Command, stewarded Japan's reconstruction from the sixth floor. Inside the inelegant, 580-square-foot presidential office, the general of the Army hung pictures of yachts on the wood-paneled walls and worked at a desk that gave a dining table aura. During this leg of our journey, we will explore how to interpret the Fourteenth Amendment to counteract the subtle, inconspicuous actions or inactions that maintain the system. Oftentimes, determining a person's commitment to the system proves difficult. In conversation with Marshall inside that office, MacArthur behaved like caste preservationists who conceal their fealty to White Supremacy, a deception that hinders caste abolitionism, a movement that prefers adversaries who advertise their objectives.

Upon arrival, Marshall conferred with General MacArthur and other high-ranking officials inside the massive Dai-ichi building. Marshall charged that the Black court-martialed soldiers "had been victims of racial bias and unfair trials and that the condition stemmed from the Army's segregation policies." MacArthur denied those accusations and allowed Marshall to access any information necessary to search for the truth.

Marshall's legwork uncovered alarming details. White officers had degraded Black soldiers, with one telling a Black soldier, "I despise 'nigger' troops and I don't want to command you and the Division is no good and you are lousy. You don't know how to fight." Although not all shared this view, enough did to both magnify distrust and erode confidence between Black soldiers and their White leaders. In barracks outside of Tokyo, Marshall interviewed thirty-four of the thirty-six court-martialed soldiers, and he spoke to others with pertinent information, unearthing exculpatory evidence. Great distances separated some of the accused from the fighting when they supposedly committed battlefield offenses. At the Army headquarters in Taegu, Korea, Marshall questioned one soldier sentenced to fifty years whose sprained ankle kept him sidelined. Another, Marshall learned, sat in a hospital at the time of his purported transgressions. When Marshall asked those with airtight defenses why they never offered them during their trials, all retorted like a soldier who said, "It wasn't worth it. We knew that when we went in that we would be convicted and we were hoping and praying that we would only get life. They gave [Lieutenant Gilbert] death solely because he was a Negro. What could we expect? We know the score."

Marshall's tabulations showed that, from August through October 1950, thirty-two Black soldiers were convicted of misbehavior offenses and sentenced to at least ten years in prison. Some of the trials took place at night, lasted fewer than fifteen minutes, and resulted in life sentences. During that same span, only two White soldiers were convicted of similar offenses, and the longer sentence assessed was for five years. One intoxicated White soldier abandoned his post, yet his five-year sentence was reduced to one year. Another White soldier fell asleep at his post but was acquitted against his commanding officer's testimony. "Justice in Korea may have been blind," Marshall wrote, "but not color blind."

Marshall concluded that an anti-Black mindset strangled the possibility of Black soldiers receiving equal justice. Strangled the possibility of them receiving due process. Their legal representation received insufficient time to mount an adequate defense. Their accusers detested them because of their race. The all-White juries were comprised of many officers who espoused this worldview. "[T]hese cases are rooted in the Jim Crow policies still persisting in the Army," Marshall observed. "There were no large number of courts martial in the Air Force, Navy or any other mixed unit. The responsibility for maintaining the color line in the Army in the Far East rests with General MacArthur. He has failed to implement the President's order for the elimination of segregation from the armed services. He could have moved promptly to that end as soon as the President announced a new policy as did the Air Force and the Navy. While there are a few mixed units in the Army in Korea the general practice is one of rigid segregation and is glaringly apparent at the headquarters of the Far East Command to which no Negroes are assigned." Marshall figured that the high casualty rates early in the war, aggravated by distrust between White officers and Black soldiers, convinced officials to scapegoat Black soldiers, the perfect foils.

Five weeks after his arrival, Marshall returned to the Dai-ichi building to present his findings to MacArthur. Marshall told him of clear evidence that would exonerate most of the soldiers and suggested that he, as the leader, bore the blame for the Army's Jim Crow energy. MacArthur dismissed the criticisms.

Marshall had heard from Japanese officials that neither the headquarters staff nor MacArthur's personal guard contained any Black soldiers. "Well, General, look—you've got all these guards out there with all this spit and polish and there's not one Negro in the whole group," Marshall said.

"There's none qualified," countered the six-foot MacArthur, two inches shorter than Marshall.

"Well, what's the qualification?"

Superlative battlefield performance, replied the Arkansan.

"Well, I just talked to a Negro yesterday, a sergeant, who has killed more people with a rifle than anybody in history. And he's not qualified?"

"No."

"Well, now, General, remember yesterday you had the big band playing at the ceremony over there?" referring to the grounds outside the building.

"Yes, wasn't it wonderful?" MacArthur replied.

"Yes. The Headquarters Band, it's beautiful. Now General, just between you and me, goddamn it, don't you tell me that there's no Negro that can play a horn," Marshall said as his eyes brightened because he had outwitted the general, whose face reddened with anger. The general told Marshall to leave.

This conversation shows how caste preservationists operate with two faces. One public. One private. The private face is the real face. The public face, the servant, exists to serve the private face, the master. The private face endorses the racial caste system. The public face feigns as much support for racial fairness as necessary but typically no more. The private face of General MacArthur backed segregation. His public face, however, disavowed bigoted intentions.

The Trinity forces caste preservationists to adopt two faces. They cannot openly declare their allegiances without putting White Supremacy's project at risk, and thus the public face deceives to protect the private face's interests. When societal commitments to racial fairness intensify, it requires increasingly elaborate ruses to satisfy the private face's objectives. During this leg of our journey, we explore how the public face reveals the existence of the private face when the public face articulates principles by which caste preservationists cannot live. Inconsistencies, we'll see, define the existence of caste preservationists. For example, a presidential candidate, whose private face cares nothing about the living standards of the Black caste, will campaign with a public face that pretends to "not have a racist bone in his body." Yet the politician, with his public face, will stumble at explaining why none of the supported policies promote equality, unveiling a caste preservationist private face.

Marshall's conversation with MacArthur confirms that he had cracked the code of this two-face paradigm. When he asked Mac-Arthur about the Headquarters Band, he appreciated that MacArthur would falter in his defense of wholesale exclusion of Black soldiers from prominent positions, considering the stereotype that Black folk are adept at musical performance. MacArthur's inability to justify such nonrepresentation spilled, to Marshall, the general's actual proclivities. Years later, Marshall remarked that MacArthur "was as biased as any person I've run across" despite the general uttering nothing explicitly racist to him. The inability to seamlessly toggle between the two faces has long exposed caste preservationists' dishonesty and *true* commitments.

In the third leg of our journey, we explored how the Court catered to Mississippi's deceit, upholding an 1890 constitution obviously birthed to annihilate Black civil and political rights. During this leg, we deepen our appreciation of the nexus between deceit and constitutional interpretation.

CASS GILBERT, THE ARCHITECT of the Supreme Court Building, designed for each associate justice a three-room office consisting of private chambers for the justice and two rooms to accommodate staff. A suite for a lean law firm. Inside Associate Justice Arthur Goldberg's oak-paneled offices, the Kennedy appointee had his law clerk, Alan Dershowitz, write a memorandum analyzing the death penalty's possible unconstitutionality. In spring 1963, Goldberg disseminated the finished product to his colleagues. "This Court has never explicitly considered whether, and under what circumstances, the Eighth and Fourteenth Amendments to the United States Constitution [proscribe] the imposition of the death penalty," it stated. "The Court has, of course, implicitly decided (in every case affirming a capital conviction) that the death penalty is constitutional. But in light of the worldwide trend toward abolition, I think this Court should now request argument and explicitly consider this constantly recurring issue."

Capital punishment had always carried the nation's legal blessing. Each of the thirteen original colonies, in fact, sanctioned it. Goldberg and Dershowitz, then, needed to convince four other justices to agree that capital punishment should surrender its long-standing status as lawful. They stabbed at an intriguing vulnerability—the executions of rapists, observing "the well-recognized disparity in the imposition of the death penalty for sexual crimes committed by whites and nonwhites." Between 1937 and 1951, they noted, 233 of the 259 persons executed for rape were Black. Puncturing the balloon here would, perhaps, deflate capital punishment statutes across the nation. Justice Goldberg's colleagues, however, snubbed his overtures to address the matter. Chief Justice Warren even advised that if he hoped to push the matter, he should scrap the race angle.

Months later, on October 21, 1963, the Supreme Court rejected hearing *Rudolph v. Alabama*, which concerned whether the death sentence assessed to Frank Lee Rudolph, a Black man, for raping a White woman violated the Eighth Amendment's prohibition against cruel and unusual punishment. With only three justices wanting to review *Rudolph*, one shy of the necessary four to grant an appeal, Goldberg took the unusual step of writing a dissent to the denial of review, or denial of certiorari. Joined by Justices Brennan and Douglas, Goldberg sidestepped how race polluted the practice of sentencing rapists to death, following Warren's guidance. Goldberg's dissent, nonetheless, excited lawyers at the nation's leading racial justice law firm.

In 1909, an interracial group of caste abolitionists founded the NAACP. A year later, the association took on its first major legal case—defending Pink Franklin, a Black South Carolina sharecropper wrongfully convicted by an all-White jury of murdering a White constable. For decades, the association invested resources and manpower into stopping lynching, whether carried out below poplar tree limbs or behind courtroom doors. In 1940, the NAACP board of directors, for tax purposes, spun the organization's legal arm into a separate entity, the NAACP Legal Defense Fund. In 1957, the LDF fully severed itself, becoming its own organization with its own board of directors.

Goldberg's memo awakened LDF attorneys into helming an anti-death-penalty initiative. Although various desegregation and Civil Rights Movement cases were hoarding LDF attorneys' attention, Jack Greenberg, Thurgood Marshall's hand-selected successor,

directed his attorneys to formulate a legal strategy that would persuade the Court to eliminate capital punishment, considered inter-
nally as another locus of racial injustice.

Triumph at the Court would require representing a death row
inmate convicted of a heinous crime.

AT ABOUT TWO IN THE MORNING of August 11, 1967, a twenty-nine-
year-old White man, William J. Micke Jr., a petty officer in the U.S.
Coast Guard, lay in bed with his wife in their Savannah, Georgia,
home. They both heard a noise that sounded as though someone
had stepped on a pan. Micke crawled out of bed and moseyed to
the kitchen, expecting to discover one of his children sleepwalking.
Instead, he surprised William Henry Furman, a mentally ill twenty-
six-year-old Black man, a burglar. Startled, Furman fled the home,
shooting backward through the closed wooden kitchen door after
escaping. He claimed that he had tripped over a cord on the porch
and accidentally fired his .22-caliber pistol. Detectives countered
that he shot intentionally. The bullet shredded through the door and
obliterated Micke's chest, slaying him instantly. At Furman's trial, the
judge instructed the jurors that they could impose the death penalty
as they saw fit. After an hour and a half of deliberation for a trial that
lasted less than a day, the jury returned with a guilty verdict and sentenced him to die in the electric chair.

Greenberg and Anthony Amsterdam, a foundational figure in the
anti-death-penalty movement, argued *Furman v. Georgia* inside the
Court Chamber. They advanced a straightforward argument—due
to a lack of standards and wide discretion given to juries under capital
punishment statutes, juries assessed the death penalty arbitrarily, violating the Eighth Amendment's prohibition against cruel and unusual
punishment and the Fourteenth Amendment's equal protection guarantee. On June 29, 1972, in a five-to-four decision, the Court struck
down every capital punishment statute in the forty-one jurisdictions
where they operated, forty states and the federal government, com-
muting about six hundred death sentences. *Furman* produced no
majority opinion. Each justice, rather, wrote his own, producing
uncertainty about what the case meant for the death penalty's future

and what style of revised capital punishment statute would satisfy five justices. Most observers reasoned that the invalidated statutes tolerated unconstitutional arbitrariness—nothing reliably distinguished between which defendants faced capital punishment and which ones did not. Justice Stewart's line, "death sentences are cruel and unusual in the same way that being struck by lightning is cruel and unusual" encapsulated the problem. If states wanted to reactivate the electric chair, therefore, they would need to enact statutes that rectified the capricious taking of life.

Georgia's staunch segregationist governor, Lester Maddox, lambasted the Court's *Furman* decision as a "license for anarchy, rape and murder." The day after *Furman*, five state legislatures announced intentions to pass new capital punishment statutes, and by 1976, thirty-five states had. This outcome surprised many observers who, in *Furman*'s wake, predicted the imminent demise of capital punishment in America. Some of these new statutes eliminated the possibility of arbitrariness by imposing mandatory death sentences for capital offenses. Other states, to similarly rid their processes of arbitrariness, adopted rules that provided juries with supposedly thorough guidance on when a crime could warrant a death sentence.

Four years later, in 1976, the Court decided five capital punishment cases jointly, generally known by the lead case, *Gregg v. Georgia*, involving these post-*Furman* statutes. The Court struck down the mandatory capital punishment statutes but affirmed those that offered juries "guided discretion." A seven-to-two majority concluded that these statutes resolved the arbitrariness issues illuminated in *Furman*. The death penalty drew fresh breath. And the LDF, convinced that race continued to corrupt decisions of life and death, needed to substantiate that these reworked statutes still permitted lightning strikes.

WHEN JACK BOGER, a White North Carolina native, graduated from the University of North Carolina School of Law in 1974, he wanted to launch his legal career practicing as a civil rights attorney. But in those days, top graduates from Harvard Law and Yale Law snatched all the openings at the most prestigious shops like the LDF and the

American Civil Liberties Union, driving him into a big New York corporate law firm. In summer 1976, though, the same summer the Court announced its *Gregg v. Georgia* decision, Boger slid into his preferred legal realm, working pro bono for the LDF on a capital punishment case, spending about five hundred hours spanning a year and a half defending Jerry Jurek, a White man sentenced to death for raping and choking a ten-year-old girl to death. Around the time Boger began his efforts on Jurek's case, Amsterdam pored over the opinions in *Gregg* for about a week, returning to LDF's Manhattan offices with a fifty-page memo exploring various legal arguments he thought might greatly reduce the number of executions or abolish the death penalty altogether. One posited that race discrimination in the administration of capital punishment statutes violated both the Eighth and Fourteenth Amendments.

On one occasion, Boger visited the LDF's office, a bit worn down and with mismatched office desks, and walked past an open room where inside a big map of the city of Denver laid on a table. "My God!" he thought to himself. "This is the room where they are planning the desegregation of Denver schools." Energy and enthusiasm pinballed through the organization's space. When one of the attorneys working on capital cases left, Greenberg asked Boger if he wanted the opening. Yes, he replied. "You've got Georgia, North Carolina, and a couple of other states," Greenberg told him. "I'm on the front line now," Boger thought to himself. He started in January 1978.

BOGER, THE NEWEST CAPITAL PUNISHMENT ATTORNEY, helped execute the LDF's anti–death penalty strategy geared toward achieving one overarching goal—saving as many fates from execution as possible. Amsterdam grew infatuated with employing rigorous statistical surveys to demonstrate that states still discriminatorily administered capital punishment statutes. Meanwhile, in 1979, David Baldus, a University of Iowa law professor, commenced his work on a complex mathematical study of Georgia's capital sentencing, investigating 156 pre-*Furman* and 594 post-*Furman* cases. This pilot study, what Baldus called the *Procedural Reform Study*, promised to present the most exhaustive post-*Furman* death penalty research findings. Baldus and his partners, law professor Charles Pulaski and statistics professor George Woodworth, did not expect their research to support litigation efforts. During this time, Boger, serving as co-counsel for various Georgia capital punishment cases, came to know Baldus.

In 1980, Jack Greenberg, armed with a quarter-of-a-million-dollar grant, scoured for a brain to conduct a new, groundbreaking, best-in-class empirical study of capital sentencing in a southern state. He selected Baldus for various reasons, including his honesty, scruples, and technical wizardry. A candid Baldus told LDF's attorneys that he expected the *Procedural Reform Study*, not yet complete, would produce unhelpful results. The Supreme Court, he figured, had successfully muscled states into adopting statutes that expunged capital punishment of arbitrariness. And, Boger further sensed, because of the progress that the Civil Rights Movement had forged, the imposition of the death penalty had reached evenhandedness. His skepticism enthused LDF attorneys—they favored a brain that doubted their thinking more than a partisan one.

After designating Georgia as the state to examine, from the middle of 1980 to spring 1981, with significant LDF guidance, Baldus, Woodworth, and Pulaski mapped out this new study's methodology. LDF attorneys expressed how crucial they considered the study's design—a proper approach, they predicted, would locate discrimination chiefly with *early* prosecutorial decisions. The design for the *Procedural Reform Study* concentrated on just two decision points— whether the prosecutor allowed the jury to consider assessing the death penalty and whether the jury assessed death. LDF attorneys wanted Baldus to conduct an even more ambitious and exhaustive study that would examine pretrial decisions. What charges did the prosecutor choose? Did the prosecutor offer the defendant a guilty plea in lieu of a possible death sentence if convicted? The idea intrigued Baldus. He and his partners tailored a questionnaire that accounted for more than four hundred variables and worked from a sample of more than one thousand cases from 1973 to 1979 where the defendant had been charged with homicide and subsequently convicted of murder or voluntary manslaughter. The approach required them to account for essentially any variable that could affect whether a defendant would receive a death sentence, implementing exacting mathematical scrutiny to determine to what extent race infected the process.

LDF attorneys, during this time, instructed lawyers throughout Georgia to plead Eighth and Fourteenth Amendment violations in any death penalty case, even providing sample language for petitions and briefs. The LDF wanted a federal judge to grant a hearing based on Baldus's still unfinished studies that they hoped would prove their thesis. With such results, the goal was to convince the federal judiciary to invalidate Georgia's capital punishment statute. When, in 1976, the Supreme Court upheld the state's new death penalty statute in *Gregg*, the justices trusted that Georgia was administering it in a nondiscriminatory fashion. LDF attorneys suspected Baldus would prove otherwise.

Like the LDF's original strategy to defeat capital punishment that prospered in 1972 with *Furman v. Georgia*, this new one, which Jack Boger would litigate, started with a death row client. This time, Warren McCleskey.

ON THE MORNING OF MAY 13, 1978, in Marietta, Georgia, McCleskey, a twenty-eight-year-old Black man, drove his dark blue 1971 Pontiac Grand Prix to pick up his three criminal associates. Ben Wright. Bernard Dupree. David Burney. They all first stopped at a friend's house to collect weapons, gloves, and other robbery gear and then parked outside a local jewelry store at about ten. They had planned to loot it at the start of the business day, but McCleskey had picked them up late and the store had already opened. Wright entered to canvass the spot then returned to the car, and the band of robbers foraged Marietta for a more palatable target. Finding nothing appetizing, the wheels on the big boxy car with an elongated hood spun southward.

In the early afternoon, they arrived at northwest Atlanta's Dixie Furniture Company, a place Wright had previously scouted. Burney ventured inside to inspect the situation. He returned, and McCleskey did the same. After the four hatched their strategy in the car, each, armed with a firearm, advanced on their mark. Wearing stocking masks, one secured the front and three entered the rear through the loading dock. A man inside the store screamed, "Call the police," before a masked robber whacked him with a sawed-off shotgun. The three in the rear bound the employees with tape, blindfolded them, and forced the manager to hand over the store's money, upward of fifteen hundred dollars. The robber in the front disarmed the private security guard and, at gunpoint, made the employees lie on the floor. The secretary, unbeknownst to the robbers, had set off the silent alarm.

MCCLESKEY, BORN ON MARCH 17, 1946, grew up with six siblings in a dangerous Marietta neighborhood. He never knew his biological father and lived, for a spell, with an aunt who physically abused him. When McCleskey was about eight years old, his mother, Willie Mae McCleskey, married John Henry Brooks, who beat her and her children during recurring episodes of inebriated furor. From an early age, McCleskey's chaotic home operated as a hub for bootlegged moonshine and illegal gambling. "My childhood was very rough," he recalled. "The hardest was the violence we grew up in as a family," violence he called "terrible and never-ending." Nearly "every weekend, someone in the neighborhood was shot and killed. Fights all the time. A dog-eat-dog world where only the strong survive."

In early December 1963, when Brooks threatened to kill Willie Mae, she fetched a pistol from under a mattress and shot her thirty-five-year-old husband. Seconds later, a seventeen-year-old McCleskey, returning home from school, opened the door to his stepfather's dying breaths. The state initially wanted to prosecute Willie Mae for a serious felony, but after authorities discovered her domestic violence victim status and that she had killed in self-defense, she pleaded guilty to a minor charge and never served time.

After graduating from his segregated high school in 1964, McCleskey married Gwendolyn Carmichael. In 1966, they welcomed their daughter, Carla, and McCleskey found work at a Lockheed Aircraft Company plant outside Atlanta. After his 1969 layoff, though, he struggled to provide, and Gwendolyn, his high school sweetheart, threatened to leave with Carla. In 1970, he turned to crime. Within weeks, police handcuffs encircled his wrists, and he pleaded guilty to committing nine robberies.

"When I got out [of prison] in 1977, I had a vision, I wanted to get back on my feet and reunited with my family," he remembered. "I thought if I could get ahold of a little money, I could get that to come to pass. The dream of being a family again—being at home with my wife and daughter—that was the happiest time of my life." Gainful employment, however, eluded the thirty-one-year-old ex-convict. A year later, his family reconciliation dream perished. He got divorced. Turned to drugs. And connected with Wright, Dupree, and Burney, ex-convicts with criminal records even longer than his.

Frank Robert Schlatt, a thirty-one-year-old five-year veteran of the Atlanta Police Department, was patrolling near Dixie Furniture in his police car that May afternoon. An ongoing cop shortage meant one officer to a car. And no backup. The police station radioed the Vietnam veteran about the triggering of the silent alarm. Schlatt motored there, parking a few minutes after the foursome stormed inside. Ordinarily cautious, Schlatt, a diminutive White man, hastily entered with his gun drawn. After walking about fifteen feet down the main aisle toward the store's rear, a voice warned him to stop.

Then bang!

Bang!

The first bullet blasted Schlatt's right eye. Destroyed his face. Exploded his brain. The second ricocheted off a pocket lighter in his chest and into a sofa. The bandits then bolted at about twenty minutes past two. Three hours after the shooting, Schlatt died at a hospital, leaving behind a wife and a nine-year-old daughter. Two and a half weeks later, the police arrested McCleskey, pinpointing him as the masked man in the front of the store who gunned down Schlatt.

On the evening of October 12, 1978, inside a Fulton County courtroom, a jury convicted McCleskey of two counts of armed robbery and one count of malice murder. The jury sentenced McCleskey, who had admitted to being one of the four robbers but denied killing Schlatt, to two life terms for the robbery convictions. Georgia law stipulated that a jury could impose the death penalty only after finding beyond a reasonable doubt that one of the statutory aggravating circumstances accompanied the murder. The jury found two—

that the murder occurred during an armed robbery and the victim was a peace officer performing his duties. Judge Sam McKenzie, per the Georgia death penalty statute, followed the jury's recommendation and set November 17 as McCleskey's final day on earth.

When Greenberg hired Boger, he admonished, "Don't let anybody get executed." If Boger could keep McCleskey alive with Baldus's research, he could save scores and open new possibilities for Black victims of castework in proving equal protection violations.

IN 1972, ATLANTA RAZED its Terminal Station, an elegant Beaux-Arts railway depot, replacing it seven years later with the nondescript twenty-six-story Richard B. Russell Federal Building that cast a long shadow on the downtown's southwestern edge. Inside a courtroom in that bland rectangle, Boger began the LDF's aggression against Georgia's new capital punishment statute.

After Baldus shared the preliminary results for his *Procedural Reform Study* with the LDF, Boger, on June 18, asked Julian Owen Forrester, a federal district court judge, for a hearing, relaying how he wished to present statistical evidence that established capital punishment in Georgia, through its statute, violated the Equal Protection Clause. Boger charged that the statute was inherently unconstitutional, and unconstitutional as specifically applied in McCleskey's case. "Through the work of Professor Baldus and his colleagues," Boger wrote, "petitioner has adduced proof that, despite Georgia's revised procedures, race continues to play an important part in determining which Georgia capital defendants will live and which will die." Boger submitted Eighth Amendment arguments too, but The Trinity guides our journey.

Chatter about Baldus's research and its pioneering methods had swirled through legal circles. On October 8, 1982, Forrester, a forty-three-year-old Reagan appointee, granted a full hearing. The Georgia native told Boger that given his science and engineering background, the study had tickled his intrigue, adding that every year he wanted to allot two weeks to matters concerning "the poor and downtrodden." Boger told Forrester, a Georgia Tech graduate, that Baldus would soon finish the second study that he was conducting for the LDF and requested a hearing date further in the future to give Baldus more time for its completion. This second study, Boger pledged, would bare the most explosive revelations. Forrester valued what *that* study promised and set the hearing date for August 1983, indefinitely staying the execution of a man seemingly on an inevitable glide path to that irreversible punishment.

Baldus and his colleagues tabulated raw numbers that revealed significant racial disparities, numbers that indicated the genre of unequal justice that Marshall had unearthed in Korea decades earlier. In 11 percent of cases, defendants charged with killing a White person received a death sentence, but only in one percent of cases did defendants charged with killing a Black person receive a death sentence. The raw numbers identified an unexpected conclusion. Black defendants were actually less likely to receive the death penalty than White defendants overall—4 percent to 7 percent—given that murders typically take place between members of the same race. The death penalty was imposed in 3 percent of cases concerning White defendants and Black victims, one percent of cases concerning Black defendants and Black victims, 8 percent of cases involving White defendants and White victims, and 22 percent of cases concerning Black defendants and White victims. Prosecutors pursued the death penalty in 19 percent of the cases concerning White defendants and Black victims, 15 percent of the cases involving Black defendants and Black victims, 32 percent of the cases involving White defendants and White victims, and 70 percent of the cases involving Black defendants and White victims.

These unexplained numerical disparities supported, yet did not confirm, the LDF's thesis. The state, after all, could present various nondiscriminatory explanations. From there, Baldus used multiple regression analysis. This complicated math had a simple purpose— enable Baldus and his team to parse out which factors really drove capital sentencing and specifically determine how much race explained these outcomes. Boger translated Baldus's results in his brief:

> Professors Baldus and Woodworth subjected the data to a wide variety of statistical procedures.... Yet regardless of which of these analytical tools Baldus and Woodworth brought to bear,

race held firm as a prominent determiner of life or death. Race proved no less significant in determining the likelihood of a death sentence than aggravating circumstances such as whether the defendant had a prior murder conviction or whether he was the prime mover in the homicide. Indeed, Professor Baldus . . . revealed that after taking into account most legitimate reasons for sentencing distinctions, the odds of receiving a death sentence were still more than 4.3 times greater for those whose victims were white than for those whose victims were black.

What became known as the "Baldus Study," which actually comprised the original *Procedural Reform Study* and then the larger *Charging and Sentencing Study* conducted for the LDF, showed that race poisoned the administration of the state's capital punishment statute in two principal ways—defendants charged with murdering White victims were more likely to receive the death sentence than defendants charged with murdering Black victims, and Black defendants of White victims were more likely to receive the death sentence than White defendants of White victims. Boger argued that because of McCleskey's race and that of his victim, a jury was *especially* likely to banish him to the electric chair.

From the prosecutor to the juror, Boger's argument implicated nearly every actor in capital sentencing. Boger even impugned the state legislature for maintaining a capital punishment statute despite it producing racially discriminatory effects. Equal protection, in other words, included inaction as well as action, Boger implied, unwittingly honoring Justice Bradley's 1870s concept. The Baldus Study could never provide direct evidence—it couldn't impugn one prosecutor or one jury in one Black death row inmate's case. Baldus's efforts, nevertheless, mounted an overwhelming circumstantial case indicating that Georgia oversaw what Boger dubbed a "'dual system' of capital sentencing."

Most observers would have expected the Baldus Study, if it found evidence of unequal justice, to expose that Black defendants received the death penalty more often than White defendants, that Georgia was electrocuting Black men wantonly but saving the necks of White murderers—the typical American would have envisioned race dis-

crimination in this two-dimensional way. Race-of-victim discrimination, in contrast, sounded awkward, abstract even, yet it supported
the racial caste system's conceit. "If the victim is white, that is the first
key to whether or not the death penalty is sought," explained Patsy
Morris, who monitored capital punishment cases in Georgia for the
ACLU. "This goes back to the whole sociocultural phenomenon of
black lives not being of equal value to white lives."

The Baldus Study showed that an illicit consideration—race—
was still manipulating post-*Gregg* capital sentencing. Judges should,
Boger thought, identify this as violating the Equal Protection Clause.
The criminal justice system failed to meet the color-blind standard
that caste preservationists were championing in the 1980s to convince the black robes to invalidate racial remedial policies.

Baldus's was not the first study to conclude that race corrupted
capital sentencing in Georgia. Two research scientists, William Bowers and Glenn Pierce, published one in 1980. Theirs determined that
a Black person murdering a White person was twenty-seven times
more likely to receive a death sentence than a Black-on-Black murderer. Unlike Baldus's, that study, however, failed to account for variables that could explain the racial disparities on nonracial grounds.
For that reason, in 1982, the Fifth Circuit held in *Smith v. Balkcom*
that Bowers and Pierce's study left "untouched countless racially
neutral variables," meaning that the study could not disprove that
nonracial variables explained the racial disparities. "Baldus has been
able to go way beyond us in two ways," Bowers later explained. "He
has looked at an incredible array of factors, where we looked at one.
And he is able to focus in on sentencing, which is where the courts
have said they want to look (for capriciousness)."

Inside the federal Atlanta courtroom, Baldus testified that "the
decision of the Court in *Gregg* [which upheld the constitutionality of
Georgia's new death penalty statute] proceeded on the assumption
that the procedural safeguards adopted . . . were adequate to ensure
that death sentencing decisions would be neither excessive nor discriminatory. . . . [M]y principal concern was [to investigate] whether
or not those assumptions . . . were valid." His results threatened the
viability of capital punishment in light of the Supreme Court's previ-

ous declaration that arbitrarily imposed death sentences violated the Constitution.

"If the case is so mitigated that the death sentence is unthinkable, the race of the victim is not going to have any effect," said Baldus, a slightly built academic who wore a wrinkled gray suit and scuffed shoes in court. And "what further happens is that when the cases become tremendously aggravated so that everybody would agree that if we're going to have a death sentence, these are the cases that should get it, the race effects go away. It's only in the mid-range of cases where the decision makers have a real choice as to what to do." Those were the cases where race really mattered. For those mid-level of aggravation cases, "the average white victim case has approximately a twenty percent higher risk of receiving a death sentence than a similarly situated black victim case."

The Baldus Study, despite its rigor, left Judge Forrester, a bespectacled White man with a round face, unmoved. "Essentially what you're saying," Forrester, behind the bench, told Baldus, "is the system is reacting less partially against the homicide committed against a black person than it is against a white person. . . . That was, it's so very speculative, you could probably argue the other side of the coin as well, either being the devil's advocate or because you really believe it, either one." Forrester showed either his poor understanding of the math, or his unwillingness to accept it. Maybe both. "That was the trouble I had with that as being a practical measure," he continued. "But in terms of the preponderant motivating factor or anything like that, could you in fairness say that what caused McCleskey to get the death penalty as opposed to anybody else, was the fact that he murdered a white person as opposed to a black person?"

"No, I can't say that was the factor, no," Baldus answered. "But what I can say, though, is when I look at all the other legitimate factors in his case, and I look to the main line of cases in this jurisdiction, statewide, that are like his . . . his case is substantially out of line with the normal trend of decision on such cases, and given that it is aberrant in that regard we are forced to ask ourselves what could cause it. I can't see any factors, legitimate factors in his case that would clearly call for it, that would distinguish it clearly from the other cases. The cases are not identical, but there's nothing that really cries out for why this case should be treated that much differently."

Baldus offered the state's counsel, Mary Beth Westmoreland, assistant attorney general of Georgia, and Forrester the chance to suggest their own variables to explain the race-of-victim discrimination. Westmoreland refused, attacking the data and data collection techniques instead, offering no strong alternate explanation for the racial disparities. Westmoreland's unwillingness to engage left Boger feeling as though he was without an adversary. Forrester, however, listed race-neutral factors he thought produced the disparities. When Baldus ran the numbers, the race-of-victim discrimination produced a result *larger* than the 4.3 death odds multiplier that Baldus's leading model had determined.

Forrester, nonetheless, found no Fourteenth Amendment violation. "The petitioner's statistics," Forrester wrote in his February 1, 1984, opinion, "do not [sufficiently support] the contention that the death penalty was imposed upon him because of his race, [or] because of the race of the victim." The Baldus Study, he concluded, "fail[ed] to contribute anything of value" to McCleskey's case. Essentially, Forrester denied that the Baldus Study proved what it clearly did. Boger expected that decision. The judge told him off the record that "there can't be that much discrimination in Georgia left. Andy Young [a Black man who worked with Dr. King and served as U.N. ambassador under President Carter] had been elected mayor in Atlanta." Forrester's misunderstanding of the Baldus Study powered his ignorant legal analysis. Boger thought that perhaps Forrester refused to allow Baldus's data to move his mind to a place he did not want it to go.

The Eleventh Circuit heard the case en banc, meaning all twelve of the circuit's judges reviewed the case. By a nine-to-three vote, the court affirmed Forrester's ruling. The majority opinion assumed that the Baldus Study proved what its lead author claimed it did yet deemed the statistics "insufficient to demonstrate discriminatory intent or unconstitutional discrimination in the Fourteenth Amendment context."

Boger then appealed to the Supreme Court despite anticipating the justices to deny certiorari:

First, I had become thoroughly convinced of the facts: the Baldus study seemed extraordinarily robust and sound, not simply because of Baldus's expertise, his careful research design, and his evident care, but because he had so transparently and thoroughly tested his methods and his findings against every proposed alternative analysis and counterhypothesis, and because none of those tests had reduced the impact or significance of the racial disparities he found. The outcomes in all his alternative quantitative and qualitative analyses triangulated consistently. Moreover, after two full years in which to consult with experts of every stripe, the State of Georgia's principal response had remained little more than a "rope-a-dope" defense; Georgia could point to no omitted variable that would reduce the impact of race, no alternative model, however far-fetched, that might justify Georgia's racially skewed sentencing patterns. Instead, all Georgia could do was recite its know-nothing mantra: "Analysis of any capital sentencing patterns is impossible."

But in July 1986, the Court granted review.

Boger suspected that he had four votes—Marshall, Brennan, Blackmun, and Stevens, meaning he needed Rehnquist, O'Connor, White, Scalia, or Powell, five justices who had railed against race-conscious decision-making by the state to redress past societal racial oppression. The public face that appeared in those remedial policy cases *should* appear when Black folk complained about race-conscious state action, too. The Baldus Study *should* unnerve anyone in the federal judiciary who presented themselves as caretakers of the color-blindness principle as had many conservative jurists, especially those influenced by the Federalist Society. If they were honestly presenting themselves, Boger simply needed to adapt a complicated, math-based Baldus Study into a legal argument that showed the Court that Georgia was race-consciously enforcing laws in violation of McCleskey's equal protection rights. Success hinged on illuminating how Supreme Court precedent supported finding an equal protection violation.

Let's visit an event reminiscent of what launched this leg of our journey—Marshall grazing a White woman while boarding a street-car, igniting an altercation with a caste preservationist. There, we will explore the Supreme Court's Fourteenth Amendment precedent prior to Marshall's appointment, precedent that Boger must master, must ply into an argument for why the Baldus Study supported the finding of an equal protection violation in McCleskey's case. Marshall's 1920s duel culminated with a beat-up adversary and his boss bailing him out of jail. This second one resolved much differently. Come now with me to downtown Dallas at around eight on the warm night of September 15, 1941.

THE STYLISH AND SLENDER BLACK MAN standing before us, L. C. Akens, arrived here after taking a southbound streetcar, Jim Crow bullying him to its rear, after finishing his shift working as a porter in North Dallas. This spot, the intersection of Commerce and St. Paul Streets, is his transfer point, where he awaits the Oak Cliff–bound car that will steer him over the Trinity River and near his South Dallas home. The twenty-six-year-old lives there with his wife, Roberta, who is confined to a wheelchair after having lost both of her legs and the use of one arm in a May 1940 train accident, and their young miracle son born five months later. On this paved road among the labyrinth of electrical wirings carrying the streetcars through Dallas and the towering buildings, his streetcar arrives. Akens steps aside to allow a Black woman to climb first, accidentally brushing against a White woman.

"Wait a minute, boy," belches Victor Leon Morris, a twenty-six-year-old White man, an off-duty police officer in plainclothes, defending his wife's honor from a Black man's skin.

Morris jerks Akens from behind three times, pulls out his service revolver, and whips him in the head with it repeatedly before shooting him, blowing a hole through Akens's right lung. Morris then fumbles his gun. A bleeding Akens gathers it and fires into Morris's back. The bullet shreds near Morris's heart.

"Darling, he got me," he wails out to his wife.

Akens runs a block away to the police headquarters inside city hall's basement. He hands the gun to the desk sergeant and exclaims,

"I've been shot and just shot a white man." Morris dies in an ambulance en route to the hospital.

The state will soon convict Akens of murder. A White Dallas attorney writes, "If the wounded survivor of the fight had been a white man, it is doubtful whether, anywhere in Texas, he would have even been indicted." Akens's case becomes another act in a long tragedy starring the Equal Protection Clause. The Supreme Court, advancing caste preservationism, has made proving equal protection violations nearly impossible for Black victims of state oppression. In forming his argument, Boger must study key equal protection cases, like the one that stems from this calamity. We have already encountered seminal ones.

In the first case we explored in our journey, *Strauder v. West Virginia*, the Supreme Court in 1880 held that a West Virginia law that forbade Black men from serving on juries infringed the Equal Protection Clause. In 1870s West Virginia, the public face mirrored the private face—both openly confessed the intentions to circumscribe Black rights. Such a facially exclusionary law, though, delivered the black robes the opportunity to hand down an easy opinion. Strauder, a criminal defendant and jury discrimination victim, could establish that the state denied him equal protection by identifying the plainly oppressive law. Public faces, consequently, discovered the peril in permitting the sunlight to illuminate the caste preservationist goals of private faces. McCleskey's case will present Boger a far more challenging undertaking. Boger must demonstrate that state actors—juries and prosecutors specifically—are violating the Equal Protection Clause in absence of a facially discriminatory law. That particular fact pattern has burdened Black claimants with a much heavier lift.

Boger should identify *Yick Wo v. Hopkins*, decided in 1886, as *the* foundational case for the legal issue of how to prove an equal protection violation in the absence of explicitly discriminatory law. As we have seen, the justices concluded that the San Francisco Board of Supervisors had unevenly enforced a city ordinance that outlawed operating a wooden laundry sans consent. The board had disallowed all two hundred Chinese laundries that applied for permission but only one of the eighty non-Chinese laundries. The black robes, in other words, relied on rather simple numerical disparities to support an equal protection violation. The public face of the Board of Supervisors avowed that anti-Chinese animus had no effect on these outcomes. The Court, though, disregarded that, and said the plaintiff need not demonstrate that any individual state actor used his Chinese ancestry as a reason for disparate treatment. "Though the law itself be fair on its face," Justice Matthews wrote, "and impartial in appearance, yet, if it is applied and administered by public authority with an evil eye and an unequal hand, so as practically to make unjust and illegal discriminations between persons in similar circumstances . . . the denial of equal justice is still within the prohibition of the constitution." A century later, Boger could quote this passage and request that the Court heed it. His far more rigorous mathematical evidence demonstrates that a similarly evil eye and unequal hand persecutes McCleskey—the Georgia capital punishment statute does not discriminate by its terms but still produces race-conscious punishments.

*Williams v. Mississippi* followed. Cornelius Jones, our third leg's protagonist, persuaded nary a black robe that Mississippi denied the equal protection rights of Williams, Jones's client convicted of murder by an all-White jury. The Court unanimously found that Jones did not demonstrate that any state actor had intentionally excluded Black men from the juries that indicted and convicted Williams, despite Black men never serving on state juries, despite a constitutional convention convened to remove Black people from political and civil society. The Court withheld the logic of *Yick Wo*, that stark numerical disparities could prove an equal protection violation, from Black criminal defendants seeking protection in jury discrimination cases, culminating in no Black jury service throughout the South. The Court forced Black criminal defendants to prove that a specific state actor intended to create all-White juries, an evidentiary alp the justices surely understood Black defendants could never surmount. Mississippi's public face denied any discriminatory intentions and received what it wanted from the black robes, the space to deny the Black population equal citizenship.

On February 27, 1903, Justice Henry Billings Brown penned a friend, confessing that he and his colleagues were emboldening southern jurisdictions to desecrate Black rights. "In some criminal cases against negroes," Brown wrote, "coming up from the Southern States, we have adhered to the technicalities of the law so strictly that I fear injustice has been done to the defendant. We have one such case before us now." That case, almost certainly *Brownfield v. South Carolina*, argued two days after the letter's date and decided about a week later, involved John Brownfield, likely innocent, convicted of murdering a White man and sentenced to death by an all-White jury. Brown's private expressions of concern meant nothing as the *Plessy* opinion author endorsed the unanimous opinion that rejected Brownfield's argument that the state violated his equal protection rights by practicing jury discrimination. Although Black men constituted 80 percent of registered voters in Georgetown County, the Court bought the state's argument that it did not intentionally exclude Black men from juries. The deceitful public face won again for the private face.

In 1935, the Court decided *Norris v. Alabama*, which marked a shift in how the Supreme Court handled jury discrimination cases. *Norris* concerned the Scottsboro Boys, nine Black youths, ranging from thirteen to twenty, convicted of raping two young White women on a freight train. The controversy drew worldwide attention, as many across the globe pictured them as casualties of a racist criminal justice system. Defense counsel showed that Black folk never served on the juries where the defendants were indicted and convicted. Still, they did not prove that any state actor had deliberately ensured all-White juries in the boys' specific grand and trial juries. How, then, could they convince the Court that the state defied its equal protection requirements?

The black robes in *Norris* held that prolonged absence of Black men from juries in a particular jurisdiction established, by itself, that jurisdiction had committed jury discrimination in the particular case under review. Without relying on direct evidence, the Court nonetheless found that Alabama deliberately excluded Black men from serving on the juries that indicted and convicted the Scottsboro Boys. The justices confronted a choice—follow precedent and assist in the denial of fundamental rights or construct the Equal Protection Clause anew to promote fairness. The Court chose fairness, deeming numerical disparities sufficient to establish that Alabama had denied equal protection, a position that would seemingly support a possible Boger argument—that the Baldus Study shows numerical disparities that only color-conscious state action explains.

In *Hollins v. Oklahoma*, decided in 1935, *Hale v. Kentucky*, decided in 1938, and *Pierre v. Louisiana*, decided in 1939, the Court obeyed this precedent, overturning the convictions of Black men sentenced to die by all-White juries sitting in jurisdictions that practiced jury discrimination by custom. Three decades passed after Brown's private correspondence acknowledging the Court's complicity with unequal justice until the Court constructed the Constitution to rectify an outrage. At last, the public face failed the private one.

In November 1940, nearly a year ago, the Supreme Court decided *Smith v. Texas*, another jury discrimination decision that added new wrinkles to the Court's equal protection jurisprudence. All-White juries indicted, convicted, and sentenced Edgar Smith to life in prison for raping a White woman. Black folk comprised about 20 percent of the Harris County population, yet very few ever served on juries. This fact differed from *Norris*, *Hollins*, *Hale*, and *Pierre*, cases involving *absolute* exclusion. "Chance and accident alone," Justice Black wrote, "could hardly have brought about the listing for grand jury service of so few negroes from among the thousands shown by the undisputed evidence to possess the legal qualifications for jury service."

At trial, jury commissioners testified that they selected few Black folk because they knew none personally, not because of race prejudice. The justices disregarded the distinction. "Where jury commissioners limit those from whom grand juries are selected to their own personal acquaintance, discrimination can arise from commissioners who know no negroes," Justice Black wrote. The Court focused on the result—the gross underrepresentation of Black jurors—not whether any state actor intentionally created that result, in assessing whether an equal protection violation had occurred. This will hold significance to Boger. The Baldus Study attests to disparate results. It does not prove that any actor intentionally discriminates against McCleskey. This precedent supports the proposition that he need not prove such intent.

———

AS WE LINGER IN DOWNTOWN DALLAS in September 1941, let's peer into the future. In June 1942, the Court will decide *Hill v. Texas*, another jury discrimination case, this one involving Henry Allen Hill, a Black man accused of raping a White woman in a Dallas County underpass. The Supreme Court, again, finds an equal protection violation, and introduces another legal argument that Boger can appropriate to McCleskey's benefit. Chief Justice Stone writes that the state must "not pursue a course of conduct in the administration of their office which would operate to discriminate in the selection of jurors on racial grounds." The Court, put another way, finds an equal protection violation when the state selects a method of operation that produces stark racial disparities relating to fundamental rights. Does not Georgia commit this sin when continuing to operate a capital punishment statute that produces significant statistical disparities in whom the state kills? In *Smith* and *Hill*, the Court endorses the theory that if a state pursues, even unintentionally, a course of action that bears far more heavily on a subjugated population, courts should find an equal protection violation. The Court speaks in the jury discrimination context, but their words translate to others.

Four years from now, in 1945, the Court will decide Akens's case, captured as *Akins v. Texas*. Typographical error. The Texas Court of Criminal Appeals reverses his first conviction because of Akens's jury discrimination claim, the state court complying with the Supreme Court's *Smith* and *Hill* decisions. Texas, thereafter, reconvicts Akens. The jury commissioners admit to intentionally selecting just one Black man to serve on the grand jury. The *Washington Post* calls him a "carefully selected, barely literate, 81-year-old." The Supreme Court, however, rejects Akens's argument that Texas intentionally limits the grand jury's Black representation. Justice Reed reasons that a grand jury with one Black member approximates the county's broader demographics. Akens contends, though, that Dallas purposefully caps Black presence on the jury. Based on precedent, *Akins* presents an easy equal protection decision the Court refuses to reach.

In response, the *Chicago Defender*, a preeminent Black newspaper, will vent that the "Court today upheld the right of the states to make deliberate token placement of Negroes on jury panels and remain within the law," underscoring the crucial point—the black robes, in *Akins*, drafted for caste preservationists a blueprint for preserving Jim Crow justice. Tokenism. Boger will express surprise that the Court chooses to hear *McCleskey* because he believes the Baldus Study demonstrates an obvious equal protection denial. Akens's case, which brought us to downtown Dallas on this day in September 1941, must caution Boger about the black robes' willingness to ignore the obvious and withhold from Black folk the full embrace of equal protection.

Marshall will join the Court in two decades. Then, the opportunity to help shape the Fourteenth Amendment's interpretation to counteract a subtler, more covert form of caste preservationism arises. What would he do with it?

INSIDE THE COURT CHAMBER on December 14, 1970, Paul A. Rosen, a young attorney representing Black plaintiffs, warned the justices that *Palmer v. Thompson* "represents but another attempt by the City of Jackson to nullify the Thirteenth and Fourteenth Amendments, to avoid the decision of *Brown versus Board of Education*, and to deny black people their rights as guaranteed by the Civil War Amendments."

In 1962, Jackson, Mississippi, was operating its public swimming pools, parks, golf links, and other facilities on a segregated basis. In *Clark v. Thompson*, a federal district court judge ruled that maintaining these Jim Crow public spaces denied the Black residents equal protection. The Fifth Circuit affirmed. Jackson then desegregated each except the pools. The city council closed the four pools that it owned and returned the lease of the fifth to the YMCA that then reserved the newly private pool for White folk only.

On May 24, 1963, a Mississippi newspaper reported that Jackson mayor Allen C. Thompson "said neither agitators nor President Kennedy will change the determination of Jackson to retain segregation." The city's leaders announced their ambitions in part to gratify the White masses, in part because they supposed they could fulfill their objectives even despite a public confession. Caste preservationism, as an ideology, yearns to fight without camouflage. Black Jackson residents, in response, sued to force the reopening and integration of the pools. The facts in *Palmer v. Thompson* raised a critical question for deciding equal protection cases. What mattered? That the city acted with discriminatory intent? Or that the decision to close the pools injured both races equally?

The five-to-four majority found that the Black plaintiffs suffered no equal protection denial. The majority, speaking through Justice Black, noted that the record did not present a situation where White folk, but not Black folk, received access to public pools. The city's decision placed both races in the same spot—without a public pool. The plaintiffs charged that the city shuttered its pools as a willful anti-Black maneuver. The majority, however, flinched from digging into the intentions of city officials, although one needn't dig far— Mayor Thompson had spilled the city's rationale. Justice Black wrote that "no case in this Court has held that a legislative act may violate equal protection solely because of the motivations of the men who voted for it." The majority deemed that compelling judges to search for the motivations of lawmakers would send judges on a quest for the often undiscoverable. "It is difficult or impossible for any court to determine the 'sole' or 'dominant' motivation behind the choices of a group of legislators. Furthermore, there is an element of futility in a judicial attempt to invalidate a law because of the bad motives of its supporters," Black asserted. He posited that should a judge nullify a law because discriminatory intentions motivated its champions, a legislative body could resurrect the dead for fresh reasons.

Rather than focusing on legislative *intent*, Justice Black hinged his decision on the *effect* of the pool closure. At one time, the city operated pools and then stopped. The facts presented during trial, Black explained, "shows no state action affecting blacks differently from whites." According to his view, the case involved a state action—the closing of pools—that produced no *disparate impact*, that is, the closure did not affect one race meaningfully more than another. The public face said, "we discriminated," and a Court majority responded, "that doesn't matter."

After *Palmer v. Thompson*, when reviewing claims of Black plaintiffs alleging an equal protection violation, lower federal courts concentrated not on the intents of state actors, but rather the effects of their decisions. Not disparate treatment but rather disparate impact. Various circuit courts concluded in a range of disputes that significant racial disparate impacts, by themselves, regardless of whether Black plaintiffs had established discriminatory intent, triggered rigorous scrutiny. Take *Hawkins v. Town of Shaw* for instance. In that 1972 decision, the Fifth Circuit concluded that despite no direct evidence of discriminatory intent, Shaw, Mississippi, a small community, had violated the Equal Protection Clause by providing significantly worse municipal services to Black residents as compared to White residents. More on this case later. If such analysis would control the Court's approach in *McCleskey*, Boger could draw upon the Baldus Study to establish an equal protection violation, given that it exposed Georgia's capital punishment process for producing substantial racial disparate impacts.

The Court heard oral argument in *Palmer* without Justice Marshall. He was at home recuperating from medical examinations. Nonetheless, he wrote a dissent that framed the case as a clearcut instance of state actors shutting down a public venue to both avoid desegregation and reaffirm the racial pecking order, which, he concluded, violated the Equal Protection Clause. Justice Douglas's dissent declared that "though a State may discontinue any of its municipal services—such as schools, parks, pools, athletic fields, and the like—it may not do so for the purpose of perpetuating or installing apartheid or because it finds life in a multi-racial community difficult or unpleasant." Marshall endorsed that proclamation. The case, to Marshall, must have recalled the traumas of his adolescence and career as an attorney. Must have felt like a White man wrenching him by his collar. Like White officers in Korea sabotaging Black officers' lives. Like more traditional, overt racism.

Jackson's city council closed the pools to preserve Black folk's status, as Chief Justice Taney said in *Dred Scott*, as "lower beings" who were "altogether unfit to associate with the white race." And Marshall seemingly believed that whether an equal protection violation occurred hinged on state actors wanting to discriminate or inflict a racial trauma. Marshall could have downplayed the importance of intent and maintained that the closing of the pool violated the equal protection rights of the Black plaintiffs because the pool closures amounted to castework.

Five years later, a new majority formed to renounce the Court's

*Palmer* holding in a case that felt nothing like the undisguised racism that marked Marshall's formative years as an American and a lawyer.

ON JUNE 7, 1976, Justice White announced his majority opinion in *Washington v. Davis*. "The principal issue in this case," he breezily read in the Court Chamber, "is whether the standard test administered to prospective civil service employees of the United States is racially discriminatory and violative of the Due Process Clause of the United States Constitution when it is administered to applicants for the positions on the Metropolitan Police Force for the District of Columbia." Recall that the Court ruled in *Bolling v. Sharpe* that the Fifth Amendment's Due Process Clause carried an implied equal protection guarantee that restricted federal action. Thus, the Court evaluated the legal issues in *Davis* as it would an equal protection dispute.

In 1966, when the Washington, D.C., police department passed over Alfred E. Davis, a Black police officer, for a promotion to sergeant, he filed a complaint with the D.C. Human Relations Commission, believing himself a casualty of departmental anti-Black antagonism. A technicality triggered the case's dismissal. In 1967, he refiled his complaint, and the Human Relations Commission sought information, but the police department refused to comply and did again when the commission later renewed its attempts to hold a hearing. As these efforts dithered, the department transferred Davis from a community relations position to a foot patrol duty, a disfavored post.

In 1970, Davis filed a federal suit against the department's employment practices. For hiring and promotion, the department considered performance on Test 21, an exam used throughout the federal service. The U.S. Civil Service Commission, a government agency instituted to select federal employees based on merit rather than favoritism, designed Test 21 to evaluate the vocabulary, verbal skills, and reading comprehension of federal employment candidates. From 1968 to 1971, 57 percent of Black test takers, but only 13 percent of White test takers, failed the test. The test, therefore, disproportionately impaired the candidacies of Black applicants, partially explaining an 8 percent Black police department in a 70 percent Black city. The Black plaintiffs argued that using the test to inform employment decisions violated Black candidates' equal protection rights. Test 21 created the significant racial disparate impact discussed in *Palmer* and that lower federal courts focused on thereafter when evaluating alleged equal protection denials. The police department, however, disclaimed any discriminatory motive.

Since the nation's inception, police departments could simply refuse Black aspirants and needed not devise any clever pretexts. But in the 1970s, with stronger anti-discrimination laws and elevated national commitment to at least the appearance of propriety, police departments hostile to integration activated the two faces paradigm. *Paradise v. United States*, where the Alabama state troopers privately endorsed racial exclusion but publicly presented themselves as open to Black membership, spoke to this. When Davis filed his lawsuit, he could not know what the department's private face looked like. The face might have valued Test 21 because it limited the number of Black officers. At the very least, though, the department stuck with the test while knowing its effect.

Following Davis's district court loss, D.C. Circuit Judge Spotswood Robinson III authored the two-to-one majority opinion that sided with him. A former NAACP attorney, Robinson followed the *Griggs v. Duke Power Co.* precedent, a 1971 Supreme Court case involving Title VII of the 1964 Civil Rights Act. "If an employment practice which operates to exclude Negroes cannot be shown to be related to job performance," the Court set forth in *Griggs*, "the practice is prohibited." When a judge deemed that a hiring criterion caused an "exclusionary effect on minority applicants," an employer carried a heavy burden to show that the discriminatory criterion "bear[s] a demonstrable relationship to successful performance of the jobs for which they were used." The D.C. Court of Appeals, then, had to answer two interlocking questions: whether Test 21 satisfied as an exclusionary criterion, and, if true, whether the department could demonstrate the test's strong relation to suitable job performance. In other words, a state action that produced a significant disparate impact could survive review only if the state could show the action's necessity. Robinson concluded that the police department could hire competent police officers absent the test, raising a key question: Why continue with a test that operated more to exclude Black candidates rather than incapable ones?

"We disagree with the Court of Appeals," Justice White announced in the Court Chamber. "We hold that to prove an unconstitutional racial discrimination under the Equal Protection or Due Process Clauses, it is essential that a racially discriminatory purpose be shown in some manner."

White penned the seven-to-two majority opinion in *Davis* that found Judge Robinson erred in applying a disparate impact standard. "We have never held that the constitutional standard for adjudicating claims of invidious racial discrimination is identical to the standards applicable under Title VII, and we decline to do so today," White wrote. The Court rejected that the discriminatory effect of a state action or law should incite a rigorous review of its constitutionality. Plaintiffs in equal protection lawsuits, the Court's majority confirmed, must prove discriminatory intent. White penned that "our cases have not embraced the proposition that a law or other official act, without regard to whether it reflects a racially discriminatory purpose, is unconstitutional solely because it has a racially disproportionate impact."

White, insisting that this reasoning squared with precedent, started his analysis with *Strauder,* which, he observed, culminated in an equal protection violation because the defendant proved intentional discrimination. He cited *Wright v. Rockefeller,* a 1964 case where the Court upheld congressional districts against charges of racial gerrymandering because the challengers unsuccessfully demonstrated that the New York legislature "was either motivated by racial considerations or in fact drew the districts on racial lines." School segregation cases like *Brown* and *Bolling v. Sharpe,* White further contended, likewise supported the need for plaintiffs to establish discriminatory purpose. In these cases, only schools segregated by law bore desegregation requirements. White framed *Yick Wo* and *Norris* as disputes where the minority party won because the state intentionally discriminated. Those parties lacked ironclad proof of discriminatory intent, White conceded, but the Court ruled in their favor because the factual record included proxies of intentional discrimination strong enough to exclude all other explanations for the stark racial disparities.

"Nevertheless," White explained, "we have not held that a law, neutral on its face and serving ends otherwise within the power of government to pursue, is invalid under the Equal Protection Clause simply because it may affect a greater proportion of one race than of another. Disproportionate impact is not irrelevant, but it is not the sole touchstone of an invidious racial discrimination forbidden by the Constitution." White tendered no real explanation why the Court dumped its *Palmer* reasoning.

The justices understood that all sorts of state actions fell far more harshly on Black folk. Disparate impact becoming the mediating principle for the Equal Protection Clause might threaten the constitutionality of a wide array of government policies, regulations, and laws. "A rule that a statute designed to serve neutral ends is nevertheless invalid, absent compelling justification," White wrote, "if in practice it benefits or burdens one race more than another would be far reaching and would raise serious questions about, and perhaps invalidate, a whole range of tax, welfare, public service, regulatory, and licensing statutes that may be more burdensome to the poor and to the average black than to the more affluent white."

Ultimately, the Court held that plaintiffs suing under the Equal Protection Clause must prove that, one, a state action was done to intentionally discriminate and, two, that the discrimination produced a discriminatory impact. In *Davis*, the plaintiffs failed to substantiate that the police department acted with discriminatory intent. The Court deemed irrelevant that the department continued administering the test even while understanding its effects. The department, to run afoul of the Equal Protection Clause, needed to have continued its behavior *because* it hurt Black candidacies. Since the Court majority found no discriminatory intent, the use of Test 21 needed to pass just the rational basis test. Seven justices found that it served a valid purpose—selecting qualified candidates.

In *Davis*, the Court officially chose the Intent Doctrine. This nearly impossible burden requires that discrimination victims prove that a state actor selected a course of action because of a discriminatory motive. We must trace the Intent Doctrine to cases like

*Williams v. Mississippi,* 1890s jury discrimination cases. The Court, in *Davis,* rejuvenated an old construction of the Equal Protection Clause, hatched during an era when White Supremacy greatly manipulated American jurisprudence. The souls of Black men executed by all-White juries haunt the Court's *Davis* opinion—Powell and the six other justices who joined him erected the Intent Doctrine on the graves of those Black men. Proof of discriminatory intent can almost always be easily hidden and will typically be unavailable. Even during a more racially hostile climate, like 1890s Mississippi, plaintiffs could not conquer the intent demon. Only when a wrongdoer confessed could the Equal Protection Clause operate as a reliable engine to alleviate racial oppression. The D.C. police department said, "we didn't discriminate," and a Court majority responded, "they can't prove otherwise." If the justices required that Boger prove intentional discrimination with clear evidence, McCleskey would die in the electric chair.

Marshall voted against the *Davis* majority. He uttered nary a word beyond "I dissent," suggesting he had not formulated a suitable response to this problem. Marshall showed no indication that he understood the disaster the *Davis* decision would provoke—the entrenching of the Intent Doctrine would return the Equal Protection Clause to a state of near uselessness in the cause of Black freedom. How could Black folk rely on the Constitution's guarantee of equality when discriminators know that hiding their intentions along with any damning evidence would allow castework to continue?

In the previous two legs of our journey, we explored how Marshall endorsed anti-stigmatization as the mediating principle for the Equal Protection Clause. This meant that affirmative action programs, although they racially classified, were constitutional because such programs did not disparage White people. But what would anti-stigmatization mean in *Davis?* Test 21 did not slur Black people. The anti-stigmatization principle held purchase in the racial remedial program context, but not here, underscoring how Marshall needed to conceive a grander construction of the Equal Protection Clause that could afford Black folk the means to combat a caste system that thrived in the absence of obvious castework.

True, the D.C. police department might have acted without discriminatory motive. But if governments, without intent to cause racial injuries, could enforce rules and laws that prolonged the racial caste system, America could not meet its obligation under The Trinity to guarantee Black freedom from caste. And, in the McCleskey case specifically, if Boger had to prove that the prosecutor who tried McCleskey or the jury that sentenced him to death intentionally discriminated, the Baldus Study felt quite useless. Marshall, the man who marched Jim Crow to the guillotine, now wearing a black robe, was in a position to address this new dilemma but only if he appreciated the stakes.

"THE JUDGMENT AND OPINION OF THE COURT," said Chief Justice Burger on January 11, 1977, "[in] *Village of Arlington Heights against Metropolitan Housing Development Corporation* will be announced by Mr. Justice Powell."

During the 1960s, the population of the overwhelmingly White Village of Arlington Heights, a Chicago suburb, boomed. The 1970 census, though, counted only 27 Black people among its 64,000 residents. The Metropolitan Housing Development Corporation, a nonprofit developer with expertise in building homes using federal housing subsidies, petitioned Arlington Heights to rezone a fifteen-acre plot of land from single-family to multiple-family classification. MHDC intended to create a housing project, Lincoln Green, which consisted of twenty two-story buildings with 190 units for low- and moderate-income families and senior citizens. About 40 percent of the Black folk residing in the six-county area around Chicago would have been eligible for residence at Lincoln Green. All observers assumed that the project would multiply the suburb's Black population.

At three well-attended public hearings in 1971, many Arlington Heights residents panned MHDC's proposal, complaining that it would lower property values in the predominantly single-family-home community, and would negatively affect the water supply, flood control, parks, schools, and traffic, all hyperbolic concerns considering the project wouldn't have increased the suburb's population *that* much. "The Village authorities after public hearings," Justice Powell said, announcing his opinion, "refused to rezone the property from single family to multi-family classification."

The MHDC, with other plaintiffs, sued Arlington Heights in federal court, arguing that the rezoning denial was racially discriminatory and thus violated the Equal Protection Clause. The district court judge sided with Arlington Heights. The Seventh Circuit reversed, finding that "the ultimate effect" of the decision to not rezone the land infringed the plaintiffs' equal protection rights. During his Supreme Court oral argument, F. Willis Caruso, the plaintiff's attorney, alleged, "This is not a garden variety zoning case. This is a case of racial discrimination." Caruso, without proof of discriminatory intent, framed the case as one where a White suburb defeated a measure that would have brought Black people into their community. This decision, he maintained, reinforced residential segregation in the Chicago era. In Caruso's narration, the public face of Arlington Heights disclaimed that the zoning decision had any racial impetus, but the private face wanted to keep its bastion of Whiteness safe from Black infiltration.

"In *Washington against Davis,*" Powell said in the Court Chamber, announcing his *Arlington Heights* opinion, "we held that official action is not invalid solely because it results in a racially disproportionate effect. We held that proof of a discriminatory intent is required to show a violation of the Equal Protection Clause." In a five-to-three opinion, the Court found no equal protection violation because the plaintiffs failed to prove that the suburb acted with discriminatory intent when denying the rezoning petition. The public face said, "we didn't discriminate," and a Court majority responded, "they can't prove otherwise."

Powell's opinion, however, offered Boger a few threads to sew into his legal analysis on behalf of McCleskey when he would argue at the Supreme Court. Powell wrote that determining whether discriminatory intent existed "demands a sensitive inquiry into such circumstantial and direct evidence of intent as may be available." Even if a plaintiff failed to provide direct evidence of discriminatory intent, "[s]ometimes a clear pattern, unexplainable on grounds other than race, emerges from the effect of the state action even when the governing legislation appears neutral on its face." Boger could explain that the Baldus Study excluded all other possible explanations for the racial disparities in death sentencing, leaving race as the only explanation.

Marshall wrote a dissent, although he again failed to provide any rhetorical tool against the Intent Doctrine. Not until a case from Memphis, Tennessee, appeared before the Court a few years later did Marshall awaken.

IN 1923, THE MEMPHIS PLANNING COMMISSION approved a plan to develop a new neighborhood, Hein Park, in midtown Memphis and advertised it to potential White residents as offering the "pleasures and benefits of country life." Decades later, Hein Park, situated just north of the massive and popular Overton Park, a leading attraction with various oft-visited places, most notably the Memphis Zoo, remained a White enclave in the heart of a southern, 40-percent-Black, city.

In 1970, the Hein Park Civil Association filed an application with the Memphis and Shelby County Planning Commission to close four streets, a move that would have restricted access to the neighborhood. The objections of the fire, police, and sanitation departments, however, nixed that plan. The HPCA, three years later, touted a narrower plan that sought the closure of just the north end of West Drive, a two-lane street, half a mile long, that cut through Hein Park. The reasons for the closure included limiting "undesirable" traffic, reducing "traffic pollution" that caused the "interruption of community living," and protecting, from traffic, children who attended a nearby school.

The city held a public hearing on the matter but neglected to alert the Black property owners north of Hein Park who took West Drive to conveniently connect to Overton Park and the rest of the city. The hearing concluded without Black participation and the commission blocked the Black residents from examining the West Drive closure file afterward. The commission then failed to notify the Black community when the city council met to further debate the matter. When Black folk discovered this council meeting already under way, they requested the opportunity to fully voice their qualms, but the council limited them to fifteen minutes. Ultimately, the city agreed to close West Drive and erected a small barrier. Although city officials portrayed this as a mundane governmental act, at no other time had the city shut a street to control traffic. Memphis blocked Black traffic from entering a White neighborhood, all through a highly irregular process with minimal Black participation.

On April 1, 1974, Nathan T. Greene, a Black man who lived north of Hein Park, along with other Black residents, sued Memphis, arguing that the West Drive closure violated their rights. The action, they argued, forced them to travel longer distances to navigate the city and decreased their home values. For Greene, the street closure recalled a childhood memory. One day, as a boy, he was walking down West Drive to visit the zoo in the days when it opened its doors to Black people on Tuesdays only, and a policeman beat him with a stick and warned him to stay off West Drive. "They wanted to prevent black people from driving as well as walking through the neighborhood," Greene claimed.

The HPCA's attorney, George E. Morrow, disputed that racial animus inspired the West Drive closure. "This is purely and simply a case of a residential subdivision without sidewalks trying to protect itself against a flood of traffic," he said, adding that "it really never entered anybody's mind that there was any racial issue." The public face uttered these words. Greene and the other Black residents thought the private face wanted to reduce Black presence in a White neighborhood. At Supreme Court oral argument, Alvin O. Chambliss, Black plaintiffs' counsel, called the closure an "action to perpetuate the past effect of discrimination." On April 20, 1981, the Court announced its decision.

"[T]he *City of Memphis against Greene*," said Justice Stevens, "arose as a result of a decision by the City of Memphis to close the north end of a street that traverses a White residential community known as Hein Park.

"Although the street closing will not cut off access to Hein Park, it will require the diversion of a substantial volume of traffic that heretofore has gone through that community on its way to the Central District of the City. In view of the fact that most of the drivers who will be inconvenienced by the closing reside in black neighborhoods

to the north of Hein Park and the fact that the benefits of the closing will inure it to the white residents of Hein Park, this action was
brought on behalf of a class of black plaintiffs who contended that
the closing violated a federal statute 42 U.S.C. Section 1982 which
provides that all citizens shall have the same right as it is enjoyed by
white citizens to inherit, purchase, sell, hold, and convey real and
personal property." Although the Black plaintiffs did not sue under
the Equal Protection Clause, the Court treated their case as essentially an equal protection matter governed by the Intent Doctrine.

"After extensive proceedings in the lower courts," Stevens said,
"the District Court ultimately found that the closing was not motivated by any racial hostility and that its adverse impact on the plaintiff
class was not sufficiently significant to constitute a violation either of
the statute or of the Thirteenth Amendment. The Court of Appeals
for the Sixth Circuit reversed without setting aside any of the specific
findings of fact made by the District Court.

"Today, we . . . hold that the closing is adequately justified by
the city's interest in managing the flow of traffic within its boundaries and attempting to preserve the comparative quiet of the residential neighborhood," Stevens concluded. In his written opinion,
Stevens argued his logic followed precedent—the plaintiffs' lawsuit
must fail because the plaintiffs neither showed they suffered a significant enough injury nor proved the city intended to discriminate.
The public face said, "we didn't discriminate," and a Court majority
responded, "they can't prove otherwise."

Marshall's dissent revealed a man increasingly aware of the central
dilemma of this leg of our journey—determining how to undermine
the racial caste system when it endures in the absence of transparent castework. Marshall devised a rule that would have offered a
decent start to a worthwhile Intent Doctrine replacement, writing,
"When, as here, the decisionmaker takes action with full knowledge
of its enormously disproportionate racial impact, I believe . . . that
the government [must] carry a heavy burden in order to justify its
action." Marshall, attempting to lift the burden from the shoulders of
Black victims and onto state and local governments, supported making Memphis prove the necessity of its actions that caused a disparate
impact.

A few years later, another Supreme Court case would provide Marshall the chance to tackle these tricky issues.

ON FEBRUARY 14, 1984, inside a Louisville, Kentucky, courtroom, public defender Doug Dowell and prosecutor Joe Gutmann carried out their roles in the jury selection process, or voir dire, as the two examined potential jurors from a larger pool, the jury venire, to choose a final trial jury. Both used "peremptory challenges," a lawyer's objection to a proposed juror from the venire made without needing to furnish an explanation. The defendant, James Kirkland Batson, a young Black man indicted for receiving stolen property, directed Dowell to object to Gutmann striking all the Black people from the jury venire. Gutmann, in particular, had removed two young Black men because he feared they would identify with Batson along racial lines.

In *Swain v. Alabama*, decided in 1965, the Court held that a prosecutor could consider race when emptying the peremptory challenge clip if the prosecutor was chasing the aspiration of convicting that defendant, rather than the goal of forbidding Black people from participating in jury service. In other words, prosecutors could strike Black jurors if they thought the state's case would fare better with a White juror instead but *not* because they deemed jury service White people's terrain. As a practical matter, this meant that the Court, after ruling in favor of the Scottsboro Boys in *Norris*, gave caste preservationists a new blueprint for reviving the all-White jury. *Akins* acquiesced to tokenism on jury venires. *Swain* empowered prosecutors to strike the tokens. And Black criminal defendants lacked recourse.

After Dowell told Batson that the law foreclosed a remedy to discriminatory exercise of peremptory challenges, Batson replied, "I don't care, object anyway."

Gutmann and Dowell stepped forward to the bench to interact with Judge George B. Ryan away from the ears of the jurors.

"Your Honor, prior to the swearing of the jury, I would like to make a motion to discharge the panel on the following grounds," Dowell said. "[T]here were four black jurors on the case. After I reviewed my notes, I noted that all four of them were struck by the

Commonwealth's pre-emptories. The jury now, as empaneled, I want the record to reflect, is an all-white panel. I submit that under these circumstances, the defendant is being denied his right to . . . equal protection of the law under the U.S. Constitution." Dowell objected to the swearing in of the jury.

"I'm going to overrule," Judge Ryan answered, "because [prosecutors] can strike anybody they want to."

The Reagan administration's brief in *Batson v. Kentucky* supported *Swain.* In the previous leg of our journey, we discussed Solicitor General Fried's *Wygant* brief, which asserted that "the Fourteenth Amendment prohibits a state from making racial distinctions in the exercise of governmental power." *Swain*, though, empowered prosecutors to make such distinctions. If the Reagan administration lawyers *truly* treasured color-blindness, they had to oppose that practice. Fried's brief, however, championed it.

The public face in the brief explained that the Court must permit a prosecutor to consider race during voir dire because unrestricted use of peremptory challenges had deep origins in criminal law. Yet, when the Jackson Board of Education wanted to employ race distinctions to integrate its teaching faculty and atone for past exclusion of Black teachers to create a better pedagogical environment, the Reagan administration's public face castigated race distinctions as unconstitutional, morally abhorrent behavior. Privately, caste preservationists wanted to both protect White racial advantages and secure better odds of convicting Black defendants. The Reagan administration failed at toggling between the two faces, revealing allegiances to White Supremacy.

A few months before granting certiorari in *McCleskey*, Boger's landmark case, the Court handed down its *Batson* opinion, which overturned *Swain.* Justice Powell, in his seven-to-two majority opinion, held that prosecutors could no longer allow race to inform their peremptory challenges. Helpful to Boger, the Court outlined how defense attorneys could prove a so-called *Batson* violation.

First, the defense had to present prima facie evidence of the prosecutor's discriminatory use of peremptory challenges—typically a simple observation that the prosecutor had stricken at least a few prospective Black jurors. Then, the burden shifted to the prosecutor to explain the strikes on nonracial grounds. If the prosecutor succeeded, the burden reverted to the defendant, who then had to convince the judge to view the prosecutor's explanation as a pretext for race discrimination.

"Such a paradigm seemed remarkably pertinent to the capital sentencing context," Boger thought, "except that Baldus's evidence had examined, not a handful of decisions by a single prosecutor, but rather thousands of decisions, looking at hundreds of factors in each decision over a seven-year period, a much more powerful prima facie showing than could ever emerge in a jury selection context, where there were often no more than a few state decisions to examine. Moreover, nothing seemed a clearer failure of the Batson paradigm than the State of Georgia's failure in McCleskey's case to offer any plausible explanation for the prima facie racial disparities that Baldus had demonstrated."

Marshall, ever more aware of the difficulty the Intent Doctrine posed to Black claimants, advocated in his concurrence that the Court should abolish the peremptory challenge altogether because judges could not trust prosecutors to abstain from discrimination, and judges would struggle to hold prosecutors accountable. In short, he doubted that Black criminal defendants could successfully play the "prove it" game, an untenable gambit when freedom hung in the balance. Marshall, therefore, advocated canceling the game entirely.

Earlier, I mentioned *Hawkins v. Town of Shaw* and told you there would be more on that case later. That time has come. Accompany me to The Promised Land, on January 23, 1971, the day a Fifth Circuit judge announced his *Hawkins* opinion that improved the world of Black inhabitants in secluded Shaw, Mississippi.

ANDREW HAWKINS, A PART-TIME HANDYMAN, lives with his wife and three children here in The Promised Land, a Black neighborhood in Shaw, a one-square-mile-sized town of twenty-five hundred—fifteen hundred Black, one thousand White—in the Mississippi Delta. The Promised Land, in the Bible, refers to land God promised Abraham and his descendants. The chosen people. Look around. *This* destitute locality is no Promised land. The homes here, dilapidated, constructed with the rugged wood of cypress trees, are poorly sealed. When holes and cracks inevitably appear, residents stuff cotton into them, futile armor against Mother Nature. Black neighborhoods like The Promised Land in Shaw receive scant municipal services. Unpaved roads. No running water. Drainage and sanitary sewers? Nonexistent. No traffic lights. Nary a streetlight. Shaw's White inhabitants, however, live a world apart. They live in comfort. In modernity. Their neighborhoods enjoy what The Promised Land wants. What The Promised Land needs. The town's government showers White folk with attention. Black folk weather the monsoon of neglect.

Three years ago, in February 1968, Hawkins, about fifty years old, walked a dirt road in The Promised Land, passing an open pit of human waste and storm water, heading to the downtown area with paved roads. He entered the post office to mail an envelope to the U.S. District Court for the Northern District of Mississippi. He was filing a class action lawsuit on behalf of himself and Shaw's Black residents. The town's mayor, clerk, and five aldermen, the lawsuit charged, were apportioning municipal services and infrastructure resources based on race.

More than a year later, in summer 1969, Judge William Keady held three days of hearings that detailed the disparities between how the races lived in Shaw and their causes. The testimony vindicated Hawkins, forcing a federal court to acknowledge that the city indeed lavished benefits on White neighborhoods and deprived Black ones. Shaw officials, however, disavowed that anti-Black impulses activated these discrepancies. The facts put into evidence, Keady determined, presented one central question—whether town officials intended to cause the problems that surround us in neglected neighborhoods like The Promised Land. The town, Keady concluded, enforced no ordinance that classified which race should receive which services, and the Black plaintiffs failed to demonstrate that officeholders had intended to manage a town where Black and White neighborhoods enjoyed vastly different experiences.

"[The town officials'] assertions that they have not discriminated because of race or poverty are supported by substantial, rational considerations explaining the quality and quantity of presently available town's services," Keady wrote in his opinion. "These facts negate plaintiffs' assertions of racial . . . discrimination." Uncovering no proof of discriminatory intent and concluding that the explanation that Shaw was simply slow to upgrade its infrastructure seemed reasonable, Keady determined no equal protection violation had occurred. Hawkins appealed. And Fifth Circuit Judge Elbert P. Tuttle, an Eisenhower appointee, handed down his opinion in *Hawkins v. Town of Shaw* on this day in January 1971.

"Nearly 98% of all homes that front on unpaved streets in Shaw are occupied by blacks," Tuttle writes in his opinion, specifying the problem. "Ninety-seven percent of the homes not served by sanitary sewers are in black neighborhoods. Further, while the town has acquired a significant number of medium and high intensity mercury vapor street lighting fixtures, every one of them has been installed in white neighborhoods. The record further discloses that similar statistical evidence of grave disparities in both the level and kinds of services offered regarding surface water drainage, water mains, fire hydrants, and traffic control apparatus was also brought forth and not disputed."

Tuttle acknowledges that "the record contains no direct evidence aimed at establishing bad faith, ill will or an evil motive on the part of the Town of Shaw and its public officials." By eschewing the Intent Doctrine, however, he still finds for the plaintiffs. The Equal Protection Clause, to Tuttle, achieves more than a mere prohibition against the state purposefully harming a racial group. After all, "thoughtlessness," Tuttle observes, "can be as disastrous and unfair to private rights and the public interest as the perversity of a willful scheme." Concluding that Shaw officials could have no compelling interest in operating a town where White, but not Black, residents reap all the benefits, Tuttle deems that the "discriminatory results of Shaw's administration of municipal services" establish an equal protection violation. A town will be obliged to improve the conditions Black residents endure because the Fifth Circuit rejects the Intent Doctrine.

In the previous leg of our journey, we learned that Reagan Justice Department lawyers will endorse the anti-classification principle in the 1980s. The principle, they profess, facilitates a color-blind society. A world free of race-conscious governance. They swear they want this. They swear the Constitution demands this. These lawyers also champion the Intent Doctrine, and, in 1987, will disseminate a piece of legal writing entitled *Report to the Attorney General Redefining Discrimination: "Disparate Impact" and the Institutionalization of Affirmative Action.*

Relying upon disparate impact, the report argues, would both disturb "naturally occurring statistical disparities between groups that are [otherwise] inevitable in a heterogeneous society such as the United States" and precipitate "the permanent institutionalization of [race]-conscious affirmative action." Put differently, Reagan Justice Department lawyers predict that judges equating disparate impact with race discrimination would lead to their embracing affirmative action as a remedy. Disparate impact, per this theory, will operate as a gateway drug that would culminate in race-conscious solutions to nonexistent discrimination. Department lawyers insist that the Equal Protection Clause forbids discrimination, which, they contend, can only involve intentional conduct. Their liberal opponents, they argue, are profaning civil rights law by redefining discrimination into disparate impacts shown through statistics, which they call examples of nondiscrimination. "As a result of this redefinition of discrimination," the report states, "many of the nation's laws incorporating the non-discrimination principle of equal treatment have, in Orwellian fashion, been turned on their heads to effectively require the very behavior that they proscribe—the [color-conscious] treatment of individuals—so that statistically proportionate representation or results for groups might be achieved. In short, through this redefinition of discrimination, the rights of individuals to equal treatment have been subordinated to a new right of proportional representation for groups."

Political conservatives accept that criminal sentencing might result in Black convicts receiving harsher sentences, and they insist that judges must not assume that anything invidious produces these outcomes absent proof of discriminatory intent. Such thinking rebuffs Boger's argument that the Baldus Study, by itself, demonstrates a Fourteenth Amendment violation. A conservative legal organization, Washington Legal Foundation, submits a McCleskey brief to the Supreme Court that articulates the arguments the Reagan Justice

Department will amplify throughout the 1980s. The brief maligns Boger for demanding "racial proportionality" in the imposition of the death penalty. "Allowing death sentences to be reversed solely on the basis of disparate impact data, and without proof of actual discriminatory motive," the brief contends, "would be unjust, unworkable, and a source of disastrous upheaval for the entire criminal sentencing process."

We mustn't separate these arguments from the broader environment in which they will be presented. The year now is 1971, the second year in the decade when the prison population will mushroom while politicians, Democrats and Republicans alike, invoke thinly veiled anti-Black language to drum up support for increasingly draconian criminal punishments. Nixon, the current president, surfs at the vanguard of this cresting wave, proclaiming that America must win the "war on drugs" as he barnstorms the nation with tough-on-crime addresses. President Reagan, in the 1980s, will escalate this rhetoric, urging a nation to condone a massive prison population.

On September 11, 1982, President Reagan will deliver a radio address on crime that fits the era. "Many of you have written to me how afraid you are to walk the streets alone at night," the president says. "As Attorney General Smith pointed out recently, an important part of the problem is that Americans are losing faith in our courts and our entire legal system. . . . We can and must make improvements in the way our courts deal with crime." Caste preservationists want judges to construct the Constitution to allow states the autonomy to deal with criminals however they see fit. In 1980, the year Reagan wins the presidency, America imprisons 329,000. When Reagan flies off in a helicopter eight years later, the number will have almost doubled, with mass incarceration leeching the blood of the Black population disproportionately.

During the two previous legs of our journey, we learned that Reagan Justice Department attorneys endorse the anti-classification principle, heralding it as the lighthouse guiding a lost nation toward the righteous shores of a color-blind society. The public face utters this. But the absence of other utterances exposes a private face that worships the racial caste system. Why would an evangelist of color-blindness tolerate a system where murderers, specifically Black murderers, of White persons, are far more likely to receive the death penalty? This being true establishes they exist in a society that values White life more. Those praying for a society where race holds no meaning cannot tolerate race predicting who the state kills and who the state lets live.

In her *City of Richmond v. J. A. Croson Company* opinion, Justice O'Connor contends that judges should employ strict scrutiny to evaluate race-conscious remedial policies to "'smoke out' illegitimate uses of race by assuring that the legislative body is pursuing a goal important enough to warrant use of a highly suspect tool." Reagan Justice Department lawyers agree. But where do we need to smoke out illegitimate uses of race more than in contexts where state action produces racial disparities, but we have little way of discerning whether illicit racial motives produce them? Why suddenly lose interest in smoking out illegitimate uses of race?

And that's how caste preservationists out themselves. The public face hails color-blindness and declares that it explains their opposition to racial remedial programs. Yet, when the issue becomes Black people complaining about hidden instances of discrimination, the same people who profess they want to exclusively breathe color-blind air only care if the Black person has proof of discriminatory intent—something nearly impossible to obtain—and they cultivate no tools to smoke out whether intentional discrimination is responsible. The public face divulges the existence of a private face. The public face's commitment to color-blindness only when progressive reformers are seeking to ameliorate past and ongoing racial oppression exposes that devotion to caste preservationism, not adherence to color-blindness, drives how they prefer to construct the Constitution.

Those hostile to race-based governmental decision-making must imagine the possibility of state actors who conceal their race-based decisions with deceit. They must imagine the possibility of what surrounds you right now. They must imagine The Promised Land. The dirt streets are bathed in sewage here, but the White folk have a sewer system. Nonetheless, town officials denied they had acted with odious motives. Those who trumpet the Intent Doctrine, if they truly care about color-blindness, must devise methodologies for discovering whether hidden biases explain places like The Promised

Land. But they *never* do. They *always* demand evidence of discriminatory intent that they know victims of discrimination rarely have. They demand photographic proof in a camera-less world. Inhale the atmosphere here one final time. Smell the funk of fraud.

Now, let's visit the Supreme Court for *McCleskey v. Kemp* oral argument.

ON THE MORNING OF OCTOBER 15, 1986, we walk the white marble floor of the Great Hall inside the Supreme Court Building, which leads to the chamber. From above, the blue and red coffered ceiling watches us, its beauty completing the magisterial experience of strolling into the highest courtroom in the land. We spot Boger. The anxiety that seizes him ambushes nearly any lawyer in these moments. As he gathers himself, let's explore each side's theory of the case.

In his brief, Boger presented why, despite losing at the trial court and on appeal, the LDF had proven its equal protection claim. He relied on the burden-shifting process the Court outlined in *Batson v. Kentucky*. McCleskey, Boger argued, carried the initial burden of presenting a prima facie case of "state-sanctioned racial discrimination." The Baldus Study, by eliminating all nonracial variables that could have explained away the disparities in outcomes, had shown that *race* poisoned the administration of the state's capital punishment statute. The burden then shifted to the state to provide an alternate theory. "[T]he State," Boger wrote, "must demonstrate that 'permissible racially neutral selection criteria and procedures have produced the . . . result.'" And Georgia failed. The state's principal expert claimed at trial that White victim cases were more likely to produce a death sentence for convicted defendants because those crimes were more aggravated. The expert never tested the hypothesis. But Baldus did. And disproved it. Georgia's failing to carry its burden meant that McCleskey had proven an equal protection violation.

Mary Beth Westmoreland, again representing Georgia, depicted the Baldus Study as unreliable because death penalty cases involved too many variables, rendering impossible the creation of a methodology that could reliably isolate the value of any singular variable. "Thus," she argued, the state "would submit that this Court should completely reject the use of this type of statistical analysis as inappropriate in this case." Deeming the Baldus Study insufficient, Westmoreland insisted that McCleskey needed to fulfill his obligation under the Intent Doctrine, and he supplied no proof of discriminatory intent. Westmoreland breezily explained away McCleskey's death sentence—he committed a crime for which death was a potential punishment, and the jury assessed it.

At ten in the morning, with Boger and Westmoreland seated at their respective tables, the gavel sounds. All in the courtroom stand, and the marshal utters his ceremonial remarks: "The Honorable, the Chief Justice and the Associate Justices of the Supreme Court of the United States. Oyez! Oyez! Oyez! All persons having business before the Honorable, the Supreme Court of the United States, are admonished to draw near and give their attention, for the Court is now sitting. God save the United States and this Honorable Court!" The nine black robes, Chief Justice Rehnquist, Justices Brennan, White, Marshall, Blackmun, Powell, Stevens, O'Connor, and Scalia, file into the chamber in groups of three and fill their leather chairs.

"We will hear arguments first this morning," Chief Justice Rehnquist says in a flat voice, in "*Warren McCleskey versus Ralph Kemp*.

"Mr. Boger, you may proceed when you are ready."

Boger walks to the rostrum, his notebook in hand. "Mr. Chief Justice and may it please the Court.

"If the State of Georgia had criminal statutes that expressly imposed different penalties, harsher penalties, on black defendants simply because they were black, or on those who killed white victims, simply because those victims were white, the statutes would plainly violate the Constitution. There was a time, of course, when the State of Georgia did have such statutes, before our nation's Civil War, when free blacks and slaves alike could be given a death sentence merely for the crime of assault on a Georgia white citizen," Boger explains, lacing his analysis with history. "With the ratification of the Fourteenth Amendment, such criminal statutes can explicitly no longer be written. Yet the old habits of mind, the racial attitudes of that time have survived, as this Court well knows, into the current century." The justices, surprisingly, ask no questions, and Boger continues following the outline of his opening remarks.

"Today, we are before the Court with a substantial body of evidence indicating that during the last decade, Georgia prosecutors and juries, in their administration of Georgia's post-*Furman* capital statutes, have continued to act as if some of those old statutes were still on the books. A black defendant convicted in the State of Georgia of the murder of a white person goes to his sentencing hearing with as serious a handicap against him on racial grounds alone as if the prosecutor had hard evidence that he had been tried and convicted previously of another murder. The color of a defendant's skin, in other words, or that of his victim, is often as grave an aggravating circumstance, in fact, in Georgia, as those expressly designated by Georgia's legislature," says Boger in a slow, methodical tone. By comparing race-conscious actions to race-conscious laws, Boger invites the justices who are aligning against 1980s race-conscious remedial programs to view Georgia's capital sentencing as another vehicle for what they profess to despise.

> We've documented below the role that's been played by racial considerations in Georgia's capital sentencing system. Our evidence demonstrates that Georgia sentences the killers of its white citizens at a rate nearly eleven times that to which it sentences to death the killers of its black citizens. And even after most of the legitimate sentencing considerations have been taken into account, a defendant remains over four times more likely to receive a capital sentence if his victim chanced to be white.
>
> Now the sources of petitioner's evidence below are two meticulous studies. They were conducted by Professors David Baldus and George Woodworth. And they have two major strengths that I think the Court should focus on at the outset. The first strength is their comprehensiveness. They provide us with a thorough picture of how the Georgia capital sentencing system operated during the 1973–1979 period covered by the studies.
>
> The second feature of these studies is the extraordinary openness of Professors Baldus and Woodworth. Their indefatigable willingness to entertain every criticism, to test every rival hypothesis, to seize upon every statistical means known to them to take their racial findings and shake them hard and see if by some sta-

tistical means or method, those findings would drop out of their analysis. In other words, Professor Baldus was not wedded at the outset to any assumptions about what he wanted to prove. He was open to all comers. He was open to the state. He was open to the court. Indeed, during our evidentiary hearing in 1983, he invited the District Judge, "please sir, you designate for us those factors you think make a difference in Georgia. You tell us a statistical method. We will with our computer here run that model. We will see whether in the test before the court we're right that race plays a part, or not." The judge accepted that test. The data were run under his model. And indeed, the racial effects, as Judge Forester saw the system in Georgia, actually increased. It's because Professor Baldus was wedded to no prior assumptions. It's because he subjected his statistical analysis to so many varieties of review. That his studies provide, I believe, such a powerful indictment of the Georgia system.

More than six minutes pass until a justice interjects. The black robes rarely afford litigators that long of a runway. But rather than ask about Boger's legal arguments, Justice White impugns the assistants who conducted the legwork for the Baldus Study, seeking to undermine its reliability. White startles Boger, who knows White lacks good faith for the question. Rehnquist then impugns Baldus's character, suggesting that bias toward the LDF, because the organization funded his work, rendered him untrustworthy. If Baldus's work were flawed, Rehnquist could point out the issue in the data. But he can't. No such flaws exist. That the two justices stoop to such an unbecoming line of questioning suggests to Boger that they're frustrated because they haven't the competency to undercut the Baldus Study. Their gambits flop, and O'Connor returns the Court's attention to the law.

"Mr. Boger," O'Connor says in a halting cadence, "if the study is utilized to support your proposition, what does a petitioner of a defendant have to show for the constitutional violation under equal protection or Eighth Amendment? Does he not have to show intentional discrimination against this particular defendant?"

"Yes," Boger responds, "I believe he does, Your Honor, and yet

I believe that we have shown that in this case. We've had to show it inferentially, of course. Juries in Georgia deliberate in secret, and there are no records kept. And prosecutors rarely confess their own—"

"Well," O'Connor interrupts, "you cited *Bazemore*, which of course was a Title VII statutory case. Are there cases involving a constitutional violation where the Court has relied on statistical proof of the type you're suggesting we use here?"

In his brief, Boger cited *Bazemore v. Friday*, a pay discrimination case. In *Bazemore*, Black plaintiffs of the North Carolina Agricultural Extension Service used multiple regression analysis, like that found in the Baldus Study, to demonstrate that Black workers, even when accounting for qualification differences, received lower pay for the same work. A case like *Bazemore*, decided a few months ago in July 1986, and *Batson*, decided in April 1986, had infused Boger with optimism that the Court was shifting in his favor. As O'Connor just noted, though, *Bazemore* concerned Title VII, not the Equal Protection Clause.

"Well," Boger replies, "there are a number of different sources of that authority, Your Honor. Both *Washington v. Davis*, of course, and *Arlington Heights*, say that the courts must be sensitive to such evidence as does exist, and acknowledge that in some cases the evidence of historical fact plus statistics may be all that does exist. In the jury discrimination cases, for example, one rarely—"

O'Connor intrudes again. "But this evidence is addressed, of course, as I understand it, to the victim. Discrimination in the sense of discrimination against the victim."

"There's also evidence of discrimination against black defendants who've murdered whites, especially in the mid-range of moderately aggravated cases," Boger replies. "In other words, the race of defendant discrimination exists, and Baldus documented it, but it's not as pervasive. It really is more of a subdivision of the cases in Georgia. But the race of victim discrimination, as Your Honor suggests, is statewide, and in all the cases."

O'Connor is downplaying the significance of race-of-victim discrimination. But Boger's brief explains that this particular evil inspired the pen of the Fourteenth Amendment's framers. "The congressional hearings and debates that led to enactment of the Fourteenth Amendment," Boger wrote, "are replete with references to this pervasive race-of-victim discrimination; the amendment and the enforcing legislation were intended, in substantial part, to stop it."

"Mr. Boger, don't you have to show that this particular jury discriminated?" Rehnquist asks, pulling the conversation, to the Intent Doctrine.

"Your Honor, I think we have shown that it's more likely than not that this jury did."

"Well," Rehnquist responds, "this particular jury was only convened once. And I think you have to show under our cases that this particular jury would have dealt differently with a black defendant who killed a black person." Rehnquist knows that Boger can't prove that the jury that sentenced McCleskey to death would have acted differently if his victim were Black.

"Well, Mr. Chief Justice, let me suggest to you why I believe we have made that showing. We of course don't have confessions from the jurors themselves. No one has come forward. But indirectly what we have is a pattern that Professor Baldus documented—"

Rehnquist interrupts, "But not a pattern on the part of this jury."

"No, this jury only assembles, as you say, for one decision," Boger responds. "If we could show, Mr. Chief Justice, that six out of ten of blacks who murdered whites are receiving death in a racially discriminatory fashion, on grounds where if there were white defendants, they wouldn't have, we would not be able to show, of course, which ones of the six they were."

"No, but . . . the institution that you're challenging is the jury here," Rehnquist replies. "And it's the jury in this defendant's case."

"Well, of course, Your Honor, it's not simply the jury," says Boger. "Professor Baldus' evidence shows dramatically that the prosecutor plays a serious role in this process."

"Well, then, do you think your evidence supports a finding that this particular prosecutor, who prosecuted this case, discriminates as between blacks who've killed whites and blacks who've killed blacks?"

"Not as between charging," Boger replies, "but as between deciding who to plead out to a lesser defense or permit not to go to trial, and who to move on to penalty."

"Okay, you say your evidence supports a finding that this particular prosecutor, in doing what you say, discriminated in the manner I described?"

"I don't believe we have to show that a particular prosecutor, as opposed to the prosecutorial office, Your Honor. What we have shown is—"

"Well," Rehnquist says, "but do you think your evidence would support a finding as to this particular prosecutor?"

We need not follow the oral argument any longer. Rehnquist knows that Boger can't possibly have evidence proving that the prosecutor acted with discriminatory intent, and, if the defendant needs that evidence, then the guarantee of equal protection effectively means nothing. In a memo he wrote for *Bakke*, Rehnquist criticized the UC Davis medical school's admissions program. "I think it as a postulate that difference in treatment of individuals based on their race or ethnic origin is at the bull's eye of the target at which the Fourteenth Amendment's Equal Protection Clause was aimed." Here, though, Rehnquist is unconcerned with the state treating people differently based on race. Like many before him, Rehnquist is asking for photographic evidence in a camera-less world.

Unbeknownst to Boger, at nine in the morning, an hour before the justices entered the chamber, Justice White gave Justices Powell, Rehnquist, O'Connor, and Scalia a twelve-page memo explaining why he would vote to affirm the Eleventh Circuit *McCleskey* decision, wildly unusual and improper. The Baldus Study "has, in fact, shown that the system operates in a predictable and largely rational fashion," White wrote. "Because of this fact, McCleskey should be held to the burden of showing that in his case the race of the victim factor influenced the imposition of his death sentence. Accepting as true the Baldus findings, they are not so stark and of such overwhelming magnitude to give rise to a permissible inference that petitioner's sentence resulted from the fact that he killed a white person. Because McCleskey has offered no further evidence in support of his claim, the judgment of [the Eleventh Circuit] should be affirmed."

When Boger leaves the Supreme Court Building, he miscalculates, thinking that "we've got a chance to get five [justices]." The next conference will verify what was decided before Boger uttered a word.

"I HAD AN INNOCENT MAN ONCE," Marshall said, seated in his high-back green-leather-and-mahogany chair, during that conference session two days after the *McCleskey* oral argument. "He was accused of raping a white woman. The government told me if he would plead guilty, he'd only get life. I said I couldn't make that decision; I'd have to ask my client. So I told him that if he pleaded guilty, he wouldn't get the death sentence.

"He said, 'Plead guilty to what?'

"I said, 'Plead guilty to rape.'

"He said, 'Raping that woman? You gotta be kidding. I won't do it.'

"That's when I knew I had an innocent man.

"When the judge sent the jurors out, he told them that they had three choices: Not guilty, guilty, or guilty with mercy. 'You understand those are the three different possible choices,' he instructed. But after the jury left, the judge told the people in the courtroom that they were not to move before the bailiff took the defendant away.

"I said, 'What happened to "not guilty"?'

"The judge looked at me, and said, 'Are you kidding?' Just like that. And he was the *judge*."

As Marshall concluded the story in the room lined with carved oak wood along its walls, he leaned toward the long mahogany conference table, pointing his finger, and said with the panache of a captivating orator executing his dismount, "E-e-e-end of story. The guy was found guilty and sentenced to death. But he never raped that woman."

Marshall stayed still then waved his hand, "Oh well, he was just a Negro."

At the end of the conference, five wanted to affirm—Rehnquist, White, Powell, O'Connor, and Scalia—and four, Brennan, Marshall, Blackmun, and Stevens, to reverse. McCleskey's case failed.

The ascending conservative intellectual movement during the 1980s claimed that the new frontier of state-sponsored discrimination created White, not Black, victims. Judges, this movement insisted, needed to extinguish the newfangled enemies of racial fairness—affirmative action, quotas, and other race-conscious programs meant to atone for past and ongoing racial injustices that needed no atoning. These policies, the argument held, violated the anti-classification principle and lured the nation away from a color-blind society. *Brown v. Board of Education*, the Civil Rights Movement, and federal Civil and Voting Rights Acts passed in the 1960s wrecked whatever separated Black folk from equality under the law. America had finished the job first started with The Trinity, the argument claimed, and renewed complaints of widespread systemic racial oppression rang hollow.

The Baldus Study, however, shattered the idyllic snow globe caste preservationists had manufactured. The black robes knew this well—Baldus's work validated the LDF's thesis that race had infected capital punishment in Georgia. A subtler, yet still pernicious, form of unequal justice, the one that beckoned Marshall to Korea, endured. A thorny task stood before the conservative members of the Court, the justices whom caste preservationists expected to pursue their ends: How could the justices who had railed against racial classifications ignore strong statistical evidence proving that a state's criminal justice system was using race as a strong factor in deciding who lives and dies? As the Court's conservative members had often done in closely divided cases, they tapped Justice Powell to write an opinion impossible to write without ignorant legal analysis.

"THE OPINION OF THE COURT in McCleskey against Kemp will be announced by Justice Powell," Rehnquist said in the Court Chamber on April 22, 1987.

"McCleskey," Powell said in a wispy Virginian drawl, "argued that the entire Georgia capital punishment system is administered in a racially discriminatory manner, based on the race of the victim and to a lesser extent on the race of the defendant. . . .

"For the reasons stated on the opinion filed today we affirm."

The issue before the Court, Powell explained in his written opinion, was whether "a complex statistical study that indicates a risk that racial considerations enter into capital sentence determinations proves that petitioner McCleskey's capital sentence is unconstitutional under the . . . Fourteenth Amendment." He replied no, and the Intent Doctrine powered his answer. McCleskey, he argued, needed to "prove that the decisionmakers in *his* case acted with discriminatory purpose." Powell's adherence to the Intent Doctrine meant that, by itself, a work that spoke to statewide discrimination lacked relevance to any individual case in that state. Powell even denied that the Baldus Study proved that discrimination had occurred in the state's administration of its capital punishment statute, writing that "at most the Baldus study indicates a discrepancy that appears to correlate with race," an ignorant description. The study, he contended, unearthed "unexplained" occurrences within Georgia's death sentencing process that the majority refused to assume had "invidious" origins.

Powell conceded that the Court had before relied on statistics to substantiate claims of discriminatory intent. In jury discrimination cases, the Court had acquiesced to statistics proving that southern states had purposefully kept juries all White. Also, in Title VII cases like *Bazemore v. Friday*, the Court allowed a multiple regression analysis to prove statutory violations of intentional discrimination. Powell differentiated those matters, however, from capital sentencing decisions. According to his logic, the result of each death penalty trial involved innumerable variables. A separate and independent jury, moreover, decided each case. A capital case's uniqueness meant that the Baldus Study could not properly capture reliable revelations about unconstitutional behavior transpiring under Georgia's capital punishment statute.

"Because discretion is essential to the criminal justice process," Powell wrote, "we would demand exceptionally clear proof before we would infer that the discretion has been abused. The unique nature of the decisions at issue in this case," he continued, "also counsels against adopting such an inference from the disparities indicated by the Baldus study. Accordingly, we hold that the Baldus study is clearly insufficient to support an inference that any of the decisionmakers in McCleskey's case acted with discriminatory purpose."

Powell's argument, of course, failed on logical grounds. Baldus's multiple regression analysis, after all, accounted for a wide array of variables across a wide array of decision-makers. Additionally, Powell leaving open the possibility of overturning a death sentence in the future if a defendant yielded "exceptionally clear proof" reeked of dishonesty, because if the Baldus Study could not clear the "exceptionally clear proof" threshold, nothing could.

The Court likewise rejected the charge that Georgia violated McCleskey's equal protection rights by continuing to administer the state's capital punishment statute despite it producing disparate impacts. Discriminatory purpose "implies more than intent as a volition or intent as awareness of consequences," Powell wrote. "It implies that the decisionmaker, in this case a state legislature, selected or reaffirmed a particular course of action at least in part 'because of,' not merely 'in spite of,' its adverse effects upon an identifiable group." For his claim to prevail, "McCleskey would have to prove that the Georgia Legislature enacted or maintained the death penalty statute because of an anticipated racially discriminatory effect."

Powell's opinion had essentially foreclosed proving race discrimination within the criminal justice system with statistics, a result that delighted caste preservationists who wished to continue leveraging the justice system to control, abuse, and mass incarcerate the Black population. Capital defendants must prove purposeful discrimination by somehow providing an admission of guilt from a partial prosecutor or a biased juror, or some other piece of evidence demonstrating intentional malfeasance. McCleskey's Fourteenth Amendment claim failed, as did his Eighth Amendment one. Marshall joined Blackmun's and Brennan's dissents but did not write one himself.

Leslie Gielow, a Powell clerk who handled the case, thought McCleskey should have prevailed. She conversed with the liberal justices' clerks, seeking arguments that might persuade Powell, although ultimately decided against pressing the matter with her boss. She understood that he had long decided to reject McCleskey's claims. Some clerks in the conservative chambers commiserated about their mutual helplessness. The strength of the Baldus Study had convinced them that McCleskey should win. Several, including one of Rehnquist's clerks, advocated the appointment of an expert to provide a neutral appraisal of the Baldus Study. Those justices refused though. They eschewed the knowledge an expert could provide. They relished ignorance. The absence of knowledge made their vote to uphold McCleskey's death sentence easier.

The public face argued that the study fell short of proving the existence of intentional racial discrimination. Those who publicly championed color-blindness could not admit publicly that they were violating their own principles. A new justice's internal memorandum, though, exposed the existence of a private face that condoned race discrimination in the imposition of the death sentence. Read Scalia's January 6 memo in full:

> I plan to join Lewis's opinion in this case, with two reservations. I disagree with the argument that the inferences that can be drawn from the Baldus study are weakened by the fact that each jury and each trial is unique, or by the large number of variables at issue. And I do not share the view, implicit in the opinion, that an effect of racial factors upon sentencing, if it could only be shown by sufficiently strong statistical evidence, would require reversal. Since it is my view that the unconscious operation of irrational sympathies and antipathies, including racial, upon jury decisions and (hence) prosecutorial decisions is real, acknowledged in the decisions of this court, and ineradicable, I cannot honestly say that all I need is more proof. I expect to write separately to make these points, but not until I see the dissent. Sincerely, Nino.

Scalia, confirmed to his seat less than a month before *McCleskey* oral argument, understood multiple regression analysis and accepted the Baldus Study. Boger figured Scalia would—he knew of his reputation as smart. Boger never fathomed, though, that Scalia would conclude that Black folk should just have to live under such conditions. Rather than deny that the Baldus Study had proved the LDF's thesis, Scalia believed that the other justices should admit the thesis was true but not construct the Constitution to thwart a system that permitted race to contaminate decisions of life and death.

Scalia never wrote that dissent. He didn't need to, and, besides, his older colleagues probably warned him against publishing an opinion wherein he admits he would not overturn a death sentence no matter how strong of a statistical study identifying race discrimination a defendant supplied. Powell's opinion sank the most comprehensive capital punishment study anyone had ever seen, dissuading another organization from funding a similar study for a constitutional challenge in another state. That likely satisfied Scalia.

Powell had composed the best opinion the public face could that gave the private face the result it craved: an opinion that allowed the state to discriminate against Black folk in the criminal justice system that did not obviously undermine the color-blindness rationale for striking down racial remedial policies. In the previous leg of our journey, we discussed how the funk of folly often indicates the existence of the funk of fraud. Identify Powell's *McCleskey* opinion, like Brown's *Plessy v. Ferguson*, like Stevens's *Parents Involved in Community Schools v. Seattle School District No. 1* as illustrations of that theory.

If the LDF won, the organization would have replicated this strategy in other states, as the Court majority surely suspected. Social scientists at the time, and since, have produced comparable studies to Baldus's work and almost all have revealed similar conclusions. Losing the case killed the civil rights groups' ambitions. Similar studies in other contexts would have shown similar results. The *McCleskey* decision neutered any such possibilities.

"I confess to being naïve," Boger wrote years after Georgia executed McCleskey in September 1991, "despite the pattern of history in this area, about the extent to which the Court might be willing to divert its eyes from, minimize, trivialize, or even acquiesce in proven patterns of racial discrimination that manifest themselves at a systemic or societal level. I was chiefly worried that the Court might not understand the study, that it might find itself lost in the details. Yet surely, I thought, if they confronted honestly what Baldus had found, knowing the stakes were life and death, they would be compelled to stay the State's hand. I should have known better."

MARSHALL HAD PLANNED on staying on the Supreme Court until a Democratic president could replace him. During the early years of the Reagan administration, he told one of his clerks, "If I die while that man's President, just prop me up and keep on voting." On

June 27, 1991, though, Marshall, in failing health, sent a retirement letter to Republican president George Herbert Walker Bush. "The strenuous demands of court work and its related duties required or expected of a Justice appear at this time to be incompatible with my advancing age and medical condition," he wrote.

The next day, reporters crammed into the Supreme Court's oak-paneled East Conference Room. Marshall, wearing a dark suit, walked into the lavishly adorned room featuring paintings of the first eight chief justices, leaning mightily on his cane, and plopped down in a mahogany chair. With his shirt undone and his tie angling to his right side, Marshall urged the president against selecting a replacement based on race.

"I don't think [race] should be used as an excuse one way or the other," Marshall said, referring to the possibility of President Bush intentionally choosing a Black replacement.

"For what, justice?" a reporter asked.

"Doing wrong. I mean for picking the wrong Negro," Marshall replied. "I think the important factor is to pick the best person for the job. Not on the basis of race." The remark landed as a thinly veiled jab at a young, Black conservative judge quickly rising through the Republican ranks who had been angling to replace him.

Another reporter asked Marshall whether Black folk had reached the mountaintop.

"I'm not free. All I know is years ago when I was a youngster, a Pullman porter told me that he had been in every city in this country," Marshall answered. "And he never had been in any city in the United States where he had to put his hand up in front of his face to find out he was a Negro."

When a reporter asked how he wanted people to remember him, he responded, "He did what he could with what he had."

ON JULY 1, 1991, President Bush exited a weatherworn, wood-shingle cottage at his family's oceanfront home in Kennebunkport, Maine, and traipsed toward a microphone. Behind him followed a dark-skinned, bespectacled Black man. Bush stopped in front of a wooden lectern, pulled out a prepared text from his navy blazer, and addressed the awaiting media.

"I am very pleased to announce that I will nominate Clarence Thomas to serve as Associate Justice of the United States Supreme Court," Bush said. The year before, Bush appointed David H. Souter from the First Circuit Court of Appeals to replace Justice Brennan to shift the Court rightward. "Clarence Thomas was my first appointee to the U.S. Court of Appeals for the District of Columbia, where he served for over a year. And I believe he'll be a great justice. He is the best person for this position," Bush vowed.

Sunlight illuminated a stocky Thomas, who stood stoically over Bush's right shoulder. As former chairman of the Equal Employment Opportunity Commission, the forty-three-year-old had alienated civil rights groups because of his opposition to various civil rights remedies, thereby ingratiating himself to the conservative political movement. By calling his sister a "welfare queen" he had alerted caste preservationists of his willingness to invoke anti-Black tropes.

"Thank you, Mr. President. I'm honored and humbled by your nomination," Thomas said after replacing Bush at the lectern. "As a child, I could not dare dream that I would ever see the Supreme Court, not to mention be nominated to it. . . .

"In my view, only in America could this have been possible. I look forward to the confirmation process and an opportunity to be of service once again to my country and to be an example to those who are where I was and to show them that, indeed, there is hope."

"Mr. President," a reporter asked, "last year you vetoed the civil rights bill, saying it could lead to quotas. Today you've made a nomination that could be easily seen as quota based. How do you explain this apparent inconsistency?"

Bush, who carried the mantle for a party and a political movement that detested affirmative action and promoted color-blindness, had cynically chosen a Black justice because he, President Bush, understood the utility of Black skin in furthering caste preservationism. When Thurgood Marshall admonished Bush to not select the "wrong Negro," Thomas raced through his mind.

Before the next, and final, leg of our journey, let's bid adieu to Thurgood Marshall on July 4, 1992, at Independence Hall in Philadelphia.

A HEART ISSUE AND AGE has disabled Marshall, enough that his eighty-four-year-old legs cannot ascend a few steps. Thus, workers place Marshall, confined to a wheelchair, on a forklift truck that raises him, along with his son John, to the podium in front of the red-brick façade of the building where the Founding Fathers framed the Constitution. John and Aloysius Leon Higginbotham Jr., the Third Circuit's first Black chief judge, slowly roll Marshall, wearing a disheveled suit, to the microphone. As the White-haired icon readies himself to deliver his remarks, a park ranger holds an umbrella over him, shading him on this warm and sunny anniversary of the Declaration of Independence.

"Do you remember Heman Sweatt?" Marshall asks of the ten thousand packed into the space between Independence Hall and the Liberty Bell.

> He was an ordinary man who had an extraordinary dream to live in a world in which Afro-Americans and whites alike were afforded equal opportunity to sharpen their minds and to hone their skills. Unfortunately, officials at the University of Texas Law School did not share his vision. Constrained by the shackles of prejudice, and incapable of seeing people for who they were, they denied Heman Sweatt admission to law school solely because his color was not theirs. It was a devastating blow and a stinging rejection, a painful reminder of the chasm that separates white from negro. . . .
>
> Heman Sweatt did not pursue liberty alone. Just a few years earlier, a couple named Shelley tried to do what white America had done for years—live in a neighborhood of their choice. But to white homeowners in Missouri, such audacity was too threatening to be tolerated in their view. Whites belonged in one world. Negroes in another. They could not see the similarities that linked them to the Shelleys—the common desire to earn a living, to raise children, to own and care for a home. They saw

only difference. I guess to them, if the United States was indeed a melting pot, then negroes either didn't get in the pot or didn't get melted down.

As I think back on these courageous people who came before, I wonder what became of the challenge the Sweatts and the Shelleys provided. They worked for liberty. They fought for freedom. They insisted on justice. They were optimistic as I was that racial interaction would breed understanding, and that understanding, in turn, would produce healing and redemption. They were hopeful as I was that over time, America would grow toward justice and expand toward equality. Had I thought in the wake of . . . *Shelley v. Kraemer* and *Brown v. Board of Education* that I would be giving a talk now on the anniversary of our Nation's independence, I would have predicted that I would have spoken with much pride and optimism of the enormous progress this Nation has made.

But as I survey the world Heman Sweatt and the Shelleys left behind, I wish I could say that racism and prejudice were only distant memories. I wish I could say that this Nation had traveled far along the road to social justice and that liberty and equality were just around the bend.

When Marshall started speaking, he sounded frail. Now his voice booms like when he argued *Brown* inside the Court Chamber.

America's diversity offers so much richness and opportunity. Take a chance, won't you? Knock down the fences that divide. Tear apart the walls that imprison. Reach out, freedom lies just on the other side. We should have liberty for all.

Marshall finishes, and tears stream among those who know him. Who respect him. Who love him. He has just delivered one of his final speeches. The sorrow wallops.

"Thank you," Higginbotham tells Marshall after he returns to the forklift.

"Judge," Marshall replies, "it's the most important thing I have ever done in my life."

Near the end of Marshall's Court tenure, a reporter asked him how racial fairness could reside in America. "[T]he Court," he responded, "could stop looking around for excuses not to enforce the Fourteenth Amendment as it was intended to be enforced." Marshall, in the same interview, bemoaned his judicial shortcomings. "I haven't done as much as I could—I don't know why," he mourned, referring to his inability to convince his colleagues to interpret the Fourteenth Amendment to complete the business he started in an office alongside his mentor, Charles Hamilton Houston. To shelter Black folk from the race hatred in which America bathed. To grant Black folk complete freedom. "I didn't persuade them on affirmative action did I? I didn't persuade them in the *Bakke* case."

As happiness floated Marshall from the Court Chamber after Chief Justice Warren announced his *Brown* opinion in 1954, anger steeled caste preservationists. Fidelity to White Supremacy inspirited their scheming of a new future for the Fourteenth Amendment. A future they could live with. A future with a racial caste system. Marshall identified an inability to persuade as his central failure. Not quite. His most critical miscalculation lay with his willingness to fight on White Supremacy's terms. The 24th Infantry Regiment that Marshall visited in Asia suffered heavy casualties because superior numbers overwhelmed them. Something similar befell Marshall behind the bench. One can understand numerical disadvantage causing defeat. But Marshall truly stumbled when not at least seeking to reimagine the broader conversation. For example, Justice White framed the question in *Washington v. Davis* as whether administering Test 21 was discriminatory and therefore did it abridge the plaintiffs' equal protection rights. Marshall accepted the framing—he accepted the Fourteenth Amendment as a vehicle for the anti-discrimination principle. Pinpoint mistakes like *that* as his most consequential.

Relying on anti-classification, colorblindness, and intent, his opponents forged a strategy to transform the Fourteenth Amendment. Employing two faces, and harnessing both ignorance and deception, they marketed a vision for the Fourteenth Amendment that would prolong the racial caste system. Marshall, as he admitted later in life, never responded with a powerful counternarrative. He needed not to have invented anything. He merely needed to return The Trinity to its abolitionist, anticaste origins. If he had positioned the Fourteenth Amendment as the Constitution's antidote to the caste system, he would have proposed an argument that would have exposed what his foes prized above all else—a White over Black existence. His opponents peddled the idea that once the nation ceased racially classifying, it would revel in a picturesque color-blind existence that caste preservationists would have detested. Marshall should have countered that Americans should only rejoice once they have satisfied the requirement under The Trinity that America purify itself of the evil of caste.

Marshall ultimately committed two fatal miscues. First, in not attempting to insert anticaste into the heart of The Trinity generally, and as the proper mediating principle for the Equal Protection Clause specifically. Second, in not conceiving of the Equal Protection Clause as forcing the state to affirmatively provide equal protection. Denying includes inaction as well as action. Weaving these two constructions into a coherent story for the Fourteenth Amendment would have allowed Marshall to explain why the state held an affirmative obligation to rid society of the racial caste system, and why any act of commission or omission that maintained that system, deliberate or not, needed to pass strict scrutiny. Society must concern itself with actions, regardless of the intention behind them, that maintain the caste system. We must regard the Georgia capital punishment statute, therefore, as presumptively unconstitutional because it, in operation, treated Black life as less valuable than White life and the state legislature, through inaction, allowed that to persist.

Marshall should have rejected the reduction of the Fourteenth Amendment to a simple anti-discrimination and anti-classification constitutional mandate. A society can maintain a caste system through discrimination and racial classification. But these are symptoms. The system itself is the true disease. Only when discrimination and classification function as castework should either trigger rigorous review under the Fourteenth Amendment. The admissions program at issue in *Bakke*, for example, racially classified but did not treat Bakke as a member of a lower caste. The Georgia capital punishment statute, however, did not racially classify, and might not have been administered with readily documentable discriminatory intent, but it still helped preserve the caste system. It was castework.

The Intent Doctrine burdened Black claimants to prove that they were discrimination victims. The state, however, should have always shouldered the evidentiary burden. In *Washington v. Davis*, the Court should have liberated the Black plaintiffs of the onerous obligation of demonstrating that the D.C. police department intended to discriminate. The department, instead, should have had to show the necessity of Test 21, which helped preserve a nearly all-White police force. Determining whether other departments hired and promoted diverse and competent officers employing other standards would have clarified the question. An equal protection construction that compelled the adoption of the *most anticaste workable alternative* would have undermined castework regardless of whether it was the product of intentional discrimination, pressing states to actively dismantle the racial caste system. Pressing states to affirmatively provide equal protection.

Marshall's adversaries claimed to treasure color-blindness yet jettisoned it whenever color-blindness would have advantaged caste abolitionism. This obliged caste preservationists to operate with two faces and compelled conservative jurists to write opinions tarred by ignorant legal analysis. Marshall proffering an anticaste construction of the Fourteenth Amendment would have left better tools to the next generation of caste abolitionists. When Thurgood Marshall dies on January 24, 1993, he crosses over a hero for the cause. An imperfect hero.

For the final leg of our journey, we say goodbye to Justice Marshall but remain here at Independence Hall and travel two centuries back in time. We have the debating of the nation's foundational document to watch.

# Eighth Leg:
## A Culture of Unfit Imposition

WHEN THURGOOD MARSHALL SPEAKS in front of the two-story building on Chestnut Street on July 4, 1992, all know it as Independence Hall, one of the nation's most storied edifices. But on this morning, Monday, June 11, 1787, locals call it the Pennsylvania State House. From most places in Philadelphia, one of the nation's largest and busiest port cities, where thirty thousand people live on the west bank of the Delaware River, we can see much of the horizon. Tall heaps of metal and the haze of pollution don't obstruct our sight line to the heavens. The broad streets, lined with leafy trees and stately brick buildings, radiate simple elegance. The gravel roads muffle the clacking and thumping of horseshoes and wagon wheels. With no modern sewage system, though, the odor on this typically hot summer day tarnishes the ambiance, a stench not unlike what we suffered through in 1970s-era The Promised Land. Before entering the statehouse, the center of Philadelphia's political life, let's probe what summoned us here.

When the "Committee of Five"—John Adams, Benjamin Franklin, Thomas Jefferson, Robert Livingston, and Roger Sherman—scribed, "We hold these truths to be self-evident, that all men are created equal, that they are endowed by their Creator with certain unalienable Rights," at this building on July 4, 1776, they broadcast that the thirteen colonies had proclaimed their autonomy from the Kingdom of Great Britain, and formally declared war. On September 3, 1783, those hostilities ended when, inside a French hotel, the two sides signed the Treaty of Paris. By then, the Articles of Confederation had been piloting the nascent national government for two years. The states, under the Articles, which entailed the thirteen separate states unifying for the common good to meet certain domestic and foreign challenges, remained sovereign. Each state, in other words, retained its own freedom and independence, except for a few limitations the Articles fixed on them, limitations that they frequently flouted anyway. Soothsayers forewarned that the Articles contained congenital defects that would endanger the viability and prosperity of a newborn yet developing country and its more than three million people. Maybe even hasten the United States toward splintering into separate regional confederations.

In September 1786, in the grand second-floor sitting room of Mann's Tavern in Annapolis, Maryland, Alexander Hamilton, a Revolutionary War military officer from New York, late of the Caribbean, and James Madison, a young Virginia politician and political thinker too diminutive to bear arms against the British redcoats, along with ten other delegates from five states, convened to debate interstate commerce. The pursuit of riches stimulated the crossing of the seas and the pillaging of the New World, but the Articles were hobbling the coin chase. At the close of the Annapolis Convention, delegates adopted a resolution "to meet at Philadelphia on the second Monday in May next, to take into consideration the situation of the United States, to devise such further provisions as shall appear to them necessary to render the constitution of the federal government, adequate to the needs of the Union." Madison preferred a national government that required an engaged citizenry that pursued the national, not just state, interest. The Articles, he lamented, could not facilitate such an outcome. Therefore, he wanted to replace it with a new text that could morph a confederation of thirteen loosely affiliated limbs into a nation of millions bonded by the titanium links of a strong federal government.

As we enter the Pennsylvania State House and amble through this cool and dark hallway, look to the right through the arches for a glimpse at the west chamber where the state's supreme court sits. Across the hall, in the handsome east chamber, fifty-three delegates from eleven states—Rhode Island will send none and New Hampshire's two delegates have yet to arrive—are charting America's future. Inside this space, the Assembly Room, the Committee of the Whole, or simply the entire body of delegates, has been deliberating in secrecy since May 25. They want to keep news from seeping out, and thereby foiling the plans to replace, and not merely improve, the Articles.

The biggest division thus far, during what's termed the Federal Convention before becoming known as the Constitutional Convention, concerns the nature of state representation in the lower house of the national legislature. In the Articles, each state had one vote in the unicameral, or one-house, Continental Congress. This arrangement conforms with the understanding that the national government sources its power from the states. Several delegates, however, want the power to rest with the people. They want to return home with a document that embraces the principle that sovereignty resides within the citizenry—popular sovereignty—and thus affords more populous states more representatives.

John Rutledge, a South Carolina delegate and future Supreme Court chief justice, rises to speak. The forty-seven-year-old slaveowner says that the delegates should base representation in the legislature "on quotas of contribution," or taxes. Southerners anticipate that slavery will vault the region to the spearhead of economic prosperity and favor a framework that would afford them more representation and thus greater influence. "The justice of that approach," the talented orator assures, "could not be contested."

Pierce Butler, an Irish-born politician and Rutledge's fellow South Carolinian, concurs, adding, "that money was power; and that the States ought to have weight in the Government in proportion to their wealth."

James Wilson, a Pennsylvania delegate and future Supreme Court justice, launches his opening gambit, the first of a two-pronged plan to convince the convention to espouse representation based on population. A lackluster speaker, Wilson offers a resolution, saying, "that the right of suffrage in the first branch of the national legislature ought not to be according [to] the rule established in the Articles of

Confederation [one state, one vote], but according to some equitable ratio of representation." He leaves what he deems equitable for his plan's second prong.

After Rufus King of Massachusetts and John Dickson of Delaware assail the pro-slavery "quotas of contribution" conception, the Scottish-born Wilson, forty-five years old, employs the wisdom of Ben Franklin, not in attendance, to sway the convention to his perspective. Franklin had written his convictions on the need for the national government to pursue the goals of *popular* majorities.

"I now think the number of Representatives should bear some proportion to the number of the Represented," Wilson says, reading Franklin's sentiments, "and that the decisions should be by the majority of members, not the majority of States."

They take a vote on Wilson's resolution. Seven states— Massachusetts, Connecticut, Pennsylvania, Virginia, North Carolina, South Carolina, and Georgia—vote in favor. New York, New Jersey, and Delaware—all vote no. Maryland delegates are deadlocked.

Rutledge moves to add to the motion just adopted. He reintroduces the pro-slavery "according to the quotas of contribution" concept, insisting that representation based on wealth offers the most equitable solution.

Wilson moves to postpone Rutledge's motion. Henry Laurens Pinckney seconds. Wilson wants the convention to instead consider *his* motion—that after "equitable ratio of representation" the words "in proportion to the whole number of white and other free citizens and inhabitants of every age, sex, and three-fifths of all other persons not comprehended in the foregoing description, except Indians not paying taxes, in each state" should follow. Wilson reminds his audience that eleven states had agreed to this rule in the Continental Congress for calculating taxes. That March 1783 proposal sought to base national taxes on a state's free population plus three-fifths of all "others," with "others" referring to enslaved people. The three-fifths formulation communicates a crude estimation of the average value each enslaved person provides the state.

Massachusetts delegate Elbridge Gerry attempts to extinguish this idea before it burns steadily. "Blacks are property," says the man who speaks in a halting, stammering cadence, "and are used as horses and cattle" are in the North. "Why should their representation be increased to the southward on account of the number of slaves, [rather] than [on the basis of] horses or oxen to the north?"

The question elicits silence, not simply because the matter incites delegates to address an unpleasantry—slavery—but because the delegates, particularly those from large and southern states, have now reached a deal, nine states in favor.

You have just witnessed the conception of the three-fifths clause, which the Committee of Style, tasked with producing the official version of the Constitution, will lay out in Article I, Section 2, Clause 3 of the Constitution: "Representatives and direct Taxes shall be apportioned among the several States which may be included within this Union, according to their respective Numbers, which shall be determined by adding to the whole Number of free Persons, including those bound to Service for a Term of Years, and excluding Indians not taxed, three fifths of all other Persons." The foundational enterprise of supplanting the concept of state sovereignty with the republican touchstone that sovereignty lies with the *people* wanted for something that could bridge the differences between enough delegates. The words of the three-fifths clause built that bridge. Because of that clause, because the delegates agree to reject the full humanity of Black people, Americans will ratify a document premised on the conception that the federal government exists because the people empowered it to exist and must therefore serve the people.

The adoption of the three-fifths clause positions *caste culture* to endure in American life. Culture simply refers to a population's ways of living taught by one generation to the next. Some genius created pizza in Naples in the 1700s, and its deliciousness inspires others to learn the recipe and impart that knowledge decade after decade, enriching Italian cuisine. Caste culture, then, is the way of living practiced by caste preservationists, taught by one generation to the next.

Three axioms in particular will form the basis of caste culture. That, one, the nation must bestow power to the White people who believe power belongs to White people. Two, that the nation must divvy the rewards of American democracy principally amongst those White people. And three, that the nation must structure society to produce such results for those White people. Caste preservationists will pass down this mindset, constantly propagating new generations.

Caste culture, which repudiates Black people as equal members of the body politic, predates the convention in this room where George Washington, elected convention president, presides in a high-backed wooden armchair. The feet of the first Africans contacting the shores of Jamestown in 1619, in addition to the presence of the Indigenous peoples, sparked the rationale for the development of caste culture. But the Founding Fathers, on this day, turn the conviction that the land branded as the United States of America belongs to White people into a contract between a nation and its White citizenry. The *White deed.* The three-fifths clause's inclusion in the Constitution will inform caste preservationists, in writing, that America has given ownership of itself to White people. *They* are We the People. The sovereign people. And caste preservationists believe that laws that violate the terms and conditions of the White deed, can and should be disregarded, for such rules are inherently illegitimate. When caste preservationists instill caste culture into their offspring, they also bequeath the White deed.

When the people ratify The Trinity, it will guarantee Black freedom, and, concomitantly, shred the White deed, at least theoretically. America, because of The Trinity, ceases to belong to its White citizenry. *All* the people, regardless of race, are sovereign. And an unwillingness to honor that, an unwillingness to treat Black people as among We the People, defies the nation's new terms and conditions. Simply put, to practice, maintain, and reproduce caste culture renders one culturally unfit for American democracy. We have constantly encountered this cultural unfitness.

When we followed states practicing jury discrimination in the first leg of our journey, we were observing people culturally unfit for American democracy. State legislators and judges clung to the belief that only White folk should participate in the administration of justice. In the second leg, when we watched the Colfax Massacre, we were witnessing people culturally unfit for American democracy showing us exactly why. Caste preservationist Louisianans rejected that Black folk and their White allies had any claim on democratic participation and concluded that they could resort to even mass murder to return the earth to its anti-Black axis. In our third leg, Cornelius Jones warred against the Mississippi Plan of 1890 *and* against the culturally unfit who installed it. Caste preservationist Mississippians, nearly the state's entire White population, sought to fortify the caste system through a new constitution because they believed that the levers of democracy belonged in their palms. Not in Black people's. Not in the palms of White people who thought Black people had a right to participate in democracy. Our fourth leg chronicled Booker T. Washington laying plans to secure Black freedom against a culturally unfit people willing to deprive Black souls of everything, including the right to benefit from their own toil. Centuries of evidence had taught caste preservationists that Black labor belonged to them, and they violated the Thirteenth Amendment in furtherance of their belief that they could appropriate for themselves the dividends of Black sweat.

We can, oftentimes, trace the disappearance of a culture to the disappearance of its people. Think of Indigenous tribes and cultures vanished by genocide. The Beothuk of Newfoundland. The Quinnipiac near Connecticut. The Tupinambá in Brazil. But a culture can also succumb when its participants no longer value the culture's practices. When participants volitionally discard a culture, lacking reasons to continue it. The Supreme Court, because it interprets the Constitution, will command great power to deprive caste preservationists of reasons to believe that caste culture has a future in America. The Court, by itself, cannot kill the culture, but it can help write its demise tale. Be one among many causes of death.

The Supreme Court, however, will shower caste preservationists with reasons to continue believing that caste culture can survive and that the White deed holds immortality. When the Supreme Court defeats the central purpose of The Trinity—securing Black freedom—it not only emboldens caste culture, it functions as an anti-democratic institution. To choose to assist the unfit is to become the unfit. Individual black robes will constantly expose themselves as culturally unfit for American democracy. Wolves masquerading as protectors. We have confronted culturally unfit justices throughout our journey in various legal contexts. Yet, none better reveals the absoluteness of the moral decay of some black robes than voting rights because caste preservationists treasure nothing more than denying Black fingertips the ballot.

In 1889, nearly two decades after the Fifteenth Amendment's ratification, James F. Claflin, then a former Illinois state legislator, will predict that although the federal government, because of cases like *United States v. Cruikshank*, might lack the legal machinery to stymie anti-Black political violence, "when the state attempts to clothe that spirit of race hatred with legality, and extend over it the shield of the state constitution, it finds its way barred by the adamantine wall of the national constitution in the first section of the fifteenth amendment—a wall that it can neither leap over nor crawl under nor batter down." Claflin expresses certainty "that we have little apprehension that any party at the south will attempt to nullify the constitution by a state enactment." By the end of the nineteenth century, caste culture will graduate from savagery, intimidation, and the stuffing of ballot boxes as the chief tool to keep power, testing Claflin's thesis.

This final leg will proceed to the early 1900s and finish in the twenty-first century. It will trace the interplay between caste culture and the Court, with an ensemble cast moving the plot forward. We will see caste preservationists fight to keep the White deed operational while we explore how the justices respond to the machinations of the culturally unfit. Positioned to help clean the stain, many black robes will spread it, become part of it, and desecrate the Supreme Court itself.

AT ELEVEN IN THE MORNING of May 22, 1901, the Greek Revival–style Alabama state capitol in Montgomery received Alabama's constitutional convention. Below the white-painted dome, the caste preservationist resolve of more than 150 delegates permeated the Hall of the House of Representatives, a spacious rectangular room on the second floor. Vessels for caste culture, the delegates focused on updating the plan to retain the White deed for their descendants, re-creating the ruse pioneered in Mississippi eleven years prior. Riding the high of political victory, the Bourbon Democrats, a fiscally conservative, laissez-faire-economics type, pressed for this constitutional convention to consolidate their power amongst competing factions of White Alabamians. From the wooden rostrum, illuminated by light gushing in from sizable windows, convention president John Barnett Knox described the mission before them.

"In my judgment, the people of Alabama have been called upon to face no more important situation than now confronts us, unless it be when they, in 1861, stirred by the momentous issues of impending conflict between the North and the South, were forced to decide whether they would remain in or withdraw from the Union," remarked the gray-haired Knox.

"And what is it that we do want to do? Why, it is, within the limits imposed by the Federal Constitution, to establish white [rule] in this State. This is our problem, and we should be permitted to deal with it, unobstructed by outside influences, with a sense of our responsibilities as citizens, and our duty to posterity." Knox's openness about the convention's objective illustrated how behaving in a manner unfit for democracy perversely infused caste preservationists with sensations of superiority. They craved power and cooked up the whopper that Black hands touching the ballot spoiled it. Then, they coerced themselves to regard the lie as unassailable, excusing, no, *demanding* righteous subterfuge.

"But if we would have white [rule], we must establish it by law— not by force or fraud," Knox explained, seemingly too inebriated on White Supremacy's liquor to discern that their conniving constituted fraud. "I submit it to the intelligent judgment of this Convention that there is no higher duty resting upon us, as citizens and as delegates, than that which requires us to embody in the fundamental law such provisions as will enable us to protect the sanctity of the ballot in every portion of the State."

When the convention ended on September 3, it had successfully conceived a disenfranchisement plan premised on stunting Black registration. The voter registration sections of the new constitution contained permanent and temporary provisions. Per the permanent provisions, prospective voters had to satisfy a literacy test which involved showing a registrar an ability to read and write parts of the U.S. Constitution, show proof of employment for a year, and meet onerous property qualifications. The permanent provisions required annual registration. Under the temporary provisions, however, open until January 1, 1903, any adult man who demonstrated to the registrar that he understood the U.S. Constitution, was a veteran of any 1800s American war, or a lineal descendant of such a veteran, acquired lifetime registration. Few Black men fought in an American war or descended from someone who did. This "grandfather clause," therefore, operated as castework to allow illiterate, unpropertied White men to become permanent electors while denying that opportunity to similarly situated Black men. Whether seeking registration under the temporary or permanent provisions, then, Black men generally had to fulfill a literacy requirement. And the Alabama plan mirrored the Mississippi Plan of 1890, tasking registrars with greatly limiting the number of Black men deemed to have met the requirements, pruning the Black vote to a feckless minority.

Stenographers transcribed the convention debates, recording the disenfranchising intent and documenting it across four volumes. Across forty-five hundred pages. The *Montgomery Advertiser*, moreover, printed transcripts of the proceedings daily. One delegate attempted to rescue his brethren's heads from the crocodile's open maw. "When this work is tested before the Supreme Court of the United States," John Ashcraft warned, "we do not want that body to search for light amid the darkness of the debates on the 14th and 15th Amendments." His opponents, nonetheless, carried the argument. And the stenographers recorded every syllable. During our last journey, we observed how and why caste preservationists create a fake public face to satisfy the longings of the real private face. In early 1900s Alabama, where caste preservationists peacocked with their castework, the self-defense instinct to don a mask rarely flickered in their minds.

Alabama's disenfranchisement scheme achieved the desired result. Of the more than 180,000 previously eligible Black voters in 1900, only about 3,000 registered under the new provisions.

LITTLE MORE THAN A YEAR LATER, on March 13, 1902, Montgomery County registrars Charles B. Teasley, Jeff Harris, and William Gunter Jr. entered the Montgomery County courthouse, strode to its right wing and into the office of the tax collector, their temporary home, to start another day's work. The state assigned the three with the duty of not registering Black men. Their counterparts across the state undertook the same mission, all performing a pivotal function in assuring that the White citizenry reaped nearly all the blessings of the state's democracy.

Jackson W. Giles, a forty-three-year-old born into slavery in 1859 on an Alabama cotton plantation, along with James L. Jeter and Edward Dale, went to the registrar's office, seeking lifetime voter registration under the temporary plan. The three Black men worked as clerks and janitors in a place we visited during the fourth leg of our journey, Montgomery's federal Post Office and Courthouse Building, and were trying to register ahead of the November elections. Giles, a widowed father of three, had paid his poll tax and had no character disqualifications under the 1901 constitution. A Republican Party activist registered since 1871, Giles had received his position inside the federal courthouse as political patronage. But the registrars refused all Black men who sought registration that day and even requested that Giles supply statements from White men attesting to his good character.

Giles departed empty-handed though primed for a fight.

ON MARCH 25, 1902, twelve days after Giles left the Montgomery County courthouse, a group of Black men who had endured the same indignity and Fifteenth Amendment rights theft gathered inside a three-story brick building owned by a local Black physician. On the third floor, the attendees resolved to fight caste culture through litigation. They founded the Colored Man's Suffrage Association of Alabama that day and elected as president Giles, a politics diehard who had voted in elections even post the state's Democratic redemption. The caste abolitionists announced a fundraising drive to collect at least $2,000 to finance multiple lawsuits against Alabama's new constitution.

"Among those who applied [to vote] and were refused," the organization's circular provided, "are some of our most worthy citizens, morally, financially and intellectually; men who pay taxes on property from $500 to $30,000. The requirements of the Board of Registrars are altogether out of harmony with law and justice." The circular further charged "that the workings of the new [state] constitution are in conflict with the Federal constitution, which declares that 'the rights of suffrage of citizens shall not be abridged on account of race, color, or previous condition of servitude.'"

The group pegged New York attorney Wilford Horace Smith for representation. Smith and Booker T. Washington surreptitiously planned the subversion of Alabama's disenfranchisement contrivances by corresponding through Emmett Jay Scott, Washington's personal secretary, via encrypted mail. On September 3, 1902, Smith filed a lawsuit against Harris, Teasley, and Gunter in federal district court for the Middle District of Alabama housed inside Montgomery's federal Post Office and Courthouse. Smith sued under two federal statutes on behalf of Giles and a class of more than five thousand Black Montgomery County citizens whom the registrars, Smith alleged, prevented from registering on account of race. The Alabama voter registration provisions, the lawsuit maintained, violated the Fourteenth and Fifteenth Amendments. As evidence, Smith leveraged the voluminous Alabama convention record, providing expansive quotations from delegates speaking candidly about following White Supremacy's decree to eradicate the Black caste from democracy. Smith's lawsuit did not seek monetary damages, praying instead for two remedies. First, void under the Fourteenth and Fifteenth Amendments the sections of the Alabama constitution that effectuated Black disenfranchisement. Second, compel the state to register Giles and his class of plaintiffs. By asking not for money but rather for the courts to right a wrong through a judicial remedy, Smith brought a so-called equity lawsuit.

On October 11, 1902, before trial, the man Washington recommended President Roosevelt appoint, Judge Thomas Goode Jones, dismissed the lawsuit. In open court, Jones expressed he lacked jurisdiction, as a federal judge, to hear the case because it did not threaten damages exceeding $2,000. Lower federal judges could "certify" a legal question to allow the Supreme Court to adjudicate the matter. Smith, believing Jones could exercise jurisdiction, urged him to certify that question. Jones obliged. On November 10, 1902, the Court granted the appeal but since the black robes committed themselves to only addressing jurisdiction, they considered the case solely on the briefs. The Court heard no oral argument.

William A. Gunter Sr., the father of one of the sued county registrars, represented the three defendants. Gunter senior begged the Court to decide the merits of the case, meaning not limit review to just the jurisdiction question, wanting the Court to answer the *real* legal question: Did the Alabama constitution voter registration provisions violate the Fourteenth and Fifteenth Amendments? "It is important, for obvious reasons, that [this question], if possible, be authoritatively settled," he wrote. The Court, in *Williams v. Mississippi*, stopped short of unequivocally affirming the Mississippi Plan of 1890. Gunter, speaking for caste preservationism, beseeched the Court to uphold the constitutionality of the Alabama constitution, and, by extension, all the southern variants modeled after the Mississippi template. Gunter, defending the Alabama constitution, wrote in his brief, with a deceitful hand, that states retained the right to protect themselves against ignorant voters and that the state achieved this through its new voting provisions. The Fourteenth and Fifteenth Amendments permitted race-neutral language that fell more heavily on Black men because of the race's inadequacies.

Using the convention delegates' words, Smith, throughout his brief, exposed how they aimed to disenfranchise Blackness, not ignorance. Smith proved an intent to discriminate and discriminatory results. Gunter, however, disputed that legislative intent even mattered. "The Convention is responsible only for its collective acts embodied in laws, and not at all for the views of individual members," he wrote. Gunter, in other words, posited that discriminatory intent did not render race-neutral laws unconstitutional. Decades later, when caste preservationists decide to wear the mask and veil their discriminatory motives, they will insist that Black claimants must prove intent, exemplifying how caste preservationists endorse whatever legal arguments shield the White deed, their claim to ownership of America. White over Black—the sole principle caste preservationists truly honor. Last, Gunter posited that an equity lawsuit provided an improper vehicle to settle "matters of a political nature."

Six months later, word came from the Court.

ON APRIL 27, 1903, inside the Court Chamber on the second floor of the Capitol's North Wing, Justice Oliver Wendell Holmes explained the Court's decision in *Giles v. Harris*. Speaking for the six-to-three majority, Holmes said he and his five colleagues "were of the opinion that the Supreme Court should not confine itself to the question of jurisdiction but should consider the case on its merits." In his fourth month wearing a robe, Holmes, in the semicircular chamber, allowed caste preservationists to rejoice, claiming that "it would be impossible to grant the relief asked." He noted that "while Giles is contending that the franchise system of Alabama is a fraud, he declares his competency as a voter under it." Holmes concluded that granting the petition "was beyond the power of a court of equity." Holmes failed, curiously, to release his written opinion that day.

A black robe anonymously told reporters later that evening that "whatever might be an individual right in an action at bar to redress a political wrong, that there was no power in a court of equity to redress a political wrong of that kind," words arranged in a mealymouthed order that resonated with the opinion that Holmes authored. The unnamed justice added that "the relief must be sought at the hands of the political department. The decision does not pass upon the validity of the constitution of Alabama, but simply held that assuming it unconstitutional a court of equity was without power." This hedging mattered not to White southerners who interpreted the *Giles* decision as the long-coveted Supreme Court rubber stamp. It effectively was.

In the text of Holmes's opinion, the funk of folly coupled with the funk of fraud, breeding an unsettling piece of ignorant legal analysis. The Court, in *Giles*, dashed Black hope of touching the ballot in the South. And the six black robes in the majority gave caste preservationists every reason to cling to their culture, every reason to believe it would persist despite The Trinity.

Holmes offered two reasons why the Court had to reject Giles's requests, both poorly thought out. First, Holmes argued, if Giles's theory that Alabama created and maintained a ruse to forestall Black voting was accurate, Giles was describing a sham. Adding Black names to the voting rolls of that sham would make the Court an accessory. "[H]ow," Holmes asked rhetorically, "can we make the court a party to the unlawful scheme by accepting it and adding another voter to its fraudulent lists?" But that analysis stank of ignorance. The fraud existed with the exclusion of Black voters. If the Court added Black names to the rolls, it would remedy the fraud, not become enmeshed with it.

Second, if Giles observed correctly that "the great mass of the white population intends to keep the blacks from voting," Holmes wrote in his opinion, the Court hadn't a remedy that could overcome it. If White Alabama conspired to disenfranchise Black men, then any judicial directive to register Giles would blink to local realities. "If the conspiracy and the intent exist, a name on a piece of paper will not defeat them," Holmes asserted. This failed to even qualify as a *legal* argument, reading more like a *political* justification for abdicating judicial responsibilities. A justice contending that the Court couldn't grant a right because the Court lacked the power to enforce its decisions meant that six black robes would rather have depicted themselves as toothless than uphold American democracy. Besides, the justices could have ordered federal officers to enforce Giles's rights. They chose not to. Holmes argued that the lack of suitable judicial options "strikingly reinforces the argument that equity cannot undertake now, any more than it has in the past, to enforce political rights." Put differently, Holmes contended that the Court, in such a political case, must relent to the White population's oath to White Supremacy. Holmes explained that Black plaintiffs, if they wished to mend such political injuries, needed to call upon the presidency, Congress, the people of the state, or the state itself. Not the feeble Supreme Court.

Holmes's opinion squares with the principle that the law must relent to the will of the dominant power holders and that voting majorities, like White Alabama Democrats, should win legal disputes. Holmes evidently believed that the movement for White rule had captured control of the South and thought, therefore, the law must reflect that victory. Black folk like Giles wanted the Court to affirm their equality and stand up to caste culture. Holmes and five other black robes, instead, curtsied.

Celebrated for his brilliance, Holmes apparently reasoned from the premise that White Alabamians had resolved to exclude Black men from the electorate, and no real dissent existed. More ignorance. Class, socioeconomic, and political lines, in fact, had left a fractured White population. Those who most pushed for the constitutional convention came from wealthy, large landowning shares of the Democratic Party. But White Republicans, populists, third party voters, and populist Democrats frowned at the suffrage changes, given how many poor White men the plan would surely, and ultimately did, disenfranchise. The *Giles* decision helped fuse the all-White single-party Democratic hegemony Holmes wrongly presumed had already been cemented.

Holmes proposed that the Supreme Court could not become a party to fraud by inserting Black names on the voting rolls. Yet, by not insisting upon Black freedom, by disregarding The Trinity, Holmes, ironically, made the Court a *true* party to fraud—the larceny of Black rights chronicled across more than four thousand pages and reprinted in Smith's brief. Holmes's decision, moreover, displayed the Court majority's cultural unfitness for American democracy. Genuflecting to the goals of caste preservationism thoroughly intertwined the black robes with the practice of protecting the White deed, the metaphorical contract embodying the belief that the United States inherently belongs to White people.

"Somewhere, somehow," the *New York Daily Tribune* observed, "there must be a way of passing on the constitutionality of State laws which plainly nullify the spirit of the federal Constitution." But no. Caste culture, operating through Montgomery County registrars, angled for the Court to allow it to proceed uninterrupted, and Justice Holmes penned a disingenuous swindle on its behalf. Holmes ventured beyond the jurisdiction question, the stated reason for the appeal, and *claimed* that he would decide the merits of the case. However, he never assessed the constitutionality of the Alabama constitution's voter registration provisions. He could not honestly uphold them as constitutional, but did not want to intervene on Black voters' behalf. He instead wrote balderdash that permitted the swiping of Black men's rights. The *Liberator*, a caste abolitionist newspaper, compared Holmes's *Giles* opinion to Chief Justice Taney's *Dred Scott*.

"Taney reasoned the Negro out of citizenship, Holmes out of his ballot."

Black folk mourned.

"THERE'S ONE MORE RIVER; there's one more river; there's one more river to cross," hummed Giles at the start of a Colored Man's Suffrage Association meeting on May 5, 1903.

At noon, 150 Black folk congregated, returning to the brick building where the campaign started mere blocks from the Alabama capitol. After expressing his refusal to delve into the Court's decision announced a week and a half before, Giles requested more donations, explaining that "we need the money" because "the fight was not lost." Giles, after all, remained the lead plaintiff in three more lawsuits challenging the constitutionality of the Alabama constitution.

Just the day before, on May 4, 1903, the Court decided *James v. Bowman*. That case, a criminal prosecution brought under the First Enforcement Act, concerned criminal defendants accused of bribing and intimidating Black men seeking to vote in the November 1898 congressional elections in Kentucky. Justice Brewer wrote the opinion that nulled a portion of the act as unconstitutional, meaning the Court could build a majority to invalidate parts of a congressional act that protected Black rights, but not parts of a southern constitution that demolished those rights. "These decisions of the Supreme Court seem to leave the question of negro suffrage and disfranchisement practically to the several states," observed the *Baltimore Sun*. "The Federal courts will not interfere, it would appear, until the States pass some law or adopt some Constitution plainly and by its terms in contravention of the Fifteenth Amendment. And in the meantime boards of registration and election judges and election workers can do anything permitted by the laws or the officials of their several States."

Besides *Giles v. Harris*, Wilford H. Smith brought two other actions that reached the Supreme Court in his campaign against the Alabama constitution. In *Rogers v. Alabama*, Smith took a stab at perfecting Cornelius Jones's master plan to nullify a state constitution's disenfranchisement scheme through a jury discrimination case. In

January 1904, Smith won his client, Dan Rogers, a new trial, but delivered no blow against disenfranchisement. A month later, in *Giles v. Teasley*, the Court rejected Smith's argument, echoing the rationale outlined in *Giles v. Harris*. Then, in April 1904, in *Jones v. Montague* and *Selden v. Montague*, cases with which Jones was not involved, the Supreme Court refused to nix Virginia's rendition of the 1890 Mississippi Plan. More on that Virginia plan later.

The first *Giles* decision invited the South to keep denying Black fingertips the ballot. Holmes looked at the Fifteenth Amendment and found that it granted "political rights" that federal courts couldn't enforce. *Giles*, even more than *Plessy*, convinced Black folk to suspend dreams of freedom and reassured caste preservationists that their culture could continue to flourish in America.

The culturally unfit, to safeguard the White deed in the voting context, pioneered other strategies.

ON MAY 24, 1932, inside the downtown Houston City Auditorium, Texas flags and forty-eight-star American flags hung from the ceiling above five thousand mingling suits. A smattering of White women also partook in the festivities alongside the White men, as the Nineteenth Amendment's 1920 ratification cleared the way for their greater political involvement. Occupying the seven-thousand-seat space, they gathered for the Texas state Democratic Party convention, which enjoyed its largest turnout in years. A celebration amid the Great Depression.

At twenty-five minutes past ten in the morning, fifty-four-year-old William Ogburn Huggins, chairman of the state Democratic executive committee, called the convention to order. Huggins, an attorney and editor of the *Houston Chronicle*, had a new, exciting proposal to rescue the key device for banishing the Black caste from the only truly competitive southern elections. He wanted to implement it that day.

DURING RECONSTRUCTION, when party leaders and insiders typically selected general election candidates at Democratic delegate conventions or caucuses, Black men had no sway in choosing nominations.

The Democrats later shifted to the direct primary, where the people—the voters—chose general election candidates. That shift encouraged use of the device that Huggins wanted to rescue for Texas Democrats. This new device had proven effective enough at keeping the Black vote a nonfactor that when one southern legislature considered a new means to disenfranchise Black voters in 1907, the *Atlanta Constitution*'s coverage quoted Georgia state representative W. J. Neel, who saw no cause for tweaks. Neel plainly acknowledged, "We already had the Negro eliminated from politics by the white primary."

By 1917, when thirty-two states had implemented the direct primary, several southern states had embraced the White primary. Eight had passed laws that stipulated that a political party's executive committee could determine voter qualifications. Those committees restricted the ballot to White fingertips. Three states executed this plan at the county level. Texas's history, though, herded state legislators down a different path. In 1918, Democratic candidates for district attorney in Bexar County competed intensely enough that both courted Black voters, largely disenfranchised through the poll tax. The race's loser pushed for legislation that would banish Black voters from the primary. The plan attracted little attention until 1923 when the Texas legislature passed a law that restricted primary participation to White voters. Because Democrats won nearly every southern general election contest, voters could most exert their will on the direction of public policy through Democratic primaries. By disallowing Black balloters from those races, caste preservationists were structuring democracy to tune out Black political needs and priorities.

On July 26, 1924, Dr. Lawrence A. Nixon, a forty-one-year-old Black physician living in El Paso, Texas, went to his polling place to do what he had reliably done—vote in the Democratic primary. Two election judges, Judges Champ C. Herndon and Charles V. Porras, stood between him and a primary ballot in the Mexican border town. Herndon and Porras, friends of Nixon, asked about his health. After pleasant conversation, Nixon showed his receipt for poll tax payment.

"Dr. Nixon, you know we can't let you vote."

"I know you can't let me vote, but I've got to try."

Nixon then presented an NAACP-prepared statement that explained how they had denied him the ballot on account of race. He asked them to sign it. Both obliged. The El Paso NAACP branch hired Fred C. Knollenberg, a White attorney, who filed suit in federal district court on Nixon's behalf, seeking $5,000 in damages. Nixon, a Black doctor un-reliant upon White dollars, offered the local NAACP an ideal plaintiff whom White folk could hardly spook with economic threats. The attorneys representing the defendants, Herndon and Porras, invoking *Giles*, convinced Judge DuVal West, an appointee of Democratic president Woodrow Wilson, to dismiss the case as a political matter over which the federal judiciary lacked jurisdiction. Nixon appealed to the Supreme Court, and on March 7, 1927, the black robes unanimously sided with him.

Justice Holmes, writing the *Nixon v. Herndon* opinion, rejected that the "political" nature of the case rendered it unreviewable by federal courts, deprecating the argument as "little more than a play upon words." The Texas statute under review stated that "in no event shall a negro be eligible to participate in a Democratic party primary election held in the State of Texas." Holmes wrote that "[i]t seems to us hard to imagine a more direct and obvious infringement of the Fourteenth Amendment." The Court nixed an obvious denial of fundamental rights, the result Jackson Giles requested two decades prior. The black robes could have similarly handled Giles's case. Their choice not to emboldened Texas and other southern states to enact a law that *flagrantly* infringed The Trinity.

On May 9, 1927, Democratic leaders in Texas regrouped in service of the White deed. The state's newly elected conservative governor, Daniel J. Moody, requested that the legislature repeal the law that the Court had invalidated and pass one that empowered the party's state executive committee to set voter qualifications. The legislature complied. Afterward, the executive committee of the state's Democratic Party adopted a resolution that provided "that all white democrats who are qualified under the constitution and laws of Texas . . . [are] allowed to participate in the primary elections."

On July 28, 1928, Nixon again attempted to participate in the primary. Election judges James Condon and C. H. Kolle denied his fingertips the ballot. On May 2, 1932, Justice Benjamin Cardozo wrote the five-to-four majority opinion that invalidated this latest ploy to conserve the White primary. *Nixon v. Condon* presented a new challenge. Remember that in the 1880s, the Court announced the state action doctrine, constructing the Fourteenth and Fifteenth Amendments as constraining state actors only. The Texas Democratic Party billed itself as a private entity. Justice Cardozo found state action, reasoning that political parties had the power to exclude Black voters because the Texas law afforded it to them.

The decision elated Black Texans. They thought they had bested their antagonists and secured the right to vote in primaries, a perch from which they might persuade politicians into considering their needs. But Cardozo included a curious line in his opinion. "Whether a political party in Texas has inherent power today without restraint by any law to determine its own membership, we are not required at this time either to affirm or to deny." These gratuitous words flipped the lightbulb in the mind of Huggins, the chairman of the state Democratic executive committee, who called the 1932 Texas Democratic Convention to order.

ON MAY 23, 1932, the day before the convention, Huggins and the rest of the executive committee assembled at the Rice Hotel in downtown Houston. There, he convinced the committee members that if the convention simply adopted a resolution that only White folk could vote in the party's primaries, in the absence of the Texas law mowed down in *Nixon v. Condon*, the Court would let *that* pathway to the White primary alone.

At the convention, Huggins, a doughy-faced White man with pince-nez eyewear, presented the new resolution. "Be it resolved, that all white citizens of the State of Texas who are qualified to vote under the Constitution and laws of the state shall be eligible to membership in the Democratic party and as such entitled to participate in its deliberations." The convention adopted it without dissension.

ON JULY 9, 1934, Albert Townsend, a balding White fifty-year-old county clerk for Harris County, Texas, was in his office when Richard Randolph Grovey, a forty-four-year-old Black man with serious eyes and a bulky jaw, entered. A college graduate, Grovey owned a barbershop, a meeting place for the Black community of Houston's Third Ward.

Grovey, who devoted much time to Democratic politics, gave Townsend, an Alabama native, his poll tax receipt and requested an absentee ballot—he expected to be away on July 28, primary day. Townsend, an elected official, refused, citing the resolution adopted by the state Democratic Party on May 24, 1932. Townsend spilled that he had received instructions that "Negro voters and electors otherwise qualified had no legal right to vote or cast absentee ballots . . . solely and only on account of their race and color as Negroes."

Grovey secured three of the approximately twenty Black Texan attorneys to represent him. On September 10, 1934, Jasper Alston Atkins, Carter Walker Wesley, and Ammon Scott Wells sued Townsend for ten dollars for Fourteenth and Fifteenth Amendment violations. The lawsuit's outcome hinged on whether Grovey could prove state action. Thus, his attorneys described Townsend as "a state officer . . . whose office functions under and by virtue of the laws of the State of Texas," who was "paid out of the tax money to which plaintiff has contributed and is required to contribute by the laws of the State of Texas," and whose duties as the county clerk for Harris County to deal with absentee voting was legally required by state law. On September 24, 1934, a Harris County justice of the peace, Campbell R. Overstreet, ruled for Townsend, dismissing the case. Grovey's attorneys sought only ten dollars in damages. Texas provided no right to appeal decisions involving such a meager sum, meaning Grovey could appeal directly to the U.S. Supreme Court, allowing for a speedy resolution.

The national NAACP opposed bringing *Grovey v. Townsend* before the Court—the association questioned Grovey's chances and knew a loss, after two historic wins, would dampen Black spirits. Having narrowly won the *Condon* case and with the Court's composition remaining the same, the twenty-five-year-old association considered Grovey and his attorneys rash. Nonetheless, they appealed to the Court, and the black robes heard the case.

———

ON APRIL 1, 1935, a few months before the Supreme Court relocated to its new home across the street, Justice Owen Roberts, a Hoover appointee, delivered his *Grovey* opinion. The case presented a simple issue. Did the Democratic Party's White primary involve state action? Clearly yes—the man entrusted with giving Grovey a ballot to vote, Townsend, held elected office and worked from a county building. The party could hardly execute its exclusionary primary absent state assistance. The Court, however, unanimously disagreed.

"We hold," Roberts said, "the party was a voluntary association and was competent to decide its membership." Grovey's attorneys, in their argument, detailed the various ways in which the primary involved state action. But the Court limited its analysis to the primary's private features, observing that the party funded its primary and tallied the votes sans state involvement. The Court, moreover, cited a separate decision from the Texas Supreme Court that explained the state legislature's prohibition from interfering with the right of citizens to form political parties and determine membership qualifications. The black robes cherry-picked a few details that favored Texas's theory of the case and disregarded all the ways the execution of the White primary hinged on state action. The state twice reworked its implementation of the White primary to comply with The Trinity, and the justices finally relented, seemingly because of what they considered a good-faith effort to comply with constitutional restrictions. In reality, though, the Court *guided* caste preservationists toward superficially skirting those restrictions while helping the culturally unfit maintain a Whites-only democracy.

The Associated Negro Press asked a Black man, William J. Thompkins, the recorder of deeds for Washington, D.C., to situate the *Grovey* outcome in historical context. "I regard this decision as being infinitely worse than the *Dred Scott* decision [because it] affects directly every colored person in the State of Texas and might eventually affect every adult man and woman in every state in the Union." Walter White, NAACP executive secretary, recounted in his biography, "It should not be difficult to imagine the gloom we all felt. Years of hard work and heavy expense appeared to have gone for naught."

That such a consequential case could reach the justices without the nation's preeminent caste abolitionist organization orchestrating the process convinced the NAACP's brain trust to invest in civil rights litigation and ram itself into a leadership role in the narrative for Black freedom. Three months after the Court's *Grovey* announcement, the NAACP plucked Charles Hamilton Houston from Howard Law School's faculty as its "special counsel," a position conceived for a brain to architect a bold litigation strategy to dismantle the legal components of oppression. The NAACP apprehended the urgency to adopt a dominant posture to present White Supremacy with a relentless and methodical adversary.

Meanwhile, as the White primary barred Black voters from the only truly competitive southern elections, a different disenfranchisement device, in a state bordering Texas, proved similarly reliable in maintaining the White deed.

BLACK MEN VOTED in the first Oklahoma Territory elections in 1890. Their presence, essential to Republican electoral viability, led to Black men receiving political appointments and winning seats in the territorial legislature. Congress conditioned Oklahoma's November 1907 admission into the Union on the state forbidding race discrimination in voting rights. A year later, the Republicans won three of the state's five House seats in the November 1908 general elections. Such ballot box disappointment spurred the Democrats to lean into caste culture, understanding that sawing off the Black stool leg would topple the Republican coalition.

In 1910, Oklahoma voters, by a nearly thirty-thousand-vote margin, adopted a Black disenfranchisement referendum. A majority of White voters approved the new law, establishing their unfitness for American democracy just as had their counterparts in Texas and throughout the South. Persons seeking voter registration, per the new law, needed to pass a literacy test. But the law exempted persons, or linear descendants of such a person, entitled to vote prior to January 1, 1866. Since very few Black folk could vote before that date, the new law almost exclusively impacted them, and they needed to satisfy a literacy requirement. Yet, in 1910, Black illiteracy stood at only about 6 percent, meaning that a fairly applied literacy test would have tripped few Black voters. The registrars, though, applied the test as intended—to silence the Black caste. On June 21, 1915, the Supreme Court, viewing it as an indisputable Fifteenth Amendment violation, voided Oklahoma's grandfather clause in *Guinn v. United States*.

Oklahoma governor Robert Lee Williams, in response, called the state legislature into a special "Jim Crow Session," with all focused on designing a new program to pilfer Black men's Fifteenth Amendment rights. On February 26, 1916, the legislature, to protect the White deed, passed a replacement registration law that grandfathered the grandfather clause. This new variant stipulated that those who voted in the 1914 general election—a near exclusively White male electorate—held lifetime registration and afforded all others an extremely brief period—from April 30 to May 11, 1916—to register or forfeit the right for life.

Thus, when Iverson W. Lane, a sixty-eight-year-old Black man, entered a Wagoner County voter registration on October 17, 1934, he was attempting to do what Black folk did before the state gained admission to the Union, but largely couldn't four decades later. Lane had relocated to Oklahoma to escape such devilry. He once owned a dry goods store in Talladega County, Alabama, where he lived as one of its wealthiest Black residents until 1908 when racial violence drove him, his wife, and five young kids away at night to Redbird, Oklahoma, one of about fifty Black towns that would emerge in Oklahoma, havens from citizens practicing a malignant culture. Lane built a life in Redbird. Owned a cotton gin, plus a construction company, and even once served as the town's mayor. He last voted in 1910, the year White voters decided those who looked like him should forfeit their Fifteenth Amendment rights. Every year since 1916 he had tried to register, but registrars stiff-armed him each time. In 1934, the registration period lasted seven days, from October 19 to October 26, and Lane displayed determination to recoup his voice. He had once exerted far more energy in search of it.

In 1928, he filed a lawsuit on behalf of himself and one hundred Black Wagoner County residents to force their registration. In 1930, pretrial, Lane said, "I have lived in Gatesville township [where Redbird is located] for twenty years. I own a home and property. I personally have sought to be registered each year since statehood.

The attempt was futile." The White folk in the county, he relayed, endorsed a slogan. "Don't let the nigger vote because he might hold office." In 1918, Robert Williams, the still-sitting governor who pressured the legislature to contrive another scheme for Black disenfranchisement after the Supreme Court invalidated the grandfather clause, accepted a nomination from Democratic president Woodrow Wilson to serve as a district judge for the Eastern District of Oklahoma. Williams presided over Lane's case, which went to trial on October 4, 1932. The scientist behind the monster, therefore, handled the inquest into his creation.

Black witnesses testified to the disenfranchisement they suffered and explained that registrars had even threatened violence for pursuing their Fifteenth Amendment rights. Yet, after one hundred of his witnesses had shuffled into the courtroom, Lane dropped the lawsuit. He lacked the finances to continue paying to bring a never-ending line of people to the witness chair. Judge Williams forced Lane to try his case in a prohibitively expensive manner—it would have cost Lane $10,000 to complete the matter. Williams tortured the rules to protect the White deed.

On that October 1934 day, when Lane, with other Black folk, trekked across the Arkansas River from Redbird to register, Marion Parks, the precinct registrar, rebuffed him. Parks told Lane that he "was instructed by the higherups," John Moss, county judge, and Jess Wilson, county register, "not to register any colored people." Registrars throughout the county had admitted that Moss and Wilson had directed them to rebuff Black folk. Three days later, on October 27, Lane's attorney, Charles Chandler, a Black Harvard Law School graduate, filed a lawsuit under the Ku Klux Klan Act against Parks, Moss, and Wilson, seeking $5,000 in damages. Lane complained to a reporter that Parks prevented him from registering "solely on account of race, color and previous condition of servitude" and maligned Wagoner County officials for employing "tricks and subterfuge."

JUDGE WILLIAMS, AFTER REFUSING to recuse himself per Lane's request, handled the trial. Ultimately siding with the defendants,

Williams further undermined the case's integrity by refusing to submit his final decision, forestalling Lane's appeal. This unethical behavior resulted in the invalidation of his decision, granting Lane a new trial with a different judge, Alfred Murrah. On April 20, 1937, inside the cream-colored two-story courtroom in the U.S. Post Office and Courthouse in Muskogee, Oklahoma, Murrah directed the jury to return a verdict in favor of the defendants.

Chandler, paid by the Wagoner County NAACP, exhorted Murrah "to look through the letter of the law and at the facts that these unfortunate citizens have been victims of discrimination." Chandler raged inside the courtroom where, above a room door, visitors could read the words "Justice Is the Great Interest of Men of Earth" inscribed on plaster panels. "How does I. W. Lane differ from Dred Scott?" he yelled. "He has no rights, no protection. This law denies him equal protection and due process. It forbids him to hold a right at the whim of another; sets up a government of men and not of laws."

"That is beautiful language, but what about the facts?" Murrah countered. "You would turn this court into a legislature."

"Lane would have been better off under the 'grandfather clause' than under the present setup. The legislature cannot by weasel words and indirection set aside the Constitution," Chandler vented. "This law is merely a revitalization of the old grandfather clause."

The Tenth Circuit affirmed Murrah's decision. "Certainly there is nothing on the face of the registration statute that even tends to support appellant's claim of discrimination between white and negro electors, nor was there proof of the conspiracy charged," wrote Judge Robert E. Lewis in his September 1938 opinion. Chandler appealed once again, and two months after the black robes heard oral argument in *Lane v. Wilson*, they announced their decision.

ON MAY 22, 1939, Chief Justice Charles Evan Hughes, Justices Harlan Stone, Owen Roberts, Pierce Butler, Stanley Forman Reed, James Clark McReynolds, Hugo Black, Felix Frankfurter, and the newly appointed William O. Douglas entered the new Court Chamber. The massive Corinthian building expressed, finally, that the federal judiciary, headed by the Supreme Court, which had never had a dedicated home, represented one-third of the federal government. Justice Felix Frankfurter, the author of the majority opinion, announced that Oklahoma's 1916 voting law, which disenfranchised thousands of Black voters for two decades, violated the Constitution.

Frankfurter "reluctantly," he wrote, seconded Lane's position that the Oklahoma law violated the Fifteenth Amendment. "[T]he legislation of 1916 partakes too much of the infirmity of the 'grandfather clause' to be able to survive." Given the original grandfather clause operated against Black voters, Frankfurter insisted that the new registration period of just twelve days in 1914 afforded them much too little time to "free themselves from the effects of discrimination to which they should never have been subjected." He ended his opinion with a racist flourish, though. "It must be remembered that we are dealing with a body of citizens lacking the habits and traditions of political independence and otherwise living in circumstances which do not encourage initiative and enterprise." Frankfurter harnessed the logic of caste culture to strike down castework.

Charles G. Watts, the attorney representing the defendants, called the Court's decision "somewhat surprising" and added that it would destroy the registration law of 1916. In 1944, five years after *Lane v. Wilson*, in *Smith v. Allwright*, the Court invalidated the Texas White primary scheme the Court condoned in *Grovey v. Townsend*. With the grandfather clause and White primary defunct, southern states, like North Carolina, counted on literacy tests to maintain the White deed.


ON MAY 5, 1956, Louise Lassiter, a thirty-six-year-old mother of three, entered her Seaboard township voting precinct housed in a country store in Northampton County, North Carolina, to register to vote. Lassiter, a bespectacled, brown-skinned Black woman, had lived in the county her entire life. Her political activist husband, Lloyd, had been registered since 1950. "If more people vote," she thought, "I think we'll have more freedom. . . . It would cause the white people to pay more attention to the rights of the colored."

Helen Hoggard Taylor, the registrar, a forty-eight-year-old

White woman, asked Lassiter to read a printed copy of the North Carolina constitution. The state's literacy test statute required that "every person representing himself for registration . . . be able to read and write . . . to the satisfaction of the registrar." Lassiter, literate, had completed one year of high school. After she finished, Taylor told her that she "mispronounced several words," including "indictment," and therefore failed.

In February 1957, Samuel S. Mitchell and James R. Walker, two Black North Carolina attorneys, filed suit in federal court, alleging that the literacy test violated the Fourteenth and Fifteenth Amendments. Seeking an injunction to bar its use, they contended that the law entrusted registrars with far too much discretion that permitted them to operate as fastidious curmudgeons, "a treatment extended only" to Black registrants. The field secretary for the local chapter of the NAACP, Charles A. McLean, told Raymond Maxwell, executive secretary to the State Board of Elections, of multiple Black folk in a county with only ten registered Black voters who had complained about wrongful registration denials.

Around the turn of the twentieth century, caste preservationists in North Carolina deliberately laid the groundwork, crafting laws designed to survive Supreme Court review and entrench the racial caste system for generations.

IN 1894, A LEFT-OF-CENTER fusionist coalition won control over the North Carolina legislature. Various populist parties, mainly comprised of small farmers wiped out by economic recessions, and the Republican Party whose key constituency remained Black men, partnered to defeat the Democrats at the polls. Two years later, in 1896, Republican Daniel Russell became the first non-Democrat to win the governorship since 1877. The same year Russell won his gubernatorial race, George Henry White, a Black Republican, won North Carolina's 2nd Congressional District, and approximately one thousand Black North Carolinians, from justice of the peace to congressman, held office across the Tarheel State.

Caste preservationists rebounded under the rallying cry of "Save the State from Negro Rule." Democrats initiated a campaign to exfoliate Black skin from the body politic. The deadliest episode of this operation happened in Wilmington, where, in 1898, members of the White Democratic power structure murdered as many as 250 Black residents, overthrew about a dozen Black officeholders, and thieved the city's government. In 1899, the Democrats united behind adding a poll tax, a grandfather clause, and a literacy test to the state constitution. This disenfranchisement plan went live in 1901 and wiped out the Black vote.

"White man," the *Raleigh News and Observer* proclaimed, "you are worthy to vote; although poor and illiterate, you have the character, the manhood, the practical education, the intelligence and the political knowledge requisite to make a good voter. Nigger-man, you have not the knowledge, nor the intelligence, nor the character, nor the manhood, nor the practical education requisite to vote. Step aside and let the white man vote." Rather than seek reelection in 1900, Congressman White moved north to practice law. "I cannot live in North Carolina and be a man," he lamented, "and be treated like a man. I used to feel at home in my State. When I practiced law at the bar of North Carolina I was not discriminated against because I was a negro. That is all in the past now."

In response to Louise Lassiter merely filing her lawsuit, the North Carolina legislature, on March 27, 1957, amended the original 1901 disenfranchisement scheme in two main ways. First, lawmakers provided those denied voter registration an administrative appeal venue, without needing to sue, a way for the legislature to route Black grievances away from federal courts where the scheme could be invalidated. Second, they repealed the grandfather clause still on the books notwithstanding the Court invalidating Oklahoma's in 1915. The month after these two alterations, inside the Century Post Office, an attractive building in downtown Raleigh, a three-judge panel heard Lassiter's lawsuit.

ON APRIL 19, 1957, before federal judges John J. Parker, Wilson Warlick, and Don Gilliam, Helen Hoggard Taylor, the registrar who rebuffed Lassiter, testified. She had served at the Seaboard precinct since 1952, she said, and had registered forty-nine Black folk over the years. She claimed that she registered twenty-one and had rejected twenty Black hopefuls the previous year, 1956. She gave the test to all regardless of race, she swore, and recalled that she rejected one White youth in 1952. The county produced White witnesses who attested that she had indeed required them to complete the literacy test. Taylor seemed like a decent White lady, not an unruly bigot. Lassiter, along with Mary Ellen Edwards and Sarah Harris, all Black women, testified to the multiple times they had tried to register with Taylor. She accused them of mistakes yet all three read the Constitution aloud during the hearing.

On June 10, 1957, the judges, in their brief *Lassiter v. Taylor* opinion, upheld the castework that rankled Black North Carolinians, and ruled that given the new administrative appeal system, Lassiter needed to first exhaust state options. The court found that "the cross examination of the three Negro women who were denied registration by the Registrar amply established adequate basis for the denial" and that Taylor administered the test to White as well as Black applicants. Nineteen states, including only seven southern states, the court noted, enforced an educational qualification, and the Supreme Court had green-lit such practices.

Walker, Lassiter's attorney, suffered racial harassment in his effort on behalf of his client. Someone destroyed his car. Authorities tormented him. He was even jailed on a trumped-up assault charge for "talking loudly and wagging his finger threateningly" at Taylor for her defiance at registering Black folk. Walker said the local public officials "don't intend to save any Negro lawyers' practice in this section. They threw the book at me to try to cripple me and drive me out. They used the criminal law to interfere with my practice of the law and as a psychological weapon to scare away clients and keep me broke."

Days after losing the case, Lassiter and Mary Ellen Edwards visited the same county store to register. Taylor tried to administer the literacy test again, but on the advice of Mitchell and Walker, the two women refused it. After losing in proceedings at the County Board of Elections, state Superior Court, and then North Carolina Supreme Court, the U.S. Supreme Court granted review for Lassiter's case.

On May 19, 1959, inside the Court Chamber during oral argument for *Lassiter v. Northampton County Board of Elections*, Isaac Beverly Lake, the counsel representing the defendants, dissembled about North Carolina history in service of the White deed.

CHIEF JUSTICE EARL WARREN TOLD LAKE, "You may proceed."

Lake had previously stood before the nine black robes. When the Court heard oral argument for *Brown v. Board of Education II*, which involved how Jim Crow schools would segregate, he told them, "I know that if a decree should be entered by this Court, or any other court, requiring the immediate intermixing of white and Negro children in the public schools of North Carolina, those schools will be in the gravest danger of abolition." He even discussed the "friendliness" between the races that would buckle to "racial tensions and bitterness and antipathies unparalleled in our state since those terrible days which called for the original Ku Klux Klan." Four years later, he returned to tout the literacy test.

"In this record which consists of stipulated facts, stipulated by counsel for the appellant who represented her in the lower court and before the Board," Lake said in a southern twang, "there is not a shadow of suggestion of any unfair arbitrary discriminatory administration of the statute by this Board or by any other election board in the State of North Carolina. Now of course in this case, I do not speak for the entire State of North Carolina, I represent the County Board of Northampton County which is the defendant in this action. But in this record, there is no suggestion of arbitrary administration of the statute anywhere in the State of North Carolina."

After Justice Frankfurter prompted Lake to explain the literacy test's purpose, Lake replied, "that in 1900, the same time when this grandfather clause was first put into the Constitution of North Carolina, it was in 1900 under the guidance of Governor [Charles Brantley] Aycock that North Carolina began a tremendous crusade for public education in public schools in North Carolina. And it has been asserted by the Supreme Court of North Carolina that the literacy test was one of the greatest boons to public education that the State ever had."

Lake continued, saying, "I think surely, this Court will not strike down a statute of the State of North Carolina which on its face is a fair test of one's ability to vote intelligently. It will not strike down such a statute which the federal court of the Eastern District of North Carolina has found to be administered fairly and without discrimination, solely on the basis of assertion by counsel outside the record without the slightest bit of evidence to support those assertions."

Lake portrayed the literacy test as a pure effort to maintain enlightened voting. Let's revisit the past to expose the funk of fraud.

AT MIDDAY ON APRIL 26, 1900, in Shelby, North Carolina, a town of about eighteen hundred, the enthusiasm of White men pervades an auditorium decorated with flower bouquets. The stage, abounding with the energy of Black hatred, has established a welcoming spot for the Democratic speakers seated in front of a one-hundred-person choir. Above them, a massive banner painted with the words "White Supremacy" stretches the width of the building.

Charles Aycock, the Democratic nominee for the gubernatorial race, will soon address loyal partisans. A charismatic speaker, Aycock carries a special duty for his party during the 1900 election campaign—convince uneducated White North Carolinians that the Democratic plan to disenfranchise Black men will spare them. The legislature has already conceived its plan to deny Black fingertips the ballot, the law that the state legislature will enact in 1901 and then modify in 1957 in response to Lassiter's lawsuit. Democrats just need to convince the White masses of the plan's wisdom and win the gubernatorial race. The Republicans are rallying White voters against it by arguing that the Supreme Court will invalidate the grandfather clause, leaving in place a literacy test that poor White men will fail. Aycock, smart and engaging, devotes much of his public remarks to marketing the party's plan for keeping democracy for the *true* We the People.

"Not only has the Democratic Party never disfranchised a white man, but it never will," Aycock promises. Applause thunders. "The only party ever to do this was the Republican party, and where it did so it enfranchised the negro." The roars grow louder.

"I want to say this. If you do elect me governor, I shall devote the entire four years of my term to the improvement of the educational system of the state. I come here to pledge the mighty Democratic Party to the education of every illiterate white child in North Carolina. They say we want to disenfranchise the white children of the state. It's a lie—a demagogue lie. We want to put into his hand the greatest power that man can have—the glorious power which comes from equal opportunity."

Aycock mentions nothing about educating Black children. In 1954, when Isaac Lake argues in *Brown II* against integration, he is endeavoring to maintain a dual school system that, intentionally, disregards Black boys and girls. Then, four years later, he will defend the literacy test as key to Governor Aycock's education efforts while omitting that this goal applies to White kids only.

On June 8, 1959, the Court will announce its *Lassiter v. Northampton County Board of Elections* decision. The black robes reason that states retain broad power for setting voter qualifications and can enforce various voting limitations, including restrictions based on residence, age, and criminal record. "[I]n our society," Justice Frankfurter writes, "where newspapers, periodicals, books, and other printed matter canvass and debate campaign issues, a State might conclude that only those who are literate should exercise the franchise." Therefore, the Court holds, literacy tests are not inherently unconstitutional.

Mitchell and Walker will launch a well-intentioned campaign against the literacy test, but their efforts ultimately strengthen it because the Court sides with North Carolina. This result matches what transpires in *Grovey v. Townsend*, the 1935 case that fortifies the White primary. In *Grovey*, the Court seemingly condones castework because the state changes its laws in response to Black plaintiffs' lawsuits. The same transpires in *Lassiter* when the state legislature fixes the law to respond to Lassiter's grievances. Texas and North Carolina both feign an interest in complying with The Trinity and thereby help save a disenfranchisement scheme. The Court's *Lassiter* decision emboldens caste preservationists to continue their culture of pathology.

In 1957, Alabama caste preservationists will showcase more creativity in their endeavors to pass down the White deed.

IN OCTOBER 1960, a first-of-its-kind lawsuit, *Gomillion v. Lightfoot*, summoned Bernard Taper, a *New Yorker* reporter, to Tuskegee, Alabama. Black folk had long vastly outnumbered White people in the city of about sixty-seven hundred, five to one, in fact, in 1960. White folk, nonetheless, controlled the instruments of power, and deluded themselves into imagining the city Booker Washington made famous as a quaint racially harmonious place. But a Black woman, Jessie P. Guzman, running for a Macon County School Board seat, awakened White Tuskegeeans. Guzman lost by a margin that reflected the disconnect between White and Black voters. "Y'see how them niggers do," a gray-haired shopkeeper told the Scottish-born Taper about the election that featured the first Black woman to pursue office in Alabama. "They'll always vote in a bloc if you give 'em a chance," she said, blind to White folk like her maintaining the caste system in lockstep. She probably struggled to recognize her hypocrisy because caste preservationists voted as a bloc to protect what they considered a birthright—the White deed. Black folk had no right to political power, and, therefore, caste preservationists like her considered Black folk working cooperatively to acquire it improper and worth remarking upon. Worth censure. With Black folk increasingly resolute on voter registration, White Alabamians perceived their caste culture as under siege. They acted swiftly.

In 1957, the Alabama state legislature redrew Tuskegee's boundaries, formerly a square, into a twenty-eight-sided polygon, placing Booker T.'s Tuskegee Institute outside the city limits along with the homes of all but four or five Black voters. The legislature excluded no White persons from this racial gerrymander. Passed unanimously, Local Act No. 140 had spawned from Sam Engelhardt, the executive secretary of the White Citizens' Councils of Alabama, part of a network of caste preservationist organizations operational throughout the South. Engelhardt advocated for such racial gerrymanders to maintain White control of cities, believing this ploy would survive judicial review. The exiled Black folk could still vote in county, state, and federal elections, where their small presence carried no risk of tilting elections.

"I don't understand why there's been such a fuss made over us," the White wife of the man who published the weekly *Tuskegee News* told Taper. "Surely it's our own business what we wish our town's boundaries to be." Her remarks laid bare the essence of caste culture—its adherents believe they can whip up whatever rules that protect the White deed. That caste culture subjugated Black people mattered not to her. Black lives held no entitlement to the fair treatment.

Tuskegee's Black community regarded Charles G. Gomillion, a Tuskegee Institute professor, as a leader. He presided as president of the Tuskegee Civil Association, the vehicle for *Gomillion v. Lightfoot*, the lawsuit against various city officials, including Mayor Philip M. Lightfoot. "We were proud of this community, just as the whites were. We think it should have been possible to move peacefully and intelligently toward a new relationship—one of true mutual respect and dignity, not just the outer forms of these," Gomillion told Taper. "There was a glorious opportunity here. With such a large pool of educated Negroes, Tuskegee could have become a model of partnership and co-operation—if the whites had only been flexible enough, realistic enough, to perceive the possibilities. Before too many years, Negroes are bound to obtain their citizenship rights. Wouldn't it be more satisfactory if they got them without becoming embittered and disillusioned in the process?

"We didn't wish to control," Gomillion explained, "merely to share—to be able to participate freely in our government, on the basis of merit and interest. In a county where Negroes are in the majority, a county that has grown prosperous with the aid of taxes paid by Negroes and money spent by Negroes, is it too much to ask that we have at least some representation in our government—somebody on the Board of Education, on the County Board of Welfare, on the City Council? Surely there must be an intelligent middle ground between the concept of no representation at all and that of total taking over." Gomillion's remarks misunderstood that caste culture, in the 1960s, insisted upon total control. And until power—something like the Supreme Court—made them change, caste preservationists would expect near absolute hegemony.

When Black folk tried to register in Macon County, registrars would fail them for unexplained technical reasons. "Some boards have resigned rather than register Negroes," Gomillion told Taper, "and despite petitions from us, Governors have been dilatory in appointing new boards, giving as a reason that they couldn't find anybody willing to serve. During a total period of four years in the past ten, Macon County has been without a Board of Registrars, and when it has had one, we've often had to hunt all over the place to find where it was meeting."

Gomillion advised Taper to expect White folk to justify the racial gerrymander. And they did, with one White businessman telling him, in response to the idea of Black folk registering in large numbers and voting, "That mustn't happen! It mustn't."

Taper asked the businessman whether Black folk might treat White people justly if they elected candidates of their liking.

The businessman replied, "Well, they wouldn't. They couldn't!"

How could he be so sure?

"Listen, if there's such a thing as hate, there's gotta be hate in the nigger heart for the white man in the South!"

The last chance to register for Tuskegeeans wanting to vote in the 1960 November presidential election—John F. Kennedy versus Richard M. Nixon—fell on October 17. The office of the United States attorney general, William P. Rogers, had accused the Macon County registrar's office of race discrimination. Taper wanted to observe the board's operation up close, and when the clock on the brick Macon County courthouse's six-story tower stuck nine, his shoes were hitting the pavement outside. He entered and ascended a slim and winding staircase, reaching a second-floor landing where about twenty, almost all Black folk, stood around or sat in the few wooden chairs, waiting to register.

Taper conversed with some of the Black people there. They knew the office would only serve a handful of them. They told him stories about how the registrars made them handwrite the Constitution, part of a process that intentionally wasted hours of time, caste preservationists playing games with citizens' constitutional rights. One Black man said, referencing the other Black folk waiting, "Nearly every one of them knows he's not going to get into the registration office today. But they all want the State of Alabama to know that they don't acquiesce in this system or approve of it, that they're not going to be kept out forever."

After a few hours of observing the machinations of the registrar's office in the drab space, where one lonely lightbulb illuminated pale green and beige walls, Taper watched a stocky White man in his mid-forties, Wheeler Dyson, chairman of the board of registrars, leave his tiny office. Its size only allowed for the registering of one or two applicants at a time. Dyson was headed for lunch, and Taper followed him out of the courthouse.

"Mr. Dyson," Taper said, "do you have any constructive proposals or suggestions for speeding up the registration procedure?"

Dyson, inside of his car, blinked as he looked at Taper suspiciously. "Them niggras ought to learn to write faster," he said through an open car window. He then paused and, in an aggrieved tone, spat out, "You ought to see some of the people they're tryin' to push through."

Taper told him that he had rejected Black folk with PhDs.

"Well, they missed some part of the questionnaire. If a fella makes a mistake on his questionnaire, I'm not gonna discriminate in his favor just because he's got a Ph.D." Dyson continued riffing despite the absurdity of the remark: "We treat everybody alike, white or black. . . . Nobody can say we're not treatin' everybody exactly equal." Speaking to an outsider, Dyson appreciated the need to speak with his public face to protect the private face that wanted to obstruct Black voting.

Taper thanked him for the interview and stepped back from the car.

"People ought to let us alone," said Dyson before darting off.

Soon thereafter, Taper boarded a plane to Washington to hear oral argument for *Gomillion*, which the Supreme Court heard the following day, October 18, 1960, and the day after. The Black plaintiffs argued that the Alabama legislature, when it revamped Tuskegee's shape to excise the city of nearly all its Black bodies, violated the Fourteenth and Fifteenth Amendments. They petitioned the courts to enjoin Alabama officials from enforcing Local Act No. 140. District Court Judge Frank Minis Johnson, who would force the integration of the Alabama state troopers, as we learned in our exploration of *United States v. Paradise*, ruled against the plaintiffs. "This Court," Johnson wrote in his *Gomillion* opinion, "has no control over, no supervision over, and no power to change any boundaries of municipal corporations fixed by a duly convened and elected legislative body, acting for the people in the State of Alabama." The Fifth Circuit affirmed Johnson's ruling.

Justice Frankfurter, in *Colegrove v. Green* decided in 1947, deemed state legislatures, not federal courts, the proper venue to contest the drawing of the boundaries for political subdivisions, like the city of Tuskegee. Would the nine black robes allow such unmistakable castework to stand?

"BUT YOU'RE RESTING ON [THE IDEA]," Justice Frankfurter said in the Court Chamber on May 19, 1960, "that the creation, the destruction, and modification of a municipality, is the political function of the State not subject to judicial review."

"I think that would be a fair statement of my position," James J. Carter, the counsel representing Tuskegee, said. "As a legal absolute and one that has become so firmly embedded in the jurisprudence of this country that I think would be getting into a real thicket if we ever got beyond it."

On November 14, 1960, Frankfurter issued his unanimous *Gomillion* opinion. He boiled the matter down to whether the Fourteenth or Fifteenth Amendment barred racial gerrymandering that deprived voting rights based on race. The Court found that the Fifteenth Amendment did bar such actions and remanded the case to Judge Johnson.

"If these allegations upon a trial remained uncontradicted or unqualified, the conclusion would be irresistible," Frankfurter wrote, "tantamount for all practical purposes to a mathematical demonstration, that the legislation is solely concerned with segregating white and colored voters by fencing Negro citizens out of town so as to deprive them of their pre-existing municipal vote." Although the Court generally considered the drawing of lines to create political subdivisions, or districting, a matter involving state power and unreviewable by the judiciary, the Court considered this an instance of a state subjugating on the basis of race. "When a legislature thus singles out a readily isolated segment of a racial minority for special discriminatory treatment, it violates the Fifteenth Amendment." The Alabama legislators were doing what their progenitors had drilled into them their entire lives, expecting the black robes to tolerate whatever contrivances they thought necessary to prolong the White deed. The black robes undermined them, suggesting a new era had dawned.

The White folk who controlled politics in post–*Brown v. Board of Education* Louisiana, as elsewhere throughout the South, similarly adopted their ancestors' protocols for oppression. Similarly expecting the black robes to bow to their caste culture. Similarly aggrieved when the bowing didn't occur.

BEGINNING ON FEBRUARY 8, 1898, inside the Mechanics Institute where the New Orleans Massacre of 1866 occurred, Louisiana launched its excursion into the increasingly cultivated fields of disenfranchisement when, during its constitutional convention, the state adopted its grandfather clause. Sitting governor Murphy J. Foster crowed that the "grandfather clause" solved the problem of denying Black fingertips the ballot "in a much more upright and manly fashion" unlike the swindle that Mississippi and South Carolina brewed of passing laws never planned to be honestly administered.

In 1921, with the Court having nullified the grandfather clause six years earlier in *Guinn v. United States*, Louisiana aped Mississippi and South Carolina after all, requiring prospective voters to "give a reasonable interpretation" of any section of the U.S. or Louisiana constitutions. This switch produced the desired result—from 1921 to 1944, Black folk never comprised more than one percent of registered voters. With Louisiana solidified as a one-party state, Black folk rarely even tried to register because the White primary barred them from the real contests. The White primary system had dissuaded Black folk from entering a registrar's office enough that the few Black folk who wandered inside never even had to pass the interpretation test. A minuscule Black vote posed no threat.

In 1944, however, when the Court, in *Smith v. Allwright*, took the same blade to the White primary as it had the grandfather clause, Black registration climbed in Louisiana. During the next dozen years, with registrars unaccustomed to administering the interpretation test, the proportion of registered voters that Black folk represented rocketed from two-tenths of one percent to *fifteen* percent by March 1956. That number felt more threatening. This, combined with the Court's *Brown v. Board of Education* decision in 1954, left the White deed more endangered than at any time since Reconstruction. Caste preservationists, in response, intensified their efforts to counteract Black progress.

Louisiana's state legislature formed the Segregation Committee, and its chairman helped create the Association of Citizens' Councils. These two entities, hand in hand, hosted mandatory seminars where registrars learned how to safeguard the White deed. In the mid-1950s, registrars in at least twenty-one parishes began rigorously enforcing the interpretation test. The State Board of Registration, working with the Segregation Committee, ordered all parishes to comply with the requirement of administering the interpretation test, but dispensed no objective standard for evaluating an applicant's performance.

On January 28, 1959, with its massive copper dome, the Calcasieu Parish Courthouse in Lake Charles accommodated a group of public officials of Louisiana's 7th Congressional District inside a courtroom. Assistant Attorney General Edward M. Carmouche, state senators, district attorneys, sheriffs, local government officials, registrars, and Citizens' Council members assembled to secure full enforcement of the interpretation test.

William M. Rainach, the forty-five-year-old chairman of the Joint Legislative Committee, commenced the meeting at thirty minutes past ten in the morning. Their treasured devices of caste preservationism, he warned them, most notably school segregation, depended on rescuing the Whites-only governing regime. If Black people could vote, the staunch segregationist admonished, the lower caste could achieve political victories, and they would relinquish their inheritance—the White deed. They couldn't let that happen. Musn't let it happen.

"In 1897," Rainach said, "our forefathers in Louisiana started a program of voter qualification law enforcement, knowing that such a program would provide the solution to their problems." Rainach, who rose from little-known state representative to prominent Louisiana leader, brought the attendees together to lecture on the need to faithfully practice caste culture in spite of The Trinity. The enterprise of restricting the ballot relied on registrars following the culture and encumbering Black registration.

"We will prove that every parish must eventually enforce our voter registration laws. The entire emphasis in the integration struggle is shifting to the field of voter qualification enforcement," Rainach explained, "and the program we are beginning here today will prove the solution to our problems, not only in this section of our country, but for the entire United States. Our committee might reduce this entire program to these questions: What is the federal position? What is the State's position? What is your position? And what shall we do?"

Parishes throughout the state held similar meetings. Federal attorneys representing the country, not civil rights attorneys representing Black plaintiffs, attacked this castework.

ON MARCH 4, 1963, inside the federal building in New Orleans, a tall White man with a full head of dark hair, John Doar, chief of the Justice Department's Civil Rights Division, stood before a three-judge panel. In a second-floor courtroom, where bronze chandeliers accentuated the polished paneled walls, Doar denounced the state's interpretation test as "a calculated scheme" to handcuff Black voter registration. The Justice Department, helmed by Attorney General Robert F. Kennedy, filed suit in the Eastern District of Louisiana against Louisiana and certain officials involved in the state's disenfranchisement project. The suit alleged that at least twenty-one parishes were enforcing unconstitutional laws that had stymied, and would continue to stymie, Black registration, violating the Fifteenth Amendment and the First Enforcement Act. Doar asked the judges to block the state from administering the test. The 1957 Civil Rights Act, which Congress amended with the 1960 Civil Rights Act, allowed the attorney general to sue local and state governments for denying voting rights on account of race. On November 27, 1963, the judges found the state's interpretation test invalid on its face and as applied, violating both the Fourteenth and Fifteenth Amendments.

The defendants appealed to the Supreme Court. On January 26, 1965, the Court heard *Louisiana v. United States*. Harry J. Kron Jr., a fifty-two-year-old Louisiana assistant attorney general, represented his state.

"YOU WOULD AGREE," said Justice Hugo Black in the Court Chamber, "would you not, that just on its face, these discrepancies show that the Fifteenth Amendment has not been observed in that state. How could you deny?" Justice Black was referring to the paltry registration numbers of Black Louisianans. A former member of the Klan who dropped his membership when he became an Alabama senator, Black goaded Kron to speak frankly. The seventy-eight-year-old justice understood his home region and why voter rolls contained a paucity of Black folk's names. He invited Kron to admit what everyone knew.

"Well, I can't deny it, but I can't completely agree either," replied Kron in a southern drawl. "But there are many, many things beyond the record in this case that do not appear in statistical tables."

"That's true with reference to voting in many places," Black replied coolly.

"The fact is," Kron retorted, Black people "just simply weren't interested in making, they simply were not interested as a class in making a start" at registering to vote. The idea that the dearth of registered Black voters had less to do with disenfranchisement than their eschewing politics out of disinterest in democracy illustrates the intimate relationship between the funk of folly and the funk of fraud.

On March 8, 1965, Justice Black announced his unanimous opinion that affirmed the district court's ruling. "This is not a test but a trap," Justice Black wrote, "sufficient to stop even the most brilliant man on his way to the voting booth. The cherished right of people in a country like ours to vote cannot be obliterated by the use of laws like this, which leave the voting fate of a citizen to the passing whim or impulse of an individual registrar." The Court could have issued this ruling in 1898 in *Williams v. Mississippi* but chose to side with caste preservationists. Six years after *Lassiter v. Northampton County Board of Elections*, the Court invalidated a literacy test variant without mentioning the dispute that had legitimated states continuing to enforce the device, suggesting discomfort with the decision.

The Justice Department and the Court, in *Louisiana v. United States*, rattled caste culture. Caste preservationists grasped that they now stood in a ring with a more strapping opponent—the federal government—willing to box. A few months later, Congress delivered the heaviest uppercut caste preservationists had sustained in the voting rights context since the Fifteenth Amendment.

ON AUGUST 7, 1965, the day after President Johnson signed the Voting Rights Act of 1965, Attorney General Nicholas Katzenbach, who worked from the Department of Justice Main Building in the Federal Triangle, dispatched a letter to South Carolina officials explaining how the anticaste law affected the state. "Until recently," he wrote, "applicants for voter registration in South Carolina have been required to read and write portions of the Constitution if they did not provide evidence of ownership of sufficient property. Under the Voting Rights Act of 1965 the reading and writing test must be discontinued, and applicants who are otherwise qualified are entitled to be registered whether or not they own sufficient property."

Although certain provisions, like that which facilitated federal poll workers watching over southern elections or that which allowed federal registrars to register voters in the South, promised to dramatically habilitate the region's democracy, Sections 2, 4, and 5 carried the most transformational capabilities. Section 2 prohibited states or political subdivisions, like cities or counties, from enforcing a voting prerequisite "to deny or abridge the right to any citizen of the United States to vote on account of race or color."

Section 5 applied only to parts of the country deemed "covered jurisdictions" that met a "coverage formula" outlined in Section 4(b)—Alabama, Alaska, Georgia, Louisiana, Mississippi, South Carolina, and Virginia, and, additionally, particular subdivisions, typically counties, in North Carolina, Arizona, Idaho, and Hawaii. The coverage formula affected jurisdictions that enforced a test or device, like a literacy test, as a prerequisite to voting as of November 1, 1964, *and* jurisdictions with either a lower than 50 percent voter registration *or* turnout in the 1964 presidential election.

Section 4, furthermore, suspended, in covered jurisdictions, the use of all tests or devices, like literacy, understanding, or knowledge tests. Section 5 forbade covered jurisdictions from altering any "voting qualification or prerequisite to voting, or standard, practice, or procedure with respect to voting different from that in force or effect on November 1, 1964," until receiving approval from the attorney general or a three-judge D.C. federal district court panel. Covered jurisdictions would gain federal blessing only upon establishing that the change "does not have the purpose and will not have the effect of denying or abridging the right to vote on account of race or color." The act's masterminds innovated Section 5 to outflank southern ingenuity in devising new nefarious disenfranchisement weapons whenever federal laws or courts confiscated the old one. As Katzenbach said during congressional hearings, the Section 5 preclearance rule existed to constrain southern legislatures from "outguessing" Congress and federal courts.

Five days later, South Carolina governor Robert McNair announced he would direct the state attorney general, Daniel R. McLeod, to sue to halt enforcement of the Voting Rights Act. "I have asked the state attorney general to proceed immediately with all proper legal steps to prevent the corruption of elections in South Carolina," McNair said. He focused his ire on the coverage formula and preclearance requirements. "It is obvious that certain terms and enforcement procedures of the federal bill attempt to impose a double standard among the states of the nation," he said, bypassing the double standard the South imposed on Black skin in most every respect. "The law is discriminatory in itself," he maintained. "We take the position it is discrimination when an illiterate cannot vote in New York but can in South Carolina. It is discriminatory not only to those in the South but to those in the North as well." Discrimination, per McNair, breached core American principles.

South Carolina's complaint declared that certain Voting Rights Act provisions, particularly the limitations placed on covered jurisdictions, violated the Constitution, and requested an injunction against Katzenbach enforcing them. The Supreme Court agreed to hear the case directly, and accelerated review to allow for a decision before the South's 1966 spring primaries. The lawsuit "was welcome," Katzenbach later wrote, "because it provided a quick way of answering any constitutional questions and putting them to rest."

THE FOLLOWING MONTH, southern governors descended upon The Cloister, a swanky beach resort in Sea Island, Georgia, for the Southern Governors' Conference. Steps from the Atlantic Ocean, southern politicians excoriated the Voting Rights Act. There, on September 13, Governor McNair held a press conference during which he explained the rationale for suing. The lawsuit was not "an attempt to deny the franchise to any South Carolinian," McNair told reporters. "We find it difficult to comprehend why South Carolina, and a few other states, has been singled out for application of a federal law which has no effect whatsoever on the other states." The act, he grumbled, "so obviously involves the application of double standards that, even if our state did not come under . . . the provisions of the law, we would feel that a challenge of its constitutionality is not only appropriate, but it is necessary for the protection of all citizens against the enactment of a discriminatory legislations." A brief history lesson explains why McNair's gripes lacked merit.

In 1819, the Supreme Court decided *McCulloch v. Maryland,* a formative constitutional law case. The backstory started in 1816, when Congress created the Second Bank of the United States to, in part, stem unregulated currency from state banks. Although many states moaned about the bank and disputed its constitutionality, Maryland took the step of imposing a tax on it. A federal cashier at the Second Bank's Baltimore branch, James W. McCulloch, declined paying Maryland's taxes. The state then sued to compel payment. Supreme Court Chief Justice John Marshall, in a unanimous opinion, deemed the bank a constitutional exercise of congressional power. The Necessary and Proper Clause of Article I, Section 8, provides that Congress can "make all Laws which shall be necessary and proper for carrying into Execution" its enumerated powers. "Let the end be legitimate," Justice Marshall famously provided, "let it be within the scope of the constitution, and all means which are appropriate, which are plainly adapted to that end, which are not prohibited, but consist with the letter and spirit of the constitution, are constitutional." In other words, if the goal, or "end," of a congressional use of power is legitimate and falls within the authority granted by the Constitution, then Congress is allowed to use all appropriate and reasonable means to achieve that goal.

South Carolina's mission to invalidate the Voting Rights Act smacked into a *McCulloch v. Maryland* impasse. The South, for nearly a century, had violated the Fifteenth Amendment, and that amendment's enforcement clause licensed Congress to protect Black folk's right to freedom from race-based denials of voting rights. Given that the Fifteenth Amendment had entitled Congress to stop South Carolina's disenfranchisement, the Voting Rights Act needed only to clear the rational basis test, an undemanding standard. South Carolina needed to convince the Court to evaluate the act under a more rigorous test. By 1965, courts had used strict scrutiny to assess when a law burdened a *person's* fundamental right, arousing South Carolina to contend that the Voting Rights Act violated a *state's* fundamental right. Settling on the state discrimination argument, South Carolina slapped fresh paint on the shopworn states' rights formulation.

"The Act violates the fundamental constitutional principles of Equality of Statehood," McLeod argued in his brief. The Constitution, he contended, guaranteed that states stand on "equal footing" in relation to the federal government, writing, "until now, there has always been equality in political rights and sovereignty. Until now, any legislation of the federal Congress affecting those political rights and sovereignty has applied equally, on a nationwide basis, to all sovereign members of the Union." The Voting Rights Act, McLeod attested, annihilated that alleged fundamental principle. "Only in these nine states are lawful voter qualifications suspended. Only in these states are the legislatures stricken dumb on election laws, the duties of local registrars usurped by federal examiners, and the supervision of elections delegated, in practical effect, to federal employees—all without any form of judicial hearing."

The Constitution and Supreme Court precedent forced McLeod

to pick an argument from a litter of runts. His argument asked the black robes to produce an opinion rife with ignorant legal analysis. Congress wrote The Trinity, the Civil Rights Act of 1866, the Civil Rights Act of 1875, and all three Enforcement Acts, understanding that each would burden the South far more than anywhere else. If an equal sovereignty existed—and it did not—The Trinity, as amendments, terminated it. But, again, it never existed.

Congress had regularly enacted legislation that benefited or hurt one state more than another. No serious mind, for instance, had ever deemed that an appropriation bill that contained funding for special programs, or earmarks, violated the Constitution. Furthermore, Congress may place a natural resource reserve on land in any state, burdening that state. No serious mind had ever deemed that a violation of the "equal sovereignty" principle, because "equal sovereignty" was never a principle. *Equal footing* was a principle. But McLeod butchered *that* to persuade the Court into subjecting the Voting Rights Act to a heightened standard of review.

The equal footing principle arose from Article IV, Section 3, Clause 1 of the Constitution, which allows Congress to admit new states into the Union. Congress conditioned Oklahoma's 1907 admission on keeping the capital in Guthrie until at least 1913. In *Coyle v. Smith*, decided in 1911, the Supreme Court ruled such a condition unconstitutional. "Has Oklahoma been admitted upon an equal footing with the original States?" Justice Horace Lurton wrote. "If she has, she, by virtue of her jurisdictional sovereignty as such a State, may determine for her own people the proper location of the local seat of government. She is not equal in power to them if she cannot." Lurton articulated a principle first announced in the 1830s, that Congress can only enforce a requirement on an admitted state that it could on an existing state. Rhode Island switched its capital to Providence in 1900. Congress could not bar that and thus could not bar Oklahoma's capital relocation.

The Constitution and precedent supported the Johnson administration's goal of defending the constitutionality of the Voting Rights Act. Yet, Wilford Smith presented the better argument in *Giles v. Harris* and lost. If a majority of the black robes wanted to endorse "equal sovereignty," thereby helping caste preservationists protect the White deed, the Court could marry the funks of folly and fraud into a shallow opinion that undermined Black freedom.

Let's use a scene that pushed Congress to pass the act to review the Court's *South Carolina v. Katzenbach* decision.

HERE IN MARION, ALABAMA, on February 18, 1965, a cold winter night, about five hundred pour from Zion United Methodist Church, a red-brick worship house with a white-painted door, and tread a half block to the city jail. A Black man, James Orange, the field secretary for the Southern Christian Leadership Conference, Dr. King's civil rights organization, sits inside behind bars, one of hundreds of civil rights workers arrested during the movement. Because Black students had been skipping school to participate in marches, police arrested him for contributing to the delinquency of minors, a pretext given that Black children regularly missed school to help White farmers pick cotton without ever rousing law enforcement reaction. Rumors swirled that the jail walls would witness his lynching. The marchers, to keep him alive, prepare to belt hymns of dissent against his unjust incarceration. The Alabama state troopers, city police officers, and sheriff's deputies have already formed a wall in front of the jail. The streetlights are not on. Either shot off or turned off. Darkness surrounds us.

A pastor kneels to pray and start the protest. The officers scold him. Stop and stand up, they snarl. When he doesn't, they beat him. Screams and the whacking of clubs against bones and muscle overrun the space. One officer bashes a man's jaw. Crack! Notice the reporters observing uniforms attacking Black flesh and sending protesters scattering in all directions like rays of light.

Follow these three protesters—a twenty-six-year-old Black man and church deacon, Jimmie Lee Jackson; his mother, Viola Jackson; and his eighty-two-year-old grandfather, Cager Lee. They scamper into nearby Mack's Café. Uniforms pursue them inside and pummel Viola and Cager Lee. The young man throws himself to aid his mother and grandfather and then suddenly, James Fowler, a trooper, shoots.

Bang!

Then again. Bang!

Two shots to the abdomen.

Jimmie Lee Jackson will die eight days later. "I never will forget as I stood by his bedside a few days ago," King says at his funeral, "how radiantly he still responded, how he mentioned the freedom movement and how he talked about the faith that he still had in his God. Like every self-respecting Negro, Jimmie Jackson wanted to be free. . . . We must be concerned not merely about who murdered him but about the system, the way of life, the philosophy which pro-duced the murderer."

This tragedy inspires both the Selma-to-Montgomery March and President Johnson to tell Attorney General Katzenbach, "I want you to write the goddamnedest toughest voting rights act that you can devise." And Katzenbach does. But his efforts will mean nothing if the Supreme Court invalidates it and safeguards the White deed once again, especially based on an ignorant legal theory.

The answer will come on March 7, 1966, inside the half-filled Court Chamber. "The Voting Rights Act was designed by Congress to banish the blight of racial discrimination in voting, which has infected the electoral process in parts of our country," Chief Justice Warren says, reading from his thirty-one-page, eight-to-one major-ity opinion. With an expressionless face, he quickly states his conclu-sion within the first minutes of his announcement when saying the sections of the act before the Court "are an appropriate means for carrying out Congress' constitutional responsibilities and are con-sonant with all other provisions of the Constitution. We therefore deny South Carolina's request that enforcement of these sections of the Act be enjoined."

The Court deems that the Voting Rights Act passes the *McCul-loch v. Maryland* test. "The language and purpose of the Fifteenth Amendment, the prior decisions construing its several provisions, and the general doctrines of constitutional interpretation," War-ren explains, "all point to one fundamental principle. As against the reserved powers of the States, Congress may use any rational means to effectuate the constitutional prohibition of racial discrimination in voting." Warren confirms Congress had a rational basis for pass-ing the act. South Carolina's effort to increase the level of scrutiny falters because the Court dismisses South Carolina's equality of states doctrine.

True, the act bears more heavily on some states. But, Justice Warren says, "The doctrine of the equality of States, invoked by South Carolina, does not bar this approach, for that doctrine applies only to the terms upon which States are admitted to the Union, and not to the remedies for local evils which have subsequently appeared." In fewer than a hundred words—the length of a judge's text typically reflects the difficulty of a legal question—Justice Warren disposes of South Carolina's argument. Warren assembles logic bulletproof enough to forever spoil this reworked rendition of states' rights, excepting jurists amenable to stomaching anything to preserve the White deed.

Jack Gremillion, Louisiana's attorney general, speaking sentimentally about his imperiled caste culture, will mourn that the Court's decision "means that the federal judiciary and the federal government have taken over the field of state registration of voters. This is really another step in the total destruction of the rights of states to regulate their internal affairs. It also undoubtedly leads to universal suffrage." The South fears this—that their ability to stop Black registration and therefore voting will have been lost forever.

"Monday's Supreme Court ruling which upheld the legality of the Voting Rights Act of 1965 was somewhat akin to Custer's Last Stand for die-hard and embittered white supremacists," a reporter for Greenville, Mississippi's, *Delta Democrat-Times* will contend. "It was not only another in a long series of Federal court decisions; it was the most important single one since segregation was unlawed in the public school system in 1954." In March 1965, less than 7 percent of the eligible Black population was registered in Mississippi. By September 1967, that number climbs to nearly 60 percent.

Caste preservationists, however, will not abide the White deed expiring without a counterstrike.

SINCE AT LEAST 1958, Mississippi's foremost newspaper, the Jackson *Clarion-Ledger*, implored the operators of the state's caste preservationist machine to "take a serious, studied look" at the racial makeup of congressional districts "in view of the NAACP's vigorous drive for Negro voting rights." With Black folk disenfranchised, that congressional districts covering the Mississippi Delta contained Black majorities meant nothing. But if Black people could vote? That would mean something. They couldn't let that happen. Mustn't let it happen.

The passage of the Voting Rights Act ultimately convinced the state legislature to heed the pleas and formulate new potions to safeguard the White deed before the Court even heard *South Carolina v. Katzenbach*. Mississippi legislators accepted that Black folk would register, and their fingertips would touch the ballot. The South had silenced the Black vote by disallowing registration. The pool of Black registered voters, however, deepened by the day. They would presumably vote.

Concern ballooned among caste preservationist Mississippians, as it did for their peers throughout the South, about losing control over city governments, police departments, courtrooms, school boards, and other administrative apparatuses that helped continue the world White Supremacy had staged. Black folk, with sudden access to the ballot, wanted representatives who would serve them, and such representatives would often look like them. In his 1965 article "From Protest to Politics," civil rights activist Bayard Rustin argued that Black folk "now sought advances in employment, housing, school integration, police protection, and so forth." Beyond holding voter registration drives, civil rights organizations angled for Black officeholding. Caste culture demanded lawmakers devise a new battle plan. And desperation begot creativity.

At noon on January 4, 1966, the all-White Mississippi legislature convened with the specter of the disappearing White deed frightening the spirit. The 174 members, many belonging to White Citizens' Councils, paced between the Indiana limestone of the Jackson capitol, under the terra-cotta dome, and behind the stained and leaded glass windows up to the House and Senate on the third floor. In 1890, Mississippi performed its constitutional convention beneath the copper rotunda dome of the Old Mississippi State Capitol to withdraw Blackness from politics. The progeny, seventy years later, chased the same outcomes as the forebears.

With *first-generation* devices like literacy tests that *prevented* Black voting invalidated, the strategies graduated to *second-generation* devices that would *nullify* or *dilute* Black voting. Legislators introduced thirty bills on the matter, most in early January, suggesting prior coordination. The bills' sponsors disproportionately represented the majority-Black Delta counties, those most vulnerable to defeat in fair elections. The hearings took place behind the curtains—the era of recording a grand conspiracy expired with Chief Justice Warren announcing his *South Carolina v. Katzenbach* opinion. The two faces paradigm would forever reign afterward. When both houses of the state legislature exited their halls on the opposite sides of the capitol, they had passed thirteen major laws that reworked the state's election systems.

Mississippi gerrymandered the state's five congressional districts, separating the Delta's majority-Black population among three of the state's five districts, avoiding Black folk holding a majority in any. At the local level, in counties with sizable, but not majority, Black populations, the state legislature switched from single-member to at-large districts. Caste preservationists preferred the latter for obvious reasons.

Imagine a county of ten thousand. Forty percent Black. Sixty percent White. And a five-member council represents the county. A single-member district plan divides the county into five districts of roughly equal sized populations. Residential segregation would guarantee at least one Black-majority district. Under at-large districts, however, where all five members are chosen by all voters, the White majority can elect all five. The legislature switched numerous counties to at-large. The state, furthermore, adopted at-large districts for state legislature elections. Black fingertips touched the ballot, but caste preservationists watered it down. In the 1968 elections, few of the 108 Black candidates who sought office won. As transpired after the Mississippi Plan of 1890, other states retraced the footprints the state left in the sand.

Although a covered jurisdiction under the Voting Rights Act, Mississippi did not seek preclearance for these changes. They were, the state argued, unrelated to voter registration and therefore did not oblige the state to seek federal approval. With the South upending long-standing voting and election laws while skirting the preclearance process, despite Black registration soaring, caste preservationists diluted the Black vote.

Black plaintiffs brought federal lawsuits under Section 5 of the Voting Rights Act, arguing that because Mississippi needed preclearance before instituting these changes, the courts should void them. On March 3, 1969, three years after the all-White Mississippi legislature walked into the central rotunda, the Supreme Court reviewed the Mississippi Plan of 1966.

CHIEF JUSTICE WARREN WROTE the seven-to-two opinion for four consolidated voting rights cases. Three from Mississippi. One, the lead case, from Virginia. *Fairley v. Patterson* concerned a Mississippi law that allowed each county's board of supervisors to switch from single-member districts to at-large elections. *Bunton v. Patterson* centered on a Mississippi law that provided that in eleven specific counties, the board of education would appoint the county superintendent of education. Before the change, the law provided those counties the option of electing or appointing the superintendent. A Mississippi law that made independent general election candidacies more difficult incited the litigation in *Whitley v. Williams.* The law targeted the Mississippi Freedom Democratic Party, a Black political party established in 1964 to contest the White supremacist Mississippi Democratic Party. Last, *Allen v. State Board of Elections,* concerned a Virginia law change that prevented illiterate voters from using stickers to vote for write-in candidates. In each dispute, new rules dwindling the victory probability for Black politicians supplanted old rules, honoring a caste culture axiom—America must bestow power to the White people who believe power belongs to White people.

Mississippi, like Virginia, argued that covered jurisdictions need not obtain preclearance for election law changes that did not bother voter registration. The two states, put differently, diminished the Voting Rights Act into a stubby-armed simpleton with limited reach. The Court rejected this restrictive interpretation. "The Voting Rights Act was aimed at the subtle, as well as the obvious, state regulations which have the effect of denying citizens their right to vote because of their race," Chief Justice Warren wrote for the majority in an opinion filed under the name of the Virginia case, *Allen v. State Board of Elections*. The Court broadly framed the right to vote, determining that voting encompassed "all action to make a vote effective."

Changing to at-large districts, the Court found, diluted the Black vote. In a democracy, each person's vote should weigh the same. "Voters who are members of a racial minority might well be in the majority in one district, but in a decided minority in the county as a whole," Warren observed. "This type of change could therefore nullify their ability to elect the candidate of their choice just as would prohibiting some of them from voting."

Making the county superintendent of education position appointive rather than elective, likewise, demanded preclearance. A discriminatory purpose, Warren reasoned, might have inspired the change. Or it could have produced a discriminatory effect in the absence of anti-Black intent. Section 5 forbade both. The Mississippi legislature, in reality, enacted the rule to prevent Black folk from electing their preferred superintendent candidates—the majority-White school boards could, if necessary, rejigger the rules to avert the election of the Black-favored contender. Changes to complicate independent candidacies likewise necessitated preclearance as did Virginia's write-in law change. After *Allen v. State Board of Elections*, the Justice Department and private complainants broadly employed Section 5.

The plaintiffs in the Mississippi cases solicited the Court to dump the results of the affected elections and order new ones given that the victors won under illegal rules. The Court, however, refused. Warren noted that the justices had yet to decide such in-depth Voting Rights Act cases—people of good faith might still mistakenly violate the unfamiliar and uncharted law—and posited that Mississippi lawmakers did not "deliberate[ly]" violate it, extending unearned grace to pupils of White Supremacy.

In eschewing preclearance, Mississippi lawmakers had postponed fair elections. Still, the South could not delay forever. In 1969, almost three-fifths of eligible southern Black folk were registered. And Section 5, because of the Supreme Court's ruling, blocked changes that could abridge or deny voting rights, now broadly defined, on account of race. The Mississippi Plan of 1890 breathed seventy-five years until Johnson signed the Voting Rights Act. The Court strangled the 1966 plan before its fourth birthday.

But Republican Richard Nixon's 1968 election predicted a rightward Supreme Court shift. Therefore, a few years after *Allen v. State Board of Elections*, when chicanery from Richmond, Virginia, reached the Court, it encountered a more conservative composition, one expected to better look after the White deed that caste preservationists had protected in the state at the turn of the twentieth century.

AT NOON ON JUNE 12, 1901, inside the Virginia state capitol, a neoclassical building in Richmond, the state's constitutional convention gathered for its first day. The delegates unanimously elected an old Confederate, John Goode, a former congressman and once President Cleveland's solicitor general, as their president.

After the delegates roared when he took the gavel, Goode, nearing eighty, said all attendees must accede to "the fear of God" when conducting the convention's work. The fate of the White deed, the perceived agreement that establishes America belongs to White people, rested on their success. "The white people of Virginia," stated Goode, standing straight and displaying a near youthful vigor, "believe that the dominant party in Congress not only committed a stupendous blunder, but a great crime against civilization and Christianity when they turned a deaf ear to the advice of their wisest leaders and required Virginia and the other Southern States under the rule of the bayonet to submit to universal negro suffrage." Goode, with white hair and a ruddy complexion, personified caste culture. "The omniscient Ruler of the universe for some wise purpose made him inferior to the White man and ever since the dawn of history," he said, "as the pictured monuments of Egypt attest, he occupied a subordinate position." By enforcing a literary test and instituting a one-dollar-and-fifty-cents poll tax that needed to be paid for three consecutive years and also six months before the election, the constitution the convention drafted snatched away Black folk's voting rights. Before the new constitution, three thousand Black voters lived in Richmond's Jackson ward. Afterward, thirty-three.

Nearly seven decades later, Richmond elected a mayor, Philip

Bagley, a vessel for the same caste preservationist worldview that abounded in the Thomas Jefferson–designed capitol during the 1901 constitutional convention. Bagley, who too operated with "the fear of God," implemented yet another ruse consistent with his culture.

DURING THE 1960s, as the Black population of Richmond grew, observers expected that it would reach an electoral majority by 1970. The suburbs felt the winds of White folk fleeing toward them as rural southern locales saw the backs of Black folk escaping toward southern cities. Atlanta. Charlotte. Richmond. They all felt the Black population boom that unnerved many White Richmonders. City council members in Richmond ran in at-large elections, an early 1900s relic adopted to foil the election of Black politicians representing Black wards. Yet, a majority-Black city could elect an all-Black city council in at-large elections. Caste preservationists in Richmond couldn't let that happen. Mustn't let it happen.

In 1964, when Black folk were 34 percent of the city's registered voters, Benjamin Cephas, a Black man, won election to the city council. A Black political mobilization organization, the Richmond Crusade for Voters, cranked up the political consciousness of Black voter-age residents. And as their registration levels rose, they desired candidates, particularly Black candidates, who vowed to pursue their interests. From 1956 to 1966, the number of registered Black voters climbed from 8,500 to 32,500. In 1966, when Black registered voters voted at a higher rate than did their White peers, the city elected two more Black candidates. Henry Marsh III. Winfred Mundle. That same year, the Supreme Court, in *Harper v. Virginia Board of Electors*, barred under the Equal Protection Clause the enforcement of the poll tax as a voting prerequisite. This promised to further lift Black voter participation.

In 1968, federal investigators observed that the panic of the Black ballot held a "tyranny over the mind of the White South, which has found continuous expression in the politics of the region." That year, Mayor Bagley declared that "niggers won't take over this town," and approached Irvin G. Horner, the executive secretary of adjoining Chesterfield County, to solve his problem. Bagley wanted Richmond to buy a portion of Chesterfield County to expand the city's boundaries, known as *annexation*. Cities typically annex to advance economically—annexation allows a city to increase its wealth, boost its capacity to fund projects, and invest in its future. Politicians clamoring for annexation often covet vacant land to develop into property that would expand the city's tax base. Bagley, however, craved just one thing—importing enough White voters into city limits to keep Richmond majority-White. During a secret meeting, Bagley said, "we don't want the city to go to the niggers. We need 44,000 bodies."

After yearlong negotiations, Bagley reached an annexation agreement with Chesterfield County. On Monday, June 30, 1969, state judge Earl L. Abbott approved the annexation. While reading his opinion, Abbott nervously sipped water like a man fearful he was violating the rules. He had grounds for trepidation. The Supreme Court, in March, had decided *Allen v. State Board of Elections*, where the black robes held that covered jurisdictions, like Virginia, needed to obtain preclearance for almost any voting change. Richmond officials failed to request preclearance for the annexation.

The city added about twenty-three square miles of land and nearly fifty thousand residents, 97 percent of them White, shriveling the Black population from 52 percent to 42 percent ahead of the 1970 city council elections. Richmond's annexation added little of economic value though. And the city failed to even annex enough schools for all its new students. Bagley privately said, "I did what I did in reference to the compromise [annexation] because the niggers are not qualified to run the city of Richmond." The annexation became effective January 1970, and in that year's elections, only one Black candidate, Marsh, won. Bagley's skullduggery appeared safe. Until events intervened.

On January 14, 1971, the Supreme Court held in *Perkins v. Matthews* that covered jurisdictions needed preclearance before annexing. Two weeks later, Richmond sought approval from the attorney general. On May 7, 1971, on account of the annexation diluting the Black vote, the attorney general's office refused preclearance. The assistant attorney general for the Civil Rights Division, David Norman, did, however, give Bagley hope of salvaging his baby. "You may," Norman wrote, "wish to consider means of accomplishing annexation which would avoid producing an impermissible adverse racial impact on voting, including such techniques as single-member districts."

On August 25, 1972, instead of switching to single-member districts, Richmond sought approval for the annexation in D.C. district court. In unrelated litigation, on March 5, 1973, the Supreme Court affirmed the judgment of *City of Petersburg v. United States*. In that case, a D.C. district court judge deemed invalid a Petersburg, Virginia, annexation, where council members were elected at-large. The district court stipulated, however, that approval could be granted if the city adopted single-member district elections as that would mitigate vote dilution.

Richmond then submitted plans to the Justice Department that adopted single-member district elections, and on August 25, 1973, the department approved a nine-ward plan that promised four majority-Black districts, four majority-White districts, and one district with a narrower White majority. A group of Black Richmonders that included the Crusade for Voters opposed the plan and intervened in the district court case, meaning the organization became an additional party to the lawsuit because of its stake in the outcome. The district court sent the dispute to a special master, Lawrence Margolis, a federal magistrate judge, to hold evidentiary hearings and offer recommendations.

Margolis concluded that Richmond, during negotiations, fixated on acquiring White bodies and little else. Mayor Bagley, in fact, sought guarantees from Chesterfield County officials that the annexation would transfer at least 44,000 White people before accepting a deal. Bagley and another council member even required that everything complete in time to permit these new White residents' participation in the 1970 city council elections.

Margolis found that, first, the city failed to satisfy its burden of establishing that the annexation did not have the goal of diluting the Black vote. Second, he determined that the single-member district plan failed to redress the annexation's racially discriminatory purpose. Margolis further concluded, third, that the city could have done more to remedy the annexation's discriminatory effects, including creating the outcome where Black voters held a majority in five of the nine districts. Such a remedy would have provided Black folk the political clout they would have enjoyed but for the annexation. Although accepting Margolis's findings, the district court did not order de-annexation, as Margolis had advised that Section 5 demanded. The case, from there, proceeded directly to the black robes.

ON JUNE 24, 1975, Justice Byron R. White announced the Court's five-to-four decision in *City of Richmond v. United States.* "We do not agree with the district court that the annexation as finely conceived had the effect of denying the right to vote," stated Justice White in the Court Chamber. "We are also sufficiently unsure that it had such a purpose that we vacate the judgment of the district court and remand the case for further proceedings with respect to the purpose of the annexation in the light of present conditions. These conclusions are more fully explained in the opinion filed with the clerk today."

The case tasked the justices with answering a straightforward question—whether the annexation, either in purpose or in effect, denied or abridged Black voter's rights. Without the annexation, Black folk would have enjoyed a majority in Richmond elections. Mayor Bagley intended to deny them that majority. And, according to Judge Margolis, the plan succeeded, diluting the Black vote. Five justices found, nonetheless, that the single-member district plan remedied any potential vote dilution injury. True, the annexation denied Black folk that voting-majority power. But Black Richmonders, White reasoned, held no legal entitlement to that result. The justices only considered whether Richmond diluted the Black vote *post-annexation.* And the city adopting single-member districts prevented dilution.

The Black intervenors wanted to force the city to create an outcome where Black folk would enjoy the majority power that they would have experienced if Richmond had never annexed. The city could have achieved that by creating five Black and four White districts as Margolis had recommended. The Court rejected Section 5 required that. "To hold otherwise," Justice White wrote, "would be either to forbid all such annexations or to require, as the price for approval of the annexation, that the black community be assigned the same proportion of council seats as before, hence perhaps permanently overrepresenting them and underrepresenting other elements in the community, including the nonblack citizens in the annexed area."

White presented shallow analysis, though. The old running back should have grappled with the special master's finding that the mayor sought annexation to deny Black folk a voting majority. An intellectually consistent White would have reasoned that when a city annexes with discriminatory purpose, the city must either de-annex or not curtail Black voting power. Such a ruling would have cohered with the majority *Washington v. Davis* opinion *he* wrote a year later which committed the Court to the Intent Doctrine.

White, instead, reasoned that the city's nine-district plan "does not undervalue the black strength in the community after annexation; and we hold that the annexation in this context does not have the effect of denying or abridging the right to vote within the meaning of [Section] 5." Regarding the discriminatory motive for the annexation, White countered that the city hadn't the full opportunity to rebut Margolis's conclusions and remanded the case for further proceedings on this matter, as though Richmond could potentially justify its mayor saying, "we don't want the city to go to the niggers. We need 44,000 bodies."

The Court's decision weakened the Voting Rights Act while gifting a blueprint for how to respond when Black folk inched closer to reaching majority status. The Court sided with caste preservationists, giving them evidence to conclude that their culture, despite the changes the Voting Rights Act had ushered, could still persist. Caste abolitionists had cheered the beefy Voting Rights Act's passage. Ten years later, however, it felt frailer because the Court, as it once had to Reconstruction-era enforcement and civil rights laws, hamstrung a congressional anticaste enactment.

After deciding *City of Richmond v. United States*, the black robes, in a subsequent critical Voting Rights Act case, again wounded the act, this time leaving in place an eight-decades-old election system.

WALTER E. URQUHART, a Birmingham state representative, fancied that he had solved Mobile's early 1900s Black voter conundrum. He in fact had, well enough that Black folk ached under it for generations.

In 1907, the Alabama legislature retooled the state's municipal government election systems. The revisions required aldermen candidates to run in single-member districts, and mayor and president of the board of aldermen candidates to run at large. In the 1908 and 1910 elections, however, enough Black fingertips in one Mobile ward touched the ballot to spook caste preservationists. Perhaps the city might elect a Black alderman. They couldn't let that happen. Mustn't let it happen.

On July 6, 1909, a group of caste preservationist Mobile residents assembled to weigh Urquhart's bill. It proposed a city commission form of government in Birmingham and Montgomery with all representatives elected in at-large contests. For a city commission, representatives serve on a small governing body that wields executive and legislative power. Distinguished Mobile residents, like Erwin Craighead, editor of the *Mobile Register*, and Albert Carey Danner, a former Confederate soldier and the meeting's chairman, concurred that "Mobile should combine with those two cities and advocate a general law permitting the citizens of the municipalities to vote on the question of adopting that system." Another participant, Laz Schwarz, a Mobile officeholder, likewise championed the commission government, "provided the question may be submitted to the white people of Mobile, and that they be permitted to elect their own commissioners."

In 1909, Frederick Bromberg, a longtime Alabama politician, penned an open letter to Alabama legislators. Bromberg, the president of the Alabama Bar Association at the time, was championing an Alabama constitution amendment that explicitly barred Black officeholding. His words illustrated how the fixation on maintaining White rule drove how the state resolved political questions, including whether to adopt the city commission form of government across Alabama. "We have always, as you know, falsely pretended that our main purpose was to exclude the ignorant vote, when, in fact, we were trying to exclude, not the ignorant vote, but the negro vote," he admitted. "At present the masses of the colored race are indifferent to the right to vote and still more indifferent to the right to hold office; by adopting remedial measures now we shall cause no discontent, because of the present apathy of our colored citizens. This is fully recognized by all statesmen."

In 1911, the legislature passed Urquhart's city commission bill. It still operated throughout Alabama, including in Mobile, when, on June 9, 1975, Wiley L. Bolden, a civil rights activist, filed a complaint in federal court on behalf of himself and other Black Mobile residents. For nearly seven decades, White folk in Mobile had been profiting off a form of governance meant to caretake the White deed before Bolden lodged his complaint that alleged Mobile's at-large elections diluted the Black vote, violating the Fourteenth and Fifteenth Amendments, and Section 2 of the Voting Rights Act. Since this governing structure predated the Voting Rights Act, Section 5 did not apply.

On October 22, 1976, District Judge Virgil Pittman sided with the Black plaintiffs' vote dilution argument. Mobile, Pittman ordered, had to shift to a mayoral system with a city council comprised of representatives elected from single-member districts. The Fifth Circuit affirmed. On March 19, 1979, Chief Justice Burger, and Justices Brennan, Stewart, White, Marshall, Blackmun, Powell, Rehnquist, and Stevens, heard oral argument for *City of Mobile v. Bolden*.


"I DON'T THINK you can decide this case in a vacuum," said a bespectacled White man with salt-and-pepper hair, sixty-six-year-old Charles Sylvanus Rhyne, who represented Mobile. "I think you have to look at the entirety of the picture, what's going on in the world today. I think that in this instance . . . there's no impediment in the voting process, whatever." Rhyne, a renowned D.C. lawyer, disputed that this matter involved Black voting rights victims because Mobile oversaw a fair electoral process. "Everybody can register," he professed, "everybody can run."

Justice Stevens interrupted. "Do you think that the *Gomillion* case would have been decided differently if there had been showing that there is no impediment to the voting process?" asked Stevens cogently, as if reading from a book. Recall in *Gomillion*, the Alabama legislature redrew the boundaries of Tuskegee to exclude nearly every Black voter from the city's elections.

"Well, the *Gomillion* case is entirely different from this," Rhyne responded. "The *Gomillion* case was an out-and-out discriminatory action, and you've got no discriminations here." Rhyne misstated the facts, but the Black plaintiffs' presentation included no detailed origin story specifying how race hatred had spawned Alabama's at-large elections.

"Well," Justice Stevens asked, "suppose this was out and out in a sense that the legislature and the commissioner said the reason we want to maintain our plan, our commission form of government, is because we do not want blacks to be elected as commissioner—would it be a different case?"

"It could be," responded Rhyne in a slight southern accent, "but you don't have that here."

ON APRIL 22, 1980, Chief Justice Warren E. Burger, in perfunctory speaking rhythm, said, "the judgment of the Court in *City of Mobile, Alabama against Bolden* will be announced by Mr. Justice Stewart."

"The City of Mobile, Alabama," Justice Stewart said, reading from his text, "has since 1911 been governed by a city commission consisting of three members elected by the voters of the city at large. The question in this case is whether this at-large system of municipal elections violates the rights of Mobile's Negro voters in contravention of federal statutory or constitutional law as held by the District Court and the Court of Appeals for the Fifth Circuit. For the reasons expressed in an opinion filed today [six justices] have concluded that Mobile's electoral and governmental system does not on the record in this case violate the United States Constitution or federal law. . . . Accordingly, the judgment before us is reversed."

Stewart rejected that the at-large system violated the plaintiffs' Fifteenth Amendment rights. The plaintiffs compared the at-large voting system to the White primary. Stewart rebuffed that analogy. "The only characteristic . . . of the exclusionary primaries that offended the Fifteenth Amendment was that Negroes were not permitted to vote in them," he wrote. Black fingertips touched the ballot, however, in Mobile's elections. "Having found that Negroes in Mobile 'register and vote without hindrance,'" Stewart concluded, "the District Court and Court of Appeals erred in believing that the appellants invaded the protection of that Amendment in the present case." Stewart argued that Section 2 achieved exactly what the Fifteenth Amendment did. That amendment restricted intentional denial of voting rights based on race. The commission form of government did not violate the Fifteenth Amendment and therefore did not violate Section 2.

Stewart, furthermore, found no evidence of discriminatory intent that would sustain an equal protection violation. A 1973 case, *White v. Regester*, served as precedent. The Court there invalidated a Texas law that turned two legislative districts in the Texas House of Representatives, one heavily Hispanic, the other heavily Black, into at-large districts. "In so holding, the Court relied upon evidence in the record that included a long history of official discrimination against minorities as well as indifference to their needs and interests on the part of white elected officials." The justices, in simpler terms, found proof of discriminatory intent. The Court distinguished *Bolden* from that case because the Court detected no hint of purposeful discrimination in Alabama.

*Bolden* exposed the folly of the Intent Doctrine. Alabama lawmakers originally deployed the city commission form of government to maintain the White deed, although historical fog secreted that truth from the black robes. A method of government instituted to harm Black people, therefore, survived. Yet, regardless of those lawmakers' decades-old intent, Black folk were now experiencing a government that muted their voices. Their concerns. We must appreciate *that* as the true consequential fact. Constitutional constructions that focused on effect not intent would have guided the justices to the result that would have freed Wiley L. Bolden from living as a member of a subordinated caste. In 1911, when Alabama lawmakers passed Urquhart's bill, they thought that they should structure democracy to funnel its fruits to White skin. They aimed to activate a caste culture axiom, and Alabama elections continued to reflect that pro-White inspiration because of the Court's interpretation of The Trinity.

In the aftermath of the black robes further hobbling the Voting Rights Act in *Bolden*, the caste abolitionists behind the case persevered in their battle against a culture capable of much more than disenfranchisement.

AT FIFTEEN MINUTES PAST ONE on the morning of February 11, 1906, a mob of twenty-five masked White men abducted a Black man from the Etowah County, Alabama, jail. They dragged him three blocks to the Louisville and Nashville railroad bridge across the Coosa River. Tied one end of a long rope to the wooden railing. Tied the other around his neck. Picked him up and threw him over. Death by strangulation arrived at the end of the twenty-foot plummet.

The lynching of Bunk Richardson spelled the nadir of race relations in the northeastern Alabama county and warned Black folk about their station—although the law forbade murder, White folk felt no duty to honor the nation's rules with respect to Black life. When the Court decided *Bolden* in 1980, White residents, forming about 80 percent of Etowah County's population, still treated Black people as an outsider race. And wanted that to continue.

Defeat inspired James Blacksher, Larry Menefee, and Edward Still, the plaintiffs' counsel in *Bolden*. If they wanted to sack the target of their ire—the state's at-large local elections—they needed to establish the discriminatory motivations behind it. Harnessing indisputable evidence, most notably Frederick Bromberg's 1909 letter, they did. On April 15, 1982, District Judge Pittman concluded that the state had intentionally implemented that electoral system to undercut Black political candidacies, and he reinstated his order mandating that Mobile adopt single-member districts.

Then, on June 29, 1982, President Reagan signed a Voting Rights Act renewal, as Presidents Nixon and Ford had before him. This renewal amended Section 2 to overturn *Bolden*. Any voting rights practice that, based on race, resulted in the denial of the "equal opportunity to participate in the political process," regardless of intent, now violated Section 2. In effect, this meant that, under Section 2, either the discovered intent behind a voting rule or its effect could invalidate it.

Armed with evidence of discriminatory intent and the updated Section 2, Blacksher, Menefee, and Still, lawyers for the Alabama Democratic Conference, a Black political league that spearheaded Black voter mobilization, conceived a strategy to topple at-large elections—from city councils to school boards—throughout Alabama. The trio chose an approach that ultimately scrapped at-large election systems in nearly two hundred political subdivisions in sixty-one of Alabama's sixty-seven counties. The paucity of Black elected officials in Alabama unnerved the ADC, and its leaders deduced, with strong evidence, that Black candidates would continue floundering until they could run in Black-majority districts. Most White ballot-ers simply refused to pull the lever for Black candidates who Black voters also favored. On November 12, 1985, ADC's lawyers filed the complaint for *Dillard v. Crenshaw County*, the case that produced game-changing success for Black candidates in local races through-out Alabama by turning at-large races into single member ones. One of the counties affected, Bunk Richardson's Etowah County, shifted to single-member contests, resulting in the 1986 election of Law-rence Presley, a Black man, to the six-member county commission.

"To be black and to be here is a milestone," Presley rejoiced after his victory, on the cusp of touching real power. They couldn't let that happen. Mustn't let that happen. In August 1987, less than nine months after Presley, the county's first Black commissioner, assumed office, the Etowah County Commission reworked its governing rules. Presley, per the former rules, would have exercised total con-trol over spending on the roads in his district. After the change, the four pre-existing members obtained control over the roads in all districts, including his. Caste preservationists hatched a novel trick to retain the White deed—stripping a Black official of power after he won.

In May 1989, when racial remedial policies were falling because a majority of the black robes extolled the color-blindness principle, Presley sued in federal district court. The county erred, he argued, in not obtaining preclearance. The D.C. district court panel rejected Presley's claim. On November 12, 1992, the Supreme Court heard oral argument for his case, which the Court consolidated with a similar controversy from Russell County, Alabama, where two Black county commissioners had *their* power likewise swiped after their victories. These cases should have rankled those black robes who framed race-conscious remedial policies like affirmative action as unconstitutional because race must never infect state decision-making. On January 27, 1992, the Court announced its *Presley v. Etowah County Commission* decision.

ASSOCIATE JUSTICES WHITE, Blackmun, Stevens, O'Connor, Scalia, Kennedy, Souter, and Thomas surrounded Chief Justice Rehnquist in the middle chair. "In an opinion filed with the clerk today," said Justice Kennedy, "we now affirm the judgment of the district court though we adapt a different rationale to determine the question, 'what constitutes a change with respect to voting as that term is used in the [Voting Rights] Act?'

"The commissioners who sued argue that these changes in decision-making structure reduced their net authority. It follows, they contend, that a vote cast for individual commissioners was made less valuable and so there was a change with respect to voting," Kennedy explained.

The six-to-three Court, with White, Blackmun, and Stevens dissenting, distinguished the changes in question from voting changes like those discussed in the cases consolidated in *Allen v. State Board of Elections*. Reducing Presley's power, the majority contended, implicated no aspect of any electoral voting procedures, did not alter how the county held elections, did not institute candidate requirements or qualifications, and left unaltered the electorate's composition.

Presley wanted the Court to hold that a governing body in a covered jurisdiction must obtain preclearance before amending rules to reduce an elected official's power. The majority rejected that as impractical. "Were we to accept [Presley's] reading of Section 5," Kennedy posited, "we would work an unconstrained expansion of the statutory coverage. Innumerable state and local enactments having nothing to do with voting, affect the power of elected officials.

"The appellants," Kennedy posited, "failed to provide a workable distinction between changes in rules governing voting and changes in the routine organization and functioning of government." Kennedy wanted to limit the Voting Rights Act to the mere act of voting, saying, "the Act by its terms covers any *voting* qualification or prerequisite to *voting*, or standard practice or procedure with respect to *voting*." Kennedy accentuated voting all three times. "The changes now at issue are not covered by this language."

The majority ignored that Congress passed the Voting Rights Act to allow Black fingertips to touch the ballot. Black voters craved the feeling of the ballot to elect candidates who would represent *them*, would wield their authority to improve *their* lives. Black Alabamians never experienced that excepting a few fleeting Reconstruction years. In *Allen v. State Board of Elections*, the Court explained that voting included "all action to make a vote effective." If city governments can simply loot the power of representatives elected by Black voters, that would drain the *effectiveness* of the Black vote. In Etowah County, Black voters' ballots held less *effectiveness* than White voters' ballots. Yet, the Court treated depriving Presley's *effectiveness* as a matter not concerning voting. Katzenbach defended Section 5 as necessary considering that the South invented new ploys whenever the old ploys met their demise. Etowah County cooked up fresh castework and the Court merely tipped the cap at the ingenuity.

Caste preservationists blasted a loophole in the Voting Rights Act. And as in the Richmond annexation case, the black robes stamped this particular scheme with its seal of approval, providing yet another blueprint for maintaining the White deed. As Justice Stevens observed in his dissent, "such a change has the same effect as a change that makes an elected official a mere figurehead by transferring his decision-making authority to an appointed official, or to a group of elected officials controlled by the majority."

The Court should have followed its vote dilution precedent. The county diluted the vote post-election rather than beforehand. The changes Etowah's White city commissioners wrought operated much like redrawing boundary lines, as in *Gomillion*, or switching elections from single-member districts to at-large elections. Presley and his Black constituents lost because the justices sided with caste preservationism, giving the unfit even more reason to believe that their culture would still prosper. The lynching of Buck Richardson reminded that White people needed not respect Black rights. The

White county commissioners who stripped away Presley's power trumpeted that same message, a message they learned to convey through centuries-long cultural teachings, a message the black robes had helped disseminate.

About forty miles east of Etowah County, a border dissects Alabama from Georgia, a state with an equally hideous racial history.

ON JULY 3, 1889, representatives and senators of Georgia's General Assembly huddled at the Kimball Opera House, where the state lodged its legislature, awaiting an update from Governor John B. Gordon. At ten in the morning, they received the news—the work on the new dedicated capitol, six blocks southwest, on Washington Street, was complete. They could relocate. From the opera house, a five-story brick building on Marietta Street in downtown Atlanta, the legislators assembled in a two-by-two line and footed it to their new workspace.

The only Black man among them, seventy-three-year-old Samuel A. McIver, a member of the legislature's lower house, trekked with his White colleagues. As they crossed the railroad tracks on the Broad Street bridge, the new building's neoclassical façade came into view. Governor Gordon, reputedly the head of the state's Ku Klux Klan, awaited their arrival. As the legislators ascended the seven steps of the west plaza and entered their new workspaces, they suffused it with caste culture where it would dwell for generations. That culture touched nearly all aspects of the work done inside the building, including how the state drew its congressional districts.

In *Wesberry v. Sanders*, decided in 1964, the Supreme Court invalidated Georgia's 1931 congressional reapportionment as violating the one-person, one-vote principle. The population of the 5th Congressional District, covering Atlanta, nearly tripled other districts. The Court held that state legislatures needed to configure roughly equal-sized congressional districts. The 1970 census presented the U.S. attorney general's office its first occasion to review how covered jurisdictions drew congressional districts that needed to comply with Section 5 of the Voting Rights Act. Georgia's final 1971 redistricting plan divided Black folk in metro Atlanta across the 4th, 5th, and 6th Districts to guarantee each a White majority. The office of Attorney General John Mitchell rejected the plan under the act. The state legislature, in response, upped the 5th District's Black percentage to 45 percent and gained preclearance.

A decade later, Black state representatives sought one at least 65 percent Black congressional district in Atlanta, computing that electing a Black congressperson required that racial composition. The legislature, instead, created nine majority-White districts and one majority-Black district, Atlanta's 5th District, whose Black total landed at fractions of a percentage point above 50. Like the 1970 redistricting plan, the 1980 version distributed Black voters in greater Atlanta among three districts. On September 23, 1981, Democratic governor George Busbee signed the Congressional Reapportionment bill and submitted it to the office of Attorney General William French Smith for preclearance. Smith's office rejected the plan for diluting the Black vote. Rather than rework the plans, the state sought preclearance from the federal district court in D.C., a choice exposing facts that White Georgia Democrats would have rather kept hidden.

FROM JUNE 28 TO JULY 1, 1982, inside the U.S. Courthouse for the District of Columbia that overlooked the National Mall, a three-judge panel heard testimony that uncovered how Lieutenant Governor Zell Miller, House Speaker Tom Murphy, and House Reapportionment Committee Chairman Joe Mack Wilson endeavored to preserve White Democratic dominance in congressional races. These politicians all belonged to the final generation of White southern Democrats who identified as helming a *White* state party with a *White* working-class base. They wanted Black votes but only to elect White candidates who represented White constituents foremost. Judges Harry T. Edwards, Aubrey Robinson Jr., and June L. Green found that Georgia's General Assembly "successfully implemented a scheme designed to minimize Black voting strength to the extent possible." Murphy and Miller "packed" the reapportion committee "with individuals who overtly opposed any plan which would unite the black population in the metropolitan Atlanta area or increase the black population."

The testimony bore alarming details of Wilson's bigotry. "[T]here are," Wilson said, "some things worse than niggers and that's Republicans." Another time, he derided legislation written to benefit Black constituents as "nigger legislation." One week after meeting with Justice Department officials, Wilson said, "the Justice Department is trying to make us draw nigger districts and I don't want to draw nigger districts." The judges concluded that "overt racial statements, the conscious minimizing of Black voting strength, historical discrimination and the absence of a legitimate non-racial reason for adoption of the plan," necessitated a finding that Georgia violated Section 5. The General Assembly, thereafter, made the 5th Congressional District 60 percent Black and received Justice Department preclearance.

Georgia state lawmakers, for 1990 census redistricting, apparently wanted to evade past ghosts and from August 19 to September 5, 1991, tackled the decennial task. Black plaintiffs, through various Section 2 lawsuits, had successfully sued the state and forced voting rule changes—mainly the switching of at-large elections to single-member district elections. This lifted the electoral fortunes for Black politicians. In 1964, Georgia had just three Black elected officials. That number snowballed to five hundred in 1990, 88 percent coming from city and county offices. But a Black congressperson represented only one of the state's ten congressional districts, John Lewis of the 5th District. The legislature first devised a redistricting plan with two majority-Black districts. The attorney general rejected it, arguing that Georgia, now with eleven House seats in a 27 percent Black state, must create *three* majority-Black districts. After initial reticence, the state ultimately complied.

Black Democrats won all three majority-Black congressional districts in the November 1992 elections. On January 13, 1994, five White voters from the 11th District, represented by Cynthia McKinney, a Black Democrat, sued in federal court. The Black district, they argued, violated *their* equal protection rights, a position, that, if vindicated at the Court, would have bolstered the phenomenon of the Equal Protection Clause offering more utility to White, not Black, claimants of race discrimination. A Supreme Court case from North Carolina, *Shaw v. Reno*, that validated this claim had landed at the Court Chamber about nine months before the White plaintiffs from Georgia filed their lawsuit.

ON APRIL 20, 1993, Robinson O. Everett, a Duke law school professor and one of five *Shaw v. Reno* plaintiffs, explained his lawsuit to the black robes. "As our complaint seeks to make clear," the tall balding man said, adopting an aggressively inflammatory framing, "this case poses the basic issue of how far a legislature may go in seeking to guarantee the election to Congress of persons of a particular race."

When courts considered questions of race and representation, they *had* focused on vote dilution. In *Shaw v. Reno*, though, White plaintiffs argued that the North Carolina legislature created its 12th Congressional District with race top of mind. Oddly shaped, the district stretched 160 miles, snaking through the state until it devoured enough Black residences to yield a majority-Black district. As amended in 1982, Section 2 made voting rules that denied or abridged the right to vote on account of race illegal, and plaintiffs need not have demonstrated an intent to discriminate. With North Carolina receiving another, a twelfth, district per the 1990 census, the attorney general's office pushed the state to create a second majority-Black district. Five White plaintiffs, including Everett, argued that the redistricting plan violated their Equal Protection rights. The underlying logic propelling the lawsuit seemed to pit Section 2 of the Voting Rights Act against the Fourteenth Amendment.

The Republican Party, for political motives, backed majority-Black congressional districts in the South. The GOP wanted to realign White southern voters into reliable Republican teammates. The party's strategists reasoned that extracting Black voters from the congressional districts of White southern Democratic congresspersons compromised their reelection prospects. Republicans wanted the elected southern Democrats to be Black, making the Democratic

Party appear like the party for Black people and the Republican Party that for White people. Republicans, in other words, thought that racial gerrymandering benefitted their long-term political priorities. The North Carolina Democratic-controlled legislature, though, created the 12th District as majority-Black but still allowed vulnerable White Democratic politicians to win reelection. This success incensed Republicans.

Two months after oral argument, Justice O'Connor released her five-to-four majority opinion, a veritable smorgasbord of ignorant legal analysis. "It is unsettling," she wrote, "how closely the North Carolina plan resembles the most egregious racial gerrymanders of the past." The plaintiffs did not argue that the redistricting plan diluted their vote. "Rather, appellants' complaint alleged that the deliberate segregation of voters into separate districts on the basis of race violated their constitutional right to participate in a 'color-blind' electoral process," O'Connor explained, disregarding that the Supreme Court had never considered "participating in a color-blind electoral process" a constitutional right.

O'Connor likened the redistricting plan to "political apartheid." When O'Connor wrote the remark, Black South Africans lived under *actual* apartheid. That governing system, premised on the same notion of Black inferiority that animated Jim Crow, another *actual* apartheid regime, started in 1948 and barred Black Africans from voting in national elections. Who, in her analogy, lived under apartheid? The White plaintiffs? Or the 12th District's Black residents who elected Mel Watt in 1992, the second Black congressperson in North Carolina since George Henry White left the House in 1899? A black robe should never proffer a comparison that clumsy and historically illiterate.

The Court, in *Shaw*, ruled that racial gerrymandering presented a valid claim under the Equal Protection Clause. For the first time, the Court held that legislative apportionment could run afoul of the Constitution without demonstrating either vote dilution as in *Allen* or vote denial as in *Gomillion*. A redistricting plan that racially classified needed to pass strict scrutiny. O'Connor cited *Gomillion* as supporting this position, misunderstanding that Alabama denied Black Tuskegeeans the right to vote in elections, and the redrawing of Tuskegee's borders to exclude only Black residents meant Black folk had no voice in the elections of the officials who provided them basic municipal services.

In *Shaw*, the state legislature denied White people no rights. O'Connor could not argue that White folk suffered from vote dilution because White North Carolinians elected candidates of their choosing, and still did under the new redistricting plan, electing ten White politicians to the House in 1992. O'Connor sprinkled buzzwords like "segregation" and "apartheid" into her opinion to mask her inability to state an injury the White plaintiffs had suffered. Her verbiage could not atone for dearth of substance and abundance of ignorance. O'Connor stretched the color-blindness principle into a parody of itself. Conservatives championed color-blindness, they insisted, because racial remedial programs were providing relief to Black nonvictims of discrimination thereby turning White folk into actual victims of discrimination. Now conservatives were championing color-blindness to protect White nonvictims of discrimination. The only consistency in how conservatives employed the color-blindness principle was that no matter what it promoted the wants of White claimants railing against governmental actions that provided supposedly undeserving Black people benefits.

The Court did not rule that the North Carolina legislature, with the drawing of the 12th Congressional District, violated the Equal Protection Clause—just that the plaintiffs presented a claim that courts must acknowledge as viable under the clause. "It really is quite reactionary," Laughlin McDonald, executive director of the ACLU, said following *Shaw v. Reno*, "in that it throws into question, I think, all the progress that's been made after the '90 census, and the '80 census and the '70 census," referring to the increasing numbers of Black officeholders.

Georgia's redistricting matter presented the Court simple interlocking questions—whether the 11th Congressional District was a racial classification under the Equal Protection Clause considering the principles announced in *Shaw*, and if so whether that district passed strict scrutiny.

———

ON JUNE 29, 1995, Justice Kennedy, announcing his *Miller v. Johnson* opinion, said, "the case involves the constitutionality of Georgia's most recent congressional redistricting plan."

The district court, Kennedy explained, had held that the 11th Congressional District violated the constitutional principles outlined in *Shaw*, reading that case as requiring strict scrutiny when race operated as the "overriding, predominant force" in a redistricting plan. Kennedy, speaking for the Court's five-to-four majority, agreed with the lower court's understanding of *Shaw*—a plaintiff must "prove that the legislature subordinated traditional race-neutral districting principles to racial considerations." Given that Georgia stipulated that it intended to create a majority-Black district to comply with the Justice Department's preclearance requirements, the Supreme Court agreed with the district court's conclusions. "On this record, we fail to see how the district court could have reached any conclusion other than that race was the predominant factor in drawing Georgia's eleventh district," Kennedy said. The majority further agreed with the district court that the Voting Rights Act did not require Georgia to create a third majority-Black district.

"The Voting Rights Act and its grant of authority to the federal courts to uncover official efforts to abridge minorities' right to vote," Kennedy read in an emotionless tone, "has been of vital importance in eradicating invidious discrimination from the electoral process and enhancing the legitimacy of our political institutions. As a nation we share both the obligation and the aspiration of working toward this end. The end is neither assured nor well served, however, by carving electorates into racial blocs. If our society is to continue to progress as a multiracial democracy, it must recognize that the automatic invocation of race stereotypes retards that progress and causes continued hurt and injury. It takes a shortsighted and unauthorized view of the Voting Rights Act to invoke that statute which had played a decisive role in redressing some of the worst forms of discrimination, to demand the very racial stereotyping the Fourteenth Amendment forbids," Kennedy said, ending his remarks.

In *Johnson*, as in *Shaw*, the Court failed to specify a harm that the plaintiffs endured. "When the state assigns voters on the basis of race," Justice Kennedy wrote in his opinion, "it engages in the offensive and demeaning assumption that voters of a particular race, because of their race, 'think alike, share the same political interests, and will prefer the same candidates at the polls.'" But those thirty-four words written to, assumedly, invoke the spirit of race equality, fail to articulate a harm—the plan simply did not injure White voters. The legislature neither took nor diluted their vote—White voters still had the ability to elect candidates of their choosing in the majority of districts, both federal and local.

*Johnson* presented an Intent Doctrine matter, which mandated that the plaintiffs prove an injury. But the plaintiffs failed. The Court, instead, conjured the language of color-blindness to protect White voters from a constitutional violation they never experienced, but didn't conjure this language on behalf of Lawrence Presley in his case against Etowah County. The Intent Doctrine also required that the plaintiffs prove an intent to discriminate, but the state legislature intended to comply with the Voting Rights Act and the Justice Department's preclearance guidance. The White plaintiffs satisfied neither of the two requirements of the Intent Doctrine, yet the Court found an equal protection violation.

Kennedy's *Johnson* opinion unmasked a caste preservationist judicial hypocrisy. Courts had examined various majority-*White* districts throughout the decades that jammed White voters into strangely shaped districts, except the concept that such districts violated the Constitution never formed. Before *Miller,* states drew districts to further the interests of White ethnic groups. Chicago's Polish Americans. Anglo-Saxons in North Georgia. San Franciscan Irish Catholics. Italian Americans of South Philadelphia. Courts had never deemed them problematic. Georgia's 95 percent White 9th Congressional District, created in 1980, maintained a unique White mountain community. The General Assembly, during 1990 redistricting, kept it. A member of the Georgia House Reapportionment Committee admitted that the residents "are predominantly of an Anglo-Saxon bloodline," and the committee drew the line "purposefully to maintain it as one district, a[n] area that has a distinct culture and heritage."

Black southerners too have a "distinct culture and heritage." Creating a congressional district for *that* ethnic group, however, incited Justice Kennedy to pontificate on the horrors of assigning voters to districts on the basis of race, underlying a troubling bias that infested the thought processes of certain black robes who professed to espouse color-blindness. This bias viewed White people, on the one hand, through the prism of their Americanness. They were We the People. And thus, when government served them, government was serving its citizenry. This bias defined Black people, on the other hand, by their race. We the *Black* People. And thus government serving *their* needs was government engaging in race-conscious decision-making on behalf of an identifiable racial group. In *Miller v. Johnson*, White noninjuries defeated Black citizens benefiting from the drawing of districts around their communities. Kennedy's opinion telegraphed a retreat from the Voting Rights Act, a law that dealt the mightiest of blows against caste culture.

A fuller retreat eventually manifested. Let's return, one final time, to the executive mansion in D.C., when President Reagan signed the Voting Rights Act's reauthorization in 1982, to investigate that retreat.


ON JUNE 29, 1982, as we ascend the marble stairway to the state floor level of the White House, we gaze rightward and spot the East Room, an ostentatious space for public events with gaudy glass chandeliers. Wearing a pin-striped navy suit, President Reagan is addressing an audience of 350 for a subdued event. "As I've said before," he remarks in the second year of his presidency, "the right to vote is the crown jewel of American liberties, and we will not see its luster diminished."

As Congress held hearings about renewing the Voting Rights Act, Reagan eschewed the bully pulpit. No public pressing of congresspeople to re-up a law. No barnstorming the nation for what introduced the ballot to all. Just silence. Only after Congress overwhelmingly passed the reauthorization bill with just twenty-four no votes in the House and eight in the Senate did the administration confirm Reagan would sign it. In addition to amending Section 2, the reauthorization extended Section 5 and the Section 4(b) preclearance formula twenty-five years.

After curt remarks, Reagan sits before a wooden desk. When

Johnson signed the Voting Rights Act, he used fifty pens and gifted them as souvenirs. As you may sense, the mood today matches none of the jubilation we encountered in the Capitol Rotunda in 1965. As the unenthusiastic eyes of Republican senators, Utah's Orrin Hatch and Kansas's Bob Dole, loom over his shoulder, Reagan signs the bill with one pen during this four-minute ceremony. He rises and mechanically declares, "It's done." The NAACP's executive director Benjamin L. Hooks tells reporters that he has "no confidence" the William Bradford Reynolds–led Civil Rights Division of the Justice Department will earnestly enforce it. "I do want to congratulate the President, however, for belatedly at least coming along with the [Voting] Rights Act," Hooks jabbed.

In 1966, when Reagan sought the California governorship, he decried the Voting Rights Act for violating states' rights. But years of the Court upholding the act that succeeded at conveying voting rights to all reshaped the political environment. Reagan, inundated by accusations of racism, cannot afford to gift-wrap ammunition for his adversaries by opposing it, especially this early in his presidency. The Supreme Court quickly validating the act in *South Carolina v. Katzenbach* deprived men like Reagan of the latitude to impugn its constitutionality. The act was clearly constitutional. The Court, by 1982, has denied caste preservationists much reason to believe that they can practice their culture in a way that would torpedo the Voting Rights Act. The Court impedes caste culture this way—by stripping the fire of necessary oxygen. But in cases like *City of Richmond v. United States* and *City of Mobile v. Bolden* the Court has dented the once pristine act, though it still proves strong, and Reagan has little choice but to sign it.

Under this 1982 reauthorization, Section 4(b) and Section 5 will continue to clog the wheels of voting castework that rolls through small southern towns mainly. In 1987, for example, the Supreme Court will uphold the denial of preclearance for two annexations sought by Pleasant Grove, Alabama, an all-White Montgomery suburb. The district court finds, and six justices subsequently agree, that the suburb annexes White but not Black areas. Pleasant Grove, the Court maintains, violates Black voting rights in an attempt to sustain an all-White democracy. In 1990, Dallas County, Alabama, will want to press the button on a voter purge program that could detonate the registrations of an untold number of Black voters, but Section 5 thwarts it. In 1993, officials in Millen, a town of nearly four thousand in eastern Georgia, will propose to delay a city council election in a majority-Black district while majority-White districts hold theirs. Under Section 5, the Justice Department kills the proposal. The city then attempts to relocate the Black district's polling places to far-away locations. Section 5 again kneecaps it.

In 2000, Albany, Georgia, will continue to redistrict the city's wards to deny a majority of Black voters. Section 5 halts this. In 2001, Section 5 blocks a Northampton County, Virginia, plan to change the method of electing the board of supervisors that would dilute Black votes. That same year, in Kilmichael, Mississippi, a town of about eight hundred, many Black candidates will run for mayor and alderperson. Three weeks before the elections, the town seeks to stop elections after learning that the population passes the majority-Black threshold. The Justice Department forces the holding of the elections, and Black candidates win the mayoral and most of the aldermen races. In 2003, after Black folk win most of the Charleston County, South Carolina, school board seats, the county proposes to shift to at-large voting, but Section 5 nixes it. The culturally unfit persist at striving to torment but yield fewer casualties because of the Voting Rights Act.

In 2005, before the expiration date of certain parts of the Voting Rights Act, Congress will consider reauthorization. One study that informs Congress's deliberations establishes that Section 2 lawsuits brought in covered jurisdictions are far more fruitful than those from noncovered jurisdictions. Covered jurisdictions account for less than a quarter of the nation's population, yet 56 percent of successful Section 2 lawsuits. Controlling for population, almost four times as many Section 2 lawsuits come from covered jurisdictions. This data convinces Congress that the coverage formula still roots out evil. Therefore, in 2006, Congress reauthorizes expiring portions of the Voting Rights Act, including, for twenty-five more years, Sections 4(b) and 5. Congress sticks with the same coverage formula. It works. That same year, Celra, a small city in Shelby County, Alabama, tries and fails to proceed with elections after eliminating its only majority-Black district without preclearance, demonstrating Section 5's ongoing efficacy.

Two years later, the nation elects its first Black president, Illinois Democratic senator Barack Obama. His election triggers immediate racial backlash from caste preservationists—a Black man in the White House presents the bogeyman they most fear. Just the mere thought of Black officeholding, had, since Black fingertips first touched the ballot after the Civil War, actuated castework. Preventing an Obama victory drove every scheme we have chronicled over this leg. If America truly belongs to White skin, how can a Black man serve as commander in chief? Many caste preservationists believe that the multiracial coalition that elects him disfigures American democracy beyond recognition, shredding the White deed. They want to restore White domination as best as practicable and believe the mission hinges on bleaching future electorates. But with the Voting Rights Act still standing, they need aid from the black robes. And the Court continues to give that aid since *Miller v. Johnson*, the Georgia redistricting case. In *Reno v. Bossier Parish School Board*, decided in 2000, and in *Georgia v. Ashcroft*, decided in 2003, the Rehnquist Court interprets Section 5 to enable covered jurisdictions to receive preclearance for vote-diluting policies. In the age of Obama, though, caste preservationists need more assistance.

Six months after a Black family opens the door to the White House, the Court will decide *Northwest Austin Municipal Utility District No. 1 v. Holder*, a case concerning a small utility district outside Austin, Texas. With no history of race discrimination in voting rights, Northwest Austin seeks either a release from preclearance requirements under Section 4(a)'s bailout provisions, *or* for the Court to declare Section 5 unconstitutional. The Court holds that Northwest Austin can seek a bailout. But in dicta, a comment in an opinion that is not necessary to resolve the case and thus does not operate as precedent in future cases, Justice Roberts curiously writes that Section 5 "imposes current burdens and must be justified by current needs." He continues, bemoaning that Section 5 "differentiates between the States, despite our historic tradition that all the States enjoy 'equal sovereignty.'" He comments that "a departure from the fundamental principle of equal sovereignty requires a showing that a statute's disparate geographic coverage is sufficiently related to the problem that it targets." Segregationist North Carolina senator Sam Ervin argued this before the passage of the Voting Rights Act as did segregationist South Carolina attorney general McLeod in *South Carolina v. Katzenbach*. The Court, however, summarily dismissed this states' rights claim. Either Roberts cannot comprehend Warren's plainly written opinion, or he intentionally misstates it. Funk of folly or funk of fraud?

In 2011, a federal judge will call conversations between Alabama state senators recorded through the course of an FBI investigation "shocking" because they uncover rank bigotry. The state senators, unaware federal agents are taping them, call Black folk "Aborigines" and discuss shuttering a gambling referendum because Black people will vote if it is on the ballot. The judge notes that the exchanges highlight how racism "remain[s] regrettably entrenched in the high echelons of state government."

Then, in May 2012, the federal district court in D.C. will side with the federal government in a lawsuit that Shelby County, Alabama, files in April 2010. Shelby County seeks a resolution of the "serious constitutional questions" regarding whether Section 5 and Section 4(b) are facially unconstitutional that the Court leaves unresolved in *Northwest Austin*.

Let's exit the White House and visit the Court Chamber, one last time, on June 25, 2013, to hear fifty-eight-year-old Chief Justice Roberts announce his *Shelby County v. Holder* opinion.

JUSTICES SCALIA, KENNEDY, and Thomas remain on the Court. The diminutive seventy-nine-year-old Justice Ruth Bader Ginsburg, the second woman justice, moved the Court leftward when Democratic president Bill Clinton tapped her, a former women's rights attorney, to replace Justice White. Clinton's second appointee, Justice Stephen Breyer, seventy-four years old, has proven a reliable liberal vote. The former Harvard Law professor served on the First Circuit Appeals Court before replacing Justice Blackmun. Justice Samuel Alito, sixty-three, took Justice O'Connor's vacated seat. We've heard his name before during our journey—the George W. Bush appointee worked in the Reagan administration and helped convert William Bradford Reynolds's historical ignorance into Constitution-is-color-blind arguments.

Obama has two appointees here, Justices Sonia Sotomayor and Elena Kagan. Sotomayor, two days before her fifty-eighth birthday, is the first Latina among the black robes. The former Second Circuit Appeals Court judge replaced Justice Souter. A former Harvard Law dean, Kagan, fifty-two, replaced Justice Stevens. Since the women supplanted two left-leaning jurists, the Court's five-to-four conservative majority holds.

"During the freedom summer of 1964 in Philadelphia, Mississippi," Roberts says, reading from his written text, "three men were murdered while working in the area to register African American voters. On bloody Sunday in Selma, Alabama in 1965, police beat and used tear gas on hundreds marching in support of enfranchising African Americans." Roberts is reciting past turmoil to argue that America's climate has moderated dramatically from the days Black folk bled for the ballot. "Today," he remarks, "both Philadelphia, Mississippi and Selma, Alabama have African American mayors." We must credit the Voting Rights Act, of course, for these gains.

"No one doubts that there is still voting discrimination in the South and in the rest of the country. As noted, when we upheld the original act, we said that exceptional conditions can justify legislative measures not otherwise appropriate."

Referring to *South Carolina v. Katzenbach*, Roberts is intimating the Court upheld the act because of unique circumstances— intractable Black disenfranchisement throughout the South. But this statement floods the funk of fraud into the chamber. Warren's *Katzenbach* opinion did not state "exceptional conditions can justify legislative measures not otherwise appropriate," and the text does not support that reading. Rather, the Court merely noted that Congress had responded to dire circumstances when it passed the Voting Rights Act. True, the law departed radically from Congress's previous lawmaking, yet that speaks nothing to its constitutionality. It merely underscores how little Congress has used its available tools to enforce Black freedom from caste.

"The question is whether the extraordinary measures of preclearance and disparate treatment of the states that were upheld forty-five years ago remained constitutional in light of today's changed conditions," Roberts says. "Now that question was before us four years ago in a case called *Northwest Austin*. In our decision, we stated that the preclearance and selective coverage features of the Act 'raised serious constitutional questions.' But we did not decide those questions at that time. . . . Those concerns were expressed in an opinion joined by eight members of the Court. Congress took no action in response."

In *Northwest Austin*, Justice Roberts inserted the zombie argument that South Carolina governor McNair articulated in September 1965 at the Cloister hotel. Justice Warren, in 1966, separated that meritless argument's head from its shoulders. Roberts reanimated a dead position and buried it in *Northwest Austin* as dicta. A justice might sign on to an opinion that contains dicta that the justice disagrees with because dicta isn't binding on future decisions. Roberts cannot rely, honestly, on Warren's *South Carolina v. Katzenbach* opinion as support for his equal sovereignty argument. Instead, he's relying on the fact that eight justices joined his *Northwest Austin* dicta that misstated Warren's words.

The third leg of our journey explored cases arising out of 1890s Mississippi. We observed how the black robes refined the deceit of a state that penned a new constitution to pillage Black men's right to vote and degrade the Black population to an inferior station. Here, Roberts is concocting his *own* deceit on behalf of a worldview that considered Black voting as illegitimate, something far worse than what we encountered with the 1890s Fuller Court.

"Today, we cannot avoid reaching the constitutional questions. The arguments that the preclearance requirement in Section 5 of the Act can no longer be justified have a great deal of force, but we do not strike down that provision. We do however find that the coverage formula in Section 4 violates the Constitution and cannot be used to decide which jurisdictions are subject to preclearance. That formula looks to conditions as they were in 1972," Roberts says, referring to the year Congress updated the formula, "and earlier, more than 40 years ago. A jurisdiction is subject to preclearance today if it employed a voting test at that time or had done so since 1964 and if voter registration or turnout in the state had been low in elections in the 1960s and early 1970s. But the Act imposes current burdens and must be based on current political conditions as we warned four years ago in *Northwest Austin*. If Congress had started from scratch when it extended the challenge provisions in 2006, it plainly could not have enacted the present coverage formula."

Roberts's ignorant legal analysis disregards that the coverage formula has proven successful, and the data before Congress verified that the covered jurisdictions still accurately identified the political subdivisions most likely to infringe voting rights. Roberts is arguing that Congress must create a new formula but offers no constitutional justification for that position other than his *Northwest Austin* dicta. He merely asserts a legal principle while offering neither supportive precedent nor sound logic.

"It would have been irrational for Congress to distinguish between states in such a fundamental way based on forty-year-old data when today's statistics tell an entirely different story," says Roberts, now dispersing the funk of fraud. The data affirms that the covered jurisdictions remain the areas most rife with successful voting rights lawsuits. "And," Roberts continues, "it would have been irrational to base coverage on the use of voting tests forty years ago when such tests had been illegal since that time, but that is exactly what Congress has done."

Congress acted irrationally, Roberts insists, when legislators continued the coverage formula first conceived in 1965, meaning the coverage formula fails the rational basis test. But laws clear that low bar in most any circumstance and cannot trip over it when Congress is reauthorizing an act previously held constitutional. If Congress had deemed the formula still effective, it acted rationally. Irrational lawmaking, for example, might have entailed determining status as a covered jurisdiction by alphabetical order. Roberts, like O'Connor in *Shaw v. Reno* when she likened creating a majority-Black district to apartheid, is tossing about buzz words to camouflage a dearth of intellectual rigor.

"When taking such extraordinary steps as subjecting state legislation to preclearance in Washington and applying that regime only to some disfavored states, Congress must ensure that the legislation it passes speaks to current conditions. The coverage formula, unchanged for forty years plainly does not do so and therefore we have no choice but to find that it violates the constitution."

Roberts regurgitates bad legal arguments into his five-to-four opinion that declared Section 4(b) unconstitutional. Because Section 5 relies on 4(b), five justices have just rendered it impotent. Nine mostly southern states are now free from needing preclearance before changing voting laws.

We opened this leg of our journey at the Constitutional Convention, where the drafters crafted a document premised on the principle that the power lies with the people. The three-fifths clause, key to establishing popular sovereignty, told White people that America belonged to them. The Voting Rights Act vexes caste preservationists because they despise the notion that they must respect Black people as legitimate members of We the People. The interpretation of the Constitution that Chief Justice Roberts just articulated inside the Supreme Court Building honors the terms and conditions of the White deed. He appeased the hearts of the culturally unfit for democracy. And they quickly honored him through castework.

EXPECTING THIS DECISION, and that North Carolina would therefore shed its status as a covered jurisdiction, the state legislature's Republican majority had already collected the necessary information to design new voter laws that would disproportionately impair Black voter participation. In 1900, Black congressman George Henry White, with Black folk disenfranchised, decided to relocate to the North rather than remain in North Carolina. A Black man, in a feat not achievable without the Voting Rights Act, won the state in a presidential election 108 years later. Like the caste preservationists a century earlier in partial response to White's victory, North Carolina Republicans went to work on conspiring the ballot from Black fingertips. "Is there any way to get a breakdown of the 2008 voter turnout, by race (white and black) and type of vote (early and Election Day)?" a Republican staffer asked in January 2012. In April 2013, a top aide to the Republican House Speaker requested "a breakdown, by race, of those registered voters in your database that do not have a driver's license number."

On June 26, 2013, a day after the *Shelby County* decision, state senator Tom Apodaca said publicly, "I guess we're safe in saying this decision was what we were expecting." He added that "now we can go with the full bill," referring to legislation written to reduce the number of Black votes cast in the state. The legislature then passed a bill that cut a week of early voting, stopped out-of-precinct voting, and required voters to show certain forms of photo ID to vote. Republicans chose these restrictions after learning they would disproportionately curtail Black voting.

With the new opportunities that the black robes provided them, caste preservationists in North Carolina fortified the White deed, clinging to their belief that America belongs to them, what they imagined the Founding Fathers promised White people, what the Supreme Court of the United States has helped them preserve in spite of The Trinity. The culturally unfit for democracy, from the statehouse to the Court Chamber, from the seventeenth to the twenty-first century, still persevere in undermining Black freedom.

# Farewell Address

AFTER TRIUMPHANT UNION HORSES galloped from Talbot County, Georgia, in 1865, Rachel Greene, for the first time, felt the breeze kissing her shoulders as a free woman. Imagine the emotions that gushed through her soul when she heard of her emancipation. Property of a master one moment. Her own master the next. The glorious reversal that spun newly freed people away from the dusk and toward the light.

On a piece of paper, Isabella Greene listed the first names, grouped by family, of those the South's embarrassment forced her to unshackle. It included Rachel, seventeen, and her two-year-old daughter, Mariah. No father included. No husband recorded. Two years later, Rachel, without forty acres, without a mule, but with one four-year-old girl needing her mother to provide, signed with an *X* a yearlong contract to work for Isabella for twenty-five dollars a month. Free but not away.

During Rachel and Mariah's time, before and after slavery, the caste preservationists who controlled the country of their birth—their homeland—looked at them and their people, saw Black skin, deemed them inferior, and chained them to the bottom of a racial caste system. Rachel and Mariah, like their lineage would in the future, sought happiness in the midst of White Supremacy, his minions and his accessories on the Supreme Court of the United States.

Mariah birthed a daughter named Daisy, who birthed a daughter named Ruth, who birthed a daughter named Stephanie, who birthed a son who shepherded you on a journey that explored how America, since its dawn, promised White people that the nation would condone their enslavement of Black people. That they could intimidate them away from the voting booth. Throw on sheets and massacre them to retake governments. Deny them a spot in the jury box. Banish them from civil society. Reduce them to peonage. Write new state constitutions to disenfranchise them. Segregate them. Miseducate them. Block them from even registering to vote. In response to these cultural practices, Black folk knelt before the Constitution. Begged for it to shield them against tyranny. Prayed for it. But the black robes wrapped their paws around three amendments that promised complete freedom and strangled the spirit out of each.

The Court has continuously emboldened caste culture, enabling White folk to amass White racial advantages, namely wealth and all its accompanying benefits. When the Civil Rights Movement grabbed the nation's ear and dragged it forward, dragged it closer to meeting its ideals, caste preservationists summoned deceit and ignorance in service of both maintaining those White racial advantages and impeding Black folk from blunting the trauma of ongoing castework. The idea that this country belongs to White people spawned all these evils. White caste preservationists believe that their racial identity entitles them to a society where they hold the favored position, and thus they can transgress whatever necessary to protect their spot atop the racial caste system.

Please appreciate that to discrown a king older than the nation itself, you must return to the abolitionist origins of The Trinity and find salvation in constitutional constructions that adopt the language of anticaste. However, as you've learned during each leg of our journey, caste preservationists care less about formulating erudite arguments steeped in sound logic than about providing the Court something, anything, to glom on to when writing opinions that promote their interests.

History teaches us much about how caste preservationists will respond to campaigns to cancel their culture. They will profess that a caste system no longer exists in America. They will conflate efforts to destroy the caste system with efforts to scathe White skin. They will rebrand *White* people as the new subordinated caste. Determining whether the funk of folly or the funk of fraud fuels these remarks might feel difficult, especially since they will make cunning use of the public face to satisfy the goals of the private face. Don't fixate too long on such matters though. Just stay attentive to how any argument they present, if followed, would conserve the caste system. They want a White-over-Black world and only care about maintaining the prized White deed that their ancestors bequeathed them and that they hope to pass forward. What they inherited has turned out durable enough that silence and inaction equate to preservationism. Before us lies a war that can tolerate neither neutral nor lazy parties.

The Thirteenth, Fourteenth, and Fifteenth Amendments could have achieved more and still can but only through the tenacity, passion, and brainpower of true caste abolitionists. If most of the black robes on the Court, at any given point in time, are willing to advance caste preservationism, the culture that Rachel Greene braved will haunt this land. Nothing we've witnessed on our journey even *slightly* suggests that caste preservationists, unless deprived of reasons to believe their culture can survive in America, will ever stop attempting to torture The Trinity and the laws meant to enforce it. You must deny them that Court majority. The depravity that we have experienced up close will linger whenever their accomplices wear black robes.

# *Acknowledgments*

Without my agent, Ayesha Pande, this book would exist only in my mind. Her guidance steered me toward boldness. Made this work more ambitious. More worthy of your time. My editor, Kristine Puopolo, guided me skillfully, pushing my focus toward the book's animating spirit and away from distractions, no matter how interesting those distractions might have been. She and Bill Thomas, Doubleday's publisher, recommended that I incorporate the Thirteenth and Fifteenth Amendments into my analytical framework. My book proposal originally concentrated on just the Fourteenth. Their suggestion dramatically enhanced this book, and any I may conceive in the future. I now appreciate what a big idea feels like.

Many assisted in the writing of this book. My memory proves good enough to recall these names: Kenneth Mack, Ana Espinoza, Walter Howell, Franita Tolson, Eva Paterson, Al Brophy, R. Volney Riser, Mindy Kent, Nancy Bean, Kimble Reynolds, and Dyana Varner. Hopefully the unmentioned, should they exist, will accept my apologies.

I couldn't have written *Their Accomplices Wore Robes* without the love and support of my wonderful wife, Wendy Ferguson, a talented attorney in her own right, to whom this book is dedicated. This project required immeasurable ambition, ambition one can never sustain absent external motivation. I would never need any more motivation than making her proud. My sons, Brave and Bond, likewise inspired me to strive above my own expectations. When they are old enough to read this book, I pray they whisper to themselves, "wow, my dad wrote these words." And I am forever grateful to the first persons I learned to love—my mom, brother, father, uncle, and late grandmother.

I dedicated my first book to "those who danced so I don't have to." My ancestors. Those who faced fires I never endured. Their spirit sustained this work and my life. To honor them, I shall never dance.

# *Notes*

## OPENING ADDRESS

1 On March 13, 2020 I pieced together the story of the killing of Breonna Taylor from a few sources. Rukmini Callimachi, *Breonna Taylor's Life Was Changing. Then the Police Came to Her Door,* NEW YORK TIMES, Aug. 30, 2020, available at: https://www.nytimes.com/; Josh Wood, *Pregnant Woman Whose Apartment Was Shot into Testifies in Hankison Trial: "I Was Scared for My Unborn Child's Life,"* LEO WEEKLY, Mar. 1, 2022, available at: https://www.leoweekly.com; Richard A. Oppel Jr., Derrick Bryson Taylor, & Nicholas Bogel-Burroughs, *What to Know About Breonna Taylor's Death,* NEW YORK TIMES, Mar. 9, 2023, available at: https://www.nytimes.com/.

2 *racial caste system* See also ISABEL WILKERSON, CASTE: THE ORIGINS OF OUR DISCONTENTS (2020) for a different discussion on racial caste.

2 In wrongful death lawsuits Some tort law scholarship speaks to how courts have allowed race to inform calculation damages. MARTHA CHAMALLAS & JENNIFER B. WIGGINS, THE MEASURE OF INJURY: RACE, GENDER, AND TORT LAW (2010); Ronen Avraham and Kimberly Yuracko, *Torts and Discrimination,* 78 OHIO STATE LAW JOURNAL 661 (2017); Ronen Avraham & Kimberly Yuracko, *The Use of Race- and Sex-Based Data to Calculate Damages Is a Stain on Our Legal System,* WASHINGTON POST, Apr. 29, 2021, available at: https://www.washingtonpost.com.

2 In March 1875 Albert V. House, *The Speakership Contest of 1875: Democratic Response to Power,* 52 JOURNAL OF AMERICAN HISTORY 252, 257 (1965).

## PART I: PRELUDE

7 Back in April BATTLES AND LEADERS OF THE CIVIL WAR BEING FOR THE MOST PART CONTRIBUTIONS BY UNION AND CONFEDERATE OFFICERS: BASED UPON "THE CENTURY WAR SERIES" 744–46 (Vol. 4 1888).

7 In late August *The Freedmen's Convention,* JOURNAL OF FREEDOM, Oct. 7, 1865, at 1; SIDNEY ANDREWS, THE SOUTH SINCE THE WAR AS SHOWN BY FOURTEEN WEEKS OF TRAVEL AND OBSERVATION IN GEORGIA AND THE CAROLINAS 121–28 (1866).

7 The delegates don handmade ANDREWS, THE SOUTH SINCE THE WAR at 131.

8   James Walker Hood LEON F. LITWACK, BEEN IN THE STORM SO LONG: THE
    AFTERMATH OF SLAVERY 503–5 (1980).

8   One man reads ANDREWS, THE SOUTH SINCE THE WAR at 128–30.

8   "The [Thirteenth] Amendment" *United States Congress, Message from the
    President of the United States, Communicating* found in COMPLIANCE WITH
    RESOLUTIONS OF THE SENATE OF THE 5TH OF JANUARY AND 27TH OF FEBRU-
    ARY LAST INFORMATION IN REGARD TO PROVISIONAL GOVERNORS OF STATES
    240 (1866).

8   The *New York Times*'s front page *The Consummation!*, NEW YORK TIMES,
    Dec. 19, 1865, at 1.

8   William Lloyd Garrison WILLIAM LLOYD GARRISON, THOUGHTS ON AFRICAN
    COLONIZATION; OR AN IMPARTIAL EXHIBITION OF THE DOCTRINES, PRIN-
    CIPLES AND PURPOSES OF THE AMERICAN COLONIZATION SOCIETY. TOGETHER
    WITH THE RESOLUTIONS, ADDRESSES AND REMONSTRANCES OF THE FREE
    PEOPLE OF COLOR 143 (Part 1 1832).

9   Republican Illinois congressman Ebon Ingersoll WILLIAM E. NELSON, THE
    FOURTEENTH AMENDMENT FROM POLITICAL PRINCIPLE TO JUDICIAL DOC-
    TRINE 67 (2009).

10  The new amendment denied state governments Ibid. at 128.

10  In those days Mark Tushnet, *Civil Rights and Social Rights: The Future of the
    Reconstruction Amendments*, 25 LOYOLA OF LOS ANGELES LAW REVIEW 1207
    (1992); James M. McGoldrick Jr., *The Civil Rights Cases: The Relevancy of
    Reversing a Hundred Plus Year Old Error*, 42 SAINT LOUIS UNIVERSITY LAW
    JOURNAL 451 (1998).

10  Schurz, a German-born Union general I pieced together the Carl Schurz
    scene with a few different sources. GEORGE M. FREDRICKSON, THE BLACK
    IMAGE IN THE WHITE MIND: THE DEBATE ON AFRO-AMERICAN CHARACTER
    AND DESTINY, 1817–1914 23, 43, 55–58 (1971); CARL SCHURZ, SPEECHES,
    CORRESPONDENCE AND POLITICAL PAPERS OF CARL SCHURZ 371–72 (1913);
    CARL SCHURZ, THE REMINISCENCES OF CARL SCHURZ 155–65 (Vol. 3 1909);
    see also IBRAM X. KENDI, STAMPED FROM THE BEGINNING: THE DEFINITIVE
    HISTORY OF RACIST IDEAS IN AMERICA (2017) for more information on the
    history of racist thought.

12  Stevens had articulated *Reconstruction Speech of the Hon. Thaddeus Stevens,
    Delivered in the City of Lancaster, September 7th, 1865.*

13  Stevens pushed for REPORT OF THE JOINT COMMITTEE ON RECONSTRUCTION,
    AT THE FIRST SESSION, THIRTY-NINTH CONGRESS III (PART 3 1866).

13  Committee chairman Lyman Trumbull BERNARD H. SIEGAN, THE SUPREME
    COURT'S CONSTITUTION: AN INQUIRY INTO JUDICIAL REVIEW AND ITS IMPACT
    ON SOCIETY 49 (1987); HENRY WILSON, HISTORY OF THE RECONSTRUCTION
    MEASURES OF THE THIRTY-NINTH AND FORTIETH CONGRESSES 1865–68
    119–29 (1868).

14  "Our fathers" THE CONGRESSIONAL GLOBE 2459 (1866).

14  the caste preservationist declared THE CONGRESSIONAL GLOBE 2538 (1866).

15  The Fourteenth Amendment, consequently *The Fourteenth Amendment and
    the Negro Race Question*, 45 AMERICAN LAW REVIEW 830, 833 (1911).

15  Two weeks after HARRISBURG TELEGRAPH, Aug. 13, 1868; KENNETH M.
    STAMPP, THE ERA OF RECONSTRUCTION: 1865–1877 189 (1967).

16  Two years later *Local Matters*, BALTIMORE SUN, Oct. 1, 1855, at 1; *The Fif-
    teenth Amendment*, BALTIMORE SUN, May 20, 1870, at 1.

16  If the former Confederacy prevented JOHN MABRY MATHEWS, LEGISLA-

TIVE AND JUDICIAL HISTORY OF THE FIFTEENTH AMENDMENT 17, 20–21 (1909).

16 On January 1, 1861 ALLEN CAPERTON BRAXTON, THE FIFTEENTH AMEND-MENT: AN ACCOUNT OF ITS ENACTMENT. A PAPER READ BEFORE THE VIRGINIA STATE BAR ASSOCIATION, AT HOT SPRINGS, VIRGINIA, ON AUGUST 22D, 1903 1–2, 16 (1903).

17 Maryland's Democratic governor *The Governor's Message,* BALTIMORE SUN, Jan. 7, 1870, at 1, 4; MARYLAND HOUSE JOURNAL 268–69 (1870); *The Comptroller's Report,* Jan. 22, 1870, at 2.

18 The spectrum's other FREDRICKSON, THE BLACK IMAGE IN THE WHITE MIND at 61, 184–85, 190.

18 That was the history The Douglass speech has been pulled together from a few sources. *Fifteenth Amendment Speech of Frederick Douglass,* https://msa .maryland.gov/; HON. EDWARD MCPHERSON, THE POLITICAL HISTORY OF THE UNITED STATES OF AMERICA DURING THE PERIOD OF RECONSTRUCTION (FROM APRIL 15, 1865, TO JULY 15, 1870) 54 (3rd ed. 1880).

19 Maintaining a caste system FREDRICKSON, THE BLACK IMAGE IN THE WHITE MIND at 64.

## FIRST LEG: THE TRINITY CONCEPTION

20 an Italianate building *Capitols of West Virginia,* https://www.wvencyclopedia .org/; DAVID HUNTER STROTHER, THE CAPITAL OF WEST VIRGINIA AND THE GREAT KANAWHA VALLEY ADVANTAGES, RESOURCES AND PROSPECTS (1872).

20 Saulsbury cautioned that John Reuben Sheeler, *The Negro in West Virginia Before 1900* 140, 149, 152, 154, 203 (PhD diss. 1954); Richard Lowe, *Another Look at Reconstruction in Virginia,* 32 CIVIL WAR HISTORY 32, 32 (1986).

20 West Virginia held a convention Richard Ogden Hartman, *A Constitution of Our Own: The Constitutional Convention of 1872 and the Resurrection of Confederate West Virginia* 58 (master's thesis 2004); *Constitutional Convention of 1872,* https://www.wvencyclopedia.org/.

21 A year later, that strain *Geo. Davenport's Death,* WHEELING DAILY INTELLI-GENCER, June 17, 1880, at 1; *Charleston Letter,* WHEELING DAILY INTELLI-GENCER, Feb. 24, 1873, at 3; *The Jury Law,* SPIRIT OF JEFFERSON, Mar. 4, 1873, at 2; *A New Question Under the Jury Law,* WHEELING DAILY INTEL-LIGENCER, July 17, 1873, at 2. *Geo. Davenport's Death,* WHEELING DAILY INTELLIGENCER, June 17, 1880, at 1; *Charleston Letter,* WHEELING DAILY INTELLIGENCER, Feb. 24, 1873, at 3; *The Jury Law,* Spirit of Jefferson, Mar. 4, 1873, at 2; *A New Question Under the Jury Law,* WHEELING DAILY INTELLI-GENCER, Jul. 17, 1873, at 2.

21 Republican congressman James Garfield confessed TALI MENDELBERG, THE RACE CARD CAMPAIGN STRATEGY, IMPLICIT MESSAGES, AND THE NORM OF EQUALITY 45 (2017); FREDRICKSON, THE BLACK IMAGE IN THE WHITE MIND at 62, 185.

22 Because of the state's poverty RONALD BUTCHART, SCHOOLING THE FREED PEOPLE: TEACHING, LEARNING, AND THE STRUGGLE FOR BLACK FREEDOM, 1861–1876 15 (2013); Harriet Beecher Stowe, *The Education of Freedmen,* 128 NORTH AMERICAN REVIEW 605, 605 (1879).

23 Stand alongside me The Strauder murder scene was pulled together from a variety of sources. Second Trial Transcript for *State v. Strauder,* Washington, D.C., National Archives; State v. Strauder, 8 W. Va. 686 (1874); State v.

Strauder, 11 W. Va. 745 (1877); HERMAN MELTON, PITTSYLVANIA COUNTY'S HISTORIC COURTHOUSE: THE STORY BEHIND *EX PARTE* VIRGINIA AND THE MAKING OF A NATIONAL LANDMARK (1999); *A Deliberate and Brutal Murder,* WHEELING DAILY REGISTER, Apr. 19, 1872, at 4; *The Strauder Murder Case!,* WHEELING DAILY REGISTER, May 9, 1873, at 4; Lucinda Thomas, 1880 Census, Wheeling, Ohio, West Virginia at 10; *Horrible Murder,* WHEELING DAILY INTELLIGENCER, Apr. 19, 1872, at 4; Robert Gillispie, 1870 Census, Wheeling Ward 2, Ohio, West Virginia at 29; Douglas S. Massey, *Residential Segregation and Neighborhood Conditions in U.S. Metropolitan Areas* in AMERICA BECOMING: RACIAL TRENDS AND THEIR CONSEQUENCES: VOL. 1 395 (2001); *Murder! $200 Reward,* WHEELING DAILY INTELLIGENCER, Apr. 22, 1872, at 2; *Arrest of Strauder,* WHEELING DAILY INTELLIGENCER, Apr. 25, 1872, at 4; NELSON, THE FOURTEENTH AMENDMENT FROM POLITICAL PRINCIPLE TO JUDICIAL DOCTRINE at 79; *The Strauder Case,* WHEELING DAILY INTELLIGENCER, Apr. 27, 1898, at 5.

25 On April 25, some Pittsburgh *Arrival of Strauder,* WHEELING DAILY INTELLIGENCER, Apr. 26, 1872, at 4.

26 The next morning Strauder I pieced together Strauder's court scene with a few different sources. Graves Registration Card for George Orrick Davenport from the Civil War; he enlisted with the Union Army in October 1861, serving as a lieutenant in the First Regiment of the Ohio Volunteer Light Artillery. He was discharged in January 1863, just months before his regiment fought in the Battle of Gettysburg in July; *Geo. Davenport's Death,* WHEELING DAILY INTELLIGENCER, June 17, 1880, at 1; WHEELING DAILY INTELLIGENCER, Oct. 4, 1865, at 4; *Strauder Discharged,* WHEELING DAILY REGISTER, May 2, 1881, at 4; *Legislative Rumpus,* SPIRIT OF JEFFERSON, Mar. 4, 1873, at 2; *What the Teetotalers Are Doing,* WHEELING DAILY REGISTER, Mar. 27, 1877, at 4; *The Register Compliments the Democracy,* WHEELING DAILY REGISTER, Nov. 5, 1880, at 1; WHEELING DAILY INTELLIGENCER, Sept. 13, 1877, at 4; WHEELING DAILY INTELLIGENCER, May 13, 1871, at 4; *That Troublesome Timepiece,* WHEELING DAILY REGISTER, Jan. 22, 1877, at 4; *The Wife Murder,* WHEELING DAILY INTELLIGENCER, Apr. 27, 1872, at 4.

27 "We the jury find" *The Strauder Murder Case!,* WHEELING DAILY REGISTER, May 9, 1873, at 4; *Murder Trial,* WHEELING DAILY INTELLIGENCER, May 6, 1873, at 4; *The Trial of Taylor Strauder,* WHEELING DAILY INTELLIGENCER, May 7, 1873, at 4; *The Strauder Murder,* WHEELING DAILY INTELLIGENCER, May 8, 1873, at 4; *The Strauder Murder Trial,* WHEELING DAILY INTELLIGENCER, May 9, 1873, at 4; *The Death Sentence,* WHEELING DAILY INTELLIGENCER, July 9, 1873, at 4.

27 But an obstacle stymied NELSON, THE FOURTEENTH AMENDMENT FROM POLITICAL PRINCIPLE TO JUDICIAL DOCTRINE at 155; JACK M. BALKIN, LIVING ORIGINALISM 191 (2014).

27 In 1869, the biracial Michael A. Ross, *Justice Miller's Reconstruction: The Slaughter-House Cases, Health Codes, and Civil Rights in New Orleans, 1861–1873,* 64 JOURNAL OF SOUTHERN HISTORY 649 (1998).

28 Campbell chased a transparent objective CHARLES LANE, THE DAY FREEDOM DIED: THE COLFAX MASSACRE, THE SUPREME COURT, AND THE BETRAYAL OF RECONSTRUCTION 116–21 (2008).

28 Writing the Supreme Court's The Slaughter-House Cases, 83 U.S. 36 (1873); Richard Aynes, *Constricting the Law of Freedom: Justice Miller, the Fourteenth Amendment, and the* Slaughter-House *Cases,* 70 CHICAGO-KENT LAW REVIEW, 628, 627–44 (1994); BALKIN, LIVING ORIGINALISM at 191.

29 Prior to the Fourteenth Amendment GERARD N. MAGLIOCCA, AMERICAN
FOUNDING SON: JOHN BINGHAM AND THE INVENTION OF THE FOURTEENTH
AMENDMENT 108 (2013).

30 We wait here I pieced together the Toliver lynching scene from a few sources.
*Horrible Murder,* SHEPHERDSTOWN REGISTER, Oct. 11, 1873, at 2; *The Talifero
Case—The Execution Postponed,* WHEELING DAILY REGISTER, July 31, 1874,
at 1; *Sentence of John Toliver,* SPIRIT OF JEFFERSON, June 9, 1874, at 2; SPIRIT
OF JEFFERSON, July 28, 1874, at 2; JUSTIN STEVENS, HAUNTED MARTINS-
BURG 22–23, 35 (2016); *The Hanging of Toliver,* SHEPHERDSTOWN REGISTER,
Aug. 22, 1874, at 3; *The Hanging by a Mob of the Negro Convict Taliferro, at
Martinsburg, Thursday Night,* WHEELING DAILY INTELLIGENCER, Aug. 17,
1874, at 1; *The Martinsburg Lynching,* SHIPPENSBURG NEWS, Aug. 22, 1874,
at 2; *Lynch Law,* SPIRIT OF JEFFERSON, Aug. 18, 1874, at 3; *The Murder Trial at
Martinsburg,* BALTIMORE SUN, Nov. 24, 1873, at 1; *The Supreme Court,* PHILA-
DELPHIA INQUIRER, Apr. 16, 1878, at 1; *Letter from Martinsburg,* WHEELING
DAILY REGISTER, Aug. 17, 1874, at 3.

32 The 1866 Civil Rights Act Martin H. Redish, *Revitalizing Civil Rights
Removal Jurisdiction,* 64 MINNESOTA LAW REVIEW 523, 526–27 (1980).

33 "[B]y virtue of the laws" *Strauder v. West Virginia,* SUPREME COURT RECORDS
AND BRIEFS.

33 In 1871, a North Carolina YORKVILLE ENQUIRER, Oct. 12, 1871, at 2; State v.
Lee Dunlap, 65 N.C. 491 (1871).

33 The proceedings then Stephen Cresswell, *The Case of Taylor Strauder,*
Archive Wheeling, available at: https://www.archivingwheeling.org/blog
/the-case-of-taylor-strauder.

33 again convicted Strauder *Taylor Strauder,* WHEELING DAILY INTELLIGENCER,
Nov. 6, 1874, at 4; *Strauder,* 11 W. Va. 745; *Taylor Strauder,* WHEELING DAILY
REGISTER, Mar. 10, 1875, at 4; WHEELING DAILY REGISTER, Mar. 11, 1875, at 4.

33 with Alpheus F. Haymond *Judge Haymond Grants a Supersedeas in the Case of
Taylor Strauder,* WHEELING DAILY INTELLIGENCER, Mar. 10, 1875, at 1.

34 At one in the afternoon *The Inauguration,* NEW YORK HERALD, Mar. 6, 1877,
at 3.

35 On November 17, 1877 *Strauder,* 11 W. Va. 745; *Taylor Strauder's Case,*
WHEELING DAILY INTELLIGENCER, Nov. 19, 1877.

35 Back in June 1876 *The Courts,* WHEELING DAILY REGISTER, June 18, 1876,
at 4.

36 On April 15, 1878 *West Virginia's Unconstitutional Law Against Colored Jurors,*
SPIRIT OF JEFFERSON, Apr. 23, 1878, at 2; *An Interesting Case,* RALEIGH
OBSERVER, Apr. 16, 1878, at 1; *Important Decision,* MEMPHIS DAILY APPEAL,
Apr. 16, 1878, at 1.

37 Later that afternoon *Writ of Error in Taylor Strauder's Case,* WHEELING DAILY
INTELLIGENCER, Apr. 16, 1878, at 4.

37 The central character I pieced together the story of the Reynolds broth-
ers from various sources. *Arrest of a County Judge,* STAUNTON SPECTATOR,
Mar. 18, 1879, at 2; PROCEEDINGS OF THE NATIONAL CONFERENCE OF COL-
ORED MEN OF THE UNITED STATES, HELD IN THE STATE CAPITOL AT NASH-
VILLE, TENNESSEE, MAY 6, 7, 8 AND 9, 1879, AT 40; *United States District Court
at Danville,* RICHMOND DISPATCH, Nov. 22, 1878, at 3; MELTON, PITTSYLVA-
NIA COUNTY'S HISTORIC COURTHOUSE at 2, 8, 11, 32; ALEXANDER BROWN,
THE CABELLS AND THEIR KIN: A MEMORIAL VOLUME OF HISTORY, BIOGRA-
PHY, AND GENEALOGY 442 (1895); A. M. Lybrook, *History of the Case of The
Commonwealth vs. Lee & Burrell Reynolds* (pamphlet 1880); RICHMOND DAILY

DISPATCH, Dec. 10, 1877, at 3; DAVID A. MOSS, DEMOCRACY 294 (2017); Lee Reynolds v. The Commonwealth, 74 Va. 834 (1880); Virginia v. Rives, 100 U.S. 313 (1880); Ex Parte Reynolds, 20 F. Ca. 586 (W.D. Vir. 1878); JOURNAL OF THE SENATE OF VIRGINIA (1877); *Virginia v. Rives*, SUPREME COURT RECORDS AND BRIEFS; Redish, *Revitalizing Civil Rights Removal Jurisdiction* at 523, 526–27; *United States District Court at Danville*, RICHMOND DISPATCH, Nov. 22, 1878, at 3; Ex Parte Reynolds et al., 3 Hughes, 559 (W.D. Va. 1878); *White and Black*, PHILADELPHIA TIMES, Dec. 4, 1878, at 4.

39 On December 4, 1878 RICHARD G. LOWE, REPUBLICANS AND RECONSTRUCTION IN VIRGINIA, 1856–70 57–61 (1991); VIRGINIA GENERAL ASSEMBLY, SENATE JOURNAL (1878).

40 vilified around the country *United States Interference in Virginia Courts*, NEW HAVEN REGISTER, Nov. 30, 1878, at 1 and Dec. 11, 1878, at 3; *Virginia*, COLUMBUS DAILY ENQUIRER, Dec. 30, 1878, at 1; *Is State Power a Nullity*, STAUNTON SPECTATOR, Dec. 10, 1878, at 2.

40 told the reporter *Virginia Juries*, NEW YORK DAILY HERALD, Dec. 11, 1878, at 3.

41 "The fourth section" LANCASTER INTELLIGENCER JOURNAL, Feb. 28, 1879, at 2; *The Indicted Virginia Judges*, NEW YORK TRIBUNE, Mar. 15, 1879, at 3.

42 *Norfolk Landmark* rebuked *A Shameful Plot*, NORFOLK LANDMARK, Mar. 5, 1879, at 2; *Federal vs. State Authority*, BALTIMORE SUN, Feb. 27, 1879, at 1; *Rives's Revenge*, RICHMOND DISPATCH, Feb. 28, 1879, at 3; *Ex Parte Virginia*, SUPREME COURT RECORDS AND BRIEFS.

43 Later that evening *Colored Men Standing Up for Their Rights*, HARRISBURG TELEGRAPH, Apr. 8, 1879, at 1; *Richmond*, PHILADELPHIA TIMES, Apr. 8, 1879, at 1; BUFFALO MORNING EXPRESS AND ILLUSTRATED BUFFALO EXPRESS, Apr. 8, 1879, at 1; *The Color Agitation in Virginia*, BALTIMORE SUN, Apr. 9, 1879, at 1.

43 Many of Thomas Jefferson's contemporaries WILLIAM JENNINGS BRYAN, THE COMMONER CONDENSED 204 (Vol. 2 1903).

43 Rives believed that *The Virginia Habeas Corpus Case Continued*, RICHMOND DISPATCH, Apr. 9, 1879, at 3; *Report on Rives's Usurpation*, RICHMOND DISPATCH, Jan. 20, 1879, at 2; *"The Equal Protection of Laws,"* SUMMIT COUNTY BEACON, Mar. 26, 1879, at 2.

44 As you look around I premised this scene for constitutional interpretation on the great book by Jack Balkin. BALKIN, LIVING ORIGINALISM.

48 On October 15, 1879 *Washington*, CHICAGO TRIBUNE, Oct. 16, 1879, at 4.

49 "stands at the front rank of second-rate lawyers" PAUL KENS, THE SUPREME COURT UNDER MORRISON R. WAITE, 1874–1888 16 (2012).

49 "The question is an exceedingly delicate one" MELTON, PITTSYLVANIA COUNTY'S HISTORIC COURTHOUSE.

49 The longest-serving justice PHILIP GREELY CLIFFORD, NATHAN CLIFFORD, DEMOCRAT (1803–1881) 14 (1922); David J. Garrow, *Mental Decrepitude on the U.S. Supreme Court: The Historical Case for a 28th Amendment*, 67 CHICAGO LAW REVIEW 995, 1006 (2000).

49 Seventy-five-year-old Republican Noah Swayne Richard L. Aynes, *The Continuing Importance of Congressman John A. Bingham and the Fourteenth Amendment*, 36 AKRON LAW REVIEW 589, 612 (2003).

49 The sixty-three-year-old Republican Samuel Miller Michael A. Ross, *Melancholy Justice: Samuel Freeman Miller and the Supreme Court During the Gilded Age*, 33 JOURNAL OF SUPREME COURT HISTORY 134, 142–44 (2008).

49 Lincoln tapped Democrat Stephen Johnson Field Speer v. See Yup Co., 13

Cal. 73 (1859); Charles J. McClain Jr., *The Chinese Struggle for Civil Rights in Nineteenth Century America: The First Phase, 1850–1870*, 72 CALIFORNIA LAW REVIEW 529, 549 (1984).

49 Although a stroke enfeebled him PETER CHARLES HOFFER, WILLIAM JAMES HULL HOFFER, & N. E. H. HULL, THE FEDERAL COURTS: AN ESSENTIAL HISTORY 195 (2006).

49 Justice John Marshall Harlan Alan F. West, *John Marshall Harlan and the Constitutional Rights of Negroes: The Transformation of a Southerner*, 66 YALE LAW REVIEW 637 (1957).

49 Virginia attorney general Field FREDERICK CLIFTON PIERCE, FIELD GENEALOGY; BEING THE RECORD OF ALL THE FIELD FAMILY IN AMERICA, WHOSE ANCESTORS WERE IN THIS COUNTRY PRIOR TO 1700 1140 (Vol. 2 1901).

50 Field moved to the empty *The Rives Mandamus*, NEW ORLEANS DAILY DEMOCRAT, Oct. 16, 1879, at 1; RESOLUTIONS ADOPTED BY THE GENERAL ASSEMBLY IN REGARD TO THE USURPATION OF POWER BY THE FEDERAL JUDICIARY IN VIRGINIA, Feb. 8, 1879, at 3; *Virginia v. Rives*, SUPREME COURT RECORDS AND BRIEFS.

51 The next day *Ex Parte Virginia*, SUPREME COURT RECORDS AND BRIEFS.

51 *Strauder v. West Virginia* SUPREME COURT RECORDS AND BRIEFS; BIOGRAPHICAL PUBLISHING COMPANY, MEN OF WEST VIRGINIA 20–25 (1903).

53 On January 27, 1880 MINNEAPOLIS MESSENGER, Feb. 6, 1880, at 8; Glenn Schwendemann, *Wyandotte and the First Exodusters of 1879*, KANSAS HISTORICAL SOCIETY, https://www.kshs.org/; BROOKS D. SIMPSON, THE RECONSTRUCTION PRESIDENTS 218 (2009); *Stalwarts and Stalwarts*, NEW YORK TIMES, Oct. 6, 1879, at 4; Roy Garvin, *Benjamin, or "Pap," Singleton and His Followers*, 33 JOURNAL OF NEGRO HISTORY 7, 12 (1948).

54 Dovener entered the Ohio County jail WHEELING DAILY INTELLIGENCER, Mar. 2, 1880, at 1.

55 When deciding any case *Strauder*, 100 U.S. 303.

56 Was the right to an impartially selected jury panel MICHAEL KLARMAN, FROM JIM CROW TO CIVIL RIGHTS: THE SUPREME COURT AND THE STRUGGLE FOR RACIAL EQUALITY 136 (2006).

56 *Ex Parte Virginia* proved easy Ex Parte Virginia, 100 U.S. 339 (1879).

56 *Virginia v. Rives*, though *Rives*, 100 U.S. 313; *Federal Jurisdiction: The Civil Rights Removal Statute Revisited*, 1967 DUKE LAW JOURNAL 136, 172–73, n181 (1967).

57 A month later Cresswell, *The Case of Taylor Strauder.*

57 Davenport, not two months after WHEELING DAILY INTELLIGENCER, Mar. 24, 1880, at 2; CINCINNATI DAILY STAR, June 9, 1880, at 5; BELMONT CHRONICLE, June 10, 1880, at 3; *Death of George O. Davenport*, WHEELING DAILY INTELLIGENCER, June 9, 1880, at 4; WHEELING DAILY INTELLIGENCER, Mar. 24, 1880, at 2; CINCINNATI DAILY STAR, June 9, 1880, at 5; BELMONT CHRONICLE, June 10, 1880, at 3.

58 Later that month *Burwell Reynolds on Trial*, NORFOLK VIRGINIAN, June 22, 1880, at 1; *Virginia News*, ALEXANDRIA GAZETTE, June 24, 1880, at 2; *Danville*, CHARLOTTE DEMOCRAT, Nov. 26, 1880, at 1; MELTON, PITTSYLVANIA COUNTY'S HISTORIC COURTHOUSE at 78–79.

58 On May 2, 1881 *Strauder*, WHEELING DAILY INTELLIGENCER, May 4, 1881, at 4.

59 Two years earlier Blyew v. United States, 80 U.S. 581 (1871); ALEXANDER TSESIS, THE THIRTEENTH AMENDMENT AND AMERICAN FREEDOM 64–66 (2004).

## SECOND LEG: THE PROTECTION RETRACTION

60 It commences *Philadelphia,* AURORA GENERAL ADVERTISER, Feb. 19, 1793, at 3; *Congress,* PENNSYLVANIA GAZETTE, Feb. 20, 1793, at 1.

60 The 1788 kidnapping of John Davis Paul Finkleman, *The Kidnapping of John Davis and the Adoption of the Fugitive Slave Law of 1793,* 56 JOURNAL OF SOUTHERN HISTORY 397, 398, 407 (1990).

61 In sin-disguising prose JACOBUS TENBROEK, EQUAL UNDER LAW 63 (1965).

61 bloodline courses through Frank W. Hackett, *Mr. Justice Bradley,* 4 GREEN BAG 145 (1892); Charles Fairman, *What Makes a Great Justice—Mr. Justice Bradley and the Supreme Court, 1870–1892,* 30 BOSTON UNIVERSITY LAW REVIEW 49 (1950); Christopher Waldrep, *Joseph P. Bradley's Journey: The Meaning of Privileges and Immunities,* 34 JOURNAL OF SUPREME COURT HISTORY 149 (2009); Ruth Ann Whiteside, *Justice Joseph Bradley and the Reconstruction Amendments* (PhD diss. 1981); WILLIAM DRAPER LEWIS, MISCELLANEOUS WRITINGS OF THE LATE HON. JOSEPH P. BRADLEY, ASSOCIATE JUSTICE OF THE SUPREME COURT OF THE UNITED STATES, WITH A SKETCH OF HIS LIFE BY HIS SON, CHARLES BRADLEY, A.M. AND A REVIEW OF HIS "JUDICIAL RECORD" (1902).

61 the Supreme Court will uphold Prigg v. Pennsylvania, 41 U.S. 539 (1842); Paul Finkleman, *Sorting Out Prigg v. Pennsylvania,* 24 RUTGERS LAW JOURNAL 605 (1993); Paul Finkleman, *Story Telling on the Supreme Court: Prigg v. Pennsylvania and Justice Joseph Story's Judicial Nationalism,* 1994 SUPREME COURT REVIEW 247 (1994).

62 Decades later, Congress will enact James Oliver Horton & Lois E. Horton, *A Federal Assault: African Americans and the Impact of the Fugitive Slave Law of 1850,* 68 CHICAGO-KENT LAW REVIEW 1179, 1180–81 (1993).

63 In 1859, Chief Justice Roger B. Taney Ableman v. Booth, 62 U.S. 506 (1858); H. Robert Baker, *The Fugitive Slave Clause and the Antebellum Constitution,* 30 LAW AND HISTORY REVIEW 1133 (2012).

64 On the afternoon of April 4, 1869 REPORT ON THE ALLEGED OUTRAGES IN THE SOUTHERN STATES BY THE SELECT COMMITTEE OF THE SENATE MARCH 10, 1871.

64 Marjorie Jones, once enslaved in North Carolina SLAVE NARRATIVES FROM THE FEDERAL WRITERS' PROJECT, 1936–1938, NORTH CAROLINA SLAVE NARRATIVES: A FOLK HISTORY OF SLAVERY IN NORTH CAROLINA FROM INTERVIEWS WITH FORMER SLAVES 144–45 (2006).

64 But after the war FONER, RECONSTRUCTION at 443–44.

65 On March 7, 1870 JAMES MICHAEL MARTINEZ, CARPETBAGGERS, CAVALRY, AND THE KU KLUX KLAN: EXPOSING THE INVISIBLE EMPIRE DURING RECONSTRUCTION 24 (2007); Loryn Clausen, *A Missed Opportunity: United States v. Hall and the Battle over the Fourteenth Amendment* (master's thesis 2007).

65 On March 23, 1870 The background information on Justice Bradley was pulled together from a few sources. Fairman, *What Makes a Great Justice* at 58; Whiteside, *Justice Joseph Bradley and the Reconstruction Amendments* at 38, 58, 75, 77, 97–100, 104, 150; JOSEPH P. BRADLEY, FAMILY NOTES RESPECTING THE BRADLEY FAMILY OF FAIRFIELD, AND OUR DESCENT THEREFROM WITH NOTICES OF COLLATERAL ANCESTORS ON THE FEMALE SIDE FOR THE USE OF MY CHILDREN 41 (1894); Waldrep, *Joseph P. Bradley's Journey* at 149; Hackett, *Mr. Justice Bradley* at 150–51; LEWIS, MISCELLANEOUS WRITINGS OF THE LATE HON. JOSEPH P. BRADLEY.

67 Put yourself XI WANG, THE TRIAL OF DEMOCRACY: BLACK SUFFRAGE AND NORTHERN REPUBLICANS, 1860–1910 60, 63 (1997).

67 On February 21, 1870 THE CONGRESSIONAL GLOBE 3613 (Forty-First Congress, Second Session 1870); SARAH VAN V. WOOLFOLK, GEORGE E. SPENCER: A CARPETBAGGER IN ALABAMA 41–43 (1966); JAMES GILLESPIE BIRNEY LETTERS, 1831–1857 (1966); Jospeh Tussman & Jacobus tenBroek, *The Equal Protection of the Laws*, 37 CALIFORNIA LAW REVIEW 341 (1949); DAVID QUIGLEY, CONSTITUTIONAL REVISION AND THE CITY: THE ENFORCEMENT ACTS AND URBAN AMERICA, 1870–1894 64 (2008); Jonathan Obert, *A Fragmented Force: The Evolution of Federal Law Enforcement in the United States, 1870–1900* 29 JOURNAL OF PUBLIC HISTORY 640, 641 (2017); Alfred Avins, *Federal Power to Punish Individual Crimes Under the Fourteenth Amendment: The Original Understanding*, 43 NOTRE DAME LAW REVIEW 317 (1968); REPORT ON THE ALLEGED OUTRAGES IN THE SOUTHERN STATES BY THE SELECT COMMITTEE OF THE SENATE, MARCH 10, 1871.

67 In the spacious rectangular Senate Chamber *Thirty-Fifth Congress*, NEW YORK DAILY HERALD, Jan. 5, 1859, at 5.

69 On May 31, 1870 Clausen, *A Missed Opportunity* at 3.

70 Ohio's Democratic Party convened The Ohio Democrats scene was pieced together with a few sources. *The Bill of Abominations*, CINCINNATI ENQUIRER, June 2, 1870, at 2; *Speech of Hon. L. D. Campbell*, GREENVILLE DEMOCRAT, June 8, 1870, at 2; *Democratic State Convention*, CINCINNATI ENQUIRER, June 2, 1870, at 1; OSMAN CASTLE HOOPER, HISTORY OF THE CITY OF COLUMBUS, OHIO FROM THE FOUNDING OF FRANKLINTON IN 1797, THROUGH THE WORLD WAR PERIOD, TO THE YEAR 1920 283 (1920); JNO. B. JEFFERY'S GUIDE AND DIRECTORY TO THE OPERA HOUSES, THEATRES, PUBLIC HALLS, BILL POSTERS, ETC. OF THE CITIES AND TOWNS OF AMERICA 219 (1883); WILLIAM HORATIO BARNES, LEWIS D. CAMPBELL, OF OHIO (1879).

71 Watch as nearly thirty men I pieced together the Boyd killing from various sources. William Warren Rogers, *The Boyd Incident: Black Belt Violence During Reconstruction*, 21 CIVIL WAR HISTORY 309 (1975); Clausen, *A Missed Opportunity* at 7–8, 21, 27, 36, 43–44, 47–48, 52, 85; TUSCALOOSA INDEPENDENT MONITOR, Dec. 28, 1869, at 2; MONTGOMERY WEEKLY ADVERTISER, Jan. 4, 1870, at 2; *The Eutaw Homicide*, SELMA MORNING TIMES, Apr. 10, 1870, at 3; Waldrep, *Joseph P. Bradley's Journey;* Melinda Meek Hennessey, *Political Terrorism in the Black Belt: The Eutaw Riot*, 1980 ALABAMA REVIEW 35 (1980).

73 Here in downtown Eutaw on the morning of October 25 ALABAMA STATE JOURNAL, Nov. 4, 1870, at 1; Clausen, *A Missed Opportunity* at 27–28, 54–55, 66, 85; Hennessey, *Political Terrorism in the Black Belt.*

75 Eight days after the riot Waldrep, *Joseph P. Bradley's Journey* at 149, 155; Whiteside, *Justice Joseph Bradley and the Reconstruction Amendments* at 179–82; GEORGE R. GOETHALS, PRESIDENTIAL LEADERSHIP AND AFRICAN AMERICANS: "AN AMERICAN DILEMMA" FROM SLAVERY TO THE WHITE HOUSE 97 (2015); *The Ku-Klux*, HARPER'S WEEKLY, Apr. 1, 1871, at 282; WANG, THE TRIAL OF DEMOCRACY at 84–85 (1997); Clausen, *A Missed Opportunity* at 84, 105–6.

79 in South Carolina they dismantled the Klan SLAVE NARRATIVES: A FOLK HISTORY OF SLAVERY IN THE UNITED STATES FROM INTERVIEWS WITH FORMER SLAVES VOL. XI PART 1 183 (1941); Lou Falkner Williams, *The Constitution and the Ku Klux Klan on Trial: Federal Enforcement and Local Resistance in South Carolina, 1871–1872*, 2 GEORGIA JOURNAL OF SOUTHERN LEGAL HISTORY 41 (1993).

79 As we enter the House Chamber on April 14, 1873 The legal analysis for this section relies on a few sources. TENBROEK, EQUAL UNDER LAW; ROBERT J.

HARRIS, THE QUEST FOR EQUALITY: THE CONSTITUTION, CONGRESS AND THE SUPREME COURT 1–56 (1977); ANDREW KULL, THE COLOR-BLIND CONSTITUTION 27 (2009); John P. Frank & Robert F. Munro, *The Original Understanding of Equal Protection of the Laws*, 50 COLUMBIA LAW REVIEW 131 (1950).

83  On January 30, 1873 1870 CENSUS RECORDS, William Garner, Matthew Faushee, and Hiram Reese.

84  He gave the inspectors *United States v. Reese*, SUPREME COURT RECORDS AND BRIEFS.

84  Garner left without voting United States v. Reese, 92 U.S. 214 (1876).

84  On December 17, 1873 LEXINGTON, KENTUCKY DIRECTORY 89 (1875).

84  He ascended the grand iron staircase *New Custom House*, LOUISVILLE DAILY JOURNAL, Aug. 6, 1858, at 3.

84  Wharton's courage courted deadly retribution ROSS A. WEBB, KENTUCKY IN THE RECONSTRUCTION ERA 76–77 (2015).

84  The Lincoln-appointed District Court judge *Blyew*, 80 U.S. 581.

85  Wharton's adversaries Patrick A. Lewis, *"All Men of Decency Ought to Quit the Army": Benjamin F. Buckner, Manhood, and Proslavery Unionism in Kentucky*, 107 REGISTER OF THE KENTUCKY HISTORICAL SOCIETY 513 (2009).

85  a Radical newspaper predicted INDIANA PROGRESS, Jan. 7, 1875, at 4.

86  On January 14 and 15, 1875 *From Washington*, RICHMOND DISPATCH, Jan. 19, 1875, at 3; *The Courts*, NATIONAL REPUBLICAN, Jan. 15, 1875, at 3; R. C. Parsons, *Franklin T. Backus*, MAGAZINE OF WESTERN HISTORY, Nov. 1885, at 9; *The Constitutionality of the Enforcement Act Argued Before the Supreme Court*, Nashville REPUBLICAN BANNER, Jan. 16, 1875, at 1.

86  Only one justice present Willard Hurst, *Review of Lincoln's Manager: David Davis*, by *Willard L. King*, 9 UNIVERSITY OF CHICAGO LAW SCHOOL RECORD 59 (1960).

86  former Republican senator from Oregon Sidney Teiser, *Life of George H. Williams: Almost Chief-Justice*, 47 OREGON HISTORICAL QUARTERLY 255 (1946).

86  Phillips supported the South's R. H. Battle, *Hon. Samuel Field Phillips, LL.D.*, 1 NORTH CAROLINA JOURNAL OF LAW 22 (1904); Robert D. Miller, *Samuel Field Phillips: The Odyssey of a Southern Dissenter*, 58 NORTH CAROLINA HISTORICAL REVIEW 263 (1981).

87  Under a thirty-seven-state flag *Franklin T. Backus*, MAGAZINE OF WESTERN HISTORY, Nov. 1885, at 9; *The Constitutionality of the Enforcement Act Argued Before the Supreme Court* at 1.

88  Some are from Grant Parish LANE, THE DAY FREEDOM DIED at 97; LEEANNA KEITH, THE COLFAX MASSACRE: THE UNTOLD STORY OF BLACK POWER, WHITE TERROR, AND THE DEATH OF RECONSTRUCTION 97 (2009).

89  William S. Calhoun, a wealthy Joel M. Sipress, *The Triumph of Reaction: Political Struggle in a New South Community, 1865–1898*, 305–18 (PhD diss. 1993).

90  Groups like the Knights of the White Camellia James G. Dauphine, *The Knights of the White Camelia and the Election of 1868: Louisiana's White Terrorists: A Benighting Legacy*, 30 JOURNAL OF THE LOUISIANA HISTORICAL ASSOCIATION 173 (1989).

90  The message beamed through Sipress, *The Triumph of Reaction* at 309–11, 315–16.

91  On March 25 HORRIBLE MASSACRE IN GRANT PARISH, LOUISIANA, TWO HUNDRED MEN KILLED, DETAILS OF THE OCCURRENCE, MEETING OF COLORED MEN IN NEW ORLEANS, ADDRESS AND SPEECHES 5 (1872); LANE, THE DAY FREEDOM DIED at 42.

92 On the night of March 31 LANE, THE DAY FREEDOM DIED at 71–72.

92 One of the men asked *The Grant Parish Prisoners*, NEW ORLEANS REPUBLICAN, May 1874, at 1.

92 Preparing for battle Sipress, *The Triumph of Reaction* at 318; KEITH, THE COLFAX MASSACRE at 88–93.

93 Those White soldiers The scene of the Colfax Massacre comes from various sources. LANE, THE DAY FREEDOM DIED at 42, 71–72, 88, 97–99, 101–4 (2008); KEITH, THE COLFAX MASSACRE at 88–93, 97, 101–5; Sipress, *The Triumph of Reaction* at 305–18; HORRIBLE MASSACRE IN GRANT PARISH, LOUISIANA; *The Grant Parish Prisoners*, NEW ORLEANS BULLETIN, May 27, 1874, at 1; PINCKNEY CHAMBERS, 1870 U.S. FEDERAL CENSUS, WARD 2, GRANT, LOUISIANA; *The Grant Parish Prisoners*, NEW ORLEANS REPUBLICAN, Mar. 4, 1874, at 1; *The Grant Parish Prisoners*, NEW ORLEANS REPUBLICAN, May 24, 1874, at 5.

96 On April 18, James Roswell Beckwith I pieced together the scene of the Colfax trials from a few different sources. *Louisiana*, CHICAGO TRIBUNE, Apr. 19, 1873, at 8; Whiteside, *Justice Joseph Bradley and the Reconstruction Amendments* at 206–8; LANE, THE DAY FREEDOM DIED at 126, 186–87; *The Grant Parish Case*, NEW ORLEANS REPUBLICAN, June 28, 1874, at 1.

97 In a calm, steady tone, Bradley LANE, THE DAY FREEDOM DIED at 161.

97 That amendment accomplished more than slavery's death John Anthony Scott, *Justice Bradley's Evolving Concept of the Fourteenth Amendment from the Slaughterhouse Cases to the Civil Rights Cases*, 25 RUTGERS LAW REVIEW 552, 558–60 (1971); Whiteside, *Justice Joseph Bradley and the Reconstruction Amendments* at 211–14.

97 Under Bradley's construction United States v. Cruikshank, 25 F. Cas. 707 (Bradley, Circuit Justice, C.C.D. La. 1874).

100 A few months after Bradley Leslie F. Goldstein, *How Equal Protection Did and Did Not Come to the United States, and the Executive Branch Role Therein*, 73 MARYLAND LAW REVIEW 190, 191 (2013); THE FOURTEENTH AMENDMENT AND THE STATES: A STUDY OF THE OPERATION OF THE RESTRAINT CLAUSES OF SECTION ONE OF THE FOURTEENTH AMENDMENT OF THE CONSTITUTION OF THE UNITED STATES 21 (1912); Michael W. McConnell, *The Forgotten Constitutional Moment*, 11 CONSTITUTIONAL COMMENTARY 115, 122–23 (1994).

101 "Under our present system of race distinctions" PHILIP DRAY, CAPITOL MEN: THE EPIC STORY OF RECONSTRUCTION THROUGH THE LIVES OF THE FIRST BLACK CONGRESSMEN 218 (2008); *Speeches of Other Black Members of Congress*, BLACK DISPATCH, June 1, 1933, at 4; CONGRESSIONAL RECORD, THE PROCEEDINGS AND DEBATES 944–45 (43rd Congress, 2nd Session Vol. 3 1875).

101 Let's submerge our heads Arthur Kinoy, *The Constitutional Right of Negro Freedom*, 21 RUTGERS LAW REVIEW 387 (1967); Paul Finkelman, *The Dred Scott Case, Slavery and the Politics of Law*, 20 HAMLINE LAW REVIEW 1 (1996); Erwin Chemerinsky, *Rethinking State Action*, 80 NORTHWESTERN UNIVERSITY LAW REVIEW 503 (1985–1986).

103 Much of White America Whiteside, *Justice Joseph Bradley and the Reconstruction Amendments* at 256; Earl M. Maltz, *The Civil Rights Act and the Civil Rights Cases: Congress, Court, and Constitution*, 44 FLORIDA LAW REVIEW 605 (1992).

103 On March 31, 1875 *Constitutionality of the Enforcement Act*, BALTIMORE SUN, Apr. 1, 1875, at 1; *The Enforcement Act Test Case*, BALTIMORE SUN, Apr. 2, 1875, at 1. The oral argument was covered in these newspaper articles.

103 Robert Hardin Marr *Biography of Judge Robert Hardin Marr*, available at: https://louisianadigitallibrary.org/.

108 The key question in *Reese* Reese, 92 U.S. 214.

109 In his majority *Cruikshank* opinion *Cruikshank*, 92 U.S. 542; James Gray Pope, *Snubbed Landmark: Why* United States v. Cruikshank (1876) *Belongs at the Heart of the American Constitutional Canon*, 49 HARVARD CIVIL RIGHTS–CIVIL LIBERTIES LAW REVIEW 386 (2014).

109 Back at the Hamburg warehouse Jenny Heckel, *Remembering Meriwether: White Carolinian Manipulation of the Memory of the Hamburg Massacre of 1876* (master's thesis 2016).

110 In 1873 WANG, TRIAL OF DEMOCRACY at 300.

110 By 1876 Ibid.

110 The era of enforcement *The Forty-Fourth Congress*, LOUISVILLE COURIER-JOURNAL, June 24, 1876, at 1.

110 During the previous leg of our journey I premised the compromise of 1877 scene on C. VANN WOODWARD, REUNION AND REACTION: THE COMPROMISE OF 1877 AND THE END OF RECONSTRUCTION (1966).

111 At ten minutes past three Scott, *Justice Bradley's Evolving Concept of the Fourteenth Amendment from the Slaughterhouse Cases to the Civil Rights Cases* at 567; Thomas Bailey Jr., *Grand Junction Saves Historic Depot from Ruin*, COMMERCIAL APPEAL, available at: https://archive.commercialappeal.com/; *The Civil Rights Cases*, SUPREME COURT RECORDS AND BRIEFS.

112 On August 4, 1880 Whiteside, *Justice Joseph Bradley and the Reconstruction Amendments* at 257; *The Civil Rights Cases*, SUPREME COURT RECORDS AND BRIEFS.

113 Gee refused and Stanley Bond on capias from *United States v. Murray Stanley*, June 7, 1876; *United States v. Murray Stanley*, RECORDS OF DISTRICT COURTS OF THE UNITED STATES, available at: https://www.docsteach.org/; *The Civil Rights Cases*, BROWN COUNTY WORLD, Oct. 25, 1883, at 2.

113 *United States v. Nichols* Demurrer from *United States v. Samuel Nichols*, Nov. 17, 1876, available at: https://www.docsteach.org/; JEFFERSON CITY STATE JOURNAL, Sept. 5, 1876, at 4.

113 On January 4, 1876 Alan F. Westin, *Ride-in!*, AMERICAN HERITAGE, Aug. 1962, available at: https://www.americanheritage.com/ride; ANNA HASSAN, LOREN MILLER: CIVIL RIGHTS ATTORNEY AND JOURNALIST 18–19 (2015); JETHRO K. LIEBERMAN, A PRACTICAL COMPANION TO THE CONSTITUTION: HOW THE SUPREME COURT HAS RULED ON ISSUES FROM ABORTION TO ZONING 92–93 (1999); Vanessa Hahn Lierley, *Badges of Slavery: The Struggle Between Civil Rights and Federalism During Reconstruction* 42–52 (master's thesis 2004).

114 Of the nine justices on the Court in 1883 *5519 Reversed*, ATLANTA CONSTITUTION, Jan. 23, 1883, at 1; United States v. Harris, 106 U.S. 629 (1883).

117 The racial landscape in America I pieced together the scene for the *Civil Rights Cases* with various works. The Civil Rights Cases, 109 U.S. 3 (1883); BARRY FRIEDMAN, THE WILL OF THE PEOPLE: HOW PUBLIC OPINION HAS INFLUENCED THE SUPREME COURT AND SHAPED THE MEANING OF THE CONSTITUTION 149 (2009); Scott, *Justice Bradley's Evolving Concept of the Fourteenth Amendment from the Slaughterhouse Cases to the Civil Rights Cases* at 568; James M. McGoldrick Jr., *The Civil Rights Cases: The Relevancy of Reversing a Hundred Plus Year Old Error*, 42 ST. LOUIS UNIVERSITY LAW JOURNAL 451 (1998); Scott, *Justice Bradley's Evolving Concept of the Fourteenth Amendment from the Slaughterhouse Cases to the Civil Rights Cases* at 552; Michael G. Collins, *Justice Bradley's Civil Rights Odyssey Revisited*, 70 TULANE LAW REVIEW 1979 (1996).

120 "What do you think of the civil rights decision?" *The Colored Race*, WHEELING DAILY INTELLIGENCER, Oct. 24, 1883, at 1.

121 "I have said that I do not despair on account of this decision" *Civil Rights*, MEMPHIS WEEKLY PUBLIC LEDGER, Oct. 23, 1883, at 2; NATIONAL REPUBLICAN, Oct. 23, 1883, at 4.

122 The fifty-year-old justice MALVINA SHANKLIN HARLAN, SOME MEMORIES OF A LONG LIFE 106–14 (2002).

123 Donning the black robe bestows *Civil Rights Cases*, 109 U.S. 3 at 26 (Harlan, J., dissenting); Kinoy, *The Constitutional Right of Negro Freedom.*

125 In *Pembina Consolidated Silver Mining Co. v. Pennsylvania* Pembina Consolidated Silver Mining Co. v. Pennsylvania, 125 U.S. 181 (1888); ADAM WINKLER, WE THE CORPORATIONS: HOW AMERICAN BUSINESSES WON THEIR CIVIL RIGHTS (2019).

## THIRD LEG: THE MISSISSIPPI INSPIRATION

127 writes a letter to James H. McKenney Cornelius Jones letter to Supreme Court April 1896, *Charley Smith v. Mississippi*, Washington, D.C., National Archives.

127 Jones practices law from his office R. VOLNEY RISER, DEFYING DISFRANCHISEMENT: BLACK VOTING RIGHTS ACTIVISM IN THE JIM CROW SOUTH, 1890–1908 46–73 (2010); *C.J. Jones Obituary*, Jones-Sadler Family Papers, Schomburg Center for Research in Black Culture; James A. Feldman, *"So Forcibly Presented by His Counsel, Who Are of His Race": Cornelius Jones, Forgotten Black Supreme Court Advocate and Fighter for Civil Rights in the* Plessy *Era*, 47 JOURNAL OF SUPREME COURT HISTORY 97 (2022).

127 Americans dub this region WILLIAM C. HARRIS, THE DAY OF THE CARPETBAGGER: REPUBLICAN RECONSTRUCTION IN MISSISSIPPI 487–88 (1979).

128 Gibson and Smith Gibson v. Mississippi, 162 U.S. 565 (1896); Charley Smith v. Mississippi, 162 U.S. 592 (1896).

129 Hiram Rhodes Revels Julius E. Thompson, *Hiram Rhodes Revels, 1827–1901: A Reappraisal*, 79 JOURNAL OF NEGRO HISTORY 297 (1994); *Visitors from Congress: Henry Wilson (1812–1875)*, MR. LINCOLN'S WHITE HOUSE, available at: https://www.mrlincolnswhitehouse.org.

129 In November 1869 HARRIS, THE DAY OF THE CARPETBAGGER at 66, 76, 257; ALBERT D. KIRWAN, REVOLT OF THE REDNECKS 67 (2015).

129 senator Henry Wilson ERNEST A. MCKAY, HENRY WILSON: PRACTICAL RADICAL, A PORTRAIT OF A POLITICIAN (1971). The speeches delivered in the Senate regarding Revels's admission to the Senate come from *The Congressional Globe*. THE CONGRESSIONAL GLOBE 1561–68 (PART 2 1866).

130 After Democratic senators LEE AND SHEPARD, CHARLES SUMNER: HIS COMPLETE WORKS, VOL. XVIII 5 (2020); CHARLES SUMNER, THE WORKS OF CHARLES SUMNER 349–51 (Vol. 2 1870); WILLIAM JAMES HULL HOFFER, THE CANING OF CHARLES SUMNER: HONOR, IDEALISM, AND THE ORIGINS OF THE CIVIL WAR (2010); CHARLES SUMNER & GEORGE FRISBIE HOAR, CHARLES SUMNER: HIS COMPLETE WORKS 74 (Vol. 3 1900).

130 Cheers and jeers ping-ponged *Congress, the Colored Member Admitted to His Seat in the Senate*, NEW YORK TIMES, Feb. 26, 1870, at 1; *Congressional*, PHILADELPHIA INQUIRER, Feb. 26, 1870, at 3.

131 Revels preached *Senator Revels' Lecture in Baltimore Last Night*, WASHINGTON DC NEW ERA, Mar. 10, 1870, at 3; *The Rise of the African Methodist Episcopal Church in Baltimore and the Bethel A.M.E. Church*, MARYLAND CENTER FOR HISTORY AND CULTURE, available at: https://www.mdhistory.org.

131 Months afterward *Cornelius Jones*, FREEDMAN'S BANK RECORDS, 1865–74,

Dec. 31, 1870, Warren County, Mississippi, Roll 15: Vicksburg, Mississippi; July 28, 1868–June 29, 1874.

131 Savor the enticing aroma of barbecue The story of what happened during the Clinton Riot comes from: BOUTWELL REPORT, MISSISSIPPI IN 1875. REPORT OF THE SELECT COMMITTEE TO INQUIRE INTO THE MISSISSIPPI ELECTION OF 1875 WITH THE TESTIMONY AND DOCUMENTARY EVIDENCE (1876); Douglas Richardson, *Incident at Moss Hill: The Clinton Riot of 1875 and the Assassination of Senator Charles Caldwell* (on file with author); *The Clinton Outrage*, WEEKLY MISSISSIPPI PILOT, Sept. 11, 1875, at 2.

132 By November 1869 I pieced together the background scene on Mississippi before the Clinton Riot from various sources. *Civil Rights Law of 1873*, Mississippi Encyclopedia, available at: https://mississippiencyclopedia.org/; NEIL R. MCMILLEN, DARK JOURNEY: BLACK MISSISSIPPIANS IN THE AGE OF JIM CROW 4 (1990); HARRIS, THE DAY OF THE CARPETBAGGER at 446, 451–52; JOURNAL OF THE SENATE OF THE STATE OF MISSISSIPPI AT A REGULAR SESSION THEREOF HELD IN THE CITY OF JACKSON, 1874 24–26 (1874); FREDRICKSON, THE BLACK IMAGE IN THE WHITE MIND at 46; BOUTWELL REPORT at 303, 352; Richardson, *Incident at Moss Hill;* VERNON LANE WHARTON, THE NEGRO IN MISSISSIPPI, 1865–1890 191 (1947).

134 Crawford spots six more suspicious-looking I pieced together the story of the Clinton Riot from various sources. BOUTWELL REPORT at 291–310, 318, 429–30, 445, 492–501, 522; Charley Caldwell, 1870 UNITED STATES FEDERAL CENSUS, Township 6, Hinds, Mississippi 59; Richardson, *Incident at Moss Hill; The Clinton Riot,* DAILY CLARION-LEDGER, Apr. 4, 1902, at 2; Charles Caldwell, *Murder,* WEEKLY MISSISSIPPI PILOT, Sept. 11, 1875, at 3.

138 Employers fired them Herbert Aptheker, *Mississippi Reconstruction and the Negro Leader Charles Caldwell,* 11 SCIENCE & SOCIETY 340, 365 (1947).

138 One man recalled BOUTWELL REPORT at 328.

138 Charley Caldwell wrote to Ames Ibid. at 33.

138 Then came Election Day Ibid. at 495–98.

139 one White Democrat explained *A Card,* MACON BEACON, Nov. 20, 1875, at 2.

139 Mississippi congressman John Roy Lynch JOHN ROY LYNCH, THE FACTS OF RECONSTRUCTION 151 (1913).

139 "What surprises me more, Mr. President" Ibid. at 147, 152–55.

140 Stay home! BOUTWELL REPORT at 435–40.

142 senator Lucius Q. C. Lamar EDWARD MAYES, LUCIUS Q. C. LAMAR: HIS LIFE, TIMES, AND SPEECHES, 1825–1893 397 (1896).

142 addressed this at the party's 1877 state convention *The New Party in Mississippi,* BUFFALO MORNING EXPRESS, Oct. 27, 1877, at 2; *Democratic State Ticket,* VICKSBURG HERALD, Aug. 17, 1877, at 1.

145 On September 2 I pieced together the scene on the Mississippi convention from a few different sources. WHARTON, THE NEGRO IN MISSISSIPPI at 213–15; *The State Convention,* WESSON MIRROR, Sept. 20, 1890, at 1; KIRWAN, REVOLT OF THE REDNECKS at 68, 75; William Alexander Mabry, *Disfranchisement of the Negro in Mississippi,* 4 JOURNAL OF SOUTHERN HISTORY 318, 327 (1938); JOURNAL OF THE PROCEEDINGS OF THE CONSTITUTIONAL CONVENTION OF THE STATE OF MISSISSIPPI (1890); Hon. E. F. Noel, *Mississippi's Primary Election Law,* 8 MISSISSIPPI HISTORICAL SOCIETY 239, 239–45 (1905).

146 "black as the ten of spades" LAFLORYA GAUTHIER, A BIOGRAPHY OF ISAIAH THORNTON MONTGOMERY (2021).

146 Only one Black Mississippian MCMILLEN, DARK JOURNEY at 20, 49; MISSIS-

SIPPI BLACK HISTORY MAKERS 156 (EDS. GEORGE A. SEWELL & MARGARET L. DWIGHT 2009).

147 Montgomery and his father JANET SHARP HERMAN, THE PURSUIT OF A DREAM 219–29 (1981).

147 Montgomery, shy and confident KIRWAN, REVOLT OF THE REDNECKS at 65; MCMILLEN, DARK JOURNEY at 20.

148 He spellbound the delegates *That Colored Orator,* NEW YORK WORLD, Oct. 1, 1890, at 1; *A Colored Cicero,* SANTA CRUZ SURF, Oct. 25, 1890, at 8; NEW YORK WORLD, Sept. 27, 1890, at 2.

148 On November 1 Mabry, *Disfranchisement of the Negro in Mississippi* at 331; MEMPHIS PUBLIC LEDGER, Oct. 20, 1890, at 2.

148 On October 21, 1890 FREDERICK DOUGLASS, GREAT SPEECHES BY FEDERICK DOUGLASS 100–3 (ED. JAMES DALEY 2013); THE NATIONAL REGISTER OF HISTORIC PLACES: VOL. 1 29 (UNITED STATES DEPARTMENT OF THE INTERIOR, NATIONAL PARK SERVICE 1976); WASHINGTON EVENING STAR, Oct. 22, 1890, at 2.

149 John Lynch, then an ex-congressman MCMILLEN, DARK JOURNEY at 51; Mabry, *Disfranchisement of the Negro in Mississippi* at 332; CLARION-LEDGER, Jan. 30, 1890, at 4; VICKSBURG HERALD, Jan. 6, 1981, at 3; VICKSBURG HERALD, June 3, 1985, at 4; VICKSBURG EVENING POST, Apr. 22, 1886, at 1.

149 In 1878 *C. J. Jones Obituary.*

150 On January 24, 1890 the CLARION-LEDGER, Jan. 30, 1890, at 4; *Opposes the Convention,* MEMPHIS DAILY COMMERCIAL, Jan. 25, 1890, at 1.

152 At about four I pieced together the killing of Stinson scene from a variety of sources. Jackson CLARION-LEDGER, Jan. 12, 1892, at 2; VICKSBURG EVENING POST, Jan. 12, 1892, at 4; *Negro Murderer Captured,* KANSAS CITY DAILY GAZETTE, Nov. 22, 1892, at 1; *He Is the Right Man,* KANSAS CITY DAILY GAZETTE, Nov. 23, 1892, at 1; *Will Leave for Mississippi Tonight,* KANSAS CITY DAILY GAZETTE, Nov. 30, 1892, at 1; *Negro Murderer Captured,* KANSAS CITY DAILY GAZETTE, Nov. 24, 1892, at 7; *He Fights a Requisition,* KANSAS CITY STAR, Nov. 28, 1892, at 2; *Gibson v. Mississippi,* U.S. SUPREME COURT RECORDS AND BRIEFS; *Gibson,* 162 U.S. 565.

154 home of Doc Thompson *Assassination,* VICKSBURG HERALD, Nov. 1, 1881, at 3; *A Murderous Affair,* GREENVILLE WEEKLY DEMOCRAT-TIMES, Nov. 5, 1881, at 2.

155 Lawrence County, Mississippi William F. Holmes, *Whitecapping: Anti-Semitism in the Populist Era,* 63 AMERICAN JEWISH HISTORICAL QUARTERLY 244, 245–48 (1974); William F. Holmes, *Whitecapping: Agrarian Violence in Mississippi, 1902–1906,* 35 JOURNAL OF SOUTHERN HISTORY 165, 166–67 (1969).

155 partner with Emanuel Molyneaux Hewlett *A Southerners Opinion of Our Courts,* WASHINGTON BEE, Mar. 14, 1896, at 4; *Rights of the Negro Argued,* WASHINGTON BEE, Dec. 21, 1895, at 1; *Two Colored Justices,* CAMBRIDGE CHRONICLE, Nov. 23, 1901, at 13.

156 On March 31, 1880 I pieced together the *Neal v. Delaware* scene from a variety of sources. *Tried Twice for His Life,* PHILADELPHIA TIMES, Dec. 5, 1881, at 1; *The Blackbird Outrage,* WILMINGTON DAILY GAZETTE, Mar. 31, 1880, at 1; WILMINGTON MORNING NEWS, Dec. 2, 1881, at 1; WILMINGTON MORNING NEWS, Nov. 24, 1883, at 2; MCMILLEN, DARK JOURNEY at 7; *Neal Wants to Be Hanged,* WILMINGTON DAILY NEWS, Aug. 28, 1880, at 1; *A Celebrated Delaware Case Recalled by Sacco-Vanzetti Appeals,* DELMARVA MORNING STAR, Aug. 28, 1927, at 11; *Waiting for the Verdict,* WILMINGTON MORNING NEWS,

DEC. 6, 1881, at 1; *See William Neal's Second Trial,* NEW YORK TIMES, Dec. 2, 1881, at 2; *Acquittal of William Neal,* BALTIMORE SUN, Dec. 7, 1881, at 1; *Neal Acquitted,* WILMINGTON MORNING NEWS, Dec. 7, 1881, at 1; *A Courageous Attorney Cheats the Gallows,* WILMINGTON MORNING NEWS, Mar. 17, 1980, at 18; *Neal v. Delaware,* SUPREME COURT RECORDS AND BRIEFS; Neal v. Delaware, 103 U.S. 370 (1880).

158 In 1878, John Bush I pieced together the *Bush v. Kentucky* scene from a variety of sources. George C. Wright, *Executions of Afro-Americans in Kentucky, 1870–1940,* 1 GEORGIA JOURNAL OF SOUTHERN LEGAL HISTORY 321, 328–330 (1991); CINCINNATI DAILY STAR, Feb. 6, 1879, at 3; Bush v. Commonwealth, 78 Ky. 268 (1880); *The Kentucky Capital,* CINCINNATI ENQUIRER, Nov. 19, 1879, at 5; *Ripening Gallows Fruit,* CINCINNATI ENQUIRER, May 30, 1879, at 5; *A Woman Accidentally Shot,* CINCINNATI ENQUIRER, Jan. 14, 1879, at 1; *Sentenced to Death,* NEW YORK HERALD, May 25, 1881, at 12; *Strauder,* 100 U.S. 303; Commonwealth v. Johnson, 78 Ky. 509 (Ky. Ct. App. 1880); *Hanged After Six Years of Trials,* DAILY GAZETTE, Nov. 22, 1884, at 1; *John Bush,* CHICAGO DAILY TRIBUNE, Nov. 22, 1884, at 6; Bush v. Kentucky, 107 U.S. 110 (1883).

160 One final case I pieced together the *Yick Wo v. Hopkins* scene from a variety of sources. ELAINE ELINSON & STAN YOGI, WHEREVER THERE'S A FIGHT: HOW RUNAWAY SLAVES, SUFFRAGISTS, IMMIGRANTS, STRIKERS, AND POETS SHAPED CIVIL LIBERTIES IN CALIFORNIA 43–45 (2009); *In re* Yick Wo, 9 P. 139 (Cal. 1885); Yick Wo v. Hopkins, 118 U.S. 356, 374 (1886).

161 As Jones toured D.C.'s courts *A Southerners Opinion of Our Courts,* WASHINGTON BEE, Mar. 14, 1896, at 4.

161 The light of precedent I premised my thinking on the legal arguments that Jones should make before the Supreme Court on a variety of sources. John Gibson v. State, 70 Miss. 554 (1893); GREENVILLE TIMES, June 23, 1894, at 5; GREENVILLE TIMES, Jan. 6, 1894, at 4; Gibson v. State, 16 so. 198 (Miss. 1894 unreported opinion).

164 In 1876, through fraud and violence I pieced together the South Carolina constitutional convention scene from a variety of sources. D. D. Wallace, *The South Carolina Constitutional Convention of 1895,* 4 SEWANEE REVIEW 348, 349–50 (1896); TERENCE FINNEGAN, A DEED SO ACCURSED: LYNCHING IN MISSISSIPPI AND SOUTH CAROLINA, 1881–1940 (2013); William V. Moore, *The South Carolina Constitution of 1895: An Introduction,* 24 JOURNAL OF POLITICAL SCIENCE 1 (1996); JOURNAL OF THE HOUSE OF REPRESENTATIVES OF THE STATE OF SOUTH CAROLINA 132 (1891); ANDERSON INTELLIGENCER, Sept. 4, 1895, at 2; ANDREW BILLINGSLEY, YEARNING TO BREATHE FREE: ROBERT SMALLS OF SOUTH CAROLINA AND HIS FAMILIES 91 (2007); SPEECHES AT THE CONSTITUTIONAL CONVENTION BY GEN. ROBT. SMALLS, WITH THE RIGHT OF SUFFRAGE PASSED BY THE CONSTITUTIONAL CONVENTION (ED. SARAH V. SMALLS 1896); George B. Tindall, *The Question of Race in the South Carolina Constitutional Convention of 1895,* 37 JOURNAL OF NEGRO HISTORY 277, 279 (1952).

165 On December 11, 1895 Johnston telegraph to Supreme Court in *Charley Smith v. Mississippi,* Washington, D.C., National Archives.

165 Johnston, the son of Amos Johnston DOROTHY OVERSTREET PRATT, SOWING THE WIND: THE MISSISSIPPI CONSTITUTIONAL CONVENTION OF 1890 120 (2017).

166 in the Magnolia *An Execution Stayed at the Last Moment,* NEW ORLEANS TIMES-PICAYUNE, July 18, 1895, at 7.

166 a gross underestimation of the number BOUTWELL REPORT at 360.

166 the first in a carriage *On the Way to the Grave*, NEW YORK TIMES, Mar. 29, 1888, at 1.

166 Observers anticipated a close JAMES W. ELY, THE CHIEF JUSTICESHIP OF MEL-VILLE W. FULLER, 1888–1910 4–8, 15–20 (2012).

168 Cleveland's second Ibid. at 9–10.

168 David Josiah Brewer J. Gordon Hylton, *David Josiah Brewer and the Christian Constitution*, 81 MARQUETTE LAW REVIEW 417, 417 (1998); J. Gordon Hylton, *The Judge Who Abstained in Plessy v. Ferguson: Justice David Brewer and the Problem of Race*, 61 MISSISSIPPI LAW JOURNAL 315 (1991); J. Gordon Hylton, *The Perils of Popularity: David Josiah Brewer and the Politics of Judicial Reputation*, 62 VANDERBILT LAW REVIEW 567 (2009).

169 Henry Billings Brown Robert J. Glennon, *Justice Henry Billings Brown: Values in Tension*, 44 UNIVERSITY OF COLORADO LAW REVIEW 553, 555–56 (1973).

169 George Shiras Jr. *George Shiras Jr.*, 2 CASE AND COMMENTARY 1 (1896); *George Shiras*, HISTORY CENTRAL, available at: https://www.historycentral.com/.

170 Edward Douglass White Walter E. Joyce, *Edward Douglass White: The Louisiana Years, Early Life and on the Bench*, 41 TULANE LAW REVIEW 751 (1966–1967); John W. Davis, *Edward Douglass White*, 7 AMERICAN BAR ASSOCIATION 377 (1921).

170 Rufus Peckham James W. Ely Jr., *Rufus W. Peckham and Economic Liberty*, 591 VANDERBILT LAW REVIEW 593 (2009).

171 After an all-White grand jury indicted Smith *Charley Smith*, 162 U.S. 592; *Charley Smith v. Mississippi*, SUPREME COURT RECORDS AND BRIEFS; FELDMAN, *"So Forcibly Presented by His Counsel, Who Are of His Race."*

173 Hewlett presented the oral argument *Gibson*, 162 U.S. 565; James H. Stone, *A Note on Voter Registration Under the Mississippi Understanding Clause, 1892*, 38 JOURNAL OF SOUTHERN HISTORY 293, 296 (1972); *Gibson v. Mississippi*, SUPREME COURT RECORDS AND BRIEFS.

173 A little after noon on a Saturday *John Gibson Executed Saturday*, NEW SOUTH, May 8, 1897, at 1; *Gibson*, 162 U.S. 565; *Charley Smith*, 162 U.S. 592.

175 The words that Justice Brown *The "Jim Crow" Case*, LOS ANGELES EXPRESS, May 18, 1896, at 1; *Plessy v. Ferguson*, SUPREME COURT RECORDS AND BRIEFS; *Plessy v. Ferguson*, 163 U.S. 537 (1896).

175 "Are you a colored man?" I pieced together the *Plessy* scene from various sources. KEITH WELDON MEDLEY, WE AS FREEMEN: PLESSY V. FERGUSON 14, 20–24, 45–55, 126, 139–47, 166 (2003); Anne Ulentin, *Free Women of Color and Slaveholding in New Orleans, 1810–1830* 34 (master's thesis 2007); Sheldon Novick, *Homer Plessy's Forgotten Plea for Inclusion: Seeing Color, Erasing Color-Lines*, 118 WEST VIRGINIA LAW REVIEW 1181 (2016).

177 writing for a seven-to-one majority Justice Brewer took no part in the case. Michael W. McConnell, *The Forgotten Constitutional Moment*, 11 CONSTITUTIONAL COMMENTARY 115, 139 (1994); Stanley J. Folmsbee, *The Origin of the First "Jim Crow" Law*, 15 JOURNAL OF SOUTHERN HISTORY 235 (1949); Gilbert Thomas Stephenson, *The Separation of the Races in Public Conveyances*, 3 AMERICAN POLITICAL SCIENCE REVIEW 180, 190–91 (1909).

180 Jones stood inside a courtroom I pieced together the Henry Williams murder and case from a variety of sources. *A Triple Murderer Arraigned*, NEW ORLEANS TIMES-DEMOCRAT, Jan. 17, 1896, at 6; *Pays the Penalty. Henry Williams Hangs After Much Delay. Known of Having Murdered Two Women*, BILOXI DAILY HERALD, Sept. 30, 1899, at 1; *Williams v. Mississippi*, 170 U.S. 213; *Williams v. Mississippi*, SUPREME COURT RECORDS AND BRIEFS.

181  held a rally in Greenville *1896 Rally Leaflet,* Jones-Sadler Family Papers, Schomburg Center for Research in Black Culture.

181  the Jackson *Daily Clarion* bragged Stone, *A Note on Voter Registration Under the Mississippi Understanding Clause* at 294.

181  petitioning the House of Representatives RISER, DEFYING DISFRANCHISE-MENT at 61–62.

182  On Catchings's behalf KIRWAN, REVOLT OF THE REDNECKS at 74; GREENVILLE WEEKLY DEMOCRAT-TIMES, Aug. 5, 1896, at 2; MISSISSIPPI CONSTITUTIONAL CONVENTION OF 1890 at 12–14; PROCEEDINGS OF THE REUNION OF THE SUR-VIVORS OF THE CONSTITUTIONAL CONVENTION OF 1890 ON THE TWENTIETH ANNIVERSARY OF THE ADOPTION OF THE CONSTITUTION, HELD IN THE SEN-ATE CHAMBER OF THE CAPITOL AT JACKSON, MISSISSIPPI, NOVEMBER 1ST, 1910. Jones also contested an election in 1898 as well. CONTESTED ELECTION CASE OF CORNELIUS J. JONES VS. T. C. CATCHINGS IN HOUSE OF REPRESENTA-TIVES OF 56TH CONGRESS OF THE UNITED STATES.

183  They all feared *The Poll Tax,* YAZOO HERALD, July 3, 1896, at 1.

184  a Black factory worker RISER, DEFYING DISFRANCHISEMENT at 55.

184  Ratliff seized Beale's bedstead Ibid. at 56.

185  The editor of the Jackson *Clarion-Ledger* JACKSON CLARION-LEDGER, Dec. 1, 1896, at 2.

185  Cooper's opinion in Henry Williams's case Ratliff v. Beale, 74 Miss. 247 (1896).

186  And hopefully coax requited Piero Gleijeses, *African Americans and the War Against Spain,* 73 NORTH CAROLINA HISTORICAL REVIEW 184, 184–88 (1996).

186  White said Ibid. at 188; CONGRESSIONAL RECORD, FIFTH CONGRESS, SECOND SESSION, VOL. XXXI 2556–57 (1898).

187  Black newspaper proved prophetic EDWARD L. AYERS, THE PROMISE OF THE NEW SOUTH: LIFE AFTER RECONSTRUCTION 332 (2007).

187  but the president stuck with McKenna ELY, THE CHIEF JUSTICESHIP OF MEL-VILLE W. FULLER at 29–30.

187  Born to an Irish immigrant father Richard J. Purcell, *Justice Joseph McKenna,* 56 RECORDS OF THE AMERICAN CATHOLIC HISTORICAL SOCIETY OF PHILADEL-PHIA 177 (1945).

187  centered the 1890 constitution convention LAWS OF THE STATE OF MISSIS-SIPPI FOR 1897 124; WEEKLY CLARION-LEDGER, May 27, 1897, at 2; *Gov-ernor's Message,* CANTON TIMES, Jan. 14, 1898, at 3; *Williams v. Mississippi,* SUPREME COURT RECORDS AND BRIEFS.

189  Here on May 12, 1898 I pieced together the Louisiana 1898 constitutional convention from various sources. George E. Cunningham, *Constitutional Disfranchisement of the Negro in Louisiana, 1898,* 29 NEGRO HISTORY BULLETIN 147, 147 (1966); ELY, THE CHIEF JUSTICESHIP OF MELVILLE W. FULLER at 30; *Yick Wo,* 118 U.S. 356; *Constitutions Are Sound,* DAILY PICAYUNE, Apr. 26, 1898, at 4; *The United States Supreme Court on the Suffrage Question,* ORLEANS SEMI-WEEKLY TIMES-DEMOCRAT, Apr. 29, 1898, at 4; *Saving the People from Themselves,* TIMES-PICAYUNE, July 24, 1898, at 4; FONER, RECONSTRUCTION at 590; *Pays the Penalty,* BILOXI DAILY HERALD, Sept. 30, 1899, at 1; C. J. Jones, *The Negro in the South,* MEMPHIS COMMERCIAL APPEAL, Nov. 10, 1901, at 10.

193  "And what is it that we want to do?" ADDRESS OF HON. JOHN B. KNOX OF CALHOUN, ON HIS INSTALLATION AS PRESIDENT OF THE CONSTITUTIONAL CONVENTION OF ALABAMA, MAY 22, 1901, 4 (1901).

193  "We are reunited. Sectionalism has disappeared," JILL LEPORE, THE STORY OF AMERICA: ESSAYS ON ORIGINS 317 (2012).

FOURTH LEG: THE SLAVERY REINTRODUCTION

194  On May 19, 1900 *A White Man Killed*, COLUMBUS DAILY ENQUIRER, May 20, 1900, at 1.

194  The unpaid advance rekindled Michael David Tegeder, *Prisoners of the Pines: Debt Peonage in the Southern Turpentine Industry, 1900–1930* 7, 14, 37–38, 86 (PhD diss. 1996).

195  Months prior PENSACOLA NEWS, Mar. 30, 1900, at 5; *The Moore Brothers*, PENSACOLA NEWS, Apr. 4, 1900, at 4.

195  The two turpentine operators had agreed *Tarrance v. State*, Trial Transcript, Escambia County, Florida, records; Tarrance v. Florida, 188 U.S. 519 (1903).

195  America remembers this period Elizabeth Sanders, *Rediscovering the Progressive Era*, 72 OHIO STATE LAW JOURNAL 1281 (2011); Nancy S. Dye, *Introduction* in GENDER, CLASS, RACE, AND REFORM IN THE PROGRESSIVE ERA 1–9 (EDS. NORALEE FRANKEL & NANCY S. DYE 1991).

196  Eliot introduces him EMMETT J. SCOTT & LYMAN BEECHER STOWE, BOOKER T. WASHINGTON: BUILDER OF A CIVILIZATION 37 (1916).

196  Weeks earlier BOOKER T. WASHINGTON'S OWN STORY OF HIS LIFE AND WORK 175–79 (ED. ALBON L. HOLSEY 1915).

197  On September 18, 1895 DEBORAH DAVIS, GUEST OF HONOR: BOOKER T. WASHINGTON, THEODORE ROOSEVELT, AND THE WHITE HOUSE DINNER THAT SHOCKED A NATION 66 (2012).

198  When Booker T. finished RODERICK BUSH, THE END OF WHITE WORLD SUPREMACY: BLACK INTERNATIONALISM AND THE PROBLEM OF THE COLOR LINE 55 (2009); Melbourne Cummings, *Historical Setting for Booker T. Washington and the Rhetoric of Compromise, 1895*, 8 JOURNAL OF BLACK STUDIES 75, 75–81 (1977). Further thinking from the scene is based on a few additional sources. Christopher E. Forth, *Booker T. Washington and the 1905 Niagara Movement Conference*, 72 JOURNAL OF NEGRO HISTORY 45, 45–47 (1987); Pero Gaglo Dagbovie, *Exploring a Century of Historical Scholarship on Booker T. Washington*, 92 JOURNAL OF AFRICAN AMERICAN HISTORY 239 (2007); Ronald E. Chennault, *Pragmatism and Progressivism in the Educational Thought and Practices of Booker T. Washington*, 44 PHILOSOPHICAL STUDIES IN EDUCATION 121 (2013).

198  "I feel like a huckleberry in a bowl of milk" ADDRESS OF BOOKER T. WASHINGTON, DELIVERED AT THE ALUMNI DINNER OF HARVARD UNIVERSITY, CAMBRIDGE, MASS., JUNE 24, 1896 (1901). I mined many sources to form my thoughts on Booker T. Washington and his ethos. They include: DAVIS, GUEST OF HONOR at 27, 42–43, 71; LOUIS R. HARLAN, BOOKER T. WASHINGTON: THE MAKING OF A BLACK LEADER, 1856–1901 110 (1972); RICHARD WOMSER, THE RISE AND FALL OF JIM CROW: THE COMPANION TO THE PBS TELEVISION SERIES (2014); RAY STANNARD BAKER, FOLLOWING THE COLOR LINE: AN ACCOUNT OF NEGRO CITIZENSHIP IN THE AMERICAN DEMOCRACY 221 (1908); WASHINGTON, THE STORY OF MY LIFE AND WORK at 154; FREDRICKSON, THE BLACK IMAGE IN THE WHITE MIND at 36; S.T.U., *What Can the Free Colored People Do for Themselves?*, THE LIBERATOR, Feb. 11, 1832, at 1; Nathan G. Alexander, *"The Curse of Race Prejudice": Debates About Racial "Prejudice" in the United States, c. 1750–1900*, 55 PATTERNS OF PREJUDICE 25 (2021); Francis H. Shaw, *Booker T. Washington and the Future of Black Americans*, 56 GEORGIA HISTORICAL QUARTERLY 193, 194–98 (1972); WINSTON JAMES, THE STRUGGLES OF JOHN BROWN RUSSWURM: THE LIFE AND WRITINGS OF A PAN-AFRICANIST PIONEER, 1799–1851 140 (2010); Board of Education v. Cumming, 103 Ga. 641 (1898).

202 *Cumming v. Richmond County Board of Education* Board of Education v. Cumming, 103 Ga. 641 (1898); Cumming v. Richmond County Board of Education, 175 U.S. 528 (1899); C. Ellen Connally, *Justice Harlan's Great Betrayal: A Reconsideration of Cumming v. Richmond County Board of Education*, 25 JOURNAL OF SUPREME COURT HISTORY 72, 73–86 (2000); *High Schools Are Abolished*, ATLANTA CONSTITUTION, July 11, 1897, at 17; AUGUSTA CHRON-ICLE, June 20, 1884, at 6; Benno C. Schmidt Jr., *Principle and Prejudice: The Supreme Court and Race in the Progressive Era. Part 1: The Heyday of Jim Crow*, 82 COLUMBIA LAW REVIEW 444, 470–72 (1982); J. Morgan Kousser, *Separate but Not Equal: The Supreme Court's First Decision on Racial Discrimination in Schools*, 46 JOURNAL OF SOUTHERN HISTORY 17, 18–44 (1980).

203 Henry William Ravenel HENRY WILLIAM RAVENEL, 1814–1887: PRIVATE JOURNAL 1865–1866 59; WHARTON, THE NEGRO IN MISSISSIPPI at 81–83.

204 On October 27, 1865 HERBERT HILL, BLACK LABOR AND THE AMERICAN LEGAL SYSTEM: RACE, WORK, AND THE LAW 65–68 (1985); JOEL WILLIAMSON, AFTER SLAVERY: THE NEGRO IN SOUTH CAROLINA DURING RECONSTRUCTION 73–74 (1965).

205 On January 15, 1900 The scene was derived from a newspaper article. *Guarding Jail in Madison*, AUGUSTA CHRONICLE, Jan. 16, 1900, at 1. More thinking on this was premised on a few sources. DAVID E. BERNSTEIN, ONLY ONE PLACE OF REDRESS: AFRICAN AMERICANS, LABOR REGULATIONS, AND THE COURTS FROM RECONSTRUCTION TO THE NEW DEAL 10–12 (2001); WILLIAM COHEN, AT FREEDOM'S EDGE: BLACK MOBILITY AND THE SOUTHERN WHITE QUEST FOR RACIAL CONTROL, 1861–1915 257 (1991); David E. Bernstein, *Thoughts on Hodges v. United States*, 85 BOSTON UNIVERSITY LAW REVIEW 811 (2005); David E. Bernstein, *Law and Economics of Post–Civil War Restrictions on Interstate Migration by African-Americans*, 76 TEXAS LAW REVIEW 781 (1997–1998); Miller Handley Barnes, *Law, Labor, and Land in the Postbellum Cotton South: The Peonage Cases in Oglethorpe County, Georgia, 1865–1940* 95–102 (PhD diss. 2000); Leo Alilunas, *Statutory Means of Impeding Emigration of the Negro*, 22 JOURNAL OF NEGRO HISTORY 148, 149–51 (1937).

206 Robert A. "Peg-Leg" Williams I pieced together the story of Williams from many newspaper articles. *City Niggers No Good*, CHARLOTTE NEWS, Mar. 15, 1890, at 2; *"Peg-Leg" in the City*, NEW BERN DAILY JOURNAL, May 28, 1890, at 1; *Local News*, NEW BERN DAILY JOURNAL, June 17, 1890, at 1; *"Peg-Leg" Williams*, NEW BERN DAILY JOURNAL, Aug. 31, 1890, at 1; State v. Moore, 113 N.C. 698 (N.C. 1893); Khayen Prentice, László Kónya, & David Prentice, *Was the African American Great Migration Delayed by Outlawing Emigrant Agents?*, JOURNAL OF THE ECONOMIC & BUSINESS HISTORY SOCIETY 4–13 (2018); *Guards Placed Around the Jail by Order of Governor Candler*, ATLANTA CONSTITUTION, Jan. 16, 1900, at 3; STATESVILLE RECORD AND LANDMARK, Sept. 5, 1889, at 1; *Peg-Leg*, WASHINGTON PROGRESS, Jan. 14, 1890, at 1; *Peg-leg on the Exodus*, CHARLOTTE NEWS, Feb. 12, 1890, at 4; *Exodus Agents Making Themselves Scarce*, WILMINGTON MESSENGER, Feb. 21, 1890, at 1; *Peg-Leg Williams Arrested*, ATLANTA CONSTITUTION, Feb. 25, 1890, at 1; *Charged with the Abduction of Two Colored Boys*, ASHEVILLE CITIZEN-TIMES, Feb. 26, 1890, at 1; *Peg Leg Williams*, ATLANTA CONSTITUTION, Mar. 1, 1890, at 5; *They Want*, BIRMINGHAM NEWS, Dec. 5, 1899, at 6; *Peg Leg Williams*, ARKANSAS DEMOCRAT, Dec. 19, 1899, at 8; *Williams Is in No Danger*, ATLANTA CONSTITUTION, Jan. 16, 1900, at 3; *Arrest of Peg-Leg Williams*, ATLANTA CONSTITUTION, Dec. 20, 1899, at 3; *Angry Mob in Madison*, AUGUSTA CHRONICLE, Jan. 15, 1900, at 1; *Mad Rush of Negroes from Middle Georgia*, AUGUSTA CHRON-

ICLE, Jan. 15, 1900, at 1; *Their Moses in Jail,* LOS ANGELES TIMES, Jan. 15, 1900, at 1; *About Twenty-Five Families Left Last Thursday Night,* ATLANTA CONSTITUTION, Jan. 16, 1900, at 3; *Guarding Jail in Madison,* AUGUSTA CHRONICLE, Jan. 16, 1900, at 1; *Judge Hart Signs Order Placing Williams in Green County Jail,* ATLANTA CONSTITUTION, Jan. 17, 1900, at 3; *The Act Is Constitutional,* AUGUSTA CHRONICLE, Jan. 17, 1900, at 1; *Madison Jail Was Guarded,* ATLANTA CONSTITUTION, Jan. 17, 1900, at 3; *Guard Placed Around Jail; Peg Leg Williams Arouses Ire of the Farmers,* SAVANNAH TRIBUNE, Jan. 20, 1900, at 1; *They Want Negroes Moved,* ATLANTA CONSTITUTION, Feb. 11, 1900, at 3; *Pegleg Williams,* ATLANTA CONSTITUTION, Jan. 26, 1900, at 10.

207    The emigrant agent law DANIEL A. NOVAK, THE WHEEL OF SERVITUDE: BLACK FORCED LABOR AFTER SLAVERY 29–41 (2015); William Cohen, *Negro Involuntary Servitude in the South, 1865–1940: A Preliminary Analysis,* 42 JOURNAL OF SOUTHERN HISTORY 31 (1976).

208    On January 16, 1900 *Madison Jail Was Guarded,* ATLANTA CONSTITUTION, Jan. 17, 1900, at 3; *The Act Is Constitutional,* AUGUSTA CHRONICLE, Jan. 17, 1900, at 1; *"Peg Leg" Goes to Federal Courts,* ATLANTA CONSTITUTION, Jan. 18, 1900, at 1; *Peg Leg Williams Again in Prison,* ATLANTA CONSTITUTION, Mar. 21, 1900, at 7.

209    In early May 1900 Isabel C. Barrows, *The Montgomery Conference,* OUTLOOK, May 19, 1900, at 160; *The Montgomery Conference,* MONTGOMERY ADVERTISER, May 3, 1900, at 4; *Brilliant Inaugural of the Southern Race Conference,* MONTGOMERY ADVERTISER, May 9, 1900, at 1; *Large Attendance at Race Conference,* PEOPLE'S WEEKLY TRIBUNE, May 5, 1900, at 1.

209    inside a newly constructed auditorium *The Great Hall Open to the Public,* MONTGOMERY ADVERTISER, Mar. 16, 1900, at 5; *The Auditorium,* MONTGOMERY ADVERTISER, Mar. 18, 1900, at 16; *The Thomas Concert,* MONTGOMERY ADVERTISER, Mar. 18, 1900, at 5; *The Auditorium Will Be Our Pride,* MONTGOMERY ADVERTISER, Feb. 4, 1900, at 13.

209    Booker T. ingested speeches Booker T. Washington, *The Montgomery Race Conference,* CENTURY MAGAZINE, Aug. 1900, at 630.

209    The night's last speaker RACE PROBLEMS OF THE SOUTH: REPORT OF THE PROCEEDINGS OF THE FIRST ANNUAL CONFERENCE HELD UNDER THE AUSPICES OF THE SOUTHERN SOCIETY FOR THE PROMOTION OF THE STUDY OF RACE CONDITIONS AND PROBLEMS IN THE SOUTH, AT MONTGOMERY, ALABAMA, MAY 8, 9, 10, A.D. 1900 25–38, 155–56, 178–94 (1900).

211    On November 30, 1900 Atlanta train depot scene: *Returning Arkansas Emigrant Tells Story of Many Trials,* ATLANTA CONSTITUTION, Dec. 1, 1900, at 5.

214    Henry Laurens Pinckney THE LIBERATOR, May 14, 1836, at 2.

215    abolitionists will view due process this way TENBROEK, EQUAL UNDER LAW at 50–53, 63–65, 119–22, 221–23, 281–95; Tussman and Jacobus tenBroek, *The Equal Protection of the Laws* at 341.

216    *Butchers' Union Co. v. Crescent City Co.* Butchers' Union Co. v. Crescent City Co., 111 U.S. 746 (1884).

216    *Allgeyer v. Louisiana* Allgeyer v. Louisiana, 165 U.S. 578 (1897).

216    On December 10, 1900 *"Peg" Williams to Get License,* ATLANTA CONSTITUTION, Dec. 13, 1900, at 7.

216    the Court addressed one main issue Williams v. Fears, 179 U.S. 270 (1900).

217    Georgia attorney general J. M. Terrell BERNSTEIN, ONLY ONE PLACE OF REDRESS at 10–25; *"Peg" Williams Must Pay Tax,* ATLANTA CONSTITUTION, Dec. 11, 1900, at 9.

218    Samuel M. Clyatt I pieced together the scene for Clyatt recapturing his

workers from various sources. BAKER, FOLLOWING THE COLOR LINE at 96; Tegeder, *Prisoners of the Pines* vii–viii, 1, 19, 88–99; Schmidt, *Principle and Prejudice* at 444, 653; PAGE SMITH, AMERICA ENTERS THE WORLD: A PEOPLE'S HISTORY OF THE PROGRESSIVE ERA AND WORLD WAR I 174–75 (1991); PAUL FINKELMAN, THE AGE OF JIM CROW: SEGREGATION FROM THE END OF RECON-STRUCTION TO THE GREAT DEPRESSION 429 (1992); Reba Ann Page, *"Wring-ing Their Bread from the Sweat of Other Men's Faces": The Persistent Use of Forced Labor in the Postbellum South* 212–25 (PhD diss. 2017).

220   At thirty minutes past three I pieced together the scene of Roosevelt becoming president from various sources. HENRY PRINGLE, THEODORE ROO-SEVELT: A BIOGRAPHY 162–64 (1932); *President Roosevelt After Taking Oath Meets Members of Cabinet,* BROOKLYN STANDARD UNION, Sept. 15, 1901, at 1; DAVIS, GUEST OF HONOR at 77, 141; HARLAN, BOOKER T. WASHINGTON at 305; DAVID W. BLIGHT, RACE AND REUNION: THE CIVIL WAR IN AMERICAN MEMORY 130–31 (2001); THOMAS G. DYER, THEODORE ROOSEVELT AND THE IDEA OF RACE 92–98, 105–9 (1992).

222   Roosevelt wrote Booker T. Washington Thomas J. Frusciano, *Theodore Roo-sevelt and the Negro in the Age of Booker T. Washington, 1901–1912* 1–14 (PhD diss. 1975); R. Volney Riser, *"The Milk in the Cocoanut": Booker T. Washington, Theodore Roosevelt, and the Fear of Conspiracy in Alabama's 1901 Constitutional Ratification Referendum,* 26 SOUTHERN HISTORIAN 30, 3–54 (2005).

222   One spring 1865 morning DAVIS, GUEST OF HONOR at 8.

223   They were free BOOKER T. WASHINGTON, UP FROM SLAVERY: AN AUTOBIOG-RAPHY 19–22 (1907).

223   debated even coming BOOKER T. WASHINGTON, MY LARGER EDUCATION: BEING CHAPTERS FROM MY EXPERIENCE 170 (1911).

223   Booker T. recommended JACKSON CLARION-LEDGER, Oct. 1, 1901, at 4; *True Story Told at Last of Booker Washington's Luncheon at White House,* WASHINGTON EVENING STAR, Nov. 15, 1915, at 4; Riser, *"The Milk in the Cocoanut."*

224   Booker T. traveled to Montgomery BRENT J. AUCOIN, THOMAS GOODE JONES: RACE, POLITICS, AND JUSTICE IN THE NEW SOUTH 117–18 (2016); DAVIS, GUEST OF HONOR at 169–81; DYER, THEODORE ROOSEVELT AND THE IDEA OF RACE at 102; WASHINGTON, MY LARGER EDUCATION at 170–72; HAR-LAN, BOOKER T. WASHINGTON at 310; WASHINGTON, UP FROM SLAVERY at 20; SCOTT AND STOWE, WASHINGTON: BUILDER OF A CIVILIZATION at 51; Riser, *"The Milk in the Cocoanut."*

225   Georgia-born mother WILLIAM ROSCOE THAYER, THEODORE ROOSEVELT: AN INTIMATE BIOGRAPHY 4 (1919).

225   On October 7 *Roosevelt Doesn't Care for Sectional Lines,* KNOXVILLE JOURNAL AND TRIBUNE, Sept. 22, 1901, at 1; WASHINGTON, MY LARGER EDUCATION at 174; *President Roosevelt's Emphatic Declaration,* WILMINGTON MORNING STAR, Sept. 22, 1901, at 4; *President Roosevelt's Appointment,* MONTGOMERY ADVER-TISER, Oct. 8, 1901, at 4.

226   On October 16, 1901 I pieced together the Roosevelt and Washington dinner scene from a few different sources. FORT PAYNE JOURNAL, Oct. 16, 1901, at 6; DAVIS, GUEST OF HONOR at 7–9, 187, 196, 200–202; WASHING-TON, MY LARGER EDUCATION at 174; *President Roosevelt's Emphatic Declara-tion,* WILMINGTON MORNING STAR, Sept. 22, 1901, at 4; *President Roosevelt's Appointment,* MONTGOMERY ADVERTISER, Oct. 8, 1901, at 4; WASHINGTON, MY LARGER EDUCATION at 175–76; HARLAN, BOOKER T. WASHINGTON at 311; Robert J. Norrell, *When Teddy Roosevelt Invited Booker T. Washington to Dine*

*at the White House,* 63 JOURNAL OF BLACKS IN HIGHER EDUCATION 70, 70–74 (2009).

227 Booker T. traveled through Florida WASHINGTON, MY LARGER EDUCATION at 176–79.

227 typically purchased a compartment BAKER, FOLLOWING THE COLOR LINE at 33, 64.

228 On October 17 *Negro Guest Entertained by Roosevelt,* ATLANTA CONSTITU-TION, Oct. 17, 1901, at 1.

228 The next day *Both Politically and Socially,* ATLANTA CONSTITUTION, Oct. 18, 1901, at 1.

228 A tornado in the South Norrell, *When Teddy Roosevelt Invited Booker T. Washington to Dine at the White House* at 70; DAVIS, GUEST OF HONOR at 210, 213, 229; Dewey W. Grantham Jr., *Dinner at the White House: Theodore Roosevelt, Booker T. Washington, and the South,* 17 TENNESSEE HISTORICAL QUARTERLY 112, 122–26 (1958).

228 The dinner happened during AUCOIN, THOMAS GOODE JONES at 119; Riser, *"The Milk in the Cocoanut."*

229 One day around 1906 ROBERT C. BANNISTER, RAY STANNARD BAKER: THE MIND AND THOUGHT OF A PROGRESSIVE 79–100 (1966).

229 Before Thomas Goode Jones's Riser, *"The Milk in the Cocoanut";* ROBERT J. NORRELL, UP FROM HISTORY: THE LIFE OF BOOKER T. WASHINGTON 242 (2011); Schmidt, *Principle and Prejudice* at 692.

230 The eighteen-year-old Federal Courthouse and Post Office I pieced together the scene of peonage arrests from various sources. *Negroes Sold into Slavery,* MONTGOMERY ADVERTISER, Mar. 22, 1903, at 1; *Statement Made by Mr. Turner,* BIRMINGHAM NEWS, Mar. 24, 1903, at 5; *About the Government Building,* MONTGOMERY ADVERTISER, Mar. 1, 1833, at 4; *The Government Building,* WEEKLY MONTGOMERY ADVERTISER, Dec. 23, 1884, at 3; *New Elevator,* MONTGOMERY ADVERTISER, Oct. 16, 1885, at 5; Alan Knight, *Mexican Peonage: What Was It and Why Was It?,* 18 JOURNAL OF LATIN AMERICAN STUDIES 41 (1986); PETE DANIEL, THE SHADOW OF SLAVERY: PEONAGE IN THE SOUTH, 1901–1969 45–49 (1972); AUCOIN, THOMAS GOODE JONES at 116–42; DOUGLAS A. BLACKMON, SLAVERY BY ANOTHER NAME: THE RE-ENSLAVEMENT OF BLACK AMERICANS FROM THE CIVIL WAR TO WORLD WAR II 201 (2009).

232 Judge Jones asked a little after noon I pieced together the scene of the *Peonage Cases* from various sources. Peonage Cases, 123 F. 671, 681 (M.D. Ala. 1903); AUCOIN, THOMAS GOODE JONES at 28, 120, 121; *Judge Jones Gives an Opinion to Grand Jury on Peonage Matters,* MONTGOMERY ADVERTISER, June 16, 1903, at 5; Schmidt, *Principle and Prejudice* at 664–65; *About the Government Building,* MONTGOMERY ADVERTISER, Mar. 6, 1833, at 1; DANIEL, THE SHADOW OF SLAVERY at 11, 21, 25, 46; BRENT J. AUCOIN, A RIFT IN THE CLOUDS: RACE AND THE SOUTHERN FEDERAL JUDICIARY, 1900–1910 58 (2007).

235 On April 11, 1904 *Saw Mill Men Take Up Fight,* ATLANTA CONSTITUTION, Apr. 12, 1904, at 2.

235 Three years earlier *Given Four Years,* WEEKLY TALLAHASSEEAN, Mar. 28, 1902, at 1.

236 Roosevelt's Justice Department DANIEL, THE SHADOW OF SLAVERY at 12, 21; Schmidt, *Principle and Prejudice* at 660; *Clyatt v. United States,* SUPREME COURT RECORDS AND BRIEFS; Clyatt v. United States, 197 U.S. 207 (1905).

237 Justice Oliver Wendell Holmes STEVEN GREEN, THE SECOND DISESTABLISHMENT CHURCH AND STATE IN NINETEENTH-CENTURY AMERICA 367 (2010).

237 Brewer addressed 150 WILLIAM ALLEN WILBUR, CHRONICLES OF CALVARY
BAPTIST IN THE CITY OF WASHINGTON 42, 94 (1914); THE SUPREME COURT
JUSTICES: ILLUSTRATED BIOGRAPHIES, 1789–1993 254 (1993); Linda Przy-
byszewski, *Judicial Conservatism and Protestant Faith: The Case of David J.
Brewer,* 91 JOURNAL OF AMERICAN HISTORY 471 (2004); David J. Brewer,
*The Right to Appeal,* INDEPENDENT, Oct. 29, 1903, at 2547–50; *United
States a Christian Nation,* WASHINGTON EVENING STAR, Feb. 10, 1905, at 17;
Dr. E. C. Rice, *Church Work for Men,* HOME MISSION MONTHLY, Oct. 1905,
at 384–86; DAVID J. BREWER, THE UNITED STATES: A CHRISTIAN NATION
70–71 (1905).

238 In his *Clyatt* opinion *Clyatt,* 197 U.S. 207.

238 "statutory privilege" MICHAEL J. BRODHEAD, DAVID J. BREWER: THE LIFE OF
A SUPREME COURT JUSTICE, 1837–1910 178 (1994).

240 Archibald H. Grimké *Beats the Big Stick,* WASHINGTON POST, Mar. 18, 1905,
at 9; Archibald H. Grimké, *Dixie's Social Evil,* NEW YORK AGE, Mar. 30, 1905,
at 1.

240 Roosevelt's Justice Department had successfully DANIEL, THE SHADOW OF
SLAVERY at 17–18.

241 At a quarter past seven *Big Welcome for President,* NEW YORK TRIBUNE, Feb. 14,
1905, at 1–2.

241 Just before ten at night EIGHTEENTH ANNUAL LINCOLN DINNER OF THE
REPUBLICAN CLUB OF THE CITY OF NEW YORK (1904); A COMPILATION OF THE
MESSAGES AND SPEECHES OF THEODORE ROOSEVELT, 1901–1905 560–66
(Vol. 1 1906).

241 Roosevelt segued into crime DYER, THEODORE ROOSEVELT AND THE IDEA OF
RACE at 92–109; see also KHALIL GIBRAN MUHAMMAD, THE CONDEMNATION
OF BLACKNESS (2010) for a longer exploration of the connection between
blackness and crime.

242 Thomas Dixon Jr. THOMAS DIXON (JR.), THE LEOPARD'S SPOTS: A ROMANCE
OF THE WHITE MAN'S BURDEN 1865–1900 338 (1902).

242 Georgia governor Allen Candler echoed Dixon *Candler on the Negro,* THE
WORLD REVIEW, May 18, 1901, at 314.

243 At ten in the morning *Whitecappers,* PINE BLUFF DAILY GRAPHIC, Aug. 23,
1903, at 12; ARKANSAS DEMOCRAT, Aug. 23, 1903, at 4.

243 William G. Whipple Bernstein, *The Law and Economics of Post–Civil War
Reconstructions on Interstate Migration by African-Americans* at 781; Pamela S.
Karlan, *Contracting the Thirteenth Amendment: Hodges v. United States,* 85
BOSTON UNIVERSITY LAW REVIEW 783 (2005); Boyett v. United States, 207
U.S. 581 (1907); David E. Bernstein, *Thoughts on Hodges v. United States*
at 811; Hodges v. United States, 203 U.S. 1 (1906); Robert J. Norrell, *Have
Historians Given Booker T. Washington a Bad Rap?,* 62 JOURNAL OF BLACKS IN
HIGHER EDUCATION 62, 62–69 (Winter 2008/2009); Page, *"Wringing Their
Bread from the Sweat of Other Men's Faces"* at 179–83.

244 Oliver Wendell Holmes Jr. Leonard A. Jones, *Oliver Wendell Holmes, The
Jurist,* 69 UNITED STATES LAW REVIEW 136 (1935); THE SUPREME COURT JUS-
TICES: ILLUSTRATED BIOGRAPHIES at 286–95; *Hon. Oliver Wendell Holmes,* 2
JOURNAL OF THE SOCIETY OF COMPARATIVE LEGISLATION 9, 9–10 (1900);
Shalom Kassan, *Oliver Wendell Holmes (1841–1935)—In Memoriam,* 11
ISRAEL LAW REVIEW 443 (1976); Edward B. Adams, *Oliver Wendell Holmes,*
15 GREEN BAG 1 (1903); Harry C. Shriver, *Oliver Wendell Holmes: Lawyer,* 24
A.B.A. JOURNAL 157 (1938).

245 William Rufus Day Harry B. Hutchins, *Justice William Rufus Day,* XI MICHI-

GAN ALUMNUS 2 (Apr. 1903); Joseph E. McLean, *William Rufus Day* (PhD diss. 1942).

245  "It is inconceivable, your honors" The oral argument transcript is included in SUPREME COURT RECORDS AND BRIEFS for Hodges v. United States, 203 U.S. 1 (1906).

249  On May 28, 1906 *Justice Brown Out*, WASHINGTON POST, May 29, 1906, at 2.

249  By a seven-to-two vote *Hodges*, 203 U.S. 1.

251  Caste preservationists insisted *The State of Negroes in Maryland*, CECIL WHIG, Dec. 22, 1866, at 2; CLARISSA OLDS KEELER, THE CRIME OF CRIMES OR THE CONVICT SYSTEM UNMASKED 3–16 (1907); Christopher Muller, *Freedom and Convict Leasing in the Postbellum South*, 124 AMERICAN JOURNAL OF SOCIOLOGY 367, 367–77 (2018).

251  As John T. Morgan James Gray Pope, *Mass Incarceration, Convict Leasing, and the Thirteenth Amendment: A Revisionist Account*, 94 NEW YORK UNIVERSITY LAW REVIEW 1465, 1468–1516 (2019).

252  "Wherever I found the lease system in the South" Collis Lovely, *The Abuses of Prison Labor*, THE SHOE WORKERS' JOURNAL 3–11 (Vol. 6).

253  In October 1906 I pieced together the story of Stirling from various sources. *Richard Barry, Slavery in the South To-Day*, COSMOPOLITAN, Mar. 1907, at 481–91; *To Investigate Peonage Practices*, SCRANTON TRIBUNE, Oct. 16, 1906, at 1; *Rich Spinster Died Alone*, LANCASTER NEW ERA, Sept. 3, 1907, at 5; *At the White House*, WASHINGTON EVENING STAR, Oct. 12, 1906, at 1; *Taste of Slavery, True Barbarism, Enthralls Many*, WASHINGTON TIMES, Oct. 13, 1906, at 1; *"Help the Slaves" Is Woman's Plea*, WASHINGTON TIMES, Oct. 14, 1906, at 10; *Florida Peonage Cases*, WASHINGTON EVENING STAR, Oct. 15, 1906, at 2; *Government Probe for Slave Story*, WASHINGTON TIMES, Oct. 15, 1906, at 10; *Moody Starts Peonage Investigation*, BOSTON EVENING TRANSCRIPT, Oct. 18, 1906, at 16; *Can It Be True?*, PENSACOLA JOURNAL, Oct. 21, 1906, at 4; *The South Florida Peonage Case*, PENSACOLA JOURNAL, Oct. 24, 1906, at 4; Julielynne Marie Anderson, *"Prosecuting Vice; etc.": Emma Stirling's Work for Children, Youth and Young Women*, 1894–95 (master's thesis 2007); Cohen, *Negro Involuntary Servitude in the South, 1865–1940; Two Cosbys Sentenced to Atlanta Penitentiary*, MONTGOMERY ADVERTISER, July 1, 1903, at 1; CHARLES W. RUSSELL, UNITED STATES DEPARTMENT OF JUSTICE, REPORT ON PEONAGE 7–8 (U.S. Department of Justice Report of 1908); Jerrell H. Shofner, *Mary Grace Quackenbos, a Visitor Florida Did Not Want*, 58 FLORIDA HISTORICAL QUARTERLY 273, 273–79 (1980); Page, *"Wringing Their Bread from the Sweat of Other Men's Faces"* at 8–13; Goldstein, *How Equal Protection Did and Did Not Come to the United States, and the Executive Branch Role Therein* at 190, 194–95.

255  On April 6, 1908 Schmidt, *Principle and Prejudice* at 675; Pete Daniel, *Up from Slavery and Down to Peonage: The Alonzo Bailey Case*, 57 JOURNAL OF AMERICAN HISTORY 654 (1970); DANIEL, THE SHADOW OF SLAVERY at 69–76.

256  The revised law stipulated Bailey v. State, 158 Ala. 18 (1910).

257  Inside Dorothy Industrial Hall Booker T. Washington, *The Training of Negro Women*, 46 SOUTHERN HARDWARE 115, 115–17 (1901).

258  Booker T. and a group of White folk AUCOIN, THOMAS GOODE JONES at 140–41; Schmidt, *Principle and Prejudice* at 677–81; DANIEL, THE SHADOW OF SLAVERY at 67–72; *Bailey*, 158 Ala. 18; Daniel, *Up from Slavery and Down to Peonage*.

260  Charles Evans Hughes, a Taft nominee MERLO JOHN PUSEY, CHARLES EVANS HUGHES 271–76 (1951).

260 "We at once dismiss from consideration" Bailey v. Alabama, 219 U.S. 219 (1911).

261 which constituted peonage and violated the Thirteenth Amendment Schmidt, *Principle and Prejudice* at 680–88.

262 although outsiders never learned of his involvement DANIEL, THE SHADOW OF SLAVERY at 79.

262 *United States v. Reynolds* United States v. Reynolds, 345 U.S. 1 (1953).

262 ignored the original racial sin *A Blow at Peonage*, 97 NEW OUTLOOK 47, 47–48 (1911); Laura I. Appleton, *The Secret History of the Carceral State*, MARYLAND LAW REVIEW (upcoming) (2024); Aziz Z. Huq, *Peonage and Contractual Liberty*, 101 COLUMBIA LAW REVIEW 351, 382–87 (2001).

263 Harry M. Daugherty ANNUAL REPORT OF THE ATTORNEY GENERAL OF THE UNITED STATES 132 (1921).

264 The all-White jury convicted *Tarrance*, 188 U.S. 519.

264 wrote to the black robes *Dave Powell letter to the Supreme Court, Tarrance v. Florida*, WASHINGTON, D.C., NATIONAL ARCHIVES.

265 It taught Black folk Brando Simeo Starkey, *Respectability Politics: How a Flawed Conversation Sabotages Black Lives*, ANDSCAPE, available at: https://andscape .com.

266 While visiting New York City *Dr. Washington Claimed by Death*, ATLANTA CONSTITUTION, Nov. 15, 1915, at 1.

## PART II: PRELUDE

269 Clarence Ellington *F.B.I. Scours Area of Negro Slaying*, NEW YORK TIMES, July 13, 1964, at 20; *Similar Incident Reported*, NEW YORK TIMES, July 12, 1964, at 54; *FP Negro Narrow Escapes in Georgia Blast at Car*, FORT PIERCE TRIBUNE, July 13, 1964, at 3; Jud Deakins, *Ellington Tells of Shooting*, PALM BEACH POST, July 13, 1964, at 13; *Racial Extremists Checked in Georgia*, PENSACOLA NEWS JOURNAL, July 14, 1964, at 2.

270 On November 4, 1944 Leslie G. Ainley, *Fenway Park Is Spectacle of Color as Leaders Rally to Chieftain*, BOSTON GLOBE, Nov. 5, 1944, at 7; Louis M. Lyons, *FDR Lashes at Dewey*, BOSTON GLOBE, Nov. 5, at 1, 6; Samuel B. Cutler, *Thousands Cheer F.D. in Boston Appearance*, BOSTON GLOBE, Nov. 5, 1944, at 1, 10; *President's Fenway Park Speech*, BOSTON GLOBE, Nov. 5, 1944, at 4; Virginia Pasley, *50,000 Bostonians Roar Welcome to F.D.R.*, NEW YORK DAILY NEWS, Nov. 5, 1944, at 36.

271 76 percent went for FDR SEAN J. SAVAGE, ROOSEVELT: THE PARTY LEADER 1932–1945 42–43 (1991).

271 had nabbed the Black vote NANCY JOAN WEISS, FAREWELL TO THE PARTY OF LINCOLN: BLACK POLITICS IN THE AGE OF F.D.R. 209–34 (2020).

272 to avert a march on Washington John H. Bracey Jr. and August Meier, *Allies or Adversaries?: The NAACP, A. Philip Randolph and the 1941 March on Washington*, 75 GEORGIA HISTORICAL QUARTERLY 1 (1991).

272 Warfare thrust Americans Robert L. Fleegler, *"Forget All Differences Until the Forces of Freedom Are Triumphant": The World War II–Era Quest for Ethnic and Religious Tolerance*, 27 JOURNAL OF AMERICAN ETHNIC HISTORY 59 64–59 (2008).

272 Gunnar Myrdal, a Swedish GUNNAR MYRDAL, AN AMERICAN DILEMMA: THE NEGRO PROBLEM AND MODERN DEMOCRACY 1015 (1944).

273 Lemuel Penn MARY PENICK MOTLEY, THE INVISIBLE SOLDIER: THE EXPERIENCE OF THE BLACK SOLDIER, WORLD WAR II 89 (ED. MARY PENICK MOTLEY

1987); BILL SHIPP, MURDER AT BROAD RIVER BRIDGE: THE SLAYING OF LEMUEL PENN BY THE KU KLUX KLAN (2017); Michal R. Belknap, *The Legal Legacy of Lemuel Penn*, 25 HOWARD LAW JOURNAL 467 (1982).

273 On July 17, 1946 *Bullets, Vote Not Connected in Taylor Death*, ATLANTA CONSTITUTION, July 26, 1946, at 4; *Lynching Foes Stage March of Protest to White House, Capitol*, EVENING STAR, July 29, 1946, at A4; *Group Hopes to See Truman for Protest on Lynchings*, EVENING STAR, July 30, 1946, at 4; *White House March by Colored Women Protests Lynchings*, EVENING STAR, July 30, 1946, at 13.

276 had penned his future wife HARRY S. TRUMAN & BESS WALLACE TRUMAN, DEAR BESS: THE LETTERS FROM HARRY TO BESS TRUMAN, 1910–1959 39 (1998).

276 And acted on it DONALD R. MCCOY & RICHARD T. RUETTEN, QUEST AND RESPONSE 45–54 (1973); J. MICHAEL MARTINEZ, A LONG DARK NIGHT: RACE IN AMERICA FROM JIM CROW TO WORLD WAR II 312 (2016); SAMUEL WALKER, PRESIDENTS AND CIVIL LIBERTIES FROM WILSON TO OBAMA: A STORY OF POOR CUSTODIANS 141 (2012).

276 At about thirty minutes past three in the morning E. Merton Coulter, *The Confederate Monument in Athens, Georgia*, 40 GEORGIA HISTORICAL QUARTERLY 230 (1956); SHIPP, MURDER AT BROAD RIVER BRIDGE; Belknap, *The Legal Legacy of Lemuel Penn*.

277 "A Scandinavian journalist tells me that throughout Europe" Walter White, *NAACP Petition to UN Emphasizes Human Rights*, AKRON BEACON JOURNAL, Oct. 24, 1947, at 6.

278 "Because freedom is indivisible and can" George Streator, *U.N. Gets Charges of Wide Bias in U.S.*, NEW YORK TIMES, Oct. 24, 1947, at 9; W. E. BURGHARDT DU BOIS, AN APPEAL TO THE WORLD: A STATEMENT ON THE DENIAL OF HUMAN RIGHTS TO MINORITIES IN THE CASE OF THE CITIZENS OF NEGRO DESCENT IN THE UNITED STATES OF AMERICA AND AN APPEAL TO THE UNITED NATIONS FOR REDRESS (1947); TO SECURE THESE RIGHTS: THE REPORT OF THE PRESIDENT'S COMMITTEE ON CIVIL RIGHTS 13 (1947); Hugh H. Smyth, *The N.A.A.C.P. Protest to UN*, 8 PHYLON 355, 355–56 (1947); MARY L. DUDZIAK, COLD WAR CIVIL RIGHTS: RACE AND THE IMAGE OF AMERICAN DEMOCRACY 44–46 (2011).

279 Around four in the morning *Text of Lackey's Statement Describing Shotgun Attack on Negroes in Car*, ATLANTA CONSTITUTION, Sept. 3, 1964, at 10; SHIPP, MURDER AT BROAD RIVER BRIDGE; Belknap, *The Legal Legacy of Lemuel Penn*.

280 On the morning of March 12, 1956 I pieced together the story of the Southern Manifesto from various sources. Brown v. Board of Education of Topeka, 347 U.S. 483; KLINKER & SMITH, THE UNSTEADY MARCH at 234–38; Brown v. Board of Education II, 347 U.S. 483 (1954); Sarah McCulloh Lemmon, *The Ideology of the Dixiecrat Movement*, 30 SOCIAL FORCES 162 (1951–1952); KARI FREDERICKSON, THE DIXIECRAT REVOLT AND THE END OF THE SOLID SOUTH, 1932–1968 2, 69 (2003); Woodrow Price, *Why Was Virginia's Mood Changed on School Plan?*, NEWS AND OBSERVER, July 13, 1956, at 1; Brent J. Aucoin, *The Southern Manifesto and Southern Opposition to Desegregation*, 55 ARKANSAS HISTORY QUARTERLY 173, 173–89 (1996); Mary L. Dudziak, Brown *as a Cold War Case*, 91 JOURNAL OF AMERICAN HISTORY 32, 32–40 (2004); Mary L. Dudziak, *Desegregation as a Cold War Imperative*, 41 STANFORD LAW REVIEW 61, 61–81 (1988); Justin Driver, *Supremacies and the Southern Manifesto*, 92 TEXAS LAW REVIEW 1053 (2014); JOHN KYLE DAY, THE SOUTHERN MANIFESTO: MASSIVE RESISTANCE AND THE FIGHT TO PRESERVE SEGREGATION 122–47 (2014); KEITH FINLEY, DELAYING THE DREAM: SOUTHERN SENATORS AND THE FIGHT AGAINST CIVIL RIGHTS, 1938–1965 138–46 (2008).

284 When the station wagon pulls SHIPP, MURDER AT BROAD RIVER BRIDGE.

284 On July 3, 1964 *Johnson Signs Broad Civil Rights Bill into Law*, BALTIMORE SUN, July 3, 1964, at 1, 4.

284 Before the bill's passage in the House HOUSE CONGRESSIONAL RECORD 15870–71 (1964); PROCEEDINGS AND DEBATES OF THE 88TH CONGRESS SECOND SESSION VOL. 110–PART 12 JUNE 29, 1964, TO JULY 21, 1964.

285 Johnson said, looking straight ahead PHILIP A. GODUTI JR. & PHILIP A. GODUTI, RFK AND MLK: VISIONS OF HOPE, 1963–1968 97–99 (2017).

286 Penn's head flops forward SHIPP, MURDER AT BROAD RIVER BRIDGE.

287 The Johnson administration's next bill STATEMENT BY ATTORNEY GENERAL NICHOLAS DEB. KATZENBACH, BEFORE THE SENATE COMMITTEE ON THE JUDICIARY ON A BILL TO ENFORCE THE FIFTEENTH AMENDMENT TO THE CONSTITUTION OF THE UNITED STATES, March 23, 1965.

289 Ervin, a former North Carolina Supreme Court justice FINLEY, DELAYING THE DREAM 140–41; JEFFREY K. SMITH, THE FIGHTING LITTLE JUDGE: THE LIFE AND TIMES OF GEORGE C. WALLACE 59 (2009); *Debate on Rights Short on Fireworks*, DAYTON DAILY NEWS, Mar. 24, 1965, at 41.

290 Johnson said in a slow *Text of Johnson Vote Rights Talk*, LOS ANGELES TIMES, Aug. 7, 1965, at 15; *"I Love Everybody": Dream of Slave Days Becomes a Reality*, PHILADELPHIA INQUIRER, Aug. 7, 1965, at 1.

290 And caste preservationism snatched it all away *Georgia Sniper Kills a Negro Educator*, NEW YORK TIMES, July 12, 1964, at 1, 54; *Educator Slain in South Buried*, NEW YORK TIMES, July 15, 1964, at 17; *Georgia: An Extreme Case*, TIME, Sept. 11, 1964, available at https://time.com/.

290 His wife told friends SHIPP, MURDER AT BROAD RIVER BRIDGE.

## FIFTH LEG: THURGOOD AND THE CASTE DERELICTION

293 plotted for it I pieced together some of the background for the *Brown* scene from various sources. RICHARD KLUGER, SIMPLE JUSTICE: THE HISTORY OF BROWN V. BOARD OF EDUCATION AND BLACK AMERICA'S STRUGGLE FOR EQUALITY 133–36 (1975); MARK V. TUSHNET, MAKING CIVIL RIGHTS LAW: THURGOOD MARSHALL AND THE SUPREME COURT, 1936–1961 12–13 (1994); JUAN WILLIAMS, THURGOOD MARSHALL: AMERICAN REVOLUTIONARY 23, 59, 62, 216 (2000); LELAND WARE, A CENTURY OF SEGREGATION: RACE, CLASS, AND DISADVANTAGE 23–24 (2018).

294 Marshall worked alongside Houston THURGOOD MARSHALL, MARSHALLING JUSTICE: THE EARLY CIVIL RIGHTS LETTERS OF THURGOOD MARSHALL 18 (ED. MICHAEL G. LONG 2011).

295 the grasshopper imparting the sensei's wisdom WILLIAMS, THURGOOD MARSHALL at 59.

295 Rather than attack public education for schoolchildren W. Edward Orser, *Neither Separate Nor Equal: Foreshadowing Brown in Baltimore County, 1935–1937*, 92 MARYLAND HISTORICAL MAGAZINE 5–36 (1997).

295 In Houston's first segregation case to reach the Supreme Court *Missouri ex rel. Gaines v. Canada* Missouri ex rel. Gaines v. Canada, 305 U.S. 337 (1935).

295 *Sipuel v. Board of Regents of the University of Oklahoma* Sipuel v. Board of Regents of the University of Oklahoma, 332 U.S. 631 (1948).

295 *Sweatt v. Painter* Sweatt v. Painter, 339 U.S. 629 (1950).

295 *McLaurin v. Oklahoma State Regents* McLaurin v. Oklahoma State Regents, 339 U.S. 637 (1950).

296 deciding to attack separate but equal directly *Association Hails Setbacks to Bias*, NEW YORK TIMES, June 28, 1950, at 25.

297 "As I understand" ARGUMENT: THE ORAL ARGUMENT BEFORE THE SUPREME COURT IN BROWN V. BOARD OF EDUCATION OF TOPEKA, 1952–55 (ORAL ARGUMENTS BEFORE THE SUPREME COURT) 37 (ED. LEON FRIEDMAN 1969).

298 Eight minutes before one WILLIAMS, THURGOOD MARSHALL at 225–27; *Brown*, 347 U.S. 483.

300 Late in the evening on New Year's Eve 1964 Daniel Geary, *The Moynihan Report: An Annotated Edition*, THE ATLANTIC, Sept. 14, 2015, available at: https://www.theatlantic.com.

300 the team emerged with a seventy-eight-page report OFFICE OF POLICY PLANNING AND RESEARCH, UNITED STATES DEPARTMENT OF LABOR, THE NEGRO FAMILY: THE CASE FOR NATIONAL ACTION (1965); DANIEL PATRICK MOYNIHAN, MILES TO GO: A PERSONAL HISTORY OF SOCIAL POLICY 177–79 (1996). See ALSO Gerald Naughton, *The Moynihan Report, the Watts Riots, and the Tropes of Reconstruction*, 20 [INTER]SECTIONS 40 (2017); WILLIAM RYAN, BLAMING THE VICTIM (1976).

301 This one-two punch coldcocked See also RICHARD ROTHSTEIN, THE COLOR OF LAW: A FORGOTTEN HISTORY OF HOW OUR GOVERNMENT SEGREGATED AMERICA (2017) for more information on residential segregation.

302 On June 4, 1965 *A New Rights Drive Needed, L.B.J. Says*, BALTIMORE EVENING SUN, June 5, 1965, at 3.

302 "You do not wipe away" Lyndon B. Johnson, *Commencement Address at Howard University*, June 4, 1965.

304 on August 17, 1965 *Dr. King Arrives Here to Study Riots Problems*, LOS ANGELES TIMES, Aug. 18, 1965, at 3; Sorin Adam Matei & Sandra Ball Rokeach, *Watts, the 1965 Los Angeles Riots, and the Communicative Construction of the Fear Epicenter of Los Angeles*, 72 COMMUNICATION MONOGRAPHS 301, 301–2 (2005); A REPORT BY THE GOVERNOR'S COMMISSION ON THE LOS ANGELES RIOTS, VIOLENCE IN THE CITY—AN END OR BEGINNING? (1965).

304 one Black college student GERALD HORNE, FIRE THIS TIME: THE WATTS UPRISING AND THE 1960s 182 (1995).

304 "I believe, and have said on many occasions" MARTIN LUTHER KING, JR., THE AUTOBIOGRAPHY OF MARTIN LUTHER KING, JR. (ED. CLAYBORNE CARSON 1998); available at: https://kinginstitute.stanford.edu/.

305 King continued Ibid.

305 Bill Moyers distributed copies MOYNIHAN, MILES TO GO at 178; Rowland Evans & Robert Novak, *See page of the Moynihan Report*, LOS ANGELES TIMES, Aug. 19, 1965, at 39.

306 White America deemed socially acceptable EDUARDO BONILLA-SILVA, RACISM WITHOUT RACISTS: COLOR-BLIND RACISM AND THE PERSISTENCE OF RACIAL INEQUALITY IN AMERICA 1–18 (2022); EDUARDO BONILLA-SILVA, WHITE SUPREMACY AND RACISM IN THE POST–CIVIL RIGHTS ERA 1–8 (2001).

306 *Meet the Press* RICK BALL, MEET THE PRESS: YEARS OF HISTORY IN THE MAKING, xv–xvi (1998).

309 On the morning WILLIAMS, THURGOOD MARSHALL at 3–14; WIL HAYGOOD, SHOWDOWN: THURGOOD MARSHALL AND THE SUPREME COURT NOMINATION THAT CHANGED AMERICA 6–7 (2015).

310 Johnson had planned Percy R. Luney Jr. *Thurgood Marshall as Solicitor General: An Opportunity to Fulfill a Dream*, 6 HARVARD BLACKLETTER JOURNAL 18 (1989).

311 On May 20, 1968 The story of the Washington protests is explored well in Marc Ariel Robinson, *The Black Power Movement and the Black Student Union (BSU) in Washington State, 1967–1970* 76–92 (PhD diss. 2012); Marc Robinson, *Black Student Union University of Washington History Notes* (on file with author).

311 Langston Hughes Sheryll D. Cashin, *Justice Thurgood Marshall: A Race Man's Race-Transcending Jurisprudence*, 52 HOWARD LAW JOURNAL 507, 975 (2009).

313 Thurgood Marshall visited Thurgood Marshall, *The Continuing Challenge of the 14th Amendment*, 1968 WISCONSIN LAW REVIEW 979 (1968); Holly Dunlop, *Justice Marshall Quiets UW Hecklers*, WISCONSIN STATE JOURNAL, Sept. 22, 1968, at 2.

314 Like many colleges and universities Richard A. Posner, *The DeFunis Case and the Constitutionality of Preferential Treatment of Racial Minorities*, 1974 SUPREME COURT REVIEW 1 (1974).

314 After oral argument DeFunis v. Odegaard, 416 U.S. 312 (1974).

315 When workers assembled I pieced together the Bakke backstory from a variety of sources. Robert Lindsey, *White/Caucasian—and Rejected*, NEW YORK TIMES, Apr. 3, 1977, at 209; JOEL DREYFUSS & CHARLES LAWRENCE, THE BAKKE CASE: THE POLITICS OF INEQUALITY 3–30 (1979); HOWARD BALL, THE BAKKE CASE: RACE, EDUCATION, AND AFFIRMATIVE ACTION 56–57 (2000); Bakke v. Regents of the University of California, 18 Cal. 3d 34 (1976).

319 Reynold Colvin Hon. Bridget Mary McCormack & Len Niehoff, *May It Displease the Court*, 44 LITIGATION 33, 37 (2018).

320 The Social Security Act of 1935 IRA KATZNELSON, WHEN AFFIRMATIVE ACTION WAS WHITE: AN UNTOLD HISTORY OF RACIAL INEQUALITY IN TWENTIETH-CENTURY AMERICA (2005).

320 Black folk received fewer *RACE—The Power of an Illusion BACKGROUND: A Long History of Affirmative Action—For Whites*, CALIFORNIA NEWSREEL, 2003, available at: https://newsreel.org.

321 On June 20, 1974 DREYFUSS & LAWRENCE, THE BAKKE CASE at 3–30; Bakke v. Regents of the University of California, 18 Cal. 3d 34 (1976); BALL, THE BAKKE CASE at 56–57.

322 The Democratic Party revamped Donald W. Beachler, *The South and the Democratic Presidential Nomination, 1972–1992*, 26 PRESIDENTIAL STUDIES QUARTERLY 402 (1996); Rick Farmer, *The Return of the Brokered Convention? Democratic Party Rules and Presidential Nominations* (2009), available at: https://www.uakron.edu/; Elaine C. Kamarck, *Delegate Allocation Rules in Presidential Nomination Systems: A Comparison Between the Democrats and the Republicans*, 4 JOURNAL OF LAW & POLICY 275 (1987–1988); David C. Paris & Richard D. Shingles, *Preference Representation and the Limits of Reform: The 1976 Democratic Convention*, 44 JOURNAL OF POLITICS 201 (1982); Jimmy Carter, *Democratic Nomination Acceptance Speech*, July 15, 1976.

322 cunning deployment of the Southern Strategy Nicol C. Rae, *The Democrats' "Southern Problem" in Presidential Politics*, 22 PRESIDENTIAL STUDIES QUARTERLY 135 (1992).

323 Heading a multiracial party forced Frank Brown, *Nixon's "Southern Strategy" and Forces Against Brown*, 73 JOURNAL OF NEGRO EDUCATION 191 (2004).

324 On June 7, 1977 JOSEPH A. CALIFANO JR., GOVERNING AMERICA: AN INSIDER'S REPORT FROM THE WHITE HOUSE AND THE CABINET (1981); Nancy Hicks, *Califano Says Quotas Are Necessary to Reduce Bias in Jobs and Schools*, NEW YORK TIMES, Mar. 18, 1977, at A1, A16; Rodger D. Citron, *A Life in the Law: An Interview with Drew Days*, 30 TOURO LAW REVIEW 153, 164 (2014).

325 nearly fifty educators David Bird, *Califano Concedes Error in Advocating Job Quotas*, NEW YORK TIMES, Apr. 1, 1977, at A1, A27.

326 On September 1, Attorney General Bell Ernest Holsendolph, *Carter Gets Draft of U.S. Stance on Reverse Discrimination Suit*, NEW YORK TIMES, Sept. 2, 1977, at A9.

327 A dismayed Califano watched as CALIFANO JR., GOVERNING AMERICA at 231–43.

328 Then on September 12 David E. Rosenbaum, *Carter Said to Back Bar to Race Quotas*, NEW YORK TIMES, Sept. 12, 1977, at A1, A24.

329 Young said STEVEN F. LAWSON, RUNNING FOR FREEDOM: CIVIL RIGHTS AND BLACK POLITICS IN AMERICA SINCE 1941 244 (2014).

329 After viewing it CALIFANO JR., GOVERNING AMERICA at 242.

330 In 1911 Fifth Avenue Coach Co. v. New York, 221 U.S. 467 (1911); Mark Tushnet, MAKING CONSTITUTIONAL LAW: THURGOOD MARSHALL AND THE SUPREME COURT, 1961–1991 94–96 (1997). See also TUSHNET, MAKING CIVIL RIGHTS LAW.

330 the Court invalidated minimum wage Adkins v. Children's Hospital, 261 U.S. 525 (1923); Lochner v. New York, 198 U.S. 45 (1905).

330 FDR's threats to add seats to the Supreme Court JOSEPH ALSOP & TURNER CATLEDGE, THE 168 DAYS (1938); LEONARD BAKER, BACK TO BACK: THE DUEL BETWEEN FDR AND THE SUPREME COURT (1967).

330 *United States v. Carolene Products Co.* United States v. Carolene Products Company, 304 U.S. 144 (1938); Felix Gilman, *The Famous Footnote Four: A History of the Carolene Products Footnote*, 46 SOUTH TEXAS LAW REVIEW 163 (2004); Sonu Bedi, *Collapsing Suspect Class with Suspect Classification: Why Strict Scrutiny Is Too Strict and Maybe Not Strict Enough*, 47 GEORGIA LAW REVIEW 301 (2013).

331 "The Japanese race is an enemy race" COMMISSION ON WARTIME RELOCA- TION AND INTERNMENT OF CIVILIANS, PERSONAL JUSTICE DENIED: REPORT OF THE COMMISSION ON WARTIME RELOCATION AND INTERNMENT OF CIVIL- IANS 66 (2012).

332 Gordon Hirabayashi GORDON K. HIRABAYASHI, A PRINCIPLED STAND: THE STORY OF HIRABAYASHI V. UNITED STATES (2013).

333 briefcase containing his diary Ibid. at 68.

333 Fred Korematsu LORRAINE K. BANNAI, ENDURING CONVICTION: FRED KORE- MATSU AND HIS QUEST FOR JUSTICE (2015).

334 *Skinner v. Oklahoma* decision Skinner v. State of Oklahoma, ex rel. William- son, 316 U.S. 535 (1942).

334 *Hirabayashi v. United States* Hirabayashi v. United States, 320 U.S. 81 (1943).

335 *Korematsu v. United States* Korematsu v. United States, 323 U.S. 214 (1944).

336 *Bolling v. Sharpe* Bolling v. Sharpe, 347 U.S. 497 (1954).

336 *McLaughlin v. Florida* McLaughlin v. Florida, 379 U.S. 184 (1964).

336 *Pace v. Alabama* Pace v. Alabama, 106 U.S. 583 (1883).

337 *Loving v. Virginia* Loving v. Virginia, 388 U.S. 1 (1967).

338 what triggers strict scrutiny For the legal analysis of this scene, I relied mainly on several sources. Owen M. Fiss, *Groups and the Equal Protection Clause*, 5 PHILOSOPHY & PUBLIC AFFAIRS 107 (1976); Greg Robinson & Toni Robinson, *Korematsu and Beyond: Japanese Americans and the Origins of Strict Scrutiny*, 68 LAW AND CONTEMPORARY PROBLEMS, 29, 29–33 (2005); Scott H. Dewey, *Of Loaded Weapons and Legal Alchemy, Great Cases and Bad (?) Law: Korematsu and Strict Scrutiny, 1944–2017*, 3 LEGAL INFORMATION REVIEW 43, 43–63 (2017–18); Eugene V. Rostow, *The Japanese American Cases—A*

*Disaster,* 54 YALE LAW JOURNAL 489, 490–92 (1945); Jack M. Balkin & Reva B. Siegel, *The American Civil Rights Tradition: Anticlassification or Antisubordination?,* 9 UNIVERSITY OF MIAMI LAW REVIEW 9 (2003).

338   In September 1977 BALL, THE BAKKE CASE at 91.

339   On the morning of October 12, 1977 Ibid. at 88. The legal arguments of the respective sides can be found in *Regents of the University of California v. Bakke,* SUPREME COURT RECORDS AND BRIEFS.

342   "The first case on today's calendar" Regents of the University of California v. Bakke, *Oral Argument,* OYEZ, available at: https://www.oyez.org.

342   William Brennan Jr. TIMOTHY L. HALL, SUPREME COURT JUSTICES: A BIO-GRAPHICAL DICTIONARY 358–61 (2001).

343   Potter Stewart Joel Jacobsen, *Remembered Justice: The Background, Early Career and Judicial Appointments of Justice Potter Stewart,* 35 AKRON LAW REVIEW 227 (2002).

343   *Milliken v. Bradley* Milliken v. Bradley, 418 U.S. 717 (1974).

343   Byron White HALL, SUPREME COURT JUSTICES at 368–71.

344   Chief Justice Burger Ibid. at 384–87.

344   Harry Blackmun Ibid. at 388–91.

344   G. Harrold Carswell of Georgia John Paul Hill, *Nixon's Southern Strategy Rebuffed: Senator Marlow W. Cook and the Defeat of Judge G. Harrold Carswell for the U.S. Supreme Court,* 112 REGISTER OF KENTUCKY HISTORICAL SOCIETY 613 (2014).

344   Lewis Franklin Powell HALL, SUPREME COURT JUSTICES at 392–95.

344   William Hubbs Rehnquist Ibid. at 396–99; MARK V. TUSHNET, A COURT DIVIDED: THE REHNQUIST COURT AND THE FUTURE OF CONSTITUTIONAL LAW 19 (2005).

345   he professed DAVID M. O'BRIEN, JUSTICE ROBERT H. JACKSON'S UNPUBLISHED OPINION IN BROWN V. BOARD: CONFLICT, COMPROMISE, AND CONSTITU-TIONAL INTERPRETATION 68 (2017).

345   John Paul Stevens HALL, SUPREME COURT JUSTICES at 401–3.

350   they met inside their elegant Conference Room I pieced together this scene from various sources. WILLIAMS, THURGOOD MARSHALL at 365; BALL, THE BAKKE CASE at 261–67; Lee Epstein & Jack Knight, *Piercing the Veil: William J. Brennan's Account of Regents of the University of California v. Bakke,* 19 YALE LAW & POLICY REVIEW 341 (2001); Powell Papers, Bakke Case, available at: https://scholarlycommons.law.wlu.edu/powellpapers/.

354   Chief Justice Burger said Regents of the University of California v. Bakke, *Opinion Announcement,* June 26, 1978, OYEZ, available at: https://www.oyez .org; Regents of the University of California v. Bakke, 438 U.S. 265 (1978); *Focus of Historic Battle in Civil Rights Law,* NEW YORK TIMES, June 29, 1978, at 1.

356   On November 18, 1978 Stuart Auerbach, *Marshall Calls Black Gains More "Myth" than Reality,* LOS ANGELES TIMES, Nov. 19, 1978, at 1; MICHAEL D. DAVIS & HUNTER R. CLARK, THURGOOD MARSHALL: WARRIOR AT THE BAR, REBEL ON THE BENCH 354–55 (1994); Robert Belton, *Justice Thurgood Marshall and the Sociology of Affirmative Action,* 6 HARVARD BLACKLETTER JOURNAL 102 (1989); WILLIAMS, THURGOOD MARSHALL at 368.

359   October 1933 lynching of George Armwood ANDOR SKOTNES, A NEW DEAL FOR ALL? RACE AND CLASS STRUGGLES IN DEPRESSION-ERA BALTIMORE 124–25 (2012).

359   he once wrote Parren Mitchell, *Economic Parity for Black Americans,* FELLOW-SHIP, Sept. 1980, at 3–4.

360  Mitchell addressed his colleagues Associated Gen. Contr., Cal. v. Secretary of Com., 441 F. Supp. 955 (C.D. Cal. 1977).

361  Mitchell's hometown daily *House Passes Jobs Bill*, BALTIMORE SUN, Feb. 25, 1977, at 1.

361  *Fullilove v. Phillip Klutznick* Fullilove v. Kreps, 443 F. Supp. 253 (S.D. N.Y. 1977); Fullilove v. Kreps, 584 F.2d 600 (2d Cir. 1978).

361  Drew Days III Drew S. Days III, *Fullilove*, 96 YALE LAW JOURNAL 453 (1987); Rodger D. Citron, *A Life in the Law: An Interview with Drew Days*, 30 TOURO LAW REVIEW 153 (2014); *Drew Days, First Black Leader of Civil Rights Unit, Dies at 79*, NEW YORK TIMES, Nov. 19, 2020.

362  Chief Justice Burger wrote the opinion THE SUPREME COURT IN CONFERENCE (1940–1985): THE PRIVATE DISCUSSIONS BEHIND NEARLY 300 SUPREME COURT DECISIONS 741–44 (ED. DEL DICKSON, 2001); Fullilove v. Klutznick, 448 U.S. 448 (1980); Powell Papers, Fullilove Case, available at: https://scholarlycommons.law.wlu.edu/powellpapers/.

### SIXTH LEG: THURGOOD AND THE IGNORANCE OBSERVATION

365  defeat provided a twenty-eight-year-old Williams v. Zimmerman, 192 A. 353 (Md. 1937).

365  A young Black girl W. Edward Orser, *Neither Separate Nor Equal: Foreshadowing Brown in Baltimore County, 1935–1937*, 92 MARYLAND HISTORICAL MAGAZINE 5–36 (1997); Thomas Anthony Gass, *"A Mean City": The NAACP and the Black Freedom Struggle in Baltimore, 1935–1975* 153–55 (PhD diss. 2014).

366  *Murray v. Pearson Barring of Negro by U. of Md. Argued*, BALTIMORE SUN, Nov. 6, 1935, at 11; Lum v. Rice, 275 U.S. 78 (1927).

366  Marshall wrote Charles Hamilton Houston Thurgood Marshall letter to Charles H. Houston, Sept. 12, 1935, NAACP Papers.

367  During the September 1936 *Admit Aim of Suit Is Negroes' School*, BALTIMORE SUN, Sept. 16, 1936; WILLIAMS, THURGOOD MARSHALL at 79–80; *Open Suit to Get Negro into School*, BALTIMORE SUN, Sept. 16, 1936, at 26; *Urge Negro's Admission to Catonsville School*, BALTIMORE SUN, Apr. 23, 1937, at 15; *Negroes Seek High School of Own in County*, BALTIMORE EVENING SUN, Mar. 14, 1936, at 18; *Negro Pupil's Plea Argued in Appeals Court*, BALTIMORE EVENING SUN, Apr. 22, 1937, at 44.

370  the seventeenth chief justice I pieced together the *Parents Involved* scene from various sources. Parents Involved in Community Schools v. Seattle School District No. 1, 551 U.S. 701 (2007); *Brown*, 347 U.S. 483; *Plessy*, 163 U.S. 537; Adam Liptak, *The Same Words, but Differing Views*, NEW YORK TIMES, June 29, 2007, available at: https://www.nytimes.com/; Goodwin Liu, *History Will Be Heard: An Appraisal of the Seattle/Louisville Decision*, 2 HARVARD LAW & POLICY REVIEW 53 (2008); Erwin Chemerinsky, *Making Schools More Separate and Unequal: Parents Involved in Community Schools v. Seattle School District No. 1*, 2014 MICHIGAN STATE LAW REVIEW 653 (2014); Parents Involved in Community Schools v. Seattle School District No. 1, *Opinion Announcement*, OYEZ, June 28, 2007, available at: https://www.oyez.org/.

376  On the morning of August 4, 1964 SETH CAGIN, WE ARE NOT AFRAID: THE STORY OF GOODMAN, SCHWERNER AND CHANEY AND THE CIVIL RIGHTS CAMPAIGN FOR MISSISSIPPI 396–400 (1988); *FBI Men Find Three Bodies*, CLARION-LEDGER, Aug. 5, 1964, at 1.

376 Sixteen years later Peggy Elam, *Just What Makes the Neshoba Fair So Darn Special?*, CLARION-LEDGER, Aug. 3, 1980, at 3; *Reagan Campaigns at Neshoba Fair,* GREENWOOD COMMONWEALTH, Aug. 4, 1980, at 1; Douglas E. Kneeland, *Reagan Campaigns at Mississippi Fair,* NEW YORK TIMES, Aug. 4, 1980, at A11.

376 regurgitated the game plan ALEXANDER P. LAMIS, THE TWO PARTY SOUTH (1990); ALEXANDER P. LAMIS, SOUTHERN POLITICS IN THE 1990S 8 (1999).

377 On November 4, 1980 I pieced together the Reagan victory scene from a few different sources. WILLIAMS, THURGOOD MARSHALL at 374; *Reagan Buoyed by National Swing to Right,* NEW YORK TIMES, Nov. 6, 1980, at 1; RAYMOND WOLTERS, RIGHT TURN: WILLIAM BRADFORD REYNOLDS, THE REAGAN ADMINISTRATION, AND BLACK CIVIL RIGHTS (2018); JAMES H. MERIWETHER, TEARS, FIRE, AND BLOOD: THE UNITED STATES AND THE DECOLONIZATION OF AFRICA 213 (2021); KYLE LONGLEY, JEREMY MAYER, MICHAEL SCHALLER, & JOHN W. SLOAN, DECONSTRUCTING REAGAN CONSERVATIVE MYTHOLOGY AND AMERICA'S FORTIETH PRESIDENT 76 (2015).

379 Beaufort County spans much *The Negroes in the South,* NEW YORK TIMES, June 14, 1869, at 5.

380 amid the stone sculptures and wood carvings Michael Kruse, *The Weekend at Yale That Changed American Politics,* POLITICO MAGAZINE, Sept./Oct. 2018, available at: https://www.politico.com.

381 In late April 1982 Marcia Chambers, *Yale Is a Host to 2 Meetings About Politics,* NEW YORK TIMES, May 2, 1982, at 53.

381 The Federalist Society I relied on a few sources for my legal analysis here. Mitchell N. Berman, *Originalism Is Bunk*, 84 NEW YORK UNIVERSITY LAW REVIEW 1 (2009); DANIELLE MCLAUGHLIN & MICHAEL AVERY, THE FEDERALIST SOCIETY: HOW CONSERVATIVES TOOK THE LAW BACK FROM LIBERALS 99–100 (2013).

383 Attorney General William French Smith I pieced together the story of the Reagan Justice Department from a few different sources. Fred Barbash, *U.S. Changes School, Job Bias Policy,* WASHINGTON POST, May 22, 1981, available at: https://www.washingtonpost.com/; *Reagan Civil Rights Policies Are Defended and Criticized,* NEW YORK TIMES, May 30, 1983, at 6; Charles E. Finn Jr., *"Affirmative Action" Under Reagan,* COMMENTARY, Apr. 1982, at 17; Neal Devins, *Affirmative Action After Reagan,* 68 TEXAS LAW REVIEW 353 (1989); *Reagan's Choice for Civil Rights Post: William Bradford Reynolds,* NEW YORK TIMES, June 8, 1981, at 26; *Rights Official Says Race-Based Policies Are "Morally Wrong,"* NEW YORK TIMES, Apr. 30, 1983, at 7; Jarvin DeBerry, *Martin Luther King Jr. Explicitly Supported What's Now Called Affirmative Action,* THE TIMES-PICAYUNE/THE NEW ORLEANS ADVOCATE, Apr. 29, 2014, available at: https://www.nola.com/; Linda Greenhouse, *Supreme Court Roundup,* NEW YORK TIMES, Oct. 13, 1982, at 19; Olatunde C. Johnson, *The Story of Bob Jones University v. United States: Race, Religion, and Congress' Extraordinary Acquiescence* in STATUTORY INTERPRETATION STORIES (EDS. WILLIAM ESKRIDGE, PHILIP P. FRICKEY, & ELIZABETH GARRETT 2010); William Bradford Reynolds, *Civil Rights Goals for the Year 2000 and the Means for Achieving Them,* DEPARTMENT OF JUSTICE, Sept. 12, 1983; Liu, HISTORY WILL BE HEARD.

392 His client, Walter Mills Mills v. Board of Education of Anne Arundel County, 30 F. Supp. 245 (D. Md. 1939).

392 Mills made MARK V. TUSHNET, THE NAACP'S LEGAL STRATEGY AGAINST SEGREGATED EDUCATION, 1925–1950 63–64 (2014); *Charles Anne Arundel Board Discriminates Against Negro Teachers,* BALTIMORE SUN, Apr. 22, 1939, at 5;

*Principal Attacks Constitutionality of Higher Wage Base for White Instructors*, BALTIMORE EVENING SUN, Dec. 12, 1938, at 36.

392 Mills later recalled Milton Kent, *Educator Recalls His Path to Roses*, BALTIMORE SUN, July 30, 1984, at 1D.

393 Judge William Calvin Chestnut WILLIAMS, THURGOOD MARSHALL at 90–91.

393 In November 1985 *Ban Upheld*, THE MACNEIL/LEHRER NEWSHOUR, Nov. 6, 1985, American Archive of Public Broadcasting, available at: https://americanarchive.org/.

393 Adopted in 1972 Richard J. Cairns, *Wygant v. Jackson Board of Education—A Question of Layoffs*, 8 PACE LAW REVIEW 159 (1988); Wygant v. Jackson Board of Education, 476 U.S. 267 (1986); Bill Wagner, *Affirmative Action*, ABA JOURNAL, May 1, 1986, at 1.

394 the 1980–81 Jackson High yearbook explained JACKSON HIGH SCHOOL YEARBOOK 67–68 (1981–82 school year).

395 The same year they married *Engagement Announcement*, WINDSOR STAR, June 8, 1953, at 25.

395 The pace of minority hiring snailed along *Wygant v. Jackson Board of Education*, SUPREME COURT RECORDS AND BRIEFS.

396 An example corroborating Author interview with Tony Dungy and Lauren Dungy.

397 one White boy complained Billy Bowles, *Jackson, Flint Calm Racial Outbreaks*, DETROIT FREE PRESS, Feb. 21, 1972, at 14.

397 what the *New York Times* described Iver Peterson, *Public Law Organizations Are Uniting to Advocate the Conservative Cause*, NEW YORK TIMES, July 28, 1985.

398 District Court Judge Charles Joiner Wygant v. Jackson Board of Education, 746 F.2d 1152 (1984).

398 In June 1985 *Wygant v. Jackson Board of Education*, SUPREME COURT RECORDS AND BRIEFS.

399 Diane L. Vaksdal Peterson, *Public Law Organizations Are Uniting to Advocate the Conservative Cause*.

400 "Mr. Chief Justice" Wygant v. Jackson Board of Education, *Oral Argument*, Nov. 6, 1985, OYEZ, available at: https://www.oyez.org.

400 Sandra Day O'Connor EVAN THOMAS, FIRST: SANDRA DAY O'CONNOR 39, 47, 113–14 (2019).

407 During their conference THE SUPREME COURT IN CONFERENCE at 750–52; *Wygant*, 476 U.S. 267; *Wygant v. Jackson Board of Education*, Powell Papers, available at: https://scholarlycommons.law.wlu.edu/powellarchives/.

412 testified a balding White man UNITED STATES CONGRESS SENATE COMMITTEE ON THE JUDICIARY, NOMINATION OF JUSTICE WILLIAM HUBBS REHNQUIST HEARINGS BEFORE THE COMMITTEE ON THE JUDICIARY, UNITED STATES SENATE, NINETY-NINTH CONGRESS, SECOND SESSION, ON THE NOMINATION OF JUSTICE WILLIAM HUBBS REHNQUIST TO BE CHIEF JUSTICE OF THE UNITED STATES, JULY 29, 30, 31, AND AUGUST 1, 1986 (1987).

413 Rehnquist participated TOVA ANDREA WANG, THE POLITICS OF VOTER SUPPRESSION: DEFENDING AND EXPANDING AMERICANS' RIGHT TO VOTE (2012).

414 In a 1986 article A. E. Dick Howard, *A Key Fighter in Major Battles*, AMERICAN BAR ASSOCIATION, June 15, 1986, at 47.

414 Antonin Scalia Stuart Taylor, *Scalia's Views, Stylishly Expressed, Line Up with Reagan's*, NEW YORK TIMES, June 19, 1986, at 27; Michael A. Spizzuco, *Adherence to the Code: Justice Antonin Scalia's Italian American Jurisprudence*, available at: https://scholarship.shu.edu/.

415 On July 7, 1986 Richard Cohen, *Pretender in Paradise*, 5 JOURNAL OF APPEL-
LATE PRACTICE AND PROCESS 87 (2003); Author interview with J. Richard
Cohen, Sept. 4, 2022; MORRIS DEES, A LAWYER'S JOURNEY: THE MORRIS DEES
STORY 270 (1991).

416 On March 16, 1968 *Negro Sheriff Arrests Police Chief, Trooper,* SHREVEPORT
TIMES, Mar. 20, 1968, at 3-A.

416 *United States v. Frazer* United States v. Frazer, 317 F. Supp. 1079 (M.D. Ala.
1970); Paradise v. Prescott, 585 F. Supp. 72 (M.D. Ala. 1983); United States v.
Paradise, 480 U.S. 149 (1987). The majority opinion in *United States v. Paradise* has a wonderful summary of the litigation that this scene was premised
on.

419 As Cohen prepared Cohen, *Pretender in Paradise;* James C. Harvey, *The Reagan Administration and Affirmative Action in Four Major Cities: Detroit, Boston,
New Orleans and Memphis,* 9 THURGOOD MARSHALL LAW REVIEW 1 (1983).

419 Marshall had delivered remarks at the conference Thurgood Marshall, *A
Colorblind Society Remains an Aspiration,* TEACHING AMERICAN HISTORY,
Aug. 15, 1987, available at: https://teachingamericanhistory.org/.

422 Cohen rode with Morris Dees Author interview with J. Richard Cohen.

423 "We will hear argument first this morning" United States v. Paradise, *Oral
Argument,* OYEZ, available at: https://www.oyez.org.

423 Cohen listened to Fried and thought Author interview with J. Richard
Cohen.

423 On February 25, 1987 Ibid.

423 O'Connor backed the position *Paradise,* 480 U.S. 149.

425 For a local Washington, D.C. I pieced this scene together from various
sources. RONALD REAGAN, AN AMERICAN LIFE: THE AUTOBIOGRAPHY 402
(1990); WILLIAMS, THURGOOD MARSHALL at 382–84; *Thurgood Marshall
Ranks Reagan Last Among U.S. Presidents He Observed,* JET, Sept. 28, 1987, at
12; Donnie Radcliffe & Marjorie Williams, *The Night of the Smiling Swedes,*
WASHINGTON POST, Sept. 9, 1987; *Marshall Puts Reagan at "Bottom" Among
Presidents on Civil Rights,* NEW YORK TIMES, Sept. 9, 1987, at 1.

426 Marshall remarked WILLIAMS, THURGOOD MARSHALL at 382.

426 Marshall said inside the luxurious Kapalua Bay Hotel Thurgood Marshall,
*The Constitution's Bicentennial: Commemorating the Wrong Document?,* 40
VANDERBILT LAW REVIEW 1337 (1987); Al Kamen, *Marshall Blasts Celebration
of Constitution Bicentennial,* WASHINGTON POST, May 6, 1987, available at:
https://www.washingtonpost.com/.

428 "Good evening" City of Richmond v. J.A. Croson Co., SUPREME COURT RECORDS
AND BRIEFS.

429 At the end of the hearing Tom Campbell, *Minority Business Ordinance Voted
by City Council,* RICHMOND TIMES DISPATCH, Apr. 12, 1983, at 1.

429 the Supreme Court heard oral argument regarding its constitutionality City
of Richmond v. J. A. Croson Co., 488 U.S. 469 (1989).

429 "We'll hear argument next" City of Richmond v. J. A. Croson Company,
*Oral Argument,* OYEZ, available at: https://www.oyez.org.

429 Anthony McLeod Kennedy THE SUPREME COURT JUSTICES: ILLUSTRATED
BIOGRAPHIES 1789–1995 516–20 (ED. CLARE CUSHMAN 1995).

429 Judge Robert Bork William T. Coleman, *Why Judge Bork Is Unacceptable,*
NEW YORK TIMES, Sept. 15, 1987, at 35A.

432 B. Drummond Ayres B. Drummond Ayres Jr., *Court Ruling Is a Bitter Irony
for Richmond,* NEW YORK TIMES, Jan. 25, 1989, at A18.

432 Justice O'Connor composed *J. A. Croson Company,* 488 U.S. 469.

434 Justice Marshall until his death HOWARD BALL, A DEFIANT LIFE: THURGOOD MARSHALL AND THE PERSISTENCE OF RACISM IN AMERICA 279 (2001).

435 *Adarand Constructors v. Pena* Adarand Constructors, Inc. v. Peña, 515 U.S. 200 (1995).

## SEVENTH LEG: THURGOOD AND THE TWO-FACED DECEPTION

438 Welcome to 1920s segregated Baltimore WILLIAMS, THURGOOD MARSHALL at 15–16.

439 Black American soldiers I pieced together the story of Thurgood in Korea from various sources. Lu Sun, *Battling the Military Jim Crow: Thurgood Marshall and the Racial Politics of the NAACP During the Korean War* (master's thesis 2014); Thurgood Marshall, *Draft of Report on Korea*, NAACP PAPERS, Mar. 12, 1951; *Doomed Officer Denies Cowardice*, NEW YORK TIMES, Oct. 15, 1950, at 9; WILLIAMS, THURGOOD MARSHALL at 169–73; MICHAEL D. DAVIS & HUNTER R. CLARK, THURGOOD MARSHALL: WARRIOR AT THE BAR, REBEL ON THE BENCH I 27–32 (1994); JAMES C. SCOTT, DOMINATION AND THE ARTS OF RESISTANCE: HIDDEN TRANSCRIPTS (1990).

444 Goldberg disseminated Arthur Goldberg, *Memorandum to the Conference Re: Capital Punishment October Term*, 1963, 27 SOUTH TEXAS LAW REVIEW 493 (1985–1986).

445 They stabbed at an intriguing vulnerability Ibid. at 505.

445 *Rudolph v. Alabama* Rudolph v. Alabama, 375 U.S. 889 (1963) (Goldberg, Douglas, & Brennan, JJ., dissenting from denial of certiorari). See also Dennis D. Dorin, *Two Different Worlds: Criminologists, Justice and Racial Discrimination in the Imposition of Criminal Punishment in Rape Cases*, 72 JOURNAL OF CRIMINAL LAW AND CRIMINOLOGY 1667, 1694 (1981).

445 defending Pink Franklin Franklin v. South Carolina, 218 U.S. 161 (1910).

446 William Henry Furman Furman v. Georgia, 408 U.S. 238 (1972).

446 On June 29, 1972 *Furman*, 408 U.S. 238.

447 "license for anarchy, rape and murder" CAROL S. STEIKER & JORDAN M. STEIKER, COURTING DEATH: THE SUPREME COURT AND CAPITAL PUNISHMENT 60–61 (2016).

447 Four years later David C. Baldus, George Woodworth, John Charles Boger, & Charles A. Pulaski, *McCleskey v. Kemp (1987): Denial, Avoidance, and the Legitimization of Racial Discrimination in the Administration of the Death Penalty* in DEATH PENALTY CASES at 233–34 (EDS. JOHN H. BLUME & JORDAN M. STEIKER 2009) [hereinafter BALDUS CHAPTER]; ROBERT M. BOHM, DEATHQUEST: AN INTRODUCTION TO THE THEORY AND PRACTICE OF CAPITAL PUNISHMENT IN THE UNITED STATES 83–99 (2016); Gregg v. Georgia, Proffitt v. Florida, Jurek v. Texas, Woodson v. North Carolina, and Roberts v. Louisiana, 428 U.S. 153 (1976).

447 When Jack Boger Author interview with Jack Boger.

448 a complex mathematical study I pieced together the scene involving the Baldus Study from various sources. BALDUS CHAPTER at 233; MICHAEL MELTSNER, CRUEL AND UNUSUAL: THE SUPREME COURT AND CAPITAL PUNISHMENT (1974); DAVID C. BALDUS, GEORGE WOODWORTH, & CHARLES A. PULASKI, EQUAL JUSTICE AND THE DEATH PENALTY: A LEGAL AND EMPIRICAL ANALYSIS (1990); John Charles Boger, *McCleskey v. Kemp: Field Notes from 1977–1991*, 112 NORTHWESTERN LAW REVIEW 1637 (2018).

450 On the morning of May 13, 1978 The story of the run-up to McCleskey's murder of Schlatt can be found in JEFFREY L. KIRCHMEIER, IMPRISONED BY

THE PAST: WARREN MCCLESKEY AND THE AMERICAN DEATH PENALTY 11–15 (2015).

451 McCleskey, born on March 17, 1946 The information on McCleskey's background comes from a few different sources. Bill Montgomery, *Schlatt a Careful Cop, Buddies Say*, ATLANTA JOURNAL-CONSTITUTION, May 14, 1978, at 22A; Dale Russakoff and Joe Dolman, *Policeman Shot Dead in Holdup*, ATLANTA JOURNAL-CONSTITUTION, May 14, 1978, at A1; KIRCHMEIER, IMPRISONED BY THE PAST at 11–40.

453 When Greenberg hired Boger Author interview with Jack Boger.

453 Boger, on June 18, asked Julian Owen Forrester Ibid. The work EDWARD LAZARUS, CLOSED CHAMBERS: THE FIRST EYEWITNESS ACCOUNT OF THE EPIC STRUGGLES INSIDE THE SUPREME COURT 184–90 (1998), gives an excellent summary of events here.

453 "Through the work of Professor Baldus and his colleagues" *McCleskey v. Kemp*, SUPREME COURT RECORDS AND BRIEFS.

453 "the poor and downtrodden" Author interview with Jack Boger.

454 would bare the most explosive revelations Ibid.; Samuel R. Gross, *David Baldus and the Legacy of McCleskey v. Kemp*, 97 IOWA LAW REVIEW 1906, 1910–11 (2012).

454 Boger translated Baldus's results *McCleskey v. Kemp*, SUPREME COURT RECORDS AND BRIEFS.

455 "'dual system' of capital sentencing" Ibid.

456 explained Patsy Morris Hal Straus, *Death by the Numbers*, ATLANTA JOURNAL, Aug. 28, 1983, at D1.

456 Baldus's was not the first study Smith v. Balkcom, 671 F.2d 858 (5th Cir. 1982); William J. Bowers, *A Tribute to David Baldus, a Determined and Relentless Champion of Doing Justice*, 97 IOWA LAW REVIEW 1879 (2012).

456 Bowers later clarified STRAUS, *Death by the Numbers*.

456 Baldus testified that *McCleskey v. Kemp*, SUPREME COURT RECORDS AND BRIEFS.

458 Forrester wrote McCleskey v. Zant, 580 F. Supp. 338 (N.D. Ga. 1984).

458 The Eleventh Circuit heard McCleskey v. Kemp, 753 F.2d 877 (11th Cir. 1985).

460 L. C. Akens I pieced together the murder scene from a variety of sources. *White Justice in Texas*, ATLANTA DAILY WORLD, Oct. 21, 1945, at 4; *Negro Seizes Policeman's Gun and Kills Him in Streetcar Fight*, DALLAS MORNING NEWS, Sept. 16, 1941, at 1; *Quick Justice Faces Slayer of Policeman*, DALLAS MORNING NEWS, Sept. 17, 1941, at 4; Akins v. Texas, NAACP PAPERS.

462 Justice Henry Billings Brown HENRY BILLINGS BROWN, MEMOIR OF HENRY BILLINGS BROWN LATE JUSTICE OF THE SUPREME COURT OF THE UNITED STATES: CONSISTING OF AN AUTOBIOGRAPHICAL SKETCH 92 (1915).

463 *Brownfield v. South Carolina* Brownfield v. South Carolina, 189 U.S. 426 (1903).

463 *Norris v. Alabama* Norris v. Alabama, 294 U.S. 587 (1935); J. F. Barbour Jr., *Constitutional Law—Equal Protection of Laws—Exclusion of Negroes from Jury Service—Effect on Defendant's Right to a New Trial*, 8 MISSISSIPPI LAW JOURNAL 196 (1935).

464 *Hollins v. Oklahoma* Hollins v. Oklahoma, 295 U.S. 394 (1935); Pierre v. Louisiana, 306 U.S. 354 (1939).

464 *Smith v. Texas* Smith v. Texas, 311 U.S. 128 (1940).

465 *Hill v. Texas* Hill v. Texas, 316 U.S. 400 (1942).

465 "Court today upheld the right" *Supreme Court Upholds Limit on Negro Jury-*

*men,* CHICAGO DEFENDER, June 9, 1945, at 3; Brando Simeo Starkey, *Criminal Procedure, Jury Discrimination & the Pre-Davis Intent Doctrine: The Seeds of a Weak Equal Protection Clause,* 38 AMERICAN JOURNAL OF CRIMINAL LAW 1 (2010).

466   *Palmer v. Thompson* I pieced together the *Palmer v. Thompson* scene from a variety of sources. Clark v. Thompson, 206 F. Supp. 539 (S.D. Miss. 1962); Palmer v. Thompson, 403 U.S. 217 (1971); Hawkins v. Town of Shaw, 461 F.2d 1171 (5th Cir. 1972); Randall Kennedy, *Reconsidering Palmer v. Thompson,* 2018 SUPREME COURT REVIEW 179 (2018); Paul Brest, *Palmer v. Thompson: An Approach to the Problem of Unconstitutional Legislative Motive,* 1971 SUPREME COURT REVIEW 95 (1971); Palmer v. Thompson, *Oral Argument,* OYEZ, Dec. 4, 1970, available at: https://www.oyez.org.

469   *Washington v. Davis* I pieced together the *Washington v. Davis* scene from a variety of sources. Davis v. Washington, 512 F.2d 956 (D.C. Cir. 1975); Griggs v. Duke Power Co., 401 U.S. 424 (1971); Washington v. Davis, 426 U.S. 229 (1976); DISTRICT OF COLUMBIA APPROPRIATIONS FOR FISCAL YEAR 1970 HEARINGS BEFORE THE SUBCOMMITTEE OF THE COMMITTEE ON APPROPRIATIONS, UNITED STATES SENATE, NINETY-FIRST CONGRESS, FIRST SESSION, ON AN ACT MAKING APPROPRIATIONS FOR THE GOVERNMENT OF THE DISTRICT OF COLUMBIA AND OTHER ACTIVITIES 407–9 (1971); Washington v. Davis, *Opinion Announcement,* OYEZ, June 7, 1976, available at: https://www.oyez.org.

474   *"Village of Arlington Heights against Metropolitan Housing Development Corporation"* I pieced together the *Village of Arlington Heights* scene from various sources. Roger Capettini, *Moderate-Income Housing Plans Told,* CHICAGO DAILY HERALD, Feb. 5, 1971, at 45; Village of Arlington Heights v. Metropolitan Housing Development Corp., 429 U.S. 252 (1977); F. Willis Caruso, *The History Beyond the Village of Arlington Heights v. Metropolitan Housing Development Corp. Case,* 5 LAW & HOUSING JOURNAL 47 (1977); Village of Arlington Heights v. Metropolitan Housing Development Corporation, *Opinion Announcement,* OYEZ, Jan. 11, 1977, available at: https://www.oyez.org.

476   Memphis Planning Commission I pieced together the *Greene* scene from various sources. City of Memphis v. Greene, 451 U.S. 100 (1981); *Memphis v Greene,* CRÈME DE MEMPH: A BLOG DEDICATED TO THE DESIGN AND HISTORY OF MEMPHIS, TN, May 25, 2019, available at: http://cremedememph.blogspot.com/; Julia Malone, *Memphis "Badge of Slavery" Case Reaches Supreme Court,* CHRISTIAN SCIENCE MONITOR, Dec. 1, 1980, available at: https://www.csmonitor.com/; City of Memphis v. Greene, *Opinion Announcement,* OYEZ, Apr. 20, 1981, available at: https://www.oyez.org.

479   On February 14, 1984 I pieced together the *Batson* scene from various sources. Batson v. Kentucky, 476 U.S. 79 (1986); Swain v. Alabama, 380 U.S. 202 (1965); *Batson v. Kentucky,* SUPREME COURT RECORDS AND BRIEFS; F.R.D., *Swain v. Alabama: A Constitutional Blueprint for the Perpetuation of the All-White Jury,* 52 VIRGINIA LAW REVIEW 1157 (1966); the Honorable Theodore McMillan & Christopher J. Petrini, *Batson v. Kentucky: A Promise Unfulfilled,* 58 UNIVERSITY OF MISSOURI KANSAS CITY LAW REVIEW 361 (1989–1990).

481   Andrew Hawkins, a part-time handyman CHARLES MONROE HAAR & DANIEL WILLIAM FESSLER, THE WRONG SIDE OF THE TRACKS: A REVOLUTIONARY REDISCOVERY OF THE COMMON LAW TRADITION OF FAIRNESS IN THE STRUGGLE AGAINST INEQUALITY 12, 28 (1986); UNITED STATES CONGRESS,

HOUSE COMMITTEE ON EDUCATION AND LABOR, GENERAL SUBCOMMITTEE ON LABOR, 1965, MINIMUM WAGE–HOUR AMENDMENTS, 1965, HEARINGS, EIGHTY-NINTH CONGRESS, FIRST SESSION, PARTS 3–4, 1901–26 (1965).

482 Three years ago, in February 1968 CHARLES MONROE HAAR & DANIEL WILLIAM FESSLER, FAIRNESS AND JUSTICE: LAW IN THE SERVICE OF EQUALITY 12 (1987).

482 Keady wrote in his opinion Hawkins v. Town of Shaw, Mississippi, 303 F. Supp. 1162 (N.D. Miss. 1969).

483 *Hawkins v. Town of Shaw* Hawkins, 437 F.2d 1286.

484 will disseminate a piece of legal writing OFFICE OF LEGAL POLICY, REPORT TO THE ATTORNEY GENERAL: REDEFINING DISCRIMINATION: "DISPARATE IMPACT" AND THE INSTITUTIONALIZATION OF AFFIRMATIVE ACTION, 1987.

485 On September 11, 1982 RADIO ADDRESS TO THE NATION ON CRIME AND CRIMINAL JUSTICE REFORM, Sept. 11, 1982.

485 with mass incarceration leeching James Cullen, *The History of Mass Incarceration*, BRENNAN CENTER FOR JUSTICE, July 20, 2018, available at: https://www.brennancenter.org/.

487 The anxiety that seizes him Author interview with Jack Boger.

488 Chief Justice Rehnquist says in a flat voice McCleskey v. Kemp, *Oral Argument*, OYEZ, Oct. 15, 1986, available at: https://www.oyez.org.

494 Marshall said, seated in his high-back Sandra Day O'Connor, *Thurgood Marshall: The Influence of a Raconteur*, 44 STANFORD LAW REVIEW 1217 (1992).

494 At the end of the conference *McCleskey v. Kemp*, Powell Papers, available at: https://scholarlycommons.law.wlu.edu/powellpapers/.

495 "The opinion of the Court" McCleskey v. Kemp, *Opinion Announcement*, OYEZ, Apr. 22, 1987, available at: https://www.oyez.org.

495 explained in his written opinion *McCleskey*, 481 U.S. 279.

497 Leslie Gielow Howard Ball, *Thurgood Marshall's Forlorn Battle Against Racial Discrimination in the Administration of the Death Penalty: The McCleskey Cases, 1987, 1991*, 27 MISSISSIPPI COLLEGE LAW REVIEW 335, 351–53 (2007–2008).

498 memo in full Scott E. Sundby, *The Loss of Constitutional Faith: McCleskey v. Kemp and the Dark Side of Procedure*, 10 OHIO STATE JOURNAL OF CRIMINAL LAW 5, 32–33 (2012).

499 If the LDF won Author interview with Jack Boger.

499 Boger wrote years Boger, *McCleskey v. Kemp*.

499 he told one of his clerks BALL, A DEFIANT LIFE at 203.

500 "The strenuous demands of court work" Ibid. at 379.

500 reporters crammed into the Supreme Court's *Thurgood Marshall Speaks with the Media About His Retirement*, June 28, 1991, YOUTUBE.

501 "I am very pleased to announce that I will nominate Clarence Thomas" *July 1, 1991—George H. W. Bush Announces Nomination of Clarence Thomas to the US Supreme Court*, YOUTUBE.

501 The year before Neil A. Lewis, *Sworn In as 105th Justice, Souter Says Shock Recedes*, NEW YORK TIMES, Oct. 9, 1990, at A22.

502 from various sources. A. Leon Higginbotham Jr., *Justice Thurgood Marshall: He Knew the Anguish of the Silenced and Gave Them a Voice*, 3 GEORGETOWN JOURNAL ON FIGHTING POVERTY LAW & POLICY, 163 (1996); Vanessa Williams, Dennis Romero, & Daniel Rubin, *City Honors Thurgood Marshall on Day of Fetes and Festivals*, PHILADELPHIA INQUIRER, July 5, 1992, at 1; Lee Linder, *10,000 See Thurgood Marshall Awarded Liberty Medal*, ASSOCIATED PRESS, July 5, 1992.

EIGHTH LEG: A CULTURE OF UNFIT IMPOSITION

507 But on this morning, Monday, June 11, 1787 I pieced together the 1787 convention from a variety of sources. EDWARD J. LARSON AND MICHAEL P. WINSHIP, THE CONSTITUTIONAL CONVENTION: A NARRATIVE HISTORY FROM THE NOTES OF JAMES MADISON 3–10, 40–41 (2005); Shirley V. Baltz, *Annapolis on the Threshold*, 81 MARYLAND HISTORICAL MAGAZINE 222, 225–26 (1986); CATHERIN DRINKER BOWEN, MIRACLE AT PHILADELPHIA: THE STORY OF THE CONSTITUTIONAL CONVENTION MAY TO SEPTEMBER 1787 1, 23–24 (1986); DAVID O. STEWART, THE SUMMER OF 1787: THE MEN WHO INVENTED THE CONSTITUTION 45–50 (2007).

511 the three-fifths clause Howard A. Ohline, *Republicanism and Slavery: Origins of the Three-Fifths Clause in the United States Constitution*, 28 WILLIAM AND MARY QUARTERLY 5 (1971).

514 James F. Claflin James F. Claflin, *The Fifteenth Amendment*, 1 LAW MAGAZINE FOR LAWYERS AND LAYMEN 82 (1889).

515 described the mission before them JOURNAL OF THE PROCEEDINGS OF THE CONSTITUTIONAL CONVENTION OF THE STATE OF ALABAMA HELD IN THE CITY OF MONTGOMERY, COMMENCING MAY 21ST, 1901 8–12 (1901).

516 John Ashcraft warned Ibid. at 47.

516 Little more than a year later I pieced together the story of Giles from a couple of sources. RISER, DEFYING DISFRANCHISEMENT at 149; Brian Lyman, *The Journey of Jackson Giles*, MONTGOMERY ADVERTISER, Jan. 27, 2022, available at: https://www.montgomeryadvertiser.com/.

517 On March 25, 1902 *The Convention Elects Its Permanent Officers*, MONTGOMERY ADVERTISER, May 22, 1901, at 1; LYMAN, *The Journey of Jackson Giles*; RISER, DEFYING DISFRANCHISEMENT at 294.

517 On October 11, 1902 *Giles v. Harris*, SUPREME COURT RECORDS AND BRIEFS.

518 On November 10, 1902 *Alabama Case Is Granted an Early Hearing*, BIRMINGHAM POST-HERALD, Nov. 11, 1902, at 1.

519 William A. Gunter Sr. RISER, DEFYING DISFRANCHISEMENT at 179.

519 Gunter senior begged the Court *Giles v. Harris*, SUPREME COURT RECORDS AND BRIEFS.

519 Smith, throughout his brief Ibid.

520 *Giles v. Harris* Giles v. Harris, 189 U.S. 475 (1903).

520 Holmes said he and his five colleagues *Cannot Settle Political Questions*, SOUTHERN WATCHMAN, May 23, 1903, at 3; *The Alabama Negroes Lose*, CHARLOTTE OBSERVER, Apr. 28, 1903, at 1.

520 A black robe anonymously told reporters *Validity of Ala. Constitution Not Question for Equity Court*, BIRMINGHAM POST-HERALD, Apr. 28, 1903, at 1.

520 In the text of Holmes's opinion *Giles*, 189 U.S. 475.

522 Celebrated for his brilliance For my legal analysis here, I leaned on a few sources. Samuel Brenner, *"Airbrushed Out of the Constitutional Canon": The Evolving Understanding of Giles v. Harris, 1903–1925*, 107 MICHIGAN LAW REVIEW 853 (2009); Richard H. Pildes, *Democracy, Anti-Democracy, and the Canon*, 17 CONSTITUTIONAL COMMENTARY 295 (2000); Richard H. Pildes, *Keeping Legal History Meaningful*, 19 CONSTITUTIONAL COMMENTARY 645 (2002); *Giles v. Harris*, 5–4 POD, available at: https://www.fivefourpod.com/.

522 The *Liberator* THE LIBERATOR, May 15, 1903, at 1.

523 On May 24, 1932 *Negroes Not to Participate in Demo Primaries*, CORSICA SEMI-WEEKLY, June 24, 1932, at 6.

525   the *Atlanta Constitution's Disfranchisement—Then and Now*, ATLANTA CONSTI-
      TUTION, July 29, 1907, at 4.

525   By 1917 Leo Alilunas, *The Rise of the "White Primary" Movement as a Means of
      Barring the Negro from the Polls*, 25 JOURNAL OF NEGRO HISTORY 161 (1940);
      Robert Wendell Hainsworth, *The Negro and the Texas Primaries*, 18 JOURNAL
      OF NEGRO HISTORY 426 (1933); Thurgood Marshall, *The Rise and Collapse of
      the "White Democratic Primary,"* 26 JOURNAL OF NEGRO HISTORY 249 (1957).

525   On July 26, 1924 WILL GUZMAN, CIVIL RIGHTS IN THE TEXAS BORDERLANDS:
      DR. LAWRENCE A. NIXON AND BLACK ACTIVISM (2015).

526   writing the *Nixon v. Herndon* opinion Nixon v. Herndon, 273 U.S. 536 (1927).

527   *Nixon v. Condon* Nixon v. Condon, 286 U.S. 73 (1932).

527   The decision elated Black Texans For more information on the White pri-
      mary and Black Texans, see GARY M. LAVERGNE, BEFORE BROWN: HEMAN
      MARION SWEATT, THURGOOD MARSHALL, AND THE LONG ROAD TO JUS-
      TICE (2010); BERNADETTE PRUITT & M. HUNTER HAYES, THE OTHER GREAT
      MIGRATION: THE MOVEMENT OF RURAL AFRICAN AMERICANS TO HOUSTON,
      1900–1941 163–70 (2013); Darlene Clark Hine, *The Elusive Ballot: The Black
      Struggle Against the Texas Democratic White Primary, 1932–1945*, 81 SOUTH-
      WESTERN HISTORICAL QUARTERLY 371 (1978); *Picture of Albert Townsend*,
      HOUSTON POST, May 7, 1944, at 11; Alan Robert Burch, *Charles Hamilton
      Houston, the Texas White Primary, and Centralization of the NAACP's Litigation
      Strategy*, 21 THURGOOD MARSHALL LAW REVIEW 95 (1995).

527   On May 23, 1932 *Dem Convention Opens in Uproar*, BROWNSVILLE HERALD,
      May 24, 1932, at 1; *Rayburn Wins Bitter Fight for Keynoter*, HOUSTON CHRON-
      ICLE, May 24, 1932, at 1; *Democratic Executive Committee After Its Session*,
      HOUSTON CHRONICLE, May 24, 1932, at 3.

527   On July 9, 1934 Grovey v. Townsend, 295 U.S. 45 (1935). The original
      pleadings for *Grovey v. Townsend* are available at: https://www.harriscounty
      archives.com/.

528   who devoted much time to Democratic politics *Negro Dems to Debate Liquor
      Question Friday*, HOUSTON CHRONICLE, May 7, 1933, at 9.

528   "Negro voters and electors otherwise qualified" *Grovey v. Townsend*, SUPREME
      COURT RECORDS AND BRIEFS.

528   Jasper Alston Atkins, Carter Walker Wesley, and Ammon Scott Wells J. CLAY
      SMITH JR., EMANCIPATION: THE MAKING OF THE BLACK LAWYER, 1844–1944
      350 (1999).

529   On April 1, 1935 I pieced together the *Grovey* decision scene from various
      sources. *Grovey*, 295 U.S. 45; Hine, *The Elusive Ballot* at 371; Marshall, *The
      Rise and Collapse of the "White Democratic Primary"* at 249; Burch, *Charles
      Hamilton Houston, the Texas White Primary, and Centralization of the NAACP's
      Litigation Strategy* at 95; *Texas Method to Bar Negro Voter Upheld*, HOUSTON
      CHRONICLE, Apr. 1, 1933, at 1; CHARLES L. ZELDEN, THURGOOD MARSHALL:
      RACE, RIGHTS, AND THE STRUGGLE FOR A MORE PERFECT UNION 47 (2013).

529   Black men voted R. Darcy, *Did Oklahoma African Americans Vote Between
      1910 and 1943*, 93 CHRONICLES OF OKLAHOMA 72 (2015); Arthur Lincoln
      Tolson, *The Negro in Oklahoma Territory 1889–1907: A Study in Racial Dis-
      crimination* (PhD diss. 1966).

530   In 1910, Oklahoma voters GERALD WILBUR HICKMAN, DISFRANCHISEMENT
      IN OKLAHOMA: THE GRANDFATHER CLAUSE OF 1910–1916 (1967).

531   *Guinn v. United States* Guinn v. United States, 238 U.S. 347 (1915).

531   Iverson W. Lane Lucille Jackson, *I. W. Lane*, OKLAHOMA HISTORICAL SOCI-
      ETY, available at: https://www.okhistory.org/; *Negroes Assail Vote Registrars*,

MUSKOGEE TIMES-DEMOCRAT, Oct. 27, 1934, at 2; *Wagoner County Negroes Fight Registration Law*, BLACK DISPATCH, Apr. 3, 1930, at 1; *Williams Won't Quit Vote Suit*, MUSKOGEE TIMES DEMOCRAT, Dec. 13, 1934, at 6; *Court Denied County Negro Registration*, RECORD-DEMOCRAT, Jan. 16, 1936, at 1; *New Trial Asked in Wagoner Co. Disfranchisement Scrap; Laws Violate 14th Amendment*, BLACK DISPATCH, Jan. 23, 1936, at 1.

532 after refusing to recuse himself *Negro Seeks Recording of Case Verdict*, WAGONER TRIBUNE, Oct. 20, 1936, at 1.

533 exhorted Murrah *Murrah Upholds Constitutionality of Election Law*, RECORD-DEMOCRAT, Apr. 22, 1937, at 1; HARLOW'S WEEKLY, May 1, 1937, at 3.

533 The Tenth Circuit affirmed *Lane v. Wilson*, 98 F.2d 980 (10th Cir. 1938).

534 violated the Constitution *Negro Case Files in Wagoner County*, TULSA WORLD, May 23, 1939, at 3; Lane v. Wilson, 307 U.S. 268, 275 (1939).

534 Louise Lassiter JOHN WERTHEIMER, LAW AND SOCIETY IN THE SOUTH: A HISTORY OF NORTH CAROLINA COURT CASES 127 (2009).

534 "If more people vote," she thought Ibid.

535 In February 1957 *Suit Charges Voting Rights Were Denied*, GREENSBORO DAILY NEWS, Feb. 26, 1957, at 12; *Highest Court May Get Suit on Vote Test*, GREENSBORO DAILY NEWS, Feb. 27, 1957, at 7; *Election Law Amendment Sought*, GREENSBORO DAILY NEWS, Mar. 30, 1957, at 1.

535 "Save the State from Negro Rule" *Issue Must Be Clean Cut*, FAYETTEVILLE OBSERVER, Oct. 3, 1898, at 2.

536 "White man," the *Raleigh News and Observer* proclaimed WERTHEIMER, LAW AND SOCIETY IN THE SOUTH at 130.

536 Congressman White moved north *White Talks Again*, CHARLOTTE OBSERVER, Sept. 5, 1900, at 8.

536 On April 19, 1957 Lassiter v. Taylor, 152 F. Supp. 295 (E.D. N.C. 1957); *Legal Moves Loom in Ballot Incident*, DURHAM HERALD-SUN, Apr. 5, 1957, at 9; *Negroes Challenge Voter Literacy Test*, GREENSBORO RECORD, Apr. 19, 1957, at 1; *Tar Heel Literacy Test Is Under Fire in Courts*, WILMINGTON MORNING STAR, Apr. 20, 1957, at 1.

537 suffered racial harassment *Vote Att'y Finds Car Cut New Louisburg*, THE CAROLINIAN, Apr. 27, 1957, at 1.

537 visited the same county store to register *Third Move Next in Chain of Legal Action*, CAROLINA TIMES, July 5, 1957, at 1.

537 the U.S. Supreme Court granted review Alexander Moseley, *Organization Formed to Carry Literacy Vote Test and Attorney Walker's Case to the U.S. Supreme Court*, CAROLINA TIMES, Nov. 15, 1958, at 1.

538 Chief Justice Earl Warren told Lake Lassiter v. Northampton County Board of Elections, *Oral Argument*, OYEZ, May 19, 1959, available at: https://www.oyez.org.

538 would segregate, he told them ARGUMENT: THE ORAL ARGUMENT BEFORE THE SUPREME COURT IN BROWN V. BOARD OF EDUCATION OF TOPEKA, 1952–55 at 460.

539 At midday on April 26, 1900 *Who Lied in 1898*, THE CAUCASIAN, May 3, 1900, at 3; *A Royal Welcome to the Candidates*, RALEIGH NEWS AND OBSERVER, Apr. 27, 1900, at 1.

540 goal applies to White kids only William Alexander Mabry, *"White Supremacy" and the North Carolina Suffrage Amendment*, 13 NORTH CAROLINA HISTORICAL REVIEW 1, 1-4 (1936).

540 On June 8, 1959 Lassiter v. Northampton County Board of Elections, 360 U.S. 45 (1959).

544 *Gomillion v. Lightfoot* Gomillion v. Lightfoot, 167 F. Supp. 405 (M.D. Ala. 1958); Gomillion v. Lightfoot, 364 U.S. 339 (1960); BERNARD TAPER, GOMIL-LION VERSUS LIGHTFOOT: THE TUSKEGEE GERRYMANDER CASE (2017). The dialogue in this scene comes from Taper's book.

545 *Colegrove v. Green* Colegrove et al. v. Green et al., 328 U.S. 549 (1946).

545 Justice Frankfurter said in the Court Chamber Gomillion v. Lightfoot, *Oral Argument*, OYEZ, Oct. 18, 19, 1960, available at: https://www.oyez.org; ROBERT J. NORRELL, REAPING THE WHIRLWIND: THE CIVIL RIGHTS MOVEMENT IN TUSKEGEE (1985); Charles Goode Gomillion, *Civil Democracy in the South* (PhD diss. 1957).

546 Beginning on February 8, 1898 OFFICIAL JOURNAL OF THE PROCEEDINGS OF THE SENATE OF THE STATE OF LOUISIANA AT THE SECOND REGULAR SESSION, May 16, 1898.

546 Sitting governor Murphy J. Foster Ibid. at 33.

546 *Smith v. Allwright* Smith v. Allwright, 321 U.S. 649 (1944).

547 Louisiana's state legislature formed Louisiana v. United States, 380 U.S. 145 (1965).

547 On January 28, 1959 MINUTES, SEVENTH CONGRESSIONAL DISTRICT CONFERENCE ON UNIFORM ENFORCEMENT OF LOUISIANA QUALIFICATION LAWS, JANUARY 28, 1959.

548 On March 4, 1963 *Briefs Are Asked in Louisiana's Voter Law Case*, SHREVEPORT JOURNAL, Mar. 5, 1963, at 1.

549 "You would agree" Louisiana v. United States, *Oral Argument*, OYEZ, Jan. 27–26, 1965, available at: https://www.oyez.org.

549 Justice Black announced his unanimous opinion *Louisiana*, 380 U.S. 145.

550 explaining how the anticaste law affected the state *South Carolina v. Katzenbach*, SUPREME COURT RECORDS AND BRIEFS. See also Andrew Kull, *Post-Plessy, Pre-Brown: Logical Exactness in Enforcing Equal Rights*, 24 JOURNAL OF SUPREME COURT HISTORY 155 (1999).

552 Katzenbach later wrote NICHOLAS DEB KATZENBACH, SOME OF IT WAS FUN: WORKING WITH RFK AND LBJ 178 (2008).

552 southern governors descended upon the Cloister Robert McHugh, *McNair: S.C. to Challenge Legality of U.S. Vote Law*, THE STATE, Aug. 13, 1965, at 1D; Al Lanier, *S.C. to Challenge Federal Voting Rights Law*, GREENVILLE NEWS, Aug. 13, 1965, at 1.

552 *McCulloch v. Maryland* McCulloch v. Maryland, 17 U.S. (4 Wheat.) 316 (1819).

553 McLeod argued in his brief *South Carolina v. Katzenbach*, SUPREME COURT RECORDS AND BRIEFS.

555 Here in Marion, Alabama STEVE FIFFER & ADAR COHEN, JIMMIE LEE & JAMES: TWO LIVES, TWO DEATHS, AND THE MOVEMENT THAT CHANGED AMERICA (2015).

556 King says at his funeral William E. Kelly, *Justice Revisited: The Catalyst of the Voting Rights Act of 1965*, 82 JOURNAL OF ALABAMA ACADEMY OF SCIENCE 14 (2011).

556 President Johnson to tell Attorney General Katzenbach YVONNE RYAN, ROY WILKINS: THE QUIET REVOLUTIONARY AND THE NAACP 149 (2013).

556 The answer will come on March 7, 1966 South Carolina v. Katzenbach, 383 U.S. 301 (1966).

557 will mourn that the Court's decision *Justices Uphold Voting Rights Act*, MONROE NEWS-STAR, Mar. 7, 1966, at 1; *Voting Rights Law Provisions Upheld*, THE STATE, Mar. 8, 1966, at 1.

557 Mississippi's, *Delta Democrat-Times Voter Impact*, DELTA DEMOCRAT-TIMES, Mar. 8, 1966, at 3.

557 In March 1965 U.S. COMMISSION ON CIVIL RIGHTS, THE VOTING RIGHTS ACT: TEN YEARS AFTER, JANUARY 1975 43 (1975).

557 By September 1967 Ibid.

557 Since at least 1958 I pieced together the scene of the Mississippi Plan of 1966 from a couple of different sources. Robert McDuff, *The Voting Rights Act and Mississippi: 1965–2006*, 17 REVIEW OF LAW AND SOCIAL JUSTICE 475 (2008); FRANK B. PARKER, BLACK VOTES COUNT 1–3, 34–66 (2011).

561 almost three-fifths of eligible southern UNITED STATES COMMISSION ON CIVIL RIGHTS, THE VOTING RIGHTS ACT, TEN YEARS AFTER: A REPORT OF THE UNITED STATES COMMISSION ON CIVIL RIGHTS 302 (1975).

562 *Allen v. State Board of Elections* Allen v. State Board of Elections, 393 U.S. 544 (1969). See also John P. MacCoon, *The Enforcement of the Preclearance Requirement of Section 5 of the Voting Rights Act of 1965*, 108 CATHOLIC UNIVERSITY LAW REVIEW 107 (1979).

562 At noon on June 12, 1901 *Constitutional Convention of Virginia Convenes*, VIRGINIAN-PILOT, June 13, 1901, at 1.

562 Goode, nearing eighty JOHN GOODE, RECOLLECTIONS OF A LIFETIME 209 (1906); *John Goode Dead*, LEXINGTON GAZETTE, July 21, 1909, at 1.

563 Bagley who too operated MARVIN T. CHILES, THE STRUGGLE FOR CHANGE: RACE AND THE POLITICS OF RECONCILIATION IN MODERN RICHMOND (2023).

563 implemented yet another ruse JOHN V. MOESER & RUTLEDGE M. DENNIS, THE POLITICS OF ANNEXATION: OLIGARCHIC POWER IN A SOUTHERN CITY 1 (1982).

563 During the 1960s I pieced together the scene of race and annexation in Richmond from a variety of sources. Thomas P. Murphy, *The Intergovernmental Dynamics of Annexation and Deannexation: The Richmond Case*, 31 ADMINISTRATIVE LAW REVIEW 385 (1979); Julian Maxwell Hayter, *From Intent to Effect: Richmond, Virginia, and the Protracted Struggle for Voting Rights, 1965–1977*, 26 JOURNAL OF PUBLIC HISTORY 534 (2014); KIMBERLY A. MATTHEWS, THE RICHMOND CRUSADE FOR VOTERS (2017); JULIAN MAXWELL HAYTER, THE DREAM IS LOST: VOTING RIGHTS AND THE POLITICS OF RACE IN RICHMOND, VIRGINIA 138 (2017).

566 On June 24, 1975 City of Richmond v. United States, *Opinion Announcement*, OYEZ, June 24, 1975, available at: https://www.oyez.org; City of Richmond v. United States, 422 U.S. 358 (1975).

568 that Black folk ached under it for generations The history of this scene can be found in the various Bolden cases. Bolden v. City of Mobile, 423 F. Supp. 384 (S.D. Ala. 1976); Bolden v. City of Mobile, 571 F.2d 238 (5th Cir. 1978); Bolden v. City of Mobile, Ala., 542 F. Supp. 1050 (S.D. Ala. 1982).

569 "I don't think you can decide this case in a vacuum" City of Mobile v. Bolden, *Oral Argument*, OYEZ, Mar. 19, 1979, available at: https://www.oyez.org.

570 On April 22, 1980 City of Mobile v. Bolden, *Opinion Announcement*, OYEZ, Apr. 22, 1980, available at: https://www.oyez.org; Mobile v. Bolden, 446 U.S. 55 (1980).

572 Bunk Richardson *Bunk Richardson Is Taken from Jail and Hanged by Gadsden Mob*, MONTGOMERY ADVERTISER, Feb. 12, 1906, at 1; AMY LOUISE WOOD, LYNCHING AND SPECTACLE WITNESSING RACIAL VIOLENCE IN AMERICA, 1890–1940 80 (2011).

572 James Blacksher, Larry Menefee, and Edward Still Jerome Gray & James U. Blacksher, *The* Dillard *Cases and Grassroots Black Political Power*, 46 CUMBERLAND LAW REVIEW 309 (2016).

572 On April 15, 1982 *Bolden*, Ala., 542 F. Supp. 1050.

572 Then, on June 29, 1982 DEPARTMENT OF JUSTICE, SECTION 2 OF THE VOT-ING RIGHTS ACT, available at https://www.justice.gov/.

573 *Dillard v. Crenshaw County* Dillard v. Crenshaw County, 640 F. Supp. 1347 (M.D. Ala. 1986).

573 "To be black and to be here is a milestone" *Etowah Enters New Era in County Governance*, BIRMINGHAM POST-HERALD, Jan. 21, 1987, at D3.

574 *Presley v. Etowah County Commission* Presley v. Etowah County Commission, 502 U.S. 491 (1992).

574 "In an opinion filed with the clerk today" Presley v. Etowah County Commission, *Opinion Announcement*, OYEZ, Jan. 27, 1992, available at: https://www.oyez.org.

575 The Court should have followed See Pamela S. Karlan, *Rights to Vote: Some Pessimism About Formalism*, 71 TEXAS LAW REVIEW 1705 (1993).

576 On July 3, 1889 TIMOTHY CRIMMINS & ANNE H. FARRISEE, DEMOCRACY RESTORED: A HISTORY OF THE GEORGIA STATE CAPITOL (2007).

576 reputedly the head of the state's Ku Klux Klan W. Todd Groc, *John B. Gordon*, NEW GEORGIA ENCYCLOPEDIA, available at: https://www.georgiaencyclopedia.org.

576 In *Wesberry v. Sanders* Wesberry v. Sanders, 376 U.S. 1 (1964).

576 its first occasion to review how See Charles S. Bullock III & Ronald Keith Gaddie, *Voting Rights Progress in Georgia*, 10 LEGISLATION AND PUBLIC POLICY 1 (2006) for an exploration of Georgia post–Voting Rights Act.

577 From June 28 to July 1, 1982 Busbee v. Smith, 549 F. Supp. 494 (D.D.C. 1982).

578 Georgia state lawmakers, for 1990 census redistricting For background, see Richard Briffault, *Race and Representation After Miller v. Johnson*, 1995 UNIVERSITY OF CHICAGO LEGAL FORUM 23, available at: http://chicagounbound.uchicago.edu/; Robert A. Holmes, *Reapportionment Politics in Georgia: A Case Study*, 45 PHYLON 179 (1984).

578 On January 13, 1994, five White voters Miller v. Johnson, 515 U.S. 900 (1995).

578 violated *their* equal protection rights *Miller v. Johnson*, SUPREME COURT RECORDS AND BRIEFS.

579 "As our complaint seeks to make clear" Shaw v. Reno, *Oral Argument*, OYEZ, Apr. 20, 1993, available at: https://www.oyez.org.

580 O'Connor likened the redistricting plan For the legal analysis here, I relied on a few sources. A. Leon Higginbotham Jr., Gregory A. Clarick, & Marcella David, *Shaw v. Reno: A Mirage of Good Intentions with Devastating Racial Consequences*, 62 FORDHAM LAW REVIEW 1593 (1994). See also Dewey Clayton, *Black Congressional Representation in the South: Making the Case for Majority Black Districts*, 28 BLACK SOCIAL ISSUES 36 (1998); Armand Derfner, *Racial Discrimination and the Right to Vote*, 26 VANDERBILT LAW REVIEW 523 (1973); Jocelyn Benson, *Turning Lemons into Lemonade: Making Georgia v. Ashcroft the Mobile v. Bolden of 2007*, 39 HARVARD CIVIL RIGHTS–CIVIL LIBERTIES LAW REVIEW 485 (2004).

582 On June 29, 1995 Miller v. Johnson, *Opinion Announcement*, OYEZ, June 29, 1995, available at: https://www.oyez.org.

582 the Court failed to specify a harm For the legal analysis here, I relied on a few sources. Laughlin McDonald, *Can Minority Voting Rights Survive Miller v. Johnson*, 1 MICHIGAN JOURNAL OF RACE AND LAW 119 (1996); Michael J. Pitts, *What Has Twenty-Five Years of Racial Gerrymandering Doctrine Achieved?*, 9

UNIVERSITY OF CALIFORNIA IRVINE LAW REVIEW 229 (2018); Miller v. Johnson, 515 U.S. 900 (1995); Robert A. Holmes, *Reapportionment Politics in Georgia: A Case Study*, 45 PHYLON 179 (1984); Briffault, *Race and Representation After Miller v. Johnson* at 23; Pitts, *What Has Twenty-Five Years of Racial Gerrymandering Doctrine Achieved?* at 229; Richard H. Pildes & Richard G. Niemi, *Expressive Harms, "Bizarre Districts," and Voting Rights: Evaluating Election-District Appearances After Shaw v. Reno*, 92 MICHIGAN LAW REVIEW 483 (1993).

584 On June 29, 1982 *Ronald Reagan, Remarks on Signing the Voting Rights Act Amendments of 1982*, RONALD REAGAN PRESIDENTIAL LIBRARY & MUSEUM, June 29, 1982, available at: https://www.reaganlibrary.gov.

585 Pleasant Grove, Alabama City of Pleasant Grove v. United States, 479 U.S. 462 (1987).

585 In 1990, Dallas County, Alabama A discussion of the proceeding cases can be found in VOTING RIGHTS ACT: SECTION 5 OF THE ACT—HISTORY, SCOPE, AND PURPOSE, HEARING BEFORE THE SUBCOMMITTEE ON THE CONSTITUTION OF THE COMMITTEE ON THE JUDICIARY HOUSE OF REPRESENTATIVES 109TH CONGRESS FIRST SESSION, OCT. 25, 2005. See also FANNIE LOU HAMER, ROSA PARKS, AND CORETTA SCOTT KING: VOTING RIGHTS ACT REAUTHORIZATION AND AMENDMENTS ACT OF 2006, HOUSE OF REPRESENTATIVES REPORT, May 22, 2006.

587 *Reno v. Bossier Parish School Board* Reno v. Bossier Parish School Bd., 528 U.S. 320 (2000).

587 *Georgia v. Ashcroft* Georgia v. Ashcroft, 539 U.S. 461 (2003).

587 *Northwest Austin Municipal Utility District No. 1 v. Holder* Northwest Austin Municipal Utility District No. 1 v. Holder, 557 U.S. 193 (2009).

588 In 2011, a federal judge United States v. McGregor, 824 F. Supp. 2d 1339 (M.D. Ala. 2011).

588 *Shelby County v. Holder* Shelby County v. Holder, 570 U.S. 529 (2013).

589 Roberts says, reading from his written text Shelby County v. Holder, *Opinion Announcement*, OYEZ, June 25, 2013, available at: https://www.oyez.org; Adam Liptak, *Supreme Court Invalidates Key Part of Voting Rights Act*, NEW YORK TIMES, June 25, 2013, available at: https://www.nytimes.com/.

591 Roberts's ignorant legal analysis For the legal analysis here, I relied on a few sources. James Blacksher & Lani Guinier, *Free at Last: Rejecting Equal Sovereignty and Restoring the Constitutional Right to Vote, Shelby County v. Holder*, 8 HARVARD LAW & POLICY REVIEW 39 (2014); Richard L. Hasen, *Shelby County and the Illusion of Minimalism*, 22 WILLIAM & MARY BILL OF RIGHTS JOURNAL 713 (2014); Wendy B. Scott, *Reflections on Justice Thurgood Marshall and Shelby County v. Holder*, 76 LOUISIANA LAW REVIEW 121 (2015); Nicholas O. Stephanopoulos, *The South After Shelby County*, 2013 SUPREME COURT REVIEW 55 (2013); Zachary S. Price, *NAMUDO'S Non-Existent Principle of State Equality*, 88 NEW YORK UNIVERSITY LAW REVIEW ONLINE 24 (2013).

592 the White deed See also Cheryl I. Harris, *Whiteness as Property*, 106 HARVARD LAW REVIEW 1707 (1993) on property rights and race.

592 Expecting this decision *Inside the Republican Creation of the North Carolina Voting Bill Dubbed the "Monster" Law*, WASHINGTON POST, Sept. 2, 2016, available at: https://www.washingtonpost.com/.

# Index

## ABOUT THE AUTHOR

Brando Simeo Starkey is a writer and scholar. A member of the New York State Bar, he taught law at Villanova University Charles Widger School of Law and wrote for several years for ESPN's Andscape. Born and raised in Cincinnati, he graduated from The Ohio State University and Harvard Law School. He lives in Southern California with his wife and two sons. He writes *The Braveverse* newsletter, about law, politics, and freedom from caste, at TheBraveverse.com.